Western Civilizations

Their History & Their Culture

Joshua Cole

Carol Symes

Western Civilizations

Their History & Their Culture

BRIEF FOURTH EDITION

VOLUME 1

W. W. NORTON & COMPANY · NEW YORK · LONDON

W. W. Norton & Company has been independent since its founding in 1923, when William Warder Norton and Mary D. Herter Norton first published lectures delivered at the People's Institute, the adult education division of New York City's Cooper Union. The firm soon expanded its program beyond the Institute, publishing books by celebrated academics from America and abroad. By midcentury, the two major pillars of Norton's publishing program—trade books and college texts—were firmly established. In the 1950s, the Norton family transferred control of the company to its employees, and today—with a staff of four hundred and a comparable number of trade, college, and professional titles published each year—W. W. Norton & Company stands as the largest and oldest publishing house owned wholly by its employees.

Editor: Jon Durbin

Project Editor: Christine D'Antonio

Associate Editor: Justin Cahill

Editorial Assistant: Travis Carr

Manuscript Editor: Michael Fleming

Managing Editor, College: Marian Johnson

Managing Editor, College Digital Media: Kim Yi

Production Manager: Andy Ensor

Media Editor: Laura Wilk

Assistant Media Editor: Chris Hillyer

Marketing Manager, History: Sarah England

Design Director: Rubina Yeh

Book Designer: Judith Abbate / Abbate Design

Photo Editor: Evan Luberger

Photo Research: Rona Tucillo

Permissions Manager: Megan Jackson

Permissions Clearer: Bethany Salminen

Composition: Cenveo Publisher Services

Cartographers: Mapping Specialists

Manufacturing: LSC Communications—Willard

Permission to use copyrighted material is included in the credits sections of this book, which begin on page A45.

The Library of Congress has cataloged an earlier edition as follows:

Library of Congress Cataloging-in-Publication Data

Cole, Joshua, 1961–

   Western civilizations : their history & their culture / Joshua Cole and Carol Symes.—Eighteenth edition.

     pages cm

   Includes bibliographical references and index.

   ISBN 978-0-393-92213-4 (hardcover)

   1. Civilization, Western—Textbooks. 2. Europe—Civilization—Textbooks. I. Symes, Carol. II. Title.

   CB245.C56   2013

   909'.09821—dc23   2013029952

This edition: ISBN 978-0-393-26533-0

W. W. Norton & Company, Inc., 500 Fifth Avenue, New York, N. Y. 10110
www.wwnorton.com

W. W. Norton & Company Ltd., 15 Carlisle Street, London W1D 3BS

3 4 5 6 7 8 9 0

To our families

Kate, Teimel, Lucas and Ruby Cole
Toan, Erin, and Connor Wilson

With love and gratitude for their support.

And to our students, who have also been
our teachers.

JOSHUA COLE (Ph.D., University of California, Berkeley) is professor of history at the University of Michigan, Ann Arbor and the former director, Center for European Studies at the University of Michigan. His publications include work on gender and the history of the population sciences, colonial violence, and the politics of memory in nineteenth- and twentieth-century France, Germany, and Algeria. His first book was *The Power of Large Numbers: Population, Politics, and Gender in Nineteenth-Century France* (Ithaca, NY: Cornell University Press, 2000).

CAROL SYMES (Ph.D., Harvard University) is associate professor of history and former director of undergraduate studies in the history department at the University of Illinois, Urbana-Champaign, where she has won the top teaching award in the College of Liberal Arts and Sciences. Her main areas of study include medieval Europe, the history of information media and communication technologies, and the history of theater. Her first book was *A Common Stage: Theater and Public Life in Medieval Arras* (Ithaca, NY: Cornell University Press, 2007). She is the founding editor of *The Medieval Globe,* the first academic journal to promote a global approach to medieval studies.

Brief Contents

Contents

Chapter 9 ▪ THE CONSOLIDATION OF EUROPE, 1100–1250   223

Chapter 10 ▪ THE MEDIEVAL WORLD, 1250–1350   255

Chapter 11 ▪ REBIRTH AND UNREST, 1350–1453   285

Maps

Documents

This new Brief Fourth Edition of *Western Civilizations* sharpens and expands the set of tools we have developed to empower students—our own and yours—to engage effectively with the themes, sources, and challenges of history. It presents a clear, vigorous, and coherent narrative, supplemented by a compelling selection of primary sources and visually striking images. At the same time, as the authors of this book's previous edition we have worked to develop a unified program of pedagogical elements that guide students toward a more thorough understanding of the past, and of the ways that historians reconstruct that past. This framework helps students to analyze and interpret historical evidence on their own, encouraging them to become active participants in the learning process. We have also worked hard to overcome one of the major shortcomings of most brief editions—the lack of a coherent narrative Here we used our innovative pedagogical tools as guides, particularly the Story Lines, Chronologies, and Core Objectives, to ensure that the chapter themes and core content remain fully present. Moreover, we cut the narrative by 25 percent, rather than the more traditional 40 percent, which again helps to retain a more coherent reading experience.

Moreover, the wide chronological scope of this book offers an unusual opportunity to trace central human developments (population movements, intellectual currents, economic trends, the formation political institutions, the power of religious belief, the role of the arts and of technologies) in a region of the world whose cultural diversity has been constantly invigorated and renewed by its interactions with peoples living in other places. Students today have a wide selection of introductory history courses to choose from, thanks to the welcome availability of introductory surveys in Latin American, African, and Asian history, alongside both traditional and innovative offerings in the history of the United States and Europe. Global history has also come into its own in recent years. But our increasing awareness that no region's history can be isolated from global processes and connec-

tions has merely heightened the need for a richly contextualized and broad-based history such as that represented in *Western Civilizations*. As in previous editions, we have attempted to balance the coverage of political, social, economic, and cultural phenomena with extensive treatment of material culture, daily life, gender, sexuality, art, science, and popular culture. And following the path laid out in the book's previous editions, we have insisted that the history of European peoples must be understood through their interactions with peoples in other parts of the world. Accordingly, our treatment of this history, attentive to the latest developments in historical scholarship, is both deep and dynamic.

Given the importance of placing human history in a global context, those of us who study the histories of ancient, medieval, and modern Europe are actively changing the ways we teach this history. The title of this book reflects the fact that, for good reasons, few historians today would uphold a monolithic vision of a single and enduring "Western civilization" whose inevitable march to domination can be traced chapter by chapter through time. This older paradigm, strongly associated with the curriculum of early-twentieth-century American colleges and universities, no longer conforms to what we know about the human past. Neither "the West" nor "Europe" can be seen as a distinct, unified entity in space or time; the meanings attributed to these geographical expressions have changed in significant ways. Moreover, historians now agree that a linear notion of any civilization persisting unchanged over the centuries was made coherent only by leaving out the intense conflicts, extraordinary ruptures, and dynamic changes that took place at the heart of the societies we call "Western." Smoothing out the rough edges of the past does students no favors; even an introductory text such as this one should present the past as it appears to the historians who study it—that is, as a complex panorama of human effort, filled with possibility and achievement but also fraught with discord, uncertainty, accident, and tragedy.

Highlights of the New Brief Fourth Edition

The new Brief Fourth Edition makes history an immersive experience through its innovative pedagogy and digital resources. InQuizitive—Norton's groundbreaking, formative, and adaptive new learning program—enables both students and instructors to assess learning progress at the individual and classroom level. The Norton Coursepack provides an array of support materials FREE TO INSTRUCTORS who adopt the text for integration into their local learning-management system. The Norton Coursepack includes valuable assessment and skill-building activities like New Primary Source Exercises, Guided Reading Exercises, Review Quizzes, and Interactive Map Resources. In addition, we've created new Office Hours and Present and Past videos that help students understand the core objectives and make history relevant for them (see page xxix for information about student and instructor resources).

We know that current and future users of our text will welcome the efforts we made in this new edition to update and reorganize the Late Medieval and Early Modern periods in order to place them in a larger Atlantic World context. The major highlight of this reorganization is a brand-new chapter, entitled "Europe in the Atlantic World, 1550–1650." It places the newly integrated space of the Atlantic at the center of the story, exploring the ways that nation building, religious warfare, economic developments, population movements, and cultural trends shaped—and were shaped by—historical actors on this dynamic frontier. Another significant result of the reorganization of these two periods is to provide a clearer chronological framework for the narrative, so that the students can better see how major topics and events emerge from their historical context. This, of course, was part of a larger effort begun across the entire text in the previous edition. These revisions demonstrate our dual commitment to keep the book current and up to date, while striving to integrate strong pedagogical features that help students build their study and history skills (see chapter-by-chapter revisions further below).

NEW AND REVISED PEDAGOGICAL FEATURES

In our ongoing effort to shape students' engagement with history, this book is designed to reinforce your course objectives by helping students to master core content while challenging them to think critically about the past. In order to achieve these aims, our previous edition augmented the traditional strengths of *Western Civilizations* by introducing several exciting new features. These have since been refined and revised in accordance with feedback from both teachers and student readers of the book. The most important and revolutionary feature is the pedagogical structure that supports each chapter. As we know from long experience, many students in introductory survey courses find the sheer quantity of information overwhelming, and so we have provided guidance to help them navigate through the material and to read with greater engagement.

At the outset of each chapter, the **Before You Read This Chapter** feature offers three preliminary windows into the material to be covered: *Story Lines*, *Chronology*, and *Core Objectives*. The *Story Lines* allow the student to become familiar with the primary narrative threads that tie the chapter's elements together, and the *Chronology* grounds these *Story Lines* in the period under study. The *Core Objectives* provide a checklist to ensure that the student is aware of the primary teaching points in the chapter. The student is then reminded of these teaching points upon completing the chapter in the **After You Read** This Chapter section, which prompts the student to revisit the chapter in three ways. The first, *Reviewing the Core Objectives*, asks the reader to reconsider core objectives by answering a pointed question about each one. The second, *People, Ideas, and Events in Context*, summarizes some of the particulars that students should retain from their reading, through questions that allow them to relate individual terms to the major objectives and story lines. Finally, *Thinking about Connections*, new to this edition, allows for more open-ended reflection on the significance of the chapter's material, drawing students' attention to issues that connect it to previous chapters and giving students insight into what comes next. As a package, the pedagogical features at the beginning and end of each chapter work together to enhance the student's learning experience by breaking down the process of reading and analysis into manageable tasks.

A second package of pedagogical features is designed to capture students' interest and compel them to think about what is at stake in the construction and use of historical narratives. Each chapter opens with a vignette that showcases a particular person or event representative of the era as a whole. Within each chapter, an expanded program of illustrations and maps has been enhanced by the addition of **Guiding Questions** that urge the reader to explore the historical contexts and significance of these visual features in a more analytical way. The historical value of images, artifacts, and material culture as types of primary sources is further emphasized in another feature we introduced in our previous edition, **Interpreting Visual Evidence**. These carefully crafted features provide discussion leaders with a provocative departure point for conversations about the key issues raised by visual sources, which students often find more approachable than texts. Once this conversation has begun, students can further develop their skills by **Analyzing Primary Sources** through close readings of primary texts accompanied by cogent interpretive questions. The dynamism and diversity of Western civilizations are also illuminated through a look at **Competing Viewpoints** in each chapter, in which specific debates are presented through paired primary source texts. The bibliographical **For Further Reading**, now located at the end of the book, has also been edited and brought up to date.

In addition to these tools that have proven very successful, we are delighted to introduce an entirely new feature with this Brief Fourth Edition. The new **Past and Present** features in the main text prompt students to connect events that unfolded in the past with the breaking news of our own time, by taking one episode from each chapter and comparing it with a phenomenon that resonates more immediately with our students. To bring this new feature to life for students, we have also created a new series of *Past and Present* Author Interview Videos in which we describe and analyze these connections across time and place. There are a number of illuminating discussions, including "Spectator Sports," which compares the Roman gladiatorial games with NFL Football; "The Reputation of Richard III," which shows how the modern forensics we see on numerous TV shows were recently used to identify the remains of Richard III; "The Persistence of Monarchies in a Democratic Age," which explains the origins and evolution of our ongoing fascination with royals from Louis XIV to Princess Diana; and "The Internet and the Enlightenment Public Sphere," which compares the kinds of public networks that helped spread Enlightenment ideas to the way today's Internet can be used to spread political ideas in movements such as the Arab Spring and Occupy Wall Street. Through this new feature not only do we want to encourage students to recognize the continuing relevance of seemingly distant historical moments, we want to encourage history-minded habits that will be useful for a lifetime. If students learn to see the connections between their world and that of the past, they will be more apt to comprehend unfolding developments and debates in a more informed and complex historical context.

A TOUR OF NEW CHAPTERS AND REVISION

Our previous edition of *Western Civilizations* featured significant changes to each of the book's first five chapters, and this process of revision has continued in the present edition. In Chapter 1, the challenge of locating and interpreting historical evidence drawn from nontextual sources (archaeological, environmental, anthropological, mythic) is a special focus. Chapter 2 further underscores the degree to which recent archeological discoveries and new historical techniques have revolutionized our understanding of ancient history. Chapter 3 offers expanded coverage of the diverse polities that emerged in ancient Greece, and of Athens' closely related political, documentary, artistic, and intellectual achievements. Chapter 4's exploration of the Hellenistic world includes an unusually wide-ranging discussion of the scientific revolution powered by this first cosmopolitan civilization. Chapter 5 emphasizes the ways that the unique values and institutions of the Roman Republic are transformed through imperial expansion under the Principate.

With Chapter 6, more-extensive revision has resulted in some significant reshaping and reorganization in order to reflect recent scholarship. The story of Rome's transformative encounter with early Christianity has been rewritten to enhance clarity and to emphasize the fundamental ways that Christianity itself changed through both its changing status within the Roman Empire and also its contact with peoples from northwestern Europe. Chapter 7, which examines Rome's three distinctive successor civilizations, now offers more-extensive coverage of the reign of Justinian and emergence of Islam. Balanced attention to the interlocking histories of Byzantium, the Muslim caliphates, and western Europe has been carried forward in subsequent chapters. Chapters 8 contains an entirely new section, "A Tour of Europe around the Year 1000," with coverage of the Viking diaspora, the formation of Scandinavian kingdoms and the empire of Cnute, early medieval Rus' and eastern Europe, and the relationships among Mediterranean microcosms. Chapter 8 also features greatly expanded coverage of economy, trade, and the events leading up to the First Crusade. Chapter 9, which now covers the period 1100–1250, features a new segment on the Crusader States and crusading movements within Europe.

Chapter 10's treatment of the medieval world between 1250 and 1350 is almost wholly new, reflecting cutting-edge scholarship on this era. It includes a fresh look at the consolidation of the Mongol Khanates, new images and maps, some new sources, and a new **Interpreting Visual Evidence** segment on seals and their users. Chapters 11 and 12 have been thoroughly reorganized and rewritten to ensure that the narrative of medieval Europeans' colonial ventures (from the western Mediterranean to the eastern Atlantic and Africa, and beyond) is integrated with the story of the Black Death's effects on the medieval world and the impetus for the intellectual and artistic innovations of the Renaissance. In previous editions of the book, these concurrent phenomena were treated as separate, as though they took place in three separate periods (the later Middle Ages, the Renaissance, and the "Age of Exploration"). This divided treatment made the connections among them almost impossible to explain or appreciate. In this Brief Fourth Edition, therefore, the voyages of Columbus are firmly rooted in their historical contexts while the religious social and cultural upheavals of the Reformation (Chapter 13) are more clearly placed against a backdrop of political and economic competition in Europe and the Americas.

This program of revisions sets the stage for the most significant new chapter in the book: Chapter 14, "Europe in the Atlantic World, 1550–1650." This chapter, the hinge between the book's first and second halves, resulted from a close collaboration between us. It is designed to function either as the satisfying culmination of a course that surveys the history of western civilizations up to the middle of the seventeenth century (like that taught by Carol Symes) or to provide a foundation for a course on the history of the modern West (like that taught by Joshua Cole). The chapter illuminates the changing nature of Europe as it became fully integrated into a larger Atlantic World that dramatically and how that integration impacted all of its internal political, social, cultural, and economic development. In addition to greatly enhanced treatment of the transatlantic slave trade and the Columbian Exchange, Chapter 14 also features new sections on the different models of colonial settlement in the Caribbean and the Americas, as well as expanded coverage of the Thirty Years' War.

The new emphasis on the emergence of the Atlantic World carries over to Chapter 15, which covers the emergence of powerful absolutist regimes on the continent and the evolution of wealthy European trading empires in the Americas, Africa, and Asia. This material has now been reorganized to clarify developments over time, as the early successes of the Spanish Empire are gradually eclipsed by the successes of the Dutch, the French, and the British Empires. A new document on the *streltsy* rebellion, meanwhile, allows students to better understand the contested nature of power under the Russian tsars during the absolutist period. We have retained the emphasis on intellectual and cultural history in Chapter 16, on the Scientific Revolution, and in Chapter 17, on the Enlightenment. In Chapter 16 we have enhanced our treatment of the relationship between Christian faith and the new sciences of observation with a new primary source document by Pierre Gassendi. In Chapter 17, meanwhile, we have sought to set

the Enlightenment more clearly in its social and political context, connecting it more explicitly to the theme of European expansion into the Americas and the Pacific. This helps, for example, in connecting a document like the American Declaration of Independence with the ideas of European Enlightenment thinkers.

Chapters 18 and 19 cover the political and economic revolutions of the late eighteenth and early nineteenth centuries. Chapter 18 covers the French Revolution and the Napoleonic empire in depth, while also drawing attention to the way that these central episodes were rooted in a larger pattern of revolutionary political change that engulfed the Atlantic world. Chapter 19 emphasizes both the economic growth and the technological innovations that were a part of the Industrial Revolution, while also exploring the social and cultural consequences of industrialization for men and women in Europe's new industrial societies. The *Interpreting Visual Evidence* feature in Chapter 19 allows students to explore the ways that industrialization created new perceptions of the global economy in Europe, changing the way people thought of their place in the world.

Chapters 20 and 21 explore the successive struggles between conservative reactionaries and radicals in Europe as the dynamic forces of nationalism unleashed by the French Revolution redrew the map of Europe and threatened the dynastic regimes that had ruled for centuries. Here, however, we have sought to clarify the periodization of the post-Napoleonic decades by focusing Chapter 20 more clearly on the conservative reaction in Europe after 1815, and the ideologies of conservatism, liberalism, republicanism, socialism, and nationalism. By setting the 1848 revolutions entirely in Chapter 21 (rather than splitting them between two chapters, as in previous editions), we've helped instructors to demonstrate more easily the connection between these political movements and the history of national unification in Germany and Italy in subsequent decades. While making these changes in the organization of the chapters, we have retained our treatment of the important cultural movements of the first half of the nineteenth century, especially romanticism.

Chapter 22 takes on the history of nineteenth-century colonialism, exploring both its political and economic origins and its consequences for the peoples of Africa and Asia. The chapter gives new emphasis to the significance of colonial conquest for European culture, as colonial power became increasingly associated with national greatness, both in conservative monarchies and in more-democratic regimes. Chapter 23 then brings the narrative back to the heart of Europe, covering the long-term consequences of industrialization and the consolidation of a conservative form of nationalism in many European nations even as the electorate was being expanded. This chapter emphasizes the varied nature of the new forms of political dissent, from the feminists who claimed the right to vote to the newly organized socialist movements that proved so enduring in many European countries.

Chapters 24 and 25 bring new vividness to the history of the First World War and the intense conflicts of the interwar period, while Chapter 26 uses the history of the Second World War as a hinge for understanding European and global developments in the second half of the twentieth century. The *Interpreting Visual Evidence* feature in Chapter 24 focuses on the role of propaganda among the belligerent nations in 1914–18, and the chapter's section on the diplomatic crisis that preceded the First World War has been streamlined to allow students to more easily comprehend the essential issues at the heart of the conflict. In Chapter 25 the *Interpreting Visual Evidence* feature continues to explore a theme touched on in earlier chapters—political representations of "the people"—this time in the context of fascist spectacles in Germany and Italy in the 1930s. These visual sources help students to understand the vulnerability of Europe's democratic regimes during these years as they faced the dual assault from fascists on the right and Bolsheviks on the left.

Chapters 27–29 bring the volume to a close in a thorough exploration of the Cold War, decolonization, the collapse of the Soviet Union and the Eastern Bloc in 1989–1991, and the roots of the multifaceted global conflicts that beset the world in the first decade of the twenty-first century. Chapter 27 juxtaposes the Cold War with decolonization, showing how this combination sharply diminished the ability of European nations to control events in the international arena, even as they succeeded in rebuilding their economies at home. Chapter 28 explores the vibrancy of European culture in the crucial period of the 1960s to the early 1990s, bringing new attention to the significance of 1989 as a turning point in European history. Finally, extensive revisions to Chapter 29 add to the issues covered in our treatment of Europe's place in the contemporary globalized world. The chapter now includes a new section on efforts to deal with climate change, as well as expanded discussion of both the impact of global terrorism and recent developments in the Arab-Israeli conflict. The discussion on the financial crisis of 2008 and the presidency of Barack Obama has been brought up to date and two new sections have been added to allow students to think about the Arab Spring of 2011 and the European debt crisis of recent years in connection with the broader history of European democracy, nation building, and colonialism in the modern period.

History becomes an immersive experience for students using Norton's digital resources with the Brief Fourth Edition of *Western Civilizations*. The comprehensive ancillary package features a groundbreaking new formative adaptive system as well as innovative interactive resources, including maps and primary sources, to help students master the core objectives in each chapter and continue to strengthen the skills they need to do the work of historians. Norton is unique in partnering exclusively with subject-matter experts who teach the course to author these resources. As a result, instructors have all of the course materials they need to successfully manage their Western Civilization course, whether they are teaching face-to-face, online, or in a hybrid setting.

INSTRUCTOR RESOURCES

LMS Coursepacks: Strong Assessment and Lecture Tools

* **New! Author Office Hour Videos:** These segments feature the authors speaking for 90 seconds on the Core Objectives of each chapter. There are nearly 100 of these new video segments.
* **New! Past and Present Author Interview Videos:** These videos connect topics across time and place and show why history is relevant to understanding our world today. Examples include "Spectator Sports," "Medieval Plots and Modern Movies," "Global Pandemics," and "The Atlantic Revolutions and Human Rights."
* **New! Guided Reading Exercises:** These exercises are designed by Scott Corbett (Ventura College) to help students learn how to read a textbook and, more importantly, comprehend what they are reading. The reading exercises instill a three-step Note-Summarize-Assess pedagogy. Exercises are based on

actual passages from the textbook, and sample feedback is provided to model responses.
* **New! StoryMaps:** These presentations break complex maps into a sequence of four or five annotated screens that focus on the *story* behind the *geography*. The ten StoryMaps include such topics as the Silk Road, the spread of the Black Death, and nineteenth-century imperialism.
* **Interactive iMaps:** These interactive tools challenge students to better understand the nature of change over time by allowing them to explore the different layers of the maps from the book. Follow-up map worksheets help build geography skills by allowing students to test their knowledge by labeling.
* **Review Quizzes:** Multiple-choice, true/false, and chronological-sequence questions allow students to test their knowledge of the chapter content and identify where they need to focus their attention to better understand difficult concepts.
* **Primary Sources:** Over 400 primary source documents and images

Instructor's Manual

The Instructor's Manual for *Western Civilizations*, Brief Fourth Edition, is designed to help instructors prepare lectures and exams. The Instructor's Manual contains detailed chapter outlines, general discussion questions, document discussion questions, lecture objectives, interdisciplinary discussion topics, and recommended reading and film lists. This edition has been revised to include sample answers to all of the student-facing comprehension questions in the text.

Test Bank

The Test Bank contains over 2,000 multiple-choice, true/false, and essay questions. This edition of the Test Bank has been completely revised for content and accuracy. All test questions are now aligned with Bloom's Taxonomy for greater ease of assessment.

Lecture PowerPoint Slides

These ready-made presentations provide comprehensive outlines of each chapter, as well as discussion prompts to encourage student comprehension and engagement.

STUDENT RESOURCES

New! Norton InQuizitive for History 🐰 This groundbreaking formative, adaptive learning tool improves student understanding of the core objectives in each chapter. Students receive personalized quiz questions on the topics with which they need the most help. Questions range from vocabulary and concepts to interactive maps and primary sources that challenge students to begin developing the skills necessary to do the work of a historian. Engaging game-like elements motivate students as they learn. As a result, students come to class better prepared to participate in discussions and activities.

New! Student Site

wwnorton.com/college/history/western
-civilizationsBrief4

Free and open to all students, Norton Student Site includes additional resources and tools to ensure they come to class prepared and ready to actively participate in discussions and activities.

- **Office Hour Videos:** These segments feature the authors speaking for 90 seconds on the Core Objectives of each chapter. There are nearly 100 of these new video segments.
- **Western Civilizations Tours powered by Google Earth:** This new feature traces historical developments across time, touching down on locations that launch images and primary source documents
- **iMaps:** Interactive maps challenge students to explore change over time by navigating the different layers of the maps from the book. Practice worksheets help students build their geography skills by labeling the locations.
- **Online Reader:** The online reader offers a diverse collection of primary source readings for use in assignments and activities.

Acknowledgments

Our first edition as members of the *Western Civilizations* authorial team was challenging and rewarding. Our second edition has been equally rewarding in that we have been able to implement a number of useful and engaging changes in the content and structure of the book, which we hope will make it even more student- and classroom-friendly. We are very grateful for the expert assistance and support of the Norton team, especially that of our editor, Jon Durbin. Christine D'Antonio, our fabulous project editor, has driven the book beautifully through the manuscript process. Travis Carr has provided good critiques of the illustrations in addition to all the other parts of the project he has handled so skillfully. Laura Wilk, our amazing new emedia editor, has assembled a great team to successfully deliver InQuizitive and all the carefully crafted new elements in the Norton Coursepack. Andy Ensor has masterfully marched us through the production process. Michael Fleming and Bob Byrne were terrific in skillfully guiding the manuscript through the copyediting and proofreading stages. Finally, we want to thank Sarah England for spearheading the marketing campaign for the new Brief Fourth Edition. We are also indebted to the numerous expert readers who commented on various chapters and who thereby strengthened the book as a whole. We are thankful to our families for their patience and advice, and to our students, whose questions and comments over the years have been essential to the framing of this book. And we extend a special thanks to, and we hope to hear from, all the teachers and students we may never meet—their engagement with this book will frame new understandings of our shared past and its bearing on our future.

REVIEWERS

Brief Third Edition Consultants
Paul Freedman, Yale University
Sheryl Kroen, University of Florida
Michael Kulikowski, Pennsylvania State University

Harry Liebersohn, University of Illinois, Urbana-Champaign
Helmut Smith, Vanderbilt University

Brief Third Edition Reviewers
Donna Allen, Glendale Community College
Marjon Ames, Appalachian State University
Eirlys Barker, Thomas Nelson Community College
Matthew Barlow, John Abbot College
Ken Bartlett, University of Toronto
Volker Benkert, Arizona State University
Dean Bennett, Schenectady City Community College
Patrick Brennan, Gulf Coast Community College
Neil Brooks, Community College of Baltimore County, Essex
James Brophy, University of Delaware
Kevin Caldwell, Blue Ridge Community College
Keith Chu, Bergen Community College
Alex D'erizans, Borough of Manhattan Community College, CUNY
Hilary Earl, Nipissing University
Karin Enloe, Arizona State University
Kirk Ford, Mississippi College
Michael Gattis, Gulf Coast Community College
David M. Gallo, College of Mount Saint Vincent
Jamie Gruring, Arizona State University
Tim Hack, Salem Community College
Bernard Hagerty, University of Pittsburg
Paul T. Hietter, Mesa Community College
Paul Hughes, Sussex County Community College
Lacey Hunter, Caldwell College
Kyle Irvin, Jefferson State Community College
Lloyd Johnson, Campbell University
Llana Krug, York College of Pennsylvania
Guy Lalande, St. Francis Xavier University
Chris Laney, Berkshire Community College
Charles Levine, Mesa Community College
Heidi MacDonald, Lethbridge University

Steven Marks, Clemson University
James Martin, Campbell University
Michael Mckeown, Daytona State University
Dan Puckett, Troy State University
Dan Robinson, Troy State University
Craig Saucier, Southeastern Louisiana University
Aletia Seaborn, Southern Union State College
Nicholas Steneck, Florida Southern College
Victoria Thompson, Arizona State University
Donna Trembinski, St. Francis Xavier University
Pamela West, Jefferson State Community College
Scott White, Scottsdale Community College
Aaron Wilson, Creighton University
Julianna Wilson, Pima Community College

Brief Fourth Edition Reviewers

Matthew Barlow, John Abbott College
Ken Bartlett, University of Toronto
Bob Brennan, Cape Fear Community College
Jim Brophy, University of Delaware
Keith Chu, Bergen Community College

Geoffrey Clark, SUNY Potsdam
Bill Donovan, Loyola University Maryland
Jeff Ewen, Sussex County Community College
Peter Goddard, University of Guelph
Paul Hughes, Sussex County Community College
Michael Kulikowski, Penn State University
Chris Laney, Berkshire Community College
James Martin, Campbell University
Derrick McKisick, Fairfield University
Dan Puckett, Troy University
Major Ben Richards, US Military Academy
Bo Riley, Columbus State Community College
Kimlisa Salazar, Pima Community College
Sara Scalenghe, Loyola University Maryland
Suzanne Smith, Cape Fear Community College
Bobbi Sutherland, Dordt College
David Tengwall, Anne Arundel Community College
Pam West, Jefferson State Community College
Julianna Wilson. Pima Community College
Margarita Youngo, Pima Community College

Western Civilizations

Their History & Their Culture

Before
You
Read
This
Chapter

Early Civilizations

CORE OBJECTIVES

- **UNDERSTAND** the challenges involved in studying the distant past.

- **DEFINE** the key characteristics of civilization.

- **IDENTIFY** the factors that shaped the earliest cities.

- **EXPLAIN** how Hammurabi's empire was governed.

- **DESCRIBE** the main differences between Mesopotamian and Egyptian civilizations.

There was a time, the story goes, when all the peoples of the earth shared a common language and could accomplish great things. They developed new technologies, made bricks, and aspired to build a fortified city with a tower reaching to the sky. But their god was troubled by this, so he destroyed their civilization by making it hard for them to understand one another's speech.

We know this as the legend of Babel. It's a story that probably circulated among peoples of the ancient world for thousands of years before it became part of the Hebrew book we call by its Greek name, Genesis, "the beginning." This story lets us glimpse some of the conditions in which the first civilizations arose, and it also reminds us of the ruptures that make studying them hard. We no longer speak the same languages as those ancient peoples, just as we no longer have direct access to their experiences or their beliefs.

Such foundational stories are usually called *myths*, but they are really an early form of history. For the people who told them, these stories helped to make sense of the present by explaining the past. The fate of Babel conveyed a crucial

3

message: human beings are powerful when they share a common goal, and what enables human interaction is civilization. To the peoples of the ancient world, the characteristic benefits of civilization—stability and safety, government, art, literature, science—were always products of city life. The very word "civilization" derives from the Latin word *civis*, "city." Cities, however, became possible only as a result of innovations that began around the end of the last Ice Age, about 13,000 years ago, and that came to fruition in Mesopotamia 8,000 years later. The history of civilization is therefore a short one. Within the study of humanity, which reaches back to the genus *Homo* in Africa, some 1.7 million years ago, it is merely a blip on the radar screen. Even within the history of *Homo sapiens sapiens*, the species to which we belong and which evolved about 50,000 years ago, civilization is a very recent development.

The study of early civilizations is both fascinating and challenging. Historians still do not understand why cities developed in the region between the Tigris and the Euphrates rivers, in what is now Iraq. Once developed, however, the basic patterns of urban life quickly spread to other parts of the ancient world, both by imitation and by conquest. A network of trading connections linked these early cities, but intense competition for resources made alliances among them fragile. Then, around the middle of the second millennium B.C.E. (that is, "Before the Common Era," equivalent to the Christian dating system B.C., "Before Christ"), emerging powers began to shape some fiercely independent cities into empires. How this happened—and how we know that it happened—is the subject of Chapter 1.

BEFORE CIVILIZATION

More than 9,000 years ago, a town began to develop at Çatalhöyük (*CHUH-tal-hih-yik*) in what is now south-central Turkey. Over the next 2,000 years, it grew to cover an area of thirty-three acres, within which some 8,000 inhabitants lived in more than 2,000 separate houses. If this seems small, consider that Çatalhöyük's population density was actually twice that of today's most populous city, Mumbai (in India). It was so tightly packed that there were hardly any streets. Instead, each house was built immediately next to its neighbor, and generally on top of a previous house.

The people of Çatalhöyük developed a highly organized and advanced society. They wove wool cloth; they made kiln-fired pottery; they painted elaborate hunting scenes on the plaster-covered walls of their houses; they made weapons and tools from razor-sharp obsidian imported from the nearby Cappadocian mountains. They honored their ancestors with religious rites and buried their dead beneath the floors of their houses. Settled agriculturalists, they grew grains, peas, and lentils and tended herds of domesticated sheep and goats. But they also hunted and gathered fruits and nuts, like their nomadic ancestors, and their society was egalitarian, another feature common to nomadic societies: both men and women did the same kinds of work. But despite their relatively diverse and abundant food supply, their life spans were very short. Men died, on average, at the age of thirty-four. Women, who bore the additional risks of childbirth, died at around age thirty.

The basic features of life in Çatalhöyük are common to all subsequent human civilizations. But how, when, and why did such settlements emerge? And how do we have access to information about this distant past? The era before the appearance of written records, which begin to proliferate around 3100 B.C.E., is of far greater duration than the subsequent eras we are able to document—and no less important. But it requires special ingenuity to identify, collect, and interpret the evidence of the distant past. In fact, historians have just begun to explore the ways that climatology, neuroscience, evolutionary biology, and genetics can further illuminate this period, augmenting the older findings of paleontology, archaeology, and historical anthropology.

Societies of the Stone Age

Primates with human characteristics originated in Africa 4 to 5 million years ago, and tool-making hominids—species belonging to the genus *Homo*, our distant ancestors—evolved approximately 2 million years ago. Because these early hominids made most of their tools out of stone, they are designated as belonging to the Stone Age. This vast expanse of time is divided into the Paleolithic ("Old Stone") and the Neolithic ("New Stone") Eras, with the break between them falling around 11,000 B.C.E.

As early as 164,000 years ago, hominids in Africa were kindling and controlling fire and using it to make tools. The Neanderthals, a hominid species that flourished about 200,000 years ago, made jewelry, painted on the walls of caves, and buried their dead in distinctive graves with meaningful objects such as horns (blown to make music)

CAVE PAINTINGS FROM LASCAUX. These paintings, which date to between 10,000 and 15,000 B.C.E., show several of the different species of animals that were hunted by people of the Ice Age. The largest animal depicted here, a species of long-horned cattle known as the *auroch,* is now extinct.

and, in one case, flowers. Could these hominids speak? Did they have a language? At present, there is no way that we can answer such questions.

However, archaeology has shown that in the last phase of the Paleolithic Era, around 40,000 B.C.E., the pace of human development began to accelerate dramatically. Human populations in Africa expanded, suggesting that people were better nourished, perhaps as a result of new technologies. In Europe, *Homo sapiens* began to produce finely crafted and more-effective tools such as fishhooks, arrowheads, and sewing needles made from wood, antler, and bone. The most astonishing evidence of this change was produced by these new tools: cave paintings like those at Lascaux and Chauvet (in France). These amazing scenes were purposefully painted in recesses where acoustic resonance is greatest, and were probably intended to be experienced as part of multimedia musical ceremonies. This is almost certain evidence for the development of language.

Despite these changes, the patterns of human life altered very little. Virtually all human societies consisted of bands of a few dozen people who moved incessantly in search of food. As a result, these groups left no continuous archaeological record. Their lifestyle also had social, economic, and political limitations which help to explain the differences—both positive and negative—between these subsistence societies and those that can be called "civilizations." Early humans had no domestic animals to transport goods, so they could have no significant material possessions aside from basic tools. And because they could not accumulate goods over time, the distinctions of rank and status created by disparities in wealth could not develop.

Hierarchical structures were therefore uncommon. When conflicts arose or resources became scarce, the solution was probably to divide and separate. And although scholars once assumed that men did the hunting and women the gathering, it is more likely that all members of a band (except for the very young and very old) engaged in the basic activity of acquiring food.

THE BUILDING BLOCKS OF CIVILIZATION

What changes allowed some hunter-gatherer societies to settle and build civilizations? The historical divide between the Paleolithic and Neolithic Ages, around 11,000 B.C.E., reflects very evident developments brought about by changes in the climate, which led to the development of managed food production, which in turn fostered settlements that could trade with one another, both locally and over long distances. For the first time, it became possible for individuals and communities to accumulate and store wealth on a large scale. The results were far-reaching. Communities became more stable, and human interactions more complex. Specialization developed, along with distinctions of status and rank. Both the rapidity and the radical implications of these changes have given this era its name: the Neolithic Revolution.

The Neolithic Revolution

The artists who executed the cave paintings at Lascaux and Chauvet were able to survive in harsh climatic conditions. Between 40,000 and 11,000 B.C.E., daytime temperatures in the Mediterranean basin averaged about 60° F (16° C) in the summer and about 30° F (–1° C) in the winter. These are very low compared to today's temperatures in the city of Marseilles, not far from Lascaux, which average about 86° F (30° C) in summer and 52° F (11° C) in winter. This means that cold-loving reindeer, elk, wild boar, bison, and mountain goats abounded in regions now famous for their beaches and vineyards. But as the glaciers receded northward with the warming climate, these species retreated with them, all the way to Scandinavia. Some humans moved north with the game, but others stayed behind to create a very different world.

Within a few thousand years after the end of the Ice Age, peoples living in the eastern Mediterranean and

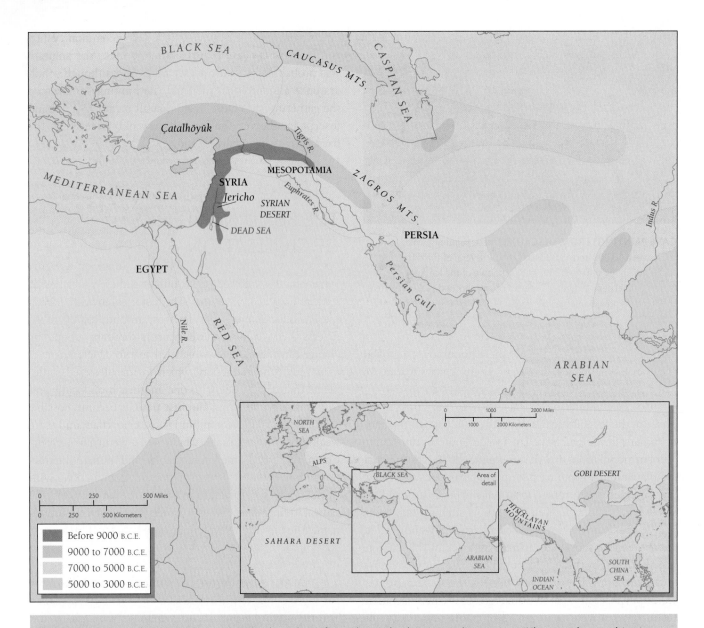

THE GROWTH OF AGRICULTURE. Examine the chronology of agriculture's development in this region. ▪ *What areas began cultivating crops first, and why?* ▪ *How might rivers have played a crucial role in the spread of farming technologies?*

some other regions of the world accomplished the most momentous transformation in human history: a switch from food-gathering for subsistence to food production. The warmer, wetter climate allowed wild grains to flourish, geometrically increasing the food supply. People began to domesticate animals and cultivate plants. Stable settlements grew into cities. This process took several thousand years, but it still deserves to be called "revolutionary." In a relatively short time, people altered patterns of existence that were millions of years old.

This revolution produced new challenges and inequalities. For example, well-nourished women in sedentary communities can bear more children than women in hunter-gatherer groups, and so the women of this era became increasingly sequestered from their male counterparts, who in turn gave up an equal role in child care. The rapid increase in population was also countered by the rapid spread of infectious diseases, while dependence on carbohydrates resulted in earlier deaths than were typical among hunter-gatherers.

Eventually, increased fertility and birthrates outweighed these limiting factors, and by about 8000 B.C.E. human populations were beginning to exceed the wild food supply. They therefore had to increase the food-growing capacity of the land and devise ways of preserving and storing grain between harvests. Some peoples had learned how to preserve wild grain in storage pits as early as 11,500 B.C.E., and they discovered that they could use this seed to produce even more grain the following year. The importance of the latter discovery cannot be overstated: deliberate cultivation could support larger populations and could also compensate for disasters (such as flooding) that might inhibit natural reseeding. Even more important, intensified seeding and storage provided humans with the stable and predictable surpluses needed to support domestic animals. This brought a host of additional benefits, guaranteeing a more reliable supply of meat, milk, leather, wool, bone, and horn, and also providing animal power to pull carts and plows and to power mills.

The Emergence of Towns and Villages

The accelerating changes of the Neolithic Revolution are exemplified by towns like Çatalhöyük and by the simultaneous rise of trade and warfare—sure signs of increased specialization and competition. Hundreds, and probably thousands, of settlements grew up in western Asia (the "Near East") between 7500 and 3500 B.C.E. Some of these can be classified as cities: centers of administration and commerce with a large and diverse population, often protected by walls. Among the earliest of these was Jericho, in the territory lying between modern Israel and Jordan. Jericho emerged as a seasonal grain-producing settlement, and by 6800 B.C.E. its inhabitants were undertaking a spectacular building program. Many new dwellings were built on stone foundations, and a massive dressed stone wall was constructed around the western edge of the settlement. It included a circular tower whose excavated remains still reach to a height of thirty feet, a powerful expression of its builders' wealth, technical prowess, and political ambitions.

Jericho covered at least eight acres and supported 3,000 people, so it was even more densely settled than Çatalhöyük. It was sustained by intensive cultivation, made possible by irrigation, of recently domesticated strains of wheat and barley. Jericho's inhabitants also produced some of the earliest-known pottery, which allowed them to store grain, wine, and oils more effectively. Pottery's most important benefits, however, were in cooking. For the first time, it was possible to produce nourishing stews, porridges, and ales. (The capacity to produce beer is a sure sign of civilization.) Pottery production was not only vital to ancient civilizations, it is vital to those who study them. As the techniques for making pottery spread throughout the Near East and Asia, identifiable regional styles also developed. By studying the different varieties, archaeologists can construct a reasonably accurate chronology and can also trace the movements of goods and people.

Jericho and Çatalhöyük illustrate the impact that stored agricultural surpluses have on human relations. For the first time, significant differences began to arise in the amount of wealth individuals could stockpile for themselves and their heirs. Dependence on agriculture also made it more difficult for individuals to split off from the community when disputes and inequities arose. The result was the construction of a much more stratified society, with more opportunities for a few powerful people to become dominant. The new reliance on agriculture also meant a new dependence on the land, the seasons, and the weather, which in turn led to new speculations about the supernatural. Different life forces were believed to require special services and gifts, and the regular practice of ritual and sacrifice ultimately produced a priestly caste of individuals or families who seemed able to communicate with these forces. Such spiritual leadership was allied to more worldly forms of power, including the capacity to lead war bands, to exact tribute from other settlements, to construct defenses, and to resolve disputes.

Trade was another important element in the development of early settlements. Local trading networks were already established around 9000 B.C.E., and by 5000 B.C.E., long-distance routes linked settlements throughout the region. Long-distance trade accelerated the exchange of ideas and information within the Fertile Crescent, and it further increased social stratification. Because status was enhanced by access to exotic goods from afar, local elites sought to monopolize trade by organizing and controlling the production of commodities within their own communities and by regulating their export. Certain people could now devote at least a portion of their labor to pursuits other than agriculture: making pottery or cloth, manufacturing weapons or tools, building houses and fortifications, or facilitating trade. Thus the elites who fostered and exploited the labor of others eventually became specialized themselves, with the leisure and resources to engage in intellectual, artistic, and political pursuits. The building blocks of civilization had been laid.

THE WHITE TEMPLE AT URUK, c. 3400 B.C.E. This temple may have been dedicated to the sky god, An, or designed to provide all the region's gods with a mountaintop home in a part of the world known for its level plains.

URBAN DEVELOPMENT IN MESOPOTAMIA

The Greeks called it Mesopotamia, the "Land between Rivers." It was a land that received only about eight inches (20 cm) of rainfall per year. Its soils are sandy, and summer temperatures exceed 110° F (44° C). The two rivers supplying water—the Tigris and Euphrates—are noted for their violence and unpredictability. Both are prone to flooding, and the Tigris was liable to change its course from year to year. It was in this challenging environment that the urban society of Sumer flourished.

Early Ubaid Settlements

The earliest cities of Mesopotamia were founded by the Ubaid peoples, so called because of their settlement at al-Ubaid (now in Iraq), which dates to around 5900 B.C.E. In this era, the headwaters of the Persian Gulf extended at least 100 miles farther inland than they do today, so some Ubaid settlements bordered on fertile marshlands, which enabled them to develop irrigation systems. Although these began as relatively simple channels and collection pools, Ubaid farmers quickly learned to build more sophisticated canals and to line some pools with stone. They also constructed dikes and levees to control the seasonal flooding of the rivers and to direct the excess water into irrigation canals. Despite the hostility of the environment, Ubaid communities were soon producing surpluses sufficient to support specialists in construction, weaving, pottery, metalwork, and trade: the typical attributes of Neolithic village life.

Yet there is also early evidence of something quite new: central structures that served religious, economic, and administrative functions, something not found in Çatalhöyük. Starting out as shrines, these structures soon became impressive temples built of dried mud brick, like the bricks described in the story of Babel—and unlike the plentiful stone used at Jericho (the scarcity of stone meant that builders in this region had to be more resourceful). Each large settlement had such a temple, from which a priestly class acted as managers of the community's stored wealth and of the complex irrigation systems that would make the civilization of Sumer possible.

Urbanism in Uruk, 4300–2900 B.C.E.

After about 4300 B.C.E., Ubaid settlements developed into larger, more prosperous, and more highly organized communities. The most famous of these sites, Uruk, became the first Sumerian city-state. Its sophistication and scale is exemplified by the White Temple, built between 3500 and 3300 B.C.E. Its massive sloping platform looms nearly forty feet above the surrounding flatlands, and its four corners are oriented toward the cardinal points of the compass. Atop the platform stands the temple proper, dressed in brick and originally painted a brilliant white.

Such temples were eventually constructed in every Sumerian city, reflecting the central role that worship played in civic life. Uruk in particular seems to have owed its rapid growth to its importance as a religious center. By 3100 B.C.E. it encompassed several hundred acres, enclosing a population of 40,000 people within its massive brick walls. The larger villages of Sumer were also growing rapidly, attracting immigrants just as the great cities did. Grain and cloth production grew tenfold. Trade routes expanded dramatically. And to manage this increasingly complex economy, the Sumerians invented the technology on which most historians now rely: writing.

CUNEIFORM WRITING. The image on the left shows a Sumerian clay tablet from about 3000 B.C.E. Here, standardized pictures are beginning to represent abstractions: notice the symbol *ninda* (food) near the top. On the right, carvings on limestone from about 2600 B.C.E. reveal the evolution of cuneiform. ▪ *Why would such standardized pictograms have been easier to reproduce quickly?*

The Development of Writing

In 4000 B.C.E., the peoples of Sumer were already using clay tokens to keep inventories. Within a few centuries, they developed a practice of placing tokens inside hollow clay balls and inscribing, on the outside of each ball, the shapes of all the tokens it contained. By 3300 B.C.E., scribes had replaced these balls with flat clay tablets on which they inscribed symbols representing the tokens. These tablets made keeping the tokens themselves unnecessary, and they could also be archived for future reference or sent to other settlements as receipts or requests for goods.

Writing thus evolved as a practical recording technology to support economic pursuits. Because it existed to represent real things, its system of symbols—called *pictograms*—was also realistic: each pictogram resembled the thing it represented. Over time, however, a pictogram might be used not only to symbolize a physical object but to evoke an idea associated with that object. For example, the symbol for a bowl of food, *ninda*, might be used to express something more abstract, such as "nourishment." Pictograms also came to be associated with particular spoken sounds, or *phonemes*. Thus when a Sumerian scribe needed to employ the sound *ninda*, even as part of another word, he would use the symbol for a bowl of food to represent that phoneme. Later, special marks were added so that a reader could tell whether the writer meant it to represent the object itself, a larger concept, or a sound used in a context that might have nothing to do with food.

By 3100 B.C.E., Sumerian scribes also developed a specialized tool suited to the task of writing, a stylus made of reed. Because this stylus leaves an impression shaped like a wedge (in Latin, *cuneus*), this script is called *cuneiform* (*kyoo-NAY-i-form*). Cuneiform symbols could now be impressed more quickly into clay. And because the new stylus was not suited to drawing pictograms that accurately represented things, the symbols became even more abstract. Meanwhile, symbols were invented for every possible phonetic combination in the Sumerian language, reducing the number of necessary pictograms from about 1,200 to 600. Whereas the earliest pictograms could have been written and read by anyone, writing and reading now became specialized, powerful skills accessible only to a small and influential minority who were taught in special scribal schools.

THE CULTURE OF SUMER

The great centers of Sumerian civilization shared a common culture and a common language. They also shared a set of beliefs. However, this common religion did not produce peace. The residents of each city considered themselves to be the servants of a particular god, whom they sought to glorify by exalting their own city above others. The result was intense competition that frequently escalated into warfare. There was also an economic dimension to this conflict, since water rights and access to arable land and trade routes were often at stake.

Much of the economic production of a city passed through the great temple warehouses, where priests

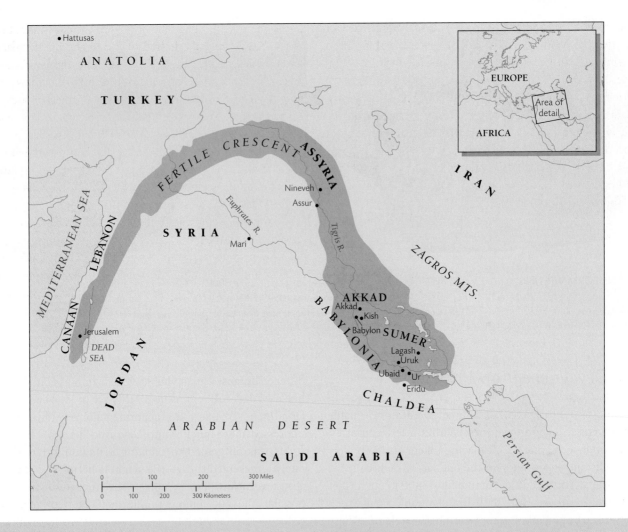

THE FERTILE CRESCENT. Notice the proximity of cities to rivers; consider the vital role played by the Tigris and Euphrates in shaping Mesopotamian civilizations. ■ *How many city-states can you identify on the map?* ■ *Why would these city-states have been clustered so closely together?* ■ *What challenges and opportunities would this present?*

redistributed the city's produce. During the third millennium, these great temples began to control the production of textiles, employing thousands of servile women and children. Temple elites also played a key role in long-distance trade, as both buyers and sellers of goods. So for any city-state to surrender its independence would not only offend the conquered city's god, it would jeopardize its entire economy and the power of its ruling class.

Each Sumerian city had its own aristocracy, the group from which priests were drawn. As much as half the population consisted of free persons who held parcels of land sufficient to sustain themselves, but the rest were dependents of the temple who worked as artisans or as agricultural laborers, and many of these dependents were slaves. Most of these slaves were prisoners of war from other Sumerian city-states whose bondage was limited to three years, after which time a slave had to be released.

But non-Sumerians could be held indefinitely, although a few might manage to buy their freedom. In either case, slaves were the property of their owners. They could be beaten, branded, bought, and sold like any other form of merchandise. Perhaps the only positive thing to say about slavery in antiquity is that it was egalitarian: anyone could become a slave. It was not until the beginning of the modern era that slavery became linked to race (see Chapter 14).

The Early Dynastic Period, 2900–2500 B.C.E.

Around 2900 B.C.E., conflicts among the growing Sumerian city-states became more acute. Competition for resources intensified and warfare became more frequent and destructive. A new type of military leadership began to emerge and eventually evolved into a form of kingship. Historians refer to this phase as the Early Dynastic Period because it was dominated by family dynasties, each headed by a war leader whose prestige earned him the title *lugal*: "big man." Unlike the priestly rulers of the Uruk Period, lugals did not see themselves as humble servants of the city's god. Rather, they believed that success in battle had earned them the right to exploit the city's wealth for their own glory.

The most striking expression of this development is the *Epic of Gilgamesh*, a series of stories recited over many generations and eventually written down on cuneiform tablets: the first literary monument in world history. It recounts the exploits of a lugal named Gilgamesh, who probably lived in Uruk sometime around 2700 B.C.E. Gilgamesh earns his legendary reputation through military conquest and personal heroism, particularly in campaigns against uncivilized—that is, nonurban—tribes. But he becomes so powerful that he ignores his own society's code of conduct; he disrespects the priesthood and commits acts of sacrilege. So the people of Uruk pray to the gods for retribution, and the gods fashion a wild man named Enkidu to challenge Gilgamesh.

The confrontation between Gilgamesh and Enkidu reveals the core values of Sumerian society. Gilgamesh is a creature of the city; Enkidu is a creature of the past, a hunter-gatherer. But then Enkidu has a sexual encounter with a beguiling woman and is unable to return to the wilderness: his urban initiation has civilized him and allowed him to befriend the lord of Uruk. Together they have many adventures. But Enkidu is eventually killed by the goddess Inanna, who punishes the friends for mocking her powers. Gilgamesh, distraught with grief, attempts to find a magical plant that will revive his friend. He finds it at the bottom of a deep pool, only to have it stolen from him by a water snake. In the end, he is forced to confront the futility of all human effort. He becomes "The One Who Looked into the Depths," the name by which his story was known to Sumerians. The larger message seems to be that not even civilization can shield humans from the forces of nature and the inevitability of death.

Sumerian Religion

In the Uruk Period, the Sumerians identified their gods with the capricious forces of the natural world. In the Early Dynastic Period, however, they came to imagine their gods as resembling the lugals who now ruled the city-states. Like these kings, the gods desired to live in the finest palaces and temples, to wear the costliest clothing and jewels, and to consume the tastiest foods. According to this new theology, which clearly reflects changes in Sumerian society, humans exist merely to provide for their gods. This was, indeed, why the gods had created people in the first place. There was thus a reciprocal relationship between humanity and divinity. The gods depended on their human servants to honor and sustain them; and in return, the gods occasionally bestowed gifts and favors.

As the gods' representatives on Earth, lugals bore special responsibilities and also enjoyed special privileges. Kings were thus set apart from all other men, including priests. But kings were also obliged to honor the gods through offerings, sacrifices, festivals, and massive building projects. Kings who neglected these duties, or who exalted themselves at the expense of the gods, were likely to bring disaster on themselves and their people. And even kings could not evade death.

Science, Technology, and Trade

The Sumerians' worldview was colored by their adversarial relationship with their surroundings. Precisely because neither their gods nor their environment were trustworthy, Sumerians cultivated a high degree of self-reliance and ingenuity. These qualities made them the most technologically innovative people of the ancient world.

For example, despite the fact that their land had no mineral deposits, the Sumerians became skilled metallurgists. By 6000 B.C.E., a number of cultures throughout

SUMERIAN WAR CHARIOTS. The earliest known representation of the wheel, dating from about 2600 B.C.E., shows how wheels were fashioned from slabs of wood. (For a later Mesopotamian wheel with spokes, see the illustration on page 51.)

The Flood: Two Accounts

> One of the oldest stories in the world tells of a great flood that devastated the lands and peoples of the earth, an event that can be traced to the warming of the earth's climate at the end of the last Ice Age. Many ancient cultures told versions of this story, and two of these are excerpted below. The first, included in the Epic of Gilgamesh, was written down during the first half of the third millennium B.C.E., making it at least 1,500 years older than the similar account in the Hebrew Bible. But both are probably the products of much older storytelling traditions. The hero of the Sumerian story is Utnapishtim. The Hebrew story's hero is Noah.

The Epic of Gilgamesh

Utnapishtim spoke to Gilgamesh, saying: "I will reveal to you, Gilgamesh . . . a secret of the gods. . . . The hearts of the Great Gods moved them to inflict the Flood. Their Father Anu uttered the oath (of secrecy). . . . [But the god] Ea . . . repeated their talk [to me, saying]: 'O man of Shuruppak, son of Ubartutu: Tear down the house and build a boat! . . . Spurn possessions and keep alive living beings! Make all living beings go up into the boat. The boat which you are to build, its dimensions must measure equal to each other: its length must correspond to its width. Roof it over like the Apsu.' I understood and spoke to my lord, Ea: 'My lord, thus is the command which you have uttered. I will heed and will do it.' . . . On the fifth day I laid out her exterior. It was a field in area, its walls were each 10 times 12 cubits in height. . . . I provided it with six decks, thus dividing it into seven (levels). . . . Whatever I had I loaded on it. . . . All the living beings that I had I loaded on it. I had all my kith and kin go up into the boat, all the beasts and animals of the field and the draftsmen I had go up.

"I watched the appearance of the weather—the weather was frightful to behold! I went into the boat and sealed the entry. . . . All day long the South Wind blew . . . , submerging the mountain in water, overwhelming the people like an attack. . . . Six days and seven nights came the wind and flood, the storm flattening the land. When the seventh day arrived . . . the sea calmed, fell still, the whirlwind and flood stopped up. . . . When a seventh day arrived, I sent forth a dove and released it. The dove went off, but came back to me, no perch was visible so it circled back to me. I sent forth a swallow and released it. The swallow went off, but came back to me, no perch was visible so it circled back to me. I sent forth a raven and released it. The raven went off, and saw the waters slither back. It eats, it scratches, it bobs, but does not circle back to me. Then I sent out everything in all directions and sacrificed (a sheep). I offered incense in front of the mountain-ziggurat. . . .

"The gods smelled the savor . . . and collected like flies over a sacrifice. . . . Just then Enlil arrived. He saw the boat and became furious. . . . 'Where did a living being escape? No man was to survive the annihilation!' Ea spoke to Valiant Enlil, saying . . . 'How, how could you bring about a Flood without consideration? Charge the violation to the

western Asia and Europe had learned how to produce weapons and tools using copper. By the Uruk Period (4300–2900 B.C.E.), trade routes were bringing this raw element into Sumer, where it was processed into weapons and tools. Shortly before 3000 B.C.E., people further discovered that copper could be alloyed with arsenic (or later, tin) to produce bronze. Bronze is almost as malleable as copper, and it pours more easily into molds; but when cooled, it maintains its rigidity and shape even better than copper. For almost two thousand years, until about 1200 B.C.E. and the development of techniques for smelting iron, bronze was the strongest metal known to man—the most useful and, in war, the most deadly. Following the Greeks (see Chapter 3), we call this period the Bronze Age.

Alongside writing and the making of bronze, the invention of the wheel was the fundamental technological violator, charge the offense to the offender, but be compassionate lest (mankind) be cut off, be patient lest they be killed.' Enlil went up inside the boat and,

grasping my hand, made me go up. He had my wife go up and kneel by my side. He touched our forehead and, standing between us, he blessed us. . . ."

Source: Maureen Gallery Kovacs, trans., *The Epic of Gilgamesh*, Tablet XI (Stanford, CA: 1985, 1989), pp. 97–103.

The Book of Genesis

The Lord saw that the wickedness of humankind was great in the earth and . . . said, "I will blot out from the earth the human beings I have created . . . for I am sorry I have made them." But Noah found favor in the sight of the Lord. . . . God saw that the earth was corrupt and . . . said to Noah, "I have determined to make an end to all flesh. . . . Make yourself an ark of cypress wood, make rooms in the ark, and cover it inside and out with pitch. . . . Make a roof for the ark, and put the door of the ark in its side. . . . For my part I am going to bring a flood on the earth, to destroy from under heaven all flesh. . . . But I will establish a covenant with you, and you shall come into the ark, you, your sons, your wife, and your sons' wives with you. And of every living thing you shall bring two of every kind into the ark, to keep them alive with you. . . . Also take with you every kind of food that is eaten." . . . All the

fountains of the great deep burst forth, and the windows of the heavens were opened. . . . The waters gradually receded from the earth. . . . At the end of forty days, Noah opened a window of the ark . . . and sent out the raven, and it went to and fro until the waters were dried up from the earth. Then he sent out the dove from him, to see if the waters had subsided from the face of the ground, but the dove found no place to set its foot, and it returned. . . . He waited another seven days, and again sent out the dove [which] came back to him . . . and there in its beak was a freshly plucked olive leaf, so Noah knew the waters had subsided from the earth. Then he . . . sent out the dove, and it did not return to him anymore. . . . Noah built an altar to the Lord . . . and offered burnt offerings. And when the Lord smelled the pleasing odor, the Lord said in his heart, "I will never again curse the ground because of humankind . . . nor

will I ever again destroy every living creature as I have done." . . . God blessed Noah and his sons.

Source: Genesis 6:5–9:1, *The New Oxford Annotated Bible* (Oxford: 1994).

Questions for Analysis

1. What are the similarities and differences between these two accounts?

2. What do these differences or similarities reveal about the two societies that told these stories? Does one seem to derive from the other? Why or why not?

3. How is the geography and climate of Mesopotamia reflected in the Sumerian version of the story?

achievement of the era. The Sumerians were using potter's wheels by the middle of the fourth millennium B.C.E. and could produce high-quality clay vessels in greater quantity than ever before. By around 3200 B.C.E., the Sumerians were also using two- and four-wheeled chariots and carts drawn by donkeys. (Horses were unknown in this region until sometime between 2000 and 1700 B.C.E.). Chariots were another new and deadly military technology, giving

warriors a tremendous advantage over armies on foot: the earliest depiction of their use, dating from 2600 B.C.E., shows one trampling an enemy. At the same time, wheeled carts dramatically increased the productivity of the Sumerian workforce.

Other inventions derived from the study of mathematics. In order to construct their elaborate irrigation systems, the Sumerians had to develop sophisticated

Past and Present

Engineering Nature

Humans have been manipulating our planet's environment since the Neolithic Revolution. The image on the left shows the irrigation canals that enabled ancient Egyptians to channel the Nile's life-giving waters into the desert. The image on the right shows a storm-surge barrier in the Netherlands, which protects reclaimed land from rising sea levels (ironically) caused by the cumulative results of man-made climate change.

Watch related author videos on the Student Site
wwnorton.com/college/history/western-civilizationsBrief4

measuring and surveying techniques as well as the art of map making. Agricultural needs may also lie behind the lunar calendar they invented, which consisted of twelve months, six lasting 30 days and six lasting 29 days. Since this produced a year of only 354 days, the Sumerians eventually began to add a month to their calendars every few years in order to predict the recurrence of the seasons with sufficient accuracy. The Sumerian practice of dividing time into multiples of sixty has lasted to the present day, not only in our notion of the 30-day month but also in our division of the hour into sixty minutes, each comprised of sixty seconds. Mathematics also contributed to Sumerian architecture, allowing them to build domes and arches thousands of years before the Romans would adopt and spread these architectural forms throughout their empire (Chapter 5).

Sumerian technology depended not only on ingenuity but also the spread of information and raw materials through trade. Sumerian pioneers traced routes up and down the rivers and into the hinterlands of Mesopotamia, following the tributaries of the Tigris and Euphrates. They blazed trails across the deserts toward the west, where they interacted with and influenced the Egyptians. By sea, they traded with the peoples of the Persian Gulf and, directly or indirectly, with the civilizations of the Indus Valley (modern Pakistan and India). And, along with merchandise, they carried ideas: stories, art, the use of writing, and the whole cultural complex that arose from their way of life. The elements of civilization, which had fused in their urban crucible, would thus come together in many other places.

THE FIRST EMPIRES

Evidence shows that competition among Sumerian city-states reached a new level around 2500 B.C.E., as ambitious lugals vied to magnify themselves and their kingdoms. Still, it seems that no Sumerian lugal ever attempted to create an empire by imposing centralized rule on the cities he conquered. As a result, Sumer remained a collection of interdependent but mutually hostile states whose rulers were unable to forge any lasting structures of authority. This pattern would ultimately make the people of Sumer vulnerable to a new style of imperial rulership imposed on them from the north in the person of Sargon the Akkadian.

Sargon and the Akkadian Empire, 2350–2160 B.C.E.

The Akkadians were the predominant people of central Mesopotamia. Their Sumerian neighbors to the south had greatly influenced them, and they had adopted cuneiform script along with many other elements of Sumerian culture. Yet the Akkadians preserved their own Semitic language, part of the linguistic family that includes Hebrew and Arabic. Sumerians tended to regard them as uncivilized, but in the case of the lugal whom the Akkadians called "great king," this probably meant not being bound by the conventions of Sumerian warfare. For Sargon initiated a systematic program of conquest designed to subject all the neighboring regions to his authority. By 2350 B.C.E., he had conquered the cities of Sumer and then moved to establish direct control over all of Mesopotamia.

From his capital at Akkad, Sargon installed Akkadian-speaking governors to rule the cities of Sumer, ordering them to pull down existing fortifications, collect taxes, and obey his will. Sargon thus transformed the independent city-states of Sumer and Akkad into a much larger political unit: the first known empire, a word derived from the Latin *imperium*, "command." This enabled him to manage and exploit the network of trade routes crisscrossing the power broader area known as the Near East. So although his political influence was felt only in Mesopotamia, his economic influence stretched from Ethiopia to India. Sargon's capital became the most splendid city in the world, and he exercised unprecedented power for a remarkable fifty-six years.

Sargon's imperialism also had a marked effect on Sumerian religion. To unite the two halves of his empire, Sargon merged Akkadian and Sumerian divinities. He also tried to lessen the rivalry of Sumerian cities by appointing a single Akkadian high priest or priestess, often a member of his own family, to preside over several local temples.

Sargon's successor, his grandson Naram-Sin, extended Akkadian conquests and consolidated trade, helping to stimulate the growth of cities throughout the Near East and binding them more closely together. By 2200 B.C.E., most people in central and southern Mesopotamia would have been able to converse in the language of either the Sumerians or the Akkadians. Indeed, the two civilizations became virtually indistinguishable except for these different languages.

The Dynasty of Ur and the Amorites, 2100–1800 B.C.E.

After Naram-Sin's death, Akkadian rule faltered. Around 2100 B.C.E., however, a new dynasty came to power in Ur under its first king, Ur-Nammu, and his son Shulgi. Ur-Nammu was responsible for the construction of the great ziggurat at Ur, a massive temple complex that originally rose seventy feet above the surrounding plain. Shulgi continued his father's work, subduing the lands up to the Zagros Mountains northeast of Ur and demanding massive tribute payments from them; one collection site accounted for 350,000 sheep per year, and Shulgi built state-run textile-production facilities to process the wool. He promulgated a code of law, calling for fair weights and measures, the protection of widows and orphans, and limitations on the death penalty for crimes. He also pursued military conquests, the centralization of government, commercial expansion and consolidation, and the patronage of art and literature. Shulgi thus established a pattern of rule that influenced the region for centuries to come.

The Empire of Hammurabi

In 1792 B.C.E., a young Amorite chieftain named Hammurabi (*hah-muh-RAH-bee*) became the ruler of Babylon, an insignificant city in central Mesopotamia. The Amorites, like the Akkadians, were a Semitic people. Until this period they had largely been nomads and warriors, but now they came to control the ancient cities of Mesopotamia.

THE ZIGGURAT OF UR. Built around 2100 B.C.E., this great temple is the best-preserved structure of its kind. It is located at Nasiriyah, in what is now Iraq. Archaeological research (see diagram) reveals that its central shrine, the most sacred part of the temple, was reached by climbing four sets of stairs and passing through a massive portal.

Hammurabi may have been the first ruler in history to understand that power need not be based on force. He recognized that military intelligence, diplomacy, and strategic planning might accomplish what his small army could not. For Hammurabi used writing itself as a weapon. He did not try to confront his mightier neighbors directly. Rather, through letters and embassies, double-dealing and cunning, he induced his stronger counterparts to fight each other. While other Amorite kings exhausted their resources in costly wars, Hammurabi fanned their mutual hatred and skillfully portrayed himself as a friend and ally to all sides. Meanwhile, he quietly strengthened his kingdom, built up his army, and, when the time was right, fell on his depleted neighbors. By such policies, he transformed his small state into what historians call the Old Babylonian Empire.

Under Hammurabi's rule, Mesopotamia achieved an unprecedented degree of political integration. Ultimately, his empire stretched from the Persian Gulf into Assyria. To help unify these territories, Hammurabi introduced another innovation, promoting the worship of the little-known patron god of Babylon, Marduk, and making him the ruler-god of his entire empire. Although he also paid homage to the ancient gods of Sumer and Akkad, Hammurabi made it clear that all his subjects now owed allegiance to Marduk.

The idea that political power derives from divine approval was nothing new, but Hammurabi's genius was to use Marduk's supremacy over all other gods to legitimate his own claim to rule in Marduk's name, because he was king of Marduk's home city. Hammurabi thus became the first known ruler to launch wars of aggression justified in the name of his primary god. This set a precedent for colonial expansion that would become a characteristic feature of Near Eastern politics, as we will see in Chapter 2, and that lies behind nearly all imperial ventures down to the present day.

Yet Hammurabi did not rely solely on religion to bind his empire together. Building on the precedents of past rulers, he also issued a collection of laws, copies of which were inscribed on stone and set up in public places throughout his realm. The example that survives (see page 19) is an eight-foot-tall *stele* (*STEH-leh*) made of gleaming black basalt, originally erected in a central marketplace. The upper portion shows Hammurabi consulting with the god of justice. The phallic form on which the laws were inscribed would have been immediately recognizable as a potent symbol of Hammurabi's authority, obvious even to those who could not read the laws themselves. (It still makes a strong impression on visitors to the Louvre museum in Paris.)

It is impossible to overemphasize the importance of Hammurabi's decision to become a lawgiver. By collecting and codifying legal precedents, like those of Shulgi, Hammurabi declared himself to be (as he stated in the code's preamble) "the shepherd of the people, the capable king"—not a lugal ruling through fear and caprice. This set a new standard of kingship, and expressed a new vision of empire as a union of peoples subject to the same laws.

Law and Society under Hammurabi

The Code of Hammurabi reveals a great deal about the structure and values of Babylonian society. Its 282 pronouncements begin with legislation against false testimony (fraud or lying under oath) and theft; followed by laws regulating business deals; laws regulating the use of public resources, especially water; laws relating to taverns and brothels, many of which appear to have been run by women; laws relating to debt and slavery; many laws dealing with marriage, inheritance, divorce, and widows' rights; and finally laws punishing murder, violent assault, and even medical malpractice. What emerges is a fascinating picture of a complex urban culture that required more formal legislation than the accumulated customs of previous generations.

The division among classes in Babylonian society was marked. As Hammurabi's code indicates, an offense committed against a nobleman carried a far more severe penalty than the same crime committed against a social equal, or against a dependent or slave; nobles were also punished more severely than were commoners for crimes they committed against other nobles. Hammurabi's code also provides evidence as to the status of women in Babylonian society, and shows that they enjoyed certain important protections under the law, including the right to divorce abusive or indigent husbands. If a husband divorced a wife "without cause," he was obliged to provide financial support for her and their children. However, a wife who went around the city defaming her spouse was subject to severe punishment, and she would risk death (as would her lover) if she were caught in adultery. The sexual promiscuity of husbands, by contrast, was protected under the law.

Hammurabi died around 1750 B.C.E., but his administrative efforts created a durable state in Mesopotamia. For another two centuries, the Old Babylonian Empire played a significant role in the Near East, until invaders from the north sacked the capital and occupied it. But even for another thousand years thereafter, Babylon remained the region's most famous city.

THE DEVELOPMENT OF CIVILIZATION IN EGYPT

At about the same time that Sumerian civilization was transforming Mesopotamia, another civilization was taking shape in a very different part of the world and in very different ways. Unlike the Sumerians, the Egyptians did not have to wrest survival from a hostile and unpredictable environment. Instead, their land was renewed every year by the flooding of the Nile River. The fertile black soil left behind every summer made theirs the richest agricultural region in the entire Mediterranean world.

The distinctiveness of Egyptian civilization rests on this fundamental ecological fact. It also explains why ancient Egypt was a narrow, elongated kingdom, running along the Nile north from the First Cataract toward the Mediterranean Sea for a distance of more than 600 miles (1,100 km). Outside this narrow band of territory—which ranged from a few hundred yards to no more than 14 miles (23 km)—lay uninhabitable desert. This contrast, between the fertile Black Land along the Nile and the dessicated Red Land beyond, deeply influenced the Egyptian worldview, in which the Nile itself was the center of the cosmos and the lands beyond were hostile.

Ancient Egyptian civilization enjoyed a remarkable continuity. Its roots date back to (at least) 5000 B.C.E. From about 3000 B.C.E., the defining element of this civilization would be the pervasive influence of a powerful, centralized, bureaucratic state headed by pharaohs who were regarded as living gods. No other civilization in world history has ever been governed so steadily, for so long, as ancient Egypt.

For convenience, historians have traditionally divided ancient Egyptian history into distinctive "kingdoms" and "periods." Following ancient Egyptian chroniclers, modern historians have also tended to portray these Old, Middle, and New Kingdoms as characterized by unity and prosperity, punctuated by chaotic interludes when central authority broke down: the so-called Intermediate Periods. Like all attempts at periodization, however, these divisions do not capture the complexities of human experience or even the real pace of historical development.

Predynastic Egypt, c. 10,000–3100 B.C.E.

The phrase *Predynastic Egypt* refers to the period before the emergence of the pharaohs and their royal dynasties—an era for which archaeological evidence is difficult to find and interpret. The first-known permanent settlement in Egypt, situated at the southwestern edge of the Nile Delta (near the modern town of Merimde Beni Salama) dates to approximately 4750 B.C.E. It was a farming community that may have numbered as many as 16,000 residents, and this number

Analyzing Primary Sources

The Code of Hammurabi

The laws of Hammurabi, published on the authority of this powerful king and set up in central places throughout the Old Babylonian Empire, were influenced both by the needs of an urban society and by older ideas of justice and punishment common among Semitic peoples. In its entirety, the code comprises 282 laws, beginning and ending with statements of Hammurabi's devotion to the gods, his peace-keeping mission, and his sense of his duties as king. The following excerpts are numbered so as to show the order in which these provisions appear on the stele that publicizes them.

hen the god Marduk commanded me to provide just ways for the people of the land in order to attain appropriate behavior, I established truth and justice as the declaration of the land. I enhanced the well-being of the people.

* * *

1. If a man accuses another man and charges him with homicide but cannot bring proof against him, his accuser shall be killed.

2. If a man charges another man with practicing witchcraft but cannot bring proof against him, he who is charged with witchcraft shall go to the divine River Ordeal, he shall indeed submit to the divine River Ordeal; if the divine River Ordeal should overwhelm him, his accuser shall take full legal possession of his estate; if the divine River Ordeal should clear that man and should he survive, he who made the charge of witchcraft against him shall be killed; he who submitted to the divine River Ordeal shall take full legal possession of his accuser's estate.

If a man comes forward to give false testimony in a case but cannot bring evidence for his accusation, if that case involves a capital offense, that man shall be killed.

* * *

6. If a man steals valuables belonging to the god or to the palace, that man shall be killed, and also he who received the stolen goods from him shall be killed.

7. If a man should purchase silver, gold, a slave, a slave woman, an ox, a sheep, a donkey, or anything else whatsoever, from a son of a man or from a slave of a man without witnesses or a contract—or if he accepts the goods for safe-keeping—that man is a thief, he shall be killed.

8. If a man steals an ox, a sheep, a donkey, a pig, or a boat—if it belongs either to the god or to the palace, he shall give thirtyfold; if it belongs to a commoner, he shall replace it tenfold; if the thief does not have anything to give, he shall be killed.

* * *

15. If a man should enable a palace slave, a palace slave woman, a commoner's slave, or a commoner's slave woman to leave through the main city-gate, he shall be killed.

* * *

53. If a man neglects to reinforce the embankment of the irrigation canal of his field and then a breach opens and allows the water to carry away the common irrigated area, the man in whose embankment the breach opened shall replace the grain whose loss he caused.

* * *

104. If a merchant gives a trading agent grain, wool, oil, or any other commodity for local transactions, the trading agent shall collect a sealed receipt for each payment in silver that he gives to the merchant.

* * *

128. If a man marries a wife but does not draw up a formal contract for her, she is not a wife.

129. If a man's wife should be seized lying with another male, they shall bind them and throw them into the water; if the wife's master allows his wife to live, then the king shall allow his subject (i.e., the other male) to live.

* * *

142. If a woman repudiates her husband, and declares, "You will not have marital relations with me"—her circumstances shall be investigated by the authorities of her city quarter, and if she is circumspect and without fault, but her husband is wayward and disparages her greatly, that woman will not be subject to any penalty; she shall take her dowry and she shall depart for her father's house.

Source: Martha T. Roth, ed., *Law Collections from Ancient Mesopotamia and Asia Minor* (Atlanta, GA: 1995), pp. 76–135 (excerpted).

THE CODE OF HAMMURABI. The laws of Hammurabi survive on an eight-foot column made of basalt. The top quarter of the column depicts the Babylonian king (standing, at left) being vested with authority by Shamash, the god of justice. Directly below, one can make out the cuneiform inscriptions that are the law code's text. ■ *How would the physical format of these laws send a powerful message about Hammurabi's kingship?*

Questions for Analysis

1. Based on these excerpts, what conclusions can you draw about the values of Old Babylonian society? For example, what types of crimes are punishable by death, and why?

2. In what ways does the Code of Hammurabi exhibit the influences of the urban civilization for which these laws were issued? What are some characteristics and consequences of urbanization? What, for example, do we learn about economic developments?

ANCIENT EGYPT AND THE NEAR EAST. Notice the peculiar geography of ancient Egypt and the role played by the Nile River. Identify the Nile on the map. ▪ *In what direction does the Nile flow?* ▪ *How did the lands on either side help to isolate Egyptian culture from outside influences?* ▪ *Consider how the Nile helped forge Egypt into a unitary state under a powerful centralized government. Yet how might Egypt's relationship to the Nile be potentially hazardous, as well as beneficial?*

suggests that some Egyptian communities were much larger than those of a comparable period in Mesopotamia. Many other Neolithic farming centers have also been discovered in or near the Nile Delta, where a degree of cultural cohesiveness was already developing, fostered by shared interests and trade. In later centuries, this northern area would be known as Lower Egypt, so called because it was downstream.

Although towns in Lower Egypt were numerous, it was in Upper Egypt that the first Egyptian cities developed. By 3200 B.C.E. (when the Sumerian city of Uruk had been thriving for a thousand years), important communities such as Nekhen, This, and Abydos had all developed high degrees of occupational and social specialization. They had encircled

themselves with sophisticated fortifications and had begun to build elaborate shrines to honor their gods. Indeed, the establishment of permanent sites of public worship may be key to explaining the growth of these towns into cities. As in Mesopotamia, a city's role as the center of a prominent religious cult attracted travelers and encouraged the growth of industries. And travel in Upper Egypt was relatively easy compared to Mesopotamia. The Nile bound cities together, and almost all Egyptians lived within sight of it.

It was due to the Nile, therefore, that the region south of the delta was able to forge a cultural and eventually a political unity, despite its enormous length. The Nile fed Egypt and was also a conduit for people, goods, and ideas.

Centralizing rulers could project their power quickly and effectively up and down its course. Within a remarkably short time, just a century or two after the first cities' appearance in Upper Egypt, they had banded together in a confederacy. The pressure exerted by this confederacy in turn forced the towns of Lower Egypt to adopt their own form of political organization. By 3100 B.C.E., the rivalry between these competing regions had given rise to the two nascent kingdoms of Upper and Lower Egypt.

The Power of the Pharaoh, c. 3100 – c. 2686 B.C.E.

With the rise of powerful rulers in these two kingdoms, Egyptian history enters a new phase, one that can be chronicled with unusual precision. The system for numbering the ruling dynasties that emerged in this era—known as the Archaic Period—was actually devised nearly three thousand years later by an historian named Manetho (*mahn-EH-thoh*), who wrote in the third century B.C.E. By and large, Manetho's work has withstood the scrutiny of modern historians and archaeologists, although recent research has added a "Zero Dynasty" of early kings who were instrumental in bringing about the initial unification of Egypt.

Manetho did not record these rulers because he didn't know about them; we know them almost exclusively from archaeological evidence. Among them was an Upper Egyptian warlord known to us as King Scorpion, because the image of a scorpion accompanies engravings that assert his authority. Another warlord, King Narmer, appears to have ruled both Upper and Lower Egypt. His exploits, too, come down to us in powerful pictures (see **Interpreting Visual Evidence** on page 22). Both of these kings probably came from Abydos in Upper Egypt, where they were buried. Their administrative capital, however, was at Memphis, the capital city of Lower Egypt and an important center for trade with the Sinai Peninsula and the Near East.

Following the political unification of Upper and Lower Egypt, the basic features of Egypt's distinctive centralized kingship took shape along lines that would persist for the next 3,000 years. The title used to describe this kingship was *pharaoh*, a word that actually means "great household" and thus refers not to an individual king but to the whole apparatus that sustains his rule. This fact, in turn, helps to explain the extraordinary stability and longevity of Egyptian civilization, which could survive even a dynastic takeover by Macedonian Greeks in the century before Manetho wrote his chronicle (Chapter 4). Indeed, it is comparable to some modern forms of government—none of which has yet lasted so long. As we have seen, kingship in Mesopotamia tended to be a form of personal rule, dependent on the charisma of a particular individual. But in Egypt, the office of the pharaoh was durable enough to survive the deaths of individual successors, facilitating the peaceful transition of power to new rulers and withstanding the incompetence of many.

This was accomplished, as we shall see, by the efficiency of palace bureaucracy, but it was also a function of the pharaoh's close identification with the divine forces credited with renewing Egypt every year. Like the seasons, the pharaoh died only to be born again, renewed and empowered. Egyptian rulers thus laid claim to a sacred nature quite different—and much more benign—than that governing Sumeria. And they were more powerful than any Sumerian lugal, who was never more than a mortal who enjoyed (an all-too-temporary) divine favor.

How the earliest kings of Egypt came to be distinguished as pharaohs and to establish their claims to divinity is still not well understood. We do know, however, that legitimating their rule over all Egypt was difficult. Local civic and religious loyalties remained strong, and for centuries Lower Egyptians would continue to see themselves as distinct from their neighbors to the south. Indeed, it seems probable that the centralization of government in the person of the pharaoh and his association with divinity were related approaches to solving the problem of political unity. And together, these measures had astonishing success. By the end of the Second Dynasty, which coincides with the end of the Archaic Period (2686 B.C.E.), the pharaoh was not just the ruler of Egypt, he *was* Egypt: a personification of the land, the people, and their gods.

The Old Kingdom, c. 2686–2160 B.C.E.

Because so few written sources from the Old Kingdom survive, historians have to rely on funerary texts from the tombs of the elite. These sources are hardly representative, and they have tended to convey the impression that Egyptians were obsessed with death; they also tell us little about the lives of ordinary people. Further complicating the historian's task is the early Egyptians' own belief in the unchanging, cyclical nature of the universe. This makes it difficult for us to reconstruct their history in detail.

However, the surviving inscriptions, papyri, and art of the Third Dynasty (c. 2686–2613 B.C.E.) do tell us a great deal about the workings of the "great household" that undergirded individual rulers' power. This power was vast because the pharaoh was considered to be the intermediary between the land, its people, and their gods, so all the resources of Egypt belonged to him. Long-distance trade

Interpreting Visual Evidence

The Narmer Palette

The Narmer Palette (c. 3100 B.C.E.) is a double-sided carving made of green silt-stone. Palettes were used to grind pigments for the making of cosmetics, but the large size (63 cm, over 2 feet) of this one is unusual. It was discovered in 1897 by archaeologists excavating a temple dedicated to the god Horus at Nekhen, the capital of Upper Egypt. Found nearby were other artifacts, including the so-called Narmer Macehead, thought to depict the marriage of Narmer, king of Upper Egypt, to a princess of Lower Egypt.

On the left, dominating the central panel, Narmer wears the White Crown of Upper Egypt (image A). He wields a mace and seizes the hair of a captive kneeling at his feet. Above the captive's head is a cluster of lotus leaves (a symbol of Lower Egypt) and a falcon representing the god Horus, who may be drawing the captive's life force (*ka*) from his body. The figure behind Narmer is carrying the king's sandals; he is depicted as smaller because he is an inferior. The two men in the lower panel are either running or sprawling on the ground, and the symbols above them indicate the name of a defeated town. On the right, the other side of the palette shows Narmer as the chief figure in a procession (image B). He now wears the Red Crown of Lower Egypt and holds a

A. Narmer wearing the White Crown of Egypt.

B. Narmer wearing the Red Crown of Egypt.

mace and a flail, symbols of conquest. Behind him is the same servant carrying his sandals, and in front of him are a man with long hair and four standard-bearers. There are also ten headless corpses. Below, the entwined necks of two mythical creatures (serpopards, leopards with serpents' heads) are tethered to leashes held by two men. In the lowest section, a bull tramples the body of a man whose city the bull is destroying.

Questions for Analysis

1. This artifact has been called "the first historical document in the world," but scholars still debate its meanings.

For example, does it represent something that actually happened, or is it political propaganda? In your view, is this proof that Narmer has united two kingdoms? Why or why not?

2. Do the two sides of the palette tell a coherent story and, if so, on which side does that story begin?

3. What might be significant about the site where the palette was found? Should the palette be interpreted as belonging with the mace found nearby? If so, how might that influence your interpretation of the palette's significance?

was entirely controlled by the pharaoh, as were systems for imposing taxation and conscripting labor. To administer these, the pharaohs installed provincial governors, known to the Greeks as *nomarchs*, many of whom were members of the pharaoh's own family.

Old Kingdom pharaohs kept tight control over the nomarchs and their armies of lesser officials in order to prevent them from establishing local roots in the territories they administered. Writing was therefore critical to internal communication and the management and exploitation of Egypt's vast wealth. This gave rise to a whole class of scribal administrators who enjoyed the power, influence, and status that went along with literacy, a skill few people could command—especially in Egypt, since only experts could master the intricacies of hieroglyphic reading or writing. Even a child just beginning his scribal education was considered worthy of great respect because the training was so difficult. But it carried great rewards. Indeed, the scribal author of a document from the Middle Kingdom called "The Satire of the Trades" exhorted the beginning student to persevere by reminding him how much better off he would be than everyone else.

The Power of Writing

Among the many facets of Egyptian culture that have fascinated generations of scholars is the Egyptian system of pictographic writing. Called *hieroglyphs* (HI-eroh-glifs) or "sacred carvings" by the Greeks, these strange and elaborate symbols remained completely impenetrable (and thus all the more mysterious) until the nineteenth century, when a French scholar named Jean-François Champollion deciphered them with the help of history's most famous decoding device, the Rosetta Stone. This *stele* preserves three versions of the same decree issued in 196 B.C.E., written in ancient Greek, demotic (a later Egyptian script), and hieroglyphics—still in use after more than 3,000 years. Because he could read the text in Greek, Champollion was eventually able to translate the demotic and hieroglyphic texts as well. From this beginning, generations of scholars have added to and refined the knowledge of ancient Egyptian language.

The development of hieroglyphic writing in Egypt dates to around 3200 B.C.E., when pictograms begin to appear in Mesopotamia. But the uses of writing for government and administration developed far more quickly in Egypt than in Sumer. And unlike Sumerian cuneiform, Egyptian hieroglyphics never evolved into a system of phonograms. Instead, the Egyptians developed a faster, cursive script for representing hieroglyphics, called *hieratic* script, which they employed for the everyday business of government and commerce. They also developed a shorthand version that scribes could use for rapid note-taking. Little of this hieratic script remains, however, due to the perishable nature of the medium on which it was usually written: papyrus.

Produced by hammering, drying, and processing river reeds, papyrus was much lighter, easier to write on, and more transportable than the clay tablets used by the Sumerians. When sewn together into scrolls, papyrus also made it possible to record and store large quantities of information in very small packages. Production of this versatile writing material remained one of Egypt's most important industries and exports throughout antiquity and into the Middle Ages. Yet even in the arid environment of Egypt, which has preserved so many ancient artifacts, papyrus is fragile and subject to decay. Compared to the huge volume of papryrus documents that would have been produced, therefore, the quantity that survives is small, and this significantly limits our understanding of Old Kingdom Egypt.

The origins of the ancient Egyptian language in which these texts were written has long been a matter of debate, and it can be plausibly linked to both the Semitic languages of the Near East and a number of African language groups. Whatever its origins, the Egyptian language has enjoyed a long history. Eventually, it became the tongue known as Coptic, which is still used today in the liturgy of the Coptic Christian church in Ethiopia.

THE ROSETTA STONE. This famous *stele*, carved in 196 B.C.E., preserves three translations of a single decree in three different forms of writing: hieroglyphs (top), demotic Egyptian (middle), and classical Greek (bottom). ▪ *Why would scholars be able to use the classical Greek text to decipher the hieroglyphic and demotic scripts?*

Imhotep and the Pyramids

One of the greatest administrative officials in the history of Egypt exemplifies both the skills and the possibilities for advancement that the consummate scribe could command. Imhotep (*im-HO-tep*) rose through the ranks of the pharaoh's administration to become a sort of prime minister to Djoser (*ZOH-ser*), a pharaoh of the Third Dynasty around 2650 B.C.E. Imhotep's learning included medicine, astronomy, theology, and mathematics—but above all he was an architect. Earlier pharaohs had already devoted enormous resources to their burial arrangements at Abydos. It was Imhotep, however, who designed the Step Pyramid, the first building in history constructed entirely of dressed stone. It was not only to be the final resting place of Djoser but an expression of his transcendent power as the pharaoh.

Built west of the administrative capital at Memphis, the Step Pyramid towers 200 feet over the desert. Surrounding this structure was a huge temple and mortuary complex, perhaps modeled after Djoser's palace. These buildings served two purposes. First and foremost, they would provide Djoser's *ka*, his spirit or life force, with a habitation and sustenance in the afterlife. Second, the design of the buildings, with their labyrinthine passageways, would (it was hoped) thwart tomb robbers, a chronic problem as pharaonic burials became more and more tempting to thieves.

Imhotep set a precedent to which all other Old Kingdom pharaohs would aspire. The pyramids on the plain of Giza, built during the Fourth Dynasty (2613–2494 B.C.E.), are a case in point. The Great Pyramid itself, built for the pharaoh Khufu (*KOO-foo*, called Cheops by the Greeks), was originally 481 feet high and 756 feet along each side of its base, constructed from more than 2.3 million limestone blocks and enclosing a volume of about 91 million cubic feet. In ancient times, the entire pyramid was encased in gleaming white limestone and topped by a gilded capstone,

STEP PYRAMID OF KING DJOSER. This monument to the pharoah's power and divinity was designed by the palace official Imhotep around 2650 B.C.E. It served as a prototype for the pyramids constructed at Giza in the following century.

as were the two massive but slightly smaller pyramids built for Khufu's successors. During the Middle Ages, the Muslim rulers of nearby Cairo had their builders strip off the pyramid's casing stones and used them to construct and fortify their new city. (The gold capstones had probably disappeared already.) But in antiquity these pyramids would have glistened brilliantly by day and glowed by night, making them visible for miles in all directions. The Greek historian Herodotus (*heh-RAH-duh-tuhs*), who toured Egypt more than 2,000 years after the pyramids were built, estimated that it must have taken 100,000 laborers 20 years to build the Great Pyramid. This is probably an exaggeration, but it is a measure of the impression these monuments made.

Once thought to have been the work of slaves, the pyramids were in fact raised by tens of thousands of peasant workers, who labored most intensively on the pyramids while their fields were under water during the Nile's annual flood. Still, the investment of human and material resources required to build the great pyramids put grave strains on Egyptian society. Control over the lives of individual Egyptians increased and the number of administrative officials employed by the state grew ever larger. So too did the contrast between the lifestyle of the pharaoh's splendid court at Memphis and that of Egyptian society as a whole.

The End of the Old Kingdom

For reasons that are not entirely clear, the Fifth and Sixth Dynasties of the Old Kingdom (2494–2181 B.C.E.) witnessed the slow erosion of pharaonic power. Although pyramid construction continued, the monuments of this period are less impressive in design, craftsmanship, and size, perhaps mirroring the diminishing prestige of the pharaohs who ordered them built. Instead, the priesthood of Ra at Nekhen, which was the center of worship for the god Horus and the place where Narmer's unification of Egypt was memorialized, began to assert its own authority over that of the pharaoh. Ultimately, it declared that the pharaoh was not an incarnation of Horus or Ra, but merely the god's earthly son. This was a blow to the heart of Egyptian political theology. More practically threatening was the growing power of the pharaoh's nomarchs, whose increased authority in the provinces allowed them to become a hereditary local nobility: precisely what the vigorous kings of earlier dynasties had refused to permit.

Scholars are uncertain as to how some priests and local officials were able to take power away from the pharaonic center. It may be that the costly building efforts of the Fourth Dynasty had overstrained the economy, while the

PYRAMIDS AT GIZA. The Great Pyramid of Khufu (Cheops) is in the center, and was completed c. 2560 B.C.E. The pyramids are not only monuments to pharaonic power, they also exemplify the enormous wealth and human resources of Egyptian society.

EGYPTIAN CULTURE AND SOCIETY

As already noted, the environment of Egypt and the special benefits it conferred on its inhabitants were construed as peculiar divine gifts, renewed each year through the mediation of the pharoah, who was god on earth. Although the Egyptians told a variety of stories that dealt with the creation of their world, these were not greatly concerned with how humanity came to exist. Rather, what mattered was the means by which all life was created and re-created in an endless cycle of renewal.

Egyptian Religion and Worldview

At the heart of Egyptian religion lay the myth of Osiris and Isis, two of the gods most fundamental to Egyptian belief. Osiris was, in a sense, the first pharaoh: the first god to hold kingship on earth. But his brother, Seth, wanted the throne for himself. So Seth betrayed and killed Osiris, sealing his body in a coffin. Then his loyal sister Isis retrieved the corpse and managed to revive it long enough to conceive her brother's child, the god Horus. Enraged by this, Seth seized Osiris' body and hacked it to pieces, spreading the remains all over Egypt. Still undeterred, Isis sought the help of Anubis, the god of the afterlife. Together, they found, reassembled, and preserved the scattered portions of Osiris' body, thus inventing the practice of mummification. Afterward, Horus, with the help of his mother, managed to defeat Seth. Osiris was avenged and revived as god of the underworld, and the cycle of his death, dismemberment, and resurrection was reflected in the yearly renewal of Egypt itself.

Life and Death in Ancient Egypt

In addition to embodying Egypt's continual regeneration, Osiris exemplified the Egyptian attitude toward death, which was very different from the Sumerians' bleak view. For the Egyptians, death was a rite of passage, a journey to be endured on the way to an afterlife that was more or less like one's earthly existence, only better. To be sure, the journey was full of dangers. After death, the individual body's *ka*, or life force, would have to roam the Duat, the underworld, searching for the House of Judgment. There, Osiris and forty-two other judges would decide the ka's fate. Demons and evil spirits might try to frustrate the ka's quest to reach the House of Judgment, and the journey might take some time. But if successful and judged worthy, the deceased would enjoy immortality as an aspect of Osiris.

continued channeling of resources to the royal capital at Memphis increased shortages and resentments in the provinces. Other evidence points to changing climatic conditions that may have disrupted the regular inundations of the Nile, leading to famine in the countryside. Meanwhile, small states were beginning to form to the south in Nubia. With better organization and equipment, the Nubians may have restricted Egyptian access to precious metal deposits, further crippling the Egyptian economy.

As a result, the pharaoh's power diminished. Local governors and religious authorities began to emerge as the only effective guarantors of stability and order. By 2160 B.C.E., which marks the beginning of what historians call the First Intermediate Period, Egypt had effectively ceased to exist as a united entity. The central authority of the pharaoh in Memphis collapsed, and a more ancient distribution of power reemerged: a northern center of influence based at Herakleopolis (*her-ah-clay-OH-polis*) was opposed by a southern regime headquartered at Thebes, with families from each region claiming to be the legitimate pharaohs of all Egypt.

Compared to the centralized authority of the Old Kingdom, this looks like chaos. But redistribution of power always leads to some important developments in any society. In Egypt, wealth became much more widely and evenly diffused than it had been, as did access to education, the opportunities for the creation of art, and the possibilities for personal advancement. Resources that the pharaoh's court at Memphis had once monopolized now resided in the provinces, enabling local elites to emerge as both protectors of society and as patrons of local artisans. Many arts and luxuries—including elaborate rites for the dead—were developed originally at the pharaoh's court, and had been limited to it. Now, however, they became available to Egyptian society as a whole.

Egyptian funerary rites aimed to emulate the example set by Isis and Anubis, who had carefully preserved the parts of Osiris' body and enabled his afterlife. This is why the Egyptians developed their sophisticated techniques of embalming, whereby all of the body's vital organs were removed and then treated with chemicals—except for the heart, which played a key role in the ka's final judgment. A portrait mask was then placed on the mummy before burial, so that the deceased would be recognizable despite being wrapped in hundreds of yards of linen. To sustain the ka on his or her journey, food, clothing, utensils, weapons, and other items of vital importance would be placed in the grave along with the body.

"Coffin texts," or books of the dead, also accompanied the body and were designed to speed the ka's journey. They contained special instructions that would help the ka travel through the underworld and prepare it for the final test. They also described the "negative confession" the ka would make before the court of Osiris, a formal denial of offenses commited in life. The god Anubis would then weigh the deceased's heart against the principle of *ma'at*: truth, order, justice. Because ma'at was often envisioned as a goddess wearing a plumed headdress, a feather from this headdress would be placed in the scales opposite the heart; only if the heart was light (empty of wrongdoing) and in perfect balance with the feather would the ka achieve immortality.

As previously noted, this manner of confronting death has often led to the erroneous assumption that the ancient Egyptians were pessimistic, but in actuality their practices and beliefs were inherently life affirming, bolstered by confidence in the renewal of creation. Binding together this endless cycle was ma'at, the serene order of the universe, and embodying ma'at on earth was the pharaoh. But when that order broke down, so too did their confidence in the pharaoh's power.

Egyptian Science

Given the powerful impression conveyed by their monumental architecture, it may seem surprising that the ancient Egyptians lagged far behind the Sumerians and Akkadians in science and mathematics, as well as in the application of new technologies. Only in the calculation of time did the Egyptians make notable advances, since their close observation of the sun for religious and agricultural reasons led them to develop a solar calendar that was far more accurate than the Mesopotamian lunar calendar. Whereas the Sumerians have bequeathed to us their means of dividing and measuring the day, the Egyptian calendar is the direct ancestor of the Julian Calendar adopted for Rome by Julius Caesar in 45 B.C.E. (see Chapter 5) and later corrected by Pope Gregory XIII in 1582 C.E.; this is the calendar we use today.

The Social Pyramid

The social pyramid of Old Kingdom Egypt was extremely steep. At its apex stood the pharaoh and his extended family, whose prestige and power set them entirely apart from all other Egyptians. Below them was a class of nobles, whose primary role was to serve as priests and officials of the pharaoh's government; scribes were usually recruited and trained from among the sons of these families. All of these Egyptian elites lived in considerable luxury. They owned extensive estates, exotic possessions, and fine furniture. They kept dogs, cats, and monkeys as pets, and hunted and fished for sport.

Beneath this tiny minority was everyone else. Most Egyptians lived in crowded conditions in simple mud-brick dwellings. During a period of prosperity, master craftsmen—jewelers, goldsmiths, and the like—could improve their own conditions and those of their familes by fulfilling the needs of the wealthy, but they did not constitute anything like a middle class. Other skilled professionals—potters, weavers, masons, bricklayers, brewers, merchants, and schoolteachers—also enjoyed some measure of respect as well as a higher standard of living. The vast majority of Egyptians, however, were laborers who provided the brute force necessary for agriculture and construction. Beneath them were slaves, typically captives from foreign wars rather than native Egyptians.

Yet despite the enormous demands the pharaohs placed on Egypt's wealth, their rule does not appear to have been perceived as particularly oppressive. Commoners' belief in the pharaoh's divinity made them willing subjects, as did the material benefits of living in a stable, well-governed society. Even slaves had certain legal rights, including the ability to own, sell, and bequeath personal property.

Unfortunately for historians, the written laws and other documentary practices produced by the lugals of Mesopotamia do not have any Old Kingdom parallels. This makes it difficult to reconstruct social values or the daily lives of commoners through reference to such sources.

The Status of Women

Despite the absence of written laws, there is evidence that Egyptian women enjoyed unusual freedoms by the standards of the ancient world. Female commoners were recognized as

Analyzing Primary Sources

The Instruction of Ptah-Hotep

Egyptian literature often took the form of "instructions" to or from important personages, offering advice to those in public life. This document declares itself to be the advice of a high-ranking official of the Old Kingdom to his son and successor, perhaps composed around 2450 B.C.E. However, the earliest surviving text dates from the Middle Kingdom period.

Be not arrogant because of your knowledge, and be not puffed up because you are a learned man. Take counsel with the ignorant as with the learned, for the limits of art cannot be reached, and no artist is perfect in his skills. Good speech is more hidden than the precious greenstone, and yet it is found among slave girls at the millstones.

... If you are a leader commanding the conduct of many, seek out every good aim, so that your policy may be without error. A great thing is *ma'at*, enduring and surviving; it has not been upset since the time of Osiris. He who departs from its laws is punished. It is the right path for him who knows nothing. Wrongdoing has never brought its venture safe to port. Evil may win riches, but it is the strength of *ma'at* that endures long, and a man can say, "I learned it from my father." ... If you wish to prolong friendship in a house which you enter as master, brother, or friend, or anyplace that you enter, beware of approaching the women. No place in which that is done prospers. There is no wisdom in it.

A thousand men are turned aside from their own good because of a little moment, like a dream, by tasting which death is reached. ... He who lusts after women, no plan of his will succeed. ... If you are a worthy man sitting in the council of his lord, confine your attention to excellence. Silence is more valuable than chatter. Speak only when you know you can resolve difficulties. He who gives good counsel is an artist, for speech is more difficult than any craft.

Source: Nels M. Bailkey, ed., *Readings in Ancient History: Thought and Experience from Gilgamesh to St. Augustine*, 5th ed. (Boston, MA: 1995), pp. 39–42.

Questions for Analysis

1. According to Ptah-Hotep, what are the most important attributes of a man engaged in public life? What are the most dangerous pitfalls and temptations he will encounter?

2. Why does Ptah-Hotep emphasize the importance of acting in accordance with *ma'at*? How does this idea of *ma'at* compare to that described elsewhere in the chapter?

3. Based on what you have learned about the changes in Egyptian politics and society, what might indicate that Ptah-Hotep lived during the time of the prosperous Fifth Dynasty of the Old Kingdom? How might these instructions have resonated differently with later readers of the Middle Kingdom?

---

persons in their own right and were allowed to initiate complaints (including suits for divorce), to defend themselves and act as witnesses, to possess property of their own, and to dispose of it, all without the sanction of a male guardian or representative, as was typically required in other ancient societies—and in most modern ones until the twentieth century. Women were not allowed to undergo formal scribal training, but surviving personal notes exchanged between high-born ladies suggest at least some could read and even write.

Normally women were barred from holding high office, apart from that of priestess and also, importantly, queen. Indeed, queens are often represented as the partners of their royal husbands and were certainly instrumental in ruling alongside them. And occasionally, a woman from the royal family might assume pharaonic authority for a time, as did Queen Khasekhemwy (*kah-sehk-KEM-wee*, d. 2686 B.C.E.) on behalf of her son Djoser before he came of age. Some may even have ruled in their own right; this was certainly the case under the New Kingdom (see Chapter 2).

Gender divisions were less clearly defined among the peasantry. The limitations of our sources, however, means that we can only glimpse the lives of peasants through the eyes of their social superiors. Whatever their status, it seems that women did not enjoy sexual equality. While most Egyptians practiced monogamy, wealthy men could and did keep a number of lesser wives, concubines, and female slaves; and any Egyptian man, married or not, enjoyed freedoms that were denied to women, who would be subject to severe punishments under the law if they were viewed as guilty of any misconduct.

The Widening Horizons of the Middle Kingdom (2055–c. 1650 B.C.E.)

After the disruption of Old Kingdom authority around 2160 B.C.E., warfare between competing pharaonic dynasties would continue for over a century. Then, in 2055 B.C.E., the Theban king Mentuhotep II conquered the northerners and declared himself the ruler of a united Egypt. His reign marks the beginning of Egypt's Middle Kingdom and the reestablishment of a unified government, but this time centered in Thebes rather than Memphis. The architect of this new government was Mentuhotep's chief supporter, Amenemhet (*ah-meh-NEHM-het*), who seized power after the king's death and established himself and his descendants as Egypt's Twelfth Dynasty.

This succession of remarkable pharaohs remained in power for nearly 200 years, and under them the Egyptians began to exploit more thoroughly the potential for trade to the south. They secured their border with Nubia and began to send mounted expeditions to the land they called Punt, probably the coast of Somalia. By the middle of the nineteenth century B.C.E., Nubia was firmly under Egypt's control. Meanwhile, diplomatic relations with the smaller states and principalities of Palestine and Syria led to decisive Egyptian political and economic influence in this region. These lands were not incorporated into Egypt; instead, Amenemhet constructed the Walls of the Prince in Sinai to guard against incursions from the Near East.

The huge fortifications built along Egypt's new frontier demonstrate the great resourcefulness of the Twelfth Dynasty, and their very different ways of allocating resources and expressing ambition. As such, they also display a marked shift in the Egyptian outlook on the world. The placid serenity epitomized by ma'at, and the shared devotion to the pharaoh that had built the pyramids, had been challenged. Egyptians could no longer be dismissive of outsiders or the world beyond their borders. Unlike their Old Kingdom ancestors, the Egyptians of the Middle Kingdom were not turned inward. Their attitude to the pharaoh also seems to have changed. Although they continued to enjoy special position as divine representatives, the pharaohs of the Middle Kingdom represented themselves as what they were expected to be—good shepherds, tenders of their flock. Only by diligently protecting Egypt from a hostile outside world could a pharaoh provide the peace, prosperity, and security desired by his

After You Read This Chapter

Go to **INQUIZITIVE** to see what you've learned—and learn what you've missed—with personalized feedback along the way.

REVIEWING THE OBJECTIVES

- The study of the distant past is challenging because written sources are rare. What other sources of information do historians use?
- All civilizations require the same basic things and share certain characteristics. What are they?
- The cities of Mesopotamia remained largely independent from one another, yet shared a common culture. Why was this the case?
- Hammurabi's empire created a new precedent for governance in Mesopotamia. How did he achieve this?
- The civilizations of ancient Mesopotamia and Egypt differed in profound ways. What were the major causes of their differences?

subjects; his alignment with ma'at was now conditional, and it had to be *earned*.

The literature of the Middle Kingdom expresses the general change in attitude. Among the most popular literary forms were manuals ostensibly written by or for kings, detailing the duties and perils of high office and offering advice for dealing with difficult situations. These include *The Instruction of Ptah-Hotep* (see **Analyzing Primary Sources** on page 27), an example of Egyptian "wisdom literature" attributed to a court official of the Old Kingdom, which achieved a wider readership in this new era. Ptah-Hotep's teaching is upbeat and practical; by contrast, the examples of this genre produced under the Middle Kingdom are bleakly pragmatic. Reading between the lines, we discern that Egyptians' sense of their own superiority—a product of their isolation and their comparatively benign environment—had been shattered. They saw themselves being drawn into a much wider world, and in the course of the next millennium, they would become more fully a part of it.

CONCLUSION

While the story of Babel records the legendary loss of communication, this chapter shows that people of the distant past can still speak to us. The marks they have left on the landscape, the remains of their daily lives, their written records, and their very bodies make it possible for historians to piece together the evidence and to make sense of it. And every year new sources come to light, meaning that we have to be ready to revise, constantly, our understanding of what happened in the past.

Although this chapter has emphasized the differences between the early civilizations of Mesopotamia and Egypt, it is worth noting some significant similarities. Both developed the fundamental technologies of writing at about the same time, and this facilitated political alliances, long-distance trade, and the transmission of vital information to posterity. During the third millennium, both underwent a process of political consolidation, an elaboration of religious ritual, and a melding of spiritual and political leadership. Both engaged in massive building and irrigation projects, and both commanded material and human resources on an enormous scale. At the same time, each of these civilizations cultivated an inward focus. Although they had some contact with each other, and some transfers of information and technology probably took place, there were few significant political or cultural interactions. For all intents and purposes, they inhabited separate worlds. This relative isolation was about to change, however. The next millennium would see the emergence of large-scale, land-based empires that would transform life in Mesopotamia, Egypt, and the lands that lay between them. These are the developments we examine in Chapter 2.

PEOPLE, IDEAS, AND EVENTS IN CONTEXT

- What fundamental changes associated with the **NEOLITHIC REVOLUTION** made early civilizations possible?
- What new technologies allowed the **SUMERIANS** to master the environment of **MESOPOTAMIA**, and how did these technologies contribute to the development of a new, urbanized society?
- By contrast, why did the Nile River foster a very different civilization and enable the centralized authority of the **PHARAOH**?
- How do the differences between **CUNEIFORM** and **HIEROGLYPHS** reflect the different circumstances in which they were invented and the different uses to which they were put?
- In what ways are the *EPIC OF GILGAMESH* and the *CODE OF HAMMURABI* rich sources of information about the civilizations of Sumer and **BABYLON**?
- How do the **ZIGGURATS** of Mesopotamia and the **PYRAMIDS** of Egypt exemplify different forms of power, different ideas about the gods, and different beliefs about the afterlife?
- Why was the worldview of ancient Egyptians, which was strongly reflected in the concept of **MA'AT** during the **OLD KINGDOM**, altered in significant ways by the time of the **MIDDLE KINGDOM**?

THINKING ABOUT CONNECTIONS

- How do the surviving sources of any period limit the kinds of questions that we can ask and answer about the distant past? In your view, are there sources for this early era that have been undervalued? For example, if writing had not been developed in Mesopotamia and Egypt, what would we still be able to know about the civilizations of these two regions?
- What features of ancient civilizations do modern civilizations share? What might be the implications of these shared ideas, social structures, and technologies?
- In particular, what lessons could we draw from humans' tendency to manipulate their environment? How should knowledge of the distant past influence current debates over sustainability and climate change?

Before You Read This Chapter

Peoples, Gods, and Empires, 1700–500 B.C.E.

CORE OBJECTIVES

- **DESCRIBE** the impact of new migrations and settlements on the ancient Near East.

- **DEFINE** the differences between Egypt's New Kingdom and the previous Old and Middle Kingdoms.

- **EXPLAIN** the workings and importance of transnational networks in the late Bronze Age.

- **IDENTIFY** the new empires and kingdoms that emerged in the Iron Age.

- **UNDERSTAND** the historical importance of monotheism.

According to Hesiod, a Greek poet who flourished during the eighth century B.C.E., all of human history falls into five ages. The dawn of time was a golden age, when men lived like gods. Everything was good then, food was plentiful, and work was easy. The next age was silver, when men took gods for granted, killed one another, and lived in dishonor. So the gods destroyed them, sending a mighty flood that spared only the family of Deucalion, who built an ark. Then came the age of bronze, when everything was made of bronze—houses and armor and weapons and tools—and giants fought incessantly from huge strongholds, causing destruction so great that no man's name survives. The time following was short but bright, a heroic age, the time of men who ventured with Theseus and fought beside Achilles and sailed with Odysseus, men whose names will live forever. But Hesiod's own age was iron: a dull age, a time of tedium and strife and bickering and petty feuds.

Hesiod's periodization captures an understanding of history that had evolved with humanity itself and that reflects actual developments. The stories he knew told of a time before cities.

31

They recalled times of environmental catastrophe. They chronicled the wars of the age we still call Bronze, when the enormous abandoned palaces visible in Hesiod's day were built. And they remembered the race of heroes whose glory was measured by their abiding fame, and who bequeathed a further round of stories. Thanks to new archaeological finds, new linguistic discoveries, and new efforts at decoding the historical record, we can both confirm and correct Hesiod's perspective on the past.

In the second millennium B.C.E., the ancient Near East was transformed by the arrival of new peoples and by the emergence of extensive land-based empires built up through systematic military conquest. These migrations and conquests caused upheaval, but they also led to cultural contact and economic integration that extended from Scandinavia to China. By the thirteenth century B.C.E., nations from the southern Balkans in Europe to the western fringes of Iran in the Ancient Near East had been drawn into a wide-ranging web of relationships.

Yet this extraordinary system proved more fragile than its participants could have imagined. Around 1200 B.C.E., a wave of mysterious invasions led to the destruction of nearly every Bronze Age civilization. As a result, around the turn of the first millennium B.C.E. we enter a new world organized along profoundly different lines. In this new age, iron would slowly replace bronze as the primary component of tools and weapons. New and more brutal empires would come to power, while new ideas about the divine and its relationship to humanity would emerge. Two of the Western world's most enduring religious traditions—Judaism and Zoroastrianism (*zoh-roh-AHS-tree-anism*)—were born, fundamentally altering conceptions of ethics, politics, and the natural world. This Iron Age would prove a fateful historical crossroads, as elements both old and new combined to reconfigure the ancient world.

INDO-EUROPEAN LANGUAGES AND PEOPLES

In 1786, a British judge serving in India made a discovery that transformed the understanding of history. Turning his spare time to the study of Sanskrit, the ancient language of South Asia, Sir William Jones discovered that it shares the same grammar and vocabulary as ancient Greek and Latin—to an extent inexplicable by sheer coincidence. He then examined the early Germanic and Celtic languages of Europe and the Old Persian language of the Near East, and found that they also exhibit marked similarities. He concluded that all of these languages must have evolved from

a common source. Within another generation, the ancient language whose existence Jones had hypothesized, and the later languages derived from it, would be labeled Indo-European, reflecting their wide distribution from India to Ireland. The Biblical story of mankind's shared language, the story of Babel, turns out to be partly true.

Since then, scholars have greatly enlarged our understanding of Indo-European languages and their speakers. Yet much remains controversial. It is certain that Indo-European linguistic forms begin to appear in the Near East and eastern Mediterranean shortly after 2000 B.C.E. Around this same time, a group of Indo-European speakers also moved into the Aegean basin, where the resulting language became an early form of Greek. Other Indo-European speakers went east; some may have reached western China.

These were not the only new peoples moving into the Near East. As we noted in Chapter 1, Semitic-speaking peoples were also making their mark, beginning with the Akkadians and the Amorites, from whose ranks Hammurabi came. The Assyrians, the Phoenicians, and the Canaanites would also become prominent. These newcomers did not wipe out existing cultures; rather, they built on established patterns of urban life and organization. But their collective impact was enormous.

New Settlers in Anatolia

By 1900 B.C.E., the nomadic Assyrians had become caravan merchants whose extensive trade networks stretched across Anatolia and Mesopotamia. They relied on the protection of local rulers and, in turn, they made these rulers rich. They also served as advisers and officials, and married into important urban families. In the process, they carried Mesopotamian civilization and its trappings into far-flung regions.

In their wake, new population groups were attracted to Anatolia, northern Syria, and Mesopotamia. The most formidable of these were the Hittites, an Indo-European-speaking people who arrived around 2000 B.C.E. In contrast to the Assyrians, the Hittites were conquerors and colonists who imposed themselves and their language on the peoples they vanquished. By 1700 B.C.E., they had integrated many city-states into a larger kingdom.

The Hittites' warrior aristocracy fielded the most fearsome army of the Bronze Age. They were quick to adopt the latest technologies, including the chariot and (eventually) the use of iron for weaponry. But the Hittites also adopted the more peaceful practices of those they conquered, using cuneiform to record their own language and laws. And they sought to control trade routes, particularly the overland trade in copper and arsenic, the raw materials for making bronze. By 1595 B.C.E., they had captured Babylon.

A century later, the Kassites, another new people, moved into that devastated city. For the next 500 years, they presided over a largely prosperous Babylonian realm. The Hittites, however, continued to destabilize the region, until they were themselves checked by the arrival of a people known as the Mitannians, whose initial advantage was their use of horses, hitherto unknown outside the steppes of Asia. Their light, horse-drawn chariots became terrifying death-machines, transporting archers rapidly around the battlefield. The Mitannians also pioneered cavalry tactics. Eventually, however, their opponents adopted these same technologies, and the Hittites once again achieved the advantage and turned their attention to Egypt.

THE NEW KINGDOM OF EGYPT

As we have seen, Egypt's Middle Kingdom had been formed by the many internal changes of the First Intermediate Period, chiefly the redistribution of wealth and power. Now it was further transformed by external forces, through the dynamic movement of new peoples. Some of these came to Egypt as immigrants; others were hired as mercenaries. And for a while, a strategy of accommodation preserved Egypt from large-scale armed attack and fostered commercial exchange with neighboring regions. But around 1700 B.C.E., Egypt was invaded for the first time since the unification of the Upper and Lower Kingdoms. These invaders' origins and identity remain mysterious; the Egyptians called them simply Hyksos (*HIHK-sohs*), "rulers of foreign lands." The Hyksos began to project their authority over most of Lower Egypt.

With this conquest, the central authority of the pharaoh once again dissolved and Egypt entered what scholars call the Second Intermediate Period (c. 1650–1550 B.C.E.). Significantly, however, the Hyksos took over the machinery of pharaonic government in Lower Egypt and took steps to legitimize their rule. In Upper Egypt, by contrast, Hyksos power was weak. Here, a native pharaonic regime maintained a tenuous independence at the traditional capital of Thebes.

Although the Hyksos established Lower Egypt as the most significant power in the Near East, their conquest also weakened the dominion of Upper Egypt over the Nubians, who eventually founded an independent kingdom called Kush. This Nubian kingdom posed a much greater threat to the native dynasty at Thebes than to the Hyksos in Lower Egypt—but it also provided additional incentive to southern pharaohs determined to oust the Hyksos. By the end of the sixteenth century B.C.E., the pharaoh Ahmose had driven them out, establishing the Eighteenth Dynasty and the New Kingdom of Egypt.

The Pharaohs of the Eighteenth Dynasty

Under the Eighteenth Dynasty, Egyptian civilization reached the height of its magnificence and power. Although many Egyptian traditions were renewed and strengthened, the dynamism of the New Kingdom—particularly its new focus on imperial expansion—changed the very fabric of Egyptian life, which had never before looked beyond the narrow world of the Nile Valley.

Among the striking developments that took place during this period was the rise of a new aristocracy whose wealth was acquired through warfare and the winning of lands (with slaves to work them), which they received from the pharaoh as rewards for service. The Eighteenth Dynasty itself was forged in battle. Ahmose, the man who expelled the Hyksos, had been reared by the warrior queen Ahhotep. His eventual successor, Thutmose I (r. 1504–1492 B.C.E.), was the son of an unknown warrior who married Ahmose's daughter.

Under Thutmose's leadership, the Egyptians subdued the Nubians to the south, seizing control of their gold mines. They also penetrated beyond their northeastern frontier, driving deep into Palestine and Syria. By the time of his death, Thutmose could claim to rule the land from beyond the Nile's Fourth Cataract to the banks of the Euphrates. Never had Egypt so clearly declared its imperial ambitions. Nor was this success fleeting. The Egyptians would sustain a strong military presence in the Near East for the next 400 years.

The Legacy of Hatshepsut

The early death of Thutmose's son and successor could have resulted in a crisis for the Eighteenth Dynasty. Instead, it led to one of the most remarkable reigns in Egypt's history, for Thutmose II (r. 1492–1479 B.C.E.) passed the power of pharaoh to his sister, wife, and co-ruler Hatshepsut (*haht-SHEHP-suht*, r. 1479–1458 B.C.E.). Such brother-sister unions were common in the Egyptian royal family, although they do not appear to have been the routine way to produce royal children: pharaohs customarily kept a harem of subsidiary wives and concubines for this purpose. However, Thutmose II and Hatshepsut did conceive at least one child together, Neferure; in fact, she may have been their designated heir. For 21 years, Hatshepsut ruled as pharaoh in her own right, while her daughter took on the usual duties of queen.

Like her great-grandmother Ahhotep, Hatshepsut was a warrior. Moroever, she was routinely protrayed on

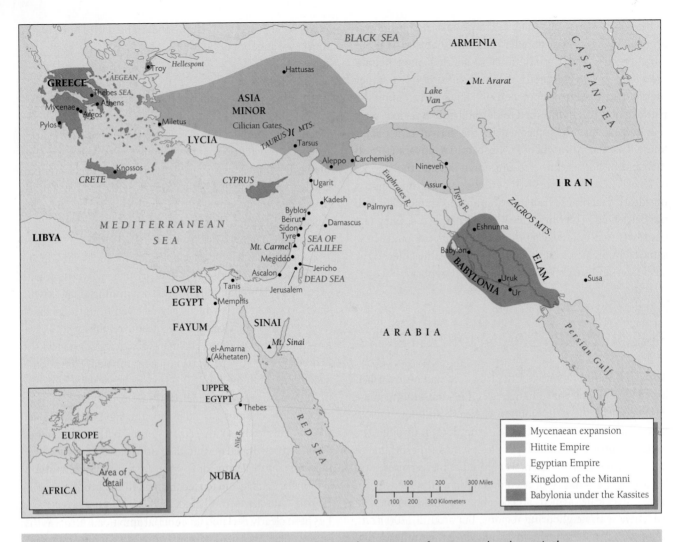

EGYPT AND ITS NEIGHBORS, c. 1400 B.C.E. ▪ *What factors appear to shape patterns of conquest and settlement in the Mediterranean?* ▪ *What political developments dominate this map?* ▪ *What developments would have enabled trade to flourish during this period?*

monuments and in statuary with the masculine figure and ceremonial beard characteristic of pharaohs. She did not pretend to be a man: inscriptions almost always indicate her sex, and she herself claimed to be the most beautiful woman in the world. But it was important to Egyptians that she use the conventional iconography of power to locate herself firmly within a long history of male dynastic rule.

Hatshepsut's statecraft proved crucial to the continuing success of Egypt. With her stepson/nephew, Thutmose III, she launched several successful military campaigns and extended trade. The arts also flourished, setting standards that would be emulated for a thousand years. Indeed, Hatshepsut was one of the most ambitious builders in Egyptian history, which is saying something. Her own mortuary temple was probably the first tomb constructed in the Valley of the Kings, the New Kingdom's answer to the pyramids.

Yet after Hatshepsut's death in 1458 B.C.E. her legacy was called into question. At some point late in her nephew's reign, attempts were made to remove her name from inscriptions and to destroy her images (see **Interpreting Visual Evidence** on page 36). Scholars used to assume that Thutmose himself was responsible for this, because he resented his stepmother/aunt's power over him. But more recent research has suggested that the culprit was his son, Amenhotep II (r. 1427–1400 B.C.E.), who was thereby blocking the claims of royal rivals, possibly Hatshepsut's daughter, Neferure.

Religious Change and Political Challenges

The great conquests of the Eighteenth Dynasty brought mind-boggling riches to Egypt. Much of this wealth went to the glorification of the pharaoh in the form of grand temples, tombs, and other monuments, including the thousands of steles that provide us with so much information about this era. Another significant portion of the plunder went to the military aristocracy that made such conquests possible. But the lion's share went to the gods as offerings of thanks. As the temples became wealthy and powerful, so too did their priests. But no temple complex was so well endowed as that of Amon at Thebes.

Thebes was not only the capital of New Kingdom Egypt, it was also the place most sacred to Amon (or Amun), the god of creation, who played an important role in the dynasty's self-image. Amon had come into prominence when the political center of gravity shifted to Thebes during the Middle Kingdom, and his cult had steadily increased in status and popularity. By 1550 B.C.E. he had become identified as another manifestation of the sun god Ra, and was believed to be the divine force behind the Eighteenth Dynasty's triumph over the Hyksos. This accounts for the favor shown to his priests at Thebes, who became a formidable political force. Eventually, they surpassed even the military aristocracy in importance and influence.

AKHENATEN, HIS WIFE NEFERTITI, AND THEIR CHILDREN. The Aten is depicted here as a sun disk, raining down power on the royal family. ▪ *What messages might this image have conveyed to contemporary Egyptians?* ▪ *How does this depiction of the pharaoh differ from earlier precedents?*

The Reign of Akhenaten (1352–1336 B.C.E.)

All of these factors are important when we consider the reign of Amenhotep IV, who inherited the vast, well-governed kingdom assembled by his predecessors. This young pharaoh showed an early inclination toward the worship of the sun, but not as an aspect of Amon. Instead, Amenhotep (whose dynastic name means "Amon Is Pleased") exalted Ra as a discrete divinity and laid aside the traditional iconography of this god as a falcon (or a falcon-headed man), replacing it with the symbol *Aten*, the hieroglyph representing the sun's rays. He then went farther, changing his own name to Akhenaten (*AH-keh-NAH-ton*), "He Who Is Profitable to the Aten," and building a new capital to honor the god. Located halfway between Memphis and Thebes, it was called Akhetaten ("The Horizon of the Aten").

Although the priesthood of Amon exalted Amon-Ra, it also recognized all the other gods of Egypt. Akhenaten's theology, by contrast, was closer to monotheism. And unlike traditional Egyptian deities, the Aten could not be imagined as taking on human or animal form. Akhenaten also celebrated his new religion by representing himself in a very unconventional way. In a complete departure from the divine virility of his ancestors—which even

his ancestor Hatshepsut had emulated—Akhenaten had himself pictured as a family man enjoying the company of his wife, Nefertiti, and their children. This emphasis on his own humanity might have been an extension of his theology, which honored the life force within every being. But it was also dangerous to the ideology of royal power. The pharaoh was not supposed to be a man with quirky personality. He was supposed to be a god on earth.

Akhenaten's spiritual revolution therefore had enormous political implications. Not surprisingly, the priesthood of Amon also put up strenuous resistance. To make matters worse, Akhenaten did not balance his theological enthusiasm with attention to Egypt's interests abroad. This cost him the support of his nobility and may even have led to his deposition. He was ultimately succeeded by one of his younger sons, Tutankhaten ("Living Image of the Aten"), a child of nine whose name was quickly changed to reflect the restoration of the god Amon and his priesthood. He became Tutankhamun (r. 1333–1324 B.C.E.), the boy king whose sumptuous tomb was discovered in 1922. After his early death, he was succeeded by a general called Horemheb, who reigned as the last pharaoh of the Eighteenth Dynasty. When he died, he passed his office to another general. This was Ramses, the founder of the Nineteenth Dynasty, who would restore Egypt to glory in the Near East.

Interpreting Visual Evidence

Remembering Hatshepsut

The pharaohs of Egypt's New Kingdom carefully controlled their public images. The visual language they used was highly symbolic, an iconography (vocabulary of images) intended to make each successive pharaoh look as much like his royal predecessors as possible: godlike, steadfast, virile, authoritative—even when the pharaoh was a woman, Hatshepsut (r. 1479–1458 B.C.E., images A and B). So many statues and portraits of her survive that nearly every major museum in the world has at least one (the Metropolitan Museum of Art in New York has a whole room set aside for them). But many of these images show signs of having been defaced during the reign of her successor, Thutmose III, who was also her nephew and stepson. Until very recently, scholars assumed that Hatshepsut must have usurped his powers, and that this was his revenge. Yet the evidence clearly shows that Hatshepsut was Egypt's legitimate ruler. Why, then, would Thutmose III or his heirs have tried to efface her memory?

The two unblemished *steles* shown here depict Hatshepsut and Thutmose III. In the *stele* on the left (image C), Hatshepsut is placed in the center of the frame, wearing a royal helmet; she is offering wine to the god Amun. Behind her stands Thutmose III, wearing the crown of Upper Egypt. In the *stele* on the right (image D), Thutmose III wears the warrior's crown, while Hatshepsut wears the double crown of Upper and Lower Egypt and wields a mace.

Questions for Analysis

1. Bearing in mind that few Egyptians could read the hieroglyphs accompanying these images, how might they

A. Defaced head of Hatshepsut.

B. Undefaced statue of Hatshepsut.

TRANSNATIONAL NETWORKS OF THE LATE BRONZE AGE

Bronze Age history must be understood within the context of what we might call international relations. Yet it is more accurate to call the political and economic networks of this period *transnational*, because this web of alliances and relationships transcended any idea of national identity.

This Late Bronze Age was an age of superpowers. The great pharaohs of the Eighteenth Dynasty had transformed Egypt into a conquering state, and the Hittites had created an empire out of the disparate city-states and kingdoms of Anatolia. The Assyrians controlled Near Eastern trade, and the Kassite kingdom of Babylonia remained a significant force in economic and military relationships. In addition to these imperial entities, numerous smaller states flourished and extended their influence. Holding it all together was a have "read" the relationship between these two royal relatives? Does this evidence support the hypothesis that Thutmose was slighted by Hatshepsut?

2. What can these images tell us about gender roles? What else would we need to know before making a judgment about masculine and feminine characteristics in ancient Egypt?

3. Given that Hatshepsut was Egypt's legitimate pharaoh, what might have motivated either Thutmose III or his son Amenhotep II to deface her image many years after her death?

C. *Stele* of Hatshepsut and Thutmose.

D. *Stele* of Thutmose and Hatshepsut, from the Red Chapel at Karnak.

network of trade that created an interdependent Afro-Eurasian world.

Transnational Diplomacy

Although warfare remained the fundamental mode of interaction, a balance of power among the larger empires gradually helped to stabilize the region. By the fourteenth century B.C.E., a wide-ranging correspondence was binding leaders together and promoting a set of mutual goals and understandings. Surviving letters show that the most powerful rulers address one another as "brother," while lesser princes and chieftains show their deference to the pharaoh, the Hittite king, and other sovereigns by using the term "father." Rulers of this period also exchanged lavish gifts and entered into marriage alliances with each other. Professional envoys journeyed back and forth, conveying gifts and handling politically sensitive missions. Some of these emissaries were also merchants, sent to explore the possibility of trading opportunities as well as to cement alliances.

Transnational Trade

Indeed, it was trade that allowed smaller communities to become integral parts of this transnational network. Seaside cities such as Ugarit and Byblos became centers for the exchange of dazzling commodities. A single vessel's cargo might contain scores of distinct items originating anywhere from the interior of Africa to the Baltic Sea, as demonstrated by the contents of a merchant ship discovered at Uluburun off the Turkish coast in 1982. The region was also supplied with goods brought in overland, via contacts reaching into India and the Far East.

Trade was not only the basis for a new economy, but the conduit for art, ideas, and technology. In the past, such influences spread slowly and unevenly; now, the societies of the late Bronze Age could keep abreast of all the latest developments. This trend was particularly marked in large coastal towns. At Ugarit, on the coast of modern-day Syria, the swirl of commerce and the multiplicity of languages spoken by traders even propelled the development of a simpler form of writing than the cuneiform still in use throughout most of the Near East. The Ugaritic alphabet consisted of about thirty symbols representing the sounds of consonants. (Vowels had to be inferred.) This system was far more easily mastered and more flexible than cuneiform, and it would become the model for the development of all modern alphabets.

The search for markets, resources, and trade routes also promoted greater understanding among cultures. After a great battle between Egyptians and Hittites near Kadesh (c. 1275 B.C.E.), the pharaoh Ramses II realized that more was to be gained through peaceful relations with his northern neighbors than through warfare. The treaty he established with the Hittites fostered stability and allowed further economic exchanges to flourish.

But greater integration also meant greater mutual dependence. If one economy suffered, the effects of that decline were sure to be felt elsewhere. And the farther this transnational system spread, the more vulnerable it became. Many of the new markets depended on emerging societies in far less stable regions, where civilization was also new.

AEGEAN CIVILIZATIONS: MINOAN CRETE, MYCENAEAN GREECE

Greek poets like Hesiod described a heroic age when great men mingled with gods and powerful kingdoms contended for wealth and glory. For a long time, modern scholars dismissed these stories as fables. Tales of Theseus and the Minotaur, the Trojan War, and the wanderings of Odysseus were regarded as reflecting no historical reality. Greek history was assumed to begin in 776 B.C.E., when the first recorded Olympic Games occurred. The Greece of the Bronze Age was considered a primitive backwater that played no significant role in the Mediterranean world or in the later, glorious history of classical Greece.

But in the late nineteenth century, an amateur archaeologist named Heinrich Schliemann became convinced that these myths were really historical accounts. Using the epic poems of Homer as his guide, he found the site of Ilium (Troy) near the coast of northwest Anatolia. He also identified a number of once-powerful citadels on the Greek mainland, including the home of the legendary king Agamemnon at Mycenae (MY-seh-nee). Soon afterward, the British archaeologist Sir Arthur Evans took credit for discovering the remains of a great palace at Knossos on the island of Crete that predated any of the major citadels on the Greek mainland. He dubbed this magnificent culture—which no modern person had known to exist—"Minoan," after King Minos, the powerful ruler whom the ancient Greeks described as dominating the Aegean, and the man for whom the engineer Daedalus had designed the Labyrinth. Although some of their conclusions have proven to be false, the discoveries of Schliemann and Evans forced scholars to revise, entirely, the history of Western civilizations. It is now clear that Bronze Age Greece—or, as it is often termed, Mycenaean Greece—was an important and integrated part of the Mediterranean world during the second millennium B.C.E.

The Minoan Thalassocracy

In the fifth century B.C.E., the Athenian historian Thucydides wrote that King Minos of Crete had ruled a *thalassocracy*, an empire of the sea. We now know that he was correct, that a very wealthy civilization began to flourish on the island of Crete around 2500 B.C.E. Thereafter, for about a millennium, the Minoans controlled shipping around the central Mediterranean and the Aegean, and may have exacted tribute from many smaller islands. At its height between 1900 and 1500 B.C.E., Minoan civilization was the contemporary of Egypt's Middle Kingdom and the Hittite kingdom. And unlike them, it was virtually unassailable by outside forces, protected by the surrounding sea.

The Diplomacy of the Mycenaeans and the Hittites

Around 1260 B.C.E., the powerful Hittite king Hattusilis III sent the following letter to a "King of Ahhiyawa," identifiable as a leader of the Mycenaean Greeks, who often called themselves Akhaiwoi, Achaeans. This fascinating document exemplifies the tangle of close ties that bound powerful men together within the transnational system of the Late Bronze Age, as well as the problems and misunderstandings that could arise from the misbehavior of men under their command. The events referenced here all occurred in western Anatolia (Turkey), a region controlled partly by the Hittites and partly by the Greeks, the same region in which Troy (Ilium) was located. (See the map on page 34.)

 have to complain of the insolent and treacherous conduct of one Tawagalawas [*tah-wah-GAH-la-wahs*]. We came into contact in the land of Lycia, and he offered to become a vassal of the Hittite Empire. I agreed, and sent an officer of most exalted rank to conduct him to my presence. He had the audacity to complain that the officer's rank was not exalted enough; he insulted my ambassador in public, and demanded that he be declared vassal-king there and then, without the formality of an interview. Very well: I order him, if he desires to become a vassal of mine, to make sure that no troops of his are found in Iyalanda when I arrive there. And what do I find when I arrive in Iyalanda?—the troops of Tawagalawas, fighting on the side of my enemies. I defeat them, take many prisoners ... scrupulously leaving the fortress of Atriya intact out of respect for my treaty with you. Now a Hittite subject, Piyamaradus [*pie-yah-ma-RA-dus*] by name, steals my 7,000 prisoners, and makes off to your city of Miletus. I command him to return to me: he disobeys. I write to you: you send a surly message unaccompanied by gift or greeting, to say that you have ordered your representative in Miletus, a certain Atpas, to deliver up Piyamaradus. Nothing happens, so I go fetch him. I enter your city of Miletus, for I have something to say to Piyamaradus, and it would be well that your subjects there should hear me say it. But my visit is not a success. I ask for Tawagalawas: he is not at home. I should like to see Piyamaradus: he has gone to sea. You refer me to your representative Atpas: I find that both he and his brother are married to daughters of Piyamaradus; they are not likely to give me satisfaction or to give you an unbiased account of these transactions. ... Are you aware, and is it with your blessing, that Piyamaradus is going round saying that he intends to leave his wife and family, and incidentally my 7,000 prisoners, under your protection while he makes continual inroads on my dominion? ... Do not let him use Achaea [in Greece] as a base for operations against me. You and I are friends. There has been no quarrel between us since we came to terms in the matter of Ilios [the territory of Troy]: the trouble there was my fault, and I promise it will not happen again. As for my military occupation of Miletus, please regard it as a friendly visit. ... [As for the problems between us], I suggest that the fault may not lie with ourselves but with our messengers; let us bring them to trial, cut off their heads, mutilate their bodies, and live henceforth in perfect friendship.

Source: Adapted from Denys Page, *History and the Homeric Iliad* (Berkeley, CA: 1959), pp. 11–12.

Questions for Analysis

1. Reconstruct the relationship between Hattusilis III and the Achaean king, based on the references to people and places in this letter. What picture emerges of their interactions, and of the connections between the Hittite Empire and Mycenaean Greece?

2. Why is Hattusilis so concerned about the disrespect shown to him by the Achaeans? Reading between the lines, what do you think he wanted to accomplish by sending this letter?

3. Based on this letter, what can you deduce about the standards of behavior expected of civilized participants in the transnational system of the Late Bronze Age? Within this code of conduct, what sanctions or penalties could be imposed on individuals or their nations?

MINOAN FRESCO, C. 1500 B.C.E. A stylized representation of bull-leaping, painted into the plaster of a wall at Knossos. ▪ *Is this likely to represent real practices?* ▪ *Why or why not?*

Thanks to its strategic position, Crete was not only a safe haven but also a nexus of vibrant economic exchange. Like its counterparts in the Near East, it acted as a magnet for the collection of resources which were then redistributed by its rulers and their emissaries. Knossos was also a production center for textiles, pottery, and metalwork. Minoan merchants traded these with Egypt, southwest Anatolia, and Cyprus for a range of exotic goods. Artistic influences also traveled along these routes; among much else, Minoan-style paintings from this period appear regularly in the Nile Delta and the Levant.

Traces of the bright colors and graceful lines of these paintings are still evident on the ruined walls of the palace at Knossos (*Kuh-NOSS-oss*). Furnished with indoor plumbing, among other luxuries, it covered several acres and comprised hundreds of rooms joined by an intricate network of winding hallways that inspired the famous story of the Labyrinth. The Minoans probably worshiped a god in the form of a bull or bull-man, and they appear to have devised an elaborate ritual sport known as bull-leaping, similar to bull-fighting but involving an element of athletic dance. There is also some evidence that they practiced human sacrifice (possibly facilitated by the dangers of bull-dancing) as a religious rite.

Despite all these fascinating remains, Minoan culture remains mysterious because its language has yet to be decoded. Its script is called Linear A, to distinguish it from Linear B, used in Mycenaean Greece—a script that *has* been deciphered. Although Linear A and Linear B represent different languages, the formal relationship between them reflects the fact that Minoan commercial activity engaged the mainland of Greece. The presence of a wide variety of Minoan objects on the Greek mainland corroborates this.

Yet the dynamics of the relationship between Minoans and Mycenaeans remains debatable. Before 1600 B.C.E., the Minoans were clearly much more sophisticated and may have dominated their Greek neighbors. One story told of Theseus describes how the hero was sent to Crete as a hostage, intending to free Athens from the heavy tribute imposed by King Minos. Given what we have already learned about the close relationship between myth and history, it is probable that this story preserves ancient memory, just as the story of Daedalus is an attempt to explain the technological marvels of the palace at Knossos.

Mycenaean Greece

When Linear B was deciphered in the early 1950s, the texts written in this script spurred scholars to reconsider the history of ancient Greece. Since then, new research shows that the Indo-Europeans whose language became Greek entered the region in several waves after the turn of the second

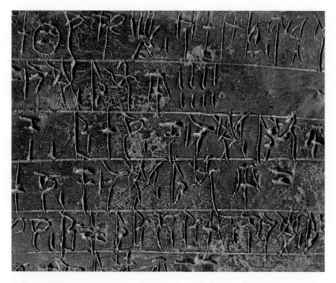

LINEAR B TABLET FROM KNOSSOS. Unlike cuneiform, whose characters are formed using the wedge-shaped tip of a reed, the scripts of Linear A and B used a sharp stylus that incised fine lines in clay or soft stone.

The basic political and commercial unit of the Mycenaean world—a powerful king and war leader, a warrior aristocracy, a palace bureaucracy, a complex economy, large territorial kingdoms—differs markedly from the Greek city-state of the classical age (Chapter 3). However, we can trace some features of this later civilization back to the Mycenaeans, including the Greek language. Linear B tablets speak of a social group with considerable economic and political rights, the *damos*; this may be the precursor of the *demos*, the urban population that sought political empowerment in many Greek cities. The tablets also preserve the names of several gods familiar from the later period, such as Zeus, Poseidon, and Dionysos. And later Greeks believed themselves to be descended from these legendary forebears, whom they credited with superhuman achievements. Although they knew little about their Mycenaean ancestors in fact, the impact of what they imagined about them was considerable.

The Sea Peoples and the End of the Bronze Age

The civilization of Mycenaean Greece seems to have collapsed around the end of the thirteenth century B.C.E. What triggered this cannot be determined with any certainty, but the consequences of the collapse are clear. Because Mycenaean Greece was an integrated part of a transnational network, the effects of its demise were felt throughout the Mediterranean and the Near East. Thereafter, a wave of devastation swept from north to south, caused by a group of people so thoroughly destructive that they obliterated everything in their path. We might know nothing about them were it not for a narrow victory by the pharaoh Ramses III around 1176 B.C.E.

In the *stele* set up to commemorate his triumph, Ramses III referred to these invaders as "Sea Peoples" and named several groups as part of a coalition. Some were familiar to the Egyptians, and it seems that many were from the Aegean. Most notable were the Philistines who, after their defeat, withdrew to populate the coast of the region named after them: Palestine.

Because the Sea Peoples' arc of annihilation started in the north, it may have been one of the factors contributing to the collapse of Mycenaean Greece. Disruption of northern commercial networks would have devastated the Mycenaean kingdoms, which could not support their enormous populations without trade. Suddenly faced with an apocalyptic combination of overpopulation, famine, and violence, bands of desperate refugees would have fled the Aegean basin. Meanwhile, the damage to commerce devastated the

millennium, dominating and displacing the indigenous inhabitants. By 1500 B.C.E., huge citadels dotted the Greek landscape, ruled by warriors whose epitaphs boast of their martial prowess and who were buried with their weapons. The power of these rulers was based on their leadership and their ability to reward followers with plunder. The most successful of them gained control of strategic sites from which they could exploit major trade routes, engaging in both trade and piracy.

Over time, and perhaps under the influence of Minoan culture, the Mycenaean citadels developed into much more complex societies. They served as both centers of government and warehouses for storage. By the thirteenth century B.C.E., some rulers had carved out territorial kingdoms with as many as 100,000 inhabitants; later, Hesiod would imagine their citadels to have been built by giants. These palace centers were adapted from Near Eastern models and their massive size was not ideally suited to the Greek landscape. In war also, Mycenaean imitation of Near Eastern examples had its limits. For example, Mycenaean kings cherished the chariots used by their contemporaries on the plains of Anatolia, yet such chariots were highly impractical on rocky terrain.

Despite these and other differences from their Mediterranean neighbors, the Mycenaean Greeks played an important role in Bronze Age networks. By about 1400 B.C.E., they had subjugated Crete, taking over Knossos and using it as a Mycenaean center. In western Anatolia, not far from Troy, at least one Mycenaean king exercised enough influence for a Hittite ruler to address him as "my brother." This evidence suggests that the Mycenaeans earned prestige as warriors and mercenaries, as the Greeks' heroic poems attest.

MYCENAEAN GREECE. ▪ *What are the main geographical features of Greece?* ▪ *How might this dry, mountainous country surrounded by the sea determine the nature of Greek civilization and economic interests?* ▪ *How might geography have allowed Mycenaean culture to spread so widely?*

economy of the Hittites, whose ancient kingdom rapidly disintegrated. Along the Mediterranean coast we find other clues. The king of Ugarit wrote a letter to a "brother" king on the island of Cyprus, begging for immediate aid because he had sent all his own warriors to help the Hittites. Poignantly, however, we have his letter only because the clay tablet on which it was written baked hard in the fire that destroyed his palace. The letter was never sent.

In the end, the Sea Peoples destroyed the civilizations that had flourished in the Near East and Mediterranean for over 2,000 years. The devastation was not total; not all cities disappeared, and trade did not cease entirely. But the Hittite Empire was gone, leaving behind it many weak, short-lived principalities. The great cosmopolitan cities of the eastern Mediterranean lay in ruins, and new groups—sometimes contingents of Sea Peoples like the Philistines—populated the coast. The citadels of Mycenaean Greece were depopulated by as much as 90 percent over the next century, and Greece entered into a period of cultural and economic isolation that would last for 250 years.

The victorious Egyptians survived, but with their major trading partners diminished or dead their civilization suffered. The Assyrians, the original architects

of the networks that had undergirded the transnational system, had to fight for their very existence. In Babylon, the peaceful and prosperous rule of the Kassites withered. In the vacuum left behind, new political configurations took shape and a new metallurgical technology began to supplant the use of bronze. Out of the ashes arose the culture of the Iron Age.

THE STATES OF THE EARLY IRON AGE

With the destruction of transnational networks, the geopolitical map of the Near East changed significantly. In Anatolia, a patchwork of small kingdoms grew up within the territories once controlled by the Hittites. Similar developments took place in the Levant: the eastern Mediterranean coastline that today comprises Israel, Lebanon, and parts of Syria. For centuries, this region had been controlled either by the Egyptians or the Hittites. With the collapse of these empires, new states began to emerge here, too. They were small, but they had a huge impact on the history of Western civilizations.

The Phoenicians

The most influential civilization of this period was that of a people whom the Greeks called Phoenicians. They are also known as Canaanites, and were speakers of a Semitic language closely related to Hebrew. During the Late Bronze Age, most Phoenician cities had been controlled by Egypt. But the erosion of Egyptian imperial power after 1200 B.C.E. gave these cities the opportunity to forge a new independence and to capitalize on their commercial advantages. One Phoenician city was a clearing house for papyrus, the highly prized Egyptian writing material. This explains why the Greek name for this city, Byblos, became the basis for the Greek word *biblion*, meaning "book." (The Bible is so called from the plural *biblia*, "the books.") Another valuable commodity came to be the name by which the Phoenicians themselves were known: a rare purple dye derived from the shells of snails culled from seabeds off the Levantine

Past and Present

The Fragility of Global Networks

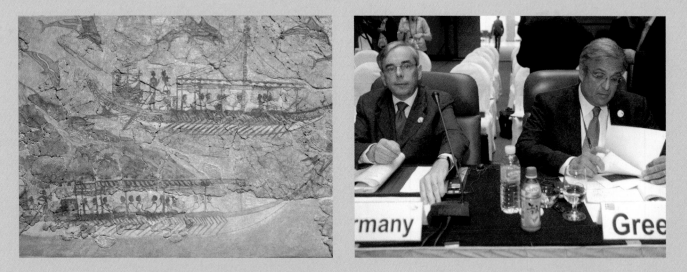

In the late Bronze Age, the destruction of transnational commercial networks had a domino effect on the interlocking civilizations of the West, plunging many into a "dark age" of isolation and impoverishment. The global economic crisis of our own day was caused by a similar phenomenon: the 2008 collapse of mutually dependent financial systems that proved more fragile than anyone had anticipated.

Watch ralated author videos on the Student Site
wwnorton.com/college/history/western-civilizationsBrief4

coast. So as far as the Greeks were concerned, those who supplied this dye were *phoinikeoi*, "purple people." The Phoenicians also became expert metalworkers, ivory carvers, and shipbuilders.

Phoenician Colonies and Cultural Influence

The Phoenicians were also aggressive colonists. By the end of the tenth century B.C.E., they had planted settlements from one end of the Mediterranean to the other and had begun to venture out into the Atlantic Ocean.

The widespread colonial and mercantile efforts of the Phoenicians meant that they influenced cultures across the Mediterranean. Among their early overseas trading partners were the Greeks, and the Phoenicians may have played an important role in reintroducing urban life

to Greece after the collapse of the Mycenaean citadels. While each city of the Phoenician mainland had its own hereditary royal government, in the Phoenicians' overseas colonies a new type of political system emerged in which power was shared among a handful of elite families. This aristocratic form of government would become a model for many other Western societies, including those of Greece and Rome.

Without question, however, the most important contribution of the Phoenicians was their alphabet. As we noted earlier, a thirty-character system had evolved at Ugarit by the end of the Bronze Age. Around 1100 B.C.E., the Phoenicians refined this writing system to twenty-two characters. This simpler alphabet further facilitated trade and accounting, and the Phoenicians may have wanted to encourage similar practices among their partners to safeguard their own interests. The Greeks certainly remained aware of their debt to the Phoenicians: their legends ascribe the invention of the

Phoenician	Hebrew	Classical Greek	Modern Alphabetic
	א	A	A
	ב	B	B
	ג	Γ	G
	ד	Δ	D
	ה	E	E
	ו	Y	V
	ז	Z	Z
	ח	H	H
	ט	Θ	TH
	י	I	Y
	כ	K	K
	ל	Λ	L
	מ	M	M
	נ	N	N
	ס	Ξ	S
	ע	O	O
	פ	Π	P
	צ		TZ
	ק		Q
	ר	P	R
	ש	Σ	S
	ת	T	T

THE EVOLUTION OF THE ALPHABET. This table shows how the shapes of letters changed as the Phoenician alphabet was adapted by the Hebrews, the Greeks, and eventually the Romans (from whom our modern alphabet derives).

alphabet to Cadmus, a Phoenician who settled in Greece. Their debt is also clear in the close relationship between the names of letters in Greek (alpha, beta, gamma, delta . . .) and Phoenician letter names (aleph, bayt, gimel, dalet . . .), and from the obvious similarities in letter shapes.

The Philistines

Southward along the Levantine coast from Phoenicia lay the land of the Philistines, descendants of the Sea Peoples defeated by Ramses III. Their bad reputation is the result of their dominance over their neighbors, the herdsmen known as the Hebrews, who used writing as an effective weapon against them: the Philistines are the great villains of the Hebrew scriptures, and the word *philistine* has accordingly come to mean a boorish, uncultured person. Because the Philistines do not appear to have made use of the same powerful technology to record their own outlook on the world, and almost everything we know about them comes from the work of archaeologists, or has to be sifted through the bad press of their detractors. We know little about their language, but their material culture, behavior, and organization exhibit close affinities with Mycenaean Greece.

Philistine power was based on five great strongholds, the so-called Pentapolis (Greek for "five cities"): Gaza, Ashkelon, and Ashdod on the coast, and the inland cities of Ekron and Gath. Again, these citadels are strikingly similar to the fortified palaces of Mycenaean civilization, and they appear to have served many of the same functions. From these strongholds, the Philistines dominated the surrounding countryside by organizing agricultural production and controlling trade routes. An independent lord ruled over each citadel, and no doubt tensions and rivalries existed among them. But much like the heroes of Greek epic, the Philistines could set aside differences when facing a common enemy.

Because we see the Philistines primarily through the eyes of their Hebrew enemies, we must be careful about drawing conclusions about them from the stories of Goliath's brutality or Delilah's sexual treachery. Yet the Hebrews had good reason to fear the Philistines, whose pressure on the Hebrew hill country was constant and who threatened the Hebrews' holy sanctuary at Shiloh, where the sacred Ark of the Covenant was said to contain the original tablets of the law given to Moses on Mount Sinai. In Hebrew tradition, the tribes of Israel had once carried the Ark before them into battle against the Philistines, only to lose it in the fray and to witness thereafter the destruction of Shiloh. The Philistines then established garrisons throughout the land of the Hebrews, exacted tribute, and denied them access to weapons.

The Hebrews and Their Scriptures

The central feature of Hebrew culture, their conception of and relationship to their god, will be discussed at greater length toward the end of this chapter. In this section, we focus our attention on the development of Hebrew society— while acknowledging that religion is always related to politics, as well as to economic conditions and the concerns of everyday life. Indeed the Hebrews, like all ancient peoples, could not have distinguished among these phenomena.

In reconstructing the early history of the Hebrews, we are indebted to an unusual textual source: a series of scriptures (literally "writings") that comprise mythology, laws

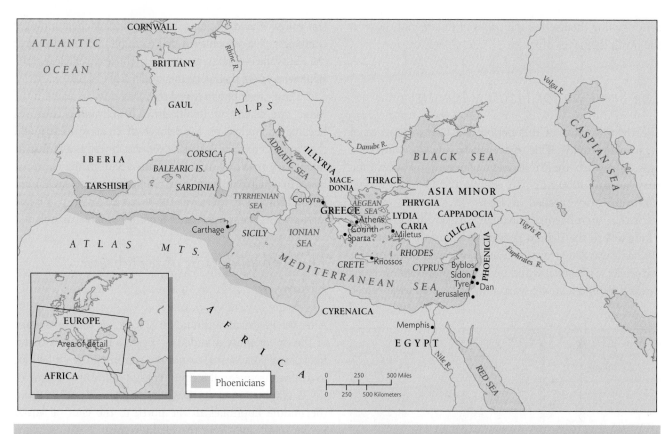

PHOENICIAN COLONIZATION. Compare this map to the more detailed one of the Hebrew kingdoms on page 46. ▪ *What part of the Mediterranean served as the homeland for the Phoenician city-states, and where did Phoenicians establish colonies?* ▪ *Why would overseas colonization be of such crucial importance to Phoenician city-states?* ▪ *What does their westward colonization imply about the Phoenicians' aims and about the different opportunities available in the West, as compared with the East?*

and ritual practices, genealogical records, books of prophecy, proverbs, poetry, and royal chronicles. These are collectively known as the Hebrew Bible or (among Christians) as the Old Testament. The books of the Bible were assembled over many centuries, mostly by unknown authors, copyists, and editors. Like other sources, they have to be treated as artifacts produced by particular historical circumstances, which also governed the way that certain texts were preserved and put together.

The first five books of the Hebrew Bible are traditionally attributed to Moses, but most of the materials in these books were borrowed from other Near Eastern cultures, including the stories of creation and the flood, which parallel those of Sumer (as we saw in Chapter 1). The story of Moses's childhood draws on a legend told about the Akkadian king Sargon the Great. And the story of the exodus from Egypt is fraught with problems. Although the later Book of Joshua claims that the Hebrews who returned from Egypt conquered and expelled the native Canaanites, archaeological and linguistic evidence suggests that the Hebrews were essentially Canaanites themselves. They may have merged with scattered refugees from Egypt in the aftermath of the

Sea Peoples' invasions, but for the most part they had been continuously resident in Canaan for centuries. In other words, the first five books of the Bible constitute a retrospective history whose purpose was to justify Hebrew traditions and claims to territory.

Among the other writings included in the Hebrew Bible are a group of texts which record events of the more recent past, those of the period we are considering now. These "historical books" are more straightforwardly verifiable, even if many details are difficult to confirm. According to the Book of Judges, the Hebrews were wandering herdsmen who had just begun to establish permanent settlements around the time of the Philistines' arrival in the Levant. They had organized themselves into twelve tribes—extended clan units whose families owed one another mutual aid and protection in times of war, but who frequently fought over cattle and grazing rights. Each tribe was ruled by a patriarch known as a judge, who exercised the typical functions of authority in a clan-based society: war leadership, high priesthood, and dispute settlement. By the middle of the twelfth century B.C.E., these tribes occupied two major territories, with those settled in the south calling themselves the tribes of Judah, and those in the north the tribes of Israel.

The Struggle for Hebrew Identity

The Hebrew tribes of this period had little experience of organized activity. This made them highly vulnerable, especially when the Philistines conquered the Levantine coast around 1050 B.C.E. To counter the Philistine threat effectively, they needed a leader. Accordingly, around 1025 B.C.E., an influential tribal judge called Samuel selected a king to lead the Hebrew resistance against the Philistines. His name was Saul. However, Saul proved to be an ineffective war-leader. So Samuel withdrew his support from Saul and threw it behind a young warrior in Saul's entourage, Saul's

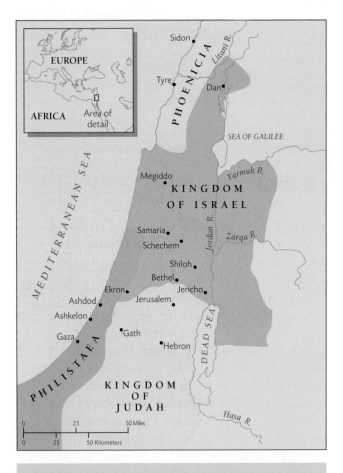

THE HEBREW KINGDOMS, c. 900 B.C.E. Notice the scale of the map and consider the comparatively small size of the Hebrews' world. ▪ *What advantages did the Philistines and Phoenicians possess, geographically and otherwise?* ▪ *Why did they present such a challenge to the Hebrews?* ▪ *What political and religious consequences might have resulted from the division of the kingdom after the death of King Solomon, given the location of Jerusalem?*

son-in-law David. Waging his own independent military campaigns, David achieved one triumph after another over the Philistines—that is, according to those chroniclers of the Bible who wrote their accounts under David's patronage.

These same books reveal that David was a man on the make; and when Saul finally drove him from his court, he became an outlaw on the fringes of Hebrew society and then a mercenary in Philistine service. It was as a Philistine mercenary that David fought against Saul in the climactic battle in which Saul was killed. Soon thereafter, David himself became king, first over the tribes of Judah, his home territory, and later over Saul's territory of Israel as well.

The Consolidation of a Hebrew Kingdom

After David's victory around 1000 B.C.E., he took advantage of the opportunity afforded by Egypt's decline to expand his control southward, eventually confining the Philistines to an inconsequential strip of coastal land. By the time of his death in 973 B.C.E., David's kingdom stretched from the middle Euphrates in the north to the Gulf of Aqaba in the south, and from the Mediterranean coast eastward into the Syrian deserts.

As David's power and prestige grew, he was able to impose on his subjects a highly unpopular system of taxation and forced labor. His goal was to build a glorious capital at Jerusalem, a Canaanite settlement that he designated as the central city of his realm. It was a shrewd choice. As a newly conquered city, Jerusalem had no previous affiliation with any of Israel's twelve tribes and so stood outside the ancient rivalries that divided them. Geographically too, Jerusalem was a strategic choice, lying between the southern tribes of Judah (David's people) and the northern tribes of Israel. David also took steps to exalt the city by making Jerusalem the resting place of the sacred Ark and reorganizing the priesthood of the Hebrew god, Yahweh. By these measures, he sought to forge a new collective identity centered on his own family and its connections to Yahweh. To this end, he also encouraged the writing of histories and prophecies that would affirm this identity and his central role in forging it.

The Reign of King Solomon (r. 973–937 B.C.E.)

Continuing his father's policies, but on a much grander scale, David's son Solomon built a great temple complex at Jerusalem to house the Ark. Such visible support of Yahweh's cult was approved by the historians whose works are included in the Bible, and who portray Solomon's reign as a golden age. However, Solomon was a ruthless and often brutal ruler whose promotion of Yahweh coincided with a program of despotism. To finance his expensive tastes and programs, Solomon instituted oppressive taxation and imposed customs duties on the lucrative caravan trade that passed through his country. With the help of the Phoenician king of Tyre, Solomon constructed a commercial fleet whose ships plied the waters of the Red Sea and beyond, trading—among other commodities—the gold and copper mined by Solomon's slaves.

Solomon also maintained a large standing army of conscripts from his own people. To undertake his ambitious building projects, Solomon required many of his subjects to perform forced labor four months out of every year. This level of oppression was too much for many Israelites, and the north seethed with rebellion against the royal capital. Within a decade or so of Solomon's death, in fact, the fragile monarchy split in two. The dynasty descended from David continued to rule the southern kingdom of Judah with its capital at Jerusalem, but the ten northern tribes banded together as the kingdom of Israel, with their capital at Shechem. In the meantime, the changing political situation of the Near East made the Hebrew kingdoms increasingly vulnerable.

THE REVIVAL OF THE ASSYRIAN EMPIRE

The Assyrians had long played an important role in spreading trade and promoting urban settlements. But like the other great powers of the Near East, their civilization had been devastated by the Sea Peoples. For several centuries afterward they struggled for survival. Then, in the ninth century B.C.E., a brilliant but brutal ruler laid the foundations of what historians call the Neo-Assyrian Empire. Under the leadership of Assurnasirpal II (*ah-sur-NAH-sur-PAHL*, r. 883–859 B.C.E.), these "new" Assyrians began to conduct aggressive military campaigns against their neighbors. Those whom they defeated either had to pay tribute or face the full onslaught of the Assyrian war machine, which under Assurnasirpal acquired a deserved reputation for savagery.

Despite their military successes, Assurnasirpal and his successors inspired stiff resistance. The northern kingdom of Israel formed an alliance with other small states to halt Assyrian expansion. This coalition ultimately forced the Assyrians to settle for smaller victories against the Armenians to the northwest and the Medes to the northeast. Thereafter, a cycle of violent oppression and rebellion continued until the reign of a military commander who took the name Sargon II (r. 722–705 B.C.E.). He claimed to be the direct successor of Sargon of Akkad, the first great king in Mesopotamian history, nearly 1,500 years earlier (Chapter 1).

Like the Hebrews, Sargon and his heirs skillfully deployed history as a political tool. And eventually, they extended the frontiers of the Neo-Assyrian Empire from western Iran to the shores of the Mediterranean. Briefly, they even subjugated parts of Egypt. Sargon himself put an end to the kingdom of Israel in 722 B.C.E., enslaving and deporting most of the population, and he terrified the southern kingdom of Judah into remaining a quiet vassal. By the seventh century B.C.E., Assyria was the unrivaled power of the ancient Near East.

Neo-Assyrian Government and Administration

The Neo-Assyrian Empire was built on the ability of its army to oppress both enemies and subjects alike. At its head was a hereditary monarch regarded as the earthly representative of the Assyrians' patron god, Assur. Supporting the

ASSYRIAN ATROCITIES. Judean captives whose city has fallen to the Assyrian king Sennacherib (r. 704–681 B.C.E.) are shown being impaled on stakes. This triumphal carving comes from the walls of Sennacherib's palace at Nineveh. ▪ *What would be the purpose of advertising these captives' fates?*

empire's centralized authority was an extensive bureaucracy of governors, high priests, and military commanders—professions by no means mutually exclusive. These administrators exercised local authority on behalf of the king. They maintained lines of transport and communication and they oversaw construction of an extensive network of roads across the Near East. The Neo-Assyrian state also deployed a system of spies and messengers to report on the activities of subjects and provincial governors.

Not surprising for a people so mindful of historical precedent, the Neo-Assyrians modeled their laws on the code of Hammurabi, though many of their penalties were more severe. Neo-Assyrian law was also rigidly patriarchal, which entailed substantial revision of Hammurabi's code: now only husbands had the power of divorce, and they were legally permitted to inflict a variety of penalties on their wives, ranging from corporal punishment to mutilation and death.

The Neo-Assyrian Military-Religious Ethos

The Neo-Assyrians' new religious, political, and military ideology took shape during the long centuries when they fought for survival. Its two fundamental tenets were the waging of holy war and the exaction of tribute through terror.

The Neo-Assyrians were convinced that their god demanded the constant expansion of his worship through military conquest. Ritual humiliation of a defeated city's gods was therefore a regular feature of Neo-Assyrian conquests. Statues of conquered gods would be carried off to the Neo-Assyrian capital, where they would remain as "hostages." Meanwhile, an image of Assur himself—usually represented as a sun disk with the head and shoulders of an archer—would be installed in the defeated city, and the conquered people would be required to worship him. Although subject peoples did not have to abandon their previous gods altogether, they were made to feel their gods' inferiority. The Neo-Assyrians were therefore strict *henotheists*, meaning that they acknowledged the existence of other gods but believed that one god should be the supreme deity of all peoples.

Rather than defeating their foes once and imposing formal obligations, the Neo-Assyrians raided even their vanquished foes each year. This strategy kept the Neo-Assyrian military machine primed for battle, but it did little to inspire loyalty among subject peoples. Assyrian battle tactics were notorious even by the standards of ancient warfare, in which the mutilation of prisoners, systematic rape, and mass deportations were all commonplace. Moreover, the Neo-Assyrian army was not a seasonal army of part-time conscripts or peasants, but a massive standing force of more than 100,000 soldiers. And because the Neo-Assyrians mastered iron-smelting techniques on a large scale, they could equip their fighting men with high-quality steel weapons that overwhelmed opponents still reliant on bronze.

The organization of this army also contributed to its success. At its core were heavily armed and armored shock troops, the main force for crushing enemy infantry in the field and for routing the inhabitants of an enemy city once inside. To harass enemy infantry, the Neo-Assyrians deployed light skirmishers with slings and javelins, combined archery and chariotry, and also developed the first true cavalry force in the West. They even trained a highly skilled corps of combat engineers to undermine city walls and to build catapults, siege engines, battering rams, and battle towers.

The Legacy of Neo-Assyrian Power

The successors of Sargon II continued Neo-Assyrian military policies while devoting great energy to promoting an Assyrian cultural legacy. Sargon's immediate successor, Sennacherib (*sen-AH-sher-ib*, r. 704–681 B.C.E.), rebuilt the ancient Assyrian city of Nineveh, fortifying it with a double wall for a circuit of nine miles. He constructed an enormous palace there, and he ordered the construction of a massive irrigation system, including an aqueduct that carried fresh water to the city from thirty miles away. His son rebuilt the conquered city of Babylon along similar lines. His grandson Assurbanipal (*ah-sur-BAHN-uh-pahl*, r. 669–627 B.C.E.) was perhaps the greatest of all the Assyrian kings. For a time, he ruled the entire delta region of northern Egypt. He also enacted a series of internal reforms, seeking ways to govern his empire more peacefully.

By Neo-Assyrian standards, Assurbanipal was an enlightened ruler, and one to whom all students of history owe a tremendous debt. Like his grandfather Sargon II, he had a strong sense of the rich traditions of Mesopotamian history and laid claim to them. But he did this much more systematically: he ordered the construction of a magnificent library at Nineveh, where all the cultural monuments of Mesopotamian literature were to be copied and preserved. This library also served as an archive for the correspondence and official acts of the king. Fortunately, this trove of documentation has survived. Our knowledge of history, not to mention all modern editions of the *Epic of Gilgamesh*, derive from the library at Nineveh.

When Assurbanipal died in 627 B.C.E., the Neo-Assyrian Empire appeared to be at its zenith. Its kings had adorned their capitals with magnificent artwork, and the Hanging Gardens of Babylon were already famous: these were artificial slopes whose cascading flowers and trees were fed by irrigation systems that pumped water uphill, an amazing marriage of engineering and horticulture. The collapse of this empire is therefore all the more dramatic for its suddenness. Within fifteen years of Assurbanipal's reign, Nineveh lay in ruins. An alliance had formed between the Indo-European Medes of Iran and the Chaldeans, a Semitic people who controlled the southern half of Babylonia. By 605 B.C.E., the Chaldeans occupied Babylon itself and had become the predominant imperial power in Mesopotamia and the Levant. In 586 B.C.E., they captured Jerusalem, destroyed the Temple, and deported the population of Judea to Babylon. Meanwhile, the Medes retired to the Iranian Plateau to extend their dominion there.

THE RISE OF THE PERSIANS

The Persian Empire emerged as the successor state to the empire of the Neo-Assyrians, after the region was ruled for a few decades by the Chaldeans and Medes. On these foundations, the Persians would construct the largest empire known to humanity up until that time.

The Persian Empire of Cyrus the Great

The Persians came to power rather suddenly, under an extraordinary prince named Cyrus who succeeded to the rule of a single Persian tribe in 559 B.C.E. Shortly thereafter, Cyrus made himself ruler of all the Persians and then, around 549 B.C.E., threw off the lordship of the Medes and began to claim dominion over lands stretching from the Persian Gulf to the Halys River in Asia Minor.

This brought the Persians into close contact with the kingdom of Lydia. The Lydians had attained great prosperity as producers of gold and silver and as intermediaries for overland commerce between Mesopotamia and the Aegean. Most important, they were the first people in the ancient Near East to use precious-metal coinage as a medium of exchange for goods and services. When Cyrus came to power, their king was Croesus (*CREE-suhs*), a man whose reputation as the possessor of untold riches survives in the expression "rich as Croesus." Distrusting his new neighbor, Croesus decided to launch a preemptive strike against the Persians to preserve his own kingdom from conquest. According to the Greek historian Herodotus, he took the precaution of asking the oracle of Apollo at Delphi whether this strategy was

a good one, and was told that he would destroy a great nation if he pursued it. The oracle's pronouncement was both ambiguous and true: the nation that Croesus destroyed was his own. Cyrus defeated his forces in 546 B.C.E.

Cyrus then invaded Mesopotamia in 539 B.C.E., striking so quickly that he took Babylon without a fight. Once in Babylon, the entire Chaldean Empire was his, and his imperial policies proved very different from those of his predecessors in that region. Cyrus freed the Hebrews who had been held captive in Babylon since 586 B.C.E. and sent them back to Jerusalem, helping them to rebuild their temple and allowing them to set up a semi-independent vassal state. Cyrus also allowed other conquered peoples considerable self-determination, especially with respect to cultural and religious practices, a marked reversal of Assyrian and Chaldean policies. Two hundred years later, a young Macedonian king, Alexander, would emulate many of his exploits and build an empire sustained by many of the same strategies (see Chapter 4).

The Consolidation of Persia

When Cyrus died in battle in 530 B.C.E., Persian expansion continued, and his son conquered Egypt in 525 B.C.E. But although Cambyses (*kam-BY-sees*) was a warrior king like his father, he left the Persian Empire a poorly organized collection of rapid conquests. After a short period of civil war, the aristocratic inner circle that had served both Cyrus and his son settled on a collateral member of the royal family as the new king. This was Darius, whose long reign of 35 years (r. 522–486 B.C.E.) consolidated his predecessors' military gains by improving the administration of the Persian state. Darius divided the empire into provinces, each of which was administered by an official called a *satrap*. Satraps enjoyed extensive powers and considerable political latitude, yet they owed absolute loyalty to the central government, as did vassal states such as the technically autonomous Hebrew kingdom.

Adhering to the tolerant policy of Cyrus, Darius allowed the various peoples of the empire to retain most of their local institutions but enforced a standardized currency and a system of weights and measures. Beyond this, he had little interest in imposing onerous taxes, martial law, or hegemonic religious practices. After centuries of Neo-Assyrian and Chaldean tyranny, the light hand of Persian rule was welcomed throughout the empire's far-reaching lands.

Darius was also a great builder. He erected a new royal residence and ceremonial capital which the Greeks called Persepolis ("Persia City"). He ordered a canal dug from the Nile to the Red Sea to facilitate trade with

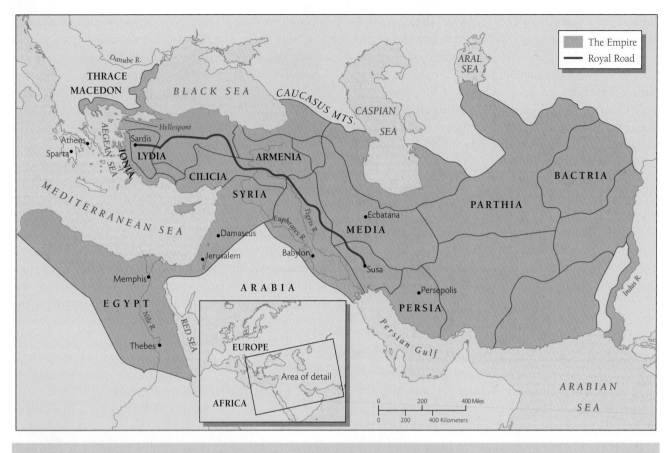

THE PERSIAN EMPIRE UNDER DARIUS I, 521–486 B.C.E. Consider the location of the Persian heartland and the four administrative centers of Persepolis, Susa, Ecbatana, and Sardis. ▪ *What older kingdoms and empires did the Persian Empire contain?* ▪ *Why is the Royal Road especially noted on this map?* ▪ *How did Darius I successfully rule such a large and complex empire?*

the Egyptian interior, and directed the installation of irrigation systems on the Persian plateau and the fringes of the Syrian desert to increase agricultural production. Darius also expanded the existing Assyrian road system to enhance trade and communications throughout his huge realm. The most famous artery was the Royal Road, stretching 1,600 miles from Susa, near the Persian Gulf, to Sardis (the old Lydian capital) near the Aegean. Government couriers along this road constituted the first postal system, carrying messages and goods in relay stages from one post to another. Each post was a day's horseback ride from the next, where a fresh horse and rider would be ready to carry the dispatches brought by the postman before him. An extensive imperial spy network also used this postal system, famed throughout Persia as "the eyes and ears of the king."

Clearly, Darius was a gifted administrator. But as a military strategist he made an enormous mistake when he attempted to extend Persian rule into Greece. Cyrus's conquest of Lydia had made the Persian king the overlord

of some long-established Greek-speaking cities on the eastern coast of the Aegean Sea, a region called Ionia. But these cities resisted even the easy terms of Persian rule, desiring instead to model themselves on the self-governing city-states across the Aegean. Consequently, between 499 and 494 B.C.E., the Greeks of Asia waged a war for independence and briefly gained the support of troops from Athens. Darius quelled this uprising and then decided to send a force to punish Athens and serve notice of Persian dominion over all Greek states. But at the battle of Marathon in 490 B.C.E., the Athenians dealt Darius the only major setback of his reign. And when his son and successor, Xerxes (*ZEHRK-zees*), attempted to avenge this humiliation in 480 B.C.E., a resistance led by both Athens and Sparta forced him to retreat and abandon his plans a year later. (We will discuss these events at greater length in Chapter 3.)

The Persians were thus compelled to recognize that they had reached the limits of their expansion. Thereafter, they concentrated on their Asian possessions and used money and diplomacy to keep the Greeks in check. This was not difficult, because the Greeks' hasty union in the face of Persian hegemony was short-lived, and they were too embroiled in wars with one another to pose any real threat to Persia.

The richness of their culture and the general tolerance they exhibited served the Persians well in maintaining their enormous empire. Unlike the Assyrians or Chaldeans, the Persians could count on the loyalty and even the affection of their subjects. In fact, their imperial model—the accommodation of local institutions and practices, consistent administration through a trained bureaucracy, and rapid communications between center and periphery—would be the one adopted by the great and lasting empires of the near and distant future.

The Spiritual Legacy of Zoroastrianism

Persia's political and cultural achievements were paralleled by a spiritual one, Zoroastrianism. This important religion was one of the three major universal faiths known to the world before Christianity and Islam, along with Buddhism and Judaism (to be discussed later in this chapter). Its founder was Zarathustra, known to the Greeks as Zoroaster, a Persian who probably lived shortly before 600 B.C.E. Zarathustra sought to reform the traditional customs of the Persian tribes by eradicating polytheism, animal sacrifice, and magic. That is, he wanted to redefine religion as an ethical practice common to all, rather than as a set of rituals and superstitions that caused divisions among people.

Zoroastrianism teaches that there is one supreme god in the universe, whom Zarathustra called Ahura-Mazda,

A CYLINDRICAL SEAL OF DARIUS THE GREAT (r. 522–486 B.C.E.). Seals were used in place of signatures to authenticate documents and correspondence. The cylindrical matrix (right) was rolled in soft wax to create an impression. This finely wrought example shows the king in a chariot, hunting lions with a bow. A winged representation of the god Ahura-Mazda rises above the scene.

"Wise Lord." Ahura-Mazda is the essence of light, truth, and righteousness; there is nothing wrathful or wicked about him, and his goodness extends to everyone, not just to one people or tribe. How, then, can there be evil and suffering in the world? Because, Zarathustra posited, there is a counter deity, Ahriman, who rules the forces of darkness. Yet he also posited that Ahura-Mazda must be vastly stronger than Ahriman.

Later teachers and priests of Zoroastrianism, the magi, placed greater emphasis on the dualism of these divine forces. They insisted that Ahura-Mazda and Ahriman are evenly matched, engaged in a desperate and eternal struggle for supremacy. Accordingly, light will not triumph over darkness until the Last Day, when the forces of Ahura-Mazda vanquish those of Ahriman forever. This vision of the universe would prove enormously influential, later informing the developing theologies of Christianity and Islam—not to mention the plots of much modern science fiction, fantasy literature, and film.

The devotion of the Persian imperial dynasty to Zarathustra's teachings made Zoroastrianism important to the conduct of Persian government, and also helps to explain the moderation of Persian rule. Unlike the Assyrians, the Chaldeans, or even the Egyptians, Persian kings saw themselves as presiding over an assemblage of different nations whose customs and beliefs they were prepared to tolerate. Whereas Mesopotamian potentates characteristically called themselves "true king," Persian rulers took the title "king of kings" or "great king," implying that they recognized the legitimacy of other kings who ruled under their canopy.

Unlike other ancient religions, then, Zoroastrianism did not exalt the power of a godlike ruler or support any particular regime. It was a personal religion, making private, spiritual demands as opposed to public, ritual ones. Its Wise Lord supported neither tribes nor states, but only individuals who serve the cause of truth and justice. According to its tenets, individuals possess free will and can choose to sin or not to sin; they are not compelled by an array of conflicting gods to act in particular ways. Zoroastrianism thus urges its adherents to choose good over evil, to be truthful, to love and help one another to the best of their powers, to aid the poor, and to practice generous hospitality. Those who do so will be rewarded in an afterlife, when the dead are resurrected on Judgment Day and consigned either to a realm of joy or to the flames of despair. In the scriptures of the Zoroastrian faith, known as the Avesta (compiled, like the Bible, over the course of many centuries), the rewards for righteousness are great, but not immediate. They are spiritual, not material.

Two Perspectives on Imperial Rule

> These two inscriptions exemplify two very different attitudes toward imperial power and two very different methods of achieving it. The first glorifies the victories of the Neo-Assyrian king Esarhaddon in Syria, and is one of the most important records of his reign (r. 681–669 B.C.E.). The second commemorates the taking of Babylon by the Persian king Cyrus the Great (r. 559–530 B.C.E.), whose empire came to encompass and surpass that of the Neo-Assyrians.

The *Stele* of King Esarhaddon at Senjirli, c. 680 B.C.E.

To Assur, father of the gods, lover of my priesthood, Anu mighty and preeminent, who called me by name, Ba'al, the exalted lord, establisher of my dynasty, Ea, the wise, all-knowing . . . Ishtar, lady of battle and combat, who goes at my side . . . all of them who determine my destiny, who grant to the king, their favorite, power and might . . . [I am] the king, the offering of whose sacrifices the great gods love . . . [he] who has brought all the lands in submission at his feet, who has imposed tribute and tax upon them; conqueror of his foes, destroyer of his enemies, the king, who as to his walk is a storm, and as to his deeds, a raging wolf; . . . The onset of his battle is powerful, he is a consuming flame, a fire that does not sink: son of Sennacherib, king of the universe, king of Assyria, grandson of Sargon, king of the universe, king of Assyria, viceroy of Babylon, king of Sumer and Akkad. . . . I am powerful, I am all-powerful, I am a hero, I am gigantic, I am colossal, I am honored, I am magnified, I am without an equal among all kings, the chosen one of Assur . . . the great lord [who], in order to show to the peoples the immensity of my mighty deeds, made powerful my kingship over the four regions of the world and made my name great.

. . . Of Tirhakah, king of Egypt and Kush, the accursed . . . without cessation I slew multitudes of his men, and him I smote five times with the point of my javelin, with wounds, no recovery. Memphis, his royal city, in half a day . . . I besieged, I captured, I destroyed, I devastated, I burned with fire. . . . The root of Kush I tore up out of Egypt and not one therein escaped to submit to me.

Source: Daniel David Luckenbill, ed., *Ancient Records of Assyria and Babylonia*, Vol. 2 (Chicago: 1926–27), pp. 224–27.

Inscription Honoring Cyrus, c. 539 B.C.E.

He [the god Marduk] scanned and looked (through) all the countries, searching for a righteous ruler who would lead him. (Then) he pronounced the name of Cyrus, king of Anshan [Persia], declared him to be the leader of the world. . . . And he (Cyrus) did always endeavor to treat according to justice the black-headed [people] whom he (Marduk) made him conquer. Marduk, the great lord, a protector of his people/worshipers, beheld with pleasure his good deeds and his upright mind, (and therefore) ordered him to march against his city Babylon. He made him set out on the road to Babylon, going at his side like a real friend. His widespread troops—their number, like the water of a river, could not be established—strolled along, their weapons packed away. Without any battle, he made them enter his town Babylon, sparing Babylon any calamity. He delivered into his hands Nabonidus, the king who did not worship him. All the inhabitants of Babylon as well as of the entire country of Sumer and Akkad, princes and governors (included), bowed to him and kissed his feet, jubilant that he (had received) the kingship, and with shining faces. Happily they greeted him as a master through whose help they had come (again) to life from death (and) had all been spared damage and disaster, and they worshiped his name.

I am Cyrus, king of the world, great king, legitimate king, king of Babylon, king of Sumer and Akkad, king of the four rims (of the earth), son of Cambyses, great king, king of Anshan, grandson of Cyrus, great king, king of Anshan, descendent of Teipes, great king, king of Anshan, of a family (which) always (exercised) kingship;

whose rule Bel and Nebo love, whom they want as king to please their hearts.

When I entered Babylon as a friend and (when) I established the seat of the government in the palace of the ruler under jubilation and rejoicing. . . . My numerous troops walked around Babylon in peace, I did not allow anybody to terrorize (any place) of the (country of Sumer) and Akkad. I strove for peace in Babylon and in all his (other) sacred cities. . . . I abolished the . . . [yoke] which was against their (social) standing, I brought relief to their dilapidated housing, putting (thus) an end to their (main) complaints. . . . All the kings of the entire world from the Upper to the Lower Sea, those who are seated in throne rooms, (those who) live in other (types of buildings as well as) all the kings of the West living in tents, brought their heavy tributes and kissed my feet in Babylon.

Source: Excerpted from James B. Pritchard, ed., *Ancient Near Eastern Texts Relating to the Old Testament*, 3rd ed. (Princeton, NJ: 1969), pp. 315–16.

Questions for Analysis

1. Both of these inscriptions constitute propaganda, but of different kinds. How do they differ? What audience(s) are they addressing? What function(s) does each inscription serve?

2. Each of these rulers claims to have a close relationship with the divine. How do those relationships differ, and what do those differences reveal about their attitudes to kingship and its sources of power?

3. Both of these kings boast of their royal lineage and their connections to past rulers. How different or similar are these perspectives? What do they reveal about these kings' awareness of history?

THE DEVELOPMENT OF HEBREW MONOTHEISM

Of all the important trends that we have traced in our study of the Iron Age Near East, perhaps none is of greater significance to the civilizations of the West than monotheism: the belief in a single god, the creator and ruler of all things. This development is traditionally associated with the Hebrews, but even the Hebrews were not always monotheists. Those who argued for the exclusive worship of Yahweh were a minority within Hebrew society, albeit a vocal and assertive one. How the Hebrews came to regard Yahweh as the only divine being in the universe, and to root their identity in such an exclusive religious outlook, is therefore a phenomenon that can only be understood within its historical context.

From Monolatry to Monotheism

For those who later advocated the exclusive worship of Yahweh, the early history of the Hebrews was full of embarrassments. Even the Hebrew scriptures reveal their propensity for the worship of many gods. Yahweh himself, in commanding that his people "have no other gods before me," acknowledged the attraction of those gods. The older, polytheistic Hebrew religion honored nature spirits such as Azazel and the Canaanite deity El, whose name is an important element in many Hebrew place-names (for example, Bethel) and became a synonym for "God." The temple built by Solomon at Jerusalem even included altars to Ba'al and his wife Asherah, a fertility goddess. Later Hebrew kings continued such practices, overriding the protests of religious purists devoted to Yahweh.

THE GODDESS ASHERAH. The Canaanite fertility goddess, Asherah, was the wife of the god Ba'al (or of his father, El), but she also figures in some inscriptions as the wife of the Hebrew god Yahweh. One Hebrew king even placed an image of her in the temple of Yahweh at Jerusalem. ■ *Why would this be viewed as controversial?*

By the beginning of the first millennium, however, the Hebrews living under the rule of David began to practice monolatry, meaning that they worshiped one god exclusively without denying the existence of others. Although the legendary prophet Moses is often credited as the first promoter of Yahweh's cult, sometime around the middle of the second millennium B.C.E., the ascendancy of Yahweh actually took place much later under the influence of the Levites, a tribe who claimed unique priestly authority and sought to enhance their own power and prestige by discrediting other gods.

The success of their campaign rested on the Levites' access to writing. The written word was especially potent in the ancient world because the skills necessary for its mastery were rare. In an age of constant threats to Hebrew religious and political sovereignty, the literacy of the Levites helped to preserve and promote Yahweh's worship. So did the political supremacy of the House of David, which bolstered its own legitimacy by allying itself with the Levites. The result was a centralized cult situated in the new royal capital of Jerusalem, which linked the political and the religious identity of the Hebrews to the worship of Yahweh as the supreme god.

Nevertheless, the worship of other gods actually increased in the eighth and seventh centuries B.C.E., perhaps in reaction to the austere morality demanded and imposed by the Yahwists. Thus, religious figures like Jeremiah (c. 637–587 B.C.E.) railed against "foreign" cults and warned of the disastrous consequences that would arise if Yahweh's people did not remain faithful to him. Moreover, Yahweh remained a somewhat conventional god, even in the eyes of his promoters. He was conceived as possessing a physical body and was often capricious and irascible. Further, he was not omnipotent; his power was largely confined to the territory occupied by the Hebrews.

Still, some of the Hebrews' most important contributions to subsequent Western religions crystallized by the middle of the eighth century B.C.E. One was their theology of Yahweh's transcendence: the teaching that God is not part of nature but exists outside of it. God can therefore be understood in purely intellectual or abstract terms, as entirely separate from the operations of the natural world.

Complementing this principle was the belief that Yahweh had appointed humans to be the rulers of nature by divine mandate. When Yahweh orders Adam and Eve to "replenish the earth and subdue it, and have dominion over . . . every living thing," his injunction stands in striking contrast to other accounts of creation in which humans are made to serve the gods. Finally, Hebrew religious thought was moving in this period toward the articulation of universal ethics—a universal theory of justice and righteousness. According to the Babylonian flood story, for example, a particularly petulant god destroys humanity because their noise deprives him of sleep. In Genesis, Yahweh sends a flood in punishment for human wickedness but saves Noah and his family, because "Noah was a just man."

The Hebrews honored Yahweh during this period by subscribing to certain moral precepts and taboos. The Ten Commandments as they now appear in Exodus 20:3–17 may not have existed, but they certainly reflect earlier ethical injunctions against murder, adultery, lying, and greed. In addition, the Hebrews observed an array of ritual practices unusual in the ancient world, such as infant circumcision, adherence to strict dietary laws, and refraining from labor on the seventh day of the week.

Yet the moral standards imposed by Yahweh on the Hebrew community were not binding when the Hebrews dealt with outsiders. Lending at interest, for example, was not acceptable among Hebrews, but was quite acceptable between a Hebrew and a non-Hebrew. Such distinctions applied also to more serious issues, such as the killing of civilians in battle. When the Hebrews conquered territories in Canaan, they took "all the spoil of the cities, and every man they smote with the sword . . . until they had

RECONSTRUCTION OF THE ISHTAR GATE. This is a reconstruction of one of the fifty-foot-high entrance gates built into the walls of Babylon by King Nebuchadnezzar around 575 B.C.E. About half of this reconstruction, in the Pergamon Museum of Berlin, is original.

destroyed them." Far from having any doubts about such a brutal policy, the Hebrews believed that Yahweh had inspired the Canaanites to resist so that the Hebrews could slaughter them: "For it was the Lord's doing to harden their hearts that they should come against Israel in battle, in order that they should be utterly destroyed, and should receive no mercy but be exterminated" (Joshua 11:20).

With the political fragmentation of the Hebrew kingdoms after Solomon's death, important regional distinctions arose within Yahweh's cult. As we noted previously, the rulers of the northern kingdom discouraged their citizens from participating in ritual activities at Jerusalem, thereby earning the disapproval of the Jerusalem-based Yahwists who shaped the biblical tradition. The erosion of a cohesive Hebrew identity was further accelerated by the Neo-Assyrians, who under Sargon II absorbed the northern kingdom as a province and enslaved nearly 28,000 Hebrews. The southern kingdom of Judah survived, but political collaboration with the Neo-Assyrians meant acceptance of the god Assur.

This was the whetstone on which the Yahwist prophets sharpened their demands for an exclusive monotheism that went beyond monolatry. Hebrew prophets were practical political leaders as well as religious figures, and most of them understood that military resistance to the Assyrians was futile. So if the Hebrews were to survive as a people, they had to emphasize the one thing that separated them from everyone else in the known world: the worship of Yahweh and the denial of all other gods. The prophets' insistence that Yahweh alone should be exalted was thus an aggressive reaction to the equally aggressive promotion of Assur by the Assyrians.

The foremost Hebrew prophets of this era were Amos and Hosea, who preached in the kingdom of Israel before it fell to the Neo-Assyrians in 722 B.C.E.; Isaiah and Jeremiah, who prophesied in Judah before its fall in 586 B.C.E.; and Ezekiel and the "second Isaiah" (the Book of Isaiah had at least two different authors), who continued to preach "by the waters of Babylon" during the exile there. Despite some differences in emphasis, these prophets' messages consistently emphasize three core doctrines:

1. Yahweh is the ruler of the universe. He even makes use of peoples other than the Hebrews to accomplish his purposes. The gods of other nations are false gods. There has never been and never will be more than this one god.
2. Yahweh is exclusively a god of righteousness. He wills only the good, and evil in the world comes from humanity, not from him.
3. Because Yahweh is righteous, he demands ethical behavior from his people. Over and above ritual and sacrifice, he requires that his followers "seek justice, relieve the oppressed, protect the fatherless, and plead for the widow."

Judaism Takes Shape

Through their insistence on monotheism as the cornerstone of Hebrew identity, the Yahwists made it possible for the Hebrews to survive under Neo-Assyrian domination. And as the Assyrian threat receded in the late seventh century B.C.E., so the Yahwists triumphed religiously and politically. The king of Judah during the waning years of the Neo-Assyrian Empire, Josiah (r. 621–609 B.C.E.), was a committed monotheist whose court employed prominent prophets, including Jeremiah. With Assyrian power crumbling, Josiah found himself in a position to pursue significant reforms. He presided over the redrafting and revision of the "Law of Moses" to bring it into line with current policies, and it was during his reign that the Book of Deuteronomy was "discovered" and hailed as Moses' "Second Law." Deuteronomy is the most stridently monotheistic book of the Hebrew Bible, and it lent weight to this new political program.

But within a generation of King Josiah's death, the Chaldeans under Nebuchadnezzar (as discussed earlier in the chapter) conquered Jerusalem, destroyed the Temple, and carried thousands of Hebrews off to Babylon in 587/586 B.C.E. This Babylonian Captivity brought many challenges, paramount among them the maintenance of the Hebrews' identity. The leading voices in defining that identity continued to be the patriotic Yahwists, the same people who would later spearhead the return to Palestine after Cyrus of Persia captured Babylon and liberated the Hebrews two generations later.

Among the Yahwists, the prophet Ezekiel stressed that salvation could be found only through religious purity, which meant ignoring all foreign gods and acknowledging only Yahweh. Kingdoms and states and empires came to nothing in the long run, Ezekiel said. What mattered for those living in exile was the creature God had made in his image—man—and the relationship between God and his creation.

The period of captivity was therefore decisive in forging a universal religion that transcended politics. Just as Yahweh existed outside creation, so the people who worshiped him could exist outside of a Hebrew kingdom. In Babylon, the worship of Yahweh therefore became something different: it became Judaism, a religion that was not tied to any particular political system or territory, for after 586 B.C.E. there was neither a Hebrew ruling class nor a Hebrew state. Outside of Judah, Judaism flourished. This was an unparalleled achievement in the ancient world: the survival of a religion that had no political power to back it and no holy place to ground it.

After 538 B.C.E., when Cyrus permitted the Hebrews of Babylon to return to their lands and to rebuild the Temple, Jerusalem became once again the central holy place of Hebrew religious life. But the new developments that had fashioned Judaism during captivity would prove lasting, despite the religious conflicts that soon erupted. These conflicts led to ever more specific assertions about the nature of Judaism, and to religious teachings that focused on ethical conduct as an obligation owed by all human beings toward their creator, independent of place or political identity. The observance of ritual requirements and religious taboos would continue, but not as the essence of religious life; rather, they would be symbolic of the special relationship binding Yahweh to the Hebrews. Eventually, the transcendental monotheism that emerged from these historical processes would become common to the worldview of all Western civilizations.

CONCLUSION

The centuries between 1700 and 500 B.C.E. were an epoch of empires. While the two great powers of the second millennium were New Kingdom Egypt and the Hittite Empire

After You Read
This Chapter

Go to **INQUIZITIVE** to see what you've learned—and learn what you've missed—with personalized feedback along the way.

REVIEWING THE OBJECTIVES

- The settlement of Indo-European peoples in the Near East had marked effects on the older civilizations there. What were some major consequences?
- Egypt's New Kingdom differed profoundly from the Old and Middle Kingdoms that preceded it. Why was this the case?
- The civilizations of the late Bronze Age were bound together by transnational networks. What were the strengths and fragilities of these relationships?
- What kingdoms and empires emerged in the Near East after the devastation caused by the Sea Peoples?
- Monotheism was a significant historical development of the first millennium B.C.E. Why is it so important?

in Anatolia, a host of lesser empires also coalesced during this period, including Minoan Crete, Mycenaean Greece, and the trading empire of the Assyrians. All were sustained by a sophisticated network of trade and diplomacy. But between 1200 and 1000 B.C.E. the devastation wrought by the Sea Peoples brought this integrated civilization to an end. These invasions cleared the way for many new, small states, including those of the Phoenicians, the Philistines, the Lydians, and the Hebrews. Many crucial cultural and economic developments were fostered by these small states, including alphabetic writing, coinage, mercantile colonization, and monotheism. Yet the dominant states of the Iron Age continued to be the great land empires centered in western Asia: first the Neo-Assyrians, then briefly the Chaldeans, and finally the Persians.

The empires of the early Iron Age were quite different from those that had formed an integrated Near East a thousand years before. These new empires were much more highly unified. They had capital cities, centrally managed systems of communication, sophisticated administrative structures, and ideologies that justified their aggressive imperialism as a religious obligation imposed on them by a single, all-powerful god. They commanded armies of unprecedented size, and they demanded from their subjects a degree of obedience impossible for any previous Bronze Age emperor to imagine or enforce. Their rulers declared themselves the chosen instruments of their gods' divine will.

At the same time, we can trace the emergence of more personalized religions. Zoroastrian dualism and Hebrew monotheism added an important new emphasis on ethical conduct, and both pioneered the development of authoritative written scriptures that advanced religious teachings. Zoroastrianism, despite its radical re-imagining of the cosmos, proved fully compatible with imperialism and became the driving spiritual force behind the Persian Empire. Judaism, by contrast, was forged in the struggle to resist the imperialism of the Neo-Assyrians and Chaldeans. Both systems of belief would exercise enormous influence on future civilizations. In particular, they would provide the models on which Christianity and Islam would ultimately erect their own traditions, just as the models of imperial governance forged in this period would become the template for future empires. In Chapter 3, we will look at the ways in which the city-states of ancient Greece both built on and departed from these models.

PEOPLE, IDEAS, AND EVENTS IN CONTEXT

- How did the Hittite Empire integrate the cultures of **INDO-EUROPEAN PEOPLES** with the older civilizations of this region?
- What do the reigns of **HATSHEPSUT** and **AKHENATEN** tell us about the continuities and limitations of pharaonic power?
- What factors produced the transnational networks of the Late **BRONZE AGE**?
- How did the civilizations of **MINOAN CRETE** and **MYCENAEAN GREECE** differ from one another, and from the neighboring civilizations of the Near East?
- In what ways do the **PHOENICIANS**, the **PHILISTINES**, and the **HEBREWS** exemplify three different approaches to state-building at the beginning of the first millennium B.C.E.?
- What was new about the **NEO-ASSYRIAN EMPIRE**? How do its methods of conquest and its military-religious ethos compare to the **PERSIAN EMPIRE** that followed it?
- How and why did monotheism develop in the Hebrew kingdoms? In what ways might **JUDAISM** have been influenced by **ZOROASTRIANISM**?

THINKING ABOUT CONNECTIONS

- In the religions of Akhenaten, Zoroaster, and the Hebrews we see a rejection of polytheism. What cultural factors may have contributed to this? What would you consider to be the long-term effects of monotheism as a motivating force in history?
- What patterns of success or failure appear to be emerging when we consider the empires that flourished in the Iron Age, particularly those of the Assyrians and the Persians? Are similar patterns visible in other periods of history, including our own?

STORY LINES

- The emergence of democracy was dependent on the historical circumstances of the ancient Greek world, including slavery and the exclusion of women from public life. It therefore differs markedly from the political system(s) described as democratic today.

- The Greeks were united only through a shared language and culture. The lack of a common political structure made it difficult for them to work toward a common goal except when faced with annihilation.

- The Athenians' leadership in the Persian Wars enabled them to dominate the Mediterranean, and also to influence our understanding of their historical legacy.

- The cultural achievements of the fifth century B.C.E. glorified the individual male and his role in the community, and also valorized Athenian imperial ambitions.

CHRONOLOGY

800–400 B.C.E.	Rise of the polis
c. 750 B.C.E.	Homeric epics transcribed
725–650 B.C.E.	Hoplite tactics become standard
c. 600 B.C.E	Militarization of Sparta
600–500 B.C.E.	Emergence of the Milesian School (pre-Socratic philosophy)
594 B.C.E.	Solon's reforms in Athens
546 B.C.E.	Cyrus of Persia conquers Lydia and controls the Greek cities of Ionia
510 B.C.E.	Overthrow of the Peisistratid tyrants in Athens
499–494 B.C.E.	Ionian Revolt
490 B.C.E.	Battle of Marathon
480 B.C.E.	Battles of Thermopylae and Salamis
479 B.C.E.	Battle of Plataea
478 B.C.E.	Formation of the Delian League
431 B.C.E.	Peloponnesian War begins
404 B.C.E.	Defeat of Athens by Sparta
399 B.C.E.	Death of Socrates

Before
You
Read
This
Chapter

The Civilization of Greece, 1000–400 B.C.E.

n the fifth century B.C.E., a Greek-speaking subject of the Persian Empire began to write a book. He had been to Egypt and along the African coast, to the Greek colonies of Italy, the cities of Persia, the wilds of Thrace and Macedonia, and all over the Aegean. He had collected stories about peoples and places even farther afield: Ethiopia, India, the Black Sea. We have already met this intrepid traveler, Herodotus (c. 484–c. 425 B.C.E.), who marveled at the pyramids of Giza (Chapter 1) and who told how the king of Lydia lost his power to the Persians (Chapter 2). His reason for compiling this information was timely: he wanted to write a history of recent events. As he put it, "Herodotus of Halicarnassus here sets forth the results of his research, with the aim of preserving the remembrance of what men have done, and of preventing the great and wonderful deeds of both Greeks and barbarians from losing their glory; and in particular to examine the causes that made them fight one another."

Herodotus's fascination with the Persians, Phoenicians, and Egyptians underscores the extent to which all Greek-speakers regarded themselves as different from other peoples. In fact, they had responded very differently to the Bronze Age collapse.

THE ACROPOLIS OF ATHENS AND THE PARTHENON. Many Greek cities were built upon mountain strongholds, but the most famous of these is the Acropolis of Athens. First settled in the Neolithic Period, during the Bronze Age it became a fortified palace—allegedly that of the hero Theseus—and then a precinct sacred to the goddess Athena, for whom the city was named. The Parthenon, its most important surviving structure, was built on the site of an older temple after the Athenian victory over the Persians at Marathon in 490 B.C.E., and then rebuilt after the Persians sacked Athens ten years later. Most of the damage it sustained thereafter occurred during modern wars. ▪ *Why was this site the focal point of so much activity?* ▪ *What do these successive events tell us about the relationship between place and identity?*

off from trade and communication. The use of writing declined to such an extent that knowledge of Linear B disappeared. Archaeological evidence suggests a world in stasis, isolated from the centers of civilization that were reemerging in the Near East.

The material realities of life in this era profoundly shaped the civilization that emerged from it. This civilization would emphasize political equality and modest display, principles that formed the basis of early democracies. At the same time, the hardships of daily life, which contrasted sharply with stories of a heroic and opulent past, made the Greeks suspicious of their gods. They came to rely far more on the power of individual human beings than on divine intervention in human affairs. They also developed an awareness that excessive pride in one's own accomplishments could be dangerous. While the gods favored those who showed initiative and daring, they would punish the *hubris* of those who failed to acknowledge their own limitations.

While they struggled to cooperate politically, they were able to unite around a common language and culture, and their shared values were distinct from those of the people they called *barbarians*: peoples whose speech, to Greek ears, sounded like gibberish ("bar-bar-bar"). They cherished individual liberty, participatory government, artistic innovation, scientific investigation, and the creative powers of the human mind. Although the practical implementation of these ideals would prove problematic—and continues to be so—our own civilization would be unimaginable without the political experiments and cultural achievements of ancient Greece.

FROM CHAOS TO POLIS

By the end of the twelfth century B.C.E., Mycenaean civilization had vanished. Except at Athens, the great citadels that had crowned the heights of mainland kingdoms were destroyed. Settlements shrank in size and moved inland, away from vulnerable coastlines, thus cutting themselves

Homer and the Heroic Tradition

Around the year 1000 B.C.E., the chaotic conditions that had contributed to the isolation of Greece were alleviated by a period of relative peace. The standard of living improved, artisans developed their crafts, and increased contact among individual settlements fostered trade. Greek pottery, in particular, became a sophisticated and sought-after commodity, which Greek merchants could exchange for luxury goods from abroad.

As trade became an increasingly important feature of the new economy, the personal fortunes of those who engaged in trade increased accordingly, leading to a new kind of social stratification based on wealth. The men who controlled that wealth were aware that their status was not founded on warfare or noble birth, as had been the case in the past. Instead, they began to justify their preeminence as a reflection of their own superior qualities as "best men" (*aristoi*). Wealth was one sign of this superiority, but it was not sufficient in itself as a claim to aristocracy, which literally means "the rule of the best." Those who aspired to this status were therefore expected to emulate, as far as possible, the heroes of old, whose stories lived on in the prodigious memories and agile voices of the singers of tales.

These singers, the guardians of a rich oral history that had never been written down, were part poets in their own right and part *rhapsodes*, "weavers of songs." The most famous is Homer, the poet credited with having woven together the mesh of stories that we know as the *Iliad* and the *Odyssey*, which crystallized around 800 B.C.E. The epics ascribed to Homer are vast encyclopedias of lore set at the end of the Bronze Age, the time his contemporary Hesiod called "the Age of Heroes" (Chapter 2): the age of Achilles and his Trojan rival, Hector; the age of Odysseus.

But these stories were not fixed in that time. Over centuries of retelling, the social and political relationships portrayed in the poems changed to reflect the assumptions and agendas of later ages. Treating these epics as historical sources, therefore, requires the historian to peel back layers of meaning. For example, Homer depicts a world in which competition and status are of paramount importance to the warrior elite, just as they were of vital concern to the aristocrats of his own day. Through the exchange of expensive gifts and hospitality, men aspiring to positions of power sought to create strong ties of guest friendship (*xenia, zeh-NEE-ah*) with one another, and thus to construct networks of influence that would support their economic, social, and political ambitions. This suggests that aristocrats in the Greek world conceived of themselves as having more in common with each other than they did with the local societies they dominated, something that is also reflected in the essential similarity of Trojans and Greeks in the *Iliad*.

However, the shared sense of a common culture among aristocratic households did not lessen the competition among them. Indeed, it led to competition over the epic past, as fledgling aristocratic clans vied to claim descent from one or another legendary hero. A hero cult might begin when an important family claimed an impressive Mycenaean tomb as that of their own famous ancestor, someone named in the *Iliad* and said to have come from that place. They would then develop a pious tradition of devotion that would extend to their followers and dependents; eventually, an entire community might come to identify itself with the famous local hero. The heroic ideal thus became a deeply ingrained feature of Greek society.

The Rise of the Polis

In the ninth century B.C.E., contacts between Greeks and Phoenicians intensified. Most crucially, the Greeks adopted the Phoenician alphabet, which replaced the long-disused Linear B. The Phoenicians also pointed the way to the revival of another lost art among the Greeks: seafaring. After the devastation of the late Bronze Age, Greek vessels hugged the shoreline and traveled only short distances. By the tenth century, however, Greeks were copying Phoenician designs for merchant vessels, which allowed them to set out on trading ventures of their own. As commercial activity increased, significant numbers of Greeks began to move to the shores of the mainland, to outlying islands, and to the eastern coast of the Aegean.

These economic and cultural developments were accompanied by dramatic growth in the Greek population, which placed heavy demands on the resources of a mountainous country with limited agricultural land. Soon, some degree of economic, political, and social cooperation among the inhabitants of rival communities became necessary. But the values that had developed during centuries of isolation did not make such cooperation easy. Each local community treasured its autonomy and independence, celebrated its own rituals, and honored its own heroes. On what basis could such communities unite?

The Greek solution to this challenge was the *polis*, the root from which we derive the words *politics* and *political*. The Greeks considered the polis to be a social collectivity, first and foremost—not a place. For this reason, our sources speak of groups of people ("the Athenians," "the Spartans") rather than individual cities. *Poleis* (the plural of *polis*) came to be so essential to Greek identity that Aristotle (see Chapter 4) would later define man as "a political animal," someone who participates in the life of the polis and who cannot survive outside it.

In practice, poleis combined both formal institutions and informal structures that could differ widely. Most poleis were organized around a social center known as the *agora*, where markets and important meetings were held. Surrounding the whole urban settlement, the *asty*, was the *khora*, "land." The khora of a large polis might support several other towns or smaller poleis, as well as numerous villages. The Greeks described this early process of community building as the "bringing together of dwellings" (*synoikismos*, synoecism).

Polis formation could also come about through the conquest of one settlement by another and/or through the gradual alliance of neighboring communities. Some poleis took shape around fortified hilltops, such as the Athenian acropolis (literally, the "high city"). Other communities may have borrowed a Near Eastern (and particularly Phoenician) practice of orienting the urban center around a temple precinct. In many Greek cities, however, temple building may have been a consequence of polis formation rather than a cause, as elites competed with one another to exalt their poleis and glorify themselves.

THE CULTURE OF ARCHAIC GREECE, 800–500 B.C.E.

Scholars date the Archaic Period of Greek history to the emergence of the polis and the return of writing, which the Greeks would put to a wide variety of uses. The Athenians, in particular, used writing to establish their cultural dominance over other Greek poleis, controlling the inscription of the Homeric canon, promoting the work of contemporary poets, and fostering the writing of prose histories, which allowed them to pass on to posterity a narrative of history in which they played the central role. It is therefore important to bear in mind that much of what we know about this early period derives from the work of later authors who wrote from this Athenian perspective: these include the Ionian-born Herodotus, who spent much of his later life in Athens; the historians Thucydides (c. 460–c. 395 B.C.E.) and Xenophon (430–354); and the philosophers Plato (c. 428–348) and his pupil Aristotle (384–322).

Colonization and Panhellenism

In the eighth and seventh centuries B.C.E., small-scale Greek trading ventures and settlements had developed into a full-fledged colonial enterprise that followed the example of the Phoenicians. Many larger poleis competed with one another to establish colonies, with Athens and Corinth being particularly successful in such ventures.

Although each of these colonies was an independent foundation, it sustained familial and affective ties to its mother polis; so it was often called upon to support the polis and could become entangled in the political and military affairs of the mainland. At the same time, these individual Greek colonies celebrated their shared language and heritage, which was exported to far-flung reaches of the known world, creating a Panhellenic ("all-Greek") culture that eventually stretched from the Black Sea to the Mediterranean coastlines of modern France and Spain.

Greek colonization permanently altered the cultural geography of the Mediterranean world. The western shores of Anatolia would remain a stronghold of Greek culture for the next 2,000 years. So many Greeks settled in southern Italy that later Romans called the region Magna Graecia, "Greater Greece"; Greek-speaking enclaves would survive there into the twentieth century of our era. By the fourth century B.C.E., more Greeks lived in Magna Graecia than in Greece itself.

Motives for colonization varied. Some poleis, such as Corinth, were blessed by their strategic location on the land bridge between Attica and the Peloponnesus (*pel-oh-poh-NEE-suss*; the large peninsula of mainland Greece), but cursed by the poverty of their land. Trade therefore became the lifeblood of this polis and of the ruling aristocracy who bankrolled the ambitious planting of colonies. Other poleis, confronted by the pressures of growing populations and political unrest, sponsored new colonies as outlets for undesirable elements or unwanted multitudes. These colonial projects parallel, in many ways, those of modern nation-states.

Colonial expansion also intensified Greek contacts with other cultures. Phoenician pottery brought new artistic motifs, while Egypt profoundly influenced early Greek sculptural representations of the human form (see *Interpreting Visual Evidence* on page 64). However, intensified contact with other cultures simultaneously sharpened Greeks' awareness of their own identity as Hellenes (the Greeks' name for themselves). Such self-conscious Hellenism did not lead to greater political cooperation, but it did encourage the establishment of Panhellenic festivals, such as the Olympic Games, and of holy sites.

The most important of these was the temple of Apollo at Delphi, home to the oracle of the sun god. Suppliants who sought to have their questions answered would offer gifts to the shrine and then wait while the god spoke through his priestess, whose mysterious answers would be translated into enigmatic Greek verse by an attending priest. The resulting advice was essentially a riddle that called for further interpretation on the part of the recipient—who often misconstrued it: as we noted in Chapter 2, Croesus of Lydia thought that he was following the advice of the oracle when he attacked the Persians, but the great nation he destroyed turned out to be his own.

At the Olympic Games, Greeks honored the king of the gods, Zeus, near the giant temple dedicated to him at Olympia. The Greeks took great pride in these athletic competitions, and only Hellenes were permitted to participate in them. Like colonization, these games did little to alleviate rivalry among the poleis; in fact, they often increased it. But they further strengthened the Greeks' awareness of their common culture, an awareness that could be harnessed when they faced a common threat.

Hoplite Warfare

In the centuries immediately following the calamities of the late Bronze Age, the defense of surviving Greek communities rested with the few elite warriors who had the resources to invest in armor, chariots, and weaponry. This monopoly on military prowess gave the aristocracy

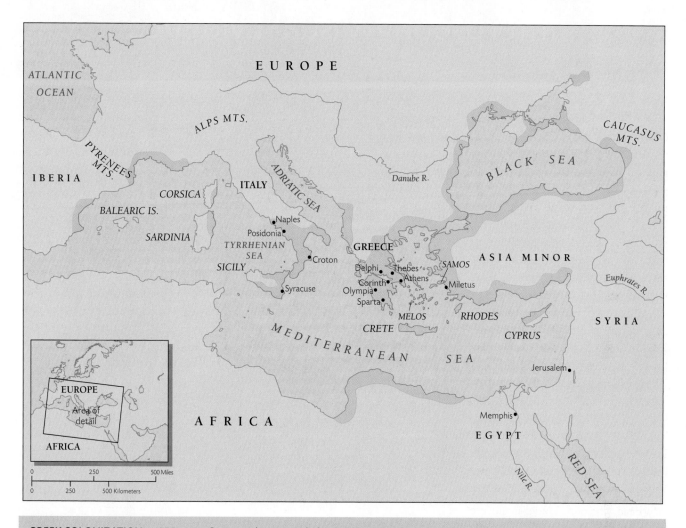

GREEK COLONIZATION, C. 550 B.C.E. Compare this map with that on page 45. ▪ *How do you account for the differences in Greek and Phoenician patterns of colonization?* ▪ *Were Greek colonies likely to compete with Phoenician colonies?* ▪ *Where were such conflicts most likely to erupt?*

tremendous political and social leverage. As a result, aristocrats dominated political offices and priesthoods in the poleis, as well as economic life.

But during the Archaic Period, a revolution in military tactics brought aristocratic military dominance to an end. Increasingly, the effective defense of a polis required that it be able to call on a standing militia. Accordingly, able-bodied citizens began to equip themselves for battle and to train alongside one another. These citizen-soldiers became known as *hoplites*, from the large round shield (*hoplon*) carried by each. In battle, hoplites stood shoulder to shoulder in a close formation called a *phalanx*, several columns across and several rows deep, with each hoplite carrying his shield on the left arm to protect the unshielded right side of the man next to him. In his right hand, each hoplite carried a spear or sword, so that an approaching phalanx presented a nearly impenetrable wall of armor and weaponry to its

opponents. If a man in the front rank fell, the one behind him stepped up to take his place; as a result, the weight of the entire phalanx was literally behind the front line, with each soldier leaning with his shield into the man in front of him.

This tight formation required only one shared skill: the ability to stay together. As long as the phalanx remained intact, it was nearly unbeatable. But like the polis itself, it could fall apart if its men did not share a common goal. The hoplite revolution was therefore bound up with a parallel revolution in politics. As a polis came increasingly to draw upon the resources of more and more citizens, it was forced to offer them a larger part in the exercise of political power. By the seventh century B.C.E., these citizen-soldiers formed a hoplite class that could demand a say in decision making and thereby challenge the hegemony of old elites.

The Ideal of Male Beauty

The Greek word *kouros* ("young man" or "youth") is now applied to a whole series of life-sized statues from the Archaic Period. The one shown here comes from Anavyssos in Attica, and was made between 540 and 515 B.C.E. (it is now in the National Archaeological Museum of Athens). Although scholars used to believe that such statues were meant to represent the god Apollo, further research has shown that most were made to commemorate the dead, especially young warriors who had fallen in battle. This one appears to be walking forward, smiling, but his eyes are closed. The accompanying inscription reads: "Stop and show your pity here for Kroisos, now dead, who once fighting in the foremost ranks of battle was destroyed by raging Ares."

Questions for Analysis

1. What aspects of the body does the kouros emphasize? If this is intended to be a model of Greek manhood, what values would it convey to contemporary youths?

2. Is this a representation of the young man as he was when living, or in death? How do your conclusions about the ideal of male beauty change if this is a glorification of death?

3. Compare this image to the values expressed in the verses by Tyrtaeus of Sparta on "The Beautiful and the Good" (page 67). How do these two perspectives complement one another?

Aristocracy, Tyranny, and Democracy

For the better part of the seventh and sixth centuries B.C.E., aristocrats continued to dominate the Greek poleis. Struggles for influence among competing families were commonplace, and these differences affected polis government at every level, not least because aristocrats were the only members of society who could afford to hold unpaid and time-consuming political offices.

The aristocrats of this period pursued not only wealth, power, and fame; they also cultivated a distinctive lifestyle. Participating in politics and holding office was part of this lifestyle. So too was the *symposium*, a "drinking party" at which elite men would enjoy wine, poetry and poetic competition, performances by trained dancers and acrobats, and the company of *hetaeras* (courtesans) who provided witty conversation, music, and physical intimacy.

Respectable women were excluded from such meetings, as they were from nearly all other aspects of public and political life (as will be discussed later). So too were non-aristocratic men. The symposium was thus an arena for the display of aristocratic masculinity.

The glorification of male sexuality was another important aspect of this homosocial aristocratic culture. Typically, a man in his late twenties to late thirties, who had just begun to make his career in political life, would take as his lover and protégé an aristocratic youth in his early to mid-teens. The two would form an intimate bond in which sexual intercourse played an important role. This benefited both partners and their families, and allowed the younger partner to learn the workings of politics while making valuable social connections. Many later philosophers, including Plato, argued that true love could exist only between such lovers, because only within such

HOPLITE INFANTRY ADVANCING INTO COMBAT. This Corinthian vase, dating from around 650 B.C.E., displays the earliest-known depiction of hoplites fighting in a phalanx formation.

a relationship could a man find a partner worthy of his affections.

A whole complex of values, ideas, practices, and assumptions thus shaped aristocratic identity. As a result, it was impossible for those outside this elite world to participate fully in the public life of the polis. By the middle of the Archaic Period, moreover, the circle of the aristocratic elite tightened even further, as smaller and smaller groups came to dominate higher offices. Many aristocrats found themselves on the outside of their own culture, looking in.

For these men, one remedy lay close at hand: an alliance with the rising class of hoplites. And occasionally, a single aristocrat with the backing of the hoplites would succeed in setting up an alternative form of government, a *tyranny*. The word *tyrannos* had been borrowed from the Lydians, and it signified someone who ruled outside the traditional framework of the polis.

A tyrant in Archaic Greece was not necessarily an abusive ruler. Indeed, tyranny often led the way to wider political enfranchisement because anyone who sought the support of the hoplite class would have to appease that class by extending further rights of political participation, while all the time striving to keep the reins of power in his own hands. But this was an inherently unstable state of affairs, because the continuance of tyranny became an obstacle to even greater power for the hoplite class. For this reason, tyrannies rarely lasted for more than two generations and could serve as a stepping-stone from aristocracy to a more broadly participatory form of government: democracy.

It is important to stress that our notion of democracy is quite different from that of the Greeks. In fact, Aristotle denegrated this form of government as "mob rule," because it gave too much power to the *demos*, a word meaning "neighborhood" or "affinity group." He saw it as a system too easily controlled by a particular faction. Our ideal of democracy is closer to what Aristotle would have called a *polity*—governance by the polis as a whole.

The Power of Poetry

The aristocracy of the Archaic Period were deeply invested in the heroic ideal enshrined in the Homeric epics. But they also strove to express their unique culture in newer poetic forms. The most characteristic of these is the lyric, a series of rhythmic verses sung to the music of the lyre. Because these songs would have been composed orally, even improvised, relatively few survive. But those that do are valuable historical sources. Because they were the focus of entertainment at gatherings, they are often politically charged, sexually explicit, or daringly subversive. For example, the poet Archilochus of Paros (c. 680–640 B.C.E.) flouts the conventions of epic poetry by mocking his own failures on the battlefield: "Some barbarian waves my shield, since I had to abandon it / . . . but I escaped, so it scarcely matters / . . . I can get another just as good." So much for the heroic ideal of returning either with one's shield, or on it! In another lyric, Archilochus

Analyzing Primary Sources

Songs of Sappho

Although Sappho of Lesbos (c. 620–550 B.C.E.) was a prolific poet and skilled musician, we know very little about her life, and only a few examples of her extraordinary verse survive. Of the nine books collected in the third century B.C.E., we now have just one complete lyric and a series of fragments, some consisting of only two or three words, often preserved because they were quoted admiringly by other authors. Astonishingly, though, a papyrus scroll containing a previously unknown part of a poem was identified in 2004. Another has since been found.

Fragment 16

Some say thronging cavalry, some say
    foot soldiers,
others call a fleet the most beautiful of
sights the dark earth offers, but I say it's
    whatever you love best.

And it's easy to make this understood by
everyone, for she who surpassed all
    human
kind in beauty, Helen, abandoning her
    husband—that best of
men—went sailing off to the shores of
    Troy and
never spent a thought on her child or
    loving
parents: when the goddess seduced her
    wits and left her to wander,
she forgot them all, she could not
    remember
anything but longing, and lightly straying
aside, lost her way. But that reminds me
    now: Anactória,

she's not here, and I'd rather see her lovely
step, her sparkling glance and her face
    than gaze on
all the troops in Lydia in their chariots
    and glittering armor.

Source: Translated by Jim Powell, *The Poetry of Sappho* (New York: 2007), pp. 6–7.

The New Fragment (2004)

Live for the gifts the fragrant-breasted
    Muses
send, for the clear, the singing lyre, my
    children.
Old age freezes my body, once so lithe,
rinses the darkness from my hair, now
    white.
My heart's heavy, my knees no longer
    keep me
up through the dance they used to
    prance like fawns in.
Oh, I grumble about it, but for what?
Nothing can stop a person's growing old.

They say that Tithonus was swept away
in Dawn's passionate, rose-flushed arms
    to live
forever, but he lost his looks, his youth,
failing husband of an immortal bride.

Source: Translated by Lachlan Mackinnon, *Times Literary Supplement*, July 15, 2005.

Questions for Analysis

1. How does Sappho use stories from the older tradition she has inherited to address her own concerns? How does the perspective of the female poet transform masculine ideas about heroism, beauty, warfare, and aging?

2. What are the challenges of working with such fragmentary sources as these? If these were the only pieces of evidence to survive from Archaic Greece, what conclusions could you draw about the society and its values?

---

castigates his faithless (female) lover and his even more faithless (male) lover with whom she has run off.

Given the male domination of Greek culture, it is paradoxical that the most famous lyric poet of this age was not a man. Rather, it was Sappho (*SAF-foh*, c. 620–550 B.C.E.), who lived in the polis of Mytilene on the island of Lesbos. Revered by her contemporaries, Sappho composed songs for a wide array of occasions and a range of moods: songs of courtship and marriage, longing and desire, loss, old age, and death. Often, they are passionately dedicated to women: both the women whom Sappho loved and the historical women who occupy the margins of masculine epic. Frequently, they take some image or incident from that inherited tradition and give it a distinctive spin. In one song, Sappho compares herself to Agamemnon, who was only able to return from Troy after he prayed to Hera, a goddess worshiped at Lesbos; Sappho now prays that her beloved will arrive safely with the goddess's help. In another, she imagines a scene not included in the *Iliad*, the joyous wedding of the Trojan Hector and his bride, Andromache. The intimacy of lyric thus reveals something that few sources from antiquity are able to convey: the feelings and desires of individuals who were often at odds with the dominant culture of their time.

Analyzing Primary Sources

"The Beautiful and the Good"

The poet known as Tyrtaeus of Sparta flourished during the middle of the sixth century B.C.E. He may originally have come from Athens, but whatever his origins he expressed ideas of honor, beauty, and virtue that were universal among the hoplite warriors of the new poleis. The key terms he uses in the following verses cannot be adequately translated into English, since these short Greek adjectives are freighted with ancient meanings: kalos *(beautiful, honorable), and* agathos *(good, brave, manly). They stand in opposition to the term* aischros *(shameful, ugly, mean).*

alos it is for an *agathos* warrior to die, fallen among the foremost fighters, in battle for his native land; but to leave his polis and rich fields and beg—that is most painful of all, as he wanders with his dear mother and aged father, his small children and his wedded wife. Detested he will be in the eyes of all those to whom he comes, constrained by need and hateful poverty. He shames his birth and belies his glorious appearance; dishonor and misery are his companions.

If no account is taken of a warrior who is a wanderer, if there is no respect for him or his family in the future, then let us fight with all our hearts for this land and die for our children, no longer hesitating to risk our lives. Young men, stand firm beside each other and fight.

Do not begin shameful flight or fear. Rather, create a mighty, valorous spirit in your breasts, and show no love for your lives when you are fighting. Do not flee, abandoning the older men, whose knees are no longer nimble.

For *aischros* it is for an older warrior to fall among the foremost fighters and lie out ahead of the young men—a man whose hair is already white and his beard grey—as he breathes out his valorous spirit in the dust, holding his bloody guts in his own hands, his body laid bare. *Aischros* is this to the eyes, and a cause of resentment to look upon.

But to the young men all is seemly, while the glorious flower of lovely youth is theirs. To men the young man is admirable to look upon, and to women lovable while he lives and *kalos* when he lies among the foremost fighters. So let a man take a firm stance and stand fast, with both feet planted upon the ground, biting his lip with his teeth.

Source: Excerpted and modified from *The Greek Polis*, eds. W. H. Adkins and Peter White (Chicago: 1986), pp. 23–24.

Questions for Analysis

1. How does Tyrtaeus characterize defeat? How does this poem exemplify the values and tactics of hoplite warfare?

2. Why is so much emphasis placed on physical beauty and youth? What other qualities are associated with the word *kalos*? Why is old age potentially *aischros*?

3. How does this ideal of male beauty compare with that made visible in the kouros of Anavyssos (page 64)?

PORTRAITS OF THREE POLEIS

The poleis of the Archaic Period developed in very different ways. To illustrate this diversity, we will examine three particularly well-documented examples: Athens, Sparta, and the Ionian city of Miletus. None of these, however, can be considered typical. There were approximately one thousand poleis in Greece, and about most of them we know almost nothing. But at least we can survey some of the features that, with variations, made each polis unique—and yet comparable, in some ways, to its neighbors.

Athens

The Athenians liked to boast that their city had been a great metropolis since the Bronze Age. But although Attica had long been a populous and prosperous region, Athens itself was of no great significance during the Mycenaean Era. When Athenians first came together to form a polis, theirs was a distinctly agricultural economy. Whatever profits aristocrats acquired through trade, they reinvested in land. Indeed, Athenian elites came to regard commerce as a disreputable means of earning a living, a mentality that persisted even when the city's excellent harbors made Athens famous as a mercantile polis.

THE ATHENIAN PNYX, WITH A VIEW OF THE ACROPOLIS. The Athenian assembly, the *ekklesia*, met on the sloping hill of the Pnyx. A speaker standing on the *bema* ("stepping stone," to the right) would have to make himself heard by all the citizens gathered in front of this platform, and all proceedings would have been plainly visible to noncitizens and foreigners in the *agora* (central marketplace) at the foot of the hill (off to the left). Overlooking it all was the temple of the city's patron goddess, Athena, on the crest of the Acropolis. ▪ *How is the relative openness and accessibility of Athenian democracy symbolized by this chosen site?*

In the Archaic Period, aristocratic dominance over this polis rested on the monopolization of elected offices and control of the city's council, the Areopagus (*ah-ree-OH-pah-gus*). By the early seventh century B.C.E., an even smaller group of aristocratic officials wielded executive authority in Athens: the *archons*, or "first men." Ultimately, nine archons presided over the entire governance of the polis. Although each served for only one year, all became lifetime members of the Areopagus. And because the Areopagus appointed the archons, it could therefore control its own future membership.

As power was consolidated by this small group, deep economic and social divisions developed. A significant proportion of the population fell into slavery through debt, while struggles among aristocratic families destabilized the government and fomented cycles of revenge killings. Finally, this situation inspired Athens' first attempt to promulgate a set of written laws. In 621 B.C.E., an aristocrat named Drakon sought to control civic violence through harsh punishments: hence our use of the term "draconian" to describe any severe penalty or regime. This attempt failed, but ultimately led both aristocrats and hoplites to an agreement. In 594 B.C.E., they elected one man, the poet Solon, as the sole archon for one year, and they gave him sweeping powers. Solon was an aristocrat, but he had made his fortune as a merchant and did not hold that vocation in

contempt; this meant that he was not allied with any single interest.

Solon's political and economic reforms laid the foundations for the later development of Athenian institutions. He forbade the practice of debt slavery and set up a fund to buy back Athenian slaves who had been sold abroad. He encouraged the cultivation of olives and grapes, thus spurring cash-crop farming and urban industries such as oil and wine production, as well as the manufacture of pottery storage jars and decorative drinking cups. He also broadened rights of political participation and set up courts in which citizens served as jurors and to which any Athenian might appeal. He based eligibility for political office on property qualifications, not birth, thus making it possible for someone not born into the aristocracy to gain access to power. Moreover, he convened an Athenian assembly, the *ekklesia* (*eh-KLAY-see-a*), and gave it the right to elect archons. Now all free-born Athenian men over the age of eighteen could participate in government. Even those who were not eligible for citizenship were able to see the workings of government for themselves, since the assembled citizens met on the slopes of the Pnyx (*pNIX*), a hill visible from the central marketplace and overlooked by the sacred precincts of the Acropolis.

Yet Solon's reforms were not widely accepted. The aristocracy thought them too radical; the people of the demos, not radical enough. In the resulting generation of turmoil, an aristocrat named Peisistratos (*pi-SIS-trah-tohs*) succeeded in establishing himself as tyrant in 546 B.C.E. Somewhat ironically, Peisistratos then proceeded to institute Solon's reforms. But the apparent mildness of his rule was undergirded by the quiet, persistent intimidation of his fellow Athenians by foreign mercenaries and the ruthlessness with which he crushed any dissent. Still, by enforcing Solon's laws, he strengthened the political role of the demos and remained a popular ruler until his death. His sons, however, were less able to control the various factions that threatened their rule: one was assassinated and the other ousted with the help of the Spartans in 510 B.C.E.

But the following period of Spartan-sponsored oligarchy ("rule of the few") was brief. Two generations of increasing access to power had left the Athenian demos with a taste for self-government. For the first time in recorded history, a group of commoners can be credited with the overthrow of a regime. The hoplites rallied behind Cleisthenes

(CLIE-sthen-ees), an aristocrat who had championed the cause of the demos after the fall of the Peisistratids. Once voted in as archon in 508/7 B.C.E., Cleisthenes took steps to limit aristocratic power. By reorganizing the Athenian population into ten voting districts, he suppressed traditional aristocratic loyalties. He also introduced the practice of ostracism, whereby Athenians could decide each year whether they wanted to banish someone for a decade and, if so, whom. With this power, Cleisthenes hoped that the demos could prevent the return of a tyrant and quell factional strife.

By 500 B.C.E., these struggles had given Athens a far more populist government than any other Greek polis, and had strengthened its political institutions. In the meantime, Athens had become the principal exporter of olive oil, wine, and pottery in the Greek world. It was poised to assume the role it would claim for itself during the fifth century B.C.E. as the exemplar of Greek culture.

Sparta

Located in the southern inland part of the Peloponnesus, Sparta took shape when four villages (and ultimately a fifth) combined to form a single polis. Perhaps as a relic of this unification process, Sparta retained a dual monarchy throughout its history, with two royal families and two lines of succession: a situation that often led to political infighting among their respective supporters.

According to local tradition, Spartan hegemony in the surrounding region of Laconia began with the conquest of Messenia, one of the mainland's few agriculturally viable territories. Around 720 B.C.E., the Spartans subjugated and enslaved the indigenous people there, the *helots*, who were forced to work under Spartan lordship. Around 650 B.C.E., however, the helots revolted, briefly threatening Sparta with annihilation. Eventually, Sparta triumphed; but the shock of this rebellion brought about a permanent transformation.

Determined to prevent another uprising, Sparta became the most militarized polis in Greece. By 600 B.C.E. everything was oriented to the maintenance of its hoplite army, a force so superior that Spartans confidently left their city unfortified. At a time when Athenian citizens spent more time legislating than fighting, Spartan society was becoming increasingly devoted to an older aristocratic ideal of perpetual warfare.

The Spartan system made every male citizen a professional soldier of the phalanx. At birth, every Spartiate child was examined by officials who determined whether it was healthy enough to raise; if not, the infant was abandoned in the mountains. This was a custom observed elsewhere in the ancient world, but only in Sparta was it institutionalized. If deemed worthy of upbringing, the child was placed at age seven in the polis-run educational system. Boys and girls trained together until age twelve, participating in exercise, gymnastics, and other physical drills and competitions. Boys then went to live in barracks, where their military training would commence in earnest. Girls continued their training until they became the mates of eligible Spartiate males.

Barracks life was designed to accustom youths to physical hardship. At age eighteen, the young man who survived this training would try for membership in a brotherhood whose sworn comrades lived and fought together. Failure to gain acceptance would mean that the young man would lose his rights as a citizen. If accepted, he remained with his brotherhood until he was thirty years of age. He was also expected to mate with a Spartiate woman, but occasions for this were few—a fact that partially accounts for the low birthrate among Spartan citizens. After age thirty, a Spartiate male could opt to live with his family, but he was still required to remain on active military duty until he was sixty.

All Spartiate males over the age of thirty were members of the citizens' assembly, the *apella*, which voted on matters proposed to it by the two kings and twenty-eight elders. This *gerousia* (*gher-oo-SEE-ah*, "council of elders") was the main policymaking body of the polis and also its primary court. Its members were elected for life, but had to be over the age of sixty before they could stand for office. Meanwhile, five *ephors* (overseers), elected annually, supervised the educational system and acted as guardians of Spartan tradition. In the latter role, ephors could even depose an errant king from command of the army while on campaign. The ephors also supervised the Spartan secret service, the *krypteia*. Agents spied on citizens, but their main job was to infiltrate the helot population and identify potential troublemakers.

Spartan policy hinged on the precarious relationship between the Spartiates and the helots, who outnumbered the Spartiates ten to one. Helots accompanied the Spartiates on campaign as shield bearers and baggage handlers. At home, however, the helots were a constant security concern. Every year the Spartans ritually declared war on them as a reminder that they would not tolerate dissent. Ironically, the threat of unrest meant that the polis was notoriously reluctant to send its army abroad.

Helot slavery therefore made the Spartan system possible, but Sparta's reliance on a hostile population of slaves was also a serious limitation. This system also limited Spartans' contact with the outside world in other respects. Spartiates were forbidden to engage in commerce, because wealth might distract them from the

THE PELOPONNESUS. Located on the Peloponnesian peninsula, the highly militarized society of Sparta dominated the region known as Laconia. ▪ *Where is Sparta located?* ▪ *How might Sparta's inland situation have influenced its outlook on foreign affairs?* ▪ *Did geography make conflict between Athens and Sparta inevitable?*

pursuit of glory. Nor did Spartiates farm their own lands, as Athenians did. Economic activity fell either to the helots or to the free residents of other Peloponnesian cities, who were known as *perioikoi* (pair-ee-OY-koy), "those dwelling round about." Unlike the residents of Attica, the *perioikoi* exercised no political rights.

The Spartans also self-consciously rejected innovation, styling themselves as the protectors of the "traditional customs" of Greece. In this role, Sparta tried to prevent the establishment of tyrannies in neighboring states and tried to overthrow them when they arose: hence their willing intervention in the affairs of Athens under the Peisistratids. Indeed, Sparta's stern defense of tradition made it an object of admiration throughout the Greek

world, even though few Greeks had any desire to live as the Spartans did.

The fatal flaw in the Spartan system was demographic. There were many ways to fall from the status of Spartiate, but the only way to become one was by birth—and the Spartan birthrate simply could not keep pace with the demand for trained warriors. As a result, the number of full Spartiates declined from perhaps as many as 10,000 in the seventh century to only about 1,000 by the middle of the fourth century B.C.E. Another flaw is historical: because the Spartans placed little value on written records, almost everything we know about them (including the summary offered here) must be gleaned from archaeological investigations or the propaganda of their rivals, notably the Athenians.

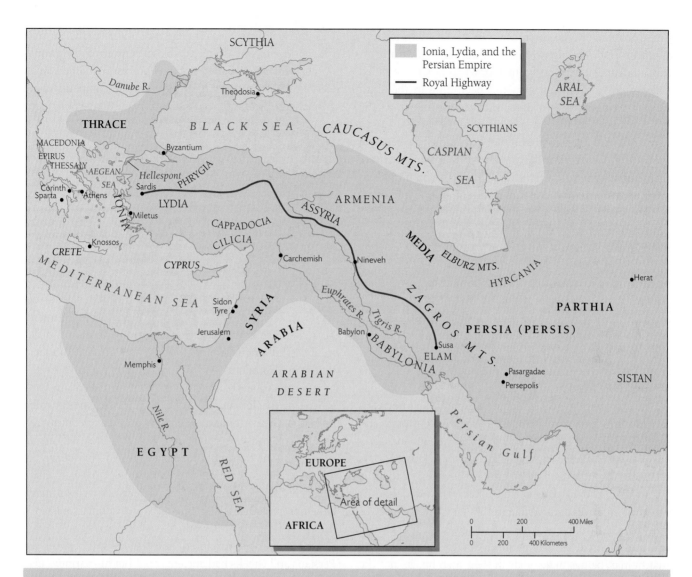

IONIA, LYDIA, AND THE PERSIAN EMPIRE. During the seventh and sixth centuries B.C.E., the Greek cities of the Ionian coast were the cultural and commercial leaders of Greece. But during the fifth century B.C.E., after the Persians conquered Lydia, they lost this position to Athens. ▪ *Where are Ionia, Lydia, and Miletus on this map?* ▪ *How does Ionia's geographical position help to explain the change in its fortunes?* ▪ *How might this change have influenced Ionian attitudes toward the Persian Empire?*

Miletus and the Ionian Revolution in Thought

Across the Aegean from the Greek mainland lay the Greek cities of Ionia on the central part of the Anatolian coast. Here, Miletus was the foremost commercial and cultural power. Long a part of the Greek world (see **Analyzing Primary Sources** in Chapter 2, page 39), it had also been shaped by Mesopotamian and Egyptian influences, and Milesian intellectuals were well aware of Near Eastern literature and learning. Some even echoed the vaunting rhetoric of Persian imperial decrees ("thus speaks Darius the Great King . . .") to make their own, quite different observations ("thus speaks Hecataeus of Miletus: the sayings of the Greeks are many and foolish").

The relationship between the Ionians of the coast and the interior kingdom of Lydia was close but difficult. It was through the Ionians that the Lydian invention of coinage was introduced to the Greek world, where it revolutionized trade, made wealth portable for the first time, and introduced a host of new philosophical and ethical problems. The Ionians, in turn, played a crucial role in Hellenizing western Asia while at the same time insisting on their independence. The major cities of Ionia ultimately banded together to form the Ionian League, a political and religious confederation of poleis pledged to support each other. This was the first such organization in the Greek world.

The Milesians founded many colonies, especially in and around the Black Sea. They were also active in Egypt.

These colonial efforts, combined with its advantageous position for trade, brought Miletus extraordinary wealth. At the same time, it became a center for what the Greeks called *philosophia*, "the love of wisdom." Beginning in the sixth century B.C.E., a series of intellectuals now known as the pre-Socratics (because they came before Socrates) raised new and vital questions about the relationship between the natural world (the *kosmos*), the gods, and men. Often, their explanations moved the direct influence of the gods to the margins or removed it altogether, something that other Greeks regarded as blasphemous. For example, Milesian philosophers sought physical explanations for the movements of the heavens, and did not presume that heavenly bodies were divine. By making human observations the starting point for their knowledge, they began to formulate scientific explanations for the working of the universe.

Stimulated by the cultural diversity of their city, Milesian philosophers also began to rethink humans' place in the cosmos. When Hecataeus (*heck-ah-TAY-us*) remarked that "the sayings of the Greeks are many and foolish," he was deriding his contemporaries' unquestioning acceptance of a narrow worldview. He set out to expand their horizons by traveling extensively and studying the customs and beliefs of other cultures. The philosopher Xenophanes (*zee-NOFF-uh-nees*) further posited that all human knowledge is relative and conditioned by experience: he observed that the Thracians (a people living north of Greece) believed that the gods had blue eyes and red hair as the Thracians themselves did, whereas Ethiopians portrayed the gods as dark skinned and curly haired, as they themselves were. He concluded that human beings make gods in their own image, not the other way around. If oxen could pray, Xenophanes declared, they would pray to gods who looked like oxen.

Such theories would become a distinctive strand in later Greek philosophy, yet they would continue to be regarded as disturbing and dangerous—dangerous enough to warrant the execution of Socrates in Athens a hundred years later (as will be discussed later). By that time, the Persian conquest of Lydia had made Miletus and its sister cities subject to that great empire. Ultimately, those poleis' resistance to Persian rule would trigger a momentous struggle for dominance and survival.

THE CHALLENGE OF THE PERSIAN WARS

The two major wars fought between the Greeks and the Persians were construed as defining events by those who witnessed and looked back on them. From the first, the contest was unequal. Persia was the largest and most efficient state the world had ever seen, capable of mustering over a million armed men. The Greeks, by contrast, remained a collection of disparate communities, fiercely competitive and suspicious of one another. An exceptionally large polis, such as Athens or Sparta, might put 10,000 hoplites in the field; but the vast majority of Greek states could only provide a few hundred each. So the threat of Persian conquest loomed large on the Greek horizon.

The Ionian Revolt (499–494 B.C.E.)

For the first time in the history of Western civilizations, we can follow the unfolding of events through the narrative of a contemporary historian. Herodotus self-consciously set out to write an account of his own times in careful, unambiguous prose, rather than in the form of heroic poetry or the boastful language of victorious inscriptions. And luckily for us, Herodotus was uniquely qualified to probe the long-term and more immediate causes of the Persian Wars. Raised in the Ionian polis of Halicarnassus, he regarded both the Greeks and the Persians as great peoples. Yet, as a Greek himself—albeit one born within the Persian dominion—he was not impartial. Indeed, his surviving account reflects the intellectual currents of Athens, where he spent the better part of his career, as well as many Athenian prejudices. This is something we must be bear in mind when reading his work.

Herodotus was careful to show that the war between the Persians and Greeks had ancient roots, but his narrative also shows that the catalyst was a political conflict in Miletus. In 501 B.C.E., the city was governed by Aristagoras (*ah-ris-TAG-or-us*), a tyrant who owed his power to the backing of the Persian emperor, Darius. But apparently Aristagoras came to believe that his days as the emperor's favorite were numbered. So he turned abruptly from puppet to patriot, rousing the Milesians and the rest of Ionia to revolt against Persian rule. As a safeguard, he also sought military support from sympathetic poleis on the Greek mainland. The Spartans refused to send their army abroad, but Athens and Eretria, on the island of Euboea, agreed to send twenty-five ships and crews. This small force managed to capture the old Lydian capital of Sardis (by then a Persian administrative center) and burn it to the ground. Then the Athenians and Eretrians went home, leaving the Ionian colonies to their own devices. In 494 B.C.E., these rebellious poleis were finally overwhelmed by the vastly superior might of Persia.

Darius realized, however, that as long as his Greek subjects could cast a hopeful eye to their neighbors across the Aegean, they would forge alliances. He therefore decided

A MODERN REPLICA OF AN ATHENIAN TRIREME. These versatile warships were much more powerful than the old 50-oared pentakonters that had been in use for centuries. As the name suggests, a trireme featured three banks of oars on each side, 170 oars in total. These were manned by citizen rowers seated on benches at three different levels in the vessel's hold. In battle, rowers could help power a ship forward, turn it, and keep it on course in a chase, even when sailing into the wind. In favorable winds, sails could be used to add speed. ■ *How does this new military technology build on some of the same strategies as hoplite warfare?*

to launch a preemptive strike against Athens and Eretria, to teach these upstart poleis a lesson. In the summer of 490 B.C.E., a punitive expedition of 20,000 soldiers crossed the Aegean. Their forces sacked and burned Eretria to the ground, sending its population into captivity in Persia. They then crossed the narrow strait to Attica, landing on the plain of Marathon, approximately 26 miles from Athens.

Marathon and Its Aftermath

In this emergency, the Athenians sought help from the only polis that could conceivably help them avoid annihilation: Sparta. But the Spartans responded that they were unable to assist—they were celebrating a religious festival. Only the small, nearby polis of Plataea offered the Athenians aid. Heavily outnumbered and without effective cavalry to counter that of the Persians, the Athenian hoplites took a position between two hills blocking the main road to the polis. After a standoff of several days, the Athenian general Miltiades (*mil-TIE-uh-dees*) received word that the Persians were watering their horses, and that the Persian infantry was vulnerable. Miltiades led a charge that smashed the Persian force and resulted in crippling losses. Almost unbelievably,

the Athenians had defeated the world's major imperial power, and they had done it without Spartan help. It was a vindication of hoplite tactics and a tremendous boost to Athenian confidence.

Yet the Athenian politician Themistocles (*theh-MIS-toh-klees*) warned that the Persians would retaliate with an even larger force. So when the Athenians discovered a rich vein of silver ore in the Attic countryside a few years later, they used the windfall to finance a fleet of 200 triremes, state-of-the-art warships.

Xerxes' Invasion

Darius the Great was succeeded by his son Xerxes (*ZERK-sees*), who almost immediately began preparing a massive invasion of Greece to avenge his father's shame. Supported by a fleet of 600 ships, this grand army set out in 480 B.C.E., crossing the narrow strait separating Europe from Asia. But unlike his father, who had dispatched talented generals to lead the earlier attack on Athens, Xerxes led this campaign himself.

Many Greek poleis capitulated immediately. But Athens, Sparta, Corinth, and some thirty others hastily formed a Hellenic League: an unprecedented alliance. In August

GREEK FORCES DEFEAT PERSIANS. This detail from a bowl commemorating the defeat of Xerxes' army depicts an Athenian hoplite poised to strike a death-blow to his Persian opponent. The artist has carefully delineated the differences between the enemies' dress and weaponry. To the Greeks, the Persian preference for trousers over short tunics seemed particularly barbaric and effeminate.

THE PERSIAN WARS WITH GREECE. Imagine that you are the Persian emperor Xerxes, planning the conquest of Greece in 480 B.C.E. ▪ *What are the two possible routes that you could take to attack Greece?* ▪ *What geographical considerations would dictate your military strategy?* ▪ *Bearing in mind that Xerxes' attempt failed, what would you have done differently?*

of 480, a major Persian offensive was held at bay when the outnumbered Greek allies, under the military leadership of Sparta, confronted Xerxes at the mountain pass of Thermopylae (*ther-MO-pih-lie*). For three days, they valiantly held off the Persian multitude. Meanwhile, a Greek fleet led by Athens engaged a Persian flotilla. The Spartans' defense of Thermopylae ultimately failed, but their sacrifice of some 300 warriors allowed the new Athenian warships to inflict heavy losses on the Persians.

However, these engagements left Athens without any men to defend their city. Themistocles therefore persuaded the entire population to abandon Athens for the island of Salamis. From there, the Athenians watched the Persians torch their city. Time, however, was on their side. Xerxes'

massive army depended on his damaged fleet for supplies, and the Persians' military tactics—which included a heavy reliance on cavalry and chariots—were not adapted for the rocky terrain of Greece.

In late September, the numerically superior Persian fleet sailed into the straits of Salamis. So confident was Xerxes that he had a throne placed above the bay, where he would have a good view of his victory. Instead, he watched as the Athenian triremes demolished the Persian fleet. This was the turning point of the war. When the allied Greek army met the Persians on favorable terrain the next spring—an open plain near Plataea—the Greeks prevailed. Against all odds, the small, fractious poleis had defeated the mightiest army of the known world.

THE GOLDEN AGE OF CLASSICAL GREECE

In the half century after the Persian Wars, Athens enjoyed a meteoric rise in power and prestige, becoming the premier naval power of the eastern Mediterranean. Athens also emerged as leader of the Delian League, a group of poleis whose representatives met on the sacred island of Delos and pledged to continue the war against Persia. The fifth century B.C.E. also witnessed the greatest achievements in Athenian culture and politics.

Periclean Athens

The reforms of the decades before the Persian Wars continued to encourage further experiments in democracy, including the selection of major officeholders by lot. Only one key position was now filled by traditional voting: the office of *strategos*, or general. This office became the career goal of Athens' most ambitious men.

Meanwhile, new voices were demanding a greater role in government. Most prominent were the *thetes* (THAY-tees), the class of free men that provided the triremes' rowers, the backbone of the all-important Athenian fleet. Like the hoplites of the Archaic Period, who had achieved citizenship because they were indispensible to the defense of the poleis, thetes wanted higher status and equal representation. The man who emerged to champion their cause was Pericles (PEHR-eh-klees), an aristocrat from one of Athens' most prestigious families.

Pericles advocated a foreign policy that was oriented away from cooperation with Sparta. In 462–461 B.C.E. he was elected strategos and immediately used his position to push through reforms that gave every Athenian citizen the right to propose and amend legislation, not just to vote yes or no in the citizens' assembly. And by paying an average day's wage for attendance, he made it easier for poorer citizens to participate in the assembly and in courts of justice. Through such measures, the thetes and other free men of modest means became a dominant force in politics—and loyal to the man who had made that dominance possible.

Athenian Literature and Drama

Pericles glorified Athens with an ambitious scheme of public building and lavish festivals honoring the gods. The most important of these was the Dionysia, a great spring feast devoted to the god Dionysus, which became a forum for the presentation of drama. From the beginning, Greek theater was closely connected to the political and religious life of the state that sponsored it. Indeed, the very format of classical tragedy replicates the tensions of democracy, showcasing the conflict among opposing perspectives. This format was perfected under the great tragedian Aeschylus (EYE-skihl-us, 525–456 B.C.E.) and his younger contemporary, Sophocles (496–406 B.C.E.). Their dramas made use of two and eventually three professional actors (each of whom could play numerous roles) and a chorus of Athenian citizens, which represented collective opinion and could comment on the action.

THE THEATER AT EPIDAUROS. Greek dramas were invariably presented in the open air, usually at dawn. Since these were civic spectacles, theaters had to be large enough to accommodate all citizens. Most, like this one at Epidauros (right), took advantage of the natural slope of a hill. The plan for the theater is shown above (left). The acting area would have been backed by a high wall, the *skene*, which housed stage machinery and enhanced the acoustics. A trained actor standing in the circular *orchestra* would have been audible even to those seated in the top tier. ■ *How would the size and setting of such a theater enhance the political character of the plays performed within it?*

Past and Present

Political Satire

In the fifth century B.C.E., the playwright Aristophanes took an older form of comedy, the satyr play, and turned it into a vehicle for what we still call satire. Instead of gently mocking the gods, he lampooned the politics, popular culture, and current events of his own day—and so made his fellow citizens take a fresh look at themselves. If he were alive today, he might be working for *The Daily Show*.

Watch related author videos on the Student Site
wwnorton.com/college/history/western-civilizationsBrief4

Tragedies were almost always set in the distant or mythical past, yet were intended to address the cutting-edge issues of their day. However, the very earliest of all surviving tragedies, Aeschylus's *The Persians*, represents events of the playwright's own lifetime. (We know for certain that he fought at Marathon, because he had this fact proudly recorded on his tomb.) Performed for the first time in 472, it tells the story of the great Athenian victory at Salamis, but through the eyes of the defeated Xerxes, who thus becomes its tragic hero.

But even when its subject matter was derived from the epics of Homer, the fundamental themes of tragedy—the conflicting demands of personal desire and public duty, the unforeseen consequences of human actions, the brutalizing effects of power—addressed problems of immediate concern. For example, *Oedipus at Colonus*, one of Sophocles' later tragedies, used a story of the mythical king of Thebes to comment bitterly on Athens' disastrous war with Sparta (to be discussed later in the chapter). Similarly, the *Trojan Women* of Euripides (485–406 B.C.E.), presented in 415, marks the tragic

turning point in the Athenians' march toward defeat in that war. By looking back at the capture, rape, and enslavement of Troy's women, Athenians were forced to look ahead to the consequences of their own imperial policies.

Comedy was even more obviously a genre of political commentary, and could deal openly with the absurdities and atrocities of current events. Indeed comedy—then as now—could be effectively deployed to deal with issues that were too hot to handle in any other form: sexual scandals, political corruption, moral hypocrisy, intellectual pretension, popular fads. Aristophanes (*EHR-ih-STOFF-ah-nees*, c. 446–386 B.C.E.), the greatest of the Athenian comic playwrights, lampooned everything from the philosophy of Socrates to the tragedies of his contemporary Euripides, and was an especially outspoken critic of Athenian warmongers and their imperialist aims. He was repeatedly dragged into court to defend himself against the demagogues he attacked, but the power and popularity of comic theater was such that politicians never dared to shut it down for long.

APOLLO OF TENEA, APOLLO OF PIOMBINO, AND THE CRITIAN BOY. These three statues, dating from about 560, 500, and 480 B.C.E., respectively, display the development of Greek statuary art. The first rather stiff and symmetrical statue (left) is imitative of Egyptian sculpture. Roughly half a century later, the second representation (middle) of Apollo begins to display motion, not unlike the *kouros* on page 64. The last figure (right), showing a boy standing in a relaxed posture with his weight resting on one leg, displays even greater naturalism.

Periclean Athens was also fertile ground for the development of new literary forms. Even though the Greeks were becoming more dependent on writing for legal and commercial transactions, intellectuals had long been used to expressing themselves through poetry, which was always intended to be sung and enjoyed in performance, not to be read. Now, though, the rise of functional literacy in Athens encouraged the emergence of prose as a distinct literary form. Herodotus found a ready market for his histories in Athens. His younger contemporary Thucydides (*thu-SID-ih-dees*) followed suit, using his time in exile to write a masterful—and scathingly critical—history of the war between his polis and Sparta.

Between them, these two historians developed a new approach to the study of the past, emphasizing the need to collect and interpret multiple sources and focusing on human agency as the driving force of history (rather than

divine intervention). Both conceived the historian's role as distinct from that of a mere storyteller. The word *historia* would continue to mean both "story" and "history" in Greek, but for Herodotus and Thucydides the historian's task was to investigate and critically reflect on the events of his own time, as well as to illuminate those of the past. These methods and goals would increasingly come to inform other prose genres, including the philosophical writings of Plato and Aristotle (see Chapter 4).

Art and Architecture

The artists of fifth-century B.C.E. Athens revealed the same range of talents in the visual arts as poets did in their dramas. Perhaps the most striking development was the new attention paid to the crafting of naturalistic figures, both clothed and nude. Nothing like it had ever been seen before, although it is a trend already discernible in the figure of the *kouros* examined earlier in the chapter (page 64). What hastened the acceptance of naturalism is a matter of intense debate, but scholars have long wanted to link this innovation to the triumphant victories over the Persians. Greeks tended to regard the Persian male's modesty of dress, preference for trousers, fondness for jewelry, and luxurious long hair as proofs of effeminacy (see the vase painting on page 73), whereas Greek men took pride in exercising, sculpting their physiques, and participating in athletic contests in the nude. A Greek might have said that only barbarians covered their shameful bodies in constricting clothes; free men celebrate their individuality in the care of the body and its representation in art.

The Athenians also made exceptional contributions to architecture in this period. All Greek temples sought to create an impression of harmony, but the Parthenon of Athens, built between 447 and 438 B.C.E., is generally considered the finest example (see page 60). Construction of this expensive and structurally ambitious building was urged on the Athenians by Pericles as a tribute to their patron goddess, Athena Parthenos ("Athena the Virgin"), and as a symbol of their own power, confidence, and genius.

The Daily Life of Athens: Men, Women, and Slaves

Toward the end of his famous funeral oration, which Thucydides quotes in his history, Pericles addresses only a few brief remarks to the women of Athens who mourn their fallen fathers, husbands, and sons in the first year of the disastrous war with Sparta. He urges them to do three things: rear more children for the support of Athens and its wars, show no more weakness than is "natural to their sex," and attract no attention to themselves. His remarks reveal widely held attitudes toward women in classical Greece, although they may not reflect complex historical realities.

The growth of democracy did not lead to greater equality between the sexes; in fact, it had the opposite result. In Mycenaean Greece, women had been viewed as possessing extraordinary funds of courage and wisdom. They were prized for their shrewd advice on political and military matters, and they played an active role in the world. Sometimes they ruled kingdoms in their own right. But as aristocratic ideals gave way to more democratic ones, Greek women increasingly spent their lives in the confinement of the home.

The importance of the hoplite infantry and its spirit of shared purpose encouraged men to train together and to develop close relationships. At the same time, that spirit of equality discouraged the political agency of women. Instead, the production of children to supply the infantry became the female imperative. Public spaces were largely restricted to male activities, while domestic spaces were reserved for female endeavors such as child care and weaving. Respectable women lived in seclusion, rarely venturing forth from their homes.

In Athens, girls could be married at age fourteen, to husbands more than twice their age. A girl's father arranged her marriage and provided a dowry that her husband could use for her support. And shortly after a wife entered her new home, a regular schedule of childbirth would begin. The average young wife would bear between four and six children before she died, usually around the age of thirty-five. Her place might then be taken by another, younger woman.

Because respectable women seldom went beyond their neighborhoods, since it was thought immodest for them to be seen by men outside their immediate families, slaves did most shopping or marketing for the household. Even at home, women were expected to withdraw into private rooms if visitors arrived. But they were not supposed to sit around idly, and their main occupation was spinning and weaving. This was true of all women, from royalty to slaves. And since women's work was basically menial, men looked down on them for it, even though their own livelihoods and comfort depended on it.

There is even evidence suggesting that husbands were not encouraged to form emotional attachments to their wives, although some obviously did. In a revealing passage, Herodotus reports of a certain Lydian king that he "fell in love with his own wife, a fancy that had strange consequences." By contrast, an Athenian orator remarked that "we have prostitutes for pleasure, concubines for daily physical attendance, and wives to bear us legitimate children and be our faithful housekeepers." However, these perspectives are offset by a range of archaeological and material evidence (such as funerary monuments) that testify to women's valued social roles, the affection of their husbands and children, and even their wider economic and legal powers.

In addition to depending on the labor and fertility of women, Athenians were as reliant on slaves as Spartans were on helots. Without slavery, none of the Athenian accomplishments in politics, philosophy, or art would have been possible. The Athenian ideal of dividing and rotating governmental duties among all free men depended on slaves who worked in fields, businesses, and homes. In fact, the Athenian democratic system began to function fully only with the expansion of Athenian commerce around 500 B.C.E., which enabled Athenians to buy slaves in larger numbers. Freedom and slavery were thus inescapably, and paradoxically, linked in this democracy—much as they would be many centuries later in the United States before the Civil War.

Although widespread, Athenian slavery was modest in scale. Slaves did not ordinarily work in teams or in factories; the only exceptions were the state-owned silver mines, where large numbers of slaves toiled in miserable conditions. Most slaves were owned in small numbers by a wide range of Athenian families, including the relatively poor. As domestic servants and farm laborers, slaves might even be considered trusted members of the household, although their masters were legally empowered to beat them or abuse them; concubines were often drawn from among this class of slaves. Yet slaves could never be entirely dehumanized, as they were in modern slaveholding societies; the misfortune of becoming a slave through debt was a reality of Athens' recent past, and the real possibility of being enslaved in war would become a widespread consequence of Athens' over-reaching ambitions.

"THE GREATEST WAR IN HISTORY" AND ITS CONSEQUENCES

Ultimately, Athens' foreign policy and imperial ambitions undermined its civic and cultural achievements. Since the 470s, Athens had begun crushing those allies who

THE PELOPONNESIAN WAR. This map shows the patchwork of colonies and alliances that bound together the supporters of Sparta and Athens at the outbreak of the Peloponnesian War in 431 B.C.E. ▪ *Which side had the geographical advantage?* ▪ *Which neutral powers might have been able to tip the balance by entering the war on one side or the other?* ▪ *What strategic and military choices did geography impose on the two combatants and their allies?*

attempted to break from its control. By the early 440s, its only rival for supremacy in the Greek world was Sparta. Rather than attempting to maintain a balance of power, however, Pericles adopted a more aggressive policy. In order to ensure that military resources would be directed toward any Spartan opposition, he concluded a formal peace with Persia. Yet the sole purpose of the Delian League had been the defense of Greece against Persian aggression, so Athens now had no justification for compelling its members to maintain their allegiance. Many remained loyal nonetheless, enjoying the economic benefits of warm relations with Athens. Others, however, did not, and Athens found itself increasingly having to force its allies back into line, often installing Athenian garrisons and planting Athenian colonists—who retained their Athenian citizenship—to ensure future loyalty.

In the context of recent history and longstanding Greek values, such behavior was disturbing. The Persian wars had been fought to preserve Greek independence. Now Athens itself was becoming an oppressive, imperial power. Foremost among its critics were the Corinthians, whose own economic standing was threatened by Athenian dominance. The Corinthians were close allies of the Spartans, who were in turn the dominant power in what historians call the Peloponnesian League. (The Greeks called it simply the "Spartans and their allies.") When war finally erupted between Athens and Sparta, Thucydides—himself an Athenian—ascribed it to the growing power of Athens and the anxiety this inspired in other poleis. No modern historian has improved on Thucydides' thesis. Yet for the Athenians and their leaders, there could be no question of relinquishing their empire, or the dream of dominating the Mediterranean world. For Sparta and its allies, meanwhile, the prospect of relinquishing their independence was equally unthinkable. Two very different ideas of Greek superiority were about to fight to the death.

The Peloponnesian War Begins

When the Athenians and Spartans found themselves at war with one another in 431 B.C.E., both sides believed a conclusion would come quickly—a delusion common to many of history's pivotal contests. Instead, the war dragged on for twenty-seven years. Thucydides, writing about it in exile, recalled that he knew from the time of its outbreak that it was going to be "the greatest war in history," amounting to the first world war. He also meant that it was the worst, so devastating to both sides that it destroyed the Greeks' proud heritage of freedom. By the time Athens was forced

to concede defeat, all the poleis were weakened to such an extent that they would never again be able to withstand outside threats.

From the beginning, Athens knew that it could not defeat Sparta on land; and neither Sparta nor its allies had a fleet capable of challenging the Athenians at sea. Pericles therefore developed a bold strategy: he would pull the entire population of Attica within the walls of Athens and not attempt to defend the countryside against Sparta. For sustenance, Athens would rely on supplies shipped in by its fleet, which would also be deployed to ravage the coasts of the Peloponnesus.

The Spartans duly plundered the farms and pastures of Attica, frustrated that the Athenians would not engage them in battle. Meanwhile, the Athenians inflicted significant destruction on Spartan territory in a series of raids and by successfully encouraging rebellion among the helots. Time appeared to be on Athens' side. But in 429 B.C.E. the crowded conditions of the besieged city gave rise to a typhus epidemic that killed over a third of the population, including the aged Pericles.

Pericles' death revealed that he had been the only man capable of managing the dangerous political forces he had unleashed. His successors were mostly demagogues, ambitious men who played to the worst instincts of the crowd (the demos). The most successful of these was Cleon, who refused a Spartan offer of peace in 425 B.C.E. and continued the war until his own death in battle four years later. It was under Cleon that Thucydides was given the impossible task of liberating a city under Spartan control; his failure in 423 led to his exile.

After the death of Cleon, a truce with Sparta was negotiated by an able Athenian leader named Nicias (*NICK-ee-ahs*). But Athenians continued to pursue a "dirty war" by preying on poleis that it feared might support the Spartans. This led to atrocities like the destruction of the entire city of Melos, an island colonized by the Spartans that had maintained its neutrality since the beginning of the war. When the inhabitants of Melos refused to compromise this position by accepting Athenian rule, Athens had the entire male population slaughtered and every woman and child sold into slavery.

Thereafter, Athens' policy of preemptive warfare proved destructive to itself. In 415 B.C.E., a charismatic young aristocrat named Alcibiades (*al-ki-BY-uh-dees*) convinced the Athenians to attack the powerful Greek city of Syracuse in Sicily, which was allegedly harrying Athenian allies in the western Mediterranean. The expedition ended disastrously, with the death or enslavement of thousands of Athenian warriors.

News of the Syracusan disaster shattered the Athenians. Many political leaders were driven from the polis as scapegoats, and in 411 B.C.E. a hastily convened assembly of citizens voted the democracy out of existence, replacing it with an oligarchy of 400 men, many of whom had been present at this vote. The remains of the Athenian fleet, then stationed in Samos on the Ionian coast, responded by declaring a democratic government in exile under the leadership of none other than Alcibiades. The oligarchy proved to be brief, and democracy was restored to Athens by 409. But a pattern of self-destruction had been established, making it difficult for anyone in Athens or outside it to believe in the possibility of restored greatness.

THE FAILURE OF ATHENIAN DEMOCRACY

The Spartans too despaired of bringing the war to an end. Even in its weakened condition, the Athenian fleet was invincible. Finally, Sparta turned to the Persians, who were glad to avenge themselves on Athens and agreed to supply the gold and expertise necessary to train an effective Spartan navy. Meanwhile, Athenians were turning against each other and making the Spartans' task easier. In 406 B.C.E., a rare Athenian naval victory ended in a sudden storm that prevented Athenian commanders from rescuing the sailors whose ships had been wrecked. A firestorm of protest was fanned by demagogues who insisted on making an example of those generals brave enough to return to Athens. One of these was Pericles' son Pericles, who died a victim of his father's policies. Through such measures, the Athenians executed or exiled the last of their able commanders.

The poorly led Athenian fleet was destroyed in 404 B.C.E. Without ships, the Athenians could neither feed themselves nor defend their city. The Spartans sailed the Aegean unopposed, installing pro-Spartan oligarchies. Finally, they besieged Athens, which surrendered. Corinth and Thebes, remembering the ruthless treatment of Melos, called for Athens' destruction. The Spartans refused, but imposed harsh terms: the dismantling of Athens' defensive walls, the scrapping of its fleet, and the acceptance of an oligarchy under Spartan supervision. These so-called Thirty Tyrants confiscated private property and murdered their political opponents. Their excesses drove committed democrats to plan a desperate coup, a bloodbath averted only through the intervention of the Spartan king.

By the end of 401 B.C.E., Athens had restored a semblance of democratic governance, but it was never more than a shadow of its former self. Meanwhile, Sparta succeeded Athens as the arbiter of the Greek world. But this

SOCRATES. According to Plato, Socrates looked like a goatman but spoke like a god.

was a thankless job, made worse by the losses the Spartans had suffered during the war and by the fact that they were even more aggressive in their control than the Athenians had been. In fact, the Spartans found themselves in a position they had avoided throughout their history, because their far-flung interests now sapped their manpower and undermined their control over the helots. They also faced a reinvigorated Persian Empire, which increased its naval presence in the Aegean.

These were the circumstances in which the Athenian philosopher Socrates (469–399 B.C.E.) attempted to reform his city's ethical and political traditions. To understand something of his accomplishments, and to assess the reasons for his tragic death, we must trace briefly the history of philosophical speculation in the half century before his birth.

The Pythagoreans and the Sophists

After the Persian conquest of Ionia, many Milesian philosophers fled to southern Italy. Philosophical speculation thus continued in the Greek "far west." A major figure here was Pythagoras (*pith-AG-or-us*), who founded a philosophical community. Pythagoras and his followers regarded the speculative life as the highest good, and believed that one must be purified of fleshly desires in order to achieve this. Just as the essence of life lay in the mind, they believed that the essence of the universe was to be found not in the natural world but in the study of abstractions. The Pythagoreans established the key properties of odd and even numbers and also proved an old Babylonian hypothesis in geometry, known today as the Pythagorean theorem. Even though they shunned the material world, they still exhibited the characteristic Greek quest for regularity and predictability in that world.

Two Views of Socrates

Socrates as a Sophist

Most people regard Socrates as the sage thinker who challenged the prevailing prejudices of his day. During his own time, however, he was not so universally admired. In Aristophanes' comedy The Clouds, *the protagonist, Strepsiades (strep-SIGH-uh-dees), goes to Socrates and his "Thought Shop" to ask that Socrates make him and his son, Pheidippides (phi-DIP-pid-ees), orators capable of winning lawsuits and growing rich. Aristophanes implies throughout that Socrates is a charlatan who teaches word games and tricks for hire.*

STREPSIADES: See that he [Pheidippides] learns your two Arguments, whatever you call them—oh yes, Right and Wrong—the one that takes a bad case and defeats Right with it. If he can't manage both, then at least Wrong—that will do—but that he must have.

SOCRATES: Well, I'll go and send the Arguments here in person, and they'll teach him themselves.

STREPSIADES: Don't forget, he's got to be able to argue against any kind of justified claim at all.

RIGHT: This way. Let the audience see you. . . .

WRONG: Sure, go wherever you like. The more of an audience we have, the more soundly I'll trounce you.

RIGHT: What sort of trick will you use?

WRONG: Oh, just a few new ideas.

RIGHT: Yes, they're in fashion now, aren't they, [*to the audience*] thanks to you idiots. . . . [*to Pheiddipides*] You don't want to be the sort of chap who's always in the agora telling stories about other people's sex lives, or in the courts arguing about some petty, filthy little dispute. . . .

WRONG: People here at the Thought Shop call me Wrong, because I was the one who invented ways of proving anything wrong, laws, prosecutors, anything. Isn't that worth millions—to have a really bad case and yet win? . . . Suppose you fall in love with a married woman—have a bit of fun—and get caught in the act. As you are now, without a tongue in your head, you're done for. But if you come and learn from me, then you can do

whatever you like and get away with it . . . and supposing you do get caught with someone's wife, you can say to him . . . "What have I done wrong? Look at Zeus; wasn't he always a slave of his sexual passions? And do you expect a mere mortal like me to do any better than a god?" . . .

STREPSIADES [*to Socrates*]: I wonder if you'd accept a token of my appreciation? But my son, has he learned that Argument we were listening to a moment ago?

SOCRATES: Yes, he has.

STREPSIADES: Holy Fraud, how wonderful!

SOCRATES: Yes, you'll now be able to win any case at all.

Source: Aristophanes, *The Clouds*, trans. Alan H. Sommerstein (New York: 1973), pp. 148–50, 154, 159–60 (slightly revised).

Socrates and the Laws of Athens

According to his pupil Plato, Socrates spent the last days of his life in conversation with his friends and followers, some of whom urged him to escape from captivity and live in exile. In the dialogue Crito, *a young aristocrat of that name argues that the very laws that have condemned Socrates are unjust, and that by choosing to obey them Socrates is giving them a legitimacy they do not deserve. Halfway through the debate, Socrates turns the tables on him.*

SOCRATES: I should like you to consider whether we are still satisfied on this point: that the really important thing is not to live, but to live well.

CRITO: Why, yes.

SOCRATES: And that to live well means the same thing as to live honorably, or rightly?

CRITO: Yes.

SOCRATES: Then in light of this agreement we must consider whether or not it is right for me to try to get away without an official pardon. If it turns out to be right, we must make the attempt; if not, we must let it drop. . . .

CRITO: I agree with what you say, Socrates. . . .

SOCRATES: Well, here is my next point, or rather question. Ought one to fulfill all one's agreements, provided they are right, or break them?

CRITO: One ought to fulfill them.

SOCRATES: Then consider the logical consequence. If we leave this place without first persuading the polis to let us go . . . are we or are we not abiding by our just agreements?

CRITO: I can't answer your question, Socrates. I am not clear in my mind.

SOCRATES: Look at it this way. Suppose that while we were preparing to run away (or however one should describe it), the Laws of Athens were to come and confront us with this question: "Now, Socrates, what are you proposing to do? Can you deny that by this act which you are contemplating you intend, so far as you have the power, to destroy us, the Laws, and the whole polis as well? Do you imagine that a city can continue to exist and not be turned upside down, if the legal judgments which are pronounced in it have no force but are nullified and destroyed by private persons?"—How shall we answer this question, Crito, and

others of the same kind? . . . Shall we say, "Yes, I do intend to destroy the Laws, because the polis has wronged me by passing a faulty judgment at my trial"? Is this to be our answer, or what?

CRITO: What you have just said, by all means, Socrates.

SOCRATES: Then supposing the Laws say, "Was there provision for this in the agreement between you and us, Socrates? Or did you pledge to abide by whatever judgments the polis pronounced? . . . [I]f you cannot persuade your country you must do whatever it orders, and patiently submit to any punishment it imposes, whether it be flogging or imprisonment. And if it leads you out to war, you must comply, and it is right that you should do so; you must not give way or retreat or abandon your position. Both in war and in the law courts you must do whatever your city and your country commands."

Source: Plato, *Crito*, excerpted (with modifications) from *The Last Days of Socrates*, trans. Hugh Tredennick (New York: 1969), pp. 87–91.

Questions for Analysis

1. Socrates actually refused to teach the art of "making the weaker argument defeat the stronger." But in *The Clouds*, Aristophanes shows him teaching how "to win any case at all." Why were the powers of persuasion considered potentially dangerous in democratic Athens? Why might Aristophanes choose to represent Socrates in this way?

2. How do the arguments of Plato's Socrates compare to those of Aristophanes' character?

3. How does Socrates' sense of honor and his duty toward the polis compare to that of Tyrtaeus of Sparta (page 67)?

Meanwhile, philosophy as it developed in mainland Greece was more attuned to questions of ethics and politics. The increasing power of individual citizens begged the question of how a man should conduct himself, in public and private life, so as to embrace "the beautiful and the good"—or at least to advance himself by the use of his wits. To answer this latter need were a new group of teachers known as Sophists, a term meaning "wise men." Unlike the Milesian philosophers or the Pythagoreans, however, the Sophists made a living from selling their knowledge. Their teachings are best exemplified by Protagoras (*pro-TAG-or-us*), an older contemporary of Socrates. His famous dictum, "man is the measure of all things," means that goodness, truth, and justice are relative concepts, adaptable to the needs and interests of human beings. They are not moral absolutes, established by the gods. Indeed, Protagoras declared that no one could know whether the gods existed

or, if they did, what they wanted. He thus concluded that there could be no absolute standards of right and wrong. Empirical facts, established by the perception of the senses, were the only source of knowledge. And because each man experienced the world in a different way, there could be only particular truths valid for the individual knower.

Such teachings struck many Athenians as dangerous. Sophists like Protagoras made everyday life a subject for philosophical discussion, but their relativism could too easily degenerate into a conviction that the wise man (or the wise polis) is the one best able to manipulate others. Both individually and collectively, this conviction could rationalize monstrous acts of brutality—like those committed by Athens in the case of Melos. Indeed, the lessons of the Peloponnesian War went a long way toward demonstrating the disastrous consequences of this self-serving logic: if justice is merely relative, then neither personal morality nor society can survive. This conviction led to the growth of a new philosophical movement grounded on the theory that absolute standards do exist, and that human beings can determine what these are, through the exercise of reason. The initiator of this trend was Socrates.

The Life and Thought of Socrates

Socrates was not a professional teacher, like the Sophists. He may have trained as a stonemason, and he certainly had some sort of livelihood that enabled him to maintain his status as a citizen and hoplite. Having fought in three campaigns as part of the Athenian infantry during the war with Sparta, he was both an ardent patriot and a sincere critic of Athenian policy. His method of instruction was conversation: through dialogue with passers-by, he submitted every presumed truth to examination in order to establish a firm foundation for further inquiry. Everything we know about Socrates' teachings comes from the writings of younger men who considered themselves his pupils, and who participated in these conversations. The most important of these followers was Plato.

According to Plato, Socrates sought to show that all supposed certainties are merely unexamined prejudices inherited from others. Socrates always said that he himself knew nothing, because this was a more secure place from which to begin the learning process. He sought to base his speculations on sound definitions of key concepts—justice, virtue, beauty, love—which he and his pupils could arrive at only by investigating their own assumptions. And he focused his attention on practical ethics rather than the study of the physical world (like the Milesians did) or abstractions (like the Pythagoreans). He urged his listeners to reflect on the principles of proper conduct, both for their own sakes and for that of society as a whole. One should consider the meaning and consequences of one's actions at all times, he taught, and be prepared to take responsibility for them. According to one of his most memorable sayings, "the unexamined life is not worth living."

It is bitterly ironic that such a man, the product of Athenian democracy, should have been put to death by democratic processes. Shortly after the end of the Peloponnesian War in 399 B.C.E., when Athens was reeling from the shock of defeat and from violent internal upheavals, a democratic faction decided that Socrates was a threat to the state. A democratic court agreed, condemning him to death for denying the gods, disloyalty to the polis, and "corrupting the youth." Although his friends made arrangements for him to flee the city and thus evade punishment, Socrates insisted on abiding by the laws, proving himself true to his own principles and setting an example for future citizens. He died calmly by the prescribed method, self-administered poison.

According to Socrates, the goal of philosophy is to help human beings understand and apply standards of absolute good, rather than to master a series of mental tricks that facilitate personal gain at the expense of others. The circumstances of his death, however, show that it is difficult to translate this philosophy into principles that can be widely accepted. This would be the task of Plato, who would lay the groundwork for all subsequent Western philosophy (see Chapter 4).

After You Read This Chapter

Go to **INQUIZITIVE** to see what you've learned—and learn what you've missed—with personalized feedback along the way.

REVIEWING THE OBJECTIVES

- The Greek polis was a unique form of government. What factors led to its emergence?
- Hoplite warfare had a direct effect on the shaping of early democracy. Why?
- Poleis could develop in very different ways. What are some of the reasons for this?
- In what ways did Athenian culture, philosophy, and art reflect democratic ideals?
- The Persian and Peloponnesian Wars affected Greek civilization in profound ways. Describe some of the consequences of Athens' victory in the former and its defeat in the latter.

CONCLUSION

There are many striking similarities between the civilization of ancient Greece and our own—and many stark differences. Perhaps the most salient example of both is the concept of democracy, which in ancient Greece was ruled by a class of propertied male citizens supported by slavery. In theory and in practice, this class amounted to only a small percentage of the population in Athens, whereas in Sparta the vast majority were subject to the rule of an even smaller class of Spartiates. At the same time, the growth of Athenian democracy meant, increasingly, the exploitation of other poleis and the spread of imperialism, a ruinous policy of preemptive warfare, and increased intolerance and paranoia. (Socrates was not the only man put to death for expressing his opinions.) Finally, the status of women in this "golden age" was lower than it had been in earlier periods of history, and women had fewer personal rights than in any of the ancient societies we have studied so far.

And yet the profound significance of Greek experiments with new forms of governance, and new ideas about the world, is undeniable. This can be seen with particular clarity if we compare the Greek poleis with the empires and kingdoms of Mesopotamia and ancient Egypt. The typical political regime of the ancient Near Eastern world was, as we have seen, that of a monarch supported by a powerful priesthood. In this context, cultural achievements were mainly instruments to enhance the prestige of rulers, and economic life was controlled by palaces and temples.

By contrast, the core values of the Greeks were the primacy of the human male and the principles of competition, individual achievement, responsibility, and human freedom. (The very word for freedom—*eleutheria*—cannot be translated into any ancient Near Eastern language, not even Hebrew.) In his history, Herodotus records a conversation between a Greek (in this case a Spartan) and a Persian, who expresses surprise that the Greeks should raise spears against the supposedly benign rule of his emperor. The Spartan retorts, "You understand how to be a slave, but you know nothing of freedom. Had you tasted it, you would advise us to fight not only with spears but with axes." The story of how the Greeks came to turn those spears on one another within a few generations of their united victory is worthy of one of their own tragedies.

Another way of appreciating the enduring importance of Greek civilization is to recall the essential vocabulary we have inherited from it: not only the word *democracy* but *politics, philosophy, theater, history*. The very notion of humanity comes to us from the Greeks. For them, the fullest development of one's potential should be the aim of existence: every free man is the sculptor of his own monument. This work of growing from childishness to personhood is what the Greeks called *paideia (pie-DAY-ah)*; the Romans called it *humanitas*. How this and other ideas came to be disseminated beyond Greece, to be adopted by the peoples and places of a much wider world, is the subject of Chapter 4.

PEOPLE, IDEAS, AND EVENTS IN CONTEXT

- How did the epics of **HOMER** transmit the values of the Bronze Age to the **ARISTOCRACY** of the new Greek **POLEIS**?
- How did the spread of **PANHELLENIC** Greek culture transform the Mediterranean, even as the adoption of **HOPLITE** military tactics transformed Greek politics?
- Compare and contrast the historical circumstances that led to the development of **ATHENS**, **SPARTA**, and **MILETUS**. What were the main differences among them?
- What were the different motives for the invasions of **DARIUS** and **XERXES**? By what methods did the Greek poleis manage to emerge victorious from the **PERSIAN WARS**?
- What were the triumphs and limitations of **DEMOCRACY** in **PERICLEAN ATHENS**?
- How did the **PELOPONNESIAN WAR** transform Athens and affect the balance of power in the Mediterranean?

THINKING ABOUT CONNECTIONS

- The trial and execution of Socrates can be seen as a referendum on the relationship between the individual and the state. What does this incident reveal about the limitations of personal power and individual rights? To what degree was this incident a product of Athenian losses during the Peloponnesian War? To what extent does it reflect long-term trends in the Greek world?
- We like to think that we can trace our democratic ideals and institutions back to Athens, but does this mean that the failings of Athenian democracy also mirror those of our own? What parallels can you draw between ancient Athens and today's United States? What are some key differences?

Before You Read This Chapter

The Greek World Expands, 400–150 B.C.E.

CORE OBJECTIVES

- **EXPLAIN** the reasons for Macedonia's rise to power and its triumph over the Greek poleis.

- **DESCRIBE** Alexander's methods of conquest, colonization, and governance.

- **IDENTIFY** the three main Hellenistic kingdoms and their essential differences.

- **DEFINE** the main characteristics of the Hellenistic world and explain their significance.

- **UNDERSTAND** how new philosophies and artistic movements reflect historical changes.

W hen the young Alexander of Macedonia set out for Persia in 334 B.C.E., he brought along two favorite books. The first was a copy of the *Iliad*, which his teacher Aristotle had given him. The second was the *Anabasis*, "The Inland Expedition," by an Athenian called Xenophon (ZEN-oh-fon, 430–354 B.C.E.). Both choices are significant. The *Iliad* recounts the story of a much earlier Greek assault on Asia, and its protagonist is the hero Achilles—a figure with whom Alexander identified: consummate warrior, favorite of the gods, a man who inspired passionate loyalty. It is also full of information useful to someone planning a long campaign in foreign lands against a formidable enemy, with a fractious army drawn from all parts of Greece and little prospect of bringing them home safely or soon. The *Anabasis* was an even more practical choice. Its author had been one of 10,000 Greek mercenaries hired by a Persian prince to overthrow his older brother, the Great King. The attempted coup failed, but Xenophon's book made the prince, Cyrus, another role model for Alexander. It also told, in detail, how Persians fought, how they lived, how they were governed, and what the terrain of their vast empire

87

was like. Moreover, it showed what a dedicated army of hoplites could accomplish on Persian soil. This book would be Alexander's bible for the next ten years.

By the time of Alexander the Great's early death, a united Greek and Macedonian army had extended Greek culture and Greek governance from Egypt to the frontiers of India. This personal empire, the empire of Alexander, could not last. But the cultural empire built upon it did. This Hellenistic ("Greek-like") civilization joined disparate lands and peoples, forming the basis of the Roman Empire and mirroring the cosmopolitan world of our own time. How this happened is the subject of Chapter 4.

THE DOWNFALL OF THE GREEK POLIS

The Peloponnesian War had left Sparta the dominant power in the Greek world. But by 395, a significant number of poleis were aligned against Sparta in the so-called Corinthian War (395–387 B.C.E.). To quell this rebellion, the Spartans turned once again to Persia, as they had done in the final stages of the Peloponnesian War. This pattern of violence, temporarily halted by the intervention of Persia, would be repeated time and again over the next fifty years.

The Struggle for Dominance

After the Corinthian War, the Spartans punished the most dangerous of their rivals, Thebes, by occupying the city for four years. But when the Thebans regained their autonomy they elected as their leader a fierce patriot who was also a military genius, Epaminondas (eh-pa-min-OHN-das, c. 410–362 B.C.E.). In imitation of the Spartan system, he formed an elite hoplite unit known as the Theban Sacred Band, made up of 150 male couples: sworn lovers who pledged to fight to the death for their polis and for each other's honor.

When the Theban and Spartan armies met at Leuctra in 371 B.C.E., the Sacred Band helped carry the Thebans to victory. Epaminondas then marched through the Spartan territory of Messenia and freed the helots. Spartan power—and the unique social system that had supported it—was thereby brought to an end. But as Theban power grew, so did the animosity of the other Greek poleis. In 362, when Epaminondas fell in battle, Athens attempted—and failed—to fill the vacuum by establishing a naval confederacy. Greece thus remained a constellation of petty warring states.

Social and Economic Crises

Meanwhile, the poleis were also riven by internal turmoil. Incessant warfare and political struggles profoundly affected their economic and social infrastructures. Many people were driven from their homes or reduced to slavery. Country towns had been ravaged, as had farmlands throughout Greece. Prices rose while standards of living declined. Taxes increased.

Unemployment was also widespread, and many men turned to mercenary service. As we have already noted, Cyrus, brother of the Persian emperor Artaxerxes II, even hired a Greek mercenary force of 10,000 men in an attempt to seize the throne in 401 B.C.E. But when Cyrus was killed in battle, the army—marooned in a hostile country—had to fight its way out under elected leaders. One of these was Xenophon, a former pupil of Socrates, and it was his account of this expedition that would become Alexander's guidebook.

RE-IMAGINING THE POLIS: THE ARTISTIC AND INTELLECTUAL RESPONSE

The year of Socrates' execution, 399 B.C.E., marks the end of an era—that of the polis. This basic engine of Greek life had continued to drive innovation and cultural production even during the Peloponnesian War. But now, the failure of democracy had a profound impact on the arts, philosophy, and especially political thought.

The Arts of the Fourth Century

As we observed in Chapter 3, the painters and sculptors of the fifth century B.C.E. were already working to achieve a heightened appearance of realism in their works. This experimentation continued in the fourth century, especially in the relatively new art of portraiture. Artists also grew bolder in their use of tricky techniques, like the casting of full-size statues in bronze. This was a medium in which the era's most famous sculptor, Praxiteles, excelled. Praxiteles (prak-SIT-el-eez) was bold, too, in his choice of subjects, and is widely regarded as the first artist to create full-size female nudes (see **Interpreting Visual Evidence** on page 91).

In contrast to the visual arts, the forms and functions of drama changed considerably. Tragedy and comedy were no

Analyzing Primary Sources

Xenophon Describes an Ideal Leader

In his history of "The Inland Expedition" undertaken by the Ten Thousand, Xenophon (430–354 B.C.E.) mourns the death of Cyrus the Younger, whom he believes would have made a better Great King of Persia than the brother he challenged, Artaxerxes II. The following description of the prince's character and leadership became very famous in its time, often circulating as a separate booklet. It is likely to have influenced the young Alexander.

hus then died Cyrus, a man who, of all the Persians since Cyrus the elder [the Great], was the most princely and the most worthy of rule, as is agreed by all who appear to have had personal knowledge of him. In the first place, while he was yet a boy, and when he was receiving his education with his brother and other youths, he was thought to surpass them all in everything. For all the sons of the Persian nobles are educated at the gates of the king, where they may learn many a lesson of virtuous conduct, but can see or hear nothing disgraceful. Here the boys see some honored by the king, and others disgraced, and hear of them, so that in their very childhood they learn to govern and to obey.

Here Cyrus, first of all, showed himself most remarkable for modesty among those of his own age, and for paying more ready obedience to his elders than even those who were inferior to him in station; and next, he was noted for his fondness for horses, and for managing them in a superior manner. They found him, too, very desirous of learning, and most assiduous in practicing, the warlike exercises of archery and hurling the javelin. When it suited his age, he grew extremely fond of the chase and of braving dangers in encounters with wild beasts. On one occasion he did not shrink from a she-bear that attacked him, but, in grappling with her, was dragged from off his horse, and received some wounds, the scars of which were visible on his body, but at last killed her. The person who first came to his assistance he made a happy man in the eyes of many.

When he was sent down by his father, as satrap of Lydia and Great Phrygia and Cappadocia, and was also appointed commander of all the troops whose duty it is to muster in the plain of Castolus, he soon showed that if he made a league or compact with anyone, or gave a promise, he deemed it of the utmost importance not to break his word. Accordingly the states that were committed to his charge, as well as individuals, had the greatest confidence in him; and if anyone had been his enemy, he felt secure that if Cyrus entered into a treaty with him, he should suffer no infraction of the stipulations. When, therefore, he waged war against Tissaphernes, all the cities, of their own accord, chose to adhere to Cyrus in preference to Tissaphernes, except the Milesians; but they feared him, because he would not abandon the cause of the exiles; for he both showed by his deeds and declared in words that he would never desert them, since he had once become a friend to them, not even though they should grow still fewer in number, and be in a worse condition than they were.

Whenever anyone did him a kindness or an injury, he showed himself anxious to go beyond him in those respects; and some used to mention a wish of his that he desired to live long enough to outdo both those who had done him good, and those who had done him ill, in the requital that he should make. Accordingly to him alone of the men of our days were so great a number of people desirous of committing the disposal of their property, their cities, and their own persons.

Source: Excerpted from Xenophon, *Anabasis*, ed. M. I. Finley in *The Portable Greek Historians* (New York: 1959), pp. 383–84.

Questions for Analysis

1. According to Xenophon, what are the attributes of a great leader? How would Alexander have applied these to his own situation?

2. What seems to be Xenophon's attitude toward the Persians? How might his portrayal of them have been influenced by his travels among them? How might it have been colored by his attitude toward his own countrymen?

3. In what ways does Cyrus the Younger appear to have followed the example of his ancestor, Cyrus the Great (Chapter 2, page 52)?

Re-Imagining the Polis: The Artistic and Intellectual Response | 89 longer mounted as part of publicly funded festivals, but were instead financed by private individuals who could exercise greater control over the content of performances. As a result, fourth-century playwrights did not have the freedom to use drama as a vehicle for political and social critique, as earlier dramatists had done. Instead, the "New Comedy" of this era relied more and more on mistaken identities, tangled familial relationships, and breaches of etiquette. Similar trends toward escapism are also apparent in a new literary genre: the prose novel. These pleasant fictions targeted an increasingly literate audience, including (as with many modern romance novels) an audience of women.

Philosophy after Socrates: The Schools of Plato and Aristotle

The intellectual and political legacy of Socrates was carried forward by Plato (429–349 B.C.E.), who as a young man witnessed the trial and death of his mentor. Plato strove to vindicate Socrates by constructing a philosophical system based on his precepts. He did this by founding an informal school called the Academy and by writing a series of dramatic dialogues that feature Socrates as the central character.

The longest and most famous of these dialogues is now known by its Latin title, the *Republic*. In it, Plato argues that social harmony and order are more important than individual liberty or equality. He imagines an ideal polis governed by a superior group of "guardians" chosen in their youth for natural attributes of intelligence and character. Those found to be the wisest would ultimately become "philosopher-kings." This imaginary system is clearly a response to the failures of Athenian democracy. But whether Plato himself believed in it is open to question. For such a system presumes that properly educated rulers will never be corrupted by power, a proposition that has yet to be sustained in practice.

The practical application of philosophy would be the preoccupation of Plato's own student, Aristotle (384–322 B.C.E.).

PLATO AND ARISTOTLE. Although many artistic representations of Plato and Aristotle were made in antiquity, the image that best captures the essential difference between their philosophies is this one, the focal point of a fresco by the Renaissance painter Raphael Sanzio (1483–1520 C.E., to be discussed further in Chapter 12). Plato is the older central figure to the viewer's left, who points with his right hand to the heavens; Aristotle is the younger man beside him, gesturing with an open palm to the earth. ▪ *How does this double portrait reflect these philosophers' teachings and perspectives?*

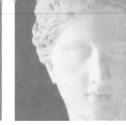

Interpreting Visual Evidence

Reconstructing an Ideal of Female Beauty

The lost statue known as the Aphrodite of Knidos was considered the most beautiful in the ancient world, but we can only study it by looking at later copies. It was the work of the fourth century's most renowned sculptor, Praxiteles, who was reputed to have modeled it after the Athenian courtesan known as Phryne, a renowned beauty who inspired several contemporary artists and many apocryphal stories. The most reliable of these concerns the riches she accrued: apparently she became so wealthy that she offered to finance the rebuilding of Thebes in 336—on the condition that the slogan "destroyed by Alexander, restored by Phryne the Courtesan" be prominently displayed on the new walls. (Her offer was rejected.)

Praxiteles' original statue is thought to have been the first monumental female nude fashioned in antiquity. According to one authority, he had initially received a commission from the island of Kos, for which he made both clothed and naked versions of Aphrodite. Apparently, the scandalized citizens approved only the draped version and refused to pay for the nude. It was purchased instead by the city of Knidos on Cyprus, where it was displayed in an open-air temple so that it could be seen from all sides. It quickly became a tourist attraction and was widely copied and emulated. Two of the more faithful replicas, made by artists working in Rome, are pictured here.

Questions for Analysis

1. As we have seen, the male nude was a favorite subject of Greek artists from the Archaic Period onward. Based on your knowledge of contemporary Greek culture and society, why was it only in the fourth century B.C.E. that a life-size female nude could be publicly displayed? Are there any precedents for statues like this?

2. Compare and contrast the ideal of female beauty suggested by the Knidian Aphrodite with the male ideals shown in Chapter 3. What can you conclude about the relationship between these ideals and the different expectations of male and female behavior in Greek society? Why, for example, would ancient sources insist that the model for the original statue was a courtesan?

3. Among the Romans, a statue like the Knidian Aphrodite was called a *Venus pudica*, a "modest Venus" (image A). Yet the citizens of Kos were allegedly shocked by its indecency, while old photographs of the copy in the Vatican Museum (image B) show that it was displayed until 1932 with additional draperies made of tin. How do you account for these very different standards of decency? To what degree do they suggest that concepts of "beauty" or "modesty" are historically constructed?

A. Roman copy of the Aphrodite of Knidos.

B. Second century C.E. copy of the Aphrodite of Knidos.

The son of a physician, Aristotle learned from his father the importance of observing natural phenomena. His own philosophical system was geared toward understanding the workings of the world through empirical knowledge—that is, information gained through sensory experience. In contrast to Plato, who taught that everything we see and touch is an untrustworthy reflection of some intangible ideal, Aristotle advocated the rigorous investigation of real phenomena. His method of instruction was also different. Unlike Socrates and Plato, whose dialogues were witty and often playful, Aristotle delivered lectures on which his students took detailed notes, and which eventually became the basis of treatises on politics, ethics, logic, metaphysics, and poetics.

Aristotle taught that the highest good consists in the harmonious functioning of the individual human mind and body. Good conduct is therefore rational conduct, and consists in acting moderately. And whereas Plato conceived of politics as a means to an end which could never be achieved in this life, Aristotle thought of politics as an end in itself: the collective exercise of moderation.

Yet Aristotle also took it for granted that some people—like barbarians—are not fully human, and so are intended by nature to be slaves. He also believed that women are not endowed with a full measure of humanity. So when Aristotle asserted that "man is by nature a political animal" (or, to be more faithful to the Greek, "a creature of the polis"), he meant only Greek males of privileged status. Nor did he believe that the best form of political organization is a democracy. Like Plato, he saw that as a "debased" form of government.

Men of Thought, Men of Action

For all their brilliance, Plato and Aristotle offered few prescriptions for reforming their own societies. But there were other intellectuals who were considering more radical alternatives. One was Xenophon, the veteran of the Ten Thousand and another product of the Socratic tradition. An exact contemporary of Plato, he spent much of his adult life in Sparta, and it is thanks to his admiring account that we know anything about the Spartiate system described in Chapter 3. He intended his description to be a rebuke to democratic Athens and a model for a different kind of ideal society.

The Athenian orator Isocrates (436–338 B.C.E.) was another direct contemporary of Plato. But rather than imagining an ideal polis, he proposed instead that the Greeks stage a massive invasion of Persia. This assault, he prophesied, should be led by a man of vision and ability who could unite the Greek world behind his cause. Isocrates spent most of his life casting about to find such a leader. Finally, he began to think that the man for the job

was someone most Greeks considered no Greek at all: the king of Macedonia, Philip II.

THE RISE OF MACEDONIA

Until the fourth century, Macedonia (or Macedon) had been a weak kingdom, regarded by most Greeks as a throwback to the "dark ages" before the emergence of enlightened poleis. As recently as the 360s, it had nearly succumbed to the even smaller kingdoms and predatory tribes that surrounded it. No one knows whether the ancient Macedonians were Greek-speaking during this period, but the royal family and nobility would at least have spoken Greek as a second language. Still, they were definitely outsiders. So when a young and energetic king consolidated the southern Balkans under his rule, many Greeks saw it as an alarming development.

The Reign of Philip II (359–336 b.c.e.)

Philip II of Macedonia was not supposed to be its ruler. Born in 382, he was the third and youngest son of King

PHILIP II OF MACEDONIA. This tiny ivory head was discovered in a royal tomb at Vergina and is almost certainly a bust of the king himself. Contemporary sources report that Philip the Great had his right eye blinded by a catapult bolt, a deformity visible here—and testimony to the unflinching realism of Greek portraiture in the fourth century B.C.E.

MACEDONIAN PHALANX. Philip of Macedonia's hoplite infantry—the model for Alexander's—was armed with two-handed pikes of graduated lengths, from 13 to 21 feet, and was massed in squares sixteen rows deep and wide. Members of the phalanx were trained to wheel quickly in step formation and to double the width of their front rank as needed, by filing off in rows of eight. The reach of their spears, called *sarissas*, extended the phalanx's fighting range.

Amyntas III, and was considered so dispensable that he was sent to Thebes as hostage when he was fourteen. This turns out to have been the making of him: he became the protégé of the brilliant Epaminondas and may even have trained in the Theban Sacred Band. By the time he returned to the Macedonian capital of Pella, he had received a more thorough education than any Macedonian before him. He was also ambitious. So when both of his older brothers died in battle, Philip was not content with the role of regent for an infant nephew. By 356, he was reigning as king, the same year that his queen, Olympias, bore him an heir. The boy was given the dynastic name Alexandros, "leader of men."

The first problem of Philip's reign was the fragility of Macedonia's northern borders. Through a combination of warfare and diplomacy, he subdued the tribes of the southern Balkans and incorporated their territory into his kingdom. His success had much to do with his reorganization of Macedonian warriors into a hoplite infantry along Theban lines, as well as access to mineral resources that he used to pay and equip a standing professional army. Philip also organized an elite cavalry squad—the Companions—who fought with and beside the king, perhaps in emulation of the Sacred Band. These young men were drawn exclusively from the nobility, and Philip thereby gained valuable young hostages to ensure the good conduct of fractious men. Their sons were now being brought up alongside Alexander and sharing his lessons with Aristotle, who had arrived at the Macedonian court in 343 B.C.E.

Isocrates saw in Philip a potential savior of Greece, but many Athenians believed that his ultimate aim was to conquer them. In actuality, he was probably trying to forge an alliance with Athens, whose fleet could facilitate an invasion of Persia by sea; in return, Philip promised to support Athens' old claim to lordship over Greece. But the Athenians refused to cooperate. This miscalculation ultimately led to war, which sent the Athenians scrambling to ally with Thebes. At the battle of Chaeronea in 338 B.C.E., an army led jointly by Philip and Alexander (aged 18) won a narrow victory, decimating the Athenian forces and destroying the Theban Sacred Band. In the aftermath, Philip called delegates from around mainland Greece to Corinth, where he established a new league whose main purpose was to provide forces for the planned invasion of Persia and maintain peace among the rival poleis.

But Philip never realized his dream of Persian conquest. Two years later, in 336 B.C.E., he was assassinated during a festival. The kingship now fell to Alexander. Among the Greeks, he would be known as Alexander, the Sacker of Cities. To the Romans, he was Alexander the Great.

THE CONQUESTS OF ALEXANDER, 336–323 B.C.E.

By the time of Alexander's early death at the age of 32, a monumental legend had already built up around him. This makes it all the more ironic that no contemporary account of his life and achievements survives. The great library assembled in his capital of Alexandria in Egypt—the repository of all Greek learning and literature—was destroyed or dispersed centuries later, and with it a great portion of assembled knowledge. So when we try to reconstruct the history of Alexander, we are depending on the writings of men who lived and worked under the Roman Empire, notably Plutarch (46–120 C.E.) and Arrian (c. 86–160 C.E.), both of whom were separated from their subject by a distance of four hundred years. Luckily, they were basing their histories on sources derived from two first-hand accounts, one written by Alexander's general (and alleged half-brother) Ptolemy (TOHL-eh-me, c. 367–c. 284 B.C.E.), who founded a new dynasty of Egyptian pharaohs, and another by Æschines Socraticus (c. 387–322 B.C.E.), an Athenian statesman.

It is a salutary reminder of how fragile the historical record of antiquity is, that the sources for the life of the era's most famous man are so hard to come by.

The Conquest of Persia

When Alexander succeeded his father in 336 B.C.E., he had to put down the revolts that erupted immediately after Philip's death—notably at Thebes, which he punished by destroying its famous walls. Two years later, he was crossing the Hellespont (literally the land bridge from Greece to Asia) to challenge the Great King of Persia.

Darius III was a minor member of the royal family who had been placed on the throne after a palace coup, at the relatively old age of 45—in the same year that

ALEXANDER'S WORLD. This view of the world, modeled on maps made in antiquity, represents what intellectuals of Alexander's own time knew about geography. ▪ *Comparing it to the map of Alexander's campaigns on page 99, how do you think this worldview affected the planning of his route?* ▪ *Based on available knowledge, why would he have traveled down the Indus river (near the marking* India) *and traveled overland to Susa?* ▪ *What similarities and differences do you find generally, comparing this ancient map with the other maps that appear in this book?*

Alexander himself became king at 20. Darius and his advisors failed to take the Macedonian threat seriously, despite the Persians' past history of defeat at the hands of Greek armies. Perhaps they assumed that the enormous forces they could rally in defense of their empire would easily overwhelm a comparatively small army of 42,000; perhaps they misunderstood Alexander's aims.

In any event, Alexander soon achieved a series of extraordinary victories, beginning in northwest Anatolia, near the site of the epic field of Troy, and continuing down the Ionian coastline. A year later, in 333 B.C.E., Darius was persuaded to engage Alexander personally. But the chosen site, on the banks of a river near Issus, favored Alexander's fast-moving infantry, not the heavy cavalry and chariots of the Persians. No warrior, Darius disgraced himself by fleeing the battlefield, abandoning not only his army but his entire household, which included his wife and his mother. (They were captured by Alexander and treated with great respect.) Darius spent the remainder of his life running from Alexander's advancing forces, until his decisive defeat at Gaugamela (near Mosul in modern Iraq) in 331, when he was killed by a local chieftain who hoped to win Alexander's favor. Instead, Alexander—acting as the new Great King— had the chieftain executed for treason. The next spring, Alexander destroyed the royal capital of Persepolis, lest it serve as a rallying point for Persian resistance.

Meanwhile, in the two years that had passed since Darius's humiliation at Issus, Alexander had completed his conquest of western Asia. One by one, the cities of Syria and Palestine surrendered. Following the example of Cyrus the Great, Alexander had developed a policy of offering amnesty to cities that submitted peacefully—but dealing mercilessly with those that resisted. The fortified city of Gaza, the last Persian stronghold on the Egyptian border, provides an example: when the fortress was finally taken, Alexander's troops slew all the adult males and enslaved the women and children. According to a later Roman historian, Alexander also dragged the body of the commander around the city's walls behind his chariot, imitating Achilles' legendary treatment of Hector.

Alexander in Egypt

After this, Alexander marched into Egypt unopposed. In fact, he was welcomed as a liberator: Egypt had been governed as a Persian satrapy since 525 B.C.E. Now Alexander himself was hailed as pharaoh and given the double crown of Upper and Lower Egypt, becoming the latest in a succession of rulers reaching back three thousand years. The "barbarian" chieftain of a backwater kingdom had become pharaoh of the oldest civilization on earth and heir to its immense riches and extraordinary history.

While the Persians had long been the Greeks' traditional enemies, the Egyptians had always been too far away to pose a threat; indeed, they were an object of awe. This may help to explain Alexander's response to the oracle of Ammon, the name the Greeks gave to the Egyptian sun god Amun-Ra, whom they identified with Zeus. At the oracle's desert oasis of Siwa, Alexander was reportedly told that he was "son of Ammon" and a god himself. Ever mindful of historical precedent, Alexander seems to have decided at this point that Egypt should be the capital of his new empire: it was in Egypt that he would build his shining new city of Alexandria. In the end, he just had time to lay out a plan for the streets before he left for the East. When he finally returned, he was in his sarcophagus.

Alexander's Final Campaigns

Over the ensuing five years, Alexander campaigned in the far reaches of the Persian Empire, in the mountainous regions that had been only loosely yoked with the more settled lands of Mesopotamia. This is the region encompassed today by Afghanistan, and a terrain famous for defeating every attempt at conquest. Here, Alexander and his army experienced the hardest fighting of their long campaign. Indeed, they never succeeded in getting more than a tenuous hold on the

THE CAMPAIGNS OF ALEXANDER. The conquests of Alexander the Great brought Greek culture to the vast expanse of the former Persian Empire, as far east as the Indus River. Trace Alexander's route with your finger. ▪ *Where did he start and end?* ▪ *What was the farthest point east that he traveled on his conquests?* ▪ *Why might Alexander have chosen to found so many cities named after him, and what can you conclude about the purposes of these cities, based on their locations?*

territory, despite Alexander's marriage to Roxane, daughter of a local chieftain. Thereafter, Alexander moved down through what is now Pakistan to the Indus Valley, meeting stiff resistance from its warlords but eventually defeating their leader, Porus, at the Battle of Hydaspes in 326 B.C.E.

This was to be the last major battle of his career, and the one in which his famous warhorse, Bucephalus ("Thundercloud"), was killed. And it was here that Alexander's exhausted army refused to go on, thousands of miles and eight years from home. He was forced to turn back, and rather than attempting to recross the mountains, he pressed southward to the shores of the Arabian Sea—what was then the end of the world. The ensuing march through the Gedrosian Desert, combined with a decade of continuous fighting, weakened him and his army considerably.

When Alexander reached the Persian royal palace of Susa he took steps that indicate how he would have tried to combine his Greco-Macedonian Empire with that of Persia, had he lived. He announced that he would

begin training Persian youths to fight alongside Greeks and Macedonians in hoplite formation. He arranged a mass marriage between hundreds of his officers and a corresponding number of Persian noblewomen. Most controversially, he showed respect for his Persian subjects by adopting Persian dress—considered by Greeks to be effeminate and barbaric—and by encouraging those around him to perform the ritual of *proskynesis* (*pros-kin-EE-sis*). This was a gesture of bodily submission performed by those of lesser social standing when they met their superiors, and by all Persians—even those of royal rank—to honor the Great King. The person paying homage would bow deeply, in some cases prostrating himself entirely. To the Greeks, this practice suggested that the Persians worshiped their king as a god. To Alexander and his close advisers, it was more likely intended to level cultural differences. In any case, it was not a success, and it fueled a mutiny among the Macedonians, which Alexander himself had to quell.

ALEXANDER DEFEATS KING DARIUS OF PERSIA AT THE BATTLE OF ISSUS (333 B.C.E.). This Roman mural, discovered at Pompeii, shows Darius fleeing from the battlefield in his chariot (right), pursued by Alexander, the mounted figure on the far left. Note the reflection of Alexander and his horse in Darius's large round shield.

Alexander's Death

Apart from these attempts to create cohesion, Alexander took no realistic steps to create an administration for his vast empire. He seems to have fixed his sights more clearly on further conquests, perhaps in Arabia, perhaps toward "Greater Greece"—Italy and Sicily. But in late May of 323 B.C.E., he began to show signs of what may have been malarial fever. Some ancient sources even suggest that he was poisoned; his closest companion, Hephaistion, had died the year before at Ecbatana, leaving Alexander without his most vigilant bodyguard. In any case, Alexander ignored the advice of his doctors. His condition worsened, and he died on June 10 or 11, 323 B.C.E., in the palace built by the Chaldean king Nebuchadnezzar in Babylon, the ancient capital of Hammurabi. He was not yet thirty-three years old.

THE HELLENISTIC KINGDOMS

According to one account—by a later Roman historian—Alexander's officers gathered around his bed as he lay dying and asked to whom he wished to leave his empire. He had replied, "To the strongest." According to other sources, he was actually incapable of speech. According to still other sources, he silently gave his signet ring to a Macedonian called Perdiccas, the leader of his cavalry.

It was certainly Perdiccas who attempted to arrange a settlement among all the possible claimants for power, albeit unsuccessfully. It was eventually decided that the infant Alexander IV, his son by Roxane, should rule jointly with Alexander's half-brother, Philip, the son of Philip II by one of his lesser wives. But this solution was never put into effect, because both the child and his uncle were soon murdered, as was Perdiccas. Meanwhile, the Persian satrapies that had been alloted to various leaders of Alexander's armies became the bases from which these men attempted to seize control.

The turmoil lasted for two generations. By about 275 B.C.E., however, three separate axes of military and political power had emerged, each headed by a Greco-Macedonian ruling class but with a distinctive character. Indeed, a striking feature of this period is the renewal of ancient political patterns within the common culture that continued to unite Alexander's fragmented empire. This is why the world created by his conquests is called Hellenistic, "Greek-like."

Ptolemaic Egypt

By far the most stable of these three Hellenistic states was Egypt, thanks in large part to the canny governance of Alexander's former general Ptolemy, who was possibly an illegitimate son of Philip II. Ptolemy decided to withdraw from the contest over the larger empire and asked only to be given Egypt as his satrapy. Clearly, he recognized Egypt's virtual invulnerability to attack. He also seems to have appreciated, as had Alexander, its historical cachet. And he may already have been planning to make Egypt an independent monarchy and a shrine to Alexander's memory. It was thanks to Ptolemy, in fact, that Alexander's embalmed body was brought to Egypt in 323 B.C.E. It was supposed to have gone to the royal burial ground in Macedonia, but Ptolemy hijacked the funeral cortege and brought it to Memphis. Later, his son Ptolemy II moved the sarcophagus to a tomb in Alexandria, where it became a pilgrimage site and an object of veneration.

The Ptolemies ruled for 300 years, until Egypt became a Roman province in 30 B.C.E. (see Chapter 5). This dynasty, the thirty-second since the fourth millennium B.C.E., would be the last. The male heirs of the line all took the name Ptolemy (hence the term "Ptolemaic Egypt"). Many of their sisters were called Cleopatra, the name of Alexander's own sister and a dynastic name among Macedonian royal women. Beginning in the reign of Ptolemy II Philadelphus ("sibling-lover"), the Ptolemies even began to follow ancient Egyptian custom by marrying their sisters. And in many other ways, they showed reverence for the culture of their kingdom while bringing it within the ambit of the wider Hellenistic world.

Analyzing Primary Sources

Alexander Puts Down a Mutiny

The following account comes from the history of Alexander's campaigns by the Greek-speaking Roman historian Arrian (c. 86–160 c.e.), who lived in the Roman province of Bythinia in northern Anatolia. This is the closest thing we have to a primary source, since histories written by Alexander's own contemporaries have not survived. The following passage describes Alexander's response to a mutiny among his troops after his return from India in 324 b.c.e.

My countrymen, you are sick for home—so be it! I shall make no attempt to check your longing to return. Go wherever you will; I shall not hinder you. But if go you must, there is one thing I would have you understand—what I have done for you, and in what coin you have repaid me. . . .

"Marching out from a country too poor to maintain you decently, [I] laid open for you at a blow, and in spite of Persia's naval supremacy, the gates of the Hellespont. My cavalry crushed the satraps of Darius, and I added all Ionia and Aeolia, the two Phrygias and Lydia to your empire. . . . I took them and gave them to you for your profit and enjoyment. The wealth of Egypt and Cyrene, which I shed no blood to win, now flows in your hands; Palestine and the plains of Syria and Mesopotamia are now your property; Babylon and Bactria and Susa are yours; you are the masters of the gold of Lydia, the treasures of Persia, the wealth of India—yes, and the seas beyond India, too. You are my captains, my generals, my governors of provinces.

"From all this that I have labored to win for you, what is left for me myself except the purple and the crown? I keep nothing for my own. . . . Perhaps you will say that, in my position as your commander, I had none of the labors and distress which you had to endure to win me what I have won. . . . Come now—if you are wounded, strip and show your wounds, and I will show mine. There is no part of my body but my back which does not have a scar; not a weapon a man may grasp or fling, the mark of which I do not carry on me . . . and all for your sakes: for your glory and your gain. Over every land and sea, across river, mountain, and plain, I led you to the world's end, a victorious army. I marry as you marry, and many of you will have children related by blood to my own. . . . But you all wish to leave me. Go then! And when you reach home, tell them that Alexander your king, who vanquished the Persians and Medes and Bactrians . . . tell them, I say, that you deserted him and left him to the mercy of barbarian men, whom you yourselves conquered. . . ."

On the Macedonians, the immediate effect of Alexander's speech was profound. . . . But when they were told [three days later that] . . . command was being given to Persian officers, foreign troops drafted into Macedonian units, a Persian corps of Guards called by a Macedonian name, Persian infantry units given the coveted title of Companions, . . . every man of them hurried to the palace . . . and [they] swore they would not stir from the spot until Alexander took pity on them.

Source: Arrian, *The Campaigns of Alexander*, trans. Aubrey de Selincourt (New York: 1958), pp. 360–65 (slightly modified).

Questions for Analysis

1. What qualities of leadership does Alexander display in this speech? How do these qualities compare to those of Cyrus the Younger, in Xenophon's description of him (page 89)?

2. Given the circumstances that precipitated this mutiny, why does Alexander use the term *barbarians* to describe the Persians and other conquered peoples? What does he hope to convey by using this word, and then by reorganizing his forces to replace Macedonians with Persians?

3. Histories written well into the nineteenth century of our era feature speeches that were allegedly spoken by historical characters on momentous occasions. How closely do you think Arrian's reconstruction of this speech reflects historical reality? How might you go about arguing that it is, in fact, an accurate reflection of what Alexander actually said?

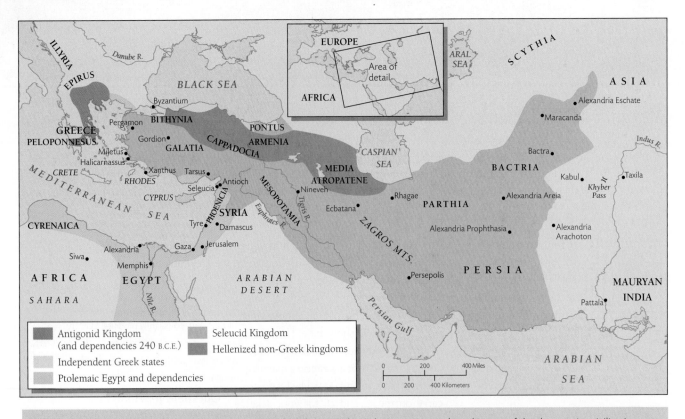

THE HELLENISTIC WORLD. Each of the three successor kingdoms to Alexander's empire was based in one of the three major civilizations we have studied so far: Egyptian, Mesopotamian, and Greek. ▪ *Based on the map above, what were the names of the three main successor states and where were they located?* ▪ *What might the division of Alexander's empire along such lines suggest about the lasting cultural differences among these regions?* ▪ *What might it suggest about the likelihood of forging a united empire, had he lived?*

They achieved this, in part, by ruling from the new city of Alexandria on the Mediterranean coast. In Alexandria, they acted as Macedonian kings toward their Greek and Macedonian citizens; outside of Alexandria, they played the role of pharaohs, surrounding themselves with the trappings and symbols of Egypt's heritage. But until the last Ptolemaic ruler, Cleopatra VII (69–30 B.C.E.), none of them bothered to learn the Egyptian language—although, as the Rosetta Stone attests (Chapter 1), they had able administrators who could communicate effectively with their multilingual and multicultural subjects.

For the Ptolemies, as for the ancient pharaohs, all of Egypt was land to be exploited for the benefit of the royal house. Supporting this tradition was the Macedonian idea that conquered land was plunder, to be used for personal enrichment and glorification. Accordingly, the Ptolemies exploited the wealth of the Egyptian countryside to the fullest. Most of this wealth ended up in Alexandria, which became the brilliant hub of the Hellenistic world. But there was little interest in improving the lives of the Egyptian peasantry, whose bread-winning labors made their rulers rich. So although the third century was a prosperous and relatively peaceful one in Egypt, future pharoahs would face regular and dangerous revolts.

Nevertheless, Ptolemaic Egypt was the most succesful of the Hellenistic kingdoms. It was also the most influential, because of its key role in preserving and transmitting the accumulated heritage of the civilizations that had preceded it: Egyptian, Mesopotamian, and Greek. The Ptolemies used much of their wealth to patronize science and the arts, and they established a great Museum ("home of the Muses") and library which attracted the greatest minds of the Hellenistic world. Many breakthroughs in astronomy, mechanical engineering, and physics occurred in Alexandria. In particular, the study of medicine advanced greatly: freed from the taboos of their homeland, Greek researchers were permitted to perform autopsies, making it possible for anatomy to become a scientific discipline in its own right. It was also in Alexandria that the texts of Greek poetry, drama, history, and philosophy were copied and preserved in the forms in which we know them, and here that the Hebrew scriptures were translated into Greek for a wider audience. Any history of Western civilizations would be impossible without these initiatives.

Seleucid Asia

The vast possessions that Alexander had accumulated in Asia—both within the Persian Empire and outside of it—eventually fell to another Macedonian, Seleucus (*seh-LOO-kus*). Seleucus had navigated the turmoil after Alexander's death successfully and exploited the connections he made through his Persian wife. At his death in 281 B.C.E., his half-Persian son Antiochus (*an-TIE-oh-kuhs*) inherited an expansive realm whose capital was the city named after him, Antioch.

Throughout its history, the dynasty founded by Seleucus (known as the Seleucids) struggled with the problem of holding the disparate parts of this realm together. Seleucus himself solved part of this problem by ceding much of the Indus Valley to the great warrior-king Chandragupta in exchange for a squad of war elephants. By the middle of the third century B.C.E., the Seleucids had also lost control of Bactria (in modern Afghanistan), where a series of Indo-Greek states were emerging with a uniquely complex culture of their own. The Seleucid heartland now became northern Syria, parts of Anatolia, Mesopotamia, and the western half of Persia: still a great, wealthy kingdom, but far less than what Alexander had left.

Like the Ptolemies, the Seleucids presented two faces to their subjects, one looking to ancient Mesopotamian tradition, another looking to Greece. In his proclamations, Antiochus used terms reminiscent of Sargon, Hammurabi, and Cyrus: "I am Antiochus, Great King, legitimate king . . . king of Babylon, king of all countries." But on his coins, he wore his hair short in the fashion of the Greeks and styled himself *basileus*, the Greek word for "king." Although the Seleucids' bureaucracy was less organized than that of the

Ptolemies, even haphazard tax collection could reap huge rewards in an empire of 30 million inhabitants. They had more than enough cash to defend their borders through the third century, a period of regular warfare with Egypt. It was not until the second century, when Antiochus III lost a costly war with a new imperial power, the Romans, that he had to plunder temples and private wealth to pay off the indemnity imposed on him.

Antigonid Macedonia and Greece

The Macedonian homeland did not possess the vast wealth of the new kingdoms carved from Alexander's conquests. It also remained highly unstable from the time of Alexander's death until 276 B.C.E., when a general named Antigonus finally established his own dynasty (known as the Antigonids). Thereafter, Macedonia drew its strength from its considerable natural resources and from its influence over Aegean trade, as well as its status as overlord of Greece. Moreover, the Macedonians continued to field the most effective army in the Hellenistic world.

Antigonus himself was influenced by a philosophical outlook called Stoicism (discussed later in this chapter) and viewed kingship as a form of noble servitude, to be endured rather than enjoyed. This perspective, combined with his modest resources, convinced him not to compete with the Seleucids and Ptolemies for dominance. Instead, Antigonid policy was to keep these other two powers at war with one another and away from the Macedonian sphere of influence. Antigonus and his successors thus pursued a strategy more reminiscent of Philip II than of his son. They secured the northern frontiers, maintained a strong standing army, and kept the fractious Greeks at heel.

The Greeks, however, were restive under the Antigonids, and two emergent powers served as rallying points for those who resented "barbarian" rule. These two forces, the Aetolian League and the Achaean League, were a departure in Greek political organization. Unlike the defensive alliances of the classical period, each represented a real political federation, with some centralization of governance. Citizens of the leagues' member poleis participated in councils of state that dealt with foreign policy and military affairs. New members were admitted on an equal footing with existing members, and all citizens of the various poleis enjoyed joint citizenship throughout the league. The same laws, weights and measures, coinage, and judicial procedures also applied throughout each federation. So effective was this mode of cooperation that James Madison, John Jay, and Alexander Hamilton employed it as one of their models for federalism in the United States.

FROM POLIS TO COSMOPOLIS

So what became of the polis, that building-block of classical Greece? As we have seen, the changes of the fourth century B.C.E. were already disrupting patterns of social and political life. Alexander's conquests hastened this process of transformation, and they also opened up a wider world—a world that came to admire all things Greek. By 300 B.C.E., a common Hellenistic culture was transcending political and geographical boundaries. It was fueled by the hundreds of thousands of adventurers who joined the Greek *diaspora* ("dispersion"), and whose emigration reduced the population of the Greek mainland by as much as 50 percent in the century after 325 B.C.E.

This exciting, urbane world was made up of interconnected cities whose scale surpassed anything imaginable in Periclean Athens. In the fifth century B.C.E., direct participation in government had meant that every male citizen had some share in his society, its institutions, its gods, its army, and its cultural life. In the huge and cosmopolitan Hellenistic city, by contrast, all these ways of defining oneself were no longer relevant. The individual male's intimate connection with the state was broken, as was his nexus of social relationships. An average Greek in one of the Hellenistic kingdoms might have only his immediate family to rely on, if that. Very often, he was alone. What resulted was a traumatic disjunction between the traditional values and assumptions of Greek life and these new realities—and a host of entirely new opportunities.

Commerce and Urbanization

The Hellenistic world was prosperous. Alexander's conquests had opened up a vast trading area stretching from Egypt to the Persian Gulf, dominated by Greek-speaking rulers and well-established merchant communities. These conquests also stimulated the economy by putting into circulation hoards of Persian gold and silver coins, jewelry, and other commodities acquired through plunder. Industries benefited too, because autocratic rulers found manufacturing to be a further means of increasing their revenues.

Every facility was provided by the Ptolemies and the Seleucids for the encouragement of commerce. Harbors were improved, warships were sent out to police the seas, roads and canals were built. The Ptolemies even employed geographers to discover new routes to distant lands. As a result of such methods, Egypt developed a flourishing commerce in the widest variety of products obtainable. Into the port of Alexandria came spices from Arabia, gold from Ethiopia and India, tin from Britain, elephants and ivory from Nubia, silver from Spain, fine carpets from Anatolia, and even silk from China.

The rapid growth of cities had both political and economic ramifications. Greek rulers imported Greek officials and especially Greek soldiers to maintain their control over non-Greek populations, making many new settlements necessary. Alexander himself had founded some 70 cities as outposts of domination and administration; in the next two centuries, his successors founded about 200 more. Urbanization also increased due to the expansion of commerce and industry, but the most significant factors were the Greek diaspora and the migration of workers from rural areas.

Population growth in some centers was explosive. At Antioch, the population quadrupled during a single century. Seleucia on the Tigris grew from nothing to a metropolis of several hundred thousand in less than two centuries. Alexandria in Egypt had half a million inhabitants; in ancient times, only imperial Rome would surpass it in size, and it would not be until the eighteenth century of our era that European cities like London and Paris were as large. Alexandria was not only populous, it was magnificent and spacious—which Rome never was. Its wide streets were paved and laid out in an orderly grid. It had splendid public buildings and parks, the great Museum, and the famous library containing half a million books. It was the storehouse and showcase of Greek culture.

Not everyone enjoyed prosperity. Agriculture remained the major occupation, and small farmers in particular suffered severely from exploitative taxation. Although industrial production increased, it continued to be based on manual labor by individual artisans, most of whom lived in poverty. Among the teeming populations of Hellenistic cities, unemployment was a constant concern. Even those who prospered in the new economy were subject to drastic fluctuations in their fortunes, owing to the precarious nature of mercantile endeavors. Merchants were also vulnerable to the boom-and-bust syndrome: an investor, thinking he could make a fortune during an upward price spiral, might go into debt to take advantage of the trend, only to find that supply exceeded demand, leaving him nothing with which to pay his creditors. The economic landscape of the Hellenistic world was therefore one of contrasting extremes. In many ways, this was also the case with respect to its culture.

HELLENISTIC WORLDVIEWS

Life in the Hellenistic boomtowns produced new worldviews and new philosophies that differed significantly from those of Plato and Aristotle. Another major departure was the separation of philosophy from scientific inquiry, which now became its own field of study. Despite these differences, however, scientists, philosophers, and religious

Past and Present

Assimilation and Difference

The Greek diaspora ("dispersion") that bound the Hellenistic kingdoms together would eventually lead to the emergence of distinctive new hybrid cultures. The mosaic on the left comes from an ancient synagogue and shows Jewish ritual objects (including a menorah and shofar) accompanied by a Greek inscription. The image on the right shows one manifestation of the modern Turkish diaspora: a clothing store in a district of Berlin called "Little Istanbul," where many Turkish "guest workers" settled in the 1960s.

Watch related author videos on the Student Site
wwnorton.com/college/history/western-civilizationsBrief4

teachers were all motivated by the same thing: the need to make human existence meaningful in a new age that lacked traditional civic structures and social values.

Two Paths to Tranquility: Stoicism and Epicureanism

The two strains of philosophy that dominated the Hellenistic world both originated in Athens around 300 B.C.E.: Stoicism and Epicureanism. Their teachings had several features in common. Both were concerned with the well-being of the individual, not with the welfare of society as a whole. Both were firmly rooted in the material world; even the soul was considered to be part of the mortal body. Both responded to the new cosmopolitan age by promoting universal values: they taught that people are the same the world over, and recognized no distinctions between Greeks and the peoples hitherto known as "barbarians."

But in other ways the two systems were radically different. The Stoics who followed Zeno of Citium (c. 335–c. 263 B.C.E.)—they took their name from the *stoa* ("colonnade") in which he regularly taught—believed that the cosmos is an ordered whole in which all contradictions are resolved for ultimate good. Evil is only relative; the particular misfortunes that befall human beings are merely incidents that will lead to the final perfection of the universe. Everything that happens is therefore predetermined. People are free only in the sense that they can accept fate or rebel against it. By freely submitting to the workings of the universe, and by acknowledging that whatever happens must be for the best, one can attain true happiness: tranquility of mind.

The Stoics' theory of ethics and social responsibility grew out of this personal philosophy. Believing that the highest good is serenity of mind, they emphasized self-discipline and the fulfillment of one's duties. They taught tolerance and forgiveness, and they also urged participation in public affairs as a special responsibility for those with able minds. They condemned slavery and violence, although they took no real actions against these evils because they saw them as inevitable— and because extreme social change might be worse.

With some later modifications, Stoic philosophy became the driving force behind the values of the Roman Republic and of early Christianity, and can be considered one of the most important products of the Hellenistic world. Even those who do not embrace its tenets or its perspective may not recognize that they have been influenced by it.

The teachings of Epicurus (341–270 B.C.E.) were based on the atomic theory of an earlier Greek philosopher called Democritus, who lived in the latter part of the fifth century B.C.E. According to his central thesis, the universe is made up entirely of atoms, and every individual object or organism is therefore the product of a combination of atoms. Studying Democritus's writings, Epicurus reached a conclusion exactly opposite to that of the Stoics: he interpreted the atomic theory to mean that there is no ultimate purpose in the workings of the universe. So the highest good cannot come of submitting oneself stoically to the endurance of hardship, because suffering is not part of a larger plan: it is merely the chance by-product of random atomic actions. The highest good, then, must be pleasure: the moderate satisfaction of bodily appetites, the intellectual pleasure of contemplating excellence and remembering past enjoyments, and serenity in the face of death. Indeed, an individual who understands that the soul itself is material, that the universe operates at random, and that no gods intervene in human affairs will have no fear of death or any other supernatural phenomena.

The Epicureans thus came by a very different route to the same general conclusion as the Stoics: nothing is better than tranquility of mind. In contrast to the Stoics, however, they did not insist on virtue as an end in itself, or on the fulfillment of one's duties. For an Epicurean, the only duty a person has is to the self, and the only reason to act virtuously is to increase one's own happiness. Similarly, Epicureans denied that there is any such thing as justice; laws and political institutions are "just" only insofar as they contribute to the welfare of the individual. Yes, certain rules have been found necessary for the maintenance of order, but these rules should be obeyed solely because that is to one's advantage. The state is, at best, a mere convenience, and the wise man should take no active part in politics. Instead, he should withdraw to study philosophy and enjoy the fellowship of a few congenial friends. Modern libertarian and anarchic movements share many characteristics with Epicureanism.

Extreme Doubt: Skepticism

The most pessimistic philosophy generated by the Hellenistic era was propounded by the Skeptics, whose name means "those on the lookout" or "the spies." Skepticism reached the zenith of its popularity in the second century under the influence of Carneades (car-ne-AH-dees, c. 214–129 B.C.E.), a man born in the Greek city of Cyrene, in North Africa, who spent his youth in Athens. His chief teaching (adopted from Aristotle) was that all knowledge is based on sense perception and is therefore limited and relative. From this, the Skeptics concluded that no one can prove anything. Moreover, because our senses can deceive us, we cannot even be certain about the truth we think we have gained by observation of the world. All we can say is that things *appear* to be such and such; we do not *know* that they really *are* that way. It follows, furthermore, that we can have no definite knowledge of the supernatural, of the meaning of life, or of right and wrong.

The only sensible course for the Skeptic is therefore to suspend judgment. If we abandon the fruitless quest for truth and cease to worry about good conduct and the existence of evil, we can at least attain a certain peace of mind, the highest satisfaction that an uncertain life affords. Needless to say, the Skeptics were even less concerned than the Epicureans with political and social problems, from which they felt wholly alienated. Their ideal was one of escape from an incomprehensible world. In some key respects they anticipated modern existentialism and nihilism.

Varieties of Religion

Like Epicureanism and Skepticism, Hellenistic religion tended to offer vehicles of escape from political commitments. When we think back to how close was the link between Greek selfhood and politics down to the middle of the fourth century B.C.E.—"man is a creature of the polis"—we can begin to appreciate what a radical change had occurred in just a few generations. In all the societies we have studied so far, religion was wholly interconnected with politics. Divine worship centered on the gods who protected a community and furthered its interests. Hence, the most serious of the charges brought against Socrates was that he had "denied the gods of the polis" and thus committed treason. Religious crimes were political crimes, and piety was the same as patriotism.

Although this sense of a vital connection between a place and its gods persisted to a certain extent during the Hellenistic period, civic-oriented worship was compromised by rootless multiculturalism. In place of a shared religion, some elite members of society gravitated toward one of the philosophies discussed above. Ordinary people, though, were more likely to embrace religious cults that offered emotional gratification or the diversion of colorful rituals, as well as some assurance of an afterlife.

Cults that stressed extreme methods of atonement, mystical union with the divine, or contact with supernatural forces accordingly attracted many followers. Among these so-called mystery religions was the cult of Dionysus, which celebrated the cyclical death and resurrection of that Greek god. The Egyptian cult of Isis (Chapter 1) also revolved around rituals of death and rebirth. So too did Zoroastrianism (Chapter 2), which became increasingly dualistic: its magi now taught that the material world was entirely evil and urged believers to adopt ascetic practices that would purify their souls and prepare them for ethereal joy in the afterlife.

Like the peoples who worshiped them, the gods of the Hellenistic world were often immigrants from other lands. Temples to Greek gods and goddesses were dedicated throughout the Near East and Egypt; conversely, temples to Near Eastern divinities were constructed in the cities of the Greek homeland. In Alexandria, scholars of religion collected Egyptian and Near Eastern mythologies, which were recorded and reformulated for Greek-speaking audiences.

Even among the Jews, who resisted assimilation and the adoption of foreign customs, Hellenistic culture put down deep roots. This was especially true among elite Jews living outside Palestine, who outnumbered the Palestinian Jewish population by a considerable margin. To meet the needs of these Greek-speaking Jews, and to satisfy the curiosity of Gentiles interested in Jewish beliefs, scholars working in Alexandria produced a Greek version of the Hebrew scriptures. It is known as the Septuagint (sep-TOO-ah-gint), from the Greek word meaning "the seventy"; legend has it that seventy scribes, each working independently, produced individual translations from Hebrew to Greek that were identical in every respect. This meant that the Septuagint could be regarded as no less a product of divine inspiration than the original books that made up the Hebrew Bible, and could be treated as an authoritative text in its own right. For Jews concerned about their social and cultural standing vis-à-vis their Greek neighbors, the Septuagint was proof of their Hellenistic values—although, ironically, some of the very portions of scripture that were now written in Greek disapproved strongly of those values.

THE SCIENTIFIC REVOLUTION OF ANTIQUITY

The Hellenistic period was the most brilliant age in the history of science before the seventeenth century of our era (see Chapter 16). There are three major reasons for this. First, there was the stimulus to intellectual inquiry caused by the fusion of Mesopotamian and Egyptian science with the philosophical methods of the Greeks. Second, as in the more famous scientific revolution, the use of a common language (in the seventeenth century it was Latin) and the ease of communication facilitated by affordable travel made the circulation of knowledge and sharing of ideas easier (in the seventeenth century, communication was greatly enabled by the printing press). Finally, as in the seventeenth century, the competition among patrons of science was intense: every ruler wanted to be thought enlightened and to be associated with new discoveries. Even purely theoretical advances were so much admired that a Hellenistic prince who had bankrolled such a breakthrough would share the glory of it. It was especially profitable to subsidize research that led to the development of new technologies, because they might have military applications.

The arts were also transformed by the economic and political conditions of the Hellenistic world. Artists working in various media strove to demonstrate their mastery of difficult techniques and so to attract the notice of potential patrons. New markets for art also changed *what* was being made, how, and for whom. In all of the civilizations we have studied so far, artists worked directly for royal or civic patrons. In the Hellenistic world, art became commodified. Sometimes a work would be made expressly for a particular patron, but many works of art were fashioned for the open market. They were also designed to suit the tastes and lifestyles of those merchant classes who had disposable income and wanted to increase their social standing through conspicuous consumption. This was as true of literature as of sculpture or the decorative arts: we know the names of over a thousand Hellenistic authors. Indeed, the number of texts and *objets d'art* that exist from this period is huge when compared to earlier eras.

Measuring and Mapping: Astronomy, Geography, and Mathematics

Hellenistic scientists took a major interest in measurements and mapmaking, whether of the heavens (astronomy), the earth (geography), or the forms occuring in nature (geometry). The most renowned—and most wronged—of the Hellenistic astronomers was Aristarchus of Samos (310–230 B.C.E.), whose major discovery anticipated that of Copernicus by 1,700 years: he deduced that the earth and other planets revolve around the sun. Unfortunately, however, this view was not accepted by many of his contemporaries or successors because it conflicted with the teachings of Aristotle, which in turn reflected the Greek conviction that humanity, and therefore the earth, must be at the center of the universe. The sad fate of his discovery was sealed in the second century C.E., when the Alexandrian scholar Claudius Ptolemaeus (known as

Competing Viewpoints

Debating the Education and Role of Women

> The drastic political, social, and economic changes of the fourth century led philosophers to reimagine the traditional structures of the polis, and to debate the proper role of women within these structures. Meanwhile, the cosmopolitan culture of the expanding Hellenistic world made it increasingly difficult to limit women's access to public spaces. The following excerpts represent two philosophical responses to these problems. The first comes from Plato's treatise on "Polis-matters" (Politeía), known to us as The Republic, the longest of his philosophical dialogues and the most influential work of political thought in history. Its conceptual narrator and protagonist is Socrates, who engages in a series of debates with his pupils. The second excerpt is taken from a philosophical treatise attributed to a female follower of Pythagoras (see Chapter 3), but it was really written around 200 B.C.E. in Hellenistic Italy, and by a man.

Plato, *The Republic*, c. 380 B.C.E.

SOCRATES: For men born and educated like our citizens, the only way, in my opinion, of arriving at a right conclusion about the possession and use of women and children is to follow the path on which we originally started, when we said that the men were to be the guardians and watchdogs of the herd.

GLAUCON: True.

SOCRATES: Let us further suppose the birth and education of our women to be subject to similar or nearly similar regulations; then we shall see whether the result accords with our design.

GLAUCON: What do you mean?

SOCRATES: ... The education which was assigned to the men was music and gymnastic[s].

GLAUCON: Yes.

SOCRATES: Then women must be taught music and gymnastic[s] and also the art of war, which they must practice like the men?

GLAUCON: That is the inference, I suppose.

SOCRATES: I should rather expect ... that several of our proposals, if they are carried out, being unusual, may appear ridiculous.

GLAUCON: No doubt of it.

SOCRATES: Yes, and the most ridiculous thing of all will be the sight of women naked in the *palaestra*, exercising with the men, especially when they are no longer young; they certainly will not be a vision of beauty, any more than the enthusiastic old men who in spite of wrinkles and ugliness continue to frequent the gymnasia. ... [Yet] not long ago, as we shall remind them, the Hellenes were of the opinion, which is still generally received among the barbarians, that the sight of a naked man was ridiculous and improper; and when first the Cretans and then the Lacedaemonians [Spartans] introduced the custom, the wits of that day might equally have ridiculed the innovation.

GLAUCON: No doubt ...

SOCRATES: First, then, whether the question is to be put in jest or in earnest, let us come to an understanding about the nature of woman: Is she capable of sharing either wholly or partially in the actions of men, or not at all? And is the art of war one of those arts in which she can or cannot share? That will be the best way of commencing the enquiry, and will probably lead to the fairest conclusion. ...

GLAUCON: I suppose so. ...

SOCRATES: And if ... the male and female sex appear to differ in their fitness for any art or pursuit, we should say that such pursuit or art ought to be assigned to one or the other of them; but if the difference consists only in women bearing and men begetting children, this does not amount to a proof that a woman differs from a man in respect of the sort of education she should receive; and we shall therefore continue to maintain that our guardians and their wives ought to have the same pursuits.

GLAUCON: Very true.

SOCRATES: Next, we shall ask ... how, in reference to any of the pursuits or arts of civic life, the nature of a woman differs from that of a man? ...

GLAUCON: By all means.

SOCRATES: ... When you spoke of a nature gifted or not gifted in any respect, did you mean to say that one man will acquire a thing easily, another with difficulty; a little learning will lead the one to discover a great deal; whereas the other, after much study and application, no sooner learns than he forgets? Or again, did you mean, that the one has a body which is a good servant to his mind, while the body of the other is a hindrance to him? Would not these be the sort of differences which distinguish the man gifted by nature from the one who is ungifted?

GLAUCON: No one will deny that.

SOCRATES: And can you mention any pursuit of mankind in which the male sex has not all these gifts and qualities in a higher degree than the female? Need I waste time in speaking of the art of weaving, and the management of pan-cakes and preserves, in which woman-kind does really appear to be great, and in which for her to be beaten by a man is of all things the most absurd?

GLAUCON: You are quite right . . . in maintaining the general inferiority of the female sex: although many women are in many things superior to many men, yet on the whole what you say is true.

Source: Excerpted from Plato, *The Republic*, Book V, trans. Benjamin Jowett (New York: 1982), pp. 170–76.

Treatise Attributed to Phintys, Third/Second Century B.C.E.

Now some people think that it is not appropriate for a woman to be a philosopher, just as a woman should not be a cavalry officer or a politician. . . . I agree that men should be generals and city officials and politicians, and women should keep house and stay inside and receive and take care of their husbands. But I believe that courage, justice, and intelligence are qualities that men and women have in common. . . . Courage and intelligence are more appropriately male qualities because of the strength of men's bodies and the power of their minds. Chastity is more appropriately female.

Accordingly, a woman must learn about chastity and realize what she must do quantitatively and qualitatively to be able to obtain this womanly virtue. I believe that there are five qualifications: (1) the sancity of her marriage bed, (2) the cleanliness of her body, (3) the manner in which she chooses to leave her house, (4) her refusal to participate in secret cults . . . , (5) her readiness and moderation in sacrificing to the gods.

Of these, the most important quality for chastity is to be pure in respect of the marriage bed, and for her not to have affairs with men from other households. If she breaks the law in this way she wrongs the gods of her family and provides her family and home not with its own off-spring but with bastards. . . . She should

also consider the following: that there is no means of atoning for this sin; no way she can approach the shrines or the altars of the gods as a pure woman. . . . The greatest glory a freeborn woman can have—her foremost honor—is the witness her own children will give to her chastity toward her husband, the stamp of the likeness they bear to the father whose seed produced them. . . .

As far as adornment of her body is concerned . . . her clothes should not be transparent or ornate. She should not put on silken material, but moderate, white-colored clothes. In this way, she will avoid being overdressed or luxurious or made-up, and not give other women cause to be uncomfortably envious. . . . She should not apply imported or artificial coloring to her face—with her own natural color-ing, by washing only with water, she can ornament herself with modesty. . . .

Women of importance leave the house to sacrifice to the leading divin-ity of the community on behalf of their husbands and their households. They do not leave home at night nor in the evening, but at midday, to attend a reli-gious festival or to make some purchase, accompanied by a single female servant or decorously escorted by two servants at most. . . . They keep away from secret cults . . . particularly because these forms of worship encourage drunkenness and ecstasy. The mistress of the house and

head of the household should be chaste and untouched in all respects.

Source: From Mary R. Lefkowitz and Maureen B. Fant, eds., *Women's Life in Greece & Rome: A Source Book in Translation*, 2nd ed. (Baltimore, MD: 1992), pp. 163–64.

Questions for Analysis

1. Follow the steps of the argument made by Socrates. How does he go about proving that women and men are different, and should have differ-ent roles in society? Are there flaws in this argument? What are they?

2. How does the author of the trea-tise seem to define "chastity," and why does "she" (actually he) say that it corresponds to more masculine qualities of courage and intelligence? Why would this author have wanted to attribute these reflections to female members of the community founded by the philosopher Pythagoras (c. 570–c. 495), three centuries earlier? How might this treatise be responding to the changes brought about by the expansion of the Greek world in the fourth and third centuries B.C.E?

3. What are main points on which these two perspectives agree? How might ideas like those expressed here have influenced contemporary ideas of female beauty and modesty (see **Interpreting Visual Evidence**, page 91)?

Ptolemy) unequivocally argued that Aristotle was correct, and that all heavenly bodies revolve around the earth. This mistaken view would not be overturned until the much later scientific revolution occurred.

Closely allied with astronomy were geography and mathematics. The most influential Hellenistic mathematician was Euclid, whose *Elements of Geometry* (c. 300 B.C.E.) remained the basic textbook of that subject until the twentieth century of our era. In the field of geography—and in a host of other pursuits, too—the most original thinker was Eratosthenes of Alexandria (*air-ah-TOS-then-ees*, c. 276–c. 196 B.C.E.). Not only did he accurately calculate the circumference of the earth (within a tiny margin of error, less than 200 miles), he was the first to suggest the possibility of reaching eastern Asia by sailing west. In addition, he founded the science of chronology by attempting to establish the dates of major events reaching back to the siege of Troy. Students of history are forever in his debt.

Medicine and Mechanics: The Sciences of Physiology and Physics

Before the third century B.C.E., physics had been a branch of philosophy. Now it became a separate, experimental science thanks to the genius of one man, Archimedes of Syracuse (c. 287–212 B.C.E.). It was he who discovered the law of floating bodies, or specific gravity, now known as 'Archimedes'

principle." According to legend, the idea came to him when he was in his bath, and the stunning insight so excited him that he lept from the water and dashed out naked into the street, shouting *"Eureka!"* ("I have found it!"). Archimedes also established the principles of the lever, the pulley, and the screw, and he invented both a compound pulley and a propeller. All of these discoveries had numerous practical uses in the construction of buildings, ships, and military machinery.

Extraordinary advances were also made in the field of medicine. Especially significant was the work of Herophilus of Chalcedon (c. 335–c. 280 B.C.E.), the greatest anatomist of antiquity and probably the first to practice human dissection. Herophilus's achievements included a detailed description of the brain, which allowed him to prove that it was the engine of human intellect (Aristotle thought that the seat of intelligence was the heart), as well as the discovery that the arteries contain blood alone (not a mixture of blood and air, as Aristotle had taught), and that their function is to carry blood from the heart to all parts of the body. His colleague Erasistratus (*air-ah-sis-STRAH-tus*) made allied discoveries, establishing that the heart was a pump and not an organ of emotion. Erasistratus also rejected the widely held theory of the physician Hippocrates (c. 460–c. 370), who had posited that the body consists of four "humors" which need to be kept in balance through bloodletting and other invasive practices. Unfortunately, this discovery went the way of the heliocentric universe posited by Aristarchus: another encyclopedist

THE CITADEL OF PERGAMON. An artist's reconstruction of Pergamon in the second century B.C.E., based on the work of nineteenth-century German archaeologists. High atop the hill is the massive altar of Zeus (now in the Pergamon Museum in Berlin) and below it slope the tiers of the theater. Other features include fortifications, terraces, and artificial landscaping for public gardens. ▪ *How does this complex of buildings compare to that of another citadel, the Acropolis of Athens (see Chapter 3, page 60)?*

DYING GAUL. The original (now lost) statue on which this Roman copy was based was sculpted in Pergamon around 220 B.C.E. The sculptor clearly wished to exhibit skill in depicting an unusual subject: the Gauls were a Celtic people about whom very little was known in this era. ▪ *How does this sympathetic representation of a "barbarian" express the new values of Hellenistic philosophy?*

of the second century C.E., Galen, preferred the erroneous theory of Hippocrates. The practice of bloodletting thus persisted into the nineteenth century of our era.

Urban Architecture and Sculpture

Hellenistic architecture drew on Greek models, but it was also influenced by tastes more characteristic of Egypt and Persia. The best surviving example comes from Pergamon, a city on the coast of Anatolia that became the capital of a new kingdom wrested from the control of the Seleucids in the second century B.C.E. It boasted an enormous altar dedicated to Zeus that crowned the heights of the city, below which an open-air theater was built into the steep slope of the hill. In Ephesus, not far away, the streets were not only paved, they were paved with marble.

But the most influential of all Hellenistic arts was sculpture, which placed even more emphasis on realism than the fourth-century sculptures discussed earlier in this chapter. And because awkward human postures offered the greatest technical challenges, sculptors often preferred to show people stretching themselves or balancing on one leg or performing other unusual feats. It is clear that the goal was to create something unique in both conception and craftsmanship—something a collector could show off as the only one of its type. It is not surprising, therefore, that complexity came to be admired for its own sake, and extreme naturalism sometimes teetered on the brink of absurdity. Yet to our eyes, such works appear familiar because of the influence they exerted on later sculptors like Michelangelo (see Chapter 12) and Auguste Rodin. Three of the most famous examples are pictured here, each exhibiting different aesthetic qualities and artistic techniques: the *Dying Gaul*, made in Pergamon around 220 B.C.E.; the *Winged Victory of Samothrace*, dating from around 200 B.C.E.; and the *Laocoön* group, from the first century B.C.E.

THE WINGED VICTORY OF SAMOTHRACE (left). This marble sculpture of the goddess Nike (Victory) may originally have been displayed on the prow of a monumental ship. It formed part of a temple complex on the island of Samothrace in the northern Aegean, and dates to around the year 200 B.C.E. It is now in the Louvre Museum, Paris. **LAOCOÖN AND HIS SONS (right).** In sharp contrast to the serene and confident *Winged Victory* is this famous sculpture group from the first century B.C.E. According to legend, Laocoön warned the Trojans not to accept the wooden horse sent by the Greeks and was accordingly punished by the sea-god Poseidon, who sent two serpents to kill him and his sons. The intense physicality of this work was an important influence on Michelangelo, a millennium and a half later.

Literary Fantasy and Historical Reality

In the sixth century B.C.E. it was the lyric, in the fifth century it was tragedy, and in the fourth century it was the novel; but in the Hellenistic era, the new literary genre was pastoral verse. These poems tapped into a strong vein of nostalgia for rural pastimes and simple pleasures, a make-believe world of shepherds and wood nymphs. The most important pastoral poet of the age was Theocritus, who flourished around 270 B.C.E. in the big-city environment of Alexandria. In the midst of urban bustle and within sight of overcrowded slums, he celebrated the charms of country life and lazy summer afternoons. He thereby founded an enduring tradition that would be taken up by poets from the Roman Virgil to the Englishman (and classical scholar) A. E. Houseman, which has provided a wealth of themes for the visual arts. Even composers like Beethoven and Debussy owe a debt to Theocritus.

By contrast, Hellenistic prose literature was dominated by historians who modeled their work on earlier pioneers, especially Thucydides. By far the most important was Polybius (c. 203–120 B.C.E.), a well-born Greek whose father was a prominent politician in the Achaean League. Polybius himself was trained as a cavalry officer at a time when the Achaean League was trying to position itself favorably in ongoing wars between the rising republic of Rome and the various kingdoms of northern Greece. In 168 B.C.E., the Romans became suspicious of the Achaeans' declared neutrality and demanded that a thousand noble hostages be sent to Rome as a guarantee of the League's good behavior. Polybius was one of those hostages, and he spent the next seventeen years living in Rome, where he became a fervent admirer of its unique form of government (see Chapter 5).

The result was a series of histories that glorified the achievements of Rome and its political system. Polybius also attempted to account for the patterns that he discerned in the history of Greece since the Peloponnesian War. He argued that historical developments follow regular cycles, and that nations pass inevitably through stages of growth and decay. Hence, it should be possible to predict exactly where a given state is heading if one knows what has happened to it in the past. Yet Polybius also argued that the special character of Rome's constitution would allow it to break the cycle, because it combined all of the different forms of government that Aristotle had outlined in his *Politics*. This view of history galvanized the framers of the United States Constitution, directly influencing their conception of our own political institutions.

CONCLUSION

Judged from the perspective of classical Greece, Hellenistic civilization seems strange. The autocratic governments of

After You Read This Chapter

Go to **INQUIZITIVE** to see what you've learned—and learn what you've missed—with personalized feedback along the way.

REVIEWING THE OBJECTIVES

- Macedonia's successful conquest of the Greek poleis can be attributed to several factors. What are they?
- Alexander the Great's imperial policies were influenced by his own upbringing, the different cultures he encountered, and some key historical precedents. Give at least one example of each type of influence.
- Explain how the three Hellenistic kingdoms reflect the differences among the three main civilizations we have studied so far.
- Why is the Hellenistic world described as "cosmopolitan"? How did this urban culture differ from that of the Greek poleis?
- The philosophies of Plato and Aristotle both derive from the teachings of Socrates, but they diverge in some important ways. What are those main differences?

the age that followed Alexander's conquests would probably appear repugnant to a staunch proponent of Athenian democracy, and the Hellenistic love of extravagance can contrast strikingly with the tastes of the fifth century B.C.E. Yet Hellenistic civilization had its own achievements that the classical age could not match. Most Hellenistic cities offered a greater range of public facilities than any Greek cities of the previous period, and the numerous advances in science and technology are astonishing when compared to anything that came before, or even after.

But the most important contribution of the Hellenistic era to subsequent historical developments was its role as intermediary between the nascent empire of Rome and the older civilizations of Mesopotamia, Egypt, and Greece. The economic and political infrastuctures that were put in place after Alexander's conquests would form the framework of Roman imperial government. The Romans would also take advantage of the common language and cultural expectations that bound the far reaches of the Greek-speaking world together. Their own Latin language would never supplant Greek as the preeminent language of scholarship and administration in the eastern portions of their empire.

The Hellenistic era must also be recognized as the bridge that connects us to the earlier ages of antiquity: most of what is contained in the first four chapters of this book is known to us because older texts and artifacts were copied and collected by the scholars of Alexandria and other Hellenistic cities. And it was Hellenistic art and architecture, Hellenistic city planning and civic culture, that the Romans strove to emulate—not those of Periclean Athens. The same can be said of drama and poetry.

For us, two further aspects of Hellenistic culture deserve special mention: its cosmopolitanism and its modernity. The word *cosmopolitan* means "universal city," and it was the Hellenistic period that came closest to turning this ideal of globalization into reality. Around 250 B.C.E. a Greek tourist could have traveled from Sicily to the borders of India—the two ends of the earth—and never have found himself among people who did not speak his language or share his basic outlook. Nor would this tourist have identified himself in ethnic or nationalist terms, or felt any exclusive loyalty to a city-state or kingdom. He would have considered himself a citizen of the world. He would also have considered himself a modern man, not bound by the old prejudices and superstitions of the past. It is for these reasons that Hellenistic civilization seems so closely related to our own. It was a world of stark contrasts and infinite possibilities, where economic instability, extremism, and authoritarian regimes existed side by side with unprecedented prosperity, rational inquiry, and extraodinary freedoms. In Chapter 5, we will see how this world adapted itself to the dominion of a single Italian city.

PEOPLE, IDEAS, EVENTS IN CONTEXT

- How did the philosophies of **PLATO** and **ARISTOTLE** respond to the crisis of the polis?
- In what ways were the military strategies of **PHILIP II OF MACEDONIA** variations on older forms of hoplite warfare? How did the rise of mercenary armies and of **THEBES** further change military strategies in the fourth century?
- To what degree did the conquests of **ALEXANDER THE GREAT** unite Mesopotamia, Egypt, and Greece?
- Why and how did the three **HELLENISTIC KINGDOMS** emerge? How were the **AETOLIAN** and **ACHAEAN LEAGUES** new models for governance and cooperation in Greece?
- In what ways were **STOICISM, EPICUREANISM**, and other new philosophies a response to **COSMOPOLITANISM** and the breakdown of traditional societies and values?
- What were the driving forces behind the **SCIENTIFIC REVOLUTION OF ANTIQUITY**? What were its main achievements?
- What are some essential characteristics of **HELLENISTIC ART**? In what ways did it differ from that of the fifth century B.C.E. (Chapter 3)?

THINKING ABOUT CONNECTIONS

- "The history of the world is but the biography of great men"—so the Scottish historian Thomas Carlyle (1795–1881) summarized the impact of figures like Alexander the Great. How would you construct an argument in support of this proposition, using what you've learned in this chapter? How would you refute it?
- In what ways do Alexander's actions demonstrate his own knowledge of history, as well as a capacity to apply that knowledge to his own circumstances? Can you identify leaders of our own day who have mobilized their understanding of history in similar ways?
- In your view, which civilization more resembles our own: classical Athens or the Hellenistic world? Why? What characteristics make an era seem "modern"?

STORY LINES

- Romans were proud of their unique history, especially the legend that they had overthrown their kings. They clung to this story even when individual men came to wield kingly powers.

- Roman identity, religion, and politics were intimately bound up in the worship of ancestors, especially male ancestors. As a result, fathers (living and dead) wielded extraordinary power in early Rome.

- Roman women enjoyed more freedoms than the women of ancient Greece, but they were still subject to the authority of their male relatives.

- Paradoxically, the Romans celebrated their farming heritage even as they built a highly urbanized society. At the same time, they regarded Greek culture as both superior and dangerous.

- The Roman army had unprecedented strength and importance in this civilization, but the army's relationship to Roman politics and society changed drastically as Rome's empire grew.

CHRONOLOGY

753 B.C.E.	Legendary founding of Rome
c. 509 B.C.E.	Roman Republic established
c. 450 B.C.E.	Law of the Twelve Tables
287 B.C.E.	"Struggle of the Orders" ends
264–146 B.C.E.	Punic Wars
134–104 B.C.E.	Slave revolts in Sicily
133–122 B.C.E.	Reforms of the Gracchi
107–86 B.C.E.	Consulship of Marius
82–79 B.C.E.	Dictatorship of Sulla
73–71 B.C.E.	Rebellion of Spartacus
52–48 B.C.E.	Struggle of Pompey and Caesar
48–44 B.C.E.	Dictatorship of Caesar
44–30 B.C.E.	Rivalry of Octavian and Antony
27 B.C.E.–14 C.E.	Principate of the Emperor Augustus
27 B.C.E.–180 C.E.	Flowering of the *Pax Romana*
79 C.E.	Eruption of Mount Vesuvius destroys (and preserves) Pompeii
117 C.E.	Roman Empire reaches its greatest extent under Trajan

Before
You
Read
This
Chapter

The Civilization of Ancient Rome

CORE OBJECTIVES

- **IDENTIFY** the factors that influenced the formation of the Roman Republic.

- **UNDERSTAND** the basic elements of Roman identity.

- **DEFINE** the classes of people who struggled for power in Rome and **EXPLAIN** their different objectives.

- **DESCRIBE** the impact of territorial expansion on Roman society.

- **TRACE** the events leading up to the establishment of the Principate.

C ould anyone be so indifferent or slow-witted as not to care how, and under what system of government, the Romans managed to bring nearly the whole inhabited world under their rule? Can anything be more important than understanding this?" So the Greek soldier Polybius (c. 203–120 B.C.E.) addresses Greek readers in a history celebrating the achievements of the Roman Republic. Polybius had witnessed some of these firsthand: on the battlefield, in Rome itself as a hostage and guest, and on a visit to newly conquered Carthage. What better testament could there be to the success of a small Italian city than the admiration of a cultivated Greek aristocrat who, having been subjected to Roman authority, wholeheartedly embraced it? None, unless we cite the equally enthusiastic endorsement of the same Jews who had rebelled against Greek influence in 164 B.C.E. They, too, could not say enough in praise of the Romans, and they willingly placed themselves under Roman protection:

> Those whom they wish to help and to make kings, they make kings, and those whom they wish they depose; and they have been greatly exalted. Yet for all that, not one of

them has put on a crown or worn purple as a mark of pride, but they have built for themselves a senate chamber and every day three hundred and twenty senators constantly deliberate concerning the people, to govern them well. (1 Maccabees 8:12–15)

The only people who could say more in praise of Rome were the Romans themselves. To them, the enormous success of their empire meant that they were divinely chosen to colonize the world. This was the message conveyed by the poet Virgil (70–19 B.C.E.), commissioned by the Emperor Augustus to tell the story of Rome's rise to glory in a manner imitating the epics of Homer. In one key passage, the father of Aeneas, Virgil's epic hero, "foretells" the future and addresses posterity: "Remember, Roman, you whose power rules / all peoples, that these are your arts: plant peace, / make law, spare subjects, and put down the proud" (*Aeneid*, Book VI, lines 851–3).

While the Greeks struggled against the Persians and against each other, a new civilization emerged beyond the northern fringes of the Greek world, on the banks of the river Tiber in central Italy. By 300 B.C.E. Rome was the dominant power on the Italian peninsula. Two centuries later, it had conquered Greece itself. For the next three centuries after that—an unprecedented period of sustained expansion—its power steadily increased. In the first century of our era, it ruled the Hellenistic world as well as a vast region that Greek culture had never touched: western Europe. Eventually, Rome's empire united the entire Mediterranean and most of Asia Minor, while at the same time embracing provinces that are now parts of France, Spain, Portugal, Britain, Belgium, Germany, Switzerland, and the Balkans. Rome thus built a historical arch that enabled Europe to share in a rich heritage reaching back to ancient Mesopotamia and Egypt. Without Rome, European culture as we know it would not exist, and neither would the political and legal institutions that formed the United States. To echo Polybius: "Can anything be more important than understanding this?"

THE TIME OF THE KINGS

Romans looked back uneasily on their early history, for this was the time when they were ruled by kings. It may have been necessary in those days: Romans had never been peaceful settlers, and their land did not yield an easy living. Although Italy had much more fertile land than Greece, its extensive coastline boasts only a few good harbors, and most of these are on the western side, away from the commercial hubs of Greece and the Near East. Nor does the length of this coastline offer secure natural defenses. So the Romans

were a warlike people from the first, continually forced to defend their own conquests against other invaders.

Early Influences

When the Romans arrived in Italy, the dominant inhabitants of the peninsula were the Etruscans, a people who remain mysterious despite the rich archaeological record they left behind. This is because their language (not a branch of Indo-European) has never been fully deciphered, even though the Etruscans used an alphabet borrowed from the Greeks. By the sixth century B.C.E., the Etruscans had established a confederation of independent city-states in north-central Italy. They were skilled metalworkers, artists, and architects, from whom the Romans later took their knowledge of the arch and the vault, among much else, including the bloody sport of gladiatorial combat.

The two most important foundation myths told by the Romans were also derived from Etruscan tradition: the story of Aeneas's escape from Troy, which became the basis of Virgil's *Aeneid*, and also the story of the infant twins Romulus and Remus, abandoned at birth and then raised by a maternal wolf, afterward founding a fledgling city. Both legends would be mined by Rome's historians for their metaphorical significance, and further details would be added to increase their relevance for a changing audience. For example, the story of Aeneas's seduction and abandonment of Dido, queen of Carthage, reflected Rome's defeat of that powerful North African civilization.

In marked contrast to Greek society, Etruscan women enjoyed a very high status and played important roles in public life. Etruscan wives even ate meals with their husbands, another departure from both Greek and Roman custom. After death, devoted couples were buried together in the same mortuary vaults, and their tombstones and sarcophagi often emphasize mutual affection. Some of these practices certainly affected the Romans, whose women were less sequestered than their Greek counterparts. Yet Rome's women did not enjoy the same freedoms as Etruscan women until very late in Roman history, and by then such freedoms were condemned as signs of decadence (as will be discussed later in the chapter).

The Romans also borrowed ideas from the Greek settlers who had begun to colonize southern Italy and Sicily during the eighth century B.C.E. From them, Romans derived their alphabet, many of their religious beliefs, and much of their art. But the Romans downplayed Greek influence in their founding mythology, preferring to emphasize their alleged descent from the Trojans and also from an Italic people called the Sabines, from whom (according to legend) Romulus and his

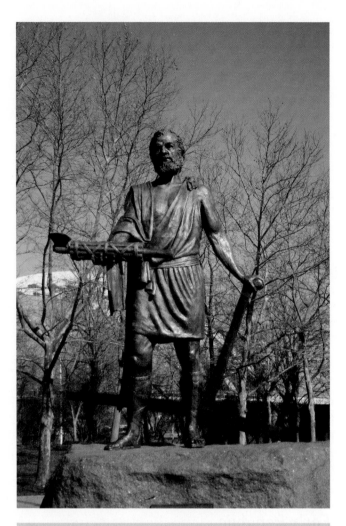

CINCINATTUS THE STATESMAN-FARMER. This bronze statue of Cincinnatus is prominent in Cincinnati, Ohio, which was named after the Roman hero (and in honor of George Washington) in 1790. In his right hand he holds the *fasces*, symbolizing his powers as dictator. In his left, he grasps the handle of a plow. ▪ *Why would this figure have fired the imagination of Americans after their War of Independence?*

commercial port and was not threatened by attack from the sea. Rome also sat astride the first good ford across the Tiber, making it a major crossroads. Further, there were strategic advantages to the seven hills among which Rome was nestled. Eventually, its central markeplace—the *forum* or "open space"—would become the beating heart of the world's most populous and powerful city, with approximately a million people crowded into an area of five square miles.

At an early date, the Romans negotiated a series of agreements with their neighbors which were collectively known as the Latin Right: a trading pact called the *commercium*, provisions for intermarriage called the *connubium*, and the *migratio*, which allowed a Latin resident of one settlement to emigrate to another and, after a year's residence, to have the full rights of a citizen there. These privileges contrast strongly with the mutual suspicion that divided the cities of ancient Sumer or Greece. Indeed, the Romans' later willingness to extend the Latin Right far beyond their homeland of Latium was a key factor in the success of their empire.

According to their own legends, the Romans' early government mirrored the structure of Roman households, with a patriarchal king whose power was checked only by a council of elders, the Senate (from the Latin *senex*, "old man"). Seven kings, including Romulus, are said to have ruled in succession. The last, Tarquinus Superbus (Tarquin the Arrogant), is reputed to have been an Etruscan who paved the way for Rome's imperial expansion by dominating the agriculturally wealthy district of Campania to the south. But his power came at the price of Roman freedom and dignity, as was made clear when Tarquin's son allegedly raped a virtuous Roman wife, Lucretia, around 510 B.C.E. When she commited suicide to avoid dishonor, the Romans—led by Lucretia's kinsman, Lucius Junius Brutus—rose up in rebellion, overthrowing not only the Etruscan dynasty but rejecting the very idea of monarchy as a legitimate form of government. Henceforth, any claim to royal authority in Rome was considered anathema, and the very word "king" (*rex*) was a term of insult. The Brutus who would be instrumental in the assassination of Julius Caesar nearly five centuries later was a descendant of that same Brutus who had driven out the Tarquin kings—something he and his contemporaries never forgot.

men had forcibly abducted their wives. This was a practice Romans would continue, as the legions who planted new colonies intermarried with indigenous populations from the Persian Gulf to the lowlands of Scotland.

The Founding of Rome

The real founders of Rome were a tribe called the Latins, descendents of Indo-European-speaking peoples who crossed the Alps into Italy and settled on the banks of the Tiber by the tenth century B.C.E. This location was advantageous. Trading ships (but not large war fleets) could navigate the river as far as the city, yet no farther; Rome could thus serve as a

THE TRIUMPH OF THE EARLY REPUBLIC

The story of Lucretia was both a patriotic myth and a potent statement of Roman attitudes toward female chastity and family honor. And it coincided with a radical change in Roman governance. This change was so radical, in fact, that it did not match any of Aristotle's political categories (Chapter 4), but instead combined elements of them all. The Romans themselves didn't know what to call their political system: they spoke of it merely as *res publica*, "the public thing."

The Territorial Expansion of Rome

The early Roman Republic was marked by almost constant warfare aimed at stitching together a patchwork of valuable territories that could support Rome's growing population. Gradually, Romans came to control the valuable port of Ostia at the mouth of the Tiber, about twenty miles from their city. They also pushed northward into Etruscan territory, and southward to Naples, another good port. By 300 B.C.E., Rome had absorbed or allied itself with all of central Italy and began to look even farther south, to the wealthy Greek colonies of Sicily.

The Romans' rapid success is remarkable when compared to the patterns familiar to us from our study of classical Greece. What was the secret of it? For one thing, the Romans did not impose heavy burdens of taxation and tribute on the settlements they conquered. More often, they demanded only that they contribute soldiers to the Roman army. Rome also extended the Latin Right to many of these conquered territories, giving them a further stake in Rome's political and military expansion.

Rome thus gained for itself nearly inexhaustible reserves of fighting men. By the middle of the third century B.C.E, its army may have numbered as many as 300,000—a huge force even by modern standards. As we have seen, the Greeks had eventually turned to paid soldiering out of economic necessity, but they fought in smaller numbers; Xenophon's army was 10,000 and Alexander's 100,000. The Great King of Persia could claim to muster a million men, but these were private or tribal armies commanded by his satraps, not a standing army loyal to him.

The Romans also devoted themselves to the discipline of warfare in ways the Greeks (except for the Spartans) and the Persians did not. Although they originally used the phalanx formation, they quickly replaced it with smaller, more flexible divisions that could adjust to the hilly conditions of central Italy. While the major unit of the Roman army was always the legion (5,000 men), the combat unit was the *maniple* ("handful"), a group of 120 infantrymen who trained together and who often performed specialized tasks or used special weaponry. The Greek Polybius could not say enough in praise of this system, which made the army adaptable to climate, terrain, and new military techniques.

The republic's early history reinforced not only the military character of the Roman nation but its commitment to agriculture as the only proper peacetime employment for a Roman. The acquisition of new lands made it possible for citizens to maintain themselves as farmers. As a result, Romans developed an interest in commerce fairly late when compared with the Greeks or Phoenicians. And they would continue—even at the height of their empire—to valorize rural life over that of the city.

The paragon of Roman heroism in this era was Lucius Quinctius Cincinnatus (519–c. 430 B.C.E.), a stout-hearted citizen-farmer who reluctantly accepted political office when Rome was threatened by attack. According to legend, he was found plowing his fields when a delegation of senators arrived to bring him to Rome, where he found that he had been named *dictator* ("decider"). This was a position of power to which the Romans elected one man during times of crisis that required decisive leadership. As legend has it, Cincinnatus dutifully performed this role, led Rome in wars with hostile neighbors—and then went back to his plow. If Lucretia was the Roman ideal of female fortitude, Cincinnatus was the paradigm of manly virtue. George Washington was frequently compared to him, to his own satisfaction.

The Constitution of the Early Republic

During this period of expansion, Rome's political system evolved accordingly. Initially, the overthrow of the monarchy had resulted in only moderate changes; instead of a king, the republic was headed by two elected officers called *consuls*. Although the consuls of the infant republic were supposedly chosen by all citizens, they were inevitably members of aristocratic families, known in Rome as *patricians* because they traced descent from a famous ancestor or *pater* ("father"). During his term of office, which lasted for one year, each consul exercised essentially the same power as a king: dealing justice, making law, and commanding the army. The only limit on power was the right of each consul to veto the actions of the other, which often led to stalemate or violent conflict. In times of grave emergency, such as that resulting in Cincinnatus's election, a dictator might be appointed for a term not longer than six months.

By the early fifth century, within a generation after the establishment of the republic, patrician dominance of the government began to be challenged by the *plebs* ("people"). This was the first stage in a centuries-long contest known as the Struggle of the Orders. The plebeian classes made up nearly 98 percent of the Roman population. Some had grown wealthy through trade, but most were smallholding farmers, artisans, or the urban poor. Their causes for grievance were numerous. Although they were forced to serve in the army, they were nevertheless excluded from holding office. They were also the victims of discriminatory decisions in judicial trials, which were judged by patricians. They did not even know what their legal rights were, because Rome had as yet no established laws: there were only unwritten customs whose meaning was interpreted by the patricians to their own advantage. The plebians were also, like the poorer citizens of Greek poleis, threatened with debt slavery.

These wrongs prompted a rebellion in the early fifth century B.C.E., when plebeians refused to join in the defense of Rome and instead seceded from the city, camping out on the Aventine hill (see the map of Rome on page 134). This general strike of military labor forced the patricians to allow the people to elect of their own officers, who were known as *tribunes* (tribal leaders). The job of each tribune was to protect his constituents from patrician injustice. Moreover, the plebeians guaranteed the safety of these officers by vowing to kill any person who hindered the exercise of their powers.

The plebs' victory led to the codification of the Law of the Twelve Tables, issued around 450 B.C.E. and inscribed on wooden tablets (hence "tables"). Although it was really a perpetuation of ancient custom, the fact that the law was now *defined* made it a significant improvement. Plebeians were made eligible to hold elected offices and they gradually gained access to the Senate. A further victory came in 287 B.C.E., when they succeeded in passing a law that made decisions enacted in their own assembly binding on the Roman government—whether the Senate approved them or not. It was at this time that the phrase *Senatus Populusque Romanum* came into regular use, abbreviated *SPQR* and designating any decree or decision made by "the Roman Senate and People." Visitors to Rome will still find *SPQR* emblazoned on everything from public buildings to the manhole covers of Rome's sewers.

These reforms had several important consequences. Successful plebeians could now work their way into the upper reaches of Roman society, which loosened the hold of patrician families. At the same time, laws prevented senators from engaging directly in commerce. This restriction had the effect of creating a new social order, that of the equestrians ("horsemen" or knights): men whose wealth made it possible for them to own and equip warhorses, and thus to provide Rome's cavalry. But the equestrians and the senators were never wholly distinct. Often, some members of a wealthy family would underwrite the political careers of their brothers and cousins. Those families who managed to win election by such means, generation after generation, became increasingly influential. Meanwhile, patricians who chose politics over wealth became impoverished and resentful. By the first century B.C.E., many were tempted to pursue their political agendas by styling themselves champions of the people (as will be discussed later in the chapter).

Later Roman patriots would regard this as a golden age of shared government, but Rome was never a democracy. A republic differs from a monarchy only because power is exercised by officers whose offices are not (at least in theory) hereditary. It is essentially a system for reserving power to an oligarchy or privileged group. The constitution that emerged in these key centuries therefore broadened and stabilized oligarchy by the balance it struck between competing institutions: the assembly, the Senate, and executive officeholders. Thanks to this distribution of powers, no single individual or clique could become overwhelmingly strong; but neither could direct expressions of the popular will affect Roman policy.

For the Greek historian Polybius, this was an ideal system, combining elements of the monarchy (executive officeholders, the consuls), the aristocracy (the Senate), and the polity (the people's assembly and the tribunes). For the framers of the United States Constitution, it was a model for the three branches of a new government designed to *prevent* the vast majority of Americans from participating directly in politics, while allowing some citizens (white men with sufficient property) a say in choosing their representatives. Polybius prophesied that such a system would break the political cycle that had destroyed the Greek poleis—that it could last forever. He was wrong.

THE ESSENCE OF ROMAN IDENTITY

Romans accepted new things reluctantly but then preserved them fiercely. The prevailing force was the *mos maiorum*, "the custom of the ancestors" or even—to use a word derived from the Latin *mos*—"morality." This unwritten code was essential to Roman identity. It accounts for the remarkable coherence of Roman culture, religion, and law, all of which rested on ancestor worship. The Latin word *pietas* ("piety") meant reverence for family traditions and for one's fathers—living and dead. What made the legendary Aeneas "pious Aeneas" was his devotion to his father, Anchises, whom he carried to safety while Troy burned. Metaphorically, this meant that Aeneas was the carrier of tradition, a man willing to shoulder the burdens of his ancestors and carry them forever.

This helps to explain why the Romans, in the ensuing centuries of their world domination, continued to identify so strongly with their homeland and its customs: to a Roman, "going native" in a foreign place was a terrible betrayal of the *mos maiorum*. It also explains the maxim of *patria potestas* ("fatherly power") upheld by the Twelve Tables. A Roman father, no matter what his social class, had absolute authority within his household. If he was too poor to raise a child, he could expose it (leaving it to perish or to charity) or sell it into slavery. If his wife or child dishonored him, he could kill with impunity. We begin to understand why Lucretia killed herself: otherwise, her father could have killed her with his own hands.

These values set the Romans apart. The Greeks, for example, never condoned anything like *patria potestas*. When fathers kill their children in Greek mythology, they are inevitably killed in revenge by another family member or by the gods. And while pride in one's ancestry is a universal human attribute, the Romans' contemporaries were awed by their extreme devotion to these principles.

Although Roman religion resembled that of the Greeks in some respects, the Roman equation of religion with family meant that all gods were essentially family gods of the Roman state. The republic was like a giant, timeless household run by "elders" (senators) and "father figures" (patricians), some of whom traced their ancestry back to these gods: the mother of Aeneas was Venus (Aphrodite). Like a Roman household, then, the Roman state could flourish only if the ancestral gods lent their continuing and active support. Committees of priests therefore functioned as branches of the government; and in stark contrast to other ancient societies, these priests were not full-time professionals who formed a special caste, but prominent men who rotated in and out of office while serving as leaders of the Senate. Their dual roles made Roman religion even more integral to political life than it had been in Greece (Chapter 3), similar in some ways to the integration of religion and politics in ancient Mesopotamia (Chapter 1).

The all-important devotion to ancestors is further reflected in Roman naming practices, another custom that separated them from other cultures. Most free men in antiquity were known by a given name and their father's name only: Alexander was "son of Philip." A free-born Roman, by contrast, had at least two names. The name that mattered was the name of his earliest ancestor. Gaius Julius Caesar, to take a famous example, would have entered public life as Julius, a member of the family of the Julii, who claimed ancestry from Iulus, the son of Aeneas. His forename, Gaius

A ROMAN PATRICIAN OF THE FIRST CENTURY B.C.E. This man, who wears the toga of an aristocrat, displays his piety by holding the busts of his ancestors. Busts, like the funerary masks described by Polybius (see page 117), commemorated the dead and served as the focus for family worship in household shrines. ▪ *How does the Roman attitude toward age and death differ from that of the Greeks (see the image on page 64)?* ▪ *What do these differences suggest about the broader values of these two societies?*

Polybius Describes the Romans' Worship of Their Ancestors

The Law of the Twelve Tables forbade excessive display at funerals, especially displays of wealth and grief on the part of women. Instead, funerals were supposed to be occasions for the display of family piety. In the following passage, the Greek historian Polybius—who had spent a formative fourteen years of his life in Rome—describes Roman burial customs and these rites' relationship to the strength of republican ideals.

quote just one example to illustrate the pains taken by the Roman state to produce men who will endure anything to win a reputation for valor in their country. Whenever one of their celebrated men dies . . . his body is carried with every kind of honor into the Forum . . . sometimes in an upright position so as to be conspicuous, or else, more rarely, recumbent. The whole mass of the people stand round to watch, and his son, if he has one of adult age who can be present, or if not some other relative, then . . . delivers an address which recounts the virtues and successes achieved by the dead man during his lifetime. By these means the whole populace . . . are involved in the ceremony, so that when the facts of the dead man's career are recalled . . . their sympathies are so deeply engaged that the loss seems . . . to be a public one which affects the whole people. Then, after the burial of the body and the performance of the customary rites, they place the image of the dead man in the most conspicuous position in the house, where it is enclosed in a wooden shrine. This image consists of a mask which is fashioned with extraordinary fidelity . . . to represent the features of these dead men. On occasions when public sacrifices are offered, these masks are displayed and decorated with great care. And when any distinguished member of the family dies, the masks are taken to the funeral, and are worn by men who are considered to bear the closest resemblance to the original, both in height and their general appearance and bearing. . . .

It would be hard to imagine a more impressive scene for a young man who aspires to win fame and practice virtue. For who could remain unmoved at the sight of the images of all these men who have won renown in their time, now gathered together as if alive and breathing? What spectacle could be more glorious than this?

Source: Polybius, *The Rise of the Roman Empire*, trans. Ian Scott-Kilvert (New York: 1979), pp. 346–47.

Questions for Analysis

1. Why does Polybius place so high a premium on the Romans' conduct of funerals? How can such rites be related to republican ideals?

2. Compare this analysis of Roman funerary rites to the image of a Roman patrician and his ancestors on page 116. How do they complement one another?

(*GUY-us*), was the most common name in Rome, the equivalent of "Joe" or "John," and he would never be addressed by this name in public, except perhaps by very intimate friends. His third name, Caesar, was a nickname he acquired in the course of his career: "Hairy" (probably a joke). And because it was the most distinctive of his names, it became the name by which he was universally known. The same goes for Marcus Tullius Cicero (Cicero means "chickpea"). The illustrious Cincinnatus was actually "Curly."

What's in a name? Everything, if you were a Roman man. And nothing, at least nothing of personal significance, if you were a Roman woman. Lucretia's name was not her own, but her father's—or forefathers': the feminine version of Lucretius. If she had a sister, they would both be called Lucretia, differentiated only as Major and Minor ("big/elder" and "little/younger") Lucretia. If there were two more girls, they would be Tertia and Quarta ("Third" and "Fourth") Lucretia, and so on. The only people in Rome who had personal names were slaves (who were named by their masters, like pets) or very low-born Romans and immigrants who had no lineage that mattered.

FROM REPUBLIC TO EMPIRE

For more than two centuries after the founding of the republic, warfare and agriculture remained the chief occupations of most Romans. The fact that Rome had no standard system of coinage until 289 B.C.E suggests strongly that commerce was an insignificant component of its economy. Apparently, Romans didn't need portable wealth; when they weren't fighting, they wanted to be home on the farm, not gadding about the world. If they had money, they put it into real estate: land or slaves.

All of this changed rapidly when Romans began to look beyond Italy. In 265 B.C.E., they controlled most of the peninsula. A year later, they were already embroiled in a war overseas. For a home-loving people with ample resources, this seems paradoxical. Indeed, historians still argue about the motives for Roman expansion. Did Rome constantly extend its rule as a matter of policy, to feed a collective appetite for warfare and plunder? Or was it an accidental empire, built up in a series of reactions to changing pressures and threats—real and imagined? No definitive answer is possible, but it is in this crucial period that the Roman Republic began to transform Western civilizations, and to transform itself into the Roman Empire.

The Punic Wars, 264–146 B.C.E.

In 265 B.C.E. Roman territory extended to the tip of Italy's "boot," but there it ended. Just off its coast, the large islands of Corsica and Sardinia and the western half of Sicily were part of another state, much older and far wealthier. This was the great maritime empire of Carthage, which stretched along the northern coast of Africa from modern-day Tunisia through the Straits of Gibraltar and into modern Spain. Carthage itself had been founded around 800 B.C.E. as a Phoenician colony (see Chapter 2). It had the largest and most effective navy of its day, and it commanded the vast resources of commercial networks that reached as far north as Britain and deep into Egypt and the Near East. In every respect but one it was far superior to Rome. Yet that one factor was decisive: Carthage had no standing army. It relied on mercenaries bankrolled by the enormous profits of its merchants.

The epic struggle between Rome and Carthage lasted well over a century. It crystallized in three periods of concentrated warfare known as the Punic Wars (because the Romans called their enemies Poeni, "Phoenicians"). The first of these wars began in 264 B.C.E. Twenty-three years of bitter fighting were protracted because the Carthaginians only needed to suffer one defeat in a land battle before resolving to engage the Romans solely at sea. There, they had the advantage—until the Romans built their own navy. Eventually, in 241 B.C.E., Carthage was forced to cede all of her Sicilian lands to Rome and to pay reparations.

Thereafter, the Romans were determined not to let Carthage revive its maritime power. So when Carthage attempted to expand its presence in Spain, Rome interpeted this as a threat and declared a new war that lasted for sixteen years: the Second Punic War. This time, Rome was thrown entirely off its guard by the brilliant exploits of the Carthaginian commander Hannibal (247–183 B.C.E), who very nearly defeated the Romans at their own game. Daringly, Hannibal raised an army in Spain and equipped it with dozens of war elephants and siege engines. He then led this entire force across the Pyrenees into Gaul (now southern France), and then over the Alps into Italy. There, he harried Roman forces in their home territories for nearly sixteen years, from 218 to 202 B.C.E.

Hannibal was challenged more by the difficulty of supplying his army than by the Romans themselves. He also seems to have counted on winning the support of the Italian provinces that Rome had conquered, but Rome's generous treatment of its Latin allies kept them loyal. As a result, Rome could call on vast resources while Hannibal had only his exhausted army and no reserves forthcoming. Nevertheless, he won several amazing victories in Italy before retreating—technically undefeated—in 203. He also won the admiration of the Romans themselves, whose own histories frankly acknowledge his genius.

This phase of warfare ended only when a Roman general, Publius Cornelius Scipio (*SKIP-ee-oh*), took a leaf out of Hannibal's book. After campaigning successfully in Spain, he crossed into Africa and met Hannibal at Zama, near Carthage, in 201 B.C.E. His victory ended the Second Punic War and won him a new name, "Africanus," in honor of his conquest.

Carthage was now compelled to abandon all of its possessions except the city itself and its immediate hinterlands, and to pay an indemnity three times greater than the already crippling reparations demanded after the First Punic War. Yet Roman suspicion remained obsessive, and by the middle of the second century, some warmongers were urging a preemptive strike. Among the most vocal was an elderly patrician called Marcus Porcius Cato, who ended every speech he gave—no matter what the topic—with the words: "And furthermore, I strongly advise that Carthage be destroyed." This won him the nickname Cato the Censor, from the Latin verb "to advise."

In 149 B.C.E. the Senate seized on a minor pretext to demand that the Carthaginians abandon their city and settle at least ten miles from the sea. Of course, this absurd mandate amounted to a death sentence for a city dependent on maritime commerce, and it was refused—as the Romans knew it would be. The result was the Third Punic War and the siege of Carthage, which ended in 146 B.C.E. Those who survived the ensuing massacre were sold into slavery, and their once-magnificent city was razed to the ground. The legend that the Romans sowed the land with salt (to make it infertile) is apocryphal, but it vividly describes the successful eradication of an entire civilization. It would stand as a warning to Rome's other potential enemies.

Roman Control of the Hellenistic World

Rome's victories over Carthage led to the creation of new colonial provinces in Sicily, North Africa, and Hispania (Spain). This not only brought Rome great new wealth, it was also the beginning of the westward expansion that became Rome's defining influence on the history of Western civilizations.

At the same time, Rome's expansion brought it into conflict with eastern Mediterranean powers. During the Second Punic War, for example, Philip V of Macedonia had entered into an alliance with Carthage. Rome sent an army to stop him, and later foiled the plans of the Achaean League

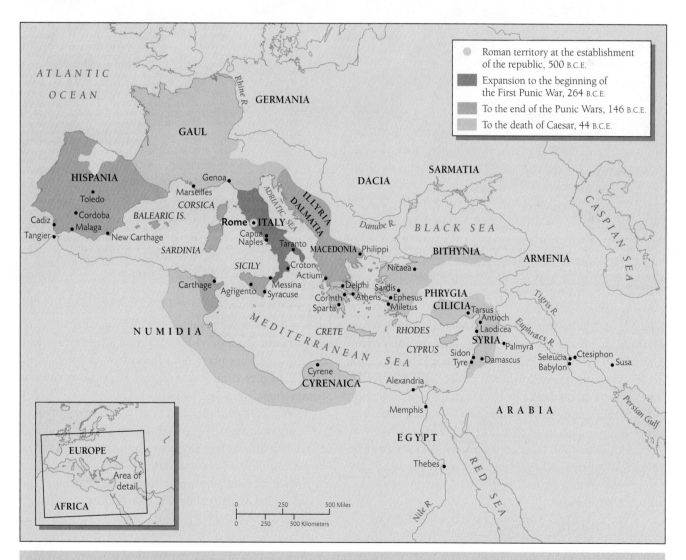

THE EXPANSION OF ROME, 264–44 B.C.E. The rapid increase of Rome's territories opened up new opportunities and challenges.
• *Looking at the phases of expansion on this map, in what directions did Roman dominion move?* • *Why was this the case?* • *What particular problems might have been created by the eventual extension of Roman rule into Gaul, well beyond the "Roman lake" of the Mediterranean?*

Past and Present

Spectator Sports

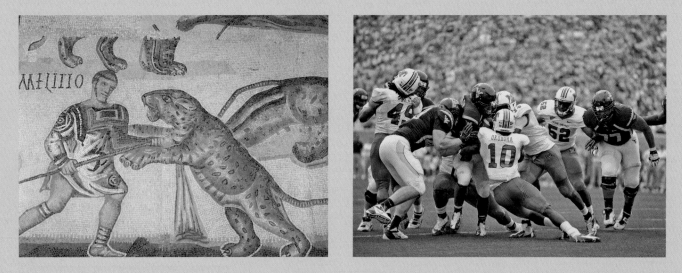

Like the Romans' love for gladiatorial combat, Americans' love of football is inextricably tied to a sense of shared identity and fascination with violence and warfare. Although American football is not a bloodsport in a technical sense, part of its allure stems from the very great physical risks taken by its players, whose careers are often cut short by injury. Both pastimes form the core of far-reaching entertainment economies that would be dismantled by any attempts at reform: concessions, advertising, merchandising, and an array of other money-making activities.

Watch related author videos on the Student Site
wwnorton.com/college/history/western-civilizationsBrief4

(see Chapter 4). This was when Polybius was sent to Rome as a hostage, and became a guest-friend in the family of Scipio Africanus, later witnessing the destruction of Carthage. Rome also thwarted similar efforts by the Seleucid monarch Antiochus III. In neither of these cases did Rome set out to conquer the eastern Mediterranean. By 146 B.C.E., however, both Greece and Macedonia had become Roman provinces, Seleucid Asia had lost most of its territories, and Ptolemaic Egypt had largely become a pawn of Roman interests.

THE CONSEQUENCES OF IMPERIALISM

Rome's seemingly inadvertent conquest of Greece and western Asia transformed the republic. New wealth poured in, increasing the inequalities within Roman society and challenging traditional values. Small farmers left the land and swelled the impoverished urban population, unable to compete with huge plantations worked by gangs of slaves. Slaves also played an increasing role in Roman cities as artisans, merchants, and household servants.

Roman rule over the Hellenistic world had a particularly pervasive impact—so much so that many Romans considered themselves to have been "conquered" by Greece. Hitherto self-assured and self-satisfied, they now felt their own language and customs to be uncouth and barbaric compared to those of their cultivated colonial subjects.

Economic Change and Social Upheaval

Like all peoples of the ancient world, Romans took slavery for granted. But they were not prepared for the huge increase in the number of slaves that resulted from these conquests. In 146 B.C.E., 55,000 Carthaginians were enslaved after the destruction of their city; not long before, 150,000 Greek prisoners of war had met the same fate. By the end of the second century B.C.E., there were a million slaves in Italy alone. Rome became one of the most slave-based economies in history, rivaling ancient Egypt or the antebellum American South.

The majority of Roman slaves worked as agricultural laborers on the vast (and growing) estates known as *latifundia*, created when Roman aristocrats absorbed the holdings of citizen-farmers who were now required to serve for years at a time on foreign campaigns and often found it impossible to maintain their farms. Consequently, they moved to the city—where there was no way for free men to sustain themselves, except through trade or violence. With abundant, cheap slaves to do all the rough work, moreover, there was no incentive for technological innovation. Meanwhile, expensive slaves did the specialized jobs: they were secretaries, bookkeepers, personal assistants, playwrights, musicians, sculptors, artists. There was little reason to employ paid labor at all, or even to train oneself in these arts, as the Greeks had. By the first century B.C.E., as a result, a third of Rome's one million inhabitants were receiving free grain from the state, partly to keep them alive and partly to keep them quiet. The poet Juvenal would later satirize the plebs as needing only "bread and circuses."

The ready availability of slaves made Roman slavery a far more impersonal and brutal institution than it had been in other ancient civilizations. The standard policy of Roman slave owners was to get as much work out of their human possessions as possible, until they died of exhaustion or were "freed" in old age to fend for themselves. The same irascible Cato the Censor who had demanded the destruction of Carthage even wrote a "how-to" book on this subject. Of course, there were exceptions. Some domestic slaves were treated as trusted family members, and slave secretaries vital to the business of Roman governance and literature could even win fame or earn enough to buy their freedom. Some slave artisans were permitted to run their own businesses, keeping some of the profits.

But the general lot of slaves was horrendous. Some businessmen owned slaves whom they trained as gladiators to be mauled by wild animals or by other gladiators for the amusement of a paying public. The luxurious lifestyles of the wealthy also meant that dozens of slaves in every household were trapped in a cycle of menial tasks as doorkeepers, litter-bearers, couriers, valets, wet-nurses, and child-minders. In some great households, designated slaves had no other duties than to rub down the master after his bath or to keep track of the mistress's social engagements. It was a life that debased both slave and owner, and undermined the values of the republic.

New Money, New Values

In the early republic, as we have seen, Roman men had nearly absolute powers over their individual households. During the second century B.C.E., however, two innovations greatly altered this pattern of patriarchal control. One was the introduction of new laws that allowed married women to control their own property: if a married woman died, her possessions would revert to her father or her father's heirs if she had no children of her own. Another was a law that allowed women to initiate divorce proceedings. These changes were intended to safeguard family wealth, but they also resulted in greater independence for women. A wife now had much more authority within the household because she contributed to its upkeep. If her husband did not show respect, she could leave him and deprive him of income.

Ironically, the growth of Rome's slave system also gave women greater freedom, for slaves took over the traditional work of child rearing, household maintenance, and the endless tasks of spinning and weaving. Women from well-to-do families now began to engage in a range of social, intellectual, and artistic activities. Indeed, women were among the chief consumers of the new Hellenistic fashions, commodities, and ideas available in Rome.

In earlier centuries, Romans had taken pride in the simplicity of their lives. Now, however, elite Romans began to indulge in creature comforts and to cultivate Hellenistic habits. Bilingualism became increasingly common, and Greek literature became the standard against which Roman authors measured themselves. For Latin was not yet a literary language. It was fine for politics or farming, but if one wanted to express lofty or beautiful thoughts one did so in Greek, which was far more flexible and sophisticated. Well-educated Greek slaves were therefore at a premium, to lend social cachet, to write letters, and to tutor Roman children.

But many Romans regarded these foreign influences with disgust. For them, the good old ways of paternal authority and stern discipline were giving way to effeminacy and soft living. Increasingly, hard-line conservatives passed laws to restore "family values" and regulate the conspicuous consumption of luxuries, especially by women. These measures were ineffectual. Rome was being irreversibly transformed into a complex cosmopolitan empire reliant on foreign slaves, foreign grain, and foreign luxuries, in which a vast gulf was widening between rich and poor, and where traditional behavioral constraints were giving way to new freedoms for elite men and women.

Spirituality and Philosophy in the Late Republic

The religious practices of Rome changed markedly in this era. The most pronounced innovation was the spread of Eastern mystery cults, which satisfied a need for more emotionally intense spiritual experiences—especially for women, who were largely excluded from the rites of the patriarchal state religion. From Egypt came the cults of Isis and Osiris, while from Asia came the worship of the Great Mother, all emphasizing the power of female sexuality and reproduction. Despite the attractions of these new cults, Romans continued to honor their traditional gods alongside these new, exotic deities. Roman polytheism could absorb them all, so long as the ancestor gods of the household and the city were paid due reverence.

The Hellenistic philosophies of Epicureanism and Stoicism both found strong adherents in Rome (Chapter 4), but more congenial to Roman values was Stoicism. Its most influential proponent was Cicero (106–43 B.C.E.), famous in his day as an orator, statesman, and staunch defender of republican virtues. Cicero based his ethical teachings on the Stoic premise that tranquility of mind is the highest good: the ideal man is rational, indifferent to sorrow and pain. Yet Cicero diverged from the Stoics in his approval of the active, political life. He became an advocate for the revival of Roman tradition through service to the state. His elegant prose style also advanced the use of Latin as a language of eloquence and became the standard model for literary composition. Students learning Latin today still begin with Cicero.

"RESTORING THE REPUBLIC": THE STRUGGLE FOR POWER

Politically, the century after the Third Punic War was one of turbulence. Bloody competitions among rival dictators and insurrections were common occurrences. Slave uprisings added to the general disorder. The most threatening revolt of all was led by Spartacus, a Thracian captive who was being trained as a gladiator. He and a band of 200 fellow slaves escaped from a gladiatorial training camp at Capua (*KAH-poo-ah,* near Naples), heavily armed, to the slopes of Mount Vesuvius, where their cause attracted a huge host of other fugitives. From 73 to 71 B.C.E. this desperate army defeated Roman forces of as many as 10,000

men before Spartacus himself was killed. The Senate, terrified of the precedent, ordered 6,000 of the captured slaves to be crucified along the length of the road from Capua to Rome—about 150 miles—as a warning to future insurgents. Crucifixion was a form of punishment reserved for slaves and non-Roman rebels, and it meant a slow, terrible, and public death from gradual suffocation and exposure.

The Reforming Efforts of the Gracchi

These waves of rebellion were mirrored by urban unrest in various forms, and the poorer classes were finding new champions among some progressive patricians. In 133 B.C.E., a grandson of Scipio Africanus, Tiberius Gracchus (*GRAH-cus*), was elected a tribune of the people. He proposed to alleviate social and economic stress by instituting major reforms, chiefly the redistribution of property. As we have noted, small farmers had been losing their lands to those whose new wealth allowed them to amass giant estates, the *latifundia.* To counter this, Tiberius Gracchus invoked old laws that had, under the early republic, limited the amount of land that could be held by a single person. His motives were not entirely populist. There was now a grave manpower shortage in the Roman army, which had been forced to expand its presence in the far reaches of the world and had left Rome itself prey to uprisings like that of Spartacus. Since a man had to meet certain property qualifications to serve in the Roman army, the available pool of citizen soldiers was contracting. So Tiberius Gracchus aimed to refresh the reserves by creating new citizens.

With the support of his brother Gaius, Tiberius Gracchus proposed a law that would restrict estates to a maximum of 300 acres per citizen, plus 150 acres for each child in his family, with the excess land to be divided among poor settlers. Not surprisingly, most senators stood to lose from this legislation, and so they engineered its veto by Gracchus's fellow tribunes. Gracchus retaliated, arguing that tribunes who opposed the people's interests were betraying their offices, and he announced plans to stand for reelection. A conservative faction in the Senate then alleged that Gracchus had his sights set on a dictatorship, and with this excuse they attacked and murdered him and his supporters on the day of the elections.

Ten years later, Gaius Gracchus renewed his older brother's struggle after being elected to the same office. Although a version of Tiberius's land reforms had finally been enacted, Gaius believed that the campaign had to go further. In 123 B.C.E. he enacted several laws for the benefit of the poor. He also imposed controls on provincial governors suspected of exploiting their subjects for personal gain. Most controversially, Gaius proposed to extend full Roman citizenship to all the allied states of Italy, a move that would have kept the army well supplied with new soldiers, but which would alter the political landscape of Rome to the detriment of the existing elite. Accordingly, the Senate proclaimed Gaius Gracchus an outlaw. In the ensuing conflict, Gaius and about 3,000 of his followers became the victims of a purge.

Rivalry among Rome's Generals

Although the reforms of the Gracchi were ultimately unsuccesful, they exposed the weakness of the Senate and increased the power of the plebs, whose favor was now courted by a succession of ambitious men. Most were professional soldiers who controlled one or more legions of the Roman army and who traded on military victories abroad to win the confidence of the people. The first of these was Gaius Marius, who had fought a successful campaign against King Jugurtha of Numidia, a small kingdom in North Africa. In 107 B.C.E. Marius's popularity catapulted him to the consulship, despite the protests of the Senate's aristocracy, and he would be elected to that office six more times.

Marius set a powerful precedent by demonstrating how easily an army command could be an alternative path to political power. He also changed the course of Rome's history by reorganizing and expanding the army. Desperate for more men to fight in Africa and in Gaul, Marius abolished the property qualification that had hitherto limited military service; the potential pool of soldiers now included the urban poor and landless peasants. As a result, a career as a Roman legionnaire became an end in itself, and a soldier's loyalty was directed toward his commander—whose success would win rewards for his men—rather than to an abstract ideal of patriotism. This change also meant that factional fighting could lead to full-blown civil war, as legions loyal to one general were pitted against those of another.

This happened in Marius's own lifetime. The aristocratic general Lucius Cornelius Sulla (*SUH-la*) had fought with distinction in the so-called Social War of 91–88 B.C.E., a conflict between Rome and her Italian allies that resulted in the extension of Roman citizenship throughout the peninsula. Thereafter, Sulla seemed the likely person to lead Rome's army to war in western Asia. Marius, however, forced the Senate to deny Sulla's claim. Sulla's response was to rally the five victorious legions that had just fought under his command and, with a Roman army at his back, to march on Rome.

Strong taboos had long prevented any armed force from entering the city limits, but Sulla argued that his actions were in keeping with the *mos maiorum*, which Marius and the Senate had betrayed. He was then given the coveted command in Asia Minor, after which Marius again seized control of the city. When Marius died soon afterward, a conservative backlash led the aristocracy to appoint Sulla to the office of dictator—and not for the traditional six months. Instead, Sulla's term had no limits, and he used this time to exterminate his opponents. He packed the Senate with men loyal to himself and curtailed the authority of the peoples' tribunes. Then, after three years of rule, he retired to a life of luxury on his country estate.

Caesar's Triumph—and Downfall

The effect of Sulla's dictatorship was to empower the aristocracy and weaken the power of the plebs. Soon, however, new leaders emerged to espouse the people's cause, once again using the army as their tool of influence. The most prominent of these military men were Gnaeus Pompeius Magnus (106–48 B.C.E.) and Gaius Julius Caesar (100–44 B.C.E.). Initially, they cooperated in a plot to "restore the republic" by forming an alliance with a third general, Marcus Junius Crassus, the man credited with finally defeating Spartacus. This alliance was known as a *triumvirate*, meaning "rule of three men," but it soon dissolved into open rivalry. Pompey (as generations of English-speaking historians have called him) had won fame as the conqueror of Syria and Palestine, while Caesar had campaigned in Gaul, adding the territories of modern France, Belgium, and western Germany to the Roman Empire, and extending its northern border the length of the Rhine.

It had become accepted that the best general should be the leader of Rome, and the example of Sulla had made it possible for that leader to be a dictator for life, a king in all but name. But it was Pompey, not Caesar, who was actually in Rome and in a position to influence the Senate directly. So in the face of tremendous popular protest and even some opposition from the aristocracy, Pompey had himself elected sole consul. Essentially, this meant that he could act as dictator. Using this authority, he declared that Caesar, who was still stationed in Gaul, was an enemy of the republic, and that his ambition was to make himself king.

The result was a pervasive and deadly civil war. In 49 B.C.E., Caesar crossed the Rubicon River, the northern boundary of Rome's Italian territories, thereby signalling his intention to take Rome by force. Pompey fled to the eastern Mediterranean in the hope of gathering an army large enough to confront Ceasar's legions. Caesar pursued him, and in 48 B.C.E. the two Roman armies met at Pharsalus in Greece. Pompey was defeated and fled to Alexandria, where he was murdered by a Roman officer attached to the court of Ptolemy XIII (62/61–47? B.C.E.). Ptolemy was then about fourteen years old and engaged in a civil war of his own—with his elder sister and co-ruler, Cleopatra VII (69–30 B.C.E.). Caesar threw his support on the side of the twenty-one-year old queen. The two must have become lovers soon after their first meeting, because their son Caesarion ("Little Ceasar") was born nine months later.

After that, Caesar returned to Rome in triumph—literally. A *triumph* was a spectacular honor awarded to a victorious Roman general by the Senate, and was the only legal occasion on which (unarmed) soldiers were allowed to parade in the streets of Rome. Triumphs had been celebrated since the earliest days of the republic and featured columns of prisoners and spoils of war, chained captives (often enemy kings) led in humiliation to their public executions, floats commemorating the achievements of the triumphant man, and thousands of cheering Romans who received extra rations of grain and gathered up coins thrown by the handful. Through it all, Caesar would have ridden in a chariot with a golden wreath held above his head, while a slave stood behind him, murmuring in his ear the words *Memento mori*: "Remember: you will die." A triumph was so glorious and—under the republic—so rarely granted that those thus honored might forget their own mortality.

Caesar's power seemed absolute. In 46 B.C.E. he was named dictator for ten years; two years later, this was changed to a lifetime appointment. In addition, he assumed nearly every other title that could augment his power. He even governed the reckoning of time: in imitation of the Egyptian calendar, he revised the Roman calendar so as to make a 365-day year with an extra day added every fourth year. This Julian calendar (as adjusted by Pope Gregory XIII in 1582) is still observed, and the seventh month is still named after Julius.

Caesar also took important steps toward eliminating the distinction between Italians and provincials within the empire by conferring citizenship on the residents of Hispania (Spain) and the newly annexed provinces in Gaul. By settling many of his army veterans in these lands, moreover, he furthered colonization. By incorporating Gaul into the Roman world he brought in a much-needed source of food and natural resources and created a new outlet for the spread of Roman influence.

In the eyes of many contemporaries, however, Caesar's achievements were further signs that he intended to make himself king: a hateful thought to those who still glorified the early days of the republic. Indeed, it was around a descendant of Lucretia's avenger, Brutus, that a faction of the Senate crystallized into conspiracy. On the Ides of March in 44 B.C.E.—the midpoint of the month, according to his own calendar—Caesar was attacked on the floor of the

CLEOPATRA VII AS EGYPTIAN PHARAOH AND HELLENISTIC RULER. Like her ancestor, Ptolemy I, Cleopatra represented herself as both enlightened Greek monarch and as pharaoh. It was perhaps due to her example that Julius Caesar was the first Roman leader to issue coins impressed with his own image. ▪ *How does Cleopatra's self-representation compare to that of Hatshepsut (see Chapter 2) or Ptolemy (Chapter 4)?*

Senate's chamber and stabbed to death by a group of men. His body would later be autopsied, the first such examination in recorded history. It was found that he had received 23 wounds.

THE PRINCIPATE AND THE *PAX ROMANA*, 27 B.C.E.–180 C.E.

In his will, Caesar had adopted his grandnephew Gaius Octavius (or Octavian, 63 B.C.E.–14 C.E.), then a young man of eighteen. On learning of Caesar's death, Octavian hastened to claim his inheritance and to avenge his slain "father," whose name he took: he was now Gaius Julius Caesar the younger. But he soon found that he had rivals among those supporters of Caesar who had not been implicated in the plot to kill him, most notably Marcus Antonius (or Mark Antony, 83–30 B.C.E.), who had served under Caesar in Gaul and was determined to make himself governor of that whole province.

Octavian engineered his own election to the office of consul (though he was far too young for this honor) and used his powers to have Caesar's assassins declared outlaws. He then pursued Antony to Gaul, at the head of an army. Antony's forces were overwhelmed, and in 43 B.C.E. he and Octavian reconciled and formed an alliance, bringing in a third man, a senator called Marcus Aemilius Lepidus, to make up a second triumvirate. They then set about crushing the faction responsible for Caesar's murder.

Their methods were brutal: prominent conspirators were hunted down and their property confiscated. The most notable of these victims was Cicero. Meanwhile, the masterminds behind the assasination, Brutus and Gaius Cassius, fled Rome and raised an army of legions from Greece and western Asia. But they were defeated by the united forces of Antony and Octavian on a battlefield near the Macedonian town of Philippi (founded by Alexander's father) in 42 B.C.E. Both Brutus and Cassius committed suicide.

With their mutual enemies destroyed, tensions mounted between Antony and Octavian. Antony went to Egypt and made an alliance with Cleopatra. Octavian, meanwhile, reestablished himself in Rome, where he skillfully portrayed Antony as having been seduced and emasculated by the female pharaoh. For ten years, Antony played the king in Egypt, fathering three of Cleopatra's children and making big plans for annexing Rome's eastern provinces. Eventually, Octavian had him declared a traitor while the Senate declared war on Cleopatra.

OCTAVIAN. Caesar's adopted heir was later granted the title "Augustus" by the Senate, and was also known as *princeps*, "first man." Eventually, he would be worshiped as a god in Rome's provinces, and idealized statues like this one would be erected in temples and public places throughout the empire.

In 31 B.C.E. Octavian's superior forces defeated those of Antony and Cleopatra in the naval battle of Actium, off the coast of Greece. Soon afterward, both Antony and Cleopatra committed suicide. Their children were taken back to Rome, and although their lives were spared they were paraded through the streets as captives. This marked the end of Egypt's independence: Cleopatra had been its last pharaoh. After more than three thousand years of

Analyzing Primary Sources

Antony and Cleopatra

In his Parallel Lives, *the Greek intellectual Plutarch (c. 46–120 c.e.) paired the biographies of famous Greeks with those of famous Romans, always to the disadvantage of the latter; for example, Julius Caesar suffers in comparison to Alexander the Great, as Romulus does when set up against Theseus. The following excerpt is from Plutarch's* Life of Mark Antony, *in which the Hellenistic ruler of Egypt, Cleopatra, plays a starring role.*

Caesar and Pompey knew Cleopatra when she was still a girl, and ignorant of the world, but it was a different matter in the case of Antony, because she was ready to meet him when she had reached the time of life when women are most beautiful and have full understanding. So she prepared for him many gifts and money and adornment, of a magnitude appropriate to her great wealth and prosperous kingdom, but she put most of her hopes in her own magical arts and charms. . . . For (as they say), it was not because her beauty in itself was so striking that it stunned the onlooker, but the inescapable impression produced by daily contact with her: the attractiveness in the persuasiveness of her talk, and the character that surrounded her conversation was stimulating. It was a pleasure to hear the sound of her voice, and she tuned her tongue like a many-stringed instrument expertly to whatever language she chose, and only used interpreters to talk to a few foreigners. . . . She is said to have learned the languages of many peoples, although her predecessors on the throne did not bother to learn Egyptian, and some had even forgotten how to speak the Macedonian dialect.

She took such a hold over Antony that, while his wife Fulvia was carrying on the war in Rome against Octavian on his behalf, and the Parthian army . . . was about to invade Syria, Antony was carried off by Cleopatra to Alexandria, and amused himself there with the pastimes of a boy. . . . Whether Antony was in a serious or a playful mood, she could always produce some new pleasure or charm, and she kept watch on him by night and day and never let him out of her sight. She played dice with him and hunted with him and watched him exercising with his weapons and she roamed around and wandered about with him at night when he stood at people's doors and windows and made fun of people inside, dressed in a slave-woman's outfit; for he also attempted to dress up like a slave. He returned from these expeditions having been mocked in return, and often beaten, although most people suspected who he was. But the Alexandrians got pleasure from his irreverence . . . enjoying his humor and saying that he showed his tragic face to the Romans and his comic one to them.

Source: Plutarch, *Life of Marcus Antonius,* cc. 25–29, excerpted in *Women's Life in Greece & Rome: A Sourcebook in Translation,* ed. Mary R. Lefkowitz and Maureen B. Fant (Baltimore, MD: 1992), pp. 147–49.

Questions for Analysis

1. How do Cleopatra's behavior and accomplishments, in Plutarch's description of her, compare to those of Roman women?

2. Given what you have learned about the values of the Roman Republic, how would a Roman reader respond to this description of Antony's behavior under the influence of the Egyptian queen? What do you think were Plutarch's motives in portraying him in this light?

---

self-rule, Egypt was now another province in Rome's empire. Octavian's power was consolidated.

The Principate of Augustus

The victory at Actium ushered in a new period of Roman history. The new Gaius Julius Caesar was now the only man left standing, with no rivals for power. For the first time in nearly a century, Rome was not embroiled in civil war. But it was no longer a republic, even though Octavian maintained the fiction that he was governing as a mere citizen. For four years he ruled as sole consul, until he accepted the titles of *imperator* (emperor) and *augustus.* Although these honorifics had been in use under the republic—*imperator* meant "commander" and *augustus* meant "worthy of honor"—they now became attached to the person of the sole ruler. Rome had long been an empire, but it was only now that it had a single emperor. To avoid confusion, historians therefore refer to this phase of Rome's history as the Principate, from the title Augustus himself preferred: *princeps*, or "first man."

Because Augustus was determined not to be regarded as a tyrant or (worse) a king, he left most of Rome's republican institutions in place—but emptied them of their power. In theory, the emperor served at the will of "the Roman Senate and People." In practice, though, he controlled the army, which meant that he also controlled the workings of government. Fortunately, Augustus was an able ruler. He introduced a range of public services, including a police force and fire brigade; he reorganized the army; and he allowed cities and provinces more substantial rights of self-government than they had enjoyed before. He instituted a new system of coinage throughout the empire, and he abolished the old, corrupt system of taxation, whereby tax collectors were compensated by being allowed to keep a portion of what they collected. Instead, Augustus appointed his own representatives, paid them regular salaries, and kept them under strict supervision. He also conducted a census of the empire's population, and it was during one of these "enrollments" that the birth of Jesus occurred, according to the gospel of Luke (see Chapter 6). Augustus also established new colonies in the provinces, encouraging the emigration of Rome's urban and rural poor, thereby removing a major source of social tension and promoting the integration of the Roman heartland with its far-flung hinterland.

Although his rule had definitively ended the republic, Augustus represented himself as a stern defender of the *mos maiorum* and traditional Roman virtues. He rebuilt many of the city's ancient temples and prohibited the worship of foreign gods. In an attempt to increase the birthrate of Rome's citizens, he penalized men who failed to marry, required widows to remarry within two years of their husbands' deaths, and rewarded women who gave birth to more than two children. He also introduced laws punishing adultery and making divorces more difficult to obtain. To hammer the message home, Augustan propaganda portrayed the imperial family as a model of domestic virtue and propriety, despite the emperor's own notorious extramarital affairs and the well-known fact that the sexual promiscuity of his daughter Julia finally forced Augustus to have her exiled.

More land was gained for Rome in the lifetime of Augustus than in that of any other ruler. His generals advanced into central Europe, conquering the modern-day territories of Switzerland, Austria, and Bulgaria. Only in Germania did Roman troops meet defeat, when three legions were slaughtered in 9 C.E., a setback that convinced Augustus to hold the Roman borders at the Rhine and Danube rivers. Subsequently, though, the emperor Claudius would begin the conquest of Britain in 43 C.E., while the Emperor Trajan (r. 98–117 C.E.) would push beyond the Danube to add Dacia (now Romania) to the empire. Trajan also conquered territories in the heartland of Mesopotamia, but in so doing aroused the enmity of the Parthians, who now ruled in Persia. His successor, Hadrian (r. 117–138 C.E.), accordingly halted Rome's expansion and embarked on a defensive policy epitomized by the construction of Hadrian's Wall in northern Britain. The empire had now reached its greatest extent; in the third century, as we shall see (Chapter 6), the tide would turn and these limits would recede.

HADRIAN'S WALL. Stretching 73.5 miles across northern England, this fortification (begun in 122 C.E.) marked the frontier of Britain as established by the emperor Hadrian. (A later wall, built farther north by Antoninus Pius in 142, was quickly abandoned.) Long stretches of the wall still exist, as do many of the forts built along it. The tree in this photograph stands on the site of a "mile castle," one of the smaller watchtowers built at intervals of a Roman mile and garrisoned by sentries.

Competing Viewpoints

Two Views of Augustus's Rule

Augustus Speaks for Himself

The emperor Augustus was a master propagandist with an unrivaled capacity for presenting his own actions in the best possible light. This list of his own deeds was written by Augustus himself and was displayed on two bronze pillars set up in the Roman forum.

Below is a copy of the accomplishments of the deified Augustus by which he brought the whole world under the empire of the Roman people, and of the moneys expended by him on the state and the Roman people. . . .

1. At the age of nineteen, on my own initiative and at my own expense, I raised an army by means of which I liberated the republic, which was oppressed by the tyranny of a faction.

2. Those who assassinated my father I drove into exile, avenging their crime by due process of law.

3. I waged many wars throughout the whole world by land and by sea, both civil and foreign. . . .

5. The dictatorship offered to me . . . by the people and by the Senate . . . I refused to accept. . . . The consulship, too, which was offered to me . . . as an annual office for life, I refused to accept.

6. Though the Roman Senate and people together agreed that I should be elected sole guardian of the laws and morals with supreme authority, I refused to accept any office offered me which was contrary to the traditions of our ancestors.

7. I have been ranking senator for forty years. . . . I have been *pontifex maximus*, augur, member of the college of fifteen for performing sacrifices, member of the college of seven for conducting religious banquets, member of the Arval Brotherhood, one of the *Titii sodales*, and a *fetial* [all priestly offices].

9. The Senate decreed that vows for my health should be offered up every fifth year by the consuls and priests. . . . The whole citizen body, with one accord, . . . prayed continuously for my health at all the shrines.

17. Four times I came to the assistance of the treasury with my own money . . . providing bonuses for soldiers who

had completed twenty or more years of service.

20. I repaired the Capitol and the theater of Pompey with enormous expenditures on both works, without having my name inscribed on them. I repaired . . . the aqueducts which were falling into ruin in many places . . . I repaired eighty-two temples. . . . I reconstructed the Flaminian Way. . . .

34. Having attained supreme power by universal consent, I transferred the state from my own power to the control of the Roman Senate and people. . . . After that time I excelled all in authority, but I possessed no more power than the others who were my colleagues in each magistracy.

35. At the time I wrote this document I was in my seventy-sixth year.

Source: "Res Gestae Divi Augusti," in *Roman Civilization, Sourcebook II: The Empire,* ed. Naphtali Lewis and Meyer Reinhold (New York: 1966), pp. 9–19.

When Octavian died in 14 C.E. he was not only Caesar, Imperator, and Augustus; he was *pontifex maximus* (high priest) and "father of the fatherland" (*pater patriae*). He was even deified by the Senate. These titles would be passed on to his successors, as would the system of government

he had devised. And even those who mourned the passing of the republic and loathed these displays of imperial *hubris* had to admit that the system worked. Rome enjoyed nearly two centuries of peace, prosperity, and stability because of it. For the true test of any political institution

The Historian Tacitus Evaluates Augustus's Reign

Writing in the first decades of the second century C.E., the senatorial historian Tacitus (c. 56–117) began his chronicle of imperial rule, the Annals, *with the death of Augustus a century earlier.*

ntelligent people praised or criticized Augustus in varying terms. One opinion was as follows. Filial duty and a national emergency, in which there was no place for law-abiding conduct, had driven him to civil war—and this can be neither initiated nor maintained by decent methods. He had made many concessions to Antony and to Lepidus for the sake of vengeance on his father's murderers. When Lepidus grew old and lazy, and Antony's self-indulgence got the better of him, the only possible cure for the distracted country had been government by one man. However, Augustus had put the State in order not by making himself king or dictator but by creating the Principate. The empire's frontiers were on the ocean, or on distant rivers. Armies, provinces, fleets, the whole system was interrelated. Roman citizens were protected by the law. Provincials were decently treated. Rome itself had been lavishly beautified. Force had been sparingly used—merely to preserve peace for the majority.

The opposite view went like this. Filial duty and national crisis had been merely pretexts. In actual fact, the motive of Octavian, the future Augustus, was lust for power. Inspired by that, he had mobilized ex-army settlers by gifts of money, raised an army—while he was only a half-grown boy without any official status—won over a consul's brigade by bribery, pretended to support Sextus Pompeius [the son of Pompey], and by senatorial decree usurped the status and rank of a praetor. Soon both consuls . . . had met their deaths—by enemy action; or perhaps in the one case by the deliberate poisoning of his wound, and in the other at the hand of his own troops, instigated by Octavian. In any case, it was he who took over both their armies. Then he had forced the reluctant Senate to make him consul. But the forces given him to deal with Antony he used against the State. His judicial murders and land distributions were distasteful even to those who carried them out. True, Cassius and Brutus died because he had inherited a feud against them; nevertheless, personal enmities ought to be sacrificed to the public interest. Next he had cheated Sextus Pompeius by a spurious peace treaty, Lepidus by spurious friendship. Then Antony, enticed by treaties and his marriage with Octavian's sister, had paid the penalty of that delusive relationship with his life. After that, there had certainly been peace, but it was a bloodstained peace. . . . And gossip did not spare his personal affairs—how he had abducted [Livia] the wife of Tiberius Claudius Nero, and asked the priests the farcical question whether it was in order for her to marry while pregnant. Then there was the debauchery of his friend Publius Vedius Pollio. But Livia was a real catastrophe, to the nation, as a mother and to the house of the Caesars as a stepmother.

Source: Tacitus, *Annals* i.9–10. Based on *Tacitus: The Annals of Imperial Rome*, trans. Michael Grant (New York: 1989), pp. 37–39.

Questions for Analysis

1. How does Augustus organize his list, and why? What does he leave out and what does he choose to emphasize?

2. Tacitus presents two contrasting views of Augustus's motives. Which does he himself seem to believe? How does his account complement or undermine that of Augustus himself?

3. Could you write a new account of Augustus's life making use of both sources? How would you strike a balance between them? What would your own conclusion be?

is its capacity to survive incompetent officeholders. Aside from one brief period of civil war in 68 C.E., the transition of power between emperors was generally peaceful and the growing imperial bureaucracy could manage affairs competently even when individual emperors proved vicious and ineffectual, as did Caligula (r. 37–41 C.E.). Nevertheless, the fact that Rome had become an autocratic state became harder and harder to conceal.

The height of the Augustan system is generally considered to be the era between 96 and 180 C.E., often known as the reign of the "Five Good Emperors": Nerva (r. 96–98 C.E.), Trajan (r. 98–117 C.E.), Hadrian (r. 117–138 C.E.), Antoninus Pius (r. 138–161 C.E.), and Marcus Aurelius (r. 161–180 C.E.). All were capable politicians, and since none but the last had a son that survived him, each adopted a worthy successor—a policy that avoided the messy family dysfunctions that absorbed Augustus and his immediate heirs. They also benefited from the fact that Rome had few external enemies left. The Mediterranean was under the control of a single power for the first time in history. On land, Roman officials ruled from Britain to Persia. Now was the *Pax Romana*, the time of Roman Peace.

MAKING THE WORLD ROMAN

Occasionally, the Roman Peace was broken. In Britannia, Roman legions had to put down a rebellion led by the Celtic warrior queen Boudica (*boh-DI-kah;* d. 60/61 C.E.), a war that ended in a massacre of the defiant tribes. Another rebellion was violently quashed in Judea, the most restive of all Roman provinces, leading to the destruction of the Temple at Jerusalem in 70 C.E. In 135 C.E., a second rebellion

completed the destruction of the city. Although Jerusalem was later refounded by Hadrian as Aelia Capitolina, a colony for veterans of Rome's army, Jews were forbidden to settle there.

Such rebellions were not the norm, however. Although the Roman Empire had been gradually achieved by conquest, it was not maintained by force. Instead, Rome controlled its territories by offering incentives to assimilation. Local elites were encouraged to adopt Roman modes of behavior and dress in order to gain entrance to political office. Local gods became Roman gods and were adopted into the Roman pantheon. Cities were constructed on a set model of urban planning, and the amenities of urban life were introduced: baths, temples, amphitheaters, aqueducts, and paved roads (see *Interpreting Visual Evidence* on page 134). Rights of citizenship were extended, and able provincials could rise far in the imperial government. Some, like the emperors Trajan and Hadrian—both raised in Hispania—came to control it. Meanwhile, tens of thousands of army veterans were settled in the provinces, marrying local women and putting down local roots. It was common for soldiers born in Syria to end their days peacefully in northern Gaul. In Camulodunum (now Colchester, England), the gravestone of a legionnaire called Longinus

SPOILS FROM JERUSALEM. A bas-relief inside the triumphal Arch of Titus in the Roman forum shows plundered treasures from the Temple at Jerusalem, including the Menorah, being carried in triumph through Rome.

Analyzing Primary Sources

Rome's Party Girls

The Satires *of the poet Juvenal circulated around the year 100* C.E. *and attacked everything from the general erosion of public morality to the effete tastes of the elite. Some of his most pointed criticism was directed at contemporary women.*

What conscience has Venus, when she is drunk? Our inebriated beauties can't tell head from tail at those midnight oyster suppers when the best wine's laced with perfume, and tossed down neat from a foaming conch-shell, while the dizzy ceiling spins round, and the tables dance, and each light shows double. Why, you may ask yourself, does the notorious Maura sniff at the air in that knowing, derisive way as she and her dear friend Tullia pass by the ancient altar of Chastity? And what is Tullia whispering to her? Here, at night, they stagger out of their litters and relieve themselves, pissing in long hard bursts all over the goddess's statue. Then, while the Moon looks down on their motions, they take turns to ride each other, and finally go home. So you, next morning, on your way to some great house, will splash through your wife's piddle. Notorious, too, are the ritual mysteries of the Good Goddess, when flute-music stirs the loins, and frenzied women, devotees of Priapus, sweep along in procession, howling, tossing their hair, wine-flown, horn-crazy, burning with the desire to get themselves laid. . . . So the ladies, with a display of talent to match their birth, win all the prizes. No make-believe here, no pretense, each act is performed in earnest, and guaranteed to warm the age-chilled balls of a Nestor or a Priam.

Source: Juvenal, *Sixth Satire* 301–26; based on *Juvenal: The Sixteen Satires*, trans. Peter Green (New York: 1974), pp. 138–39 (modified).

Questions for Analysis

1. Compare Juvenal's account of female behavior to the legend of Lucretia, on the one hand, and Plutarch's description of Cleopatra, on the other. What can you conclude about attitudes to women and to sexual morality? Why and on what grounds would men living under the Principate hold women responsible for society's ills?

2. In your view, what are the benefits and the drawbacks of the *Satires* as a historical source?

---

sketches a typical career: born in Serdica (modern Sofia, in Bulgaria) to a local man named Szdapezematygus, he rose through the ranks to become sergeant of the First Thracian Cavalry under the emperor Claudius and one of the first Roman colonists of Britannia.

Even the outer fringes of the empire need to be understood as part of Rome's orbit. Although historians speak of the empire's "borders" for the sake of convenience, these were in fact permeable zones of intensive interaction. Roman influence reached far beyond these zones, into the heartland of Germania and lands farther to the east. By the middle of the third century C.E., when some frontier garrisons were withdrawn to take part in civil wars within the empire, many of these peoples moved southward, too, sometimes as plunderers but more often as aspiring Romans (see Chapter 6).

The Entertainments of Empire

The cultural and intellectual developments of the late republic came to fruition during the Principate, and are richly reflected in its literature. For the first time, Latin began to replace Greek as a language of learning and poetry—much of it, not surprisingly, propagandistic: its purpose was to advertise and justify Rome's achievements. The poetry of Publius Virgilius Maro (Virgil, 70–19 B.C.E.) is typical, and we have already noted his strategic use of "prophecy" in the story of Aeneas. Other major poets of the Augustan age were Quintus Horatius Flaccus (Horace, 65–8 B.C.E.) and Publius Ovidius Naso (Ovid, 43 B.C.E.– 17 C.E.): the former a master of the lovely short lyric and the latter our major source for Greek mythology, which he retold in a long poem called the *Metamorphoses* ("Transformations").

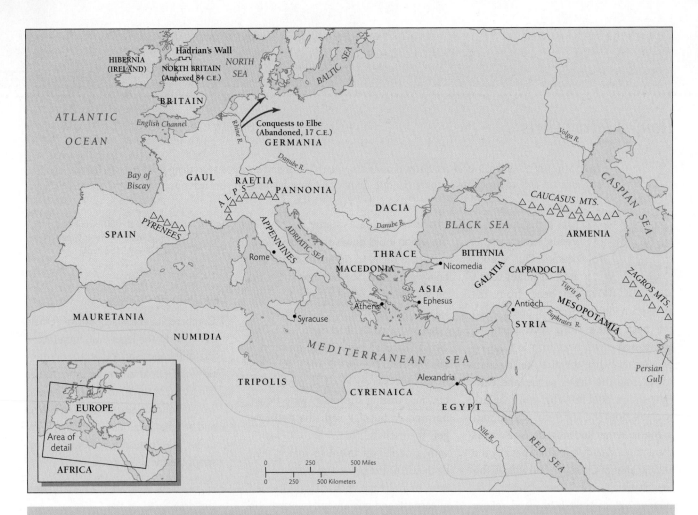

THE ROMAN EMPIRE AT ITS GREATEST EXTENT, 97–117 C.E. ▪ *How much farther north and west does the empire now reach compared to its earlier extent (see map on page 119)?* ▪ *How did geography influence the process of expansion?* ▪ *How did it dictate its limits?* ▪ *For example, what role do major river systems seem to play?*

After Augustus's death, Roman authors had more license and became important cultural critics. The tales of Petronius and Apuleius describe the more bizarre and sometimes sordid aspects of Roman life, and the satirist Juvenal (60?–140 C.E.) wrote with savage wit about the moral degeneracy he saw in his contemporaries. A similar attitude toward Roman society characterizes the writings of Tacitus (55?–117? C.E.), an aristocratic historian who describes the events and people of his age largely for the purpose of passing judgment on them. His *Annals* offer a subtle but devastating portrait of the political system constructed by Augustus and ruled by his heirs; his *Germania* contrasts the manly virtues of northern barbarians with the effeminate vices of the decadent Romans.

To many people today, the most fascinating (and repellant) aspect of Roman culture during the Principate was its spectacular cruelty. Gladiatorial contests were not new, but they were now presented in ampitheaters built to hold tens of thousands. Everyone, even emperors, attended these events, and they became increasingly bloody and brutal as people demanded more and more innovative violence. Individual gladiators fought to the death with swords or the exotic weapons of their homelands. Teams of gladiators fought pitched battles, often simulating historic Roman victories. Occasionally, a wealthy entrepreneur would fill an arena with water and stage a naval battle. Hundreds of men would die in these organized slaughters. On other occasions, hundreds of half-starved animals imported from Africa, India, or the forests of Germania would tear one another—or their human victims—apart. When a fighter went down with a disabling wound, the crowd would be asked to decide whether to spare his life or to kill him. If the arena floor became too slippery with blood, a fresh layer of sand would be spread over the gore so that the performance could continue.

Roman Art, Architecture, and Engineering

Like Latin literature, Roman art assumed its distinctive character during the Principate. Before this time, most artworks displayed in Roman homes were Hellenistic imports. As demand for such works increased, hundreds of copies were made by Roman artisans. In many cases, these copies proved more durable than their originals; in Chapter 4, for example, we were able to examine the lost *Aphrodite of Knidos*, courtesy of Roman sculptors.

Encouraged by the patronage of Augustus and his successors, artists began to experiment with more distinctively Roman styles and subjects. The relief sculpture of this period is particularly notable for its delicacy and naturalism, and sculptors also became adept at portraiture. Painting, however, was the Romans' most original and most intimate art. Romans loved intense colors, and those who could afford it surrounded themselves with brilliant wall paintings and mosaics made of tiny fragments of glass and stone, which were often set into the floors of houses or which formed the centerpieces of gardens. Lavish mosaics have been found in the remains of Roman

ROMAN AQUEDUCT IN SOUTHERN GAUL (FRANCE). Aqueducts conveyed water from mountains and lakes to the larger cities of the Roman Empire. The massive arches shown here were originally part of a 31-mile-long complex that supplied water to the city of Nemausus (Nîmes). It is now known as the Pont du Gard (Bridge of the Gardon), reflecting the use to which it was put after the aqueduct ceased to function, some eight centuries after its construction in the first century C.E. Many Roman aqueducts remained operational into the modern era: the one at Segovia, Spain was still in use at the end of the twentieth century. ▪ *What does the magnitude and longevity of such projects tell us about Roman power and technology?*

villas in all the territories of the empire, and similar design features indicate that many were mosaic "kits" that could be ordered from a manufacturer, who would ship out all the necessary components, along with a team of workmen to assemble them.

Augustus liked to boast that he had found Rome a city of clay and left it a city of marble. But in reality, marble was too precious to be used in common construction. Instead, marble panels or ornaments were added to the facings of buildings that were otherwise made of concrete. For the Roman had discovered how to make a mixture of quicklime, volcanic ash, and pumice, and it was this—along with superior engineering skills—that allowed them to build massive structures like the Colosseum, which could accommodate 50,000 spectators at gladiatorial combats.

Roman engineers also excelled in the building of roads and bridges, many of which were constructed by Rome's armies as they moved into new territories. Like the Persian Royal Road of the sixth century B.C.E. or the German Autobahn of the 1930s and the interstate highways of the United States begun in the 1950s, roads have always been, first and foremost, a device for moving armies and then, secondarily, for moving goods and people. Many of these Roman roads still survive, or form the basis for modern European highways. In Britain, for example, the only major thoroughfares before the building of high-speed motorways were based on Roman roads, to which the motorways now run parallel.

THE COLOSSEUM. Constructed between 75 and 80 C.E., this was the first amphitheater in Rome purposely built to showcase gladiatorial combats. Prior to this, gladiators would often fight in improvised arenas in the Forum or in other public places. ▪ *How does this fact change your perception of Roman history?*

Interpreting Visual Evidence

Roman Urban Planning

Prior to Roman imperial expansion, most cities in the ancient world were not planned cities—with the exception of the new settlements established by Alexander the Great, notably Alexandria in Egypt. Rome itself was not carefully planned, but grew up over many centuries, expanding outward and up the slopes of its seven hills from the nucleus of the Forum. By the time of Augustus, it was a haphazard jumble of buildings and narrow streets. Outside of Rome, however, the efficiency of Roman government was in large part due to the uniformity of imperial urban planning. As their colonial reach expanded, Romans sought to ensure that travelers moving within their vast domain would encounter the same amenities in every major city. They also wanted to convey, through the organization of the urban landscape, the ubiquity of Roman authority and majesty.

A. Imperial Rome

B. Roman settlement in Aelia Capitolina (Jerusalem) after 135 C.E.

The inhabitants of Roman cities also enjoyed the benefits of a public water supply. By the early decades of the second century C.E., eleven aqueducts brought water into Rome from the nearby hills for drinking and bathing and for flushing a well-designed sewage system. These amenities were common in cities throughout the empire, and the homes of the wealthy even had indoor plumbing and central heating. Water was also funneled into the homes of the rich for private gardens, fountains, and pools. The emperor Nero (54–68 C.E.) built a famous Golden House with special pipes that sprinkled his guests with perfume, baths supplied with medicinal waters, and a pond "like a sea." "At last," said Nero on moving day, "I can live like a human being."

The Reach of Roman Law

Roman architecture and engineering are impressive, but the most durable and useful of this civilization's

Questions for Analysis

1. Looking closely at the map of Rome (map A), how have topographical features—like the river Tiber and the seven hills—determined the shape and layout of the city? What are the major buildings and public areas? What were the functions of these spaces, and what do they reveal about Roman society and values?

2. Compare the plan of Rome to those of Roman Jerusalem (map B) and London (map C). What features do all three have in common, and why? What features are unique to each place, and what might this reveal about the different regions of the empire and the needs of the different cities' inhabitants?

3. Given that all Roman cities share certain features, what message(s) were Roman authorities trying to convey to inhabitants and travelers through urban planning? Why, for example, would they have insisted on rebuilding Jerusalem as a Roman city—Aelia Capitolina—after the rebellion of 135 C.E.?

C. London under the Romans, c. 200 C.E.

legacies was its legal system. Over the course of several centuries, the primitive code of the Twelve Tables was largely replaced by a series of new laws that reflect the changing needs of Rome's diverse and ever-growing population.

The most sweeping legal changes occurred during the Principate. This was partly because the reach of Roman law had to match the reach of the empire. But the major reason for the rapid development of Roman legal thinking during these years was the fact that Augustus and his successors appointed a small number of eminent jurists to deliver opinions on the issues raised by cases under trial in the courts. The five most prominent of these experts flourished in the second century C.E.: Gaius (only this most common of his names is known), Domitius Ulpianus (Ulpian), Modestinus, Aemelianus Papinianus (Papinian), and Paulus. Taken together, their legal opinions constitute the first philosophy of law and the foundation for all subsequent jurisprudence, a word derived from the Latin phrase meaning "legal wisdom."

As it was developed by the jurists, Roman law comprised three great branches: civil law, the law of nations, and natural law. Civil law was the law of Rome and its citizens, both written and unwritten. It included the statutes of the Senate, the decrees of the emperor, the edicts of magistrates, and ancient customs that had the force of law (like the *mos maiorum*). The law of nations was not specific to Rome but extended to all people of the world regardless of their origins and ethnicity: it is the precursor of international law. This law authorized slavery; protected the private ownership of property; and defined the mechanisms of purchase and sale, partnership, and contract. It supplemented civil law and applied especially to those inhabitants of the empire who were not citizens, as well as to foreigners.

The most interesting (and in many ways the most important) branch of Roman law was natural law, a product not of judicial practice but of legal philosophy. Roman Stoics, following in the footsteps of Cicero, posited that nature itself is rationally ordered, and that careful study will reveal the laws by which the natural world operates, including natural justice. They affirmed that all men are by nature equal, and that they are entitled to certain basic rights that governments have no authority to transgress. Accordingly,

no person or institution has the authority to infringe on this law, repeal it, or ignore it. This law supersedes any state or ruler; a ruler who transgresses it is a tyrant.

Although the practical law applied in local Roman courts often bore little resemblance to the law of nature, the development of a concept of abstract justice as a fundamental principle was one of the noblest achievements of Roman civilization. It has given us the doctrine of human rights, even if it has not resulted in ending abuses of those rights.

CONCLUSION

The resemblances between Rome's history and that of Great Britain and the United States have often been noted. Like the British Empire, the Roman Empire was founded on conquest and overseas colonization intended to benefit both the homeland and its colonial subjects, who were seen as the beneficiaries of a "civilizing mission." Like America's, the Roman economy evolved from agrarianism to a complex system of domestic and foreign markets, problems of unemployment, gross disparities of wealth, and vulnerability to financial crisis. And like both the British and the American empires, the

After You Read
This Chapter

Go to **INQUIZITIVE** to see what you've learned—and learn what you've missed—with personalized feedback along the way.

REVIEWING THE OBJECTIVES

- The founding of the Roman Republic was both a cherished myth and a series of events. What factors contributed to this unique system of government?
- The shared identity and values of the Roman people differed in many ways from those of other ancient civilizations. What were some of these major differences?
- Rome's population was divided among classes of people who often struggled with one another for power. Identify these classes and their points of contention.
- The expansion of Rome's empire had a profound impact on Roman society. Why?
- The establishment of the Principate ushered in a new era in the history of Rome. What events led to this?

Roman Empire justified itself by celebrating the peace its conquests allegedly brought to the world.

Ultimately, however, such parallels break down when we remember that Rome's civilization differed profoundly from any society of the modern world. It was not an industrialized society. Its government never pretended to be representative of all its citizens. Roman class divisions are not directly comparable to ours. The Roman economy rested on slavery to a degree unmatched in any modern state. As a result, technological advances were not encouraged, social stratification was extreme, and gender relations were profoundly unequal. Religious practice and political life were inseparable.

Nevertheless, the civilization of ancient Rome continues to structure our everyday lives in ways so profound that they often go unnoticed. Our days are mapped onto the Roman calendar. The constitution of the United States is largely modeled on that of the Republic, and Roman architecture survives in the design of our public buildings. Roman law forms the basis of most European legal codes, and American judges still cite Gaius and Ulpian. Virtually all modern sculpture is inspired by Roman sculpture, and Roman authors continue to set the standards for prose composition in many Western countries. Indeed, most European languages are either derived from Latin—Romance languages are so called because they are "Roman-like"—or have borrowed Latin grammatical structures or vocabulary. As we shall see in the following chapters, the organization of the modern Roman Catholic Church can be traced back to the structure of the Roman state: even today, the pope bears the title of Rome's high priest, *pontifex maximus*.

But perhaps the most important of all Rome's contributions was its role as mediator between Europe and the civilizations of the ancient Near East and Mediterranean. Had Rome's empire not come to encompass much of Europe, there would be no such thing as the concept of Western civilization and no shared ideas and heritage to link us to those distant places and times. Although we shall pursue the history of Rome's fragmentation and witness the emergence of three different civilizations in the territories once united by its empire, we shall see that they all shared a common cultural inheritance. In this sense, the Roman Empire did not collapse. But it was transformed, and the factors driving that transformation will be the subject of Chapter 6.

PEOPLE, IDEAS, AND EVENTS IN CONTEXT

- In what ways were the early Romans influenced by their **ETRUSCAN** neighbors and by their location in central **ITALY**?
- What were the components of the **REPUBLIC'S CONSTITUTION**? What was the relationship between **ROMAN CITIZENSHIP** and the **ROMAN ARMY** in this era?
- How do the stories of **AENEAS**, **LUCRETIA**, and **CINCINNATUS** reflect core Roman values? How did those values, summarized in the phrase *MOS MAIORUM*, set the Romans apart from the other civilizations we have studied?
- Why did the Romans come into conflict with **CARTHAGE**? How did the **PUNIC WARS** and Rome's other conquests change the balance of power in the Mediterranean?
- How did **IMPERIALISM** and contact with **HELLENISTIC CULTURE** affect the core values of Roman society, its economy, and its political system? What role did **SLAVERY** play in this civilization?
- What were the major crises of the late republic, and what were the means by which ambitious men achieved power? How did **JULIUS CAESAR** emerge triumphant, and why was he assassinated?
- In what ways did the **PRINCIPATE** differ from the **REPUBLIC**? What were the new powers of the **EMPEROR**, and how did **AUGUSTUS** exemplify these?
- How did the Romans consolidate their **EMPIRE** during the *PAX ROMANA*? By what means did they spread Roman culture?

THINKING ABOUT CONNECTIONS

- Polybius believed that the Roman Republic would last forever, because it fused together aspects of monarchy, aristocracy, and polity. What were the chief factors that led to its demise in the first century B.C.E.? Could these have been avoided—and if so, how?
- In what ways does the Roman Empire share the characteristics of earlier empires, especially that of Alexander? In what ways does it differ from them?
- The Roman Empire could be said to resemble our own civilization in different ways. What features does today's United States share with the Republic? With the Principate? What lessons can we draw from this?

CONSTANTINVS MAIOR IMPERATOR
HERACLII ET TIBERII IMPERATOR

ARCADIVS

PRIVILEGIA

STORY LINES

- In a little over three centuries, Christianity grew from obscure beginnings in a small Roman province to become the official religion of the empire.

- Meanwhile, the Roman Empire was becoming too large and diverse to be governed by a single centralized authority. Significant political, military, and economic changes occurred during the third century in response to these challenges.

- In the fourth century, the founding of a new capital at Constantinople shifted the focus of imperial administration to the East. At the same time, mass migrations of frontier peoples created new settlements within the western half of Rome's empire.

- Christianity's eventual association with political power changed the religion in profound ways. At the same time, Christian intellectuals adapted Rome's traditional culture to meet Christian needs.

CHRONOLOGY

c. 4 B.C.E.– c. 30 C.E.	Lifetime of Jesus
46–67 C.E.	Paul's missionary career
66–70	Jewish rebellion
132–135	Expulsion of Jews from Jerusalem
203	Death of Perpetua at Carthage
235–284	Rule of the "barracks emperors"
284–305	Diocletian divides the empire
312	Constantine's victory at the Battle of the Milvian Bridge
313	Edict of Milan
325	Council of Nicaea convened
c. 370–430	Careers of Jerome, Ambrose, and Augustine
c. 376	Frontier migrations begin
391	Pagan religion outlawed
410	Visigoths sack Rome
476	Odovacer deposes Romulus Augustulus
493–526	Rule of Theodoric the Ostrogoth
c. 500–583	Careers of Boethius, Benedict, and Cassiodorus

Before
You
Read
This
Chapter

The Transformation of Rome

In the year 203 C.E., a young woman was arrested and brought before the Roman governor at Carthage. She was twenty-two years old, from a respectable family. She had an infant child who was still nursing and a father who doted on her. She must have had a husband, too, but he is conspicuously absent from Perpetua's own firsthand account. Instead, Perpetua emphasizes her father's grief and the efforts he made to free her. But, clearly, he had failed as a father: a Roman *paterfamilias* should kill his daughter with his own hands if she disgraced the family. For Perpetua's crime was terrible, punishable by a death so debasing that it was reserved for slaves and barbarian prisoners—to be stripped naked before a holiday crowd and mauled by wild beasts in the arena of her own city. That was the death Perpetua died. Perpetua was a Christian.

Early Christianity posed a challenge to the Roman Empire at almost every level. To be a Christian was to be, by definition, an enemy of Rome, because Christians refused to venerate the emperor as the embodiment of Rome's gods. Moreover, Jesus Christ had himself been a criminal duly tried and put to

139

death by the Roman state. Also disturbing was the way that Christians flouted the conventions of Roman society. Perpetua was young, yet she defied her father. She was well born, yet she chose a common jail. She was a woman, yet she died in the dust like a gladiator. If this was what it meant to be a Christian, then being a Christian was incompatible with being a Roman.

How, then, did a Roman emperor become a Christian just a century or so after Perpetua's death? What changes did both Rome and Christianity have to undergo in order for this to happen? The Rome in which Perpetua was raised stretched from central Asia to the British Isles, from the Rhine to her own province of North Africa. But the governance of this enormous state and its diverse population was straining the bureaucracy built on the

foundations of the old Republic. By the fourth century, Rome itself even ceased to be the capital and hub of the empire. At the same time, Rome's settled provinces were coming under increased pressure from groups of people who had long lived along its borders but who now moved toward its center. These peoples would also challenge what it meant to be Roman, and they too would contribute to the transformation of the Roman world.

THE CHALLENGE OF CHRISTIANITY

Like the Hebrew monotheism that undergirds Judaism (see Chapter 2), Christianity was (and is) the product of historical processes. It began with the teachings of Jesus, who lived and worked among his fellow Jews around the year 30 C.E. It took root, however, in the Hellenistic world we studied in Chapter 4: the cosmopolitan, Greek-speaking cities around the eastern Mediterranean, which had been absorbed into the Roman Empire.

The Career of Jesus

Yeshua bar Yosef (Joshua, son of Joseph), known in Greek as Jesus, is one of the few figures of the ancient world about whose life we know a great deal. The earliest writings that mention him are the letters of Paul, a Hellenized Jew who was active during the 50s and 60s C.E. There were also many different narratives of Jesus's life written between c. 70 and 100 C.E. Four such accounts were eventually included in the New Testament, a collection of Christian scriptures codified around the third century C.E. In their original Greek, they were called *evangelia* ("good messages"); we know them as *Gospels*, an Old English word that means the same thing.

Jesus was born around the year 4 B.C.E., a generation or so after Augustus came to power in Rome. (He was not born precisely in the first year of the Common Era as we now reckon it.) When he was about thirty years old, he was endorsed by a Jewish preacher, John the Baptist, whom some considered to be a prophet. Thereafter, Jesus traveled around rural areas of Galilee and Judea, teaching and displaying unusual healing powers. He accumulated a number of disciples, some of whom had political ambitions.

Around the year 30 C.E., Jesus staged an entry into Jerusalem during Passover, a major religious holiday.

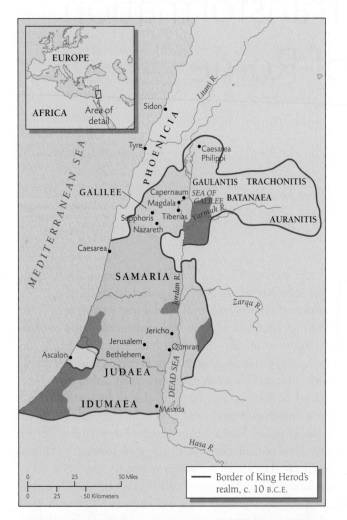

JUDEA AND GALILEE IN THE TIME OF JESUS. ▪ *What are the major Judean cities in first century C.E.?* ▪ *What do they indicate about the effects of Roman occupation on the lives of Jews?* ▪ *Given what you have learned about their history, why would some Jews resist Roman rule?*

This was interpreted as a bid for political power by both the Roman colonial government and the high-ranking Jews of the Temple. Gospel accounts say that Jesus also drew attention to himself by attacking merchants and bankers within the Temple. The city's religious leaders therefore arrested him and turned him over to the Roman governor, Pontius Pilatus (Pilate).

Pilate's main concern was to preserve peace during a volatile religious festival. His authority depended on maintaining good relations with local Jewish elites and with Herod, a recent convert to Judaism who ruled the province of Galilee as a client king of the Roman Empire. And because Jesus was a resident of Galilee, not a citizen of Roman Judea, Pilate sent Jesus to Herod for sentencing. But Herod sent him back, indicating that dealing with Jesus fell under Roman jursidiction. So Pilate chose to make an example of Jesus by condemning him to death by crucifixion, the standard penalty for those judged guilty of sedition.

That might have been the end of the story. But soon after Jesus's execution, his followers began to assert that he had risen from the dead. Moreover, they said that Jesus had promised to return again at the end of time. Meanwhile, he had promised spiritual support to his followers, who now reinterpreted the meaning of his entire career. In life, Jesus had been a teacher and healer; in death, he had been revealed as divine. The evidence of this reinterpretation has come down to us in the letters of Paul and in the Gospel narratives.

Jesus and Judaism

In the decade after 1947, many extraordinary parchment and papyrus scrolls were discovered in caves near Qumran, on the shores of the Dead Sea. Written in Hebrew, Greek, and Aramaic, at various times between 100 B.C.E. and 70 C.E., they have revolutionized our understanding of religious practice in the lifetime of Jesus, a period of intense competition among groups of Jewish believers.

Roman rule in this region was controversial. Jewish elites reaped the rewards of participation in the Roman economy and administration, but there was talk of rebellion among rural communities and the urban poor. Many hoped for a messiah, an inspired leader who would establish a new Jewish kingdom. The most extreme were the Zealots, who eventually led two disastrous revolts. The first, between 66 and 70 C.E., ended in the Romans' destruction of the Temple that had been rebuilt after Cyrus the Great released the Jews from Babylon (see Chapter 2). The second, in 132–35 C.E., destroyed Jerusalem itself and prompted the Romans to expel the entire population.

Whereas the first exile of the Jews had ended after fifty years, this new diaspora would not be reversed until the modern state of Israel was established in 1948. For over 500 years, Jerusalem even ceased to exist; on its ruins, the Romans built the colony of Aelia Capitolina (see Chapter 5). It was only in 638, when the Islamic Caliphate restored Jerusalem as a holy site, that Jews were allowed to settle there again (see Chapter 7).

This context is essential to understanding the circumstances of Jesus's death and the different messages conveyed by his words and actions. Significant divisions had arisen among the various Jewish communities with whom Jesus interacted. The hereditary Temple priesthood was controlled by a group known as the Sadducees, who collaborated closely with Rome; the high priest was even appointed by the Roman Senate. Their chief rivals were the Pharisees, who were teachers of religious doctrine. Although the Sadducees claimed the right to control the interpretation of the Torah, the Pharisees argued that Yahweh had given Moses an oral Torah as well as a written one, and that this had been handed down from teachers to students and was now the special inheritance of the Pharisees.

The oral Torah of the Pharisees enabled the flexible application of religious law to daily life. It also supported belief in a life after death, a day of judgment, and the damnation or reward of individual souls. The Pharisees even actively sought out converts and looked forward to the imminent arrival of the Messiah. In all these respects they differed significantly from the Sadducees, who interpreted the Torah more strictly, considered Judaism closed to anyone who had not been born a Jew, and who had a vested interest in maintaining the political status quo.

Even more radical than the Pharisees was a faction known as the Essenes, a separatist group that hoped for spiritual deliverance through repentance and self-denial. Although some scholars see Essene influence behind the career of Jesus, his Jewish contemporaries probably saw him as some sort of Pharisee: a similar emphasis on the ethical requirements of the law, rather than its literal interpretation, is reflected in many of his teachings. Jesus's apparent belief in the imminent coming of "the kingdom of God" also fits within a Pharisaic framework, as does his willingness to reach out to people beyond the Jewish community. But he seems to have carried these principles considerably further than did the Pharisees.

For most Jews at this time, Judaism consisted of going up to the Temple on holy days; paying the annual Temple tax; reciting the morning and evening prayers; and observing fundamental laws, such as circumcision (for men), ritual purity (especially for women), and prohibitions on the consumption of certain foods. Jesus deemphasized such observances, and it may have seemed that he wished to abolish them. But what made him most controversial was his followers' claim that he was the promised Messiah.

Such claims grew more assertive after Jesus's death, yet they never persuaded more than a small minority of Jews. But when Jesus's followers began to preach to non-Jewish audiences, they found many willing listeners. So they began to represent Jesus in terms that made sense to Greek-speaking communities. Jesus, his followers now proclaimed, was not merely a savior for the Jews. He was the "anointed one" (in Greek, *Christos*), the divine representative of God who had suffered and died for the sins of all humanity. He had now ascended into heaven, and he would return to judge all the world's inhabitants at the end of time.

Christianity in the Hellenistic World

The key figure to develop this new understanding of Jesus's divinity was his younger contemporary, Paul of Tarsus (c. 10–c. 67 C.E.). Named Saul when he was born in the Roman province of Cilicia (now south-central Turkey), he was the son of a Pharisee. The Acts of the Apostles, a major source for Saul's early life, says that he was dedicated to stamping out the cult of the crucified Jesus. But at some point in his mid-twenties—a few years after Jesus's death—he underwent a dramatic conversion, changed his name to Paul, and devoted his life to spreading the new faith to Greek-speaking, mainly non-Jewish communities.

Unlike Peter and his other early followers, Paul had never met Jesus. Instead, he claimed to have received a direct revelation of his teachings. This led to a number of major disputes. For example, the disciple Peter and his companions believed that followers of Jesus had to be Jews. Paul declared that Jewish religious law was now irrelevant; Jesus had made a new covenant possible between God and humanity, and the old covenant between God and the Jews no longer applied. This position was also vehemently opposed by the Jewish Christians of Jerusalem, a group led by Jesus's brother, James. But after a series of difficult debates that took place around 49 C.E., Paul's position triumphed. Although some early Christians would continue to obey Jewish law, most of the converts who swelled the movement were not Jews. Paul began to call this new community of believers an *ekklesia*, the Greek word for a legislative assembly (see Chapter 3). The Latinized form of this word is translated as "church."

These early converts were attracted to Christianity for a variety of reasons. Some were Hellenized Jews like Paul himself, who had already begun to adapt their lifestyles and beliefs through contact with other cultures. Christianity also appealed to groups of non-Jews who admired the Jews for their loyalty to ancestral tradition and their high ethical standards. Christianity was even attractive to those who saw Jesus as living by Stoic principles (Chapter 4) or as the embodiment of Ahura-Mazda, the good god of Zoroastrianism (Chapter 2). Others were already devotees of mystery religions, like the very old cult of the Egyptian goddess Isis (Chapter 1) or the newer worship of the warrior-god Mithras, popular among Rome's professional soldiers. Both of these religions revolved around stories of sacrifice, death, and regeneration that prepared their adherents to embrace the worship of Jesus. At the same time, there were significant differences between Christianity and these other religions. Most mystery cults stressed the rebirth of the individual through spiritual transformation, but Christianity emphasized the importance of community.

Women were especially prominent in these churches, not only as patrons and benefactors (a role Roman women often played in religious cults) but also as officeholders. This high status was unusual: in other ancient religions, women could be priests only in cults open solely to women; they never took precedence over men and many cults denied them access entirely. The fact that Christianity drew its adherents from a broad range of social classes also distinguished it from other cults. In time, these unusual features were distorted by Christianity's detractors, who alleged that Christians were political insurgents like the Jesus they worshiped.

As both Christianity and Judaism redefined themselves, they grew further apart. Judaism was adapting to the Romans' destruction of the Temple and the mass exile of Jews from Jerusalem. By and large, the scholars who reshaped Jewish doctrine during these difficult years ignored Christianity. Christians, however, could not ignore Judaism. Their religion rested on the belief that Jesus was the savior promised by God to Israel in the Hebrew Bible.

For Christians, the heroes of Jewish scripture prefigured Jesus, while the major events of Hebrew history could be read, allegorically, as Christian paradigms. Christ was the new Adam, reversing man's original sin; wood from the fateful Tree in Eden became the wood of the Cross on which Jesus died. Christ, like Abel, had been slain at the hands of a brother. Christ was the new Noah, saving creation from its sins. Christ was prefigured in Isaac, Joseph, and Moses. According to Christians, all the words of the Hebrew prophets pointed to Jesus, as did the Psalms and the Proverbs.

In short, Christian theologians argued that the Christian church is the true Israel and that when the Jews rejected Jesus, God rejected the Jews. The Hebrew Bible was henceforth the Old Testament, vital to understanding Christianity but superseded by the New Testament. At the end of time, the Jews would see their

The Prosecution of a Roman Citizen

The Acts of the Apostles *was written by the same author as Luke's Gospel and was intended as a continuation of that book. It recounts the adventures and ministry of Jesus's original disciples and also follows the career of Paul, a Hellenized Jew who became a missionary to Gentiles throughout the Roman world. It offers fascinating glimpses into the workings of the Roman legal system because Paul, depicted here as a Roman citizen, would have had special rights under Roman law (as Jesus had not). In this passage, Paul has been accused of treason against the emperor by a group of Pharisees and has been sent to Felix, the governor of Judea. These events took place between 57 and 59* C.E.

 o the soldiers, according to their instructions, took Paul and brought him by night to [the city of] Antipatris. The next day, they let the horsemen go on with him, while they returned to the barracks. When they came to Caesarea and delivered the letter to the governor, they presented Paul also before him. On reading the letter, he asked what province he belonged to, and when he learned that he was from Cilicia he said, "I will give you a hearing when your accusers arrive." Then he ordered that he be kept under guard in Herod's headquarters.

Five days later, the high priest Ananias came down with some elders and an attorney, a certain Tertullus, and they reported their case against Paul to the governor. When Paul had been summoned, Tertullus began to accuse him, saying: "Your Excellency, because of you we have long enjoyed peace, and reforms have been made for this people because of your foresight. We welcome this in every way and everywhere with utmost gratitude. But, to detain you no further, I beg you to hear us briefly with your customary graciousness. We have, in fact, found this man a pestilent fellow, an agitator among all the Jews throughout the world, and a ringleader of the sect of the Nazarenes. He even tried to profane the temple, and so we seized him.

By examining him yourself you will be able to learn from him concerning everything of which we accuse him." The Jews also joined in the charge by asserting that all this was true.

When the governor motioned to him to speak, Paul replied: "I cheerfully make my defense, knowing that for many years you have been a judge over this nation. As you can find out, it is not more than twelve days since I went up to worship in Jerusalem. They did not find me disputing with anyone in the temple or stirring up a crowd either in synagogues or throughout the city. Neither can they prove to you the charge that they now bring against me. But this I admit to you, that according to the Way, which they call a sect, I worship the God of our ancestors, believing everything laid down according to the law or written in the prophets. I have hope in God—a hope that they themselves also accept—that there will be a resurrection of both the righteous and the unrighteous. Therefore I do my best always to have a clear conscience toward God and all people. . . ."

But Felix, who was rather well informed about the Way, adjourned the hearing with the comment, "When Lysias the tribune comes down, I will decide your case." Then he ordered the centurion to keep him in custody, but to let him have some liberty and not to prevent any of his friends from taking care of his needs.

When some days later Felix came with his wife Drusilla, who was Jewish, he sent for Paul and heard him speak concerning faith in Christ Jesus. And as he discussed justice and self-control and future judgment, Felix was alarmed and said, "Go away for the present; when I have an opportunity I will summon you." At the same time he hoped that money would be given him by Paul. So he sent for him often and conversed with him. But when two years had elapsed, Felix was succeeded by Porcius Festus; and desiring to do the Jews a favor, Felix left Paul in prison.

Source: Acts of the Apostles 23:31–24:27, in *The New Oxford Annotated Bible*, New Revised Standard Version, ed. Bruce M. Metzger and Roland E. Murphy (New York: 1994).

Questions for Analysis

1. Based on this account, what legal procedures are in place for dealing with any Roman citizen accused of a crime?

2. What seems to be the relationship between the Jewish elite of Judea and the Roman governor? What is the role of their spokesman, Tertullus?

3. What is the nature of the accusation against Paul, and how does he defend himself?

PAUL'S MISSIONARY JOURNEYS. Quite apart from its religious importance, Paul's career offers fascinating glimpses into the life of a Hellenized Roman citizen from one of the empire's eastern provinces. ▪ *What were the main phases of Paul's travels in the eastern Mediterranean?* ▪ *How were his itineraries shaped by geography and by various modes of transport?* ▪ *What conclusions about his mission can you draw from the extent of his travels and his major destinations?*

error and convert. From a Christian perspective, the Jews' own impiety had caused their exile from the Holy Land and would continue to bring suffering down on their descendants.

Christianity and the Roman State

Unlike Christianity, though, Judaism remained a legally recognized religion and many Jews were further protected by their Roman citizenship. Indeed, the Acts of the Apostles represents Paul as a Roman citizen who could not be put to death without trial (as the noncitizen Jesus had been) when brought up on charges of treason. Instead, Acts follows Paul's progress through the Roman judicial system, until he is finally brought to

trial at Rome and executed (by beheading) under Nero. Even after their rebellion, the Jews of the diaspora were allowed to maintain the special status they had always had under Roman rule.

Christianity, by contrast, was an upstart religion and raised suspicions on many levels. It encouraged women and slaves to hold office; it revolved around the worship of a criminal condemned by the Roman state; its secret meetings could be breeding grounds for rebellion. Nevertheless, the official attitude toward Christians was largely one of indifference. There were not enough of them to matter, and few of them had any political power. During the first and second centuries, therefore, Christians were tolerated by Roman officials, except when local magistrates chose to make an example of someone who flouted authority.

THE CHALLENGE OF IMPERIAL EXPANSION

The emergence of Christianity coincided with the Roman Empire's most dramatic period of growth and a variety of challenges. For a long time, Rome's administrators clung to methods of governance put in place under Augustus, methods based on a single centralized authority. In reality, however, Rome's empire was no longer centered on Rome, or on Italy. It embraced ethnicities, cultures, economies, and political systems of vastly different kinds. More and more people could claim to be Roman citizens, and more and more people wanted a share of Rome's power. This placed enormous stress on the imperial administration. The fact that the empire had few defensible borders was another problem. Hadrian had attempted to establish one after 122, by building a wall between Roman settlements in southern Britannia and the badlands of northern tribes (see Chapter 5); but this act was more symbolic than effective.

For much of the second century, such stresses had been masked by the peaceful transfer of power among the so-called Five Good Emperors: Nerva, Trajan, Hadrian, Antoninus Pius, and Marcus Aurelius. This was partly accidental. None of these first four rulers had a surviving male heir, and so a custom developed whereby each adopted a young man of a good family and trained his successor in the craft of government. This sensible practice changed with the death of Marcus Aurelius in 180 C.E.

Although he was the closest Roman equivalent to Plato's ideal of the philosopher-king, Marcus was not wise enough to recognize that his own son, Commodus, lacked the capacity to rule. After his father's death, Commodus alienated the army by withdrawing from costly wars along the Danube. This move was also unpopular with the Senate, as were Commodus's violent tendencies and his scorn for the traditional norms of aristocratic conduct, including an alleged appearance as a gladiator in the Colosseum. In 192, a conspiracy was hatched inside his own palace, where he was strangled to death by his wrestling coach.

The Empire of the Severan Dynasty

Because Commodus had no obvious successor, the armies stationed in various provinces of the empire raised their own candidates. Civil war ensued, as it had during the crises of the late republic and again in 68 C.E., when three men had struggled for imperial power. In this case, there were five major contenders. The eventual victor was a North African general called Septimius Severus (r. 193–211 C.E.).

Under Severus (*SEH-ver-uhs*) and his successors, the administration of Rome's empire changed to a greater extent than it had since the time of Augustus. In many respects, changes were long overdue. Even the "Five Good Emperors" had been somewhat insulated from the realities of colonial rule. But Severus had been born and raised in Leptis Magna (in present-day Libya) and identified strongly with his father's Punic ancestors. Unlike Trajan and Hadrian, who had also grown up in the provinces, Severus did not regard Rome as the center of the universe.

Severus represents the degree to which the Roman Empire had succeeded in making the world Roman—succeeded so well that Rome itself was becoming practically irrelevant. One could be as much a Roman in Britannia or Africa as in central Italy. Severus's second wife, Julia Domna, exemplifies this trend in a different way. Descended from the Aramaic aristocracy who ruled the Roman client kingdom of Emesa (Syria), her father was the high priest of its sun-god, Ba'al. She was highly educated and proved an

Competing Viewpoints

The Development of an Imperial Policy toward Christians

> It was not until the third century that the Roman imperial government began to initiate full-scale investigations into the activities of Christians. Earlier, the official position had been akin to a policy of "don't ask, don't tell." Local administrators handled only occasional cases, and they were often unsure as to whether the behavior of Christians was illegal or criminal. The following letter was sent to the emperor Trajan by Gaius Plinius Caecilius Secundus (Pliny the Younger), the governor of Bithynia-Pontus (Asia Minor), around 112 C.E. Pliny was anxious to follow proper procedures in dealing with the new sect and wanted advice about this. His letter indicates what Romans did and didn't know about early Christian beliefs and practices.

From Pliny to Trajan

It is my regular custom, my lord, to refer to you all questions which cause me doubt, for who can better guide my hesitant steps or instruct my ignorance? I have never attended hearings concerning Christians, so I am unaware what is usually punished or investigated, and to what extent.... In the meantime, this is the procedure I have followed in the cases of those brought before me as Christians. I asked them whether they were Christians.

If they admitted it, I asked them a second and a third time, threatening them with execution. Those who remained obdurate I ordered to be executed, for I was in no doubt ... that their obstinacy and inflexible stubbornness should at any rate be punished. Others similarly lunatic were Roman citizens, so I registered them to be sent back to Rome.

Later in the course of the hearings, as usually happens, the charge rippled outwards, and more examples appeared.

An anonymous document was published containing the names of many. Those who denied that they were or had been Christians and called upon the gods after me, and with incense and wine made obeisance to your statue ... and who moreover cursed Christ ... I ordered to be acquitted.

Others, who were named by an informer, stated that they were Christians and then denied it. They said that they had been, but had abandoned their

effective governor during her husband's almost perpetual absence from Rome.

Severus largely ignored the politics of the Senate. He preferred to rule through the army, which he reorganized and expanded. Two of his reforms had long-term consequences. The first was a drastic raise in army pay, probably as much as 100 percent, which had the effect of securing the soldiers' absolute loyalty and reducing their need to augment their wages through plunder. The other was a relaxation of the long-standing rule forbidding soldiers to marry while in service. This dispensation encouraged men to put down roots in local communities, but it also made them reluctant to move when their legion was called up. On the one hand, this domesticated the army (hitherto a highly mobile fighting machine) and may have made it less effective. On the other, it gave the army a stake in the peaceful governance of Rome's colonies and further contributed to the decentralization of power.

Severus spent most of his imperial career with his army. He died at Eboracum (York, England) in 211, after negotiations with tribes north of Hadrian's Wall. On his deathbed, he is reported to have said to his two sons, "Get along together, keep the soldiers rich, and don't bother about anyone else." His elder son, Caracalla, didn't heed the first of these injunctions for long: by the end of the year, he had assassinated his brother, Geta, and attempted to erase him from the historical record by declaring a *damnatio memoriae* ("a condemnation of memory") that banned the mention of Geta's name and defaced his image on public monuments. The second of his father's orders he obeyed in a certain sense, by extending the rights of Roman citizenship to everyone, including the entire army. His father's final piece of advice helped to shorten allegiance some years previously. . . . They maintained, however, that all that their guilt or error involved was that they were accustomed to assemble at dawn on a fixed day, to sing a hymn antiphonally to Christ as God, and to bind themselves by an oath . . . to avoid acts of theft, brigandage, and adultery. . . . When these rites were completed, it was their custom to depart, and then reassemble again to take food, which was, however, common and harmless. They had ceased, they said, to do this following my edict, by which in accordance with your instructions I had outlawed the existence of secret brotherhoods. So I thought it all the more necessary to ascertain the truth from two maidservants [i.e., slaves], who were called deaconesses, even by employing torture. I found nothing other than a debased and boundless superstition. . . .

From Trajan to Pliny

You have followed the appropriate procedures, my Secundus. . . . No general rule can be laid down which would establish a definite routine. Christians are not to be sought out. If brought before you and found guilty, they must be punished, but in such a way that a person who denies that he is a Christian, and demonstrates this by his action . . . may obtain pardon for his repentance, even if his previous record is suspect. Documents published anonymously must play no role in any accusation, for they give the worst example, and are foreign to our age.

Source: Excerpted from *Pliny the Younger: The Complete Letters*, trans. P. G. Walsh (Oxford: 2006), pp. 278–79 (X.96–97).

Questions for Analysis

1. How does Pliny's treatment of Christians differ according to their social class? How does it differ from Felix's treatment of Paul (p. 143)?

2. Why would Trajan insist that anonymous accusations, like those discussed by Pliny, should not be used as evidence? Why is this "foreign to our age"?

3. What do you conclude from this exchange about the relationship between religion and politics under the Roman Empire?

Caracalla's reign significantly, since he alienated everyone who disagreed with him. He was assassinated in 217.

Caracalla's true successor was his mother's sister, Julia Maesa, who ruled through her adolescent grandson. This youth was known as Heliogabalus (or Elagabalus, r. 218–22) because of his devotion to the sun-god. But when Heliogabalus caused controversy by attempting to replace Jupiter, Rome's patron god, with a Latinized version of this eastern deity, Sol Invictus ("Invincible Sun"), his own grandmother engineered his assassination. Another of her grandsons, Alexander Severus (r. 222–35 C.E.), took his place. Alexander, in turn, was ruled by his mother Julia Mamea, the third in a succession of strong women behind the Severan dynasty, who even traveled with her son on military campaigns. This eventually proved fatal. The new prominence of the

army made Rome's legions engines of political advancement, and many aspiring generals could harness this. In 235, in consequence, Alexander and his mother were murdered at Moguntiacum (Mainz) in Upper Germania, when the army of the region turned against them. Nearly fifty years of civil unrest ensued.

The Test of Rome's Strength

From 235 to 284 C.E. there were no fewer than twenty-six "barracks emperors": military commanders, each backed by a few loyal legions, who struggled with one another and an array of problems. This period is sometimes called the "Third-Century Crisis" and interpreted as a time when the Roman Empire was nearly destroyed. It is more accurately interpreted as a time when the consequences of Roman imperialism made themselves acutely felt. Those aspects of the empire that were strong survived. Those that had always been fragile were further strained.

For example, inflation caused by the devaluation of currency under Severus nearly drained Roman coinage of its value. Meanwhile, rival emperors levied exorbitant taxes on civilians in their provinces, while warfare destroyed crops and interrupted trade, causing food shortages. Because Rome itself was almost entirely dependent on Egyptian grain and other goods shipped in from the East, its inhabitants suffered accordingly. Poverty and famine even led to a new form of slavery in Italy, as free artisans, local businessmen, and small farmers were forced to labor on the estates of large landholders in exchange for protection and food.

In 251, a terrible plague, probably smallpox, swept through the empire's territories and recurred in some areas for almost two decades. A similar plague had ravaged Rome a century earlier, but its effects had been mitigated by sound governance. Now, with an estimated 5,000 people dying every day in the crowded city, people sought local scapegoats. Christians were among those targeted. Beginning in the short reign of Decius (r. 249–51), all Roman citizens were required to swear a public oath affirming their loyalty to Rome, which meant worshiping Rome's gods. Large numbers of Christians were implicated when this edict was put into effect and the enlightened policies of earlier emperors were abandoned.

The Reorganized Empire of Diocletian

As it happens, the most zealous persecutor of Christians was also responsible for reining in these destructive forces. Diocletian (*die-oh-KLEE-shan*, r. 284–305) was a cavalry officer from the Roman province of Dalmatia (modern Croatia).

THE EMPEROR SEPTIMIUS SEVERUS. This statue, carved during the emperor's lifetime, emphasizes his career as a military commander, showing him in the standard-issue uniform of a Roman legionnaire. How does this image of Severus compare to that of Augustus (see Chapter 5, page 125)? ▪ *What do these differences suggest about the emperor's new role in the third century?*

THE TETRARCHY: DIOCLETIAN AND HIS COLLEAGUES. This grouping, carved from a valuable purple stone called porphyry, shows the two augusti, Diocletian and Maximian, embracing their younger caesars, Galerius and Constantius. ▪ *Why do you think that these rulers are portrayed with identical facial features and military regalia?* ▪ *What message does this convey?*

He could have been another "barracks emperor." Instead, he embraced the reality of Rome as a complex state that could not be governed from one place by one centralized bureaucracy. He appointed a fellow officer, Maximian, as co-emperor, putting him in charge of the western half of the empire and retaining the wealthier eastern half for himself. In 293, he delegated new authority to two junior emperors or "caesars," Galerius and Constantius. The result was a tetrarchy, a "rule of four," with each man governing a quarter of the empire, further subdivided into administrative units called *dioceses*.

This system not only responded to the challenges of imperial administration, but was also designed to secure a peaceful transfer of power, since the two young "caesars" were being groomed to take the place of the two senior "augusti." Diocletian apparently recognized that disputes over succession had been a fatal flaw of the Augustan system. Also unlike Augustus, who had cloaked the reality of his personal power in the trappings of the republic, Diocletian presented himself as an undisguised autocrat. His title was not *princeps* ("first man"), but *dominus* ("lord"). In fact, his style of imperial rule borrowed more from the Persian model than it did from the Roman. Gone were the days of simplicity and the scorn of kingly pomp: Diocletian wore a diadem and a purple gown of silk interwoven with gold. Under the Principate, the emperor's palace had been run like the household of any well-to-do Roman, only on a large scale. Diocletian, however, introduced Persian-style ceremonies in his lavish palace. Too much familiarity with their soldiers had bred contempt for the "barracks emperors." Diocletian was able to avoid this mistake.

Although Diocletian retained close personal control over the army, he took steps to separate military from civilian chains of command. To control the devastatingly high rates of inflation that were undermining the economy, Diocletian stabilized the currency and reformed the tax system. He even moved the administrative center of the empire from Italy to Nicomedia in the Roman province of Bithynia (modern Turkey). Rome remained the symbolic capital of the empire, not least because the Senate continued to meet there. But Diocletian had little need for the Senate's advice. The real power lay elsewhere.

THE CONVERSION OF CHRISTIANITY

By the beginning of the fourth century, the number of Christians living within the jurisdiction of Rome was statistically insignificant: probably no more than 5 percent of the total population in the West and possibly 10 percent of the Greek-speaking East. Still, one of Diocletian's methods for promoting unity was to take a proactive stance against any group perceived as subversive. Those who could not show proof of their loyalty to Rome's gods were stripped of their rights as citizens. Christians who had been serving in the army or in government offices were dismissed. So were Manicheans, followers of the Persian prophet Mani (c. 216–276), whose teachings paralleled Zoroastrianism by positing an eternal struggle between the forces of good and evil. Indeed, Christianity and Manichaeism must have seemed very similar, and both were implicated in a full-scale purge of religious dissidents in 303. This was the Great Persecution, a time when many became martyrs—a Greek word meaning "witnesses"—to their faith.

Christianity and Neoplatonism

Ironically, the very crises that prompted Diocletian's Great Persecution were contributing to a growing interest in Christianity. Its message of social justice and equality was attractive to those suffering from hardship. It also appealed to followers of a new and influential philosophy called Neoplatonism ("New Platonism"), which drew upon the more mystical aspects of Plato's thought. Its founder was Plotinus (204–270 c.e.), a Hellenistic philosopher from Egypt who had many followers among the Roman upper classes.

Plotinus taught that everything has its source in a single supreme being. The material world is part of this creation, but it is merely the residue of divinity. Human beings are composed of matter (bodies) and emanations of the divine (souls). This means that the individual soul, originally a part of God, is separated from its divine source. The highest goal of life is therefore to attain spiritual reunion with the divine through acts of self-denial that will liberate the soul from its earthly bondage. Asceticism (from the Greek word meaning "exercise" or "training") was therefore a major focus, because the body could be tamed by fasting and other forms of self-denial and thus made a more fitting vessel for the soul.

Neoplatonism became so popular in Rome that it almost supplanted Stoicism. (Although the two philosophies shared some fundamental characteristics, Stoicism did not hold out the hope of union with the divine.) Neoplatonism also struck a blow at traditional Roman worship of ancestors and the devotion to the empire's gods. It was thus a natural ally of Christianity, and many important Christian theologians would be influenced by it, while many educated Romans found their way to Christianity because of it. This was not, however, the path by which Christianity's first imperial convert reached the new faith.

Constantine's Vision

In 305, Diocletian built a palace near his hometown of Split, on the Adriatic coast, and retired there—the first time a Roman ruler had voluntarily removed himself from power since Sulla had resigned his dictatorship, nearly four centuries earlier (see Chapter 5). Diocletian obliged Maximian to retire at the same time, and the two caesars Galerius and Constantius moved up the ladder of succession, becoming augusti of the East and West, respectively. But the transfer of power was not as orderly as Diocletian had intended. One of the candidates to fill the vacant post of caesar was Constantius's son, Constantine, who was being trained at Galerius's court. But he was passed over, and Galerius pursued his own imperial agenda. So Constantine left the court at Nicomedia and joined his father in Gaul. From there, father and son went to Britannia and campaigned on the northern borders until 306, when Constantius died and named Constantine as his successor. This left Constantine in control of a large army: the legions of Gaul and the Rhineland, as well as Britannia.

Meanwhile, war had broken out among several other claimants to imperial power. Constantine remained aloof from this struggle, waged mostly in Italy, and concentrated on securing his quarter of the empire. Beginning around 310, he also began to promote himself as a favored devotee of the sun-god Sol Invictus, whose cult had been revived by the emperor Aurelian (r. 270–75). This was a smart move. Increasingly, the "Invincible Sun" was associated not only with the Roman gods of light and war, Apollo and Mars, but also with Mithras, whose cult was popular with soldiers. It was increasingly popular in Rome as well, where the feast long dedicated to the sky-god Saturn, the Saturnalia, was now being celebrated as the rebirth of the sun after the winter solstice, on December 25.

From the worship of Sol Invictus to the worship of Christ was, for Constantine, a small step (see **Interpreting Visual Evidence** on page 151). In 312, Constantine decided to march on Italy, which was now in the hands of a general called Maxentius, who had declared himself emperor and was trying to build up a coalition whose supporters included the Christian community of Rome. It may have been this that inspired Constantine to emblazon Christian symbols on his banners and shields the night before a battle north of Rome, at the Milvian Bridge over the Tiber. According to later legend, Constantine had seen a vision of two intertwined Greek letters inscribed on the sky, the first two letters in the name of Christ, and was told that "In this sign, you will conquer." He did.

In gratitude for his victory, Constantine showered benefits on the Christian clergy of Rome and patronized the construction of churches throughout the empire. He also forced

Licinius, the augustus of the East, to join him in promoting religious tolerance when they met at Milan in 313. This Edict of Milan guaranteed freedom of worship to all Rome's citizens, Christian and non-Christian. But it was apparent that Christianity was the favored faith and thus the pathway for anyone with political ambitions. Almost overnight, then, Christians ceased to be members of an illegal and despised cult and became affiliates of a prestigious and profitable religion. The entire basis of Christianity's appeal had changed.

From Illegal Sect to Imperial Institution

Early Christianity had grown organically; it had not been designed as a religious system. It had no absolute teachings, and not all Christian communities had access to the same scriptures. Some churches had a few of Paul's letters; others had none. Some had bishops, priests, and deacons; others had only a handful of believers. Some counted women as their leaders; others disapproved of women in authority. Some had come under the influence of Neoplatonism or Manichaeism; others considered these to be perversions.

In every respect, then, the Christianity that emerged after Constantine's conversion had to reinvent itself. Doctrines formulated to suit the needs of small, scattered communities had to be reconciled. Members of this new institutional Church needed to agree on a shared set of beliefs. They needed a chain of command. All of these fundamentals had to be hammered out in a painful process that never quite managed to forge a common understanding, because the different varieties of Christianity had been too separate for too long: products of the same diversity that made the Roman Empire hard to govern.

The Hierarchy of the Church

When it came to organization, Rome's administration provided practical models. Because the empire's basic unit of governance was the city, the city became the basic unit of ecclesiastical administration. Each major city now had a bishop (from the Greek for "overseer") who also oversaw the rural areas of his diocese (a term borrowed from Diocletian). Bishops of the oldest and most prestigious Christian communities were called *patriarchs*, and their cities also jockeyed for preeminence. The main contenders were Rome, Alexandria, and Constantinople, a new city founded by Constantine (as will be discussed later).

Which of these Roman cities should be the capital of the Roman Church? Rome had long been venerated as the place where both Peter and Paul were martyred.

Interpreting Visual Evidence

The Power of the Invincible Sun

oman emperors often linked their power with those of Rome's traditional gods, and they were also worshiped as gods in their own right. Look carefully at the following images and consider the visual language of power that came to be associated with Sol Invictus, "the Invincible Sun," and eventually with Jesus Christ.

Questions for Analysis

1. How did Constantine invoke the iconography of Sol Invictus (image A)? What messages does this image convey?

2. How might Constantine's use of this imagery—after his initial conversion to Christianity—have been interpreted by Christians? How might it have been interpreted by followers of Rome's other religions? Do you think it was designed to be ambiguous?

3. Scholars dispute both the dating and the significance of this mosaic found beneath St. Peter's Basilica in Rome (image B). Is it likely that this is a representation of Jesus as Sol Invictus? If not, how would you explain the later association of this pagan deity with the Christian God?

A. This gold medallion was issued by Constantine in 313, a year after his victory at the Battle of the Milvian Bridge. The legend calls him "Invincible Constantine."

B. This mosaic comes from a necropolis (cemetery) found beneath St. Peter's Basilica in Rome. Its precise dating is in dispute, but it was made sometime between the mid-third and mid-fourth century.

And according to one of the Gospels (Matthew 16:18–19), Jesus had designated Peter as his representative on earth. Peter's successors, the subsequent bishops of Rome, thus claimed to exercise the same powers. Rome's bishop also enjoyed some political advantages over other patriarchs. Unlike the bishop of the new imperial capital at Constantinople, he could act with more freedom because he didn't have to deal directly with the emperor. But as far as eastern bishops were concerned, the patriarch of Constantinople should be the one to exercise control over the entire Church. This division—the product of cultural differences and contemporary politics—would continue to affect the development of Christian institutions. In time,

it would lead to a very real division within Christianity that has never been resolved.

Orthodoxy, Heresy, and Imperial Authority

Christianity's new prominence raised the stakes of disputes over its basic teachings. While followers of Jesus had disagreed about such matters since the time of his death, these were of little political consequence. Under Constantine, however, doctrinal disputes had the potential to undermine the emperor. It was imperative, therefore, that these disputes be resolved.

DIOCLETIAN'S DIVISION OF THE EMPIRE, C. 304 C.E. ▪ *What areas did each of the four divisions of the empire cover?* ▪ *What seems to be the strategy behind the location of the four major capitals, both within their respective quarters and in relation to one another?* ▪ *What is the status of Rome itself, according to this map?*

The most divisive issue concerned the nature of God. Jesus had taught his followers that he was the Son of God, and that after his death he would leave behind a comforting spirit that would also be an emanation of God. Accordingly, many Christians believed that God encompassed a Trinity of equal persons: Father, Son, and Holy Spirit. But other Christians, influenced by Neoplatonism, rejected the idea that Jesus could be equal with God. Instead, they maintained that Jesus was part of God's creation and shared in his divine essence, but was not equal to God. This belief was called Arianism, after the Christian teacher Arius who espoused it. (It should not be confused with Aryanism, a modern racial concept.) After protracted struggles, Arianism was condemned as a heresy, a word that comes from the Greek verb meaning "to choose for oneself." This became the Church's term for false beliefs punished with damnation. Yet many Christians continued to adhere to the Arian view.

This new emphasis on orthodoxy (Greek for "correct teaching") was another major consequence of Christianity's conversion. So was the growing complexity of Christian theology, because Christian intellectuals had to demonstrate that Christianity was superior to Hellenistic philosophy. Just as there were many different schools of Greek and Roman thought, so there arose many different interpretations of Christian doctrine. Before Christianity became a legal religion, these differences could only be addressed informally, by small groups of bishops that had no power to enforce their decisions. In the fourth century, doctrinal disputes had real political consequences.

As a result, the Roman state became increasingly enmeshed in the governance of the Church. Constantine began this process in 325 C.E., when he summoned Christian representatives to the first ecumenical ("worldwide") meeting of the Christian community, the Council of Nicea, where Arianism was condemned and discrepancies over the canon of the Christian Bible were resolved. Constantine's successors carried this intervention much further. Gradually, they claimed to preside over Church councils as Christ's

CONSTANTINE'S CHRISTIAN SYMBOL. This fourth-century fresco shows the chi-rho symbol that Constantine claimed to have seen in the sky before his victory at the Milvian Bridge. (Chi and rho are the first two letters in the Greek word *Christos*.) Flanking this monogram are the first and last letters of the Greek alphabet, alpha and omega, which also refer to Jesus, "the beginning" and "the end."

representatives. Some even violently suppressed Christian groups who refused to accept imperial mandates. Essentially, these interventions were an extension of Augustan policies, which had made the emperor *pontifex maximus*, Rome's high priest. It began to look as though secular and spiritual authority would be combined in the person of the emperor. But this would change in later centuries, as we shall see.

New Attitudes toward Women and the Body

Women were conspicuously absent from the new hierarchy of the Christian Church. Even though they had long been deacons and may even have performed priestly duties, women were now firmly and completely excluded from any position of power.

This was perhaps the largest change brought about by Christianity's conversion. Jesus had included many women among his close followers, yet one of the gospels now rejected from the biblical canon was ascribed to Mary Magdalene. Paul had relied on women to organize and preside over churches and to finance his missionary journeys; he had declared in one letter (Galatians 3:28) that there should be no distinctions of gender, rank, or ethnicity among Christians. Women like Perpetua were prominent among the early martyrs and were often regarded as prophets. These strong female roles had always set Christianity apart from the traditional values of Roman society and had also been one of its main attractions.

What accounts for this drastic change? Three factors can be clearly identified. When Christianity was absorbed into the staunch patriarchy of Rome, it could no longer promote the authority of women. As the Church came to mirror the imperial administration, it replicated the structures of governance that had been the province of men since the founding of the republic. The Church now had the capacity to exclude or censor writings that represented women as the companions of Jesus and cofounders of the religion based on his teachings. These efforts were so successful that it was not until the very end of the nineteenth century that a gospel attributed to Mary Magdalene (among other writings) was known to exist.

The second factor leading to the marginalization of women was the growing identification of Christianity with Roman cults that emphasized masculinity, particularly the worship of Sol Invictus and the soldier-god Mithras. This was a deliberate strategy: it is easier to convert people to a new religion if that religion embraces elements of other religions. In common with many of the other religions we have studied, Christianity emphasized the heroic suffering and death of a male god and his eventual victory over death. Christ was increasingly identified with Sol Invictus, and his birthday came to be celebrated on the old Roman Saturnalia of December 25, which marked the passing of the winter solstice and the return of lengthening days.

The third factor contributing to women's exclusion from power was a growing emphasis on asceticism ("self-denial"), which changed attitudes toward the body. As we noted earlier, Neoplatonism taught that the goal of life was to liberate the soul from the tyranny of bodily desires, a teaching it shared with Stoicism. None of this was emphasized in the teachings of Christ. Quite the contrary: the body was celebrated as God's creation, and Christ himself had encouraged feasting, touching, bathing, and marriage. His followers insisted that he had been bodily resurrected, and that the bodies of all the faithful would be resurrected, too. Although early Christians had to be willing to sacrifice their lives, if need be, they were not required to renounce pleasures.

After Christianity became legal, however, there were few opportunities to "bear witness" to the faith through martyrdom. Instead, some Christians began to practice asceticism as an alternative path to sanctity. This meant renunciation of the flesh, especially sex and eating, activities both associated with women, who were in charge of any household's food supply and who were (obviously) sexual partners. A new spiritual movement, monasticism, also took hold, providing an alternative lifestyle for men who wanted to reject the world entirely; the word *monasticism* comes from the Greek word *monos*, "alone." Early monks lived as hermits and practiced extraordinary feats of self-abasement. Some tried to eke out a life in the desert; others penned themselves into small

SAINT SIMEON THE STYLITE. This gold plaque dating from the sixth century depicts the exertions of the ascetic saint who defied the devil (shown as a huge snake) by abusing his own body. Admirers wishing to speak to the saint could climb the ladder shown on the left. ▪ *What do you make of the relationship between the precious medium of this image (gold) and the message it conveys?*

cages; still others hung heavy weights around their necks. A monk named Cyriacus would stand for hours on one leg, like a crane. Another, Simeon "the Stylite," lived on top of a high pillar for thirty-seven years, punishing his lice-infested flesh while crowds gathered below to marvel.

This extreme denial of the body was a departure from most previous Christian practices and from those of many ancient religions, which often celebrated sexuality as a delight as well as a necessity. Even Roman religion had a place for priestesses and female prophets. Moreover, marriage was so important that Romans had regarded citizens' bodies as being at the service of the state: men as soldiers and fathers, women as mothers and wives. Now, however, some elite Christians were asserting that their bodies belonged to God, and that to serve God fully meant not bearing children.

Virginity for both men and women was accordingly preached as the highest spiritual standard, with celibacy for those who had once been married valued almost as highly. Marriage remained acceptable for average people, the laity, but was often represented as a second-best option. Moreover, because Aristotle had posited that women were inherently

more lustful than men, the denigration of sexuality had a disproportionately negative effect on attitudes toward women.

Christians and Pagans

The urban focus of Christianity is reflected in the Latin word referring to a non-Christian: *paganus*, someone who lives in the countryside. It implies that only an uncivilized rustic would cling to the old Roman religion and thus spoil his chances of advancement. As Christians came to occupy positions of power within the empire, men with political ambitions were increasingly forced to convert—or at least conform—to Christian norms.

Constantine had retained both pagan and Christian officials in his court, but his successors were less inclined to tolerate competing faiths. An interesting exception was Julian "the Apostate" (r. 360–63), Constantine's nephew, who abandoned Christianity and attempted to revive traditional Roman piety. But when Julian was killed in a battle with the Persians, his pro-pagan edicts were allowed to lapse. By 391, the emperor Theodosius (r. 379–95 c.e.) had prohibited pagan worship of any sort within the empire. In just three generations, Christianity had gone from being a persecuted faith to a persecuting religion. Theodosius even removed the sacred altar of the goddess Victory from the Senate chamber in Rome, prompting pagan loyalists to prophesy the end of the empire. Fifteen years later, Rome fell to a barbarian army.

SHIFTING CENTERS AND MOVING FRONTIERS

In 324, Constantine broke ground for the capital city he named after himself. It was built on the site of a settlement called Byzantium, chosen for its strategic location at the mouth of the Black Sea and at the crossroads between Europe and Asia: the Hellespont (literally "the bridge to Greece"). This site gave Constantinople commanding advantages as a center for communications and trade. It also made the city readily defensible, surrounded on three sides by water and protected on land by walls. It would remain the political and economic center of the Roman Empire until 1453, when the city was conquered by the Ottoman Turks (see Chapter 11).

East or West?

The founding of Constantinople epitomizes the shift in Rome's center of gravity from Italy and western Europe to the eastern

Mediterranean. It also signaled Constantine's intention to abandon the political precedents set by Diocletian. Instead, imperial succession became hereditary. Even more ominously, he divided the empire among his three sons. Civil war ensued, each son aligned with a different faction within the Church. In the meantime, the empire became more and more fragmented. The last ruler who could claim to govern a united Rome was the same Theodosius who outlawed its venerable religion. Then he, too, divided the empire between his sons.

As we have seen, there had always been linguistic and cultural differences between the Greek- and Latin-speaking regions under Roman rule. Now, however, these differences became heightened. The eastern empire was becoming more populous, more prosperous, and more central to imperial policy; the western provinces were becoming poorer and more peripheral. Many western cities now relied on transfers of funds from their eastern counterparts, and they suffered when these funds dried up, when trade or communication failed, or when Roman legions were transferred elsewhere. Rome itself, which had been demoted to provincial status under Diocletian, now lost even that nominal position: the Italian city of Ravenna on the Adriatic coast became the new capital of the region and a more convenient stopping place for those traveling from Constantinople to the administrative centers of Milan and Trier. Only two of Constantine's successors ever visited Rome itself, and none of them lived there.

Internal and External Pressures

The new center of the empire and the widening gap between the eastern and western provinces were not the only fault lines emerging in this period. Beneath the surface of imperial autocracy, the empire was slowly dissolving into its constituent parts. It was also coming under renewed pressure from its borders. Since the third century, the growing power of a new Persian dynasty, the Sassanids, had prompted a shift of Roman military weight to the eastern frontier, reducing the number of troops stationed elsewhere. During the fourth century, relations between assimilated Romans and their barbarian neighbors along the porous frontier of Germania were generally peaceful. But starting in the early fifth century, a new wave of settlers moved in.

From the Periphery to the Center

The tribes that lived along the empire's northern frontiers were barbarians in the pure sense of that term: they did not speak either of the empire's civilized languages and they did not live in cities. But they were sophisticated agriculturalists and metalworkers who had enjoyed trading relationships with the Roman world for centuries. Many had been settled within Roman provinces for generations. Legionnaires from the hinterlands of Germania were core components in Roman armies. In some frontier areas, entire tribes had become Roman *foederati*: allied troops in the service of the empire. Many of these tribes even adopted the form of Christianity preached by disciples of Arius. Although this made them heretics from the perspective of the institutional Church, it also tied them more closely to Roman civilization.

What altered this relatively peaceful coexistence? Our study of previous civilizations has prepared us to answer this question: the arrival of new peoples and the subsequent struggle for land and resources. During the mid-fourth century, a group of nomadic herdsmen known as the Huns began to migrate westward from central Asia, into the region north of the Black Sea. Around 370, their arrival forced a number of other groups, notably the Goths, to migrate south and west. The Goths had been clients of the Roman state for several centuries, but now they were refugees. The Romans permitted them to cross the Danube River and settle within the empire. In return for food and other supplies, they were to guard the region against other migrant groups. Local officials, however, failed to uphold their end of the bargain. Instead, they forced the starving Goths to sell themselves and their children into slavery in return for food. In 378, the Goths revolted and the Roman army sent to suppress them was defeated at the battle of Adrianople.

Peace was restored by accommodating the Goths' demands for goods and farmland and by enrolling them in the Roman army under their own military leaders. This provided an opening for Alaric, a young leader of the Goths. Taking advantage of the fact that the empire was divided, he targeted the wealthier eastern provinces and led his army into Greece, looting and capturing many ancient cities, including Athens. In a desperate attempt to halt these incursions, Alaric was offered a Roman military command and encouraged to move into Italy, meaning that the price of peace in the eastern empire was Rome itself.

Meanwhile, the Huns had arrived in the region corresponding to modern-day Hungary, forcing several other peoples westward toward the Rhine. On New Year's Eve in the year 406, a people known as the Vandals crossed the frozen Rhine and invaded Gaul. To repulse them, the imperial military commander in the West, Flavius Stilicho (whose own father had been a Vandal) made an alliance with Alaric and his Goths. But when Stilicho fell from imperial favor just a few months later, there was no one else who could restrain Alaric.

Analyzing Primary Sources

A Senator Defends the Traditional Religion of Rome

In 382, the Emperor Theodosius ordered the removal of the ancient altar dedicated to the goddess of Victory (Nike) from the Senate chamber in Rome as part of his efforts to make Christianity the dominant religion in the empire. This controversial move sparked heated debate and elicited strong protests from Rome's senatorial elites. The following statement of their case was made by Quintus Aurelius Symmachus (c. 345–402), who was at that time prefect of the city of Rome. It is principally addressed to the young Western emperor, Valentinian.

o what is it more suitable that we defend the institutions of our ancestors, and the rights and destiny of our country ... than to the glory of these times, which is all the greater when you understand that you may not do anything contrary to the custom of your ancestors? We demand then the restoration of that condition of religious affairs which was so long advantageous to the state.... Who is so friendly with the barbarians as not to require an Altar of Victory? ... But even if the avoidance of such an omen were not sufficient, it would at least have been seemly to abstain from injuring the ornaments of the Senate House. Allow us, we beseech you, as old men to leave to posterity what we received as boys. The love of custom is great.... Where shall we swear to obey your laws and commands? By what religious sanction shall the false mind be terrified, so as not to lie in bearing witness? All things are indeed filled with God, and no place is safe for the

perjured, but to be urged in the very presence of religious forms has great power in producing a fear of sinning. That altar preserves the concord of all, that altar appeals to the good faith of each, and nothing gives more authority to our decrees than that the whole of our order issues every decree as it were under the sanction of an oath....

Let us now suppose that Rome is present and addresses you in these words: "Excellent princes, fathers of your country, respect my years to which pious rites have brought me. Let me use the ancestral ceremonies, for I do not repent of them. Let me live after my own fashion, for I am free. This worship subdued the world to my laws, these sacred rites repelled Hannibal from the walls, and the Senones [Gauls] from the capital. Have I been reserved for this, that in my old age I should be blamed? I will consider what it is thought should be set in order, but tardy and discreditable is the reformation of old age." We ask, then, for peace for the gods of our fathers and of our country. It is just that all worship

should be considered as one. We look on the same stars, the sky is common, the same world surrounds us. What difference does it make by what pains each seeks the truth? We cannot attain to so great a secret by one road; but this discussion is rather for persons at ease, we offer now prayers, not conflict.

Source: Excerpted from *A Select Library of the Nicene and Post-Nicene Fathers,* 2nd Series, Vol. X (New York: 1896), pp. 411–14.

Questions for Analysis

1. How does Symmachus's defense exemplify the traditional values of the Roman Republic?

2. How does Symmachus justify the co-existence of Christianity and Rome's state religion? How would a Christian refute his position?

3. Less than a decade after the altar's removal, Theodosius outlawed all religions but Christianity. Based on your reading of this letter, how would that edict have affected Romans like Symmachus?

Like Stilicho, Alaric seems to have wanted to win a permanent place for himself in the imperial hierarchy. But unlike Stilicho—and many other generals—he did not understand how to use military power as a means toward that end. His assault on Rome made him Rome's destroyer, not its conqueror. In 410, after a protracted period of siege, Alaric's army captured and sacked the city. Many of the

Goths then moved on, eventually settling in southern Gaul and Hispania, where they established what came to be known as the Visigothic kingdom. Others, later labeled as the Ostrogoths, remained in Italy. The Vandals ultimately crossed the Strait of Gibraltar to settle in North Africa. Other tribes, including the Franks and the Burgundians, then followed the Vandals across the Rhine into Gaul and

THE MIGRATIONS OF ROME'S FRONTIER PEOPLES. ▪ *What do the routes followed by these different peoples suggest about their destinations and motives?* ▪ *Why did so many converge on Rome, even though the city was no longer the capital even of the Western Roman Empire?* ▪ *Why did the Romans refer to them as "barbarians"?*

established kingdoms of their own. A generation later the Huns—whose migrations had set all of these gears in motion—themselves invaded Roman territory under the leadership of their warlord, Attila.

In Britannia, meanwhile, remaining legions were hastily withdrawn in 410, sent to embattled territories in Rome's older provinces. In the ensuing centuries, a mixed population of Romans and Celts eventually intermingled with invaders from northwestern Germania and Scandinavia: Angles, Saxons, and Jutes. These tribes' movements were so far-reaching that they dominated all but the westernmost and northern portions of the island within a few generations. Many Celts retreated to the regions where Celtic languages are still spoken in Britain today, including Wales and Scotland. The rest of Britain would become Angleland: England.

The last western Roman emperor was an ineffectual usurper known derisively as Romulus Augustulus ("Little Romulus Augustus"). In 476 he was deposed by Flavius Odovacer, a chieftain who headed a mixed band of barbarians, Huns, and disgruntled Romans. From the perspective of the East, this event was decisive: now Constantinople was not only "New Rome," it was the only viable capital. And the best way for its imperial agenda to be carried forward in the western provinces was through a

strong barbarian ruler. Luckily, the emperor Zeno (r. 474–91) knew just the man: Theodoric, the son of a Gothic king, who had been sent to Constantinople as a hostage and raised in the civilized surroundings of the imperial court. After a decade of fierce fighting, Theodoric and his imperially equipped Gothic army managed to drive the Huns from Italy and establish a kingdom based in Ravenna, which he ruled (with imperial support) until his death in 526.

The Impact of the Fifth-Century Migrations

The migrations of the fifth century penetrated to Rome's core western provinces: Italy, Gaul, Hispania, North Africa. Yet the groups that moved through these territories were small, never more than war bands. Why couldn't long-established imperial cities defend themselves?

As the strongest legions were withdrawn from frontier western provinces, they were dispatched to protect richer eastern ones. Those that remained were integrated into local civilian populations, staffed by married men who grew their own food and lived with their families, making it difficult to move troops in an emergency. And even

Shifting Centers and Moving Frontiers | 157

Resisting Imperialism

Attempts at conquest are always met with resistance. In the Roman province of Britannia, a Celtic warrior queen named Boadicea led an armed uprising against the imperial army that is still celebrated as a proud example of British independence—as this modern statue in London indicates. A more peaceful uprising against American imperialism took place in Manila on the eve of President Barack Obama's first inauguration in 2008.

Watch related author videos on the Student Site
wwnorton.com/college/history/western-civilizationsBrief4

if the citizens of Rome's western provinces had been able to maintain a crack fighting force on the frontier, there would have been little reason for them to think that it was necessary. Their "barbarian" neighbors hadn't seemed threatening for generations. Many were so Romanized that differences between the groups are difficult to detect in surviving archaeological evidence.

In the eastern Roman Empire, by contrast, a thriving economy made it easier to equip and maintain a strong fighting force. Cities remained centers of commerce and industry, which meant that citizens possessed greater taxable wealth and could sustain the burdens of the imperial bureaucracy more easily. Moreover, potential invaders could be bought off or bribed to direct their attention elsewhere—as Alaric had been. For all these reasons, the eastern empire prospered during the fifth century, while the western empire floundered. After the fifth-century migrations, these differences were exacerbated. Ten years

after the Goths sacked Rome, the area was capable of producing only 15 percent of the revenues it had generated before. Similar reductions in revenues resulted from attacks on Gaul and Hispania. After 420 or so, as the newcomers began to set up their own kingdoms, these areas ceased to pay any taxes at all to imperial authorities. When the Vandals captured North Africa in 439, the richest of all Rome's western provinces was lost.

The consequences of these structural changes were far-reaching. In the year 400, the economy of the western Roman Empire was characterized by the mass production of low-cost, high-quality consumer goods that circulated in massive quantities. Although regional and local systems of exchange continued after 500, long-distance trade in bulk goods could be sustained only in the Mediterranean. As markets disappeared in northwestern provinces, skilled artisans either had to find other ways to make a living or had to emigrate. Standards of living gradually declined, and

THEODORIC THE OSTROGOTH. This coin shows the king in Roman dress but with the long hair characteristic of a barbarian nobleman. The inscription reads REX THEODERICVS PIVS PRINCIS—"King Theodoric, pious prince." ▪ *How does this image compare to that of Constantine (see page 151)?*

so did the overall population. It is likely that the population of western Europe did not return to its fourth-century levels for a thousand years, until just before the Black Death (see Chapter 10).

Other aspects of Roman life in these regions changed, too, but almost imperceptibly. Roman bureaucracies often survived, although the proceeds from taxes now went into the purses of the new barbarian rulers or Christian bishops. Roman agricultural patterns continued in most areas, local Roman elites continued to dominate civic life, and Roman cities continued to dominate their surrounding regions. Nor did the invasions bring an end to Roman culture or to the influence of Roman values. As King Theodoric the Goth was fond of remarking: "An able Goth wishes to be like a Roman; but only a poor Roman would want to be like a Goth."

THE SHAPING OF A NEW WORLDVIEW

As the empire sustained attack from external forces and began to fragment along old fault lines, it seemed that a new age was beginning. Christ had promised to come again at the end of time, when all human souls would be judged. How, then, should Christians live in this new world and prepare for that imminent event? The men who forged answers to this question were contemporaries who knew

and influenced one another, though they did not always agree. They are now regarded as "fathers" of the Church: Jerome (c. 340–420), who came from the northeastern edge of Italy; Ambrose (c. 340–397), who grew up in Trier and was eventually named bishop of Milan; and Augustine (354–430), born and raised in North Africa.

Jerome: Translating the Christian Message

Jerome's signal contribution to the culture of the Roman West was his translation of the Bible from Hebrew and Greek into Latin. Known as the Vulgate or "common" version, it was not the first attempt to produce a Latin Bible—but it quickly became the standard, and remained so until the sixteenth century (see Chapter 13). Jerome was also an influential commentator on the Bible's interpretation, arguing that pagan learning could and should be adapted to Christian aims. The perennial problem, of course, was that one was always tempted to appreciate classical literature for its own sake, and not for the light it shed on Christian truths. Jerome himself never entirely succeeded in subordinating his love for classical authors, especially Cicero, to his love for God. Perhaps in an effort to compensate for this, Jerome became a rigorous ascetic and a fervent promoter of monasticism. He also held a narrow view of women's roles that exercised a strong influence on some later Christian teachers.

Ambrose and the Authority of the Church

Jerome was primarily a scholar. Ambrose, by contrast, was an aristocratic man of the world who helped to define the relationship between the sacred authority of the Church and the secular authority of worldly rulers. As patriarch of the imperial administrative capital at Milan, he fearlessly rebuked the pious emperor Theodosius. On matters of faith, he declared, "The emperor is within the Church, not above the Church."

Ambrose was also an admirer of Cicero—but because of Cicero's Stoicism, not his prose. Ambrose wrote an ethics handbook, *On the Duties of Ministers*, which drew heavily on Cicero's treatise *On Duties*, written nearly four centuries earlier for the senatorial elite of the Roman republic. Unlike Cicero, however, Ambrose argued that the goal of human conduct should be reverence for God, not social or political advancement. Even more fundamentally, Ambrose argued that God assists all Christians by sharing with them the power of divine grace, but extends more grace to some Christians than to others. This doctrine would be refined and amplified by his disciple, Augustine.

The Salvation of Saint Augustine

Apart from Jesus, Augustine is often considered the greatest of all Christianity's founders. He may be the most important Christian thinker of all time. His theology is essential to the doctrine of the medieval Church and thus to modern Roman Catholicism, and it also had a profound effect on Martin Luther and on the development of Protestant Christianities (see Chapter 13). Even today, many Christian philosophers describe themselves as neo-Augustinians.

Augustine's understanding of Christianity was the result of a long process of self-discovery, which he described in a remarkable book, the *Confessions*, a series of autobiographical reflections addressed to God. Augustine was not, as Jerome and Ambrose were, a confident Christian from the cradle. His father was not a Christian, and although his mother was, he scorned her influence and refused baptism. Full of ambition, he left North Africa for Italy as a young man, winning early fame as a teacher and charismatic orator. All the while, he gravitated from one philosophical system to another without finding intellectual or spiritual satisfaction. He regarded Christianity as a religion for fools, and only the appeal of Ambrose's teachings drove him to enquire further. After a spiritual epiphany described in his *Confessions*, Augustine decided to embrace Christianity. Yet his struggle to grasp and explain its paradoxes occupied him for the rest of his life. His skills as a preacher and commentator led to his rapid advancement in the Church hierarchy, and he returned to North Africa as the bishop of Hippo Regis in 395.

Although he led an extremely active life—when he died in 430, he was defending Hippo against the Vandals—Augustine still found time to write more than a hundred treatises analyzing the problems of Christian belief. All of these grapple with a basic question: if humanity is the creation of an omnipotent God whose nature is entirely good, why are human beings so profoundly sinful? Augustine adduced himself as a supreme example. In the *Confessions*, he remembers that he and a few other boys once stole some pears from a neighbor's garden, simply for the sake of doing something bad. He also recounted his many sexual adventures as a young man and recalled that he had prayed, "O God, give me chastity—but not yet!" In short, he argued that the human inclination toward evil is innate. But how, if we are the creatures of a good God?

Augustine traced the origin of evil back to the Garden of Eden, where God had given Adam and Eve, the first human couple, the freedom to follow his will or their own. He concluded that all the evils of the world are the result of this Original Sin: the human propensity to place our own desires ahead of God's. This fact alone would justify God's condemnation. But because God is merciful, he chose instead to save some human beings through the sacrifice of his son, Jesus.

Why only some? Because human beings are inherently sinful, Augustine reasoned, they cannot achieve salvation on their own; they need to be led to accept Jesus by an act of God's grace—hence the power of Augustine's own transformative experience, which led him to embrace Christianity *against his own will* but in accordance with God's. God alone makes this choice, and by granting grace to some and not to others he allows a portion of the human race to achieve salvation. If this seems unfair, Augustine would answer that strict fairness would condemn everyone to hell and that the basis for God's choice is a mystery far beyond the realm of human comprehension.

Defending the City of God

After the sack of Rome in 410, Augustine knew that some staunchly traditional Romans blamed Christianity for it. According to them, the attack on their city resulted from the removal of the altar of Victory from the Senate chamber. In response, Augustine wrote one of his most famous works, *The City of God*, a new interpretation of human history. He argued that mankind has always been divided into two opposing societies: those who live for the world and those who seek eternal life. The former belong to the City of Man, and their rewards are the riches, fame, and power they may win on earth, all tainted by sin. Only those who live in the City of God will be saved on Judgment Day.

CLASSICAL LEARNING AND THE CHRISTIAN LIFE

Jerome, Ambrose, and Augustine were members of the first generation to grow up in a world where Christianity was legal, even normal. For three centuries there had been no such thing as a Roman Christian: this was a contradiction in terms. Now, however, many Romans *were* Christians. How could these identities be reconciled? None of these influential teachers wanted to discard the heritage of the past. Since the time of Socrates, philosophy had been characterized by its capacity to absorb and blend many competing ideas. Christian intellectuals wanted to be regarded as philosophers, but they also wanted to replace the doctrines of pagan philosophy with the doctrine of Christ. To do this, they needed to make pagan learning applicable to a Christian way of life.

Preserving and Recycling the Classics

Reinterpreting classical culture for a Christian audience involved careful selection. Those pagan authors whose works were most immediately useful to Christians, like Cicero and Virgil, enjoyed continued celebrity. Those texts that had long educated students in the liberal arts were also preserved, alongside major classics of Latin poetry as well as histories that recorded the errors of Rome's pagan past. But texts that could not be readily adapted to Christian purposes were subjected to rigorous editing. One of the men who undertook this task was Anicius Manlius Severinus Boethius (*boh-EE-thee-uhs*, c. 480–524), an aristocrat attached to the court of Theodoric. His goal was to preserve the best aspects of ancient learning by compiling a series of handbooks and anthologies that packaged pagan texts in ways he deemed appropriate for Christian readers.

This is most evident in *The Consolation of Philosophy*, which Boethius wrote in prison after Theodoric condemned him to death for treason. (The justice of the charge is unclear.) In this treatise, he concludes that happiness is not found in earthly rewards such as riches or fame but in the "highest good," which is God. He comes to this realization through a series of imaginary conversations with "Lady Philosophy," the embodiment of wisdom. For the next millennium, Boethius's *Consolation* was one of the most read and imitated books in the West: the ultimate example of classical philosophy's absorption into the Christian worldview.

Monastic Education

The vital work of preserving selected classics was increasingly done by monks, whose way of life had undergone some significant changes. Leaders of the monastic movement recognized that few men were capable of ascetic feats, and some disapproved of them. Rather, they advocated a more moderate approach and emphasized the benefits of communal life.

In the Roman West, the most influential proponent of the monastic movement was a contemporary of Boethius, Benedict of Nursia (c. 480–c. 547), the son of a

Roman aristocrat. Benedict founded a monastery at Monte Cassino, southeast of Rome, where he urged his followers to adopt "a simple rule for beginners." Benedict's *Rule* is notable for its brevity and practicality. It established a carefully defined cycle of daily prayers, lessons, and worship. Physical labor was encouraged—idleness, Benedict declared, was "an enemy of the soul"—but there was also time for private study and contemplation. In all such matters, Benedict left much to the discretion of the leader of the monastery. This man was the abbot, from the Syriac word *abba*, "father."

Cassiodorus and the Classical Canon

Benedict believed that monks must study the Bible in order to participate fully in a life of worship. And because many monks entered religious life as children, the monastery would need to provide schooling. Through this somewhat roundabout path, classical learning entered the monastic curriculum.

The man largely responsible for this was Flavius Magnus Aurelius Cassiodorus Senator (c. 490–c. 583), a younger contemporary of Benedict. Like Boethius, Cassiodorus (*cass-ee-oh-DOHR-uhs*) was attached to Theodoric's court

CASSIODORUS. This frontispiece from a Bible, produced in a monastery in Britain around the year 700, depicts Cassiodorus as a copyist and keeper of books. Monasteries were instrumental in changing the form of the book from the ancient scroll to the modern codex. Because their parchment pages were heavy, codices were customarily stored in cupboards, lying flat, as we see them here.

and was for many years the secretary in charge of the king's correspondence. He also wrote a *History of the Goths*, which depicted Theodoric's people as part of Rome's history. After Theodoric's death, Cassiodorus founded an important monastery where he composed his most influential work, the *Institutes*.

Cassiodorus believed that study of classical literature was an essential preliminary to a proper understanding of the Bible. The *Institutes* is essentially a syllabus, a list of readings arranged to begin with simpler, straightforward works before moving on to more difficult studies and finally to the demanding study of theology. Cassiodorus thereby defined a classical canon that formed the basis of Christian education in the Roman West.

In order to ensure that his monks had access to the necessary readings, Cassiodorus also encouraged the copying of books. Under his influence, monasteries thus became engines for the collection, preservation, and transmission of knowledge. It is worth noting that nearly all the Greek and Latin texts on which we rely for our study of western civilizations survive because they were copied in monasteries.

Monasteries also developed and disseminated an important new information technology: the codex. For millennia, the book had been a scroll, a clumsy format that made searching for a particular passage difficult and confined the reader to one passage at a time. The codex facilitates indexing (from the Latin word for "finger") because a reader can flip back and forth among various pages and keep a finger in one place while looking at another. Codices also store information more safely and efficiently, because they compress many hundreds of pages within protective bindings. They are less wasteful, too, because texts can be copied on both sides of a page. They even make finding a given book easier, since titles can be written on the codex's spine. It's arguable, in fact, that the invention of the codex was more revolutionary than the invention of printing a thousand years later. Unless you are scrolling through a digital version, your copy of *Western Civilizations* is a codex.

After You Read This Chapter

Go to **INQUIZITIVE** to see what you've learned—and learn what you've missed—with personalized feedback along the way.

REVIEWING THE OBJECTIVES

- A number of historical factors shaped the way that Jesus's teachings were received. Describe the most important of these.
- The expansion of Rome and the strain on its central government posed significant challenges in the third century. How did Roman emperors respond?
- Christianity's acceptance as a legal religion changed it in profound ways. Why was this?
- In the fourth and fifth centuries, a new wave of migrations penetrated to the very heart of the empire. What made this possible?
- The differences between traditional Roman and Christian cultures were gradually reconciled through the efforts of Christian intellectuals. Why was this considered necessary?

CONCLUSION

Since the English historian Edward Gibbon published the first volume of *The Decline and Fall of the Roman Empire* in 1776, a year when Britain's own empire suffered a setback, more has been written about "the fall of Rome" than on the passing of any other civilization. Gibbon himself blamed Christianity, depicting it as a debilitating disease that sapped the empire's strength. Others have accused the barbarians whose movements put pressure on Rome's frontiers. But even in the time of Julius Caesar, Roman moralists had declared that Rome was in decline. Any self-respecting Roman republican would say that Rome fell when Augustus came to power.

More recent scholarship has argued that transformation is a more accurate model for understanding this period. No civilization is static and unchanging; civilizations, like human beings, are living organisms. Indeed, any evidence of Rome's decline can also be read as evidence of its adaptability. The imperial policies of Septimius Severus and Diocletian responded to the realities of Rome's size and diversity. The settlement of frontier peoples in Rome's western provinces gave rise to hybrid polities that found new uses for Roman buildings, political offices, and laws. Through Christianity, the Latin language as well as the administrative structures and culture of ancient Rome were preserved and extended. The flexibility of the Roman political system made this possible, because it was inclusive to a degree that no modern empire has ever matched.

Still, this transformation changed what it meant to be Roman, to the extent that historians now call this period "late antiquity" to distinguish it from the classical world that preceded it. By the seventh century, indeed, so much had changed that the contours of three distinctive civilizations can be discerned, each one exhibiting different aspects of Roman influence and crystallizing around different regions of the former empire. We will explore each of these civilizations in Chapter 7.

PEOPLE, IDEAS, AND EVENTS IN CONTEXT

- What were the main differences between **JESUS** and the Jewish leaders of his day?
- How did **PAUL OF TARSUS** reach out to the peoples of the Hellenistic world? How did his teachings influence the development of early Christianity?
- In what ways did **DIOCLETIAN**'s division of the empire and his institution of the **TETRARCHY** respond to longstanding problems?
- How and why was Christianity changed under **CONSTANTINE**? What effects did this have on attitudes toward women and their role in the church?
- How did the relocation of the imperial capital to **CONSTANTINOPLE** contribute to the growing divide within the Roman Empire? How did the mass migrations of frontier peoples then transform the Latin West?
- What were the key contributions of **JEROME**, **AMBROSE**, and **AUGUSTINE** to the development of a specifically Christian outlook by the end of the fourth century?
- How did **BOETHIUS**, **BENEDICT**, and **CASSIODORUS** reshape classical culture in the fifth century?

THINKING ABOUT CONNECTIONS

- In your opinion, which phenomenon had a more profound impact on Rome: the overextension of imperial power or the mass migration of peoples from Rome's frontier? Why?
- Few historians would now agree with the judgment of Edward Gibbon, who posited that Christianity destroyed the Roman Empire. But to what extent did Christianity alter the traditional values and infrastructure of the Roman state? Were these alterations inevitable?

STORY LINES

- Justinian's attempt to reconquer the western territories of the Roman Empire was actually more destructive than the mass migrations of the previous centuries.

- Byzantine culture combined Roman legal and political systems with the learning of classical Greece while being shaped by Orthodox Christianity.

- The close connections among religion, politics, and commerce helped to drive the rapid expansion of Islam in the eighth century.

- In western Europe, the disintegration of Roman political and economic infrastructures had a destabilizing effect, but this was countered by the success of the Frankish kingdom and the spread of monasticism.

- The empire of Charlemagne unified vast portions of northwestern Europe under a single centralized government, fostering important administrative, economic, and cultural developments.

CHRONOLOGY

481–511	Reign of Clovis, king of the Franks
527–565	Reign of Justinian
570–632	Lifetime of Muhammad
590–604	Papacy of Gregory the Great
636–651	Arab conquests of Persia, Palestine, Egypt, and North Africa
661–750	Dominion of the Umayyad dynasty in the Islamic world
717–787	Iconoclast Controversy in Byzantium
717–751	The Carolingian dynasty shares power with Merovingian kings
730	The Venerable Bede completes his history of the English church
750–930	Dominion of the Abassid dynasty in Baghdad and the Umayyad dynasty in Al-Andalus (Spain)
751	Pepin becomes king of the Franks
768–814	Reign of Charlemagne
800–1000	Period of Viking invasions
871–899	Reign of Alfred the Great in England

Before You Read This Chapter

Rome's Three Heirs, 500–950

Around the year 600, the peoples of Britain were approached by missionaries from Rome. These Latin-speaking evangelists had to find a way to translate the central ideas of their faith into languages and concepts that made sense in a new context. So they looked for ways to meld Roman practices with indigenous ones, building churches on sacred sites and turning the worship of pagan gods into Christian rituals. An account of these negotiations comes down to us in a remarkable book written several generations later. In *The History of the English Church and People*, a monk named Bede (c. 672–735) described how Celtic and Anglo-Saxon tribes were uneasily united under the Roman Church. But he also shows how Roman Christian ideals were changed in the process.

This is just one example of the way that Rome's legacy was transmitted and transformed during the era known as the Middle Ages. This term is a problematic one because it is a later invention: in the seventeenth century, intellectuals began to argue that an intermediate, "medieval period" (*medium ævum*) separated their own "modern age" from the empire of ancient Rome, which many European states were trying to emulate. But it is arguable that the period between 500 and 1500 was the beginning of that "modern age." It was during this millennium that the foundations of modern states were laid and when the relationships among Judaism, Christianity, and Islam were first negotiated. In fact, three new civilizations became heirs of the Western civilizations formerly encompassed by Rome: the New Rome of Byzantium, the new religious empire of Islam, and the western European territories loyal to the Roman Church. Each of these interlocking civilizations preserved and modified different aspects of their shared Roman inheritance. Our world is still being shaped by the interactions among them.

JUSTINIAN'S IMPERIAL AMBITIONS

As we observed in Chapter 6, the eastern and western territories of Rome's empire were becoming divided along linguistic, cultural, and economic lines. By the end of the

fourth century, this division also started to become political, as the imperial capital at Constantinople exercised less and less influence over the emerging barbarian kingdoms of western Europe. And when a new emperor attempted to reverse that trend and reunify the disparate parts of the empire, his efforts actually made that division permanent.

Justinian's Attempted Reconquest

Justinian (r. 527–65) was the most ambitious emperor since Constantine, and his drive for reunification was at least partly driven by his own background. Although the territories that he ruled were largely Greek-speaking, Justinian himself came from the Latin-speaking province of Dardania (now Serbia) and was an outsider to the elite Hellenistic culture of his capital. He became even more of an outsider when he married a former entertainer, Theodora, who alienated the cultivated aristocrats of the court.

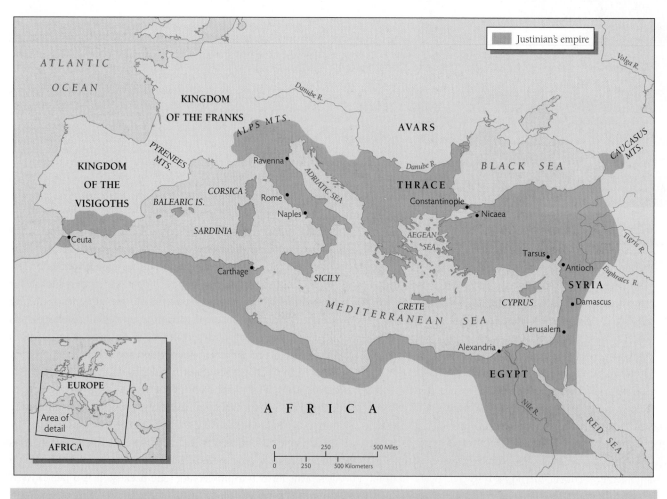

THE MEDITERRANEAN WORLD UNDER JUSTINIAN, 527–565. Compare this map with the one on page 152. Here, the green shading represents those regions controlled by Justinian. ▪ *What was the geographical extent of Justinian's empire?* ▪ *Which areas of the former Roman Empire did Justinian not attempt to reconquer?* ▪ *What may have been the strategy behind these campaigns?*

In 533, Justinian sent his general Belisarius to conquer the Vandal kingdom of northwest Africa, and his initial victory led to campaigns in Ostrogothic Italy and Visigothic Spain. But these early victories were illusory, because they drastically strained imperial resources and destroyed the very infrastructures of old Roman heartlands: roads, aqueducts. Justinian's need to levy soldiers led to oppressive taxes on vitally important regions like Egypt and Syria, which undermined support for his imperial project. These campaigns also distracted attention from dangers closer to Constantinople: the developing strength of the Persian Sassanids, which began to encroach on the eastern frontier.

The pressures of war were further exacerbated by the outbreak of a terrible plague pandemic in 541–42, now considered the first global catastrophe of this kind. Indeed, researchers in 2013 confirmed that it was caused by the same bacterium that spawned the terrible Black Death of the fourteenth century (see Chapter 10). It may have been just as deadly, affecting regions from central Asia to Scandinavia and reaching down into Africa and the Indian Ocean. It is estimated to have killed a large portion of the world's population at that time, some 25 million people; and it would recur in some places every generation or so for the next 200 years. Justinian himself was stricken with the disease, and though he recovered from it, this pandemic is still known as the Justinianic Plague.

Justinian's Impact on the West

Justinian's wars proved more devastating to Italy than the previous incursions of barbarian peoples had been. Around Rome, vital water supply lines were cut as the elaborate system of conduits and reservoirs were damaged and never repaired. Parts of the Italian countryside returned to marshland, and some areas would not be drained again until the twentieth century. In 568, a new people, the Lombards, took advantage of the situation and occupied the northern third of the peninsula. Thereafter, Italy would be divided between Lombard territories in the north and imperial territories in the southeast, with the city of Rome and its region precariously sandwiched between them. This tripartite division remained the essential political configuration of Italy until the nineteenth century. In fact, it still divides Italian politics to this day.

Imperial control over North Africa lasted only a few generations longer. Weakened by religious conflict and heavy taxation, this area fell to invading Muslims in the seventh century, along with Egypt and the rest of Roman Africa (as will be discussed later). When it did, Christianity in these regions largely disappeared, too, although a vibrant Christian community continued to flourish in Ethiopia. Meanwhile, tensions between the Visigoths and their Roman subjects in Spain continued, making it another territory easily absorbed by Islam.

The Codification of Roman Law

Justinian's most positive and lasting accomplishment to the legacy of imperial power was his codification of Roman law. This was project long overdue: since the time of the third-century jurists (see Chapter 5), the number of statutes, edicts, and legal decisions had multiplied, and the resulting body of law was both massive and self-contradictory. Moreover, conditions had changed so radically within the empire that many legal principles could no longer be applied. When Justinian came to power in 527, one of his first initiatives was to bring existing precedents into harmony with actual historical conditions and thereby to restore the prestige and power of the law.

This work was undertaken by a team of Latin-speaking lawyers under the supervision of a jurist called Tribonian. Its first publication was the Code, a systematic compilation of older imperial statutes. This was later supplemented by another book, the Novels (*Novellae,* "new laws"), containing the legislation of Justinian and his immediate successors. The commission also completed a summary of the writings of Rome's great legal authorities, the Digest. Its final product was the *Institutes,* a textbook of legal principles. Together, these four volumes constitute the *Corpus Juris Civilis,* the "body of civil law."

The *Corpus* was an extraordinary achievement, and it became the foundation on which all subsequent imperial law would rest. It eventually influenced the legal systems of many nations. The nineteenth-century Napoleonic Code—still the basis of law in France, Spain, much of Latin America, and the state of Louisiana—is essentially based on the *Corpus* of Justinian. The canon law of the medieval Roman Church would too be influenced by it (see Chapter 9).

The *Corpus* also had a profound impact on political philosophy. Starting from the maxim that "what pleases the prince has the force of law," it granted unlimited powers to the emperor and would therefore become a foundation for absolutism (see Chapter 15). Yet the *Corpus* also provided support for constitutional forms of government, because it maintained that a sovereign's powers are delegated by the people. Equally important is the fundamental principle that the state is a corporate body, not the extension of an individual's private property. The modern conception of the state as a public entity derives from the Roman law codified in the *Corpus.*

THE ROMAN EMPIRE OF BYZANTIUM

With the failure of imperial reunification, the history of the eastern Roman Empire enters a new phase. Indeed, it has usually been regarded as a new entity, the Byzantine Empire, a name derived from the ancient port where Constantinople was situated. But according to the citizens of this empire, it never ceased to be Rome, and they were never anything but Romans—even though their official language was Greek. It was they who carried forward Roman traditions, values, and institutions.

Initially, however, this new Rome was struggling for survival. By 610, its influence extended only as far west as the Adriatic and a few parts of southern Italy. On its southeastern border, the Persians had conquered almost all of Syria and Palestine. They had even plundered Jerusalem. With an enormous effort, the emperor Heraclius (r. 610–41) rallied his remaining military powers and routed the Persians, recapturing Jerusalem in 627. But these gains were short-lived. A wave of Arab armies, inspired by the new religion of Islam, soon occupied the recently reconquered territories and claimed Jerusalem as a holy site for Muslims, too. They also absorbed the entire Persian Empire and rapidly made their way westward to North Africa.

The Arabs then took to the sea and, in 677, attempted a naval conquest of Constantinople. Repulsed, they made another attempt in 717 by means of a concerted land and sea operation. This new threat was countered by the emperor Leo III (r. 717–41). Deploying keen strategy and a secret incendiary mixture known as "Greek fire," imperial forces were able to defeat the Arabs. Over the next few decades, Byzantium reconquered most of Asia Minor, which became the core of the empire.

in times of upheaval. No polity in western Europe had anything resembling such effective mechanisms of government until a much later period.

Strong, self-perpetuating political institutions thus constituted a major source of stability in the eastern Roman Empire, which survived for more than a thousand years after the founding of Constantinople (see Chapter 12). The imperial bureaucracy regulated prices and wages, maintained systems of licensing, and controlled exports and trade. Its highly educated officials also supervised many aspects of social and cultural life, overseeing schools, the organization of the Orthodox Church, and the observance of religious rites and holidays. Even the popular sport of chariot racing—New Rome's exciting answer to gladiatorial combat—fell under strict supervision, as did the regulation of the various teams' fiercely competitive fans. Efficient bureaucracies also regulated the army and navy, the courts, and the diplomatic service, endowing these agencies with organizational strengths incomparable in their time.

Another source of stability was Byzantium's well-managed economy, which was far superior to that of western Europe. Commerce and cities continued to flourish as they had done in late antiquity. Constantinople became a central emporium for exotic eastern luxury goods and western raw materials. The empire also nurtured and protected its own industries, most notably the manufacture and weaving of silk, and it was renowned for its stable gold and silver coinage. Nor was Constantinople the only great urban center. The Hellenistic capital Antioch and the bustling cities of Thessalonica and Trebizond were very large and prosperous. Any one of them would have dwarfed any western European city; Constantinople may have had a population of close to a million. In the West at this time, Paris was a tiny village and Rome had a few thousand people living among the ruins.

Sources of Stability

In some ways, the internal politics of the Byzantine Empire were as tumultuous as its changing neighborhood. All power was concentrated in the imperial court, around emperors who claimed to rule autonomously, and this meant that opposition usually took the form of intrigue, treason, and violence. (The very word byzantine has come to denote cloak-and-dagger machinations or elaborate systems of hierarchy and bureaucracy.) In reality, though, many able rulers wielded their powers very effectively, through a centralized government that continued to function even

Orthodoxy, Iconoclasm, and Identity

Strong governance and a healthy economy: viewed from our perspective, these seem to be the most important aspects of a thriving society. Yet the inhabitants of New Rome also placed a high value on religious cohesion. In old Rome, the mos maiorum had undergirded Roman pride and superiority; in New Rome, Orthodox Christianity occupied the same fundamental place. The stakes of Byzantine doctrinal disputes were therefore high, and they were further heightened because emperors took an active role in them.

The most contentious issue was the meaning and use of religious images, and in the eighth century this broke out in a violent clash known as the Iconoclast ("image-breaking") Controversy. Christians had been accustomed to expressing their devotion to Christ and the saints through the making and veneration of images. At the same time, however, there was always an awareness that any representation of a holy person came close to being a form of idolatry—something that Jewish tradition strongly condemned, as did the new religion of Islam. Although Christians insisted that images were only *aids* to worship, not *objects* of worship, the line between the two was very fine.

In Byzantium, the veneration of icons was an especially potent part of daily devotion; any attempt to suppress them was bound to be contentious. But that is precisely what the Iconoclasts advocated. They argued

that honoring images was blasphemous. For their part, traditionalist Iconodules ("image servants") retorted that images were never objects of worship; rather, icons were windows through which a glimpse of Heaven might be granted to humans.

The Iconoclast movement was initiated by the same Emperor Leo III who had saved Constantinople from invasion by Muslims, and it is even possible that Muslim doctrine played a role in his thinking; by cracking down on icons, he may have been attempting to answer a major Muslim criticism of Christianity. There may also have been political and financial considerations behind the campaign, as the emperor tried to strengthen his control over the Orthodox Church and combat the growing power of monasteries, which were major producers of icons. So when the monasteries rallied to protect icons, Leo and his successors retaliated by confiscating much of their wealth.

The Iconoclast Controversy was resolved toward the end of the eighth century in favor of the Iconodules. But it had some long-lasting effects. One was the destruction of many artworks produced or preserved in Byzantium. This means that examples of Christian artistry from the first eight centuries after Jesus's death are very rare and can be found mainly in Italy, Palestine, or Egypt, which were beyond the reach of the Iconoclast emperors. A second consequence was the widening of a religious and political breach between the Greek East and the Latin West. Prior to Emperor Leo's initiatives, the patriarch of Rome—known familiarly as "papa" in Latin slang—had often been a close ally of Byzantium's rulers. But iconoclasm called into question not only the veneration of images but the cult of the saints, and by extension the claims of papal primacy that were based on the Roman patriarch's claim to be Saint Peter's successor (see Chapter 6).

The ultimate defeat of iconoclasm crystallized some aspects of belief and practice that came to be characteristic of Byzantine identity. One was a renewed emphasis on the Orthodox faith as the key to political unity and military success. This subsequently enforced the hegemony of Constantinople's own Christian traditions, marginalizing those of Syria and Armenia. Fear of heresy also tended to inhibit freedom of expression, and not just in religious matters.

Tradition and Innovation

If Orthodoxy was central to the identity of Byzantium, so was its direct link with the Hellenistic past and the heritage of ancient Greece. Byzantine schools based their instruction on classical Greek literature to a degree that might seem

Competing Viewpoints

Debating the Power of Icons

> *The Iconoclast Controversy of the eighth century divided Byzantine society and was a factor in the growing division between the Latin Church of Rome and the Greek Orthodox Church. The excerpts below are representative of the two main arguments voiced at the time. The first is from a treatise by John of Damascus (c. 675–749), a Christian in the service of the Muslim Umayyad caliphs. The second is an official report issuing from the synod convened by the emperor Constantine V (r. 741–75) in 754. Constantine was carrying forward the iconoclastic policies of his father, Leo III.*

John of Damascus, On Holy Images

Now adversaries say: God's commands to Moses the law-giver were, "Thou shalt adore the Lord thy God, and thou shalt worship him alone, and thou shalt not make to thyself a graven thing that is in heaven above, or in the earth beneath." . . .

These injunctions were given to the Jews on account of their proneness to idolatry. Now we, on the contrary, are no longer in leading strings. . . . We have passed the stage of infancy, and reached the perfection of manhood . . . and know what may be imaged and what may not. . . . An image is a likeness of the original with a certain difference, for it is not an exact reproduction of the original. Thus, the Son is the living, substantial, unchangeable Image of the invisible God, bearing in Himself the whole Father, being in all things equal to Him, differing only in being begotten by the Father. . . . That which is divine is immutable; there is no change in Him, nor shadow of change. . . . God has noted and settled all that He would do, the unchanging future events before they came to pass. In the same way, a man who wished to build a house, would first make and think out a plan. Again, visible things are images of invisible and intangible things, on which they throw a faint light. Holy Scripture clothes in figure God and the angels. . . . If, therefore, Holy Scripture, providing for our need, ever putting before us what is intangible, clothes it in flesh, does it not make an image of what is thus invested with our nature, and brought to the level of our desires, yet invisible? . . . For the invisible things of God since the creation of the world are made visible through images. We see images in creation which remind us faintly of God, as when, for instance, we speak of the holy and adorable Trinity, imaged by the sun, or light, or burning rays, or by a running fountain, or a full river, or by the mind, speech, or the spirit within us, or by a rose tree, or a sprouting flower, or a sweet fragrance. . . .

Source: Excerpted from *St. John Damascene on Holy Images*, trans. Mary H. Allies (London: 1898), pp. 6–12.

surprising given the more tentative attitude toward classical learning in western Europe (see Chapter 6). Educated people around the Byzantine court who quoted only a single line of Homer could expect their listeners to recognize the entire passage from which it came. In the English-speaking world, only the King James Bible has ever achieved the same degree of cultural saturation. For the intellectuals of Byzantium, indeed, Homeric epics were a kind of sacred text.

Byzantine scholars also intensively studied the philosophy of Plato and the historical prose of Thucydides. By contrast, Aristotle's works were less well known, while many other philosophical traditions of antiquity were deemed dangerous to Orthodox belief. Somewhat paradoxically, Justinian—who had presided over the codification of ancient Roman (and thus pagan) law—registered his distrust of philosophy by shutting down the Athenian academies that had existed since Plato's day. Eventually, the emperor Alexius Comnenus (d. 1118) would ban the teaching of Aristotelian logic. The traditions of Greek scientific inquiry and the advances of Hellenistic science were also neglected.

Canons of the Synod of 754

It is the unanimous doctrine of all the holy Fathers and of the six Ecumenical Synods, that no one may imagine any kind of separation or mingling in opposition to the unsearchable, unspeakable, and incomprehensible union of the two natures in the one *hypostasis* or person. What avails, then, the folly of the painter, who from sinful love of gain depicts that which should not be depicted—that is, with his polluted hands he tries to fashion that which should only be believed in the heart and confessed with the mouth? He makes an image and calls it Christ. The name *Christ* signifies *God and man*. Consequently it is an image of God and man, and consequently he has in his foolish mind, in his representation of the created flesh, depicted the Godhead which cannot be represented, and thus mingled what should not be mingled. Thus he is guilty of a double blasphemy—the one in making an image of the Godhead, and the other by mingling the Godhead and manhood . . . like the Monophysites, or he represents the body of Christ as not made divine and separate and as a person apart, like the Nestorians.

The only admissible figure of the humanity of Christ, however, is bread and wine in the holy Supper. This and no other form, this and no other type, has he chosen to represent his incarnation. Bread he ordered to be brought, but not a representation of the human form, so that idolatry might not arise. And as the body of Christ is made divine, so also this figure of the body of Christ, the bread, is made divine by the descent of the Holy Spirit; it becomes the divine body of Christ by the mediation of the priest who, separating the oblation from that which is common, sanctifies it. . . .

Source: Excerpted from *The Seven Ecumenical Councils of the Undivided Church*, trans. H. R. Percival, in *Nicene and Post-Nicene Fathers*, 2d Series, ed. P. Schaff and H. Wace (repr. Grand Rapids, MI: 1955), pp. 543–44.

Questions for Analysis

1. To what other phenomena does John of Damascus compare the making of images? How do these comparisons help him to make his argument in favor of them?

2. To what phenomena do the theologians of the synod compare the making of images? Why do they declare the bread and wine of the Eucharist to be the only legitimate representations of Christ?

3. What is the significance of the fact that John of Damascus did not fall under the jurisdiction of the emperor of Byzantium but that of the Muslim Umayyad caliph? What conclusions can you draw about the relative freedoms in these two realms?

Tradition was more highly prized than innovation. The benefit of this, for posterity, was the rescue of Greek and Hellenistic writings for later ages. The vast majority of ancient Greek texts known today survive only because they were copied by Byzantine scribes.

In further contrast to western Europe, as we shall see, the Byzantine educational system extended to many commoners and was open to women as well as to men. Although most girls from aristocratic or prosperous families were educated at home by private tutors, they nevertheless mingled freely with their male counterparts at court or on social occasions, and many female intellectuals were compared to Plato or Pythagoras. There were even female physicians in the Byzantine Empire, another extraordinary departure both from ancient tradition and from the practices of western Europe until the latter part of the nineteenth century.

Byzantine achievements in the realms of architecture and art are also remarkable. The finest example of both may be the church of Hagia Sophia ("Holy Wisdom") in Constantinople, constructed at enormous cost under the patronage of Justinian. It quickly came to define an architectural style unique to Byzantium. Its purpose was to symbolize the mysteries of the Christian religion and the holy knowledge imparted by Christ to the soul of the believer. For this reason, the architects paid little attention to the external appearance of the building. The interior, however, was decorated with richly colored mosaics, gold leaf, colored marble columns, and bits of tinted glass set on edge to refract rays of sunlight, like sparkling gems. Light appeared to be generated from within. The magnificent dome over its central square represented an unprecedented engineering feat and was upheld by four great arches springing from pillars at the four corners of the square. Its effect is heightened by the many windows placed around the dome's rim, which convey the impression that it floats in mid-air.

Many aspects of Byzantine arts and learning exerted strong influence on the craftsmen and scholars of western Europe through continued economic and cultural contact. The basilica of San Marco in Venice (c. 1063) reflects this influence distinctly, as do medieval mosaics in such cities as Ravenna and Palermo. Greek-speaking monasteries in southeastern Italy maintained especially close ties with their counterparts in the eastern empire, and many were allowed to practice the rituals of the Orthodox Church. Greek books—including the comedies of Aristophanes (Chapter 4)—were copied and preserved there. But much of the heritage of Western civilizations that was cultivated in Byzantium was largely inaccessible elsewhere in Europe, as the knowledge of Greek became increasingly rare.

MUHAMMAD AND THE TEACHINGS OF ISLAM

The civilization that formed around the religion of Islam mirrors the Roman Empire in its global reach and longevity; in this, it is truly one of Rome's heirs. Islam (Arabic for "submission") also resembles the early republic of Rome in that it was based on adherence to certain social and cultural norms. But whereas the Roman Empire was the vehicle for the spread of Christianity, the Islamic faith was itself the engine of imperial expansion. It has created empires, rather than depending on them.

The Revelations of Muhammad

Islam had its beginnings in Arabia, a desert land that neither the Romans nor the Persians had ever tried to conquer.

Arabian society was tribal; it did not revolve around urban settlements, and many Arabs were herdsmen living off the milk of their camels and the produce of desert oases. But like the Hittites in the second millennium B.C.E. (Chapter 1), their very mobility and ingenuity made them excellent explorers and long-distance traders. In the second half of the sixth century, when constant wars between Byzantium and Persia made travel dangerous, the Arabs quickly established themselves as guides and guardians of land routes between Africa and Asia.

As part of this process, towns began to emerge. The most prominent of these was Mecca, an ancient sacred site that lay at the crossroads of major caravan routes. Mecca was home to the Kaaba (*KAH-ah-bah*), a shrine housing the Black Stone. (It may be an ancient meteorite.) This was a powerful object of devotion, and the tribe that controlled this shrine, the Quraish (*kur-AYSH*), thus came to dominate the region, forming an aristocracy of traders and religious leaders.

Muhammad, the founder of Islam, was a member of this tribe. He was born in Mecca around 570 C.E. Orphaned early in life, he entered the service of a rich widow whom he later married. Until middle age he lived as a prosperous merchant. Then, around 610, he experienced a spiritual epiphany: the gods of his people were not many, they were one. This supreme God (in Arabic, *Allah*) was the sole ruler of the universe, like the Hebrews' Yahweh. But whereas the Hebrews' embrace of monotheism had been a long and gradual process, Muhammad's conversion was sudden and led to further revelations and his calling as a prophet.

At first, he was not successful in gaining converts. In Mecca, tribal leaders feared that his teachings would

HAGIA SOPHIA. This great monument to the artistry, engineering skill, and spirituality of Byzantium was built during the reign of Justinian. The four minarets at its corners were added in 1453, after Constantinople was absorbed into the empire of the Ottoman Turks. Hagia Sophia is now a mosque and a museum.

diminish the importance of the Kaaba. But the town of Yathrib, to the north, had no such concerns. Its representatives invited Muhammad to live among them, to serve as judge and arbiter in local rivalries. Muhammad and a few loyal friends accepted this invitation in the year 622. Because this migration—in Arabic, the Hijrah (*HIJ-ruh*)—marks the beginning of Muhammad's wider influence, Muslims regard this year as the first of their religion, just as Christians date all events to the birth of Jesus (see Chapter 6).

Muhammad changed the name of Yathrib to Medina ("City of the Prophet") and organized his followers into a community held together by shared economic ambitions as well as by a shared set of beliefs. Yet he did not abandon his desire to exercise political and prophetic authority among his own people. So he and his followers began raiding Quraish caravans traveling beyond Mecca. The Quraish could not continue to operate an extensive commercial enterprise in the face of these threats, and by 630 Muhammad had triumphed. He was invited back to Mecca and his kinsmen submitted themselves to his authority. Muhammad responded by promoting the Kaaba as Islam's holiest place, a status it maintains today. And because Mecca had long been a pilgrimage site for tribes throughout Arabia, many people were exposed to his teachings when they assembled there. At the time of Muhammad's death in 632, Islam had become an established faith.

Muhammad and the Qur'an

As its name indicates, Islam calls for submission to Allah, the same God worshiped by Jews and Christians. The Muslim saying "there is no god but Allah" is more accurately translated as "there is no divinity but God." For Muslims, the history and prophecies of the Hebrews are important components of their religion, as are the teachings of Jesus, who is venerated as a great prophet. But they consider Muhammad to be the last and greatest prophet, and the closest to God.

Muhammad's teachings are preserved in the sacred scripture of Islam, the Qur'an (*kuhr-AHN*), an Arabic word meaning "recitations." This is because Muhammad recited his revelations to listeners, who eventually gathered them together and transcribed them. This process continued after Muhammad's death and is renewed each time a Muslim memorizes and recites verses from the Qur'an. Unlike the Christian Gospels, which offer different perspectives on Jesus's ministry recorded a generation or two after his death, the Qur'an is considered a direct link with Muhammad. It is also unlike most books of the Bible because it is highly poetic, drawing on ancient genres of Arabic song.

Like Christianity, Islam teaches that a day of judgment is coming—soon. On this day, the righteous will be granted eternal life in a paradise of delights, but wrongdoers will be damned to a realm of eternal fire. Every person is therefore offered a fundamental choice: to begin a new life of divine service or to follow their own path. If they choose to follow God, they will be blessed; if they do not, God will turn away from them. The only sure means of achieving salvation is observance of the Five Pillars of the faith: submission to God's will as described in the teachings of Muhammad, frequent prayer, ritual fasting, the giving of alms, and an annual pilgrimage to Mecca (the *Hajj*).

Unlike Christianity, Islam is a religion without sacraments or priests. Although Muslims value the opportunity to come together for prayer, there is no prescribed liturgy. Islam more closely resembles Judaism as it developed after the Diaspora, when Jews no longer had access to the Temple priesthood but instead gathered around a master teacher (*rabbi*). Similarly, Muslims rely on a community leader (*imam*) or scholar qualified to comment on matters of faith. Like Judaism, Islam also emphasizes the inextricable connection between religious observance and daily life, between spirituality and politics. There is no opposition of sacred and secular authority, as in Christianity. But in marked contrast to Judaism, Islam is a religion that aspires to unite the world in a shared faith. This means that Muslims, like Christians, consider it their duty to engage in the work of conversion.

THE WIDENING ISLAMIC WORLD

The death of any charismatic leader is a moment of crisis. Muhammad and Alexander the Great represent very different types of leadership, but both were at the center of ambitious enterprises created by that leadership. Neither designated a successor, and both left behind close followers determined to inherit their power. Although the very survival of Islam seemed unlikely after Muhammad's death, within a generation it had come to encompass the oldest Western civilizations.

The Arabic Conquest of the West

Muhammad's closest allies were his father-in-law, Abu-Bakr (*ah-boo-BAHK-uhr*), and an early convert named Umar. After Muhammad's death, these two men agreed that Abu-Bakr

Analyzing Primary Sources

A Sura from the Qur'an

The Qur'an *preserves the teachings of Muhammad in a series of* suras, *or chapters. Composed in verse forms that draw on much older traditions of Arabic poetry, they are meant to be sung or chanted. Indeed, the word* Qur'an *means "recitations," referring both to Muhammad's method of revealing divine truths and to the Muslim practice of memorizing and repeating portions of this sacred scripture.*

Sura 81: The Overturning

In the Name of God the Compassionate
   the Caring

When the sun is overturned
When the stars fall away
When the mountains are moved
When the ten-month pregnant camels
   are abandoned
When the beasts of the wild are herded
   together   5
When the seas are boiled over
When the souls are coupled
When the girl-child buried alive is asked
   what she did to deserve murder
When the pages are folded out
When the sky is flayed open
When Jahím [the Day of Reckoning] 10
   is set ablaze
When the garden is brought near

Then a soul will know what it has prepared
I swear by the stars that slide,   15
   stars streaming, stars that sweep
   along the sky
By the night as it slips away
By the morning when the fragrant air
   breathes
This is the word of a messenger ennobled, empowered, ordained before
   the lord of the throne, holding sway
   there, keeping trust
Your friend [Muhammad] has not gone
   mad
He saw him on the horizon clear
He does not hoard for himself the
   unseen   20
This is not the word of a satan struck
   with stones
Where are you going?

This is a reminder to all beings
For those who wish to walk straight
Your only will is the will of God lord of all
   beings   25

Source: From *Approaching the Qur'an: The Early Revelations*, trans. Michael Sells (Ashland, OR: 1999), pp. 48–50.

Questions for Analysis

1. What impressions of Arab culture emerge from this sura? What does the litany of unlikely or mystical events reveal about the values of Muhammad's contemporaries?

2. How does Muhammad speak of himself and his role in society?

---

should be the prophet's *caliph*, a word meaning "deputy" or "representative," and began a campaign to subdue those Muslims unwilling to accept the caliph's authority. Abu-Bakr's forces began to move beyond the borders of Arabia, where they met only minimal resistance from Byzantine and Persian armies.

When Abu-Bakr died two years later, Umar succeeded as caliph and his followers continued northward. In 636, they routed a Byzantine army in Syria and quickly swept over the entire region, occupying the cities of Antioch, Damascus, and Jerusalem. In 637, they destroyed the main army of the Persians and took the Persian capital. By 651, the Arabian conquest of the ancient Persian Empire was virtually complete.

Muslim forces also turned westward toward North Africa, capturing Byzantine Egypt and extending their control throughout the rest of North Africa. Unable to take Constantinople from the sea, they crossed from North Africa into Visigothic Spain in 710, and quickly absorbed most of that territory. Within less than a century, followers of Islam had conquered the Near East and much of the Roman Mediterranean; in the process, the desert-dwelling Arabs had transformed themselves into the world's most daring seafarers.

How can we explain this achievement? On a basic level, the motivations are familiar: the search for richer territory and new wealth. There is little evidence that Arab Muslims attempted to convert subject peoples to the faith of Islam at this time. Instead, they aimed to establish themselves as a superior ruling class. Yet religion certainly played a crucial role in forging a shared identity among tribes used to fighting one another. This identity and sense of superiority must have been further strengthened by the absence of any serious opposition. Many peoples living within the Persian and Byzantine empires were restive and exhausted by the demands of far-reaching imperial bureaucracies. Moreover, Muslim leaders were more tolerant of different Christian sects and of their Jewish subjects. For all these reasons, Islam quickly spread over the territory between Egypt and Iran, and has been rooted there ever since.

The Shi'ite–Sunni Schism

But as these conquests widened the reach of Islam, disputes divided the Muslims of Mecca. When the caliph Umar died in 644, he was replaced by a member of the Umayyad (*oo-MY-yad*) family, a wealthy clan that had resisted Muhammad's authority. Opponents of this new caliph, Uthman, rallied instead around Muhammad's son-in-law, Ali, whose family ties to Muhammad made him seem a more appropriate choice. When Uthman was murdered in 656, Ali's supporters declared him the new caliph. But Uthman's powerful family refused to accept this. Ali was murdered and another member of the Umayyad family replaced him. From 661 to 750, this Umayyad dynasty ruled the Islamic world, establishing the caliphate's new capital at Damascus in Syria.

Ali's followers, however, did not accept defeat. They formed a separate group known as the Shi'ites (from *shi'a*, the Arabic word for "faction"). The Shi'ites insisted that only descendants of Ali and Muhammad's daughter Fatimah could legitimately rule the Muslim community. Moreover, the Shi'ites did not accept the customs (*sunna*) that had developed under the first two caliphs. Those Muslims who supported the Umayyad family and followed these customs were therefore known as Sunnis. This division between Shi'ites and Sunnis has lasted until the present day. The Shi'ites predominate

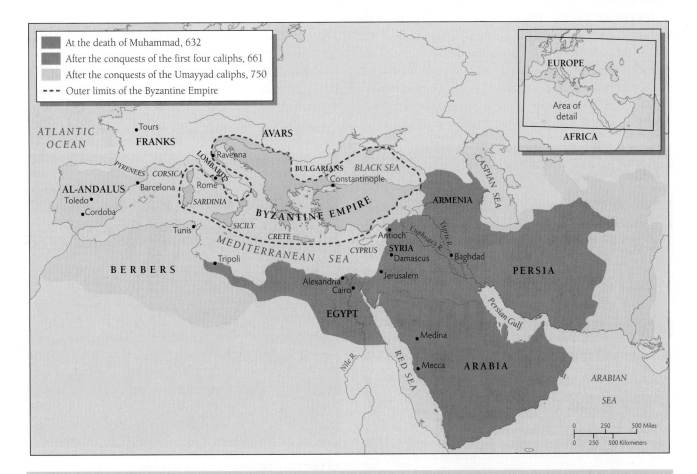

THE EXPANSION OF ISLAM TO 750. This map shows the steady advance of Islam, through Arab conquests, from the time of Muhammad to the middle of the eighth century. ▪ *What was the geographical extent of Islam in 750?* ▪ *What role did the Byzantine Empire play in the expansion of Islam?* ▪ *What conclusions can you draw regarding the period of especially rapid expansion in the generation after Muhammad's death?*

in Iran and are the largest single Muslim group in Iraq, yet they constitute only one-tenth of the world's Muslims and are often persecuted minorities in Sunni states.

The Umayyad and Abbasid Dynasties

The Umayyad capital at Damascus was a major Hellenistic and Roman city. And in many ways, the Umayyad Caliphate functioned as a Roman successor state; it even continued to employ Greek-speaking bureaucrats trained in the techniques of governance. But the failure of Umayyad attacks on Constantinople checked their power, which was also being challenged by a rival Sunni dynasty. The Abbasid clan claimed descent from one of Muhammad's uncles, and in 750 they led a successful rebellion that forced the Umayyads to retreat westward to their territories in Al-Andalus: the name for Muslim Spain.

In contrast to the Umayyads, the Abbasid Caliphate stressed Persian influences over Roman ones. Symbolic of this change was the shift in capitals from Damascus to Baghdad, where a new city was built near the ruins of the old Persian capital. The Abbasid caliphs also modeled their behavior on that of Persian princes and their administration on the autocratic rule of the former Persian Empire, imposing heavy taxation to support a large professional army and presiding over an extravagantly luxurious court. This is the

caliphate that produced the *Arabian Nights*, a collection of stories written in Baghdad under the Abbasids. A dominating presence in these tales is Harun al-Rashid (r. 786–809), whose reign marked the height of Abbasid power.

Meanwhile, the Umayyad dynasty continued to rule Al-Andalus and to claim legitimate descent from Muhammad. Relations between the Muslims of Spain and Persia were therefore very cold; but because their realms were far apart, the hostility between them rarely erupted into war. Instead, the two courts competed for preeminence through literary and cultural patronage, much as the Hellenistic kingdoms had done. Philosophers, artists, and especially poets flocked to both. The *Arabian Nights* was one product of this rivalry in Baghdad. Meanwhile, the caliphs at the Spanish capital of Córdoba amassed a library of more than 400,000 volumes— at a time when a European monastery with 100 books qualified as a major center of Christian learning.

Islamic Commerce and Industry

The Arabs' adaptation to life in highly urbanized regions was swift, and it allowed them to build on the long-established commercial infrastructures of the Persian, Hellenistic, and Roman empires. By the tenth century, Arab merchants had penetrated into southern Russia and equatorial Africa and had become masters of the caravan

THE GREAT UMAYYAD MOSQUE AT DAMASCUS. This mosque was built by Caliph al-Walid between 705 and 715. Byzantine influence is apparent in its arched colonnades, its mosaics, and its series of domes, all of which were replicated in much subsequent Islamic architecture. The mosaic over the central doorway, shown here, indicates that the visitor is entering paradise. The mosque was constructed on the foundations of a Roman temple and also incorporates a later Christian shrine dedicated to Saint John the Baptist. ▪ *Why would the caliph have chosen this site for his mosque?*

ARABIC CALLIGRAPHY. Muslim artists experimented with the art of calligraphy to make complex designs, sometimes abstract but often representing natural forms. This ink drawing on paper actually incorporates Arabic words. It dates from the seventh century, and also represents the Muslim mastery of papermaking.

routes that led eastward to India and China. Muslim ships established new trade routes across the Indian Ocean, the Persian Gulf, and the Caspian Sea, and dominated the southern Mediterranean as well.

The growth of Muslim commerce in this period was driven and sustained by a number of important new industries. Mosul, in Iraq, was a center for the manufacture of cotton cloth; Baghdad specialized in glassware, jewelry, pottery, and silks; Damascus was famous for its fine steel and for its woven-figured silk known as "damask"; Morocco was noted for leather-working; Toledo produced excellent swords. Drugs, perfumes, carpets, tapestries, brocades, woolens, satins, and a host of other products turned out by skilled artisans were carried throughout the Mediterranean world and into central Asia along the network of roads to China that came to be known as the Silk Road. With them went the faith of Islam, which took root among peoples of India, Pakistan, and Afghanistan.

One commodity in particular deserves special mention: paper. Arabs and Persians had learned papermaking from the Chinese and became masters of the art. By the end of the eighth century, Baghdad alone had more than a hundred shops where blank paper or books written on paper were sold. Paper was cheaper to produce, easier to store, and far easier to use than papyrus or parchment. As a result, paper replaced papyrus in the Muslim world by the early eleventh century—even in Egypt, the heartland of papyrus production for almost 4,000 years.

The ready availability of paper brought about a revolution. Many of the characteristic features of Islamic civilization—bureaucratic record keeping, high levels of literacy and book production, even the standard form of cursive Arabic script—would have been impossible without the widespread availability of paper. Europeans would continue to rely on the more durable, but much more expensive, parchment made from animal hides for the copying of most books and documents. It was not until the advent of print that paper began to replace parchment as the reading and writing material of western Europe (see Chapter 12).

Mobility, Opportunity, and Status

The preeminence of trade and ease of travel in the cosmopolitan Muslim world not only increased geographical mobility, it fostered social mobility too. The Qur'an stressed the equality of all Muslim males, and all careers were open to men of talent, regardless of birth or wealth.

For those men wishing instead to embrace a religious life, Islam offered two main alternatives. One was that of the *ulama*, an influential class of learned men qualified to offer advice on aspects of religious law and practice. The other was that of the Sufis, mystics devoted to the cultivation of spiritual ecstasy. Some were Dervishes known for their trancelike whirling dances; others were *faqirs* whose powers of concentration are associated with snake charming; still others were quiet, meditative men. Sufis were usually organized into brotherhoods and eventually made many successful efforts to convert the peoples of Africa and India. The coexistence of the ulama and the Sufis is testimony to the cultural pluralism of Islam.

There were no comparable careers for Muslim women, parallel to the (admittedly narrow) options of their Christian counterparts. There are significant exceptions, of course. For example, Muhammad's favored wife, Aisha (*ah-EE-sha*, d. 678), was revered as a scholar and played an important role in the creation and circulation of *hadith*: stories and sayings that shed light on the Prophet's life and teachings. But in general, women could not take advantage of widening opportunities. They were considered valuable as indicators of a man's wealth and status.

The Qur'an allowed any Muslim man to marry as many as four wives, which meant that the number of women suitable for marriage was far smaller than the number of men who desired to marry. This made for intense competition, and men who had wives and daughters needed to ensure that their prized assets were safeguarded. So women were usually kept away from men who were not members of the family or trusted friends. Along with female servants and the concubines also owned by a wealthy man, they were housed in a segregated part of the residence called the *haram* ("forbidden place"), guarded by eunuchs (men, usually sold as slaves, who had been castrated prior to adolescence). Within these enclaves, women vied with one another for precedence and worked to advance the fortunes of their children. This was often the only form of power they could exercise.

Islam's Neighbors

For the inhabitants of Byzantium, the triumph of the Abbasid Caliphate alleviated the pressures of Umayyad expansion. Farther west, the Franks of Gaul also benefited from the Abbasids. Because an Umayyad dynasty controlled Al-Andalus, the great Frankish ruler Charlemagne (*SHAHR-leh-mayn*, r. 768–814) could counter neighboring Muslims' power by maintaining strong diplomatic and commercial relations with the more distant caliphate in Baghdad. The most famous symbol of

Past and Present

The Meanings of Medievalism

The people who lived during the thousand-year period that we call the Middle Ages didn't think of themselves as "medieval." And indeed, this modern term tends to be used to describe modern phenomena—whether things that we seek to condemn (terrorism, persecution) or that we wish to glorify. The romantic image of Joan of Arc, on the left, was used to rally Americans to the cause of France and its allies during World War I. The image on the right shows warfare as imagined by the game called *Arthur II*.

Watch related author videos on the Student Site
wwnorton.com/college/history/western-civilizationsBrief4

---

this connection was an elephant called Abul Abbas, a gift from Harun al-Rashid to Charlemagne. More important, however, was the flow of silver that found its way from the Abbasid Empire north through Russia and the Baltic into the Rhineland, where it was exchanged for Frankish exports of furs, wax, honey, leather, and especially slaves—Europeans, often Slavic peoples, who were captured and sold for profit by other Europeans. Through these channels, jewels, silks, spices, and other luxury goods from India and the Far East flowed north and west into Frankish territory. These trading links with the Abbasid world helped fund the extraordinary achievements of Charlemagne's own empire, which had a lasting effect on the culture and politics of Europe.

THE CONVERSION OF NORTHWESTERN EUROPE

At the end of the sixth century, the chronicler Gregory of Tours (c. 538–594) considered himself a Roman, living in a Roman world. He was proud of his family's senatorial status and took it for granted that he and his male relatives should be bishops who ruled, by right of birth and status, over their cities and the surrounding countryside. Although Gregory was aware that his own ruler was a Frankish warlord, he regarded barbarian kings as Roman successors. In the case of the Franks, the king even ruled with the approval of the Roman emperor in Constantinople. It was also a source of satisfaction to Gregory that these barbarian kings had converted to Roman Christianity. This, too, reinforced their *romanitas* and lent legitimacy to their rule.

Two hundred years later, the greatest of all Frankish kings, Charlemagne (742–814), was crowned as a new kind of Roman emperor in the West. By this time, there was no longer a sense of direct continuity with the earlier Roman world or a sense of obligation to the Roman emperor in Byzantium. When intellectuals at Charlemagne's court set out to rejuvenate cultural life, they sought a *renovatio Romanorum imperii*, "a renewal of the empire of the Romans." This awareness of a break with the Roman past developed during the seventh century, and was the consequence of profound economic and political changes.

Economic and Political Instability

Even though the Roman economy became increasingly regionalized after the third century C.E. (see Chapter 6), the Mediterranean remained a crucial nexus of trade and communication. Gold coinage continued to circulate; luxuries like silks and spices moved westward while staples like slaves, wine, grain, and leatherwork moved eastward. But this integrated Mediterranean world became increasingly disjointed after Justinian's failed efforts to reconquer the empire's western territories. Temporary disruptions to traditional trade routes were also caused by Arab raiders—temporary, because Muslim merchants and rulers would soon do much to reconstruct and extend patterns of commerce.

The most significant causes of economic instability in northwestern Europe were internal. The cities of Italy, Gaul, and Hispania could no longer maintain their walls, their public buildings, and their urban infrastructures. Although Christian bishops and their aristocratic kin still governed from these cities, barbarian kings and their followers were moving to the countryside, living off the produce of their own estates. At the same time, some agricultural land was passing out of cultivation. The slaves or servile peasants who had farmed Rome's large plantations for hundreds of years had no efficient state to enforce their obedience. They were able to become more independent—yet they were also less effective, working just a few acres by themselves. Productivity declined, and so did tax revenues.

The systems of coinage that circulated in western Europe were also breaking down, which meant that wealth ceased to be readily portable: a hindrance to long-distance exchange. The supply of gold available in western

Europe was now being channeled eastward to Muslim realms. But in any case, gold coins were too valuable to be useful in a local market economy. When we find evidence of such coins in western Europe at this time, they are more likely to have been plundered or given as gifts than to have been used for commerce. Those rulers who were still in a position to mint money and guarantee its value shifted from gold to silver coinage. Europe would remain a silver-based economy for the next thousand years, until the supply of gold from European conquests in Africa and America once again made a gold standard viable (see Chapter 12).

As a result of these processes, western Europe came to rely on a two-tier economy of a kind that had not been necessary for centuries. Gold, silver, and luxury goods circulated among the very wealthy, but most people relied on barter and various substitute currencies. Lords collected rents in food or labor, but then found it difficult to convert these payments into the weapons, jewelry, and silks that brought prestige in aristocratic society. This was problematic not only for social reasons but for political ones: the power of lords depended on their ability to bestow rich gifts on their followers (see **Interpreting Visual Evidence** on page 182). When they could not acquire these items through trade, they had to win them through plunder and extortion. Either way, the process led to violence.

The successful chieftains of this era therefore tended to be those whose areas of influence adjoined wealthy but poorly defended territories that could be easily attacked or subjugated. Such "soft frontiers" provided warlords and kings with land and booty which they could then distribute to their followers. Successes of this sort would bring more followers to a lord's service, allowing him to further extend his influence; and as long as more conquests were made, the process of amassing power and wealth would continue. But power acquired through plunder was inherently unreliable and it did not secure long-term loyalties.

Another factor contributing to the instability of power was the difficulty of ensuring its peaceful transfer. The barbarian rulers who had established themselves after the mass migrations of the fifth and sixth centuries did not come from the traditional royal families of their peoples, and thus they faced opposition from many of their own warriors. Moreover, the groups who took possession of territories were usually made up of many different tribes, including a sizable number of Romans. Whatever unity they possessed was largely the creation of the charismatic chieftain who led them, and this charisma was not easily passed on to heirs.

The Prosperous Kingdom of the Franks

Of all barbarian kingdoms planted in western Europe in this era, only the Franks were able to establish a dynasty from which leaders would be drawn for 250 years. This family reached back to Clovis (r. c. 481–511), a warlord who established an alliance with the powerful bishops of Gaul by converting to Roman Christianity. Clovis's lineage came to be known as the Merovingians, after his legendary grandfather Merovech, said to have been fathered by a sea monster (meaning that no one really knew where he came from). Clovis's own name proved even more long-lasting than his dynasty. As the Germanic language of the Franks merged with the Latin of Gaul, the name "Clovis" lost its hard *C* and *V* and became "Louis," the name borne by French kings up to the time of the French Revolution over a millennium later (see Chapter 18).

The Merovingians' success was due, in part, to the successful transfer of power between generations. Among Europe's barbarian peoples, the right of inheritance was not limited to the eldest male. All sons—and frequently all male kin and even daughters—could consider themselves rightful heirs. So even when rule was not threatened by outsiders, the transfer of power was almost always bloody. In Gaul, however, the often brutal conflicts between rival Merovingian claimants did not materially disrupt their governance. Many elements of late Roman local administration therefore survived throughout this period.

Latin literacy, fostered by a network of monasteries linked to the Frankish court, remained an important element in this administration. These monasteries grew remarkably during the seventh century and made Merovingian Gaul wealthier and more stable than other regions of northwestern Europe. Approximately 550 monasteries were thriving by the year 700, more than 300 of which had been established in the preceding century alone. Frankish bishops also prospered, amassing vast estates from which their successors would continue to profit—again, until the time of the French Revolution.

Such massive redistributions and concentrations of wealth reflected a fundamental shift in the economic gravity of the Frankish kingdom. In the year 600, the wealth of Gaul was concentrated in the south, as it had been throughout the late Roman period. By the year 750, however, the economic center of the kingdom lay north of the Loire, in the territories that extended from the Rhine westward to the North Sea. It was here that most of the new monastic foundations of the seventh century were established.

Behind this shift in prosperity lay a long and successful effort to bring under cultivation the rich, heavy soils of northern Europe. This effort was largely engineered by the new monasteries, which harnessed the peasant workforce and pioneered technologies adapted to the climate and terrain. The most important invention was a heavy, wheeled plow capable of cutting grassland sod and clay: soils very different from those of the Mediterranean. This innovation in turn necessitated the development of more efficient devices for harnessing animals (particularly oxen) to these plows. Gradually warming weather also improved the fertility of northern lands. As food became more plentiful, the population began to expand. Although much of Frankish Gaul remained a land of scattered settlements separated by dense forests, it was far more populous by 750 than it had been in the time of Clovis. All of these developments would continue during the reign of Charlemagne, and beyond (see Chapter 8).

The Power of Monasticism

Although monasteries had existed since the fourth century, most were located in highly Romanized areas. Then, in the fifth century, a powerful monastic movement began in Ireland, and eventually spread to the Celtic regions of Britain and from there to the Continent. The Irish missionary Columbanus (540–615), for example, was the founder of Merovingian monasteries in what is now France. Important monasteries were also established on the island of Iona, off the western coast of Scotland, and at Lindisfarne, off Britain's northeastern coast. In all of these cases, close ties were forged between monks and local tribal leaders or kings, much to the political and economic gain of all parties.

Most of these new monastic foundations were deliberately located in rural areas and at strategic crossroads, where they played a crucial role in trade. Indeed, the material advantages of monastic innovation were a powerful incentive to Christian conversion in the communities directly affected by improved living conditions. Prosperity was also a powerful advertisement for authority: a lord or chieftain who had the support of a monastery and its wealth was obviously worthy of loyalty. Because monasteries played such a key role in economic and political development, lords often granted them special privileges, helping to free them from the control of local bishops and giving them jurisdiction over their own lands. Thus monasteries became powerful not only because of their wealth and alliances, but because they were lordships in their own right.

Frequently, these monasteries housed women as well as men. Often they were established for women only.

In either case, they were often ruled by abbesses drawn from noble or royal families. Monasticism thus became a road to political power for women. It also gave women—commoners as well as queens—freedoms they did not have elsewhere, or at any other time in history up to this point. In a monastery, women had control over their own minds and bodies. They could also wield enormous influence, promoting their families' diplomatic and dynastic interests. And they were guaranteed salvation, at a time when salvation outside the cloister seemed perilously uncertain. Indeed, the prayers of holy women were regarded as particularly effective in securing divine support. This further enriched female monasteries through donations of land and wealth, although it could not always safeguard them from violence.

THE LINDISFARNE GOSPELS. This page from one of the astonishing illuminated ("light-filled") books produced by the monastery at Lindisfarne shows the opening of the Gospel of John. ▪ *Why would monastic scribes have devoted so much time, energy, and skill to the decoration of a text? How do these artistic motifs compare to those featured on the metalwork found at Sutton Hoo (pages 182 and 184)?* ▪ *What conclusions can you draw from these similarities?*

Because monasteries for women also served the interests of men, kings and lords supported them. These dynamic repositories of prayer were regarded as essential to furthering the ambitions of male benefactors. They also provided a dignified place of retirement for inconvenient but powerful women, such as the sisters and daughters of rivals or the widow of a previous ruler. And by limiting the number of powerful women who could reproduce, female monasteries also reduced the number of male claimants to power. Supporting aristocratic and royal nuns was thus an important way of controlling successions and managing disputes.

Monasticism also played an important role in missionary activity, as noted earlier. The work of Irish monks was crucial to the spread of Christianity in northern parts of Britain and in other areas of northern Europe virtually untouched by the Roman Empire. But missions were also sponsored by the fledgling papacy in Rome and by the Frankish royal family—especially its women. The best example of this is the conversion of Britain's Anglo-Saxon tribes, which we glimpsed in the opening paragraph of this chapter. In 597, a group of forty Benedictine monks was sent by Pope Gregory I (r. 590–604) to the southeastern kingdom of Kent, where their efforts were assisted by Frankish translators—and by the fact that the local king, Æthelbehrt (*ETH-el-bert*), had married a Frankish princess who was already a Christian.

The Papacy of Gregory the Great

Pope Gregory I, also known as Gregory the Great, was the first bishop of Rome to envision a new role for the papacy in northwestern Europe. We have seen that the Roman *papa* had begun to assert his superiority over other Christian patriarchs in the fourth century; but in reality, he was subordinate to the emperors in Constantinople and to the greater prestige of its patriarch. As Byzantine power in Italy declined, however, Gregory sought to create a more autonomous Latin Church by focusing attention on the untapped resources of the wild West.

Gregory was also an influential theologian, and among his teachings was an emphasis on the necessity of penance for the forgiveness of sins, and the concept of Purgatory as a place where the soul could be purified before it was admitted into heaven—instead of being sent immediately to perpetual damnation. Alongside this concern for proper penance, Gregory emphasized the importance of pastoral care: the proper instruction, encouragement, and control of the laity. He also sought to increase the affective power

Interpreting Visual Evidence

The Ship Burial of Sutton Hoo

The two most impressive finds in the history of British archaeology have been made by amateurs. The most recent, in the summer of 2009, was the largest hoard of worked gold and silver ever found in one place (more than 5 kilograms of gold and 2.5 kilograms of silver; image A), discovered by a man in Staffordshire walking over a neighbor's farm with a metal detector. The hoard's extraordinary value and range of artifacts—and their historical implications—can only be guessed at now; even the dating is inconclusive.

The other find, made in 1939, was a royal gravesite dating from the seventh century (image B), which many scholars believe to be the tomb of King Redwald of East Anglia, described by Bede as a baptized Christian who refused to give up the worship of his ancestral gods. The king's body was placed in a wooden structure in the middle of a ninety-foot-long ship that had been dragged to the top of a bluff (a *hoo*), eleven miles from the English Channel. The ladder in the photograph of the original excavation reaches into the burial chamber.

The contents of the grave included:

• a lamp and a bronze bucket that had been suspended from a chain

• a ceremonial helmet (image C) modeled on those worn by Roman cavalry

A. The Staffordshire Hoard, found in 2009.

B. The original excavation of the burial chamber at Sutton Hoo, 1939.

of Christian worship by promoting the performance of music. Song has always been essential to religious ritual, but Gregory encouraged it to such a degree that the very style of singing that emerged in this period is known as Gregorian chant.

Gregory was also a statesman. Within Italy, he ensured the survival of the papacy against Lombard invaders by clever diplomacy and expert management of papal estates and revenues. He maintained good relations with Byzantium while asserting his authority over the other officers just before the withdrawal of the legions from Britain in 410—but decorated like helmets found in eastern Sweden

- a sword and a large, circular shield, resembling those found in Swedish burial sites

- exquisitely crafted belt buckles and shoulder clasps (image D), made of gold and garnet, and worked with designs.

- a pair of silver spoons with long handles, possibly crafted in Byzantium, and inscribed in Greek with the names PAULOS and SAULOS (Paul and Saul)

- a large silver dish (72 cm in diameter) made in Byzantium between 491 and 518

- a bronze bowl from the eastern Mediterranean

- a six-stringed lyre in a bag made of beaver skin, similar to lyres found in Germany

C. A Sutton Hoo helmet.

- a purse containing thirty-seven gold coins, each from a different Merovingian mint, the most recent datable to the 620s

- heaps of armor, blankets, cloaks, and other gear.

Questions for Analysis

1. What do these artifacts, and the context in which they were found, reveal about the extent of Anglo-Saxon contact with the rest of the world? Which regions are represented, and why?

2. Based on this evidence, what conclusions can you draw about Anglo-Saxon culture and values?

3. Do any of these graves' goods indicate that the occupant was a Christian king? Why or why not?

D. Sutton Hoo buckles.

bishops of the Latin Church. His support of communities living under the *Rule* of Saint Benedict (Chapter 6) helped make Benedictine monasticism the predominant monastic force in the West. Yet Gregory's influence was not always benign. He was the first prominent theologian to articulate

the Church's official policy toward Jews, which became increasingly negative. Building on Gregory's example, later popes would insist that the Jews' alleged role in Christ's crucifixion and their denial of his divinity had deprived them of their rights in a Christian world.

THE EMPIRE OF CHARLEMAGNE

Toward the end of the seventh century, tensions among noble families in the Frankish kingdom were increasing. Those located along the "soft frontier" east of the Rhine had been steadily acquiring wealth and military power. The Merovingian royal family, by contrast, had given a considerable portion of their land to monasteries, which decreased their wealth and their capacity to attract followers. A succession of short-lived kings then led to a series of civil wars, and finally to a decisive challenge.

Kings and Kingmakers

In 687, a Frankish warlord called Pepin (c. 635–714) forced his way to power by making himself the Frankish king's right-hand man. He took the title *maior domus*, "great man of the house," and began to exercise royal authority while maintaining the fiction that he was merely a royal servant. After his death, his son Charles Martel ("the Hammer," 688–741) further consolidated control over Merovingian domains and the Frankish royal administration.

For two generations then, Merovingian kings were largely figureheads—and their claim to legitimacy was threatened when Charles Martel did the job of king by repelling a Muslim force that had ventured into Frankish territory. He met them in battle at Tours in 732, some 150 miles from the Merovingian stronghold at Paris. Although the Arab-led contingent was a raiding party rather than a full-scale army, this incursion may have been regarded as an attempted conquest by the Umayyad dynasty of Al-Andalus, on the other side of the Pyrennes. Meanwhile, Charles was also developing an alliance with Benedictine missionaries from England, who were attempting to convert the Low Countries and central Germany to Christianity. Charles's family had long been active in the drive to conquer and settle these areas, and he understood clearly how missionary work and Frankish expansion could go hand in hand. Charles assisted these missionaries. In return, their leader Boniface (c. 672–754) brought him into contact with the papacy.

Although Charles never sought to become king himself, he was so clearly the effective ruler of Gaul that the Franks did not bother to choose a new king when the reigning Merovingian died in 737. But then Charles himself died a few years later, in 741. His sons Carloman and Pepin were forced to allow the election of a new king, a compromise that did not last long; in 750, Carloman withdrew to a monastery and Pepin made a bid for kingship. However, this turned out to be harder than he had expected. Frankish

identity had been forged by loyalty to Clovis's descendants; although tribal leaders had the power to elect a new king, they were reluctant to do so. Pepin therefore turned to his family's new ally, the pope, who wanted a more powerful and able Frankish king to help protect the papacy and its lands around Rome from the Lombards in northern Italy.

So Boniface, acting as papal emissary, anointed Pepin king of the Franks in 751. This was a ritual new to the Franks, but with a powerful biblical precedent: it was the ceremony by which the prophet Samuel had made Saul the first king of Israel, by anointing him with holy oil (see Chapter 2). To contemporary observers, however, the novelty of the process was unsettling: how could a legitimate king be deposed and a new king created, just like that, without a traditional election by Frankish chieftains? As we will see, the precedent established by this king-making process would lead future popes to claim the power to create and depose kings. Ultimately, it would limit the power of later medieval kings and their modern successors, because it established the principle that kingship is an office that can be held by anyone—and that if a ruler is ineffectual or tyrannical, he can be deposed and replaced by someone more competent.

The Reign of Charlemagne

Pepin's position as king was tenuous, and when he died it seemed likely that the Frankish kingdom would break up into mutually hostile regions. That it did not was the work of Pepin's son, Charles, known to the French as Charlemagne and to the Germans as Karl der Grosse—"Charles the Great." It is from him, as well as from his grandfather Charles Martel, that this new Frankish dynasty takes the name "Carolingian" (from *Carolus*, the Latin form of "Charles").

When Charlemagne came to power in 768, he managed to unite the Franks by the tried and true method of attacking a common, outside enemy. In a series of conquests, the Franks succeeded in annexing the Lombard kingdom of northern Italy, most of what is now Germany, portions of central Europe, and Catalonia (in northeastern Spain). These conquests seemed to set a seal of divine approval on the new dynasty. More important, they provided the victorious Franks with spoils of war and vast new lands that enabled Charlemagne to reward his followers and earn their loyalty.

Many of the peoples whom Charlemagne conquered were already Christians. In pagan Saxony, however, Carolingian armies campaigned for twenty years before subduing the inhabitants and forcing their conversion. This created another precedent with momentous consequences, because it linked military conquest with

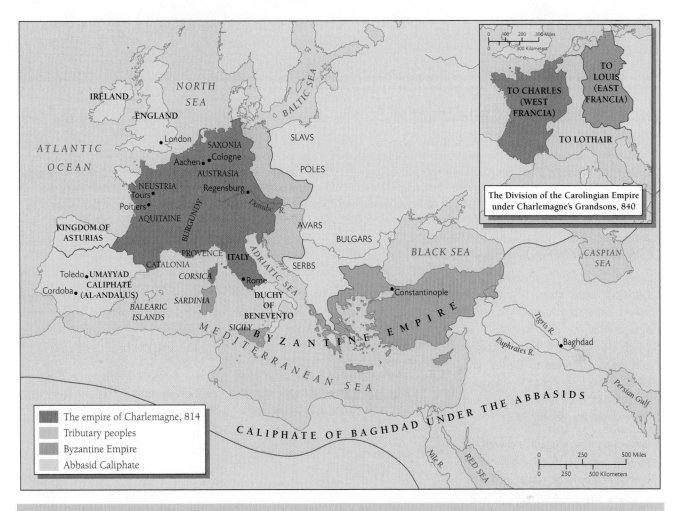

THE EMPIRE OF CHARLEMAGNE IN 814. When Charlemagne died in 814, he had created an empire that embraced a large portion of the lands formerly united under the western Roman Empire. ▪ *What were the geographical limits of his power?* ▪ *How were these limits dictated by the historical forces we have been studying?* ▪ *Along what lines was Charlemagne's empire divided after his death?*

religious conformity. It became a settled assumption that the subjugation of a vanquished people should be accompanied by their religious conversion, and this became the settled policy of Europeans even in the New World (see Chapter 14).

To rule his enormous empire, Charlemagne enlisted the help of the Frankish warrior class he had enriched. These counts (*comites*, "followers") were given the task of supervising local governance within their territories, overseeing justice, and raising armies. Charlemagne also established a network of officials who convened local courts, established tolls, administered royal lands, and collected taxes. To facilitate transactions and trade, he created a new coinage system based on a division of the silver pound into units of twenty shillings, each worth twelve pennies—a system that would last in parts of continental Europe and in Britain into the 1970s (when it was replaced by a decimal-based currency). Much of the silver for this new

coinage originated in the Abbasid Caliphate, and was payment for furs, woolen cloth, and especially slaves captured in Charlemagne's wars, who were now being transported to Baghdad. The silver, in turn, circulated as far north as Scandinavia and the Baltic Sea.

Like Carolingian administration generally, this new monetary system depended on the regular use of written records, which means that sources supporting historical research on Charlemagne's empire are relatively abundant. But Charlemagne did not rely on the written word alone. Periodically, his court sent special messengers, known as *missi*, to relay his instructions and report back on the conduct of local administrators throughout the realm. This was the most thorough system of governance known in Europe since the height of the Roman Empire, reaching many parts of the Continent that the Romans had never occupied. It set a standard for royal administration that would be emulated and envied for centuries.

The Capitularies of Charlemagne

Charlemagne's careful governance of his domains would set a high standard for other rulers far into the future. One of the means by which this governance was carried out was through capitularies (from a Latin word denoting a document divided into chapters), which contained instructions issued by the central administration of the court to local counts and other authorities. The following are directives addressed in 785 to the administrators of Saxony, a region recently conquered by Charlemagne, whose inhabitants were forcibly converted to Christianity.

Capitulary Concerning the Parts of Saxony

1. Decisions were taken first on the more important items. All were agreed that the churches of Christ which are now being built in Saxony and are consecrated to God should have no less honor than the temples of idols had, but rather a greater and more surpassing honor.

2. If anyone takes refuge in a church, let no one presume to drive him out of that church by force; rather let him be in peace until he is brought to plead his case, . . . and after this let him be brought to the presence of our lord the king. . . .

3. If anyone makes forcible entry to a church, and steals anything from it by violence or stealth, or if he sets fire to the church, let him die.

4. If anyone in contempt of the Christian faith should spurn the holy Lenten fast and eat meat, let him die; but let the priest enquire into the matter, lest it should happen that someone is compelled by necessity to eat meat.

* * *

6. If anyone is deceived by the devil, and believes after the manner of pagans that some man or some woman is a witch and eats people, . . . let him pay the penalty of death.

7. If anyone follows pagan rites and causes the body of a dead man to be consumed by fire, . . . let him pay with his life.

8. If there is anyone of the Saxon people lurking among them unbaptized, and if he scorns to come to baptism, . . . let him die.

9. If anyone sacrifices a man to the devil, . . . let him die.

* * *

12. If anyone rapes the daughter of his lord, he shall die.

13. If anyone kills his lord or his lady, he shall be punished in the same way.

* * *

18. On Sundays there are to be no assemblies or public gatherings, except in cases of great need or when an enemy is pressing; rather let all attend church to hear the word of God. . . .

* * *

33. With regard to perjury, the law of the Saxons is to apply.

34. We forbid the Saxons to come together as a body in public gatherings, except on those occasions when our *missus* [messenger] assembles them on our instructions; rather, let each and every count hold court and administer justice in his own area. And the clergy are to see to it that this order is obeyed.

Source: From *The Reign of Charlemagne: Documents on Carolingian Government*, ed. and trans. H. R. Loyn and John Percival (New York: 1975), pp. 31–34.

Questions for Analysis

1. What types of behavior does this capitulary attempt to regulate? What seem to be the major challenges faced by Charlemagne's administrators in this new territory?

2. In only one case does this capitulary mention the law of the Saxon people themselves, in the clause relating to perjury (number 33). Why would Charlemagne's administrators consider it advisable to punish this particular crime in accordance with Saxon custom?

3. How would you characterize Charlemagne's method of dealing with a conquered people? In your estimation, is this policy likely to be effective?

Christianity and Kingship

Charlemagne took his responsibilities as a Christian king very seriously. As his empire expanded, he came to see himself as the leader of a unified Christian society, Christendom, which he was obliged to defend. Like his contemporaries in Byzantium and the Muslim world—as well as his Roman predecessors—he recognized no distinction between religion and politics. He conceived kingship as a sacred office created by God to protect the Church and promote the salvation of his people. Religious strength was therefore as central to proper kingship as justice and warfare.

These ideas were not new, but they took on a new importance because of the extraordinary power Charlemagne wielded. Like other rulers of this period, Charlemagne was able to appoint and depose bishops and abbots, just as he did his counts and other officials. He further extended his authority by glorifying the rituals of churches, reforming the rules of worship in monasteries, ruthlessly prohibiting pagan practices, and forcibly imposing basic Christian observances on all his subjects, especially the restive Saxons. As the dominant political power in northern and central Italy, Charlemagne was also the protector of the papacy, and he dealt with the bishop of Rome much as he did with other bishops in his empire. He supervised and approved papal elections, and he also protected the pope from his many enemies.

The Carolingian Renaissance

Bolstering these political, economic, and religious institutions was a phenomenon known as the Carolingian Renaissance: a cultural and intellectual flowering that took place around the Carolingian court and radiated from it. Like their biblical exemplars David and Solomon, Charlemagne and his son Louis the Pious considered it a crucial part of their role to be patrons of learning and the arts. In doing so, they created a courtly ideal that would profoundly influence European culture until the First World War (see Chapter 24).

Behind the Carolingians' support for learning was the conviction that education was essential to salvation. Charlemagne therefore recruited talented men from all over Europe to further the cause of scholarship. Foremost among these was the Anglo-Saxon monk Alcuin, whose command of classical Latin established him as the intellectual leader of Charlemagne's court. Under Alcuin's direction, Carolingian scholars produced much original Latin poetry and an impressive array of writings on many subjects. But their primary efforts were devoted to collating, correcting,

CHARLEMAGNE'S IMAGE OF AUTHORITY. A silver penny struck between 804 and 814 in Mainz (as indicated by the letter *M* at the bottom) represents Charlemagne in a highly stylized fashion, as a Roman emperor with a military cloak and laurel wreath. The inscription reads *Karolus Imp Avg* (Charles, Emperor, Augustus). Charlemagne's portrait is closely modeled on both Hellenistic and Roman coins.

and recopying ancient Latin texts, including, most importantly, the text of the Latin Bible, which had accumulated many generations of copyists' mistakes in the 400 years since Jerome's translation (see Chapter 6).

To detect and correct these errors, Alcuin and his associates gathered as many different versions of the biblical text as they could find and compared them, word by word. After determining the correct version among all the variants, they made a new, corrected copy and destroyed the other versions. They also developed a new style of handwriting, with simplified letter forms and spaces inserted between words, so as to reduce the likelihood that subsequent copyists would misread the corrected texts. Reading was further facilitated by the addition of punctuation. This new style of handwriting, known as Carolingian miniscule, is the foundation for the typefaces of most modern books—including this one.

The Revival of the Western Roman Empire

On Christmas Day in the year 800, Charlemagne was crowned emperor by Pope Leo III. Centuries later, popes would cite this event as precedent for the political superiority they claimed over all rulers. In the year 800, however, Pope Leo was entirely under Charlemagne's thumb. Yet Charlemagne's biographer, Einhard, would later claim that the coronation was planned without the emperor's knowledge.

This may have been true, or it may have been advantageous to insist that it was. For one thing, the crowning of a new emperor of the Romans was certain to anger the Roman imperial government in Constantinople, with which Charlemagne had strained relations. Nor did the imperial title add much to Charlemagne's position; he was already an emperor in his own right. Why, then, did he accept the title and, in 813, transfer it to his son Louis?

Historians are still debating this question. But the symbolic significance of the action is clear. Although the Romans of Byzantium no longer influenced western Europe directly, they continued to regard it (somewhat vaguely) as an outlying province of their empire. Charlemagne's assumption of the title was therefore a clear slight to the reigning empress Irene (r. 797–802), whose occupation of the imperial throne was controversial because she was a woman. It also deepened Byzantine suspicion of Charlemagnes' cordial relationship with Harun al-Rashid, the Abbasid caliph in Baghdad.

But for Charlemagne's followers—and for all the medieval rulers who came after him—the imperial title was a declaration of independence and superiority. With only occasional interruptions, western Europeans would continue to crown Roman emperors until the nineteenth century, while many territorial claims and European concepts of national sovereignty continued to rest on Carolingian precedent. Whatever his own motives may have been, Charlemagne's revival of the western Roman Empire was crucial to the developing self-consciousness of western Europe.

DISPUTED LEGACIES AND NEW ALLIANCES

When Charlemagne died in 814, his empire descended to his only surviving legitimate son, Louis the Pious. When Louis died in 840, however, the empire's unity had dissolved and it was divided among his three sons. Western Francia (the core of modern France) went to Charles the Bald; eastern Francia (which became key principalities of Germany) went to Louis the German; and a third kingdom (stretching from the Rhineland to Rome) went to Lothair, along with the imperial title. But when Lothair's line died out in 856, this fragile compromise dissolved into open warfare, as the East and West Franks fought over Lothair's former territories and the imperial power that went with them. The core of this disputed domain, known to the Germans as Lotharingia and to the French as Alsace-Lorraine, would continue to be a site of bitter contention until the end of the Second World War (see Chapter 26).

The Collapse of the Carolingian Empire

Louis faced an impossible situation of a kind we have studied many times before: the task of holding together an artificial constellation of territories united by someone else. Charlemagne's empire had been built on successful conquest, but it had pushed beyond the practical limits of his administration. To the southwest, he now faced the Umayyad rulers of Al-Andalus; to the north, the pagan inhabitants of Scandinavia; and in the east, the Slavic lands that lay beyond. At the same time, the pressures that had driven these conquests—the need for land and plunder to secure the allegiance of followers—had become ever more pronounced as a result of their very success. The number of counts had tripled, and each of them wanted more wealth and power.

Frustrated by their new emperor's inability to reward them, the Frankish aristocracy turned against him and on each other. Smoldering hostilities, which Charlemagne had stifled by directing their energies elsewhere, flared up again. As centralized authority broke down, the vast majority of the empire's free inhabitants found themselves increasingly dominated by local lords who treated them as if they were unfree serfs. At the same time, internal troubles in the Abbasid Caliphate caused a breakdown in the commercial system through which Scandinavian traders brought Abbasid silver into Carolingian domains. Deprived of their livelihood, these traders turned to raiding, which is what the Norse word *viking* means. Under these combined pressures, the Carolingian Empire fell apart, and a new political map of Europe began to emerge.

The Impact of the Viking Invasions

Scandinavian traders were already familiar figures in the North Sea and Baltic ports of Europe when Charlemagne came to power. They had begun to establish strategic settlements from which they navigated down the rivers to Byzantium (through the Black Sea) and to the Abbasid Caliphate (through the Caspian Sea). But when the power of the Abbasids declined, Viking raiders turned to plunder, ransom, and slaving. At first, these were small-scale operations. But soon, some Viking attacks involved organized armies numbering in the thousands. The small tribal kingdoms of the Anglo-Saxons and Celts made the British Isles easy targets, as were the divided kingdoms of the Franks.

By the tenth century, the Vikings controlled independent principalities in eastern England, Ireland, the islands of Scotland, and the region of France that is still called "Norseman-land"—Normandy. A Viking people known as

PATTERNS OF VIKING ACTIVITY AND SETTLEMENT, C. 700–1100. The Vikings were instrumental in maintaining commercial contacts among northern Europe, Byzantium, and Islam until the eighth century, when changing historical forces turned them into raiders and colonists. ▪ *What area was the original homeland of the Vikings?* ▪ *What geographic region did the Vikings first conquer, and why?* ▪ *The areas marked in green show territories that were later targeted by pillagers. Why would the Vikings have avoided settlement in these areas?*

the Rus' established the beginnings of a kingdom that would become Russia. At the end of the tenth century, Vikings ventured farther west and colonized Iceland, Greenland, and a distant territory they called Vinland (Newfoundland, Canada). In 1016, a Viking army placed a Danish king on the English throne.

The threat of Viking attacks began to lessen with Scandinavia's conversion to Christianity, which proceeded rapidly from the late tenth century onward. But it was more effectively mitigated by the fact that Viking populations quickly assimilated into the cultural and political world of northwestern Europe. By 1066, when the "Norsemen" of Normandy conquered England, the English—many of whom were descended from Vikings themselves—perceived them to be French. Driving this rapid assimilation may have been the raids of the Magyars, a non-Indo-European people who crossed the Carpathian Mountains around 895 and carried out a number of devastating campaigns in central

and eastern Europe before settling in what is now Hungary (which Hungarians call *Magyarország*).

The overall effect of the Vikings on Europe continues to be a matter of scholarly controversy. The mayhem they caused is undeniable, and many settlements and monasteries were destroyed—along with countless precious books and historical artifacts. Yet the Vikings were not a source of disorder only. In Ireland and eastern England, Vikings founded a series of new towns. As long-distance traders, Vikings transported large quantities of silver into western Europe, fueling the European economy. In those few regions where people did succeed in fending off Viking attacks, the unifying force of victory was strong. The best example of this phenomenon is England, which had never been part of Charlemagne's empire and which had remained divided into small kingdoms at war with one other—despite Bede's wishful history of "an English church and people." Yet in a direct response to the Viking threat, a loosely unified kingdom emerged for the first time under Alfred the Great (r. 871–99).

Alfred's success in defending his own small kingdom from Viking attacks, combined with his emulation of Charlemagne's governance, allowed him and his heirs to assemble effective armed forces, institute mechanisms of local government, found new towns, and codify English laws. In addition, Alfred established a court school and fostered a distinctive Anglo-Saxon literary culture. While the Anglo-Saxon vernacular had been a written language since the time of the Roman missions, it now came to rival Latin as a language of administration, history, scholarship, and spirituality. Moreover, oral traditions of poetic composition and storytelling were preserved and extended, as exemplified by the epic *Beowulf*. Until the eleventh century, Anglo-Saxon was the only European vernacular used for regular written communication.

The Disintegration of the Islamic World

As we noted above, the declining power of the Abbasid dynasty in Baghdad contributed to the escalation of Viking raids. A major cause of this decline was the gradual impoverishment of the Abbasids' economic base, the agricultural wealth of Mesopotamia, which resulted from ecological crises and a devastating revolt by the enslaved African workforce there. Tax revenues were also declining as provincial rulers in North Africa, Egypt, and Syria defiantly retained larger and larger portions of those revenues for themselves. As sources of income became depleted, the Abbasids were unable to support either their large civil service or the mercenary army on which they relied for defense. Massively expensive building projects further exacerbated the fiscal, military, and political crisis.

Behind the Abbasid decline lay two significant developments: the growing power of regional rulers and the sharpening religious divisions between Sunnis and Shi'ites, and among the Shi'ites themselves. In 909, regional and religious hostilities came together when a Shi'ite clan known as the Fatimids seized control of Abbasid North Africa. In 969, the Fatimids succeeded in conquering Egypt also. Meanwhile, another Shi'ite group, rivals of both the Fatimids and the Abbasids, attacked Baghdad in 927 and Mecca in 930, seizing the Kaaba. Although an Abbasid Caliphate would continue to exist in Baghdad until 1258, when invading Mongol armies conquered it (see Chapter 10), its empire had effectively disappeared. In its place a new order began to emerge, centered around an independent Egyptian kingdom and a new Muslim state based in Persia, with North Africa and Syria forming an embattled middle ground.

After You Read This Chapter

 Go to **INQUIZITIVE** to see what you've learned—and learn what you've missed—with personalized feedback along the way.

REVIEWING THE OBJECTIVES

- Justinian's attempted reunification of the Roman Empire proved destructive. What were its effects in the East? In the West?
- What were some important features of Byzantine culture, and how did it build on that of Rome?
- The rapid expansion of Islam can be explained with reference to several historical factors. What were they?
- What accounts for the close relationship between monasticism and secular power in early medieval Europe?
- What was the Carolingian Empire, and why is it important?

In Al-Andalus, disputes over succession within the Umayyad dynasty were matched by new external pressures. Beginning in the mid-ninth century, the small Christian kingdoms of northern and eastern Iberia began to encroach on Muslim territory. By the opening years of the eleventh century, the Umayyad Caliphate had been replaced by a host of smaller Muslim kingdoms, some of which paid tribute to the Christian rulers of the north.

These fractures deepened divisions that had always existed. While Islamic rulers were extremely tolerant of religious and cultural differences when dealing with their Jewish and Christian subjects, dissent within Islam itself was another matter. Under the strong rule of the caliphates, some different groups had learned to coexist; but with the disappearance of these centralized states it would be difficult to reconcile the ideal of universality with the realities of regional and ethnic differences.

CONCLUSION

The three civilizations that emerged as Rome's heirs each exhibit aspects of Roman civilization. Which was Rome's true successor? It depends on the criteria used to make this evaluation. If imperial Rome's most fundamental characteristics were the maintenance of legal and political institutions, the answer is Byzantium. If one is looking for a civilization that combines the rich legacies of the ancient Near East, Egypt, and the Hellenistic world, the answer is Islam, which also emulated Rome in promoting commerce and cultural exchange. If one associates Rome chiefly with the city itself and the Latin language of the first Romans, the answer is northwestern Europe.

There were also many connections among these heirs of Rome. Muslim traders were common in the ports of southern Italy and Gaul. Anglo-Saxon merchants were regular visitors to the Mediterranean. Jewish merchants in the Rhineland were carrying on an active trade with the communities of Muslim Egypt, while Viking traders had opened routes from the Baltic to the Black Sea and were busily founding cities from Novgorod to Dublin.

But developments of the ninth and tenth centuries would disrupt these networks and create new centers of power, as western Europe became a society mobilized for war to a degree unmatched in either Byzantium or the Islamic world. In the centuries to come, this militarization was to prove a decisive factor in the shifting relationship among Rome's heirs.

PEOPLE, IDEAS, AND EVENTS IN CONTEXT

- In what ways do **JUSTINIAN'S CODE OF ROMAN LAW** and the building of **HAGIA SOPHIA** reflect his desire to revive the glories of ancient Rome?
- What were **BYZANTIUM**'s sources of stability, and of dissent? What effect did the **ICONOCLAST CONTROVERSY** have on Byzantine society?
- What factors contributed to **MUHAMMAD**'s rise to power? What are the **FIVE PILLARS OF ISLAM**, and what is the role of the **QUR'AN**?
- To what extent were the **UMAYYAD** and **ABBASID CALIPHATES** heirs of Rome? What made Islamic culture of this period distinctive?
- How did the **MEROVINGIAN** kings of the Franks acquire and hold power? How did **BENEDICTINE MONASTICISM** contribute to the economy of western Europe, and how was it linked to politics?
- How did **CHARLEMAGNE** build an empire, and how did the **CAROLINGIAN RENAISSANCE** revive and extend **CLASSICAL LEARNING**?
- How did the **VIKINGS** contribute to the developments of the ninth and tenth centuries?

THINKING ABOUT CONNECTIONS

- Arguably, each of these three civilizations could claim the mantle of the Roman Empire. In your view, which one has the strongest claim to carrying forward the legacies of the classical past?
- How do the historical circumstances in which Islam emerged compare to those that shaped early Christianity? What are some key similarities and differences?

STORY LINES

- Around the year 1000, new agricultural technologies and new social groupings transformed the economy and landscape of Europe.

- The rejuvenation of towns and trade created new opportunities for advancement. But at the same time, the decentralization of political power led to the violent rule of lords who could marshal human and material resources to their own advantage.

- Meanwhile, a reforming movement within the Church increased the authority of the papacy, which attempted to assert its supremacy over secular rulers and to control violence by directing it against Europe's neighbors.

- One manifestation of this Church-sanctioned violence was the First Crusade, which began when a Muslim attack on Byzantium became the pretext for a holy war.

- Crusading broadened cultural and economic contacts with the East, but it also led to increased intolerance of "others," both outside Europe and within it.

CHRONOLOGY

900–1050	Monastic reform movement
911–989	The peoples of Rus' are converted to Orthodoxy
930	Establishment of the Althing in Iceland
936–973	Reign of Otto I "the Great"
980–1037	Lifetime of Avicenna
1035	Death of Cnut the Great
1050	Medieval agricultural revolution at its height
1066–1087	Reign of William the Conqueror in England
1073–1085	Papacy of Gregory VII
1075–1122	Investiture Conflict
1081–1118	Reign of Alexius I Comnenus in Byzantium
1095–1099	First Crusade
c. 1100	*The Song of Roland* is written down

Before You Read This Chapter

The Expansion of Europe, 950–1100

n the version of history popularized by medieval minstrels, Charlemagne and his knights are able to defeat a Muslim army in the mountainous borderlands between France and Spain. Their remaining obstacle is the castle of a Muslim king whose courage commands the Christians' respect. So when ambassadors from the king promise his conversion in exchange for the safety of his people, Charlemagne readily agrees. One of his men must now negotiate the terms of surrender. Roland, Charlemagne's bravest knight, suggests that his stepfather Ganelon be the chosen messenger. But Ganelon secretly resolves to betray his hated stepson and his liege lord: he convinces the Muslim king that Charlemagne's offer is a trick, and incites him to attack the Christian warriors as they travel homeward through the Pyrenees. Ganelon knows that Roland will volunteer to command the rear guard.

And so it happens. Roland's men are ambushed and his companion, Olivier, urges him to blow his horn and call for help. But Roland refuses: he will never endanger his lord by any such dishonorable deed. Instead, he will fight to the death and, with his last ounce of strength, break his sword. For it would never do to have this sacred gift of Charlemagne—made holier still by the relic in its pommel—fall into the hands of heathens. As Roland reminds Olivier, "We must not be the theme of mocking songs."

Like Homer's *Iliad*, *The Song of Roland* is the product of an oral storytelling tradition that took shape over hundreds of years. Written down around the year 1100, it reflects the many ways in which the world had changed since the time of the real Charlemagne. Its very language exemplifies one such change: the language we call French, no longer the Frankish tongue of Charlemagne. In Charlemagne's time, moreover, there was no such thing as knighthood, there were no major castles, there was no holy war against Muslims. All of these features were added to the story over time, to mirror a new reality and the ethos of the First Crusade (1095–99).

In this chapter, we will begin to trace the processes that transformed western Europe into the premier power among the three successor civilizations of the Roman Empire. In the centuries after the year 1000, European Christendom came to embrace the formerly outlying provinces of Scandinavia, Hungary, Poland, and Bohemia. Christian colonists would also push eastward into Prussia, Lithuania, Livonia, and the Balkans. Crusading knights would establish (and eventually lose) a Latin kingdom centered on Jerusalem. This expansion would be accompanied by a revolution in agricultural production, significant urbanization, and population growth. It would foster the rise of territorial monarchies, create a new social order, and spur remarkable intellectual and cultural achievements.

A TOUR OF EUROPE AROUND THE YEAR 1000

We have seen that many of Europe's territories were gradually brought into the orbit of Western civilizations through trade and imperial conquest. Meanwhile, the Jewish diaspora, the spread of Islam, and waves of immigration from the steppes of Asia increased the already rich ethnic and cultural diversity of Europe, as did the movements of the Vikings. While Charlemagne had tried to promote an idea of Europe as Christendom, Europe was not (and could never be) wholly Christian; and it was certainly not unified. So what was it?

This chapter is entitled "The Expansion of Europe" for two main reasons: because the very idea of Europe gained increasing coherence during this period and because

Europeans' forceful annexation of neighboring territories is a crucial development. Some influential historians argue that Europe was actually invented in this era, through an ongoing process of internal and external colonization. New kingdoms and communities were being created by conquest and settlement within Europe, but also well beyond it. Europeans were becoming the agents of imperialism, not its targets. This is a striking change. The West's center of gravity had always been the Mediterranean and its adjacent lands; it was from there that influences flowed farther west and north. Now that trajectory was being reversed.

Viking Initiatives

After the Viking invasions, new polities began to emerge. Some were formed when the Vikings became colonists: Iceland, Greenland, and (briefly) Newfoundland. Indeed, Iceland can claim to be Europe's oldest state and the world's first parliamentary democracy. In the year 930, its settlers formed a legislative assembly called the Althing, a Norse word with the same meaning as the Latin *res publica*. Icelanders would also produce a fascinating and influential body of poetic forms and literary entertainments, notably the *sagas*: sprawling family histories that unfold over generations, ranging from the hilarious to the ruthless. Modern action films and movie epics are heavily indebted to the sagas.

In regions where Vikings settled among more established groups—throughout the British Isles and the Low Countries—they both absorbed and affected these cultures. In Normandy, for example, the descendants of Vikings maintained alliances and kinship ties with the rest of the Norse world while at the same time intermarrying with the Franks and adopting their language.

The Rise of Rus' and the Kingdoms of Eastern Europe

One group of Vikings established an important kingdom in a region that still bears their name: Russia. The Rus' were active raiders and traders in the Baltic region, where they came to dominate the Finns and Slavic peoples who lived along the seaboard. They extended their reach through the navigation of Eurasian waterways while also moving farther inland, to Novgorod. By the year 1000, they had conquered the fortress of Kiev.

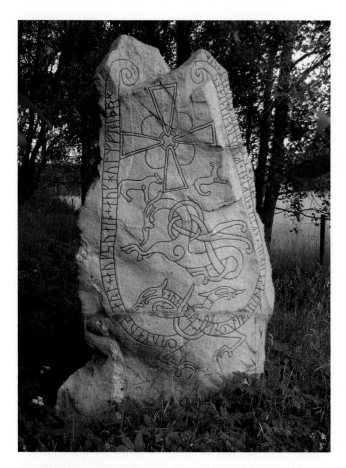

LINGSBERG RUNESTONE. This is one of two commemorative runestones erected at Lingsberg, Sweden, at the beginning of the eleventh century. The runic inscription records that a woman named Holmfríðr had it placed here in memory of her husband, Halfdan, whose father had been a Viking raider in England. Runic alphabets were in use among Germanic-speaking peoples of the North prior to the adoption of the Latin alphabet. Some runic letters survive in Anglo-Saxon and Old Norse, including the *edh*—the letter ð in the name of Holmfríðr—which is pronounced *th* as in *the*.

Kiev was a key outpost on the frontier controlled by the Khazars, a Turkic people with a trading empire along the Silk Road to China. From Kiev, on the shores of the river Dneiper, the Rus' also had easy access to the Black Sea and thence to Constantinople and Baghdad. They were thus in a position to trade directly and indirectly with much of Eurasia. Through a series of strategic intermarriages, moreover, they forged further connections with many powerful European families. This placed Kievan Rus' at the heart of the medieval world.

Yet the dominion of the Rus' was countered by the crystallization of Slavic kingdoms farther to the south: Serbia and Croatia on the Adriatic, which grew up within provinces of the old Roman Empire, and Poland. The ruling families of Croatia embraced the Latin Christianity of

Rome in this period; so did those of Poland. The Serbians, however, were drawn into the orbit of Byzantium and Greek Orthodoxy. Between them, and on the borders of Rus', was Hungary, comprising the former Roman province of Pannonia and stretching eastward toward the Carpathian mountains. It had been conquered by the Huns in the late fourth century and had since attracted new immigrants: the Magyars, a nomadic people from the region of the Urals whose language, like that of the Finns, was non-Indo-European.

The Magyars were expert herdsmen and horsemen. They also served as mercenaries fighting for various warring states. Around 895, they united under a leader called Arpád and settled in the fertile land of the Danube river basin, where they became farmers and ranchers. Arpád's descendants would embrace Latin Christianity, and would integrate the kingdom of Hungary with its neighbors through dynastic marriage and diplomacy.

New Scandinavian Kingdoms and the Empire of Cnut the Great

Meanwhile, powerful Norse lords were establishing control over parts of the Vikings' homeland. Around the year 1000, three strong kingdoms had emerged: Norway, Sweden, and Denmark. Each built on their kings' reputation for fearlessness in battle and generosity afterward, their capacity to dominate seas and riverways, and their canny practices of adaptation and intermarriage.

What made these new states distinctive was their rulers' very deliberate manipulation of this heritage, blended with the strategic decision to convert their followers to Christianity and to the political conventions of the Continent. They simultaneously glorified their own culture and achievements while tying them to newer models of government. For these reasons, scholars have often spoken of this as the "Viking Age." On the one hand, older Western civilizations can be said to have colonized Scandinavia; on the other hand, it was really Scandinavians who were doing the colonizing.

The empire forged by Cnut (*kuh-NOOT*) the Great is a good example of this. At the time of his death in 1035, Cnut ruled over Norway, much of Sweden, and England as well as his native Denmark; he had a controlling interest in large parts of Ireland and portions of the Low Countries; and he also had diplomatic and family ties to the independent principalities of Flanders and Normandy, the new kingdom of Poland (his mother was a Polish princess), and to the imperial family of Germany (through his daughter, who became empress). Although his was a short-term personal empire, it had long-term effects on the political organization of Europe.

Mediterranean Microcosms

The dynamism of these new states stands in contrast to the very different dynamics that governed relations in the medieval Mediterranean. No map could convey the political, religious, cultural, and economic affinities of this maritime world. It is more useful to imagine coastal regions and islands as interlocking components of the same civilization, and to further imagine that a community on the shores of North Africa—say, Muslim Tunis—would have more in common, and more contact, with Christian Barcelona than with another African community farther inland. The medieval Mediterranean was thus made up of diverse microcosms whose contours and interrelationships were more determined by prevailing winds, trading patterns, and climate than by the control of a particular ruler. In many places, it made little difference who the rulers were, especially since the forms of rule changed so often.

Take Sicily, for example: the first overseas colony of Rome (Chapter 5), it had been part of the Phoenician maritime empire of Carthage and, before that, a major Greek settlement (Chapters 2 and 3). All of those elements would still have been part of Sicily's historical DNA when it was invaded by the Vandals in the fifth century and afterward by the Goths. It was then reconquered by Justinian and became part of Byzantium—so important a part that one Byzantine emperor tried to move the capital from Constantinople to Palermo. Then, in the course of the tenth century, it became an emirate of the Fatimid Caliphate based in Egypt. In the eleventh, it was progressively infiltrated by Norman mercenaries who established a Norman (but only nominally Christian) kingdom there in 1072. So who were the Sicilians? More important, who did they think they were—and how stable was that identity over this long period of continual change? These are not easy questions to answer.

In any such case, it is better to think in terms of influences, connections, and orbits of exchange than about stable borders or identities; this holds true of many areas of Europe in this period but is especially true when speaking of regions joined by water. Gaining "control" of any Mediterranean community meant harnessing its commercial power, something not best done through violent conquest or military occupation. An exemplary light-handed interference was what enabled the Venetians to build a successful and long-lived trading empire in the Adriatic and then in the eastern Mediterranean and Aegean Seas.

The Heirs of Charlemagne

What had become of the former Carolingian empire? The Saxon kings of eastern Francia (now part of Germany) modeled themselves on Charlemagne, who had conquered Saxony, by extending their domains farther eastward, into Slavic lands. They also nurtured their image as guardians of Christendom: in 955, King Otto I defeated the then-pagan Magyars while carrying a sacred lance that had belonged to Charlemagne. In 962, he went to Rome to be crowned emperor by Pope John XII, who hoped Otto would help him defeat his own enemies. But Otto turned the tables on the pope, deposing him and selecting a new pope to replace him.

Otto thereby laid the foundation for his successors' claims to imperial autonomy. He also advertised his inheritance of Carolingian and Roman power through his patronage of arts and learning. The first known female playwright, Hrotsvitha of Gandersheim (c. 935–c. 1002), was raised in his court, and grew up hearing the works of classical authors read aloud. When she entered a royal convent, she wrote plays blending Roman comedy with the stories of early Christian martyrs, for the entertainment and instruction of her fellow nuns. Otto also presided over the establishment of cathedral schools and helped the bishops of his domain turn their own courts into cultural centers.

However, Otto could not control either the papacy or the independent towns of northern Italy unless he maintained a permanent presence there. And if he remained in Italy too long, his authority in Saxony broke down. The result was a gradually increasing rift between local elites and the king in his guise as emperor. This conundrum would deepen in the eleventh century, when the imperial crown passed to a new dynasty, the Salians, based in neighboring Franconia. When this Salian emperor attempted to assert control over Saxony, he touched off a war that was to have momentous repercussions (as will be discussed later).

Aspects of Charlemagne's legacy also survived in the highly effective administration of Anglo-Saxon England and in parts of the Mediterranean world. In Catalonia, counts descended from Carolingian appointees continued to administer justice in public courts of law and to draw revenues from tolls and trade. The city of Barcelona grew rapidly as both a long-distance and a regional market under the protection of these counts. In Aquitaine (southwestern France), the counts of Poitiers and Toulouse also continued to rest their authority on Carolingian foundations.

EUROPE, C. 1000. This map shows the patchwork of political power in western Europe after the millennium, although it cannot accurately illustrate the degree of fragmentation within these major territories, especially those of the Holy Roman Empire. ▪ *What factors account for the close relationship between Italy and the German principalities?* ▪ *How are they related to the northwestern regions of the Continent and the British Isles?* ▪ *Which geopolitical entities would you expect to emerge as dominant in the following centuries?*

In Charlemagne's own west Frankish kingdom, however, Carolingian rule collapsed under the combined weight of Viking raids, economic disintegration, and the growing power of local lords. A few Carolingian institutions—such as public courts and a centrally minted coinage—survived in new, autonomous principalities such as Anjou and Flanders. The Norse-Frankish rulers of Normandy also used these techniques effectively. But in the Franks' heartland, even this modicum of authority disappeared. The local count, Hugh Capet, had managed to defend his territory against the Vikings and, in 987, this modest feat earned him the title King of the Franks. Marooned on this Ile de France (literally, "island of France"), a tiny territory around Paris, the Capetian kings clung to the fiction that they were the heirs of Charlemagne's greatness. It would be another 200 years before one of them made this fiction a political reality (see Chapter 9).

AN AGRICULTURAL REVOLUTION

Like all economies prior to the nineteenth century, the medieval economy rested largely on agriculture. But, as we noted in Chapter 7, that economy was undergoing a revolution. Technological advances that boosted agricultural productivity—such as the heavy-wheeled plow—were now rendered even more effective through improved methods of harnessing, making it possible for plow animals to pull heavy loads without choking themselves. The development of iron horseshoes (around 900) and the tandem harnessing of paired teams (around 1050) were further innovations that enabled the transport of goods to new markets.

Labor-saving devices spurred another boost in productivity. The widespread use of iron for hoes, pitchforks, shovels, and scythes made work faster and easier for humans, too, and so did the wheelbarrow and the harrow (a tool drawn over plowed fields to level the earth and mix in the seed). The watermill was perhaps the most revolutionary invention. Although the Romans had known that running water was a potential power source, they had relied mainly on slave- and animal-powered wheels to grind grain. But the lack of slave labor led medieval engineers—usually monks—to experiment with new ways of harnessing water. Mills were then adapted to a variety of purposes: they drove saws for lumber, processed cloth, pressed olive oil, and provided power for the forging iron. They thus became a source of political and economic power, because those who controlled them could impose tolls and regulate the supply of food and weapons. Mills would remain the only mechanical power sources for manufacturing until the invention of the steam engine (see Chapter 19).

New Conditions for Growth

Although many of these technologies had been invented in the early Middle Ages, it was only in the eleventh century that they became sufficiently widespread to have a decisive impact. Climate change played a role in this. Starting in the late eighth century, average temperatures in Europe gradually rose by about 1° or 2°C (3.6°F). The warming climate benefited northern Europe by drying the soil and

EMPEROR OTTO THE GREAT. In this opening from a deluxe set of Gospels he commissioned for himself, Otto is shown seated on a throne and vested with the regalia of imperial and royal authority, surrounded by clerical and secular counselors, and receiving tribute from a procession of deferential women representing the four regions of his domain: Slavinia, Germania, Gallia, and Roma. ▪ *What claims to power is Otto making through this imagery?*

lengthening the growing season, while hotter summers and diminishing rainfall hurt Mediterranean agriculture in equal measure. For several centuries, it was possible to raise crops as far north as Greenland.

These new technologies also took hold because the settlement of Viking and Magyar peoples decreased the threat of invasion and the disruption of planting cycles. Left in relative peace, monasteries could develop and implement the tools described above, which were then copied by entrepreneurial peasants and local lords who saw the benefits of managing their own lands more efficiently, rather than raiding others'.

Harnessing People

All of this productivity led to population increases, fundamental changes in patterns of settlement, and the organization of the peasant workforce. In the centuries after the fragmentation of Roman imperial power, most people lived on individual plots of land that they worked by themselves and with their families. Starting in the ninth century, however, many of these individual holdings merged into large, common fields that could be farmed collectively by the inhabitants of entire villages. The resulting complex is sometimes called a *manor* (from the Latin verb *manere*, meaning "to dwell").

In many cases, the impetus for consolidation came from the peasants themselves. Large fields could be farmed more efficiently and investment costs could be shared: a single plow and a dozen oxen might suffice for an entire village, obviating the need for every farmer to maintain his own plow and team. Common fields were potentially more productive, allowing villagers to experiment with new crops and to support larger numbers of animals on common pastures. In time, prosperous peasants might be able to establish a parish church, a communal oven, a blacksmith, a mill, and a tavern. They could socialize and assist their neighbors.

In other cases, a manor could be created or co-opted by a local lord or a monastery. Manors were attractive because their greater productivity meant that lords could take a larger share of the peasants' surplus; it was also easier to control and exploit peasants who lived together in villages and who were bound by ties of kinship and dependence. Over time, some lords were able to reduce formerly free peasants to the status of serfs. Like slaves, serfs inherited their servile status; unlike slaves, they were attached to the lands they worked. Practically speaking, there may have been little difference between a serf and a free peasant—indeed, some serfs may have been better off. But, as we have seen, social mobility is often tied to geographical mobility; the inability of serfs to move freely would prevent them from achieving the liberties of those who could (as will be discussed later).

The Conquest of the Land

For centuries, farmers had known that sowing the same crop in the same field year after year would eventually exhaust the soil. The traditional solution was to divide one's land, planting half and leaving the other half to lie fallow. In the dry, thin soils of the Mediterranean, this remained the most common cropping pattern throughout the Middle Ages. In the more fertile soils of northern Europe, however, the organization of labor opened up more land for cultivation, and made that cultivation more efficient. Farmers discovered that a three-field crop-rotation system could produce a sustainable increase in overall production. One-third of the land would lie fallow or be used as pasture, so that manure would fertilize the soil; one-third would be planted with winter wheat or rye, sown in the fall and harvested in the early summer; and one-third would be planted in the spring with another crop to be harvested in the fall. These fields were then rotated over a three-year cycle.

This system increased the amount of land under cultivation, while the two separate growing seasons provided some insurance against loss due to natural disasters or inclement weather. The system also produced higher yields per acre, particularly if legumes or fodder crops like oats were a regular part of the crop-rotation pattern to replace the nitrogen that grains leach out of the soil. Both humans and animals could eat oats, and legumes provided a source of protein to balance the intake of carbohydrates from bread and beer, the two main dietary staples in northern and central Europe. Additional fodder supported more and healthier animals, increasing the efficiency of plow beasts and providing an additional source of protein through meat and milk. The new crop-rotation system also helped spread labor more evenly over the course of the year.

THE GROWTH OF TOWNS AND TRADE

As we observed in Chapter 7, the urban infrastructure of the western Roman Empire was weakened in the course of the fifth and sixth centuries. A few Roman cities

1. Cathedral
2. Alt St. Thomas
3. Alt St. Peter
4. Jung St. Peter
5. St. Nikolaus
6. St. Johann
7. St. Wilhelm
8. St. Stephen

0 50 100 200 300m

Roman fortification, the 'city'

Frankish settlement, called 'New City', walled at end of ninth century

Extension of Frankish settlement before 1200 to include Alt St. Peter's parish

Jung St. Peter's parish, walled 1202–1220

St. Nikolaus parish, walled thirteenth and fourteenth centuries

St. Johann Parish, walled 1374–1390

St. Wilhelm parish, walled 1387–1441

THE METAMORPHOSIS OF A MEDIEVAL CITY. The city of Strasbourg, on the long-disputed border between modern Germany and France, exemplifies the multilayered dynamics of urban change throughout the Middle Ages. It began as a Roman settlement, which became the nucleus for an episcopal see—hence the cathedral (1) located in the ancient precinct. It was fortified with new walls at the end of the ninth century, as the Carolingian Empire was collapsing and the Vikings were on the move. It then responded to the renewed prosperity of the eleventh and twelfth centuries, far outgrowing its original bounds, and continued to expand for several centuries thereafter. ■ *Note the scale of the map. What can you conclude from this about the density of settlement in a medieval city?*

continued to thrive, but many—including Rome itself—crumbled. Their depleted populations could no longer maintain public buildings, services, and defensive walls. In most areas of northwestern Europe, monasteries replaced cities as the nuclei of civilization. Then, under Charlemagne and his successors, towns were planted as centers for markets and administration. In Anglo-Saxon England, too, King Alfred and his heirs established new towns in strategic locations while at the same time fostering older Roman cities.

Fostering Commerce

Although many of towns were devastated by the Viking raids of the tenth century, the agricultural revolution helped to revitalize them. The rapid urbanization of the eleventh and twelfth centuries was also fostered by monasteries and secular lords who provided safe havens for travelers and trade. This was especially true in the principalities of the Rhineland, the Low Countries, and the independent counties of Flanders and Champagne. In southwestern Europe, existing towns prospered from their status as ports or their location along the overland routes connecting the Mediterranean with the Atlantic.

In Italy, which had been decimated by five centuries of warfare and invasion, renewed prosperity initially depended on the Byzantine emperors' suppression of piracy in the eastern Mediterranean. Around the turn of the millenium, therefore, the most successful cities were situated in Byzantine-controlled areas: Venice in the north and Amalfi, Naples, and Palermo in the south. These were the trading posts that brought silks, spices, and other luxuries into western Europe. In the eleventh century, however, the Norman conquests of southern Italy frequently disrupted this trade, while Turkish invasions of Asia Minor turned Byzantium's attention to the empire's eastern frontier. This opened new opportunities to the northern ports of Genoa and Pisa, whose merchant navies took over the task of policing the eastern Mediterranean.

From Italy and other Mediterranean ports, exotic goods flowed northward to the towns of Flanders and to the organized system of fairs—international markets convened at certain times of the year—that enriched the county of Champagne. Flemish towns, in turn, kept up a brisk trade with England, processing English wool into cloth.

"Town Air Makes You Free"

To our eyes, most medieval towns would have seemed half rural. Streets were unpaved, houses had gardens for raising vegetables, and animals were everywhere. Sanitary conditions were poor, and the air reeked of excrement, both animal and human. (Even in 1900, this was also true of New York, where 150,000 horses produced 45,000 tons of manure each month.) Under these conditions, disease could spread rapidly. Fire was another omnipresent danger, because wooden and thatched buildings were clustered close together.

But these inconveniences were far outweighed by the advantages of urban life. As a German adage puts it, "Town air makes you free" (*Stadtluft macht Frei*). This is because the citizens of most medieval towns were not subject to the arbitrary power of a lord—or if they were, the lord realized that rewarding initiative with further freedoms fostered still more initiative and produced more wealth. Many towns accordingly received charters of liberty from local rulers and were given the right to govern themselves. Others seized that right: in 1127, for example, the people of Flemish Arras declared that they were no longer the serfs of the local monastery and they banded together to form a commune, setting up their own form of representative government. The monastery was forced to free them and was then free to tax them. By the end of the century, Arras was the wealthiest and most densely populated town in northern Europe.

Urban areas further expanded through the constant immigration of free peasants and escaped serfs in search of a better life. For once a town had established its independence, newcomers could claim the status of citizens after a year and a day. For this reason, some powerful lords and rulers resisted the efforts of towns to claim independence. Almost inevitably, though, they paid a high price for this. In Rome, the pope's claim to secular authority over the city led to frequent uprisings. In the French city of Laon, the bishop who asserted his lordship over a newly formed commune was murdered in 1112. In 1127, the count of Flanders was assassinated in Bruges by a family of powerful officials who denied that they were his serfs.

Portable Wealth: Money and Credit

The growth of these medieval towns depended on initiative, social mobility, and surplus goods. It also depended on money: reliable currencies and the availability of credit. It is no accident that the wealthiest cities were located in regions whose rulers minted and regulated a strong coinage: Byzantium, Al-Andalus and the Christian kingdoms of Spain, the old Roman region of Provence (southern France), Anglo-Saxon England, and Flanders. Yet precisely because there were so many currencies in circulation, the medieval economy also depended on moneychangers and on bankers who could extend credit to merchants.

Many sophisticated financial mechanisms for extending credit had long been in place throughout the Islamic world and Byzantium. In western Europe, though, much of this crucial activity was carried forward by Jewish bankers situated within a close-knit network that connected cities like Constantinople, Baghdad, and Córdoba to the burgeoning cities of the north. In many regions, Jews had a virtual monopoly on these activities, because Christians were technically forbidden to lend money at interest or to make a profit from investments: a practice called *usury* (from the Latin word for "interest"). In reality, however, the Roman Church turned a blind eye to such practices. Indeed, many prominent churchmen, including bishops, made fortunes lending money—especially in banking towns like Arras and Florence.

Still, the moral stigma attaching to this necessary practice meant that Jews were often the ones targeted in times of crisis, just as they were the people to whom rulers would turn most readily when they needed funds. This helps to explain why many rulers protected the Jewish communities in their realms and often extended special privileges to them in exchange for money. The unfortunate result of this Christian hypocrisy was the circulation of conspiracy theories harmful to Jews, who were perceived as exercising control over finance. Jewish communities' reliance on the protection of powerful men also made

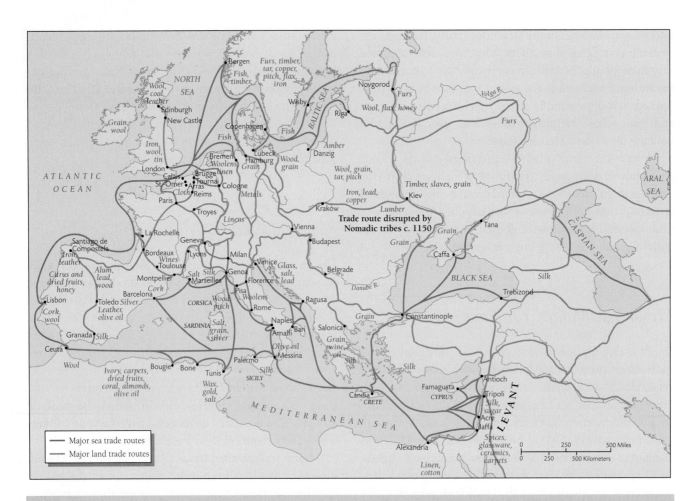

MEDIEVAL TRADE ROUTES. ■ *What does this map reveal about the relationship between waterways and overland routes during the eleventh and twelfth centuries?* ■ *Which regions appear to be most extensively interconnected, and why?* ■ *How does the trade in certain specialized goods create unique commercial patterns?*

them vulnerable when those men withdrew their support or were incapable of controlling the violence unleashed by their own policies.

VIOLENCE, LORDSHIP, AND MONARCHY

The new wealth of medieval Europe fostered social mobility, yet it also created a more stratified society. During the tenth and eleventh centuries, territorial lords and princes came to rival and often to surpass older aristocratic families in power and wealth. Some were descended from lesser officeholders in the Carolingian royal administration, men who had established independent powers after the empire collapsed and

who used their public offices for private gain. Others were successful interlopers who seized control of undefended manors and sustained war-bands of treasure-hungry young men.

Tools of Power: Castles and Knights

The predatory lords who emerged in this period protected their territories, their families, and their followers by building strongholds: castles, from the Latin word *castellum*, "little fortress." The stone castle, a structure seldom known in Europe before the Viking invasions, was both defensive and offensive. It rendered its keeper more secure from attack—though it was vulnerable to siege—and it enabled him to dominate the surrounding countryside, literally: the territory of a lord (*dominus*) was his dominion.

Indeed, castles often formed the nucleus of a new town by providing protection for the peasants and merchants who clustered close to its walls. In case of attack, these outliers could move inside.

Although most early castles were modest structures built of wood, situated on earthwork mounds surrounded by a ditch or moat, stone walls and keeps (fortified towers) soon replaced wooded palisades as the level of competitive violence increased. In Italy, rival families even built castles and towers in the middle of towns. Eventually, some castellans ("castle-holders") acquired enough power and booty to challenge more-established lords. These new lords didn't descend from Roman senators or Carolingian counts; instead, they boasted of lineages reaching back to successful warlords like Rollo the Viking, whom the Normans claimed to be their first duke (from the Latin word *dux*, "leader").

Both the older aristocracy and these self-made lords needed the help of warriors to enforce their claims to power. Accordingly, each lord maintained a private army of men heavily equipped with the new weaponry and armor made possible by the widespread availability of iron and new techniques for smelting it. These men fought on horseback and were therefore called "horsemen": in French, *chevaliers*, and in English, *knights*.

Knighthood was a career that embraced men of widely varying status. Some eleventh-century knights were the younger sons of noblemen who sought wealth by attaching themselves to the household of a great warlord. Others were youths recruited from the peasantry, mounted and armed. All that bound them together was their function, which was the violent prosecution of their lord's interests. Gradually, though, they came to regard themselves as belonging to a special military caste with its own rules of conduct. The beginnings of this process are discernible in *The Song of Roland*, a process that transformed the meaning of chivalry from "horsemanship" to something more refined (as will be discussed later).

Kings, Lords, and Vassals

Despite the emergence of self-governing cities and predatory lordships, the idea of kingship remained a powerful one. The weak Capetian rulers of Paris pretended that the lands once ruled by Frankish kings still owed allegiance to them, while the Ottonians claimed to be kings in northern Italy as well as in their own Saxon domain. In practice, however, neither was able to control the territories

YORK CASTLE (ENGLAND). This fortification exemplifies some of the major phases of medieval castle-building. The large mound is the remains of an earthwork erected on the orders of William the Conqueror in 1068, when it would have been crowned by a wooden palisade: this most basic type of construction is called a motte-and-bailey castle. York's castle remained a wooden tower until it was destroyed by fire and rebuilt in stone after 1245. It is now known as Clifford's Tower, after a rebel leader called Sir Roger Clifford, who was held prisoner there prior to his execution in 1322.

they claimed to rule. Real power lay in the hands of dukes, counts, castellans, and knights, all of whom channeled the increasing wealth of the countryside into their own hands. From their castles, these lords maintained the rights to mint money, dispense justice, raise troops, wage war, collect taxes, and impose tolls.

The Problem of "Feudalism"

The diffused distribution of power in this era is conventionally known as *feudalism*, but this term is misleading. For one thing, it is a modern construct that would have meant nothing to the people whose history we are discussing. Moreover, it has been used to mean many different things. Those influenced by the work of Karl Marx (1818–1883; see Chapter 20) used the term to describe an economic system based entirely on agriculture; as we have seen, this does not reflect the historical reality of medieval Europe or explain the importance of cities and trade. For others, "feudalism" means an aristocratic social order in which propertied men are bound together by kinship and shared interests; again, this does not match the varieties of power wielded in this period. Still others have seen "feudalism" as a system of landholding in which lesser men hold land from greater men in return for military service; and yet it was not always the greater men who held the most land.

Although people living at this time would never have heard the term *feudalism*, they would have understood the

Interpreting Visual Evidence

The Graphic History of the Bayeux Tapestry

One of the most famous historical documents of all time is not a document at all: it is an embroidered strip of linen 231 feet long (originally much longer) and 20 inches wide. It is also not an actual tapestry, as its name misleadingly implies, but an elaborate exercise in needlepoint. It tells the story of the Norman Conquest of England and the events leading up to it. The circumstances of its making remain mysterious, but it was certainly commissioned by someone close to William the Conqueror (1027–1087), the Norman duke who claimed the throne of England in 1066. Indeed, its purpose was to demonstrate the truth of William's claim and to justify his invasion of England when Harold Godwinson (c. 1022–1066), was crowned king of England in his place (image B). One likely patron is Queen Edith of England, the widow of the late King Edward (r. 1042–66) and sister of Harold, who became a friend and adviser to William. Edith was noted for her skill in embroidery as well as for her political acumen, and she would have been able to oversee the making of this visual history by the women of her household. Two of its evocative scenes, with translations of accompanying Latin texts, are reproduced here.

A. Here Harold Sails the Sea. In this scene from the first portion of the Tapestry, Harold has been sent on an embassy by King Edward. He feasts with friends in a hall on the English coast before crossing the Channel.

B. Here Is Seated Harold, King of the English. Although Harold may have promised to relinquish his claim to the English throne in William's favor, the central scene of the tapestry is his coronation. Stigant, the archbishop of Canterbury, stands on his right. Outside the cathedral, the people of London look on curiously. Some appear to be surprised or alarmed.

Questions for Analysis

1. Like a graphic novel or a comic strip, the Bayeux Tapestry tells its story through images; words (in very simple Latin) play a minor role. What do the Tapestry's artists choose to express exclusively through visualization? When do they choose to state something verbally? What might be the motivation behind these choices? What is left out of the story, or left ambiguous? What might be the reason(s) for this?

2. In addition to being a source for political and military historians, the Bayeux Tapestry provides us with fascinating glimpses into the daily life and material culture of the Middle Ages. What, for example, can you conclude about the necessary preparations for a voyage by sea? About the history of clothing, or weaponry, or animals?

3. If Queen Edith is responsible for making the Tapestry, it would constitute one of the few surviving historical accounts by a woman prior to the twentieth century. Would the fact of the creator's gender change your perception of this artifact or of these particular scenes? Why or why not?

word at its root: *feudum*, usually translated as "fief" (FEEF). A fief is a gift or grant that creates a kind of contractual relationship between the giver and receiver. This gift could be land, but it could also be the revenues from a toll or a mill, or an annual sum of money. In return, the recipient owed the giver loyalty or services of some kind.

In many cases, the recipient of a fief was subordinate to the giver and was said to be the giver's *vassal*, from a Celtic word meaning "boy." This relationship was dramatized in an act of *homage*, a ceremony that made the vassal "the man" (in French, *homme*) of his lord. Typically, the vassal would kneel and place his hands together in a position of prayer, and the lord would cover the clasped hands with his own. He would then raise up his new man and exchange a kiss with him. The symbolic importance of these gestures is clear: the lord could protect and elevate his man—but could also discipline him or bring him down.

In regions where no centralized authority existed, such relationships were essential to creating and maintaining order. However, these relationships were not understood in the same ways all over Europe. Many castellans and knights held their lands freely, owing no service whatsoever to the count or duke within whose territories their lands lay. Nor were these relationships neatly hierarchical. "Feudalism" created no "feudal pyramids," in which knights held fiefs from counts, and counts held fiefs from kings, all in an orderly fashion. Sometimes, kings would insist that the world *should* be structured this way, but they were seldom able to enforce this.

A New Type of Monarchy: England

The first place where we can observe a king's attempt to dominate other powerful lordships is England. In 1066, Duke William of Normandy claimed that he was the rightful successor of the Anglo-Saxon king, Edward, who had just died. But the English ignored this claim and elected a new king, Harold. So William crossed the English Channel to take the kingdom by force, defeating Harold's army at the Battle of Hastings (see **Interpreting Visual Evidence** on page 204). Now, however, William had to subjugate all of the Anglo-Saxon chieftains who held power in England, many of whom also aspired to be king.

William accomplished this by asserting that he was king by imperial conquest as well as by succession, and that all the land of England thereby belonged to him. Then William rewarded his Norman followers with fiefs: extensive grants of land taken from their Anglo-Saxon holders, which the Norman lords were allowed to exploit and

subdue. In return, William received their loyalty and a share of their revenues.

The Norman conquerors of England were already accustomed to holding land in return for service to their duke, back in Normandy. But in England, their subordination to the king was further enforced by the effective machinery of the previous Anglo-Saxon state. As king of England, therefore, William was able to exercise a variety of public powers that he could not have enjoyed in Normandy. In England, only the king could coin money and only the king's money was allowed to circulate. As kings of England, William and his successors also inherited the sole right to collect a national land tax, the right to supervise justice in royal courts, and the right to raise an army. They also retained the Anglo-Saxon officers of local government, known as sheriffs, to help them administer and enforce these royal rights.

William was thereby able to insist that all the people of England owed ultimate loyalty to the king, even if they did not hold a scrap of land from him. William's kingship thus represented a powerful fusion of Carolingian-style traditions of public power with the new forms of lordship that had grown up in the tenth and eleventh centuries, bolstered by indigenous Anglo-Saxon forms of governance. It was a new type of monarchy.

The Struggle for Imperial Power

We can contrast the wide-ranging powers of the new Norman kings of England with those of Germany. Any German king who claimed the title of emperor owed his imperial authority to a close alliance with the Church; he had no authority over any German principality but his own. For this reason, the emperor relied heavily on ecclesiastical leaders: his chief administrators were archbishops and bishops whom the emperor appointed and installed in their sacred offices, just as Charlemagne had done. Even the pope was frequently an imperial appointee. The fact that leading churchmen were often members of the emperor's own family also helped to counter the power of regional rulers.

But in the latter half of the eleventh century, this close cooperation between imperial and ecclesiastical authority was fractured. In 1056, the six-year-old Henry IV (1050–1106) succeeded his father as king of Saxony and emperor of the Romans. As we will observe, political competition among the advisers of underage rulers often escalates into larger conflicts. In this case, the German rulers of various other regions—led by some members of the Saxon nobility—tried to gain control of the royal government.

MATILDA OF TUSCANY MEDIATES BETWEEN EMPEROR AND POPE. Matilda was one of the most powerful rulers in eleventh-century Europe, controlling many strategic territories in northern Italy. Fluent in German as well as Latin and Italian, she was a key mediator in the struggle between the emperor and the pope and a supporter of the reforming movement within the Church. The Latin inscription accompanying this manuscript miniature reads: "The King entreats the Abbot [i.e., the pope] and even humbles himself before Matilda." ▪ *How does this image represent the relationships among these figures?* ▪ *Which appears to be the most powerful, and why?*

When Henry began to rule in his own right, in 1073, these hostilities escalated into a civil war.

At the same time, the newly elected pope, Gregory VII (r. 1073–85), began to insist that no layman—not even a king—should have any influence within the Church. (This movement toward increased papal power will be discussed further in the next section.) For King Henry, this meant that he could no longer select his own key administrators—and course, he resisted. So Pope Gregory allied himself with the rebellious Saxon nobility, and together they moved to depose Henry. In order to save his crown, Henry was therefore forced to acknowledge the pope's superiority. Crossing the Alps into Italy in 1077, in the depths of winter, he found

Gregory installed at the castle of Canossa under the protection of one of Europe's most powerful rulers, Matilda of Tuscany.

Encouraged by Matilda, who interceded on his behalf, Henry performed an elaborate ritual of penance, standing for three successive days outside the gates of the castle, barefoot, stripped of his imperial trappings, clad in the sackcloth of a suppliant. This performance forestalled his deposition, but it did not resolve his dispute with the nobility. And it also symbolically reversed the relationship between secular power and religious power. Since the time of Constantine, popes had been dependent on the rulers who protected them. Now an emperor had been bested by the pope. For the other kings and lords of Europe, Henry's humiliation was a chilling example of what could happen when a king became a vassal of the Church.

RELIGIOUS REFORM AND PAPAL POWER

The increased power of the papacy in the eleventh century was a result of the processes we have been surveying in this chapter. In the wake of the Viking invasions and the redistribution of power within the former Carolingian Empire, no ruler could maintain Charlemagne's hold on the Church. Many local churches had been abandoned or destroyed, while those that survived were often regarded as the personal property of some local family. Bishoprics, too, were co-opted by families who regarded Church lands and offices as their private property. Monasteries also underwent a process of privatization. Meanwhile, the holders of papal office were its worst abusers. Most were incompetent or corrupt, the sons or tools of powerful Roman families. Many fathered sons who themselves succeeded to high ecclesiastical office, including that of pope. The bishop of Rome had long occupied a privileged position, as the successor of St. Peter and the guardian of his tomb. Now, however, the papacy's credibility had been severely compromised.

The Monastic Reform Movement

The first successful attempts to restore the spiritual authority of the Roman Church can be traced to the founding of a new kind of monastery in Burgundy (now southeastern France). In 910, a Benedictine abbey called Cluny freed itself from any obligation to local families by placing itself under the direct protection of the papacy. And although it had a wealthy benefactor, that benefactor relinquished control over Cluny's property; instead, Duke William of Aquitaine and his family gained the spiritual support of the monks, whose prayers might save warlike men from eternal damnation.

This arrangement set a new precedent for the relationship between monasteries and powerful families, as Cluny began to sponsor other monasteries on the same model. This was another innovation: prior to this, all Benedictine monasteries had been independent of one another, united only by their observance of Benedict's *Rule* (Chapter 6). Now, Cluny established a network of Cluniac "daughter" monasteries across Europe, all of which remained subordinate to the mother house. By 1049, there were sixty-seven such priories, each one performing the same elaborate liturgy for which Cluny became famous, and each one entirely free from the control of local lords.

Cluniac influence was strongest in the former Frankish territories and in Italy, where the virtual absence of effective kingship allowed monastic power to thrive unchecked. In Germany and England, by contrast, fostering monastic reform emerged as an essential responsibility of any Christian ruler whose role model was the pious Charlemagne. Yet because these rulers were the guarantors of the monasteries' freedom, it was they who appointed the abbots, just as they also appointed the bishops of their kingdoms. As a result of this and of the Norman conquest, kings of England would have more direct control over Church lands than other European rulers. In Germany, as we have already noted, a prince's right to appoint spiritual leaders would be the central cause of Henry IV's strife with the papacy.

Despite the differences in sponsorship, these parallel reform movements made monasticism the dominant spiritual and intelletual force in western Europe. Monasteries also had an important influence on the piety of ordinary people, because many monastic communities maintained parishes that ministered directly to the laity. The spiritual practices that had been unique to monks and nuns in earlier centuries therefore came to influence daily life outside the cloister.

Relics and Pilgrims

One potent example of this new popular spirituality was the growing devotion to relics. Monasteries were the repositories of cherished objects associated with saints, such as fragments of bone or pieces of cloth cut from the garments of some holy person. These souvenirs were believed to possess special protective and curative powers. A relic was always buried beneath the altar of a church during the ceremony of its consecration, and relics were also collected and displayed in elaborate vessels (reliquaries) made of precious metals and studded with jewels. Indeed, relics were so valuable that monasteries and cathedral churches competed with one another for their acquisition and even plotted the "holy theft" of a particularly prized treasure. For instance, the relics of Nicholas, a fourth-century bishop of Myra (in Turkey), were stolen from the saint's tomb during the eleventh century. These were brought to Bari in southeastern Italy, where Benedictine monks built a magnificent church to house them. It became a major—and lucrative—attraction for pilgrims.

The possession and display of relics thus became a way to attract attention and generate revenue, since those who sought cures or favors at the shrine of a saint would often make a donation to the church in the saint's honor. If a saint was especially famous for a particular type of miracle, pilgrims might travel thousands of miles to visit a shrine. Saint Nicholas was famous for increasing the wealth of his suppliants, and for bestowing gifts—hence his later nickname, Santa Claus. The relics of Sainte Foy ("Saint Faith") of Conques (southern France) were renowned for their power to rectify injustices, restore order, and heal the maladies that afflicted the poor. Those of the apostle James at Compostela (in northwestern Spain) became the chief destination on a major pilgrimage route, rivaling even the holy sites of Rome and Jerusalem.

The Reform of the Secular Clergy

Eventually, the movement toward spiritual renewal in the monasteries of Europe began to influence the sees of bishops as well. This was a major change: bishops and the priests who served in their dioceses were secular clergy, living in the world (*saeculum* in Latin); it had long been expected that they would share some worldly preoccupations. But as the values and priorities of monasticism began to spread outward, abbots were more frequently appointed to episcopal office. Meanwhile, other bishops were forced to adopt stricter standards of personal conduct.

As their influence grew, the monasteries under the sway of Cluny began to push for even larger reforms, amounting to a fundamental dismantling of customs that reached back to the organization of the Church under Constantine, seven centuries earlier. They centered their attacks on the practice

Analyzing Primary Sources

A Miraculous Reliquary

Although pilgrimages had been a part of Christian religious practice for centuries, they became much more central elements of popular piety from the tenth century on. Pilgrims brought money and spiritual prestige to the monasteries and cathedrals that housed miracle-working relics, and competition among monastic houses sometimes led one house to steal the relics of another. But some critics worried that these newly popular shrines were encouraging idolatry. Bernard of Angers (c. 960–1028) was one such critic. His account of a visit to the shrines of several saints, including that of Sainte Foy ("Saint Faith") at Conques, reveals the negative impression that ornate reliquaries made on him—and the power of wonder-working relics to correct that impression.

t is an ancient custom in all of Auvergne, Rodez, Toulouse, and the neighboring regions that the local saint has a statue of gold, silver, or some other metal . . . [that] serves as a reliquary for the head of the saint or for a part of his body. The learned might see in this a superstition and a vestige of the cult of demons, and I myself . . . had the same impression the first time I saw the statue of Saint Gerard . . . resplendent with gold and stones, with an expression so human that the simple people . . . pretend that it winks at pilgrims whose prayers it answers. I admit to my shame that turning to my friend Bernerius and laughing, I whispered to him in Latin, "What do you think of the idol? Wouldn't Jupiter or Mars be happy with it?" . . .

Three days later we arrived at [the shrine of] St. Faith. . . . We approached [the reliquary] but the crowd was such that we could not prostrate ourselves like so many others already lying on the floor. Unhappy, I remained standing, fixing my view on the image and murmuring this prayer, "St. Faith, you whose relics rest in this sham, come to my assistance on the day of judgment." And this time I looked at my companion . . . because I found it outrageous that all of these rational beings should be praying to a mute and inanimate object. . . .

Later I greatly regretted to have acted so stupidly toward the saint of God. This was because among other miracles [that] Don Adalgerius, at that time dean and later . . . abbot [of Conques], told me [was] a remarkable account of a cleric named Oldaric. One day when the venerable image had to be taken to another place, . . . he restrained the crowd from bringing offerings and

The Reliquary of Sainte Foy, Early Tenth Century.

he insulted and belittled the image of the saint. . . . The next night, a lady of imposing severity appeared to him: "You," she said, "how dare you insult my image?" Having said this, she flogged her enemy with a staff. . . . He survived only long enough to tell the vision in the morning.

Thus there is no place left for arguing whether the effigy of St. Faith ought to be venerated since it is clear that he who reproached the holy martyr nevertheless retracted his reproach. Nor is it a spurious idol where nefarious rites of sacrifice or of divination are conducted, but rather a pious memorial of a holy virgin, before which great numbers of faithful people decently and eloquently implore her efficacious intercession for their sins.

Source: Bernard of Angers, "The Book of the Miracles of St. Faith," in *Readings in Medieval History*, 3rd ed., ed. and trans. Patrick J. Geary (Peterborough, ON., Canada: 2003), pp. 333–34 (slightly modified).

Questions for Analysis

1. Why does Bernard initially object to the display of relics in ornate reliquaries? Why would he consider this practice blasphemous? How does he become reconciled to it?

2. Can you think of present-day practices that resemble the medieval fascination with collecting, displaying, and venerating relics? What do such practices reveal about any society?

of simony (*SIGH-mony*), a term describing the use of ecclesiastical office for personal gain, including the purchase or sale of a bishopric. In other words, the reform movement targeted the very structure of the Roman Church as a network of lordships held by powerful men in trust for their families.

Even more radical was the reformers' demand that secular priests share the lifestyles of monks, taking vows of personal poverty and celibacy. Although some early councils of the Church had attempted to regulate the marriage of bishops and priests, these efforts had largely been abandoned. For a thousand years, it had been conceded that to demand priestly celibacy was unreasonable, and would also deprive a priest's parishioners of an additional resource and ministry—that of his wife. In the eleventh century, therefore, the vast majority of priests all across Europe were married. Married bishops were rarer, but not unknown. In Brittany, the bishop of Dol and his wife publicly celebrated the marriages of their daughters, endowing them with lands belonging to the bishopric; in Milan, the archbishops flatly rejected reformers' calls for celibacy on the grounds that their patron saint, Ambrose (see Chapter 6), had been married, too.

The Reform of the Papacy

In Rome, the most powerful bishopric of all remained resolutely unreformed until 1046, when the German king Henry III, who also bore the title of emperor, deposed three rival Roman nobles who claimed to be pope and appointed instead his own cousin, a monk who adopted the name Leo IX (r. 1049–54). Leo and his supporters began to promulgate decrees against simony and clerical marriage. They then took steps to enforce these decrees by traveling throughout the Continent, disciplining and removing from office priests deemed guilty of simony or obstinately determined not to "put away" their wives—whom the reformers insisted on calling "concubines."

Implicit in Leo's reforming efforts was a new vision of the Church as a type of monarchy, with the pope at the apex of a spiritual pyramid. Not surprisingly, therefore, Leo and his successors met with considerable opposition from powerful leaders within the Church itself, and they could only enforce their claims in regions where they had the support of secular rulers. Chief among these was the pious emperor Henry III, whose protection insulated papal reformers from the Roman nobility, who would otherwise have deposed or assassinated them.

But when Henry III died in 1056, the regents of his child heir Henry IV (whose reign we discussed above) were neither able nor willing to stand behind the reforming movement. In 1058, the Roman aristocracy seized this opportunity to regain control of the papal throne. By this time, however, the reform movement had gathered momentum; a year later, a new pope had been installed and was determined to counter any interference from either the German or Italian nobility. To this end, Nicholas II (r. 1059–61) created a new legislative body, the College of Cardinals (the Latin for "gathering of leaders"). The College became the nexus for creating papal policy and it also ensured the continuity of the papal office by overseeing elections, a role it still plays today.

Needless to say, this novel arrangement infuriated the advisers of the young Henry IV, since it removed the emperor's prerogative to oversee the process of papal elections himself. And it set the stage for the confrontations that were to follow.

The Investiture Conflict

In 1073, a few years after Henry IV began his adult rule, the new College of Cardinals elected a zealous reformer called Hildebrand, a Cluniac monk of Tuscan origins who took the name Gregory VII. Two years later, relations between papacy and empire were riven by a conflict that would permanently alter the political and religious landscape of western Europe. Superficially, the issue that divided Gregory and Henry was that of investiture: the right to appoint bishops and to invest them with the trappings of office. Since the time of the Carolingians, this had been the prerogative of the emperor—as it was in Byzantium. But to Pope Gregory, this practice smacked of simony, since a lay lord would obviously choose bishops who would be politically useful to him, regardless of their spiritual qualifications.

The real issue, however, was not the political power of bishops; it was the control of that power. For the papal reform movement under Gregory was predicated on liberating the Church from powerful influences in order that the papacy itself might become more powerful. This was the principle that lay behind the discouraging of clerical marriage, too: Church offices and Church property had to be protected by the Church for the Church. Allowing priests to marry might encourage the handing down of offices to sons, just as allowing rulers to appoint bishops encouraged these bishops to act as the rulers' agents. These practices tainted the austere authority that Gregory was trying to cultivate, and it also threatened to alienate property and power that he wanted to harness for the papacy.

Gregory therefore took the reform movement to a new level, insisting that adherence to these principles was not just a matter of policy but a matter of religious dogma, a term defined as "a truth necessary for salvation." When Henry IV refused to accept this and proceeded to invest the new archbishop of Milan, Gregory reminded him that he himself had the power to save or damn all souls as the successor of Saint Peter and the representative of Christ on earth. To drive the point home, Gregory excommunicated a number of Henry's advisers, including several of the bishops who had participated in the investiture at Milan. Henry countered by renouncing his obedience to Gregory, calling on him to resign. Gregory responded by excommunicating Henry, along with his supporters.

In itself, the excommunication of a king was not terribly unusual. Gregory, however, went much further by equating excommunication with deposition: since Henry was no longer a faithful son of the Church, he was no longer a king or the emperor, and his subjects had a sacred duty to rebel. It was this that occasioned Henry's humiliating stand before the castle at Canossa in January of 1077. But the story does not end there, because Henry used his restored powers to crush his Saxon opponents and to drive Gregory from Rome. In 1085, the aged pope died in exile in southern Italy.

By then, however, Gregory had established the principles on which papal governance would be based until the Reformation (see Chapter 13). In 1122, the conflict over investiture was provisionally resolved through compromise at the Concordat of Worms (VOHRMS) in Germany. Its terms declared that the emperor was forbidden to invest prelates with the *religious* symbols of their office but was allowed to invest them with the symbols of their rights as *temporal* rulers, in his capacity as their overlord. In practice, then, the rulers of Europe retained a great deal of influence over ecclesiastical appointments. But they also had to acknowledge that bishops were now part of a clerical hierarchy headed by the pope, and that they owed loyalty to the Church in Rome and not to the ruler of the region in which they lived.

CRUSADING CAUSES AND OUTCOMES

Gregory VII's equation of excommunication with deposition had given the pope a powerful new weapon, but his immediate successors would struggle to establish the

credibility of his claims. In the end, it took the appeal of a Byzantine emperor and the preaching of a crusade to unite western Christendom under the papal banner.

The Expansion and Limitations of Byzantium

As Europe expanded, the eastern Roman Empire was undergoing its own series of transformations. The decline of the Abbasid Caliphate in Baghdad had relieved some of the pressures on its borders, but Muslims from North Africa had captured the Byzantine islands of Sicily and Crete, which later fell to the Normans. Meanwhile, the migration of pagan Slavs was undermining Byzantine control of the Balkans; and a formidable power was also emerging in the north, as the Viking Rus' established themselves along the river systems that fed into the Black and Caspian Seas. In 860, a fleet of them sailed into the Black Sea and sacked Constantinople.

The Byzantine response was to make these new enemies into allies. Missionaries began the process by converting some of the Balkan Slavs to Orthodox Christianity, devising for them a written language known as Old Church Slavonic and creating the Cyrillic alphabet (based on Greek) still used in Bulgaria, Serbia, and Russia. The empire also established a military and commercial alliance with the kingdom centered on Kiev. In 911, hundreds of Rus' served with the Byzantine navy in an attack on Muslim Crete. In 957, a Kievan princess named Olga was lavishly entertained on a state visit to Constantinople. And in 989, Vladimir of Kiev helped Basil II win a civil war against an imperial rival; in exchange, Basil married him to his sister Anna and Vladimir accepted baptism into the Orthodox Church.

The eastern Roman Empire simultaneously strengthened and weakened its position by reconquering territories that had been lost to the Abbasids since the seventh century. Although most peoples of this region had remained Christian through three centuries of Islamic rule, the Armenians and the Syrians had their own distinctive and ancient Christian traditions that were at odds, doctrinally and linguistically, with the Greek-speaking church at Constantinople. Reincorporating these "heretics" into the empire strained the limits of Orthodoxy and also created centers of power that lay outside the imperial capital. Rivalries divided the eastern nobility and the imperial court, eventually erupting into warfare.

By the eleventh century, these projects of reconquest and expansion were overextending the Byzantine military and treasury. In an effort to raise cash, some emperors began to debase the gold coinage that had kept the empire competitive with the Islamic Caliphate in Baghdad, thus undermining Byzantine commerce at the very moment when Venice, Genoa, and Pisa were consolidating their control in the eastern Mediterranean and taking over the lucrative trade between Muslim North Africa and western Europe.

A failing economy, ongoing dynastic civil war, a weakened army, and uneasy relations with the new kingdoms of the Balkans proved nearly fatal to Byzantine sovereignty. And then the empire was confronted with yet another threat. The Seljuq Turks, a powerful dynasty of Sunni Muslims who were building their own empire based in Persia, began to move westward. In 1071, they captured Armenia and moved swiftly into the Byzantine heartland of Anatolia (Turkey), where they destroyed a Byzantine army. In the same year, the Seljuqs captured Jerusalem, which had been part of the Shi'ite caliphate based in Egypt, ruled by the Fatimids. By 1081, when the eastern nobility of Byzantium finally emerged triumphant in their ongoing bid for the imperial throne, the new emperor Alexius Comnenus (r. 1081–1118) found himself at the head of a crippled state.

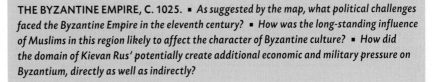

THE BYZANTINE EMPIRE, C. 1025. ▪ *As suggested by the map, what political challenges faced the Byzantine Empire in the eleventh century?* ▪ *How was the long-standing influence of Muslims in this region likely to affect the character of Byzantine culture?* ▪ *How did the domain of Kievan Rus' potentially create additional economic and military pressure on Byzantium, directly as well as indirectly?*

The Call for a Crusade

In the first decade of his rule, Alexius managed to shore up the failing economy and secure his hold over Bulgarian territory in the Balkans. He then began to plan a campaign against the Seljuqs. But with what forces? In 1085, the Byzantine army in Greece had been challenged by a far superior cavalry of Norman knights—for by this time, the Normans had established independent principalities in southern Italy and Sicily and were moving farther east. As it happened, this encounter convinced Alexius that such heavily armed horsemen would be successful if pitted against the lightly armored Seljuqs.

In the hopes of recruiting a mercenary force, Alexius approached Pope Urban II (r. 1088–99). Urban was trying to realize some of the powerful claims that Gregory VII had made on behalf of papal authority, and this seemed like a golden opportunity: by coming to the aid of the eastern Roman Empire, he could show the restive princes of western Europe that the papacy was a force to be reckoned with. At the same time, he could show that Latin military

Competing Viewpoints

Preaching the First Crusade: Two Accounts

> We owe the following account of Urban II's call for a crusade to Fulcher of Chartres, a priest who was present at the Council of Clermont in 1095 and who later served as a chaplain to the first Norman king of Jerusalem, Baldwin. It forms part of Fulcher's contemporary chronicle of the First Crusade. The second account of the motives behind the crusade comes from a biography of the Byzantine emperor Alexius I Comnenus, written by his daughter Anna (1083–1153), who also lived through these events.

Pope Urban II's Call at Clermont, November 1195

Most beloved brethren: Urged by necessity, I, Urban, by the permission of God chief bishop and prelate over the whole world, have come into these parts as an ambassador with a divine admonition to you, the servants of God....

Although, O sons of God, you have promised more firmly than ever to keep the peace among yourselves and to preserve the rights of the Church, there remains still an important work for you to do. Freshly quickened by the divine correction, you must apply the strength of your righteousness to another matter which concerns you as well as God. For your brethren who live in the east are in urgent need of your help, and you must hasten to give them the aid which has often been promised them. For, as most of you have heard, the Turks and Arabs have attacked them and have conquered the territory of Romania [the Byzantine Empire] as far west as the shore of the Mediterranean and the Hellespont.... They have occupied more and more of the lands of those Christians, and have overcome them in seven battles. They have killed and captured many, and have destroyed the churches and devastated the empire.

If you permit them to continue thus for a while with impunity, the faithful of God will be much more widely attacked by them. On this account I, or rather the Lord, beseech you as Christ's heralds to publish this everywhere and to persuade all people of whatever rank, footsoldiers and knights, poor and rich, to carry aid promptly to those Christians and to destroy that vile race [and remove it] from the lands of our friends. I say this to those who are present, but it is meant also for those who are absent. Moreover, Christ commands it.

All who die by the way, whether by land or by sea, or in battle against the pagans, shall have immediate remission of sins. This I grant them through the power of God with which I am invested. O what a disgrace, if such a despised and base race, which worships demons, should conquer a people which has the faith of omnipotent God and is made glorious with the name of Christ! With what reproaches will the Lord overwhelm us if you do not aid those who, with us, profess the Christian religion!

Let those who have been accustomed to wage unjust private warfare against the faithful now go against the infidels and end with victory this war which should have been begun long ago. Let those who for a long time have been robbers now become knights. Let those who have been fighting against their brothers and relatives now fight in a proper way against the barbarians. Let those who have been serving as mercenaries for small pay now obtain the eternal reward. Let those who have been wearing themselves out in both body

and spiritual might was greater than that of the weakened Greeks of Byzantium, thereby realizing the centuries-old dream of a united Christian Church based in Rome, with the pope at its head. In addition, Urban could support another reform that had gained momentum in recent years: a peace movement that was attempting to quell the violence unleashed by competitive bands of knights and their rapacious lords. What better way to defuse the situation than to ship those violent energies overseas, deploying them against a common enemy?

So Alexius received a favorable reply, but he got far more than he had asked for—or wanted. He had needed a modest contingent of a few thousand troops, to help him reconquer Anatolia. What he got was a vast and soul now work for a double honor. Behold! On this side will be the sorrowful and poor, on that, the rich; on this side, the enemies of the Lord, on that, his friends. Let those who go not put off the journey, but rent their lands and collect money for their expenses; and as soon as winter is over and spring comes, let them eagerly set out on the way with God as their guide.

Source: S. J. Allen and Emilie Amt, eds., *The Crusades: A Reader* (Peterborough, ON, Canada: 2003), pp. 39–40.

Anna Comnena Describes the Beginnings of the First Crusade

[Alexius] had no time to relax before he heard a rumour that countless Frankish armies were approaching. He dreaded their arrival, knowing as he did their uncontrollable passion, their erratic character and their irresolution, not to mention . . . their greed for money. . . . So far from despairing, however, he made every effort to prepare for war if need arose. What actually happened was more far-reaching and terrible than rumour suggested, for the whole of the West and all the barbarians who lived between the Adriatic and the Straits of Gibraltar migrated in a body to Asia, marching across Europe country by country with all their households. The reason for this mass-movement is to be found more or less in the following events. A certain Kelt, called Peter [the Hermit] . . . left to worship at the Holy Sepulchre and after suffering much ill-treatment at the hands of the Turks and Saracens who were plundering the whole of Asia, he returned home with difficulty. Unable to admit defeat, . . . he worked out a clever scheme. He decided to preach in all the Latin countries. A divine voice, he said, commanded him to proclaim to all the counts in France that all should depart from their homes, set out to worship at the Holy Shrine, and . . . strive to liberate Jerusalem. . . . Surprisingly, he was successful. . . . Full of enthusiasm and ardour they thronged every highway, and with these warriors came a host of civilians, outnumbering the sand of the sea shore or the stars of heaven, carrying palms and bearing crosses on their shoulders. There were women and children, too, who had left their own countries. . . .

The upheaval that ensued as men *and* women took to the road was unprecedented within living memory. The simpler folk were in very truth led on by a desire to worship at Our Lord's tomb and visit the holy places, but the more villainous characters . . . had an ulterior purpose, for they hoped on their journey to seize the capital [Jerusalem] itself, looking upon its capture as a natural consequence of the expedition. . . .

Source: Excerpted from Anna Comnena, *The Alexiad*, trans. E. R. A. Sewter (New York: 1969), pp. 308–11.

Questions for Analysis

1. Given Urban II's explanation of the problems confronting the Byzantine Empire, how do you account for the fact that the Crusades were directed toward the Holy Land and not to the relief of Byzantium?

2. How does Anna Comnena represent the motives of Peter the Hermit and the crusaders? What distinctions does she make among the participants?

3. Are there points of comparison between these two accounts? On what do they agree? How would you explain the differences between them?

army of 100,000 men, charged to retake the holy city of Jerusalem for Christendom. For Urban appears to have interpreted Alexius's request very loosely. Speaking before an assembled crowd at an ecclesiastical council at Clermont (central France) in 1095, he announced that he fully supported the peace movement. He said, furthermore, that any knights who wished to fight for a just and Christian cause could liberate the Holy Land from its Muslim captors. At home, said Urban, most knights were riffraff and marauders, destined for damnation; abroad, fighting or dying in the service of Christ would win absolution for sins. By taking up the cross (*crux*, hence "crusade"), a warrior might attain salvation, as well as booty and glory.

ROLAND AS A CRUSADING KNIGHT. The association between knighthood and crusading helped to raise the social status of knights and contributed to the refinement of a chivalric ethos. Here, a crusading knight, dressed head to foot in expensive chain mail, is shown kneeling in homage to his lord, God.

Consequently, the ultimate response to Urban's call exceeded all expectations. Indeed, his message was amplified by other preachers, including a zealous priest called Peter the Hermit, who claimed (falsely) that he had been prevented by the Seljuqs from visiting the Holy Land. Within a year, thousands of seasoned warriors and a large number of untrained, untried men were on the march toward Constantinople, where they intended to gather before departing for Jerusalem. As with any large enterprise, the participants' motives must have varied. Some may have hoped to win lands for themselves. Others were drawn by the prospect of adventure. Many were the dependents of greater men, who had no choice but to accompany their lords; some hoped to free themselves from dependence by fighting. Most had no idea how long the journey would be or knew anything about the places for which they were destined.

But except for a few of the warlords—mostly Normans from Sicily and southern Italy—the prospect of winning new territory was both unlikely and even undesirable. In fact, one of the greatest challenges facing the Christian kingdom established in Jerusalem after 1099 was that crusaders so rarely wanted to stay. After fulfilling their vows, the vast majority went home. So why did they go crusading in the first place? The risks of dying on the journey were high; the costs of embarking were enormous. Crusading knights needed a minimum of two years' revenues in hand to finance the journey. To raise such sums, most were forced to mortgage lands and borrow heavily from family, friends, monasteries, and merchants. They then had to find some way to pay back these loans if and when they returned home. By any rational assessment, the Crusade was a fool's errand.

The seeming irrationality of this endeavor underscores the importance of reckoning with the crusaders' piety, and their desire to emulate legendary heroes like Roland. Crusading was the ultimate pilgrimage, the holy places of Jerusalem the ultimate Christian shrines. If anyone could receive special blessings by traveling to Compostela, Conques, or Bari, how much more blessed would be those who fought their way through to the Holy Land? Urban II made this point explicit at Clermont, and some agitators went even further, promising that the souls of those who died on crusade would go straight to heaven.

Crusade preaching also emphasized the vengeance that Christ's soldiers should exact on his pagan enemies. To some crusaders, accordingly, it seemed absurd to wait until they arrived in the Holy Land to undertake this aspect of their mission. Muslims might hold Jesus's property at Jerusalem, but Christian theology held Jews responsible for the death of Jesus himself. Assaults against Jewish communities therefore began in the spring of 1096 and quickly spread eastward with the crusaders. Hundreds of Jews were killed in the German towns of Mainz, Worms, Speyer, and Cologne. Many individual churchmen attempted to prevent these attacks, among them the bishops in whose dioceses Jews lived. But the Church's own negative propaganda thwarted these efforts, and pogroms against Europe's Jews would remain a regular and predictable feature of Christian crusading.

The Christian Conquest of Jerusalem

Surprised by the scale of the response to his appeal, Emperor Alexius did his best to move the crusaders

Population predominantly Christian
Population predominantly Muslim
→ First Crusade (1096–1099)
→ Second Crusade (1147–1149)
→ Third Crusade (1189–1192)
→ Fourth Crusade (1202–1204)
Boundaries shown are those at time of First Crusade

THE ROUTES OF THE CRUSADERS, 1096–1204. Compare the routes followed by participants in the first three Crusades. ▪ *What were the three main routes followed by crusaders?* ▪ *What geographical and political factors appear to be determining these trajectories?*

quickly through Constantinople and into battle with the Seljuqs. But he had little interest in an expedition to Jerusalem, and insisted that the expedition's leaders promise to restore any territory they captured to him. To the crusaders, this seemed like treachery. Furthermore, they did not understand the Byzantine emperor's willingness to make alliances with some Muslim rulers (the Shi'ite Fatimids of Egypt and the Abassids of Baghdad) against other Muslim rulers (the Sunni Seljuqs). Some warlords ignorantly concluded that the Byzantines were supporting the Muslims against them. These suspicions fed a growing conviction that the eastern Roman Empire was itself an obstacle to the recovery of Jerusalem.

Viewed from the perspective of Alexius, the Crusade was a disaster. But from that of the crusaders themselves,

it was a triumph. In 1098, crusaders captured the old Hellenistic city of Antioch and with it most of the Syrian coast. At the end of 1099, they took Jerusalem, indiscriminately slaughtering Muslim, Jewish, and Christian inhabitants. Their quick success stemmed mainly from the fact that their Muslim opponents were at that moment divided among themselves: the Fatimids had in fact recaptured Jerusalem just months before the crusaders arrived, and the defeated Seljuqs were at war with one another. Western military tactics, in particular the dominance of heavily armored knights, also played an important role in the crusaders' success. Equally critical was the naval support offered by Genoa and Pisa, whose merchant adventurers hoped to control the Indian spice trade that passed through the Red Sea and on to Alexandria in Egypt. The Crusade

Past and Present

Ideas of Crusade

The launching of the First Crusade was the beginning of a trend that decisively shaped the relations between western Europeans and their neighbors, and that continues today. The very use of the word "crusade" is apt to cause trouble—as when President George W. Bush spoke of "this crusade, this war on terrorism" to which he pledged the United States after September 11, 2001.

Watch related author videos on the Student Site
wwnorton.com/college/history/western-civilizationsBrief4

thereby contributed to the further decline of Byzantine commerce and decisively altered the balance of power between Byzantium and western Europe.

The Consequences of Crusade

For Byzantium, the consequences of the crusading movement were clearly negative. On the Muslim world, however, the impact was more modest. The crusader kingdoms established by victorious Norman and Frankish warlords were never more than a sparsely settled cluster of colonies along the coastline of Syria and Palestine. Because the crusaders did not control the Red Sea, the main routes of Islamic commerce with India and the Far East were unaffected by the change in Jerusalem's religious allegiance.

In any case, those crusaders who remained to settle in the region did not *want* to interfere with the caravan routes that wound through their new territories. Trade brokered by Arab, Persian, and Jewish merchants therefore continued. But the greatest economic gains went to the Italian maritime republics of Venice and Genoa, and to the western markets now open to Muslim merchants for their goods. Both sides also gained in military terms: western Europeans learned new techniques of fortification, and Muslims learned new methods of siege warfare and the uses of heavy cavalry.

The larger impact of the Crusades on western Europe is more difficult to assess. On the one hand, the establishment of the short-lived crusader states represents the limits of Europe's expansion during this otherwise extraordinary period of growth. On the other, trade with the Islamic world, and beyond it with India and the Far East, brought enormous prosperity to some. And yet these trading links had existed before the Crusades, and continued after they ended.

In the long run, the most lasting consequence of the First Crusade was the deadly escalation of both Christian and Muslim doctrines of holy war. Almost immediately, crusading rhetoric began to dictate the terms of western Europeans' attitudes toward the wider world and even toward one another, as we shall see in the following chapters. By 1108, it fostered a new ideology that would justify warfare against the Slavs, and it would continue to inform the "reconquest" of the Iberian Peninsula by the Christian rulers of Spain, leading to the massacre or forced conversion of Muslims and Jews. It would later fuel English wars against the Welsh and the Scots, and foment the massacre and dispossession of "heretics" in southern France by northern French colonists. It justified the conquest of the Baltic region and, later, the subsequent conquest of the Americas and the colonization of Asia, Africa, and Australia. And it has continued to exacerbate global animosities to this day.

THE CULTURE OF THE MUSLIM WEST

Not all the consequences of crusading were negative. The positive outcomes were hugely important, especially for western Europe. Increased intellectual and cultural contact with the Islamic world had an enormous impact on learning, literature, music, and art. Even Christian theology was transformed by contact with Islam. Europeans had been almost entirely ignorant of Muslim beliefs prior to the Crusade, assuming that Muslims were pagans who worshiped a god called Mahomet or Mahoun. But by 1143, a scholar called Robert of Ketton (c. 1100–c. 1160), originally from a small town in England, had completed a Latin translation of the Qur'an, working in Spain with the encouragement of the abbot of Cluny. In the 1130s, he and a friend, Hermann of Carinthia (in Slovenia), had traveled to Byzantium and the crusader kingdoms, where they became students of Arabic. And because Muslim scholars had inherited, preserved, and developed not only Hellenistic medicine and science but the teachings of Aristotle, this learning would form the basis of a new Christian philosophy.

Muslim Philosophy and Christian Theology

As we noted in Chapter 7, the scholars of Byzantium had taken a conservative approach to Greek philosophy, in every sense of the word. The dialogues of Plato and some works of Aristotle were copied and studied, but the latter's ideas were so hard to reconcile with Orthodox theology that Emperor Alexius eventually banned the teaching of Aristotelian logic. Ironically, then, it was through Arabic translations that western European intellectuals became acquainted with these ideas—thanks to the labor of Arabists like Robert and Hermann.

Even before the rise of Islam, a number of Greek philosophical texts had been translated into Syriac, a Semitic language closely related to Arabic. Arabic translations soon followed, many sponsored by the Abbasid court at Baghdad, which established a special school for this purpose: the House of Wisdom. By the end of the tenth century, Arabic translations of Greek authors were widely available and intensively studied throughout the Muslim world. Even in the remote Persian city of Bukhara, the great Muslim philosopher and physician Avicenna (Ibn Sīnā, 980–1037) was able to read all of Aristotle's works before he reached the age of eighteen.

Like their counterparts in Byzantium, Muslim philosophers strove to reconcile Greek and Hellenistic philosophical traditions and to match them with the tenets of their theology. Reconciling Aristotelianism and Neoplatonism was the easier task, because these schools of thought shared a number of common assumptions, including the eternity of the world and the capacity of the human mind to understand the principles that govern the world's workings. Both traditions also stressed the freedom of individual humans to choose between good and evil.

But combining Greek philosophy with Islamic theology was more difficult. Like Judaism and Christianity, Islam holds that a single omnipotent God created the world; this runs counter to the classical Greek view of the world as eternal. Moreover, both Christian and Islamic theology emphasize the immortality of the individual human soul, another doctrine in conflict with Aristotelian and Neoplatonic thought. With respect to the concept of free will, Muslims and Christians also had more in common with one another than with Greek tradition. Muslim philosophers had already adopted an array of different intellectual tactics to deal with these challenges, and thereby laid the groundwork for the Christian theologians who relied on them (see Chapter 9).

Analyzing Primary Sources

....

An Arab Aristocrat Encounters the Crusaders

Usama ibn Munqidh (1095–1188) was an Arab Muslim from Syria, whose family maintained a prominent place in the local administration even after the conquests of the Seljuqs and the Christian crusaders. He traveled widely and worked in various Islamic cities as a diplomat and scholar. He ended his life in the service of Salāḥ ad-Dīn (Saladin), the great Muslim leader who reconquered Jerusalem the year before Usama's death. The following excerpt is from Usama's memoir, which he called The Book of Contemplation. *The Templars mentioned in the account are the Christian military order of the Knights of the Temple, who dedicated themselves to protecting pilgrims in Jerusalem and guarding the holy sites. Their headquarters was in the main mosque of the city, which stood on the Temple Mount.*

nyone who is recently arrived from the Frankish lands is rougher in character than those who have become acclimated and have frequented the company of Muslims. Here is an instance of their rough character (may God abominate them!):

Whenever I went to visit the holy sites in Jerusalem, I would go in and make my way up to the al-Aqsa Mosque, beside which stood a small mosque that the Franks had converted into a church. When I went into the al-Aqsa Mosque—where the Templars, who are my friends, were—they would clear out that little mosque so that I could pray in it. One day, I went into the little mosque, recited the opening formula 'God is great!' and stood up in prayer. At this, one of the Franks rushed at me and grabbed me and turned my face towards the east, saying, 'Pray like *this*!'

A group of Templars hurried towards him, took hold of the Frank and took him away from me. I then returned to my prayers. The Frank, that very same one, took advantage of their inattention and returned, rushing upon me and turning my face to the east, saying, 'Pray like *this*!'

So the Templars came in again, grabbed him and threw him out. They apologized to me, saying, 'This man is a stranger, just arrived from the Frankish lands sometime in the past few days. He has never before seen anyone who did not pray towards the east.'

'I think I've prayed quite enough,' I said and left. I used to marvel at that devil, the change of his expression, the way he trembled and what he must have made of seeing someone praying towards Mecca.

Source: Usama ibn Munqidh, *The Book of Contemplation: Islam and the Crusades*, trans. Paul M. Cobb (New York: 2008), p. 147.

Questions for Analysis

1. What does Usama's account reveal about the variety of relationships among Christians and Muslims in the crusader kingdom of Jerusalem?

2. Who is the true outsider in this scenario? What does Usama's treatment by the Templars suggest about the policy of Christian leaders toward the city's Muslim residents?

Muslim Science, Medicine, and Mathematics

Many Muslim philosophers were also distinguished physicians and scientists. Both astrology and medicine were applied sciences that relied on careful, accurate observation of natural phenomena. Muslim observations of the heavens were so accurate, indeed, that some astronomers had corroborated the findings of Hellenistic scientists, positing that the earth must rotate on its axis and revolve around the sun (Chapter 4). But because these theories conflicted with the (mistaken) assumptions of Aristotle—that the earth remained stationary with the sun and planets revolving around it—they were not generally accepted in the Muslim world or in Europe.

Muslim accomplishments in medicine were equally remarkable. Avicenna discovered the contagious nature

MUSLIM ARCHITECTURE AND GARDEN DESIGN. Both images display how Muslim architects and designers borrowed features from many cultures but combined them in distinctively graceful ways.

of tuberculosis and noted that many diseases could spread through contaminated water and soil. His *Canon of Medicine* would remain an authoritative medical textbook in the Islamic world and Europe until the seventeenth century. Muslim physicians also studied cauterization and the use of styptic agents, diagnosed cancer, prescribed antidotes in cases of poisoning, and made notable progress in treating eye diseases. They recognized the infectious character of plague, pointing out that it could be transmitted by clothing. Muslim physicians were even pioneers in medical administration. At least thirty-four great hospitals were located in the principal cities of Persia, Syria, and Egypt, each with separate wards for particular illnesses, a dispensary for giving out medicine, and a library. Chief physicians and surgeons lectured to students, examined them, and issued licenses to practice medicine. Even the owners of leeches (used for bloodletting, a standard medical practice of the day) had to submit their medicinal worms for inspection at regular intervals.

Islamic scientists made important advances in optics and chemistry, but their most significant contribution was to the study of mathematics. Using Arabic numerals—actually adopted from the Hindus—mathematicians developed a decimal arithmetic based on place values and hinged on the concept of the zero. Their work enabled fundamental advances in entirely new areas, both of which bear Arabic names: algebra and algorithms. These advances revolutionized both the theoretical and practical applications of mathematics in Europe. They were first promoted beyond the Islamic world by the son of a Pisan merchant who grew up in Algeria, Leonardo Fibonacci

(c. 1170–c. 1250), and they made an indispensable contribution to the burgeoning European economy. The sophisticated accounting systems that supported commerce would have been impossible if merchants and bankers had continued to use the clumsy numerical system of the Romans. Thanks to Arabic mathematics, western Europeans could now add, subtract, divide, and multiply quickly and accurately, with or without the help of another Muslim invention, the abacus.

Muslim Literature and Art

Poetry was integral to Muslim culture. It had been a highly developed Arabic art form long before the emergence of Islam, and it became even more important because it was the form in which Muhammad framed the Qur'an (see Chapter 7). Like medicine and astronomy, poetry was also a route to power. Particularly around the Abbasid court, poets composing in both Arabic and in Persian enjoyed great renown. The best known of these is Umar Khayyam (d. 1123), whose *Rubaiyat* was turned into a popular English verse cycle by the Victorian poet Edward Fitzgerald (1809–1883). Fitzgerald's sensual translation ("a jug of wine, a loaf of bread—and thou") reflects themes that were common to much Muslim poetry, but it masks the fact that much of this poetry was addressed by men to other men. Jews also participated in this elite literary world, especially in Al-Andalus, where their Hebrew and Arabic lyrics celebrated wine, sexual intimacy, and the art of poetic composition.

The distinctive architectural and decorative arts of Islam also flourished at this time, and created the spaces in which poets and scientists interacted with their patrons. Many characteristic elements of Muslim architecture (the dome, the column, and the arch) had been adapted from Byzantine models, but were then combined with the intricate tracery and ambitious scale of Persian buildings to form a new architectural vocabulary. Building styles were further inflected by the many different cultures that embraced Islam, from Spain to Egypt to India and beyond. Muslim artistry was also expressed in the magnificent gardens and fountains that adorned palaces, and in the portable magnificence of gorgeous carpets, tooled leather, brocaded silks and tapestries, inlaid metalwork, enameled glassware, and painted pottery—all decorated with Arabic script, interlacing geometric designs, plants, fruits, flowers, and fantastic animal figures (another Persian influence). These complex designs anticipate the abstract forms that were considered new in the twentieth century and can often seem strikingly modern.

The Muslim Influence on Western Europe

Prior to the contacts facilitated by crusading, the cultural, economic, and intellectual achievements of Muslim civilization completely overshadowed those of western Europe. Thereafter, Europeans would continue to rely heavily on what they had learned from the Islamic world, and this is reflected in the large number of Arabic and Persian words that passed into European languages. Essential words for commerce and trade include *traffic*, *tariff*, *alcohol*, *muslin*, *orange*, *lemon*, *alfalfa*, *saffron*, *sugar*, *syrup*, and *musk*, to name just a few. The word *admiral* also comes from Arabic (from the title *emir*), as do words that tell the story of Europe's reliance on Muslim science and technology: *alchemy*, *algebra*, *algorithm*, *alkali*, *almanac*, *amalgam*, *cipher*, *soda*, *magazine*, and *zero*—not to mention the names of stars, such as Aldebaran and Betelgeuse.

After You Read This Chapter

Go to **INQUIZITIVE** to see what you've learned—and learn what you've missed—with personalized feedback along the way.

REVIEWING THE OBJECTIVES

- The fragmentation of power in the ninth and tenth centuries created a world very different from that of Charlemagne. Describe some of the key changes. What were their causes?
- The agricultural revolution of the Middle Ages had far-reaching economic, social, and political consequences. What were they?
- The reforming movement with the Church changed the relationship between the papacy and the secular rulers of Christendom. Explain why. What were the larger implications of this shift?
- The motives behind the First Crusade were political as well as religious. Why was this the case?
- The crusading movement had profound effects on western Europe and Byzantium, as well as on the relationship between the Latin Christian and Muslim worlds. In what ways were these three civilizations transformed?

The Muslim world also had an enormous influence on the imagination of Christian Europe. Western Christians tended to look down on the Byzantine Greeks, but they respected and feared the civilization that brought Arabs, Persians, Turks, Egyptians, Africans, Indians, and Asians together in a common cultural and religious system, creating a diverse society and a splendid legacy of original discoveries and accomplishments. The expanding Europe of the Middle Ages reaped the benefits of its interactions with this rich culture.

CONCLUSION

Before the year 1000, western Europe was the least powerful, least prosperous, and least sophisticated of the three civilizations that had emerged from the Roman world. A hundred years later, it was a force to be reckoned with. This metamorphosis rested on economic foundations: increasingly efficient agriculture, a growing population, and expanding trade. These changes produced a dynamic, mobile society. No less important, however, were the political and military changes that began to alter the map of Europe in these centuries. By 1100, the mounted, heavily armored knight had emerged as the most formidable military weapon of the day, and new conceptions of power—both spiritual and temporal—were being articulated and contested.

Where, then, do the emerging kingdoms of medieval Europe fit into this picture? How would the struggle for the control of western Europe's expanding resources be carried forward in the wake of the Crusades? And what cultural, spiritual, social, and intellectual innovations would result? These are the questions we address in Chapter 9.

PEOPLE, IDEAS, AND EVENTS IN CONTEXT

- How was Europe affected by **VIKING** raids and settlements? Which territorial rulers imitated **CAROLINGIAN** models in the wake of these initiatives?
- What new technologies drove the **AGRICULTURAL REVOLUTION** of the Middle Ages? Why did the organization of labor on **MANORS** sometimes lead to **SERFDOM**?
- What conditions led to the growth of medieval **TOWNS** and why did the formation of urban **COMMUNES** foster new types of liberty? How were money and credit essential to medieval commerce?
- Why is **FEUDALISM** a problematic concept? How did the ceremony of **HOMAGE** symbolize the relationship between a **VASSAL** and his lord?
- What were the causes of the **INVESTITURE CONFLICT**?
- Why did **ALEXIUS COMNENUS** ask **POPE URBAN II** for assistance? Why did the pope use this as a pretext for urging the **FIRST CRUSADE**?
- How and why did **MUSLIM LEARNING AND CULTURE** exercise a profound influence on western Europeans?

THINKING ABOUT CONNECTIONS

- In what ways does the Investiture Conflict reflect the unique historical circumstances of the late eleventh century, and in what ways can it be viewed as an extension of longer-term phenomena?
- Based on what you have learned about the relationship between political power and religious power in previous chapters, would you say that the clash between the papacy and the Holy Roman Empire was inevitable?
- Given the many negative aspects of the crusading movement—and its eventual failure—how might you explain the continuing appeal of crusading rhetoric down to the present day?

STORY LINES

- The power of Europe's new monarchies and of the papacy depended on new methods of oversight, administration, and documentation.

- Continued crusading movements in the twelfth and thirteenth centuries intensified contacts between Latin Christendom and the Muslim world while posing a threat to many minority groups within Europe, and to the Byzantine Empire.

- The Church's presence in the daily lives of the laity produced vibrant forms of spirituality yet placed strict limitations on women, religious dissidents, and non-Christians.

- Schools and universities were crucial to the development of secular and ecclesiastical institutions, and they also provided ambitious men with unprecedented intellectual, social, and political opportunities.

- Meanwhile, Europe's princely courts, wealthy towns, universities, and cathedrals fostered new forms of entertainment, art, and architecture.

Before You Read This Chapter

CHRONOLOGY

1079–1142	Lifetime of Peter Abelard
c. 1090–c. 1164	Lifetime of Heloise
1098–1179	Lifetime of Hildegard of Bingen
1099	First Crusade ends
1122–1204	Lifetime of Eleanor of Aquitaine
c. 1140	Gratian's *Concordance of Discordant Canons*
1152–1190	Reign of Frederick II Barbarossa
1180–1223	Reign of Philip II Augustus
1187	Muslim reconquest of Jerusalem
1192–1194	Alfonso II of Aragon compiles the *Liber feudorum maior*
1194–1250	Lifetime of Emperor Frederick II
1198–1216	Reign of Pope Innocent III
1204	Capture and sack of Constantinople
1209	Franciscan order established
	Beginning of the Albigensian Crusade
1215	Magna Carta and the canons of the Fourth Lateran Council are both formulated
1216	Dominican order established

The Consolidation of Europe, 1100–1250

CORE OBJECTIVES

- **IDENTIFY** and **UNDERSTAND** the differences among Europe's emerging monarchies.

- **DESCRIBE** the ongoing effects of crusading and their importance.

- **UNDERSTAND** the connections between new religious movements and the power of the papacy.

- **DEFINE** scholasticism and **TRACE** its development.

- **EXPLAIN** the changing meaning of *chivalry* and its cultural consequences.

At the turn of the twelfth century, the eldest son of a nobleman did something unusual: he traded lordship for scholarship. His name was Peter Abelard, and after besting all the teachers in Paris he was appointed master of the cathedral school: the highest academic post of the time. There he met Heloise, the niece of a priest called Fulbert.

Heloise had received an excellent education in a nearby convent, but the path of higher learning—Abelard's school— was closed to her. Instead, she became his private pupil and, in time, his intellectual partner, lover, and wife. This last step was particularly problematic, because marriage was no longer an option for clerics like Abelard, and would ruin his chances of a brilliant career. So it remained a secret, as did Heloise's pregnancy and the birth of their son. But then her uncle found out and took revenge on Abelard, sending some local thugs to castrate him. What we know of these events comes from letters exchanged by the couple years later, when Heloise was the leader of a new religious community and Abelard was laying the intellectual foundations of the first university.

ABELARD AND HELOISE. This image from a thirteenth-century manuscript shows Abelard in a scholar's gown and cap and Heloise wearing a nun's habit; their gestures indicate that they are engaged in debate. The story of their fervent attraction and doomed marriage was already famous during their lifetimes, and by the time this manuscript was copied, theirs had become the ultimate example of star-crossed love.

The twelfth and thirteenth centuries witnessed the emergence of large-scale territorial monarchies as dominant political forces, with cathedral schools and the new universities turning out the skilled clerical professionals needed to run these growing bureaucracies, and that of the Church. But at the same time that new opportunities for advancement were available to men, those open to women were being closed down. Meanwhile, deepened connections between Europe and the wider medieval world were creating an integrated and far-reaching economy of goods and ideas. Novel literary forms took shape as the spoken vernaculars of Europe came to challenge Latin, becoming languages of commerce, devotion, and entertainment. By the middle of the thirteenth century, the political institutions and cultural identities that still define Europe had been formed.

THE MAKING OF MEDIEVAL MONARCHIES

As we learned in Chapter 8, power was highly decentralized and diffused for much of the tenth and eleventh centuries. Independent towns and lords often refused to acknowledge royal authority and kings could no longer rely on close-knit kin groups or the broad powers wielded by Charlemagne. How, then, did some rulers build the foundations of states that continue to exist today? For crucially, the *idea* of a national state—a state that consolidates a shared identity and destiny—was an idea forged in the twelfth and thirteenth centuries. Thereafter, it become so vital for modern European states to trace their origins to the medieval past that those nations without a medieval pedigree would be obliged to invent one.

England: From Lordship to Government

After 1066, the conquest of England (Chapter 8) allowed its first Norman ruler, William, to experiment with a new type of kingship. In theory, he commanded the allegiance of every person dwelling in his kingdom. In practice, however, William needed to impose his will on his new subjects, either through force or through the highly effective administrative structures of his Anglo-Saxon predecessors, which he adapted to his own needs. This process was carried forward by his son Henry I (r. 1100–35), whose approach to kingship was unusual in its focus on governance rather than warfare. Henry strengthened local administration and instituted a system of traveling judges to administer royal justice. He also introduced a method of fiscal accounting carried out by an office known as the Exchequer, so called because clerks moved counters around on a checkered cloth to calculate receipts and expenditures.

But Henry's hands-on approach to royal lordship was both new and unpopular. Then, as now, those opposed to "big government" could react violently against it, and after Henry's death those reactions provoked a civil war that lasted throughout the reign of his cousin and successor, Stephen (r. 1135–54). Yet this period of relative chaos merely underscored the need for strong, centralized rule, a need that was finally met by Henry's grandson and namesake.

Henry II and the Extension of Royal Power

At the age of twenty-one, the new King Henry II (b. 1133, r. 1154–89) was already the duke of Normandy and the lord of two other independent French counties, Anjou and Maine. He also controlled the Aquitaine, thanks to his recent marriage to its powerful and brilliant ruler, Eleanor (1122–1204), who had annulled her first marriage to the French king Louis VII in order to create this alliance.

Map Legend

- Angevin Empire under Henry II, c. 1180
- French Royal domain, 1180
- Disputed frontier, 1180
- Holy Roman Empire, 1180

France at the Death of Philip Augustus 1223

- Royal domain
- Under English rule

ENGLAND

ATLANTIC OCEAN

Paris
FRANCE

Compostela

Bay of Biscay

AQUITAINE

LÉON

SCOTLAND

NORTH SEA

Edinburgh

Carlisle

Tyne R.

Durham

Ure R.

Stamford Bridge

York

IRELAND

Dublin

WALES

Severn R.

Hereford

Gloucester

ENGLAND

Ely

Cambridge

Oxford

Thames R.

Runnymede

London

Southampton

Winchester

Canterbury

Calais

English Channel

Bruges

Ypres

Lille

Antwerp

Brussels

FLANDERS

Arras

Amiens

Meuse R.

Rhine R.

HOLY

ATLANTIC OCEAN

Bayeux

Rouen

Beauvais

VERMANDOIS

Caen

Seine R.

St. Denis

Rheims

Verdun

ROMAN

Mont-St. Michel

NORMANDY

Paris

Marne R.

LORRAINE

Mosel R.

Main R.

BRITTANY

MAINE

Chartres

Brétigny

ÎLE DE FRANCE

CHAMPAGNE

Troyes

EMPIRE

Danube R.

ANJOU

BURGUNDY

Nantes

TOURAINE

Poitiers

Bourges

Loire R.

Dijon

POITOU

Autun

Allier R.

Saône R.

Bay of Biscay

AQUITAINE

Geneva

Lyon

Bordeaux

Angoulême

Garonne R.

Perigueux

Rhône R.

PROVENCE

Po R.

GASCONY

Albi

Avignon

TOULOUSE

Montpellier

Aigues-Mortes

Marseilles

NAVARRE

LANGUEDOC

Narbonne

Ebro R.

ARAGON

MEDITERRANEAN SEA

CORSICA

CATALUNYA

EUROPE

Area of detail

AFRICA

HENRY II'S ANGEVIN EMPIRE AND THE KINGDOM OF FRANCE, 1180–1223. ▪ *What areas did Henry II's empire control in 1180?*
▪ *What advantages would the king of France have when challenging English control over continental territories—even though his own power was confined to the "island" (Ile) of France around Paris?*

Henry II restored his grandfather's administration and began, steadily, to extend its reach. He organized trusted men from every locale into juries (the Latin *jus* means both "law" and "oath") and commissioned them to adjudicate civil cases and to report every major crime that occurred in their districts. Henry also made it easier for common people to seek justice in the royal courts. These innovations represent the origin of our modern legal system.

They also brought Henry into conflict with the Church, because royal justice began to impinge on that of ecclesiastical courts: bishops' tribunals for the trial and punishment of clerics. Henry had declared that churchmen convicted of serious crimes should lose their clerical status and be handed over to his royal court for sentencing; in other words, clerics were English subjects before they were servants of Rome.

But in this, Henry was opposed by one of his own longtime friends and supporters: Thomas Becket, the archbishop of Canterbury. Thomas was a self-made man, the son of immigrants who had benefited from the social mobility of town life (he grew up in London) to obtain an education and rise through the ranks of the Church. When Thomas tried to defend the clergy's allegiance to the papacy, Henry responded by exiling him. When the archbishop returned to England in 1170, he was assassinated in his own cathedral by four of Henry's knights. Henry proclaimed his innocence, but the papacy pronounced Thomas to be a martyr. His tomb at Canterbury quickly became an important pilgrimage site, and Henry was compelled to do public penance at his tomb.

The Meaning of Magna Carta

Although Henry was forced to acknowledge the limits of royal power, the success of his legislative efforts ensured that England's government continued to work very efficiently even after his death: his crusading son Richard "the Lionheart" (r. 1189–99) could nominally rule for ten years even though he spent only six months in England during all that time.

When Richard was killed while besieging a castle, he was succeeded by his brother John (r. 1199–1216), a far more efficient administrator. But military losses forced John to cede nearly all of his father's Continental possessions to the powerful young French king, Philip II; only the Aquitaine, the inheritance of his mother Eleanor, remained of his father's original empire. This was politically disastrous for John. Not only did it deplete his resources, it angered the most powerful Norman lords of England, who lost their

ancestral lands when Normandy was lost to France. John's response was to attempt a recovery by raising taxes to equip an army, thereby enraging the barons further. In 1215, they forced John to set his seal on a "great charter" that defined their own rights while limiting those of the king.

Magna Carta established some general principles that still undergird the laws of England and its former colonies. It stipulated that the king should levy no taxes without the consent of those he taxed, that no free man should be punished until he had been judged guilty by a jury of his peers, that no one should be arrested or imprisoned without a warrant, and that no unqualified person should hold public office. The great charter also established a representative body of barons called Parliament (derived from the French word for "speaking together").

In sum, Magna Carta expressed the extraordinary idea that a king should be subject to the rule of law. And further, Magna Carta normalized the idea that strong representative government is a good thing. Since no taxation could be imposed without common consent, English kings had to convene Parliament in order to justify its necessity. In time, Parliament became a legislative body that helped to govern the kingdom, and its meetings were used to hear judicial cases, review local administration, and promulgate new laws. Gradually, England was becoming a constitutional monarchy grounded in representative government, rather than a conquered territory within a larger Norman empire.

Philip II and the Emergence of France

Compared to England's rulers, the king of the Franks exercised little control in his tiny domain of Paris and its immediate hinterland. Most of Charlemagne's institutions of governance in that region had collapsed, further weakened by Viking raids and pressure from the Viking state of Normandy. When the empire of England's Henry II was at its height, the kingdom of Louis VII (r. 1137–80)—who had lost both his wife Eleanor and her lands to that same Henry—was insignificant.

But the French dynasty that had been established by Hugh Capet (Chapter 8) was fortunate. Against all biological odds, it managed to produce an unbroken line of able male heirs for nearly 350 years (from 987 to 1328)—men who were also long-lived. On average, each Capetian king ruled for thirty years, which contributed greatly to political stability. And this kingdom, though small, was a rich center of agriculture and trade. Its prestige was also enhanced by royal patronage of the arts and of the new university of

Paris founded by Abelard, which made Paris the intellectual capital of Europe (as will be discussed later).

Beyond all this, the Capetians proved to be shrewd politicians. Louis VII's son Philip II (r. 1180–1223) styled himself "Augustus" and was the first to use the title "King of France": king of a sovereign state (rather than "King of the Franks," leader of a tribe). Philip came to the throne at the age of eighteen, having witnessed the struggles of his father against the superior strength of Henry II. He understood that he could not win a direct military confrontation. Instead, Philip declared that John owed him homage and allegiance in return for Normandy and its adjacent territories, and then took advantage of his position as John's overlord to undermine John's control over these lands. When John objected, Philip declared all his lands to be forfeit to the French crown and backed this declaration with armies that won decisive victories.

In the new territories of his domain, Philip wisely maintained the bureaucratic structures put in place by generations of Anglo-Norman rule. But he also appointed royal overseers, known as *bailiffs*, who had full judicial, administrative, and military authority there. Philip drew these men from among the needy knights and lesser nobility of his own domain and rotated them frequently from region to region. This ensured their loyalty to Philip and also prevented them from developing personal ties to the regions they governed.

France and England Compared

Philip's administrative pattern, which recognized regional diversity while promoting centralized royal control, would continue to characterize French government until the time of the French Revolution (see Chapter 18). But the French Parlement never played the crucial role in French government that Parliament did in England. A fundamental reason for this was the French nobility's successful claim to exemption from taxation, something that would long remain a political and financial problem for the crown.

Other significant points of comparison between England and France still mark their intertwined histories. England, a far smaller country, was much more tightly unified at a much earlier date; English nobles could and did rebel against their kings, but they could rarely count on sustained regional support. In France, however, regional separatism and resentment of Parisian control remained (as it also remains) a significant force. English kings could rely on local men to do much of the work of local government without pay. This made English administration

inexpensive, and it also meant that royal policies had to be popular in order to be implemented. French kings, by contrast, ruled through salaried officers who had little connection to local communities. As a result, their government lacked effective mechanisms for mobilizing public support. Eventually, these features would be the undoing of the French monarchy.

Frederick Barbarossa and the Holy Roman Empire

We have seen that struggles with the papacy ultimately led to the weakening of imperial authority in Germany and northern Italy. But in the middle of the twelfth century, a newly elected emperor made an ambitious attempt to free his office from papal control. This was Frederick, later known as Barbarossa ("Red Beard," r. 1152–90). Frederick coined the term "Holy Roman Empire" to describe his realm, asserting that its holiness derived directly from God and did not depend on the blessing of the pope.

Frederick forged a close alliance with other German princes by supporting their efforts to control their own territories. In exchange, he exacted their support of his efforts to reassert imperial control over the wealthy cities of northern Italy. This strategy worked, but it sparked a series of destructive wars. Sanctioned by the pope, the cities of northern Italy formed an alliance, the Lombard League, which finally forced Frederick to guarantee their political independence in return for large cash payments.

Meanwhile, Frederick attempted to bypass the papacy by supporting a series of rival popes (or "antipopes"). This move was successfully countered by the reigning pope, Alexander III (r. 1159–81), who drove a shrewd bargain: if Frederick would concede the sovereignty of the pope's rule within Rome and its adjacent territories—lands that came to be known as the Papal States—then Alexander would concede the emperor's sovereignty within his domains, and even his overlordship of the Church in those domains. Frederick agreed and so gained the pope's support for his rule in northern Italy.

When Frederick left for the Holy Land in 1189—joining Richard the Lionheart and Philip Augustus on a (failed) crusade to reconquer Jerusalem (to be discussed later)—he left his realm in a powerful position. Although he died on that venture, his son, Henry VI, succeeded to the throne without opposition and enjoyed a huge income from the northern Italian towns; he ultimately became the king of Sicily, too. This strengthened the empire's position even further, for now the Papal States were surrounded by

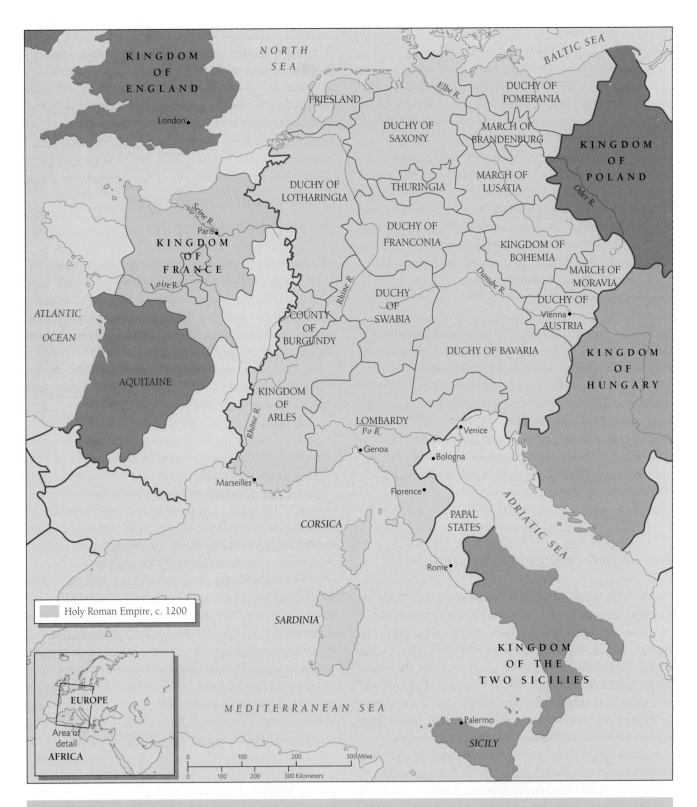

KINGDOM OF ENGLAND

NORTH SEA

BALTIC SEA

London

FRIESLAND

Elbe R.

DUCHY OF POMERANIA

DUCHY OF SAXONY

MARCH OF BRANDENBURG

KINGDOM OF POLAND

DUCHY OF LOTHARINGIA

THURINGIA

MARCH OF LUSATIA

Oder R.

Seine R.

Paris

KINGDOM OF FRANCE

DUCHY OF FRANCONIA

KINGDOM OF BOHEMIA

MARCH OF MORAVIA

Loire R.

Rhine R.

DUCHY OF SWABIA

Danube R.

DUCHY OF AUSTRIA

Vienna

ATLANTIC OCEAN

COUNTY OF BURGUNDY

DUCHY OF BAVARIA

KINGDOM OF HUNGARY

AQUITAINE

Rhône R.

KINGDOM OF ARLES

LOMBARDY

Po R.

Venice

ADRIATIC SEA

Genoa

Bologna

Marseilles

Florence

CORSICA

PAPAL STATES

SARDINIA

Rome

Holy Roman Empire, c. 1200

KINGDOM OF THE TWO SICILIES

EUROPE

Area of detail

AFRICA

MEDITERRANEAN SEA

Palermo

SICILY

0   100   200   300 Miles
0   100   200   300 Kilometers

THE HOLY ROMAN EMPIRE AND ITS NEIGHBORS, c. 1200. ▪ *How would the borders of the Holy Roman Empire have been defined during the Middle Ages?* ▪ *Why were the German states not able to unify during this period?* ▪ *Why would the prospect of a single heir to the Holy Roman Empire and to the kingdom of the Two Sicilies have been a threat to the papacy?*

the lands of a single powerful ruler. However, Henry VI died in 1197 at the age of thirty-two, leaving only a three-year-old son, the future Frederick II, as his heir apparent.

The Reign of Frederick II and the Fragmentation of Imperial Power

Frederick II is one of the most fascinating of all medieval rulers. Having grown up in Sicily, at the heart of the multicultural Mediterranean, he spoke Arabic and Italian as well as Latin, German, and French. He was both a patron of learning and a scholar, author of a treatise on falconry that is still considered a model of scientific investigation. He maintained a menagerie of exotic animals, a troop of Muslim archers, and a harem of women, all of whom traveled with him on his journeys.

Frederick was devoted to pursuing his grandfather's policies, supporting the territorial princes in Germany while enforcing imperial rights in Italy. Much had changed, however, as a result of the two decades' civil war that followed his own father's death. In Germany, the princes had become so autonomous that all Frederick could do was confirm their privileges in exchange for their loyalty. In Italy, the cities of the Lombard League had ceased to pay their taxes and were striving for independence. Meanwhile, the powerful administrative structure of Sicily had fallen into chaos.

Frederick tackled all these problems and restored control over the disparate territories of his empire. In 1237, though, he asserted his right to rule the northern Italian cities directly, bypassing their own independent governments. The result was a lengthy war, which continued until Frederick's death in 1250. The papacy took every advantage of this situation, even excommunicating Frederick and, after his death, denying the rights of his heirs. When Frederick's last legitimate son died in 1254, the prospect of effective imperial rule died with him. For the next 500 years, until the founding of the modern German and Italian states, political power in the lands of the Holy Roman Empire would be divided among several hundred territorial princes.

The "Reconquest" of Spain

By the end of the Middle Ages, a unified kingdom of Spain would emerge as the most powerful monarchy in Europe and the wider Atlantic world (a process we will continue to trace in subsequent chapters). The key to this development lay in the successful alliances forged among the peninsula's

Christian rulers as well as their eventual defeat of neighboring Muslim kingdoms. This process is somewhat misleadingly termed the *Reconquista*, the "reconquest" of Christian lands. In reality, the Roman province of Hispania was only barely Christian when the Visigoths settled there in the fifth century (Chapter 6), and the Visigoths had barely converted before the Muslims arrived in 711 (Chapter 7). But conceptualizing this struggle as a holy war to "reconquer" Christian territory allowed Christian propagandists to cast it as another Crusade and thereby win support for these efforts.

There were four major Christian kingdoms in Iberia by the mid-twelfth century. In the far north was Navarre, which straddled the Pyrenees. In central Iberia were León and Castile, states that were governed as a united kingdom after 1037. Beyond these kingdoms' frontiers lay a broad swathe of Muslim territory. In the northeast was the Christian Crown of Aragon, formed in 1137 when the count of Barcelona, who ruled Catalonia, married the queen of Aragon. Farthest to the west was the new kingdom of Portugal, which had been the first new territory gained by Christian conquests and which won independence from León-Castile in 1139.

Like their counterparts elsewhere in Europe, the kings of Spain struggled to control the power of great lords. Centuries of warfare between Muslims and Christians and among competing Christian clans had left the landscape dotted with enormous castles that could be used as power bases. A ruler seeking to establish sovereignty thus had to use a combination of force and political cunning to bring rivals to heel. We have already seen these tactics at work in England: violent conquest followed by the establishment of effective administrative structures that made royal power a fact of daily life.

This pattern is exemplified by King Alfonso II of Aragon (r. 1162–96), who was also the count of Barcelona and the first to rule the united Crown of Aragon. Alfonso used documentation as the ultimate tool of power, presiding over the compilation of a richly illuminated "big book of fiefs" (*Liber feudorum maior*) between 1192 and 1194 (see **Interpreting Visual Evidence** on page 231). This book recounted property transactions and family lineages dating back centuries, citing documents in the royal archives. Alfonso thereby grounded his authority on his command of written records.

Papal Dominion and the Development of Canon Law

Like secular rulers, the popes of this era were attempting to establish greater authority by building up bureaucratic structures that increased the visibility of papal power. The pope in Rome began to send out specially commissioned

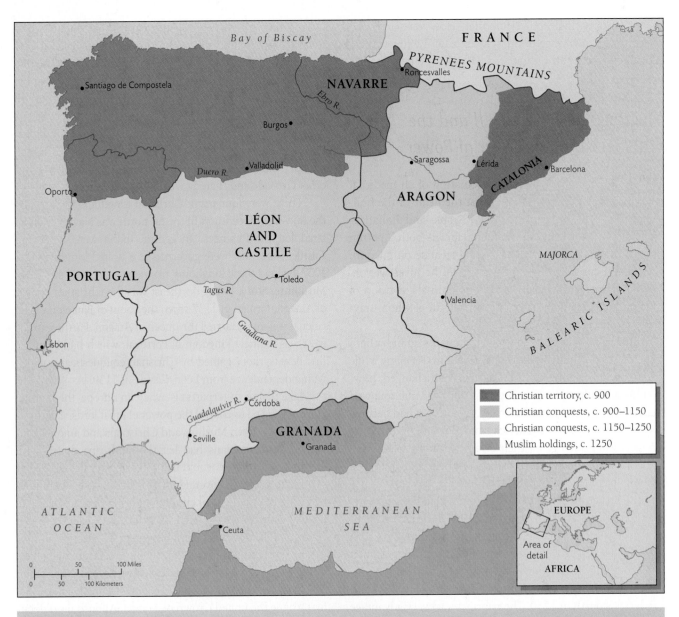

THE "RECONQUEST" OF SPAIN, 900–1250. ▪ *Where were the frontiers of the Christian kingdoms in 900? 1150? 1250?* ▪ *What geographical factors might have helped to sustain these small kingdoms?* ▪ *Why might Castile have become the largest of the Christian kingdoms over time?* ▪ *How could Aragon and Catalonia have maintained important positions as wealthy and significant powers?*

papal legates ("legal representatives") to convey and enforce papal commands, many of which arose from the legal cases that poured into Rome as the pope sought to establish a reputation for justice.

This extension of the papacy's jurisdiction required the development of a systematic body of law. A crucial step in this process was the codification of papal decrees and the decisions of Church councils reaching back to the second century—a thousand years. These formed a body of legal precedents known as *canons*, from the Greek word meaning "rules" or "supports." The problem, though, was that these precedents often contradicted one another, and so any usable

compilation had to determine which was most authoritative. The resulting *Concordance of Discordant Canons*, first redacted around 1139 and later known as the *Decretum*, is attributed to a jurist known as Gratian, who may have been from Bologna.

Significantly, Gratian's codification was influenced by the *Corpus Juris Civilis* codified under Justinian (Chapter 7). This was another outcome of the Crusades and of increased contact with Byzantium, and it revitalized the study of Roman law in western Europe. The *Decretum* was also made possible by the new intellectual trends that were simultaneously giving rise to the universities of Europe (as will be discussed later).

Interpreting Visual Evidence

Picturing Legal Transactions

Between the years 1192 and 1194, King Alfonso II of Aragon (r. 1162–96) and his court scribes compiled a remarkable book. The codex known today as "the big book of fiefs" (*Liber feudorum maior*) may have been made to assist Alfonso and his descendants in legitimizing their authority over the many areas they controlled. But it was also a way of expressing that authority: its very existence represented a new claim to royal power. In its original form, it consisted of 888 parchment folios (1,776 pages) on which 903 separate documents were copied.

This "big book" represents a new trend in Europe. In most places, claims to property were made on the basis of custom and memory, not on documentation. When property changed hands, the chief witnesses were people, and when questions arose it was these people (or their heirs) whose testimony proved ownership. In Catalonia, the habit of documenting things had a long history, and it was not unusual for individual families to keep archives of documents. At the same time, however, documentation was never sufficient on its own: verbal exchanges of agreement and the public performance of transactions constituted legally binding ceremonies meaningful to the entire community, and the validity of these actions was not dependent on the making of a written record.

With all this in mind, it is striking that seventy-nine of the documents copied into the book are accompanied by images that convey important messages about documentation and its limitations.

On the book's opening frontispiece (image A), King Alfonso consults with his chief archivist, Ramón de Caldes. Ramón discusses one of the charters taken from a large pile at his elbow, while a scribe makes copies behind him—perhaps to aid in the compilation of the "big book." The king is backed by men who look on approvingly.

One of the charters copied into the "big book" is accompanied by the second image (B). It records that the viscount of Nîmes betrothed his daughter, Ermengarde of Carcassone, to the count of Roussillon. Ermengarde, her flowing hair uncovered as a sign of her maidenhood, stands between her bearded father and her seated mother, Cecilia of Provence.

Questions for Analysis

1. Why would a book designed to document property transactions contain images, too? What functions could they have served?

2. Why would the artist of the "big book" have depicted the king consulting his archivist in the very first image? How does he depict the relationship between them? Why does he include a group of men as witnesses to their discussion?

3. Women figure prominently in many of the book's images, including the one below. On what basis could you argue that their active presence is crucial to the transactions being described?

A. King Alfonso and Ramón de Caldes.

B. Betrothal of Ermengarde to the Count of Roussillon.

The *Decretum* claimed ecclesiastical jurisdiction for many vital matters, including marriage and inheritance. Although such cases were often heard in local ecclesiastical courts overseen by bishops, popes increasingly insisted that they alone could issue dispensations that established precedents—such as the annulment of Eleanor's marriage to Louis VII—and that the papal court should function as a final court of appeals in all cases touching the Church. Thinking back to the dispute between Henry II of England and Archbishop Thomas Becket, we can better understand what was at stake: both secular and ecclesiastical rulers now defined their power in terms of law, and they naturally sought to defend their rights against encroachment. And just as kings had to become more skillful administrators, so the popes of this era were almost invariably trained as canon lawyers, which was a real departure from the monastic origins of the reforming movement discussed in Chapter 8. One of this new breed of popes was Alexander III, who dealt so skillfully with Frederick Barbarossa. Another was Innocent III (r. 1198–1216), who combined an expertise in canon law with a zeal for continuing the work of the Crusades.

CONTINUING THE CRUSADES

In 1095, when Pope Urban II urged the quarrelsome knights of northwestern Europe to take up the cross against the enemies of Christ, he was responding to the Byzantine emperor's request for reinforcements in his war with the Seljuq Turks. But the crusaders' reach quickly extended beyond the frontiers of Byzantium to the great cities of Antioch and Jerusalem. And as we saw in Chapter 8, many crusaders acted on a still broader interpretation of their mission by attacking the Jewish communities of the Rhineland.

So from the first, both the reasons for crusading and the outlets for aggression were apt to change. In the centuries following the First Crusade, violence was directed against many different kinds of people who could be construed as "enemies of Christ." While historians, for convenience, often speak of the Crusades as divided into seven or more distinct phases (the Second Crusade, the Third Crusade, etc.), the people of the time—both aggressors and victims—experienced crusading as a continuous, snowballing movement.

Crusader States and Crusading Orders

On the coasts of Palestine and Syria, the fragile principalities known as the Crusader States laid a thin veneer of

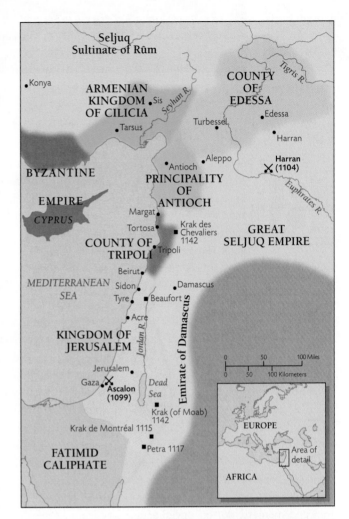

THE CRUSADER STATES. This map shows the fragile colonies known as the Crusader States at their greatest extent, around 1100. ■ *What geographical, political, and military factors would make these states vulnerable?*

western European influence on top of the much older western civilizations whose development we have been studying since Chapter 1. The relatively few veterans of the First Crusade who stayed and flourished were those who were able to adapt themselves. Most probably retained some aspects of their former identities, but they quickly became intertwined with local peoples, intermarrying and adopting their fashions, food, and outlook. Soon they had more in common with their immediate neighbors (Syrian and Armenian Christians, Shi'ite and Sunni Muslims) than with their distant families "back home." Second- and third-generation settlers might never visit western Christendom in the course of their lives.

The four main Crusader States were thus very different from the bureaucratic monarchies that were being consolidated in Europe at this time. They were more like the loosely configured, combative lordships of the tenth and eleventh centuries, and they were mostly short-lived. The largest, the inland county of Edessa, stretched as far east as the Tigris River and had to be heavily fortified against internal uprisings and external threats. Its Latin Christian population was a tiny minority, and by 1150 it had been mostly subsumed into the empire of the Seljuq Turks, with some portions reverting to Byzantium.

Edessa's position was precarious because its Frankish rulers had friendlier relations with their Armenian subjects (with whom they intermarried) than with the crusader principality of Antioch to the west, which comprised parts of what is now Syria and Turkey. Antioch also had a minority Latin Christian population and was largely dependent on Constantinople, and later Armenia, for protection from the Seljuqs. It ceased to exist in 1268, when its lands became part of a vast new empire, that of the Mongols (see Chapter 10).

The third major state, the county of Tripoli, was founded in 1109 to link these two northern states with the kingdom of Jerusalem. But its strategic commercial position exposed it to constant raids, and so its rulers entrusted its defense to a new military order dedicated to perpetual crusading: the Knights Hospitaller. Originally charged with care of pilgrims in the Hospital of St. John at Jerusalem, founded in 1023, members of this religious community became militarized after 1099 and came to control the islands of Rhodes and Malta as well as many strategic fortifications in Syria, like the massive *Krak des Chevaliers* ("Castle of the Knights," so called in a mixture of Arabic and French). In fact, the Hospitallers long outlived the Crusader States they served, maintaining a sovereign presence in the eastern Mediterranean into the early nineteenth century; the order is now headquartered in Rome.

The Kingdom of Jerusalem and the Conquest of Saladin

The kingdom of Jerusalem, the fourth and most symbolically important of the Crusader States, was really a network of cities and fortresses that constantly changed hands. Its cosmopolitan population testifies to the number of peoples who claimed it for their own: Muslims (both Sunni and Shi'a), Orthodox Christians (Greek and Syrian), alongside smaller communities (Jews, Samaritans)—all of whom dwarfed the Latin Christian population. As a result, those who claimed kingship in Jerusalem were heavily dependent on support from other Crusader States as well as from Europe; yet the cachet of Jerusalem was

KRAK DES CHEVALIERS. The necessity of securing hard-won territory in the Holy Land led to the construction of enormous castles like this one in present-day Syria, built by the Knights Hospitaller in the early twelfth century. When crusading movements were launched in Europe itself, similar castles would be built to subjugate peoples deemed rebellious or heretical.

such that ambitious allies often attempted to seize power there. Once again, defense of the kingdom came to rest on another new crusading order, the Knights Templar. Founded during the reign of King Baldwin II (r. 1118–31), the Templars were based in a wing of the captured Al-Aqsa Mosque, which was now the royal palace and thought to be part of King Solomon's original Temple complex: hence the order's name.

Although the kingdom of Jerusalem persisted in theory for almost two hundred years, it ceased to have any purchase on Jerusalem itself after 1187. In this year, a remarkable Kurdish chieftain called Salāḥ ad-Dīn (c. 1138–1193), who had become the Sunni sultan of both Egypt and Syria, succeeded in recapturing the Holy City. He became the target of a renewed crusading effort (the Third Crusade, 1189–92), which spurred three kings to take the cross: Richard the Lionheart, Philip Augustus, and Frederick Barbarossa. (Frederick was killed, Philip left early, and Richard was captured on the way back.)

Meanwhile, the victorious Saladin (as he was known in Europe) became celebrated among crusaders, who considered him a paragon of chivalry. Richard even considered arranging a marriage between his own sister, the widowed Queen Joan of Sicily, and Saladin's brother, to establish joint rule in Jerusalem. But this never happened, and the city of Acre (Akko, in northern Israel) became the new capital of the Christian kingdom. Its fall in 1291 marked the end of any viable western European presence in the region until the short-lived conquests of Napoleon at the end of the eighteenth century (see Chapter 18).

Analyzing Primary Sources

The Canons of the Fourth Lateran Council

In 1215, Innocent III presided over an ecumenical assembly of Church leaders in the papal palace and church of Saint John Lateran in Rome. The resulting canons both reaffirmed older legislation and introduced a number of new laws that responded to widespread social, economic, and cultural changes. Published in the same year as Magna Carta, they too became a standard set of principles and continued to be applied within the Church until they were modified by the Council of Trent in the sixteenth century.

Canon 1

... There is one Universal Church of the faithful, outside of which there is absolutely no salvation. In which there is the same priest and sacrifice, Jesus Christ, whose body and blood are truly contained in the sacrament of the altar under the forms of bread and wine; the bread being changed *(transsubstantiatio)* by divine power into the body, and the wine into the blood, so that to realize the mystery of unity we may receive of Him what He has received of us. And this sacrament no one can effect except the priest who has been duly ordained in accordance with the keys of the Church, which Jesus Christ Himself gave to the Apostles and their successors. . . .

• • •

Canon 3

We excommunicate and anathematize every heresy that rises against the holy, orthodox, and Catholic faith . . .

condemning all heretics under whatever names they may be known, for while they have different faces they are nevertheless bound to each other by their tails, since in all of them vanity is a common element. Those condemned, being handed over to the secular rulers of their bailiffs, let them be abandoned, to be punished with due justice, clerics being first degraded from their orders.

• • •

Canon 9

Since in many places within the same city and diocese there are people of different languages having one faith but various rites and customs, we strictly command that the bishops of these cities and dioceses provide suitable men who will, according to the different rites and languages, celebrate the divine offices for them, administer the sacraments of the Church and instruct them by word and example.

Canon 10

... It often happens that bishops, on account of their manifold duties or bodily infirmities, or because of hostile invasions or other reasons, to say nothing of lack of learning, which must be absolutely condemned in them and is not to be tolerated in the future, are themselves unable to minister the word of God to the people, especially in large and widespread dioceses. Wherefore we decree that bishops provide suitable men, powerful in work and word, to exercise with fruitful result the office of preaching; who in place of the bishops, since these cannot do it, diligently visiting the people committed to them, may instruct them by word and example. . . .

Canon 11

Since there are some who, on account of the lack of necessary means, are unable to acquire an education or to meet opportunities for perfecting themselves, the Third Lateran Council in a salutary

The Extension of Crusading Ideas within Europe

Once unleashed, the crusading ethos could not be contained by efforts to liberate the Holy Land. Within a decade after the First Crusade, it was being applied to a host of other initiatives that could open new lands for

European settlement and bring more peoples into the orbit of the Roman Church. In 1108, a crusade was called against the Slavs. In the 1160s, the rulers of Denmark and German Saxony began to colonize the Baltic coast and lands between the Elbe and Oder Rivers, again using the rhetoric of crusade.

These were represented as missionary efforts, but they were not carried forward peacefully and their goals were decree provided that in every cathedral church a suitable benefice be assigned to a master who shall instruct *gratis* the clerics of that church and other poor students, . . . we, confirming the aforesaid decree, add that, not only in every cathedral church but also in other churches where means are sufficient, a competent master be appointed . . . who shall instruct *gratis* and to the best of his ability the clerics of those and other churches in the art of grammar and in other branches of knowledge.

• • •

Canons 14–16

That the morals and general conduct of clerics may be better, let all strive to live chastely and virtuously, particularly those in sacred orders, guarding against every vice of desire. . . .

. . . All clerics shall carefully abstain from drunkenness. . . .

We forbid hunting and fowling to all clerics; wherefore, let them not presume to keep dogs and birds for these purposes. . . .

Clerics shall not hold secular offices or engage in secular and, above all, dishonest pursuits. They shall not attend the performances of mimics and buffoons, or theatrical representations. They shall not visit taverns except in case

of necessity, namely, when on a journey. They are forbidden to play games of chance or be present at them. They must have a becoming crown and tonsure and apply themselves diligently to the study of the divine offices and other useful subjects. Their garments must be worn clasped at the top and neither too short nor too long. They are not to use red or green garments or curiously sewed-together gloves, or beak-shaped shoes . . .

• • •

Canon 68

In some provinces a difference in dress distinguishes the Jews or Saracens from the Christians, but in certain others such a confusion has grown up that they cannot be distinguished by any difference. Thus it happens at times that through error Christians have relations with the women of Jews or Saracens, and Jews and Saracens with Christian women. Therefore, that they may not, under pretext of error of this sort, excuse themselves in the future for the excesses of such prohibited intercourse, we decree that such Jews and Saracens of both sexes in every Christian province and at all times shall be marked off in the eyes of the public from other peoples through the character of their dress. . . .

Moreover, during the last three days before Easter and especially on Good Friday, they shall not go forth in public at all, for the reason that some of them on these very days, as we hear, do not blush to go forth better dressed and are not afraid to mock the Christians who maintain the memory of the most holy Passion by wearing signs of mourning. . . .

Source: Excerpted from H. J. Schroeder, *Disciplinary Decrees of the General Councils: Text, Translation, and Commentary* (St. Louis, MO: 1937), pp. 236–96.

Questions for Analysis

1. Based on this selection of canons, how would you characterize the main concerns of the Fourth Lateran Council? What is it attempting to regulate, and why? What changing historical circumstances do the canons reflect?

2. In what ways do the canons distinguish between clergy and laity? How does legislation work to maintain those distinctions?

3. Why do the canons place so much emphasis on clothing and appearance? Why would it be important for both clerics and "infidels" (Jews and Muslims) to dress in distinctive ways?

the conquest and occupation of pagan lands. At the same time, the English were launching crusades against the "infidel" Irish and Welsh (who were actually Christian), justifying this on the grounds that Celts were barbarians who would benefit from a superior civilizing influence. It had been a short step from the calling of a crusade against foreigners to those aimed at fellow European Christians.

Venice and the Crusade against Constantinople

The First Crusade had begun as an attempt to aid Constantinople; the Fourth Crusade (1202–4) ended in its destruction. The object of this expedition, called by Pope

Innocent III in 1198, was Egypt, where Saladin's successors continued to hinder European colonial efforts. This meant launching an attack by sea, because the remaining crusader outposts were too weak to support the movement of land armies.

The natural embarkation point was Venice. A major player in maritime trade since the ninth century, Venice had benefited enormously from the Crusades, supplying ships and supplies while reaping the benefits of closer ties with Byzantium. But relations with Constantinople worsened throughout the twelfth century, as the Crusades damaged Byzantine trade and threatened its security. In 1182, enraged citizens of Constantinople had attacked enclaves of Italian merchants and seamen; those who were not killed were banished, the Venetians among them.

The Venetians therefore had a reason for desiring revenge, and they were now confronted with an army of impoverished crusaders who could not pay for passage to Cairo. So instead, the crusaders paid the Venetians with the services they could render. Rather than sailing for Egypt, the expedition was diverted to Zara on the Dalmatian coast of the Adriatic, a former Venetian port that had rebelled and sought protection from the king of Hungary. Despite the fact that Hungary was loyal to Rome, the city was attacked and taken.

From there, the crusaders moved on to Constantinople. After a terrible siege, the city was savagely overrun in 1204, its people killed or left homeless, its churches and public buildings damaged, and its books and artworks consigned to flames or seized as loot. (See, for example, the porphyry statue shown in Chapter 6 on page 148, which is still in Venice). Then the Venetians colonized the city, controlling its shipping as well as that of Byzantine Crete and many Greek ports. Only in 1261 was imperial rule reestablished in the capital; but by that time, the eastern Roman Empire had shrunk to a fraction of its former size.

Innocent III's Crusade for a Unified Christendom

Pope Innocent III expressed alarm at the turn taken by his crusade, but he accepted the spoils of war and approved Venetian occupation of Byzantine territory. He was an ambitious man. Newly elected to the papacy at the age of thirty-seven, probably the youngest holder of the office in history, his goal was to unify all Christendom—and the wider world—under papal hegemony. But unlike Gregory VII (Chapter 8), Innocent never questioned the rights of secular rulers. Instead, he saw his role as regulatory and disciplinary: when rulers sinned, they should be reprimanded or excommunicated, thereby calling their legitimacy into question. Indeed, Innocent insisted that every Christian was obliged to obey the pope as Jesus Christ's representative on earth.

Innocent pressed these claims in many different ways. He made the papacy financially and politically independent by expanding and consolidating papal territories in central Italy. He proclaimed his power as king-maker and king-breaker by brokering the selection of the Holy Roman Emperor and compelling John of England to grant England to the papacy, as a fief. Innocent also asserted lordship over Aragon, Sicily, and Hungary. He even levied the first income tax on the clergy, in order to support the crusade against Constantinople and its Orthodox Christians.

His crowning achievement was the ratification of his agenda at a representative assembly of the Roman Church, the Fourth Lateran Council of 1215 (held in the Roman palace and church of St. John Lateran). This council defined the central dogmas of Christianity and made one of them the acknowledgment of papal supremacy. Since a dogma is defined as "a truth necessary for salvation," this meant that all Christians had to acknowledge the pope's ultimate power; those unwilling to do so (including the Christians of Byzantium) were, by definition, heretics—and as heretics, they could be punished.

In a further effort to achieve unity within Christendom, the Fourth Lateran Council (known as Lateran IV) took an unprecedented interest in the religious education of average men and women. It responded to the urbanization of Europe by establishing free primary schools (for boys) in all major cities, requiring bishops to recruit effective preachers, and outlawing all kinds of clerical misbehavior. It also sought to increase the distance between Christians and their Muslim and Jewish neighbors by discouraging social relationships, economic exchanges, and intermarriage. Most disturbingly, Innocent's council mandated that "infidels" be visibly distinguished from Christians by the wearing of distinctive clothing: the origins of the infamous "Jewish badge" (see Chapter 26).

The Crusade against Heresy

Innocent's reign marks the height of papal power, but it also sowed seeds of dissent. When Innocent's immediate successors came into conflict with Frederick II over control of Italian territories, the emperor opposed them; and instead of excommunicating him and encouraging rebellion, they called a crusade against him.

Innocent himself had paved the way for this move by launching a series of crusades against heretics, now defined as any group or individual who did not fall into line with the papacy's policies. The most notorious of these campaigns was the Albigensian Crusade, launched in 1209 and ostensibly directed against a heretical sect called the Cathars. In reality, it justified the colonization of what is now southern France by land-hungry knights from northern France, and its terrible violence created lasting tensions that would lead the inhabitants of this devastated region to ally with the English during the Hundred Years' War (see Chapter 10) and to embrace Protestant religion during the Reformation (see Chapter 13). In order to understand how this happened, we must turn to some larger religious developments in Europe as a whole.

UNITY AND DISSENT IN THE WESTERN CHURCH

The Investiture Conflict (Chapter 8) had engaged both clergy and laity in debates over the papacy's claim to supremacy, and in many places there was resistance to its encroachment on centuries-old regional customs and social networks. Bishops had been drawn from local elites since the time of Constantine, and it was normal for these offices to be controlled by certain families. Meanwhile, priests had been married men since the establishment of the first Christian churches, and the wives of priests were not only their husbands' partners, they were also ministers to their communities. When the papacy preached against "fornicating priests" and "concubines," it was condemning relationships that had been essential and accepted for generations.

On the one hand, then, the reforms that culminated in the reign of Innocent III gave the common people an important role to play, by urging them to reject certain practices and weed out offenders. Combined with the fervor that had been whipped up by the Crusades, the result was more widespread interest and increased participation in religious life—as well as increased violence in the name of religion. On the other hand, the reforming movement severely limited the laity's ways of expressing their spirituality, and it placed more controls on daily life.

THE MYSTERY OF THE MASS. In this manuscript illumination, the visionary Hildegard of Bingen (to be discussed later) illustrates the doctrine of transubstantiation. In the lower register, the bread and wine of the Mass have been placed on the altar and are being transformed into the body and blood of the crucified Christ, depicted in the upper register. Paired scenes from Christ's life (his birth and death, his ministry and resurrection) emphasize the fact that earthly substances—bread and wine—participate in a divine cycle of regeneration. Note that Hildegard does not imagine the mediating figure as a priest, but as the (female) Church, represented as a crowned queen and associated with the Virgin Mary. ■ *What might be the significance of this choice?*

The New Monasticism

One manifestation of the new popular piety was the growth and diversification of monastic movements. Many of these rejected the worldliness of Cluny and its daughter monasteries, which had (ironically) started the reforming movement by becoming independent lordships and acquiring extensive lands and enormous wealth. Those seeking holiness had to look elsewhere. The result was the founding of new monastic orders.

The most influential of these was founded at the monastery of Cîteaux in 1098. Cistercian monks followed Benedict's *Rule* in the most austere way possible, founding monasteries in wildernesses and remote areas. They also shunned all unnecessary decoration and elaborate rituals. Instead, they practiced private prayer and committed themselves to hard manual labor. Under the charismatic leadership of Bernard of Clairvaux (1090–1153), a spellbinding preacher and one of the most influential personalities of his age, the Cistercian order grew exponentially, from 5 houses in 1115 to 343 by 1153. This astonishing increase meant that many more people were becoming professional religious, and that still more were donating funds and lands to share indirectly in a life of devotion.

The Magic of the Mass

Another manifestation of popular piety was a new focus on the sacrament of the Mass: the liturgical reenactment of Christ's last meal with his disciples. This celebration, also known as the Eucharist, had always been an important Christian practice (Chapter 6); but in the twelfth century it became the central act of worship in the western Church. Bernard of Clairvaux was instrumental in making it so, by developing and popularizing the doctrine of transubstantiation. According to this teaching, every Mass is a miraculous event because the priest's blessing transforms the bread and wine on the altar into the body and blood of Christ: hence the term *transubstantiation*, since earthly substances thereby become the substance of Christ's divine body.

Popular reverence for the Eucharist became so great that the Church initiated the practice of elevating the consecrated bread, known as the Host, so that the whole congregation could see it. Not incidentally, this new doctrine further enhanced the prestige of the priesthood by seeming to endow it with wonder-working powers. In later centuries, the Latin words spoken at the consecration of the

Host, *Hoc est corpus meum* ("This is my body"), were understood as a magical formula: *hocus pocus*.

The Cult of the Virgin

Popular devotion to the Eucharist was matched by another new and hugely influential religious practice: the veneration of Jesus's mother, Mary. Bernard of Clairvaux played an important role in this, too, traveling around Europe to promote a theology that made Mary the very embodiment of the Church. Eventually, Catholic teaching would hold that Mary had not only given birth to Jesus while still a virgin but that she remained a virgin even after Jesus's birth—and, more radically, that she herself had been conceived without sin. This made Mary the exact opposite of Eve, the woman whose disobedience had (according to Judeo-Christian tradition) brought sin into the world for the first time; for through God's grace, Mary had given birth to

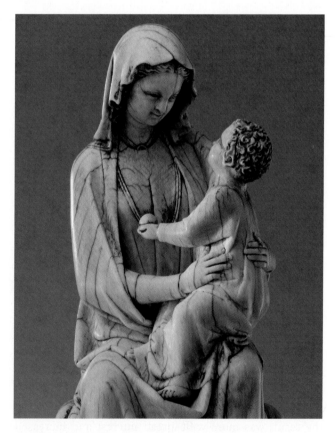

VIRGIN AND CHILD. This exquisite ivory sculpture (just over seven inches high) was carved in Paris in the mid to late thirteenth century as an aid to private devotion and prayer. The mother of Jesus, Mary, was also regarded as the mother of all humanity, the *alma mater* ("nourishing mother") who could be relied on to protect and heal those who asked for her help.

Christ, a second Adam, whose sacrifice of himself atoned for that Original Sin.

This theology raised Mary from the position of God's humble servant to that of heaven's queen, with the power to intercede on behalf of even the worst sinners. Her soaring reputation as a miracle worker and advocate is amply testified by the thousands of devotional images created during this period, the many stories and hymns celebrating her miracles, and the fact that practically all the magnificent new cathedrals of the age were dedicated to "Our Lady." This explains the many churches of Notre Dame in France, the Frauenkirchen of Germany, and so on.

The burgeoning cult of the Blessed Virgin had two contradictory effects. First, it elevated a female figure to a prominent place in the official Church for the first time, and thereby celebrated virtues associated with femininity: motherhood, healing, nourishment, mercy, kindness. But at the same time, it made Mary an unobtainable model of female perfection: she alone could be both virgin and parent, mother and bride. No real woman could emulate her, and thus real women were increasingly compared to Eve and perceived as weak and deceitful. Moreover, the veneration of a lone idealized woman coincided exactly with the suppression of most real women's access to positions of power within the Church. As the cult of the Blessed Virgin grew, so the opportunities for aspiring holy women shrank.

Heloise, Hildegard, and the Challenge to Women

This did not go unremarked at the time. The career of Heloise (c. 1090–1164), sketched at the beginning of this chapter, exemplifies both the avenues of advancement for women and the successful blocking of those avenues by new constraints on women's activities. Heloise's exact contemporary, Hildegard of Bingen (1098–1179), also struggled to make a place for herself and her female followers, and she was more outspoken than Heloise in her criticism of these trends. Like Heloise, she was an abbess and a highly original thinker. She was also a mystic who claimed to receive regular revelations from God.

Hildegard expressed these visions in writings on subjects as diverse as cosmology and medicine, which were transcribed and illustrated under her close supervision. She also composed hymns and ambitious musical dramas for her nuns—music now widely available. Her advice was frequently sought by religious and secular leaders, including Bernard of Clairvaux and Frederick Barbarossa, and she even received a special papal dispensation that allowed her to preach publicly.

Despite all this, Hildegard had to fight constantly for her rights and those of her nuns during her lifetime, and after her death efforts to have her recognized as a saint were thwarted by the papacy. A new canonization process was instituted by the papal curia (court) as a way of controlling the popular veneration of charismatic figures whom the Church considered threatening. Hildegard was one of them. It would take 800 years for her to be officially canonized, in 2012.

Heresy or Piety?

For a thousand years, as we have seen, Christianity had been transmitted to many different civilizations and had changed to absorb new influences. In this era, however, the medieval Church began to lose its capacity to respond

HILDEGARD OF BINGEN'S DIVINE INSPIRATION. This portrait of Hildegard and her male secretary, Volmar, appears in her book *Scivias* ("Know the Ways"). It shows Hildegard as the recipient of a divine vision (represented by tongues of heavenly fire) which she transcribes onto a wax tablet using a stylus—a common method for creating the first draft of a written work. Volmar is placed outside the frame in which her vision occurs, but he is prepared to copy it onto parchment. ▪ *What does this image tell us about medieval ideas of authorship and authority?* ▪ *What does it suggest about the relationship and status of the two figures?*

inclusively to change. This trend would eventually lead to a challenge so intense that it could not be contained: the Protestant Reformation (see Chapter 13). In the twelfth and thirteenth centuries, resistance was manifested in waves of popular opposition to centralized authority, which prompted the calling of crusades aimed at harnessing popular piety to that same authority.

The best way to understand this is through Innocent III's very different treatment of rather similar popular movements. On the one hand, the pope resolved to crush all disobedience; on the other, he wanted to support idealistic groups that could be made to acknowledge papal authority. So, as we already noted, Innocent condoned a crusade against the "heretics" of southern France, the Cathars (from the Greek word for "purity"); the fact that many Cathar leaders were women made the movement heretical by definition. Another related movement, Waldensianism, was also condemned. Its teachings can be traced back to a merchant called Waldes who wished to imitate the life of Christ and whose followers were active in the vernacular translation and study of the Gospels, and dedicated to lives of poverty. But when they began to preach without authorization they were branded as heretics. Many of their leaders, too, were women.

At the same time, however, Innocent embraced two other popular movements and turned them into new religious orders: the Dominicans and the Franciscans. Like the Waldensians, the friars ("brothers") of these orders imitated the life of Jesus by wandering the countryside and establishing missions in Europe's growing towns, preaching and offering assistance to the poor. They also begged for a living, hence their categorization as *mendicants*, from the Latin verb "to beg" (*mendicare*). In the end, what set these orders apart from "heretics" was their willingness to subject themselves to papal authority.

New Religious Orders

The Dominican order, formally known as the Order of Preachers, was founded by Dominic of Osma (1170–1221), a Castilian theologian. Approved in 1216, it was particularly dedicated to the prosecution of heretics and the conversion of Jews and Muslims. At first, the Dominicans hoped to achieve these ends by preaching and public debate, and so many of its members pursued academic careers in the new universities (as will be discussed later). The most influential intellectual of the Middle Ages, Thomas Aquinas (1225–1274), was a Dominican. But the Dominicans soon became associated with the use of other persuasive techniques through the administration of the Inquisition.

(It is now called the Congregation for the Doctrine of the Faith and is still staffed by members of the order.)

The Franciscans, formally known as the Order of the Friars Minor ("Little Brothers"), were committed to the welfare of the poor and the cultivation of personal spirituality. Whereas Dominic and his followers had been priests, the founder of the Franciscans was the ne'er-do-well son of an Italian merchant, Francis of Assisi (1182–1226), who eventually rebelled against the materialistic values of his father. Stripping himself (literally) of his possessions, he began to preach salvation in town squares. And he did this without official approval, thereby risking the same fate as a heretic. But when he showed himself willing to profess obedience in 1209, Innocent granted Francis and his followers permission to preach. Many Franciscans continued to engage in revivalistic outdoor preaching and to offer a model for apostolic living.

This was not, however, an approved religious lifestyle for women. Francis's most important female follower, Clare of Assisi (1194–1253), wanted to emulate Francis's example, but the Order of Poor Ladies (also known as the Poor Clares) was not allowed to work directly among the people and instead lived in cloistered convents. In northwestern Europe, however, there were communities of laywomen who did minister directly to the poor: the Beguines. But their relationship with Church was always strained. The Beguines embraced many of the practices associated with heresy, including the translation and study of the Bible. The fact that they were women made them even more suspect.

Christians against Jews

Violence and exploitation shaped the experiences of Europe's Jewish communities after the First Crusade. The Church never explicitly endorsed this, yet it did little to combat it. As a result, many Christians came to believe that their Jewish neighbors were capable of crucifying and eating Christian children, profaning the Eucharist, and poisoning wells. Stories of Jewish wealth added an economic element to these fears, as did the fact that Jewish social networks were the engine of the medieval economy. Conspiracy theorists inferred the existence of organized Jewish plots to undermine Christendom, and cited these as justifications for violence.

This situation worsened throughout the twelfth and thirteenth centuries, as both secular and ecclesiastical authorities devised more systematic mechanisms for policing undesirable segments of society: not only heretics but the indigent poor, prostitutes, "sodomites," and lepers. The Fourth Lateran Council had mandated that Jews be exposed through the wearing of the Jewish badge, and this made them easier targets in times of unrest. Meanwhile, the protections which Europe's rulers had once extended to their Jewish subjects were gradually withdrawn. In Spain, the Reconquista absorbed many of the Muslim kingdoms in which Jews had enjoyed a measure of tolerance, and they were not easily accommodated within the emerging monarchies of Christian Spain. Starting in the 1280s, rulers elsewhere in Europe began to expel their Jewish subjects from their kingdoms altogether, in most cases because they could no longer pretend to repay the enormous sums they had extorted from Jewish moneylenders: this was the case in the kingdoms of Sicily (1288), England (1290), and France (1306). The Jews were finally expelled from Spain in 1492 (see Chapter 12). By 1500, only northern Italy, parts of Germany, and central and eastern Europe were home to sizable Jewish communities.

AN INTELLECTUAL REVOLUTION

The Fourth Lateran Council mandated the education of the laity and more rigorous training for all clergy. These measures responded to a number of factors that were transforming the cultural landscape of Europe. The growth of towns had led to the growth of schools in those towns, for the most part founded by local bishops or monasteries. Meanwhile, the crusades became conduits for the transmission of Muslim learning and, through Muslim mediation, the precepts of ancient Greek philosophy. The infusion of these new ideas created an extraordinary new forum for intellectual endeavor: the university. In much the same way that ease of travel and communication had fostered a scientific revolution in the cities of the Hellenistic world (see Chapter 4), so the conditions that gave rise to the university mark the beginning of a revolution in the intellectual history of Europe.

Access to Education

In 1179, Pope Alexander III decreed that all cathedrals should set aside income for at least one schoolteacher, whose task would be to accept all comers, rich or poor, without fee. He predicted, correctly, that this measure would increase the number of well-trained clerics to staff the growing bureaucracy of the Church. The recently martyred Thomas Becket had been an early beneficiary of such schooling.

At first, cathedral schools existed almost exclusively for the training of parish priests, but their curriculum was soon broadened to provide more men with sophisticated skills. The most fundamental elements of learning were known as the *trivium*, "the three ways": grammar, logic, and rhetoric. This meant a thorough grounding in Latin and training in the formulation of sound arguments. Those who mastered the trivium could move on to the *quadrivium* or "four ways": arithmetic, geometry, astronomy, and music. Together, these seven liberal arts—so called because they promised liberation from menial labor—were the prerequisites for advanced study in philosophy, theology, law, and medicine.

Until about 1200, most students would have belonged to the minor orders of the clergy. This means that they took vows of obedience and were immune from prosecution by secular authorities, but they were not required to remain celibate—unlike priests and bishops, who were in major orders. Even those who hoped to become lawyers or bureaucrats found it advantageous to "take orders" in case powerful ecclesiastical offices became open: Heloise tried to discourage Abelard from marrying for this very reason. Abelard, a nobleman's son, is by no means typical of the men who rose to prominence in this era through education. His contemporary and rival, Suger, is more representative: an orphan of obscure origins, he became abbot of the royal monastery of Saint-Denis and chancellor of two French kings.

Later, in the thirteenth century, boys who entered schools were usually not members of the clergy and never intended to be. Some regarded Latin literacy as a badge of status and a practical necessity. Others were future notaries, estate managers, and merchants who wanted to succeed in these careers. Many alternative schools were established to cater to these vocational students and, in many cases, Latin ceased to be the language of instruction and was replaced by the vernacular language of the region.

Formal schooling remained restricted to males. Yet many girls and women reared in convents or princely courts became highly learned. Heloise had clearly received excellent preparatory training in the convent before she began her studies with Abelard. Most laywomen were taught at home, sometimes by private tutors but more often by other women. In fact, laywomen were more likely to be literate than laymen, and it is for this reason that women were often the patrons of poets and the primary readers and owners of books.

Abelard and the Rise of Scholasticism

This educational revolution led to the development of new critical methods for framing and resolving complex intellectual and practical problems. These methods are collectively known as *scholasticism*, because they had their origins in the medieval schools. Scholastic methods are highly systematic and respectful of authority, but they also rely on rigorous

Competing Viewpoints

Two Conversion Experiences

> Both Peter Waldo (or Waldes), later branded as a heretic, and Francis of Assisi, later canonized as a saint, were moved to take up a life of preaching and poverty after undergoing a process of conversion. These experiences exhibit some striking similarities, despite the different fates of these two men. The first account is that of an anonymous chronicler in Peter's home town of Lyons; the second is by Francis's contemporary and hagiographer, Thomas of Celano (c. 1200–c. 1260/70).

The Conversion of Peter Waldo

At about this time, in 1173, there was a citizen of Lyons named Peter Waldo, who had made a great deal of money by the evil means of usury. One Sunday he lingered by a crowd that had gathered round a traveling storyteller, and was much struck by his words. He took him home with him, and listened carefully to his story of how St. Alexis had died a holy death in his father's house. Next morning Waldo hastened to the schools of theology to seek advice about his soul. When he had been told of the many ways of coming to God he asked the master whether any of them was more sure and reliable than the rest. The master quoted to him the words of the Lord, "If thou wilt be perfect, go sell what thou hast and give it to the poor, and thou shalt have treasure in heaven. And come follow me."

Waldo returned to his wife and gave her the choice between having all his movable wealth or his property in land. . . . She was very upset at having to do this and chose the property. From his movable wealth he returned what he had acquired wrongly, conferred a large portion on his two daughters, whom he placed in the order of Fontevrault without his wife's knowledge, and gave a still larger amount to the poor.

At this time a terrible famine was raging through Gaul and Germany. . . . Waldo generously distributed bread, soup, and meat to anyone who came to him. On the [Feast of the] Assumption of the Virgin [August 15] he scattered money among the poor in the streets saying, "You cannot serve two masters, God and Mammon." The people around thought he had gone out of his senses. Then he stood up on a piece of high ground and said, "Friends and fellow-citizens, I am not mad as you think. . . . I know that many of you disapprove of my having acted so publicly. I have done so both for my own sake and for yours: for my sake, because anybody who sees me with money in future will be able to say that I am mad; for your sake, so that you may learn to place your hopes in God and not in wealth." . . .

1177: Waldo, the citizen of Lyons whom we have already mentioned, who had vowed to God that he would possess neither gold nor silver, and take no thought for the morrow, began to make converts to his opinions. Following his example they gave all they had to the poor, and willingly devoted themselves to poverty. Gradually, both in public and in private they began to inveigh against both their own sins and those of others. . . .

1178: Pope Alexander III held a council at the Lateran palace. . . . The council condemned heresy and all those who fostered and defended heretics. The pope embraced Waldo, and applauded the vows of voluntary poverty which he had taken, but forbade him and his companion to assume the office of preaching except at the request of the priests. They obeyed this instruction for a time, but later they disobeyed, and affronted many, bringing ruin on themselves.

Source: Excerpted from *Chronicon universale anonymi Laudunensis*, ed. and trans. Robert I. Moore in *The Birth of Popular Heresy* (London: 1975), pp. 111–13 (slightly modified).

The Conversion of Francis of Assisi

There was a man by the name of Francis, who from his earliest years was brought up by his parents proud of spirit, in accordance with the vanity of the world. . . . These are the wretched circumstances among which the man whom we venerate today as a saint, for he is truly a saint, lived in his youth; and almost up to the

242 | CHAPTER 9 *The Consolidation of Europe, 1100–1250*

twenty-fifth year of his age, ... he outdid all his contemporaries in vanities and he came to be a promoter of evil and was more abundantly zealous for all kinds of foolishness.... And while, not knowing how to restrain himself, he was ... worn down by a long illness, [he] began to think of things other than he was used to thinking upon. When he had recovered somewhat and had begun to walk about the house with the support of a cane to speed the recovery of his health, he went outside one day and began to look about at the surrounding landscape with great interest. But the beauty of the fields, the pleasantness of the vineyards, and whatever else was beautiful to look upon, could stir in him no delight. He wondered therefore at the sudden change that had come over him.... From that day on, therefore, he began to despise himself....

Now since there was a certain man in the city of Assisi whom he loved more than any other because he was of the same age as the other, and since the great familiarity of their mutual affection led him to share his secrets with him; he often took him to remote places, places well-suited for counsel, telling him that he had found a certain precious and great treasure. This one rejoiced and, concerned about what he heard, he willingly accompanied Francis whenever he was asked. There was a certain grotto near the city where they frequently went and talked about this treasure. The man of God, who was already holy by reason of his holy purpose, would enter the grotto, while his companion would wait for him outside; and filled with a new and singular spirit, he would pray to his Father in secret....

One day, however, when he had begged for the mercy of God most earnestly, it was shown to him by God what he was to do.... He rose up, therefore, fortified himself with the sign of the cross, got his horse ready and mounted it, and taking with him some fine cloth to sell, he hastened to the city called Foligno. There, as usual, he sold everything he had with him ... and, free of all luggage, he started back, wondering with a religious mind what he should do with the money. ... When, therefore, he neared the city of Assisi, he discovered a certain church ... built of old in honor of St. Damian but which was now threatening to collapse because it was so old.... And when he found there a certain poor priest, he kissed his sacred hands with great faith, and offered him the money he had with him, ... begging the priest to suffer him to remain with him for the sake of the Lord....

When those who knew him ... compared what he was now with what he had been ... they began to revile him miserably. Shouting out that he was mad and demented, they threw the mud of the streets and stones at him.... Now ... the report of these things finally came to his father ... [who] shut him up mercilessly in a dark place for several days.... It happened, however, when Francis' father had left home for a while on business and the man of God remained bound in the basement of the house, his mother, who was alone with him and did not approve of what her husband had done, spoke kindly to her son. ... and loosening his chains, she let him go free....

He [the father] then brought his son before the bishop of the city, so that,

renouncing all his possessions into his hands, he might give up everything he had.... Indeed, he [Francis] did not wait for any words nor did he speak any, but immediately putting off his clothes and casting them aside, he gave them back to his father. Moreover, not even retaining his trousers, he stripped himself completely naked before all. The bishop, however, sensing his disposition and admiring greatly his fervor and constancy, arose and drew him within his arms and covered him with the mantle he was wearing....

Source: Excerpted from Thomas of Celano, "The First Life of Saint Francis" in *Saint Francis of Assisi: Writings and Biographies*, ed. Marion A. Habiq (Chicago: 1973), pp. 229–41.

Questions for Analysis

1. How do the conversions of Peter and Francis reflect the social and economic changes of the twelfth century? What new sources of tension and temptation are evident?

2. How do these two accounts describe these new converts' relationship(s) with their families, communities, and Church authorities? What are the similarities and differences, and why would these be important factors in determining the sanctity of either?

3. The story of Peter's conversion is written by an anonymous chronicler of Lyons, that of Francis by his follower and official biographer. How do these different perspectives shape these two accounts? Which is the more reliable, and why?

questioning and argumentation. They therefore place great emphasis on evidence derived from reason. Indeed, scholasticism can be defined as the creation of knowledge through logical debate, often called *dialectic*.

The earliest practitioner of the scholastic method is often considered to be Anselm of Canterbury (1033–1109), a Benedictine monk from northern Italy who became archbishop of Canterbury. The central premise of Anselm's teaching was that the human mind can combine knowledge gained through education and experience with divine revelation. Building on the writings of Augustine and Boethius (Chapter 6), Anselm developed various rational proofs for the underlying truths of Christian doctrine. The most famous of these is his proof for the existence of God, known as the ontological proof ("proof from the fact of existence") because it reasons that human beings could not have ideas of goodness or truth or justice unless some higher being had instilled these ideas in us. He further reasoned that God must be "that than which nothing greater can be conceived" and, as such, must exist.

The philosopher who popularized the scholastic method was Abelard, and it was largely thanks to him that Paris became the intellectual capital of Europe. As a cathedral town and seat of the French monarchy, it had a number of schools when Abelard arrived there, but it was his appointment to the schoolmaster's chair at Notre-Dame that made Paris a magnet for ambitious young men attracted to his unorthodox teaching style. We can glimpse it through an audacious treatise called the *Sic et Non* ("Yes and No"), in which Abelard gathered a collection of contradictory statements from the Church Fathers, organized around 150 key theological problems. Like his contemporary Gratian, the codifier of canon law, his ultimate ambition was to show that these divergent authorities could be reconciled—in this case, through the skillful use of dialectic. Yet Abelard did not propose any solutions in this work, which caused grave concern. More inflammatory still were his meditations on the doctrine of the Trinity, which circulated in a book of lectures that was denounced and burned as heretical in 1121. Twenty years later, Bernard of Clairvaux had Abelard condemned for heresy a second time.

Bernard's own mystic spirituality stood in direct opposition to Abelard's tireless quest for reasoned understanding. Abelard, for his part, found no solace in the monastic life beloved by Bernard: teaching was the activity that nurtured his faith. Luckily, teaching also expanded his fame and allowed him to train many pupils who eventually vindicated his teachings. After Abelard's death, his student Peter Lombard would ask the same fundamental questions that his master had done, but he took care to resolve the tensions which the *Sic et Non* had left open-ended. His great work, known as the *Sentences*, became the standard theological textbook of the medieval university, on which all aspirants to the doctorate were required to comment.

The Birth of the University

The emergence of the university—a unique forum for advanced study and the questioning of received wisdom—was the natural extension of Abelard's teachings. His reputation and that of his students attracted many other intellectuals to Paris, and together they began to offer more varied and advanced instruction than anything obtainable in the average cathedral school. By 1200, this loose association of teachers had formed themselves into a *universitas*, "a union of diversity," and the resulting faculty began to collaborate in higher academic study, with a special emphasis on theology. At about the same time, the students of law based in Bologna came together in a *universitas* whose speciality was law.

Paris and Bologna provided the two basic models on which all medieval universities were based. In southern Europe, universities at Montpellier, Salamanca, and Naples were patterned after Bologna, where the students themselves were the university: they hired the teachers, paid their salaries, and fined or discharged them for poor instruction. The universities of northern Europe were like that of Paris: guilds of teachers who governed themselves and established fees for tuition and rules of conduct. They eventually embraced four faculties—liberal arts, theology, law, and medicine—each headed by a dean. By the end of the thirteenth century, the northern universities also expanded to include separate, semi-autonomous colleges, which provided housing for poorer students and were often endowed by a private benefactor. Over time, these colleges became centers of instruction, too. The universities of Oxford and Cambridge still retain this pattern of organization.

Medieval Student Life

Most of the degrees granted in our own universities derive from those awarded in the Middle Ages, even though the courses of study are very different. No university curriculum included history or vernacular languages or anything like the social sciences prior to the nineteenth century. The medieval student was assumed to know Latin grammar thoroughly before admission; he had learned it in the primary (or "grammar") schools discussed above. He was then required to spend about four years studying the basic liberal arts, which meant doing advanced work in Latin rhetoric and the rules of logic. If he passed his examinations, he received the apprentice degree: bachelor

THE SPREAD OF UNIVERSITIES. This map shows the geographical distribution of Europe's major universities and indicates the dates of their foundation. ▪ *Where were the first universities founded, and why?* ▪ *Notice the number and location of the universities founded in the fourteenth and fifteenth centuries.* ▪ *What pattern do you see in these later foundations?* ▪ *What might explain this?*

of arts. If he wanted a professional career, he had to devote additional years to the pursuit of an advanced degree, the master of arts or the doctorate in law, medicine, or theology. This was accomplished by reading and commenting on standard texts such as Peter Lombard's *Sentences* (theology), Gratian's *Decretum* (law), or Aristotle's *Physics* (medicine). The requirements for the degree of doctor of philosophy included even more specialized training, and those for the doctorate in theology were particularly arduous: it could take twelve or thirteen years to earn this degree, over and above the eight years required to earn the MA.

Student life in medieval universities was rowdy. Since many students began their studies between the ages of twelve and fifteen, they were working through all the challenges of adolescence and early adulthood as they worked toward their degrees; this helps to explain the many prohibitions against drunkenness, gambling, and sexual pursuits included among the canons of Lateran IV. Moreover, because university students constituted an independent and privileged community apart from the towns in which they lived (technically immune to prosecution by secular authorities), there were often riots or pitched battles between "town" and "gown."

That said, study had to be intensive. Because handcopied books were expensive, the primary mode of instruction was the lecture (Latin for "public reading") in which a master would perform an authoritative work and comment on it, while the students took notes. As students advanced in their disciplines, they were expected to develop their own skills of analysis and interpretation in formal, public disputations. Advanced disputations could become extremely complex; sometimes they might last for days. Often they sparked debates of great magnitude. The Ninety-Five Theses posted by Martin Luther in 1517 were actually a set of debating points organized along these lines (see Chapter 13).

Classical Thought, Arabic Philosophy, Jewish Learning, and Christian Theology: The Synthesis of Thomas Aquinas

The intellectual revolution of the Middle Ages was hugely indebted to the learning and legacy of Muslim scholars. As we saw in Chapter 8, Muslim philosophers had been honing an array of different techniques to deal with the challenge of reconciling classical thought with Islamic belief, and these techniques contributed fundamentally to the development of Christian theology in the wake of the Crusades.

The most influential of these Muslim philosophers was Ibn Rushd, known to his Christian disciples as Averroès (ah-VER-oh-ayz, 1126–1198). Born in the Andalusian capital of Córdoba, Averroès single-handedly advanced the study of logic by publishing a series of careful commentaries that sought to purge Aristotle's works of all later and confusing influences. Soon translated from Arabic into Latin, these commentaries were received in western Europe alongside new translations of Aristotle's texts and fundamentally influenced the way all subsequent scholars

understood Greek philosophy. The prestige of Averroès was so great that Christian intellectuals called him simply "the Commentator," just as they called Aristotle "the Philosopher"—as if there were no others.

Ultimately, Averroès's learning was suppressed by the new Muslim dynasty that came to power in his lifetime, the Almohads, who demanded that all philosophy be subordinated to orthodox belief. After burning several of Averroès's works, they exiled him to Morocco. The greatest Jewish scholar of this period, Moses Maimonides (my-MAHN-eh-dees, c. 1137–1204), was also driven into exile by the Almohads; he traveled first to North Africa and then to Egypt, where he became famous as a teacher, jurist, and physician. Like Averroès, he exercised great influence on Christian theologians through his systematic exposition of Jewish law, the *Mishneh Torah*.

Because many aspects of the rabbinic tradition, Greek philosophy, and Arabic learning were not readily compatible with Christian doctrine, they all had to be filtered through the dialectical methods pioneered by Abelard and his pupils. The greatest proponent of this endeavor was Thomas Aquinas (1225–1274), a Dominican who became the leading theologian at the University of Paris. Thomas was committed to the defense of the Roman Church, but he also believed that the study of the physical world was a way of gaining knowledge of the divine. Thomas worked quietly and steadily on his two great summaries of theology, the *Summa contra Gentiles* (a compendium of arguments for refuting non-Christian religions) and the comprehensive *Summa Theologiae*. The theology of the modern Roman Catholic Church still rests on Thomistic methods, doctrines, and principles.

COURTS, CITIES, AND CATHEDRALS

In the eleventh century, it would have been possible to describe European society as divided among those who worked, those who prayed, and those who fought. By 1200, such a description no longer bore much relationship to reality. New elites had emerged, and the wealthiest members of society were merchants and bankers; aristocrats either had to best them by engaging in trade or join them through strategic intermarriage. The aristocracy still fought, but so did upwardly mobile knights, rural archers, citizen militias, and peasant infantries. Meanwhile, the pupils of the new schools made up a growing professional class that further defied categorization. We have already observed that careers in the Church or royal bureaucracies were open to self-made, educated men. But princely courts and cities also provided opportunities for advancement.

From Chevalerie to Chivalry

The transformation of chivalry and the emergence of medieval court culture were connected to the growing wealth of Europe, the competition among territorial rulers, and contemporary developments in military technology. In 1100, a knight could get by with a woolen tunic and leather corselet, a horse, and a sword. A hundred years later, a knight needed full-body armor made of iron, a visored helmet, a broadsword, a spear, a shield, several warhorses capable of carrying all this gear, and a groom or squire to care for everything. By 1250, a knight also had to keep up appearances at tournaments, which meant maintaining a string of horses, sumptuous silk clothing for himself and caparisons for his steeds, and a retinue of liveried servants. As the costs of a warrior's equipment rose, the number of men who could personally afford it declined dramatically, which made knightly display something increasingly prized by the nobility and upstart merchants alike. Knights who did not inherit property or gain sufficient wealth to support themselves had to seek wealthy brides or the protection of a lord who could afford to equip them.

There were still other factors contributing to the prestige of knighthood. As part of the larger effort to control violent competition for land, both secular and ecclesiastical rulers had begun to promote a new set of values that would redefine chivalry: bravery, loyalty, generosity, and civility. This new chivalry appealed to knights because it distinguished them from all the other "new men" who were emerging as powerful in this period, especially merchants and clerics. It also appealed to the nobility whose status in this socially mobile world no longer depended on descent from high-born ancestors. Families who *did* have such ancestors did not necessarily have the wealth to maintain a noble lifestyle.

What, then, was "nobility"? Was high status a matter of birth or was it the result of individual achievement? The amalgamation of knighthood and nobility offered something to those on both sides of the question. To the older aristocracy, it was a visible sign of good breeding. To professional warriors like many crusaders, and to the merchants and bureaucrats who later adopted its language and customs, chivalry offered a way of legitimizing social positions attained through bravery or skill. As a result, mounted combat—whether on the battlefield, in tournaments, or in the hunt—would remain the defining pastime

MAKING A KNIGHTLY APPEARANCE. The costs of maintaining a chivalric lifestyle rose steeply in the twelfth and thirteenth centuries, not only because a knight needed the most up-to-date equipment but also because he was expected to cut a gallant figure at tournaments and to dazzle female spectators. This image is one of many sumptuous full-page illuminations in the Manesse Codex, made in Zurich in the early fourteenth century and preserving the compositions of earlier courtly poets.

of European gentlemen until the end of the First World War (see Chapter 24).

The Culture of the Court

Closely linked to this new ideology of chivalry was a new emphasis on *courtoisie*, "courtliness," the refined behavior appropriate to a court. This stemmed in part from practical necessity. Those great lords who could support a knightly retinue would have households full of energetic, lusty young men whose appetites had to be controlled. Hence, the emerging code of chivalry encouraged its adherents to view noble women as objects of veneration who could only be wooed and won by politesse, poetry, and valiant deeds;

Past and Present

Medieval Plots and Modern Movies

From westerns to science fiction to action movies to romantic comedies, most of the films that draw big audiences today are based loosely or closely on literary genres that were popularized during the Middle Ages: tales of chivalry and heroism, forbidden love, supernatural events, and magical adventures.

Watch related author videos on the Student Site
wwnorton.com/college/history/western-civilizationsBrief4

they had to be courted. Non-noblewomen, though, were fair game and could be taken by force if they did not yield willingly to the desires of a knight.

Whole new genres of poetry, song, and storytelling emerged in the twelfth century to celebrate the allied cultures of chivalry and courtliness. These stand in marked contrast to the older entertainments of Europe's warrior class, the heroic epics that are often the earliest literary artifacts of various vernacular languages: the Anglo-Saxon *Beowulf*, *The Song of Roland*, the Norse sagas, the German *Song of the Nibelungs*, and the Spanish *Poem of the Cid*. These epics portray a virile, violent society. Gore flows freely; skulls are cleaved; manly valor, honor, and loyalty are the major themes. If women are mentioned, it is often as prizes to be won in battle.

The courtly entertainments introduced in the twelfth century are very different in style, subject matter, and authorship. Many of them were addressed to, and commissioned by,

women. In some cases, they were even composed by women or in close collaboration with a female patron. An example of the former is the collections of *lais* (versified stories) of Marie de France, who was active during the reigns of Henry II and Eleanor of Aquitaine, and who may have been an abbess as well as a member of the Anglo-Norman aristocracy. An example of the latter are the Arthurian tales composed by Marie's contemporary, Chrétien de Troyes (*KRAY-tyan duh TWAH*, fl. 1165–90), who spent time working under the patronage of Eleanor's daughter (by her first husband, Louis VII), Marie of Champagne.

Romances were engaging tales of love and adventure, often focusing on the exploits of King Arthur and his knights or some other heroic figure of the past, like Alexander the Great. But they were also attuned to the interests and concerns of women: threats to women's independence, enforced or unhappy marriages, disputed inheritances, fashion, fantasies of power. The heroine of one anonymous romance is a woman who dresses as a knight and travels the world performing valiant deeds. Other heroines accompany their husbands on crusades or quests, or defend their castles against attack, or have supernatural powers. Following in Chrétien's footsteps, the German poets Wolfram von Eschenbach and Gottfried von Strassburg vied to produce romances that retained the scope and complexity of heroic epics while featuring women in strong, central roles: Wolfram's *Parzival*, the story of the search for the Holy Grail, and Gottfried's *Tristan*, which retold the Celtic story of the adulterous love between Tristan and Isolde. Both inspired the operatic reconceptions of Richard Wagner (1813–1883).

The poetic tradition initiated by the southern French troubadours and northern French trouvères (terms deriving from the verbs *trobar/trouver*: "to discover, to invent") also contributed to the culture of chivalry and inspired the work of German *minnesänger* ("love singers"). Much troubadour poetry displays sensitivity to feminine beauty and the natural world. Take, for example, a lyric of Bernart de Ventadorn (c. 1135–1195), one of Eleanor's protégés:

> When leaves and grass are lush with renewed growth
> The beauty of my Lady blossoms forth . . .
> I am her slave, her vassal, she my lord;
> I pay her homage, hope to have a word
> Of kindness, or of love, exchanged for mine
> But she is cruel: she will not make a sign.

Other troubadour songs celebrated old-fashioned warlike virtues, as in the verses of Bernart's contemporary, Bertran de Born (c. 1140–1214), a friend of Eleanor's son Richard the Lionheart:

> It pleases me to hear the mirth and song
> Of birds, filling the wood the whole day long.
> But more it pleases me to see the fields
> All planted thick with tents, to see the shields
> And swords of my companions ranged for war,
> To hear the screams, to see the blood and gore.

To what extent do courtly entertainments reflect reality? Certainly, as the first song reveals, there were women throughout this period who wielded tremendous power, particularly in Scandinavia and parts of southern Europe, where women could inherit property, rule in their own right, and be treated as lords in fact and in name (as in Bernart's song). Queen Urraca ruled the combined kingdom of León-Castile from 1109 until 1126. Ermengarde

of Narbonne (c. 1127–1197) ruled her strategically placed county from early adolescence to the time of her death. Eleanor remained sole ruler of Aquitaine throughout her long life, and she played a crucial role in the government of England at various times. The strong-willed Blanche of Castile (1188–1252), Eleanor's granddaughter, ruled France during the minority of her son Louis IX and again when he went on crusade.

Queens are not, of course, typical, but their activities in this period reflect some of the opportunities open to well-born women—and the freedoms that set most western European women of this time apart from their counterparts in the Byzantine and Muslim worlds. A striking symbol of this is the figure of the queen in the game of chess. In the Muslim courts where the game originated, the equivalent of the queen was a male figure, the king's chief minister, who could move only diagonally and only one square at a time. In twelfth-century Europe, this piece became the queen. She was the only figure versatile enough to move all over the board.

Urban Opportunities and Inequalities

In 1174, a cleric called William FitzStephen wrote a biography of his former employer, Thomas Becket, who had recently been canonized. In it, William went out of his way to extoll the urban culture of London that had produced this saintly man and other men of superior quality, as well as all the splendid sights and pastimes to be had there. Towns were crucibles of activity, and as such became cultural powerhouses as well as economic ones.

As we noted in Chapter 8, many of the towns that had emerged in the eleventh century were governed by associations of citizens who undertook a wide variety of civic responsibilities. But urban governance was also apt to fall into the hands of oligarchs, a trend that became increasingly marked during the thirteenth century when the enormous wealth generated by some forms of commerce led to stark social inequalities. In Italy, some cities sought to control the resulting violence by turning to an outsider who would rule as a dictator. Other cities adopted the model of Venice and became formal oligarchies, casting off all pretense to egalitarianism. Some cities remained republics in principle, like Florence, but became increasingly oligarchical in practice.

But even in places where town governance was controlled by a powerful few, there were many meaningful opportunities for collective activity. Urban manufacturing was regulated by professional associations known as guilds or (in some regions) confraternities. Guilds promoted the interests of their members by trying to preserve monopolies and limit

Illicit Love and the Code of Chivalry

Little is known about Marie de France, author of a series of popular verse tales that are among the earliest chivalric romances, but she may have been a nun or abbess living in the Anglo-Norman realm of Henry II and Eleanor of Aquitaine. The following excerpt is from her Lais (Ballads), adapted from stories told in the Franco-Celtic county of Brittany (Abelard's home).

 he Bretons, who lived in Brittany, were fine and noble people. In days gone by these valiant, courtly and noble men composed lays for posterity and thus preserved them from oblivion. . . . One of them, which I have heard recited, should not be forgotten. It concerns Equitan, a most courtly man, lord of Nantes, justiciary, and king.

Equitan enjoyed a fine reputation and was greatly loved in his land. He adored pleasure and amorous dalliance: for this reason he upheld the principles of chivalry. Those who lack a full comprehension and understanding of love show no thought for their lives. Such is the nature of love that no one under its sway can retain command over reason. Equitan had a seneschal, a good knight, brave and loyal, who took care of his entire territory, governing it and administering its justice. Never, except in time of war, would the king have forsaken his hunting, his pleasures, or his river sports, whatever the need might have been.

As his wedded wife the seneschal had a woman who was to bring great misfortune to the land. She was a lady of fine breeding and extremely beautiful with a noble body and good bearing. Nature had spared no pains when fashioning her: her eyes sparkled, her face and mouth were beautiful, and her nose was well set. She had no equal in the kingdom, and the king, having often heard her praised, frequently sent her greetings and gifts. . . . He went hunting in her region on his own and on returning from his sport took lodging for the night in the place where the seneschal dwelt, in the very castle where the lady was to be found. He had ample occasion to speak with her, to express his feelings and display his fine qualities. He found her most courtly and wise, beautiful in body and countenance. . . .

That night he neither slept nor rested, but spent his time reproaching and reprimanding himself. "Alas," he said, "what destiny brought me to this region? Because of this lady I have seen, my heart has been overwhelmed by a pain so great that my whole body trembles. I think I have no option but to love her. Yet, if I did love her, I should be acting wrongly, as she is the seneschal's wife. I ought to keep faith with him and love him, just as I want him to do with me. . . ."

Source: From "Equitan," in *The Lais of Marie de France*, trans. Glyn S. Burgess and Keith Busby (Harmondsworth, UK: 1985), pp. 56–57.

Questions for Analysis

1. Despite the king's initial misgivings, he and the seneschal's wife eventually have an affair and plot to murder her husband, only to be caught in their own trap. Given this outcome, how would you interpret Marie's remarks about courtliness and "the code of chivalry"? What are the tenets of this code, according to the king?

2. What social tensions does this story reflect, and how might it shed light on historical realities? What moral might contemporary readers draw from it?

outside competition. To these ends, terms of employment and membership were strictly regulated. If an apprentice or a journeyman worker (from the French *journée*, meaning "day" and, by extension, "day's work") wished to become a master, he had to produce a "masterpiece" to be judged by the masters of the guild. If the market was considered too weak to support additional master craftsmen, even a masterpiece would not secure a man the coveted right to set up his own shop and earn enough to marry. Most guilds were closed to Jews and Muslims and they also restricted the opportunities available to women.

Guilds and confraternities were therefore instruments of economic control, but they were also important social, political, and cultural institutions. Most combined the functions of religious association, drinking club, and benevolent society, looking after members and their families in hard times, supporting the dependents of members who died, and helping to finance funerals. Guilds also empowered their members in much the same way that unions do today, providing them with political representation and raising their social status. In the wealthy city of Arras, there was even a guild of professional entertainers, the confraternity of jongleurs, which became the most powerful organization in the town.

The Varieties of Urban Entertainment

Like courts, towns fostered new kinds of vernacular entertainment. Even the genres of Latin poetry, song, and drama produced in this period can be considered "vernacular" because they made use of vernacular elements (like rhyme, not a feature of classical Latin poetry), dealt with current events, and were popular with a wide audience. In one of Heloise's letters to Abelard, she recalls that he was so renowned for his love songs that "every street and

tavern resounded with my name." It's possible that some of Abelard's songs were sung in French but more probable that they used the edgy, colloquial Latin popular among the student singer-songwriters known as "goliards," which means something like "daredevils." Their lyrics glorified the carefree life of youth, the pleasures of drinking and dice, the joys of love, and the agonies of poverty.

Perhaps the genre most representative of urban culture is the fabliau—a short story in verse with a salacious or satirical ending. Medieval fables lampooned the different types of people who were striving to reinvent themselves in the permissive world of the town: the oafish peasant, the effete aristocrat, the corrupt priest, the sex-starved housewife, the wily student, the greedy merchant, the con man. Gender-bending and reversals of fortune are common themes. In one fabliau, a young noblewoman is forced by her impoverished father to marry a buffoonish shopkeeper who thereby gains a knighthood. To shame him, she dresses herself as a knight and beats her husband in a jousting match. In another, a priest tricks a poor peasant out of his cow by promising that God will reward him by doubling his "investment" in the Church. When the cow breaks out

ROMANESQUE AND GOTHIC. Some distinguishing features of the Romanesque and Gothic styles are exhibited in these two churches, both dedicated to the Virgin Mary and built within a century of one another. On the left is the west front of the Church of Notre-Dame-la-Grande in Poitiers, the ancestral domain of Eleanor of Aquitaine. Constructed between 1135 and 1145, it featured rounded arches, strong stone walls, massive supporting pillars, and small windows. On the right is the cathedral of Notre-Dame at Reims in Champagne, built between 1220 and 1299. The emphasis on stolid, horizontal registers is here replaced by soaring, vertical lines. The gabled portals, pointed arches, and bristling pinnacles all accentuate the height of this structure, while the multitude of stained-glass windows—chiefly the enormous rose window—flood the vast interior with colored light.

of the priest's pasture and runs for home, she brings the priest's cow along, too, and the peasant is delighted by the fulfillment of the promised miracle.

The Medieval Cathedral

The cathedrals constructed in Europe's major cities during this period exemplify the ways in which the cultural communities of the court, the schools, and the town came together. For although any cathedral-building campaign would have been spearheaded by a bishop looking to glorify his episcopal see, it could not be completed without the support of the nobility, the resources of the wealthy, the learning of trained theologians, and the talents of urban craftsmen. And cathedrals were not merely edifices: they were theaters for the performance of liturgy, music, drama, and preaching.

Cathedrals were not, in themselves, new: the seat of a bishop had long been known as his *cathedra*, his throne, and the church that housed it was the principal church of the diocese. But the size, splendor, and importance of cathedrals increased exponentially in the twelfth and thirteenth centuries alongside the growing power of the Church, the population of cities, and the wealth and knowledge necessary for their construction. Indeed, the cathedrals of this period are readily distinguishable from their predecessors by their architectural style, which came to be called "Gothic," while the style of earlier buildings is known as "Romanesque."

As the term suggests, Romanesque buildings use the basic elements of public architecture developed under the Roman Empire: massive stone walls, the rounded arch, and sturdy supporting columns. These features convey stability, and they also enabled churches to be fortified and defended in troubled times. By contrast, the structural elements of Gothic architecture are the pointed arch, groined and ribbed vaulting, and the flying buttress, an external support that strengthened the much thinner stone walls and enormous stained-glass windows whose light illuminated elaborate decorative programs that made the cathedral a microcosm of the medieval world and an encyclopedia of medieval knowledge.

These new Gothic cathedrals were not buildings that could be defended in wartime and, it was thought, they would never have to be: they were manifestations of urban pride, expressions of practical and intellectual genius, symbols of a triumphant and confident Church. Their builders would have been dismayed to learn that the modern term *Gothic* was actually intended to be derogatory, the name for art forms that Renaissance artists—who favored Roman models—considered barbaric (see Chapter 12). They would have been still more shocked to learn that cathedrals were among the first monuments targeted for destruction during the Reformation, the revolutions of the

After You Read This Chapter

Go to **INQUIZITIVE** to see what you've learned—and learn what you've missed—with personalized feedback along the way.

REVIEWING THE OBJECTIVES

- The emerging monarchies of Europe shared certain features but differed from one another in significant ways. What were the major similarities and differences of kingship in England, France, and Spain? Why are they important?
- How did the meaning and purposes of crusading change in the twelfth and thirteenth centuries?
- The growth of papal power made religion an important part of daily life for all Christians in unprecedented ways, but it also limited lay spirituality and the rights of non-Christians. How?
- Scholasticism was the method of teaching and learning fostered by medieval schools and it was also a method of debating and resolving problems. How did scholasticism assist in the reconciliation of classical and Christian thought?
- Why did the meaning of chivalry change in the twelfth century? What new literary genres and art forms of the High Middle Ages were fostered by courts, universities, and towns?

eighteenth and nineteenth centuries, and the wars of the twentieth. One of the prime examples of Gothic architecture, the cathedral dedicated to the Virgin Mary at Reims (shown on page 251), was almost entirely destroyed during World War I; what visitors see today is a reconstruction.

CONCLUSION

A century ago, the American medievalist Charles Homer Haskins described the intellectual, religious, and cultural changes of this era as "the Renaissance of the twelfth century" and the beginning of northwestern Europe's enduring cultural prestige. A generation later, his student Joseph Strayer located "the medieval origins of the modern state" in this same period and, with them, the modern ideas of national sovereignty and national identity. In recent decades, the British medievalists R. I. Moore and Robert Bartlett have also argued that this era marks the beginning of the modern world, though not in positive ways. Moore sees the growth of strong institutions like the Church and the state as leading to "the formation of a persecuting society" in which governmental bureaucracies are used to identify, control, and punish groups of people deemed threatening to those in power through a never-ending "war on heresy." Bartlett views this era as the key phase in a brutal process of "conquest and colonization" visible in the eastern expansion of the Holy Roman Empire, the Norman conquest of England, the growth of papal power, the Crusades, and other movements.

Common to all of these different paradigms is a recognition that the expansion of European power began around the year 1000, continued into the twelfth century, and was consolidated in the thirteenth. By 1250, Europe had taken on the geographic, political, linguistic, and cultural characteristics that continue to define it today. Many European states still look to these centuries for their origins and for the monuments of their cultural heritage. The doctrines crystallized in medieval canon law and scholastic theology are still the core doctrines of the Roman Catholic Church, and devotion to the Virgin Mary is still central to the piety of millions. The religious orders that emerged to educate and curb a burgeoning medieval population continue their ministries. The daughter houses of medieval monastic orders continue to proliferate in lands unknown to medieval Europeans: Japan, Australia, New Zealand, the Americas. Students still pursue the degrees granted in medieval universities, and those who earn them wear the caps and gowns of medieval scholars. Meanwhile, poets aspire to the eloquence of troubadours, singers record the music of Hildegard, and Hollywood films are based on chivalric romances. It is difficult to tell where the Middle Ages end and the modern world begins.

PEOPLE, IDEAS, AND EVENTS IN CONTEXT

- What was at stake in the clash between **HENRY II** of England and **THOMAS BECKET**?
- What was **MAGNA CARTA** and why was it made? How did **PHILIP AUGUSTUS** consolidate royal authority in France, and why were the German emperors unable to do so?
- Why were the **CRUSADER STATES** short-lived and fragile? How did the **RECONQUISTA** continue the Crusades?
- What were the main goals of **INNOCENT III**? How did the **FRANCISCANS** and **DOMINICANS** advance his agenda?
- How do the **CULT OF THE VIRGIN** and the careers of **HILDEGARD OF BINGEN** and **HELOISE** exemplify the ideals and realities of women's roles in the Church?
- Why were **PETER ABELARD'S** teachings condemned by the Church? In what sense can he be considered the founder of the **UNIVERSITY OF PARIS**?
- What is **SCHOLASTICISM**? How did **THOMAS AQUINAS** respond to the influence of Classical and Muslim philosophies?
- How did noblewomen like **ELEANOR OF AQUITAINE** contribute to the emergence of a new vernacular culture? What types of entertainment are characteristic of medieval cities?

THINKING ABOUT CONNECTIONS

- The growth of towns, monarchies, and the Church increased the degree of control that those in power could exercise; but this growth also increased access to education and new forms of social mobility. Is this a paradox, or are these two phenomena related?
- The U.S. Constitution is based on the legal principles and institutions that emerged in medieval England, but it also drew on Roman models. Which do you consider to be more influential, and why?
- Some historians have argued that the extent and methods of persecution discernible in the Middle Ages are unprecedented in the history of Western civilizations. How would you support or refute this thesis? For example, does the persecution of Jews in medieval Europe differ from their treatment under the neo-Assyrians and Chaldeans, or under the Roman Empire? Why or why not?

Before You Read This Chapter

The Medieval World, 1250–1350

W hen Christopher Columbus set out to find a new trade route to the East, he carried with him two influential travel narratives written centuries before his voyage. One was *The Book of Marvels*, composed around 1350 and attributed to John de Mandeville, an English author (writing in French) who claimed to have reached the far horizons of the globe. The other was Marco Polo's account of his journey through the vast Eurasian realm of the Mongol Empire to the court of the Great Khan in China. The Venetian merchant had dictated it to an author of popular romances around 1298, when both men were in prison—in Columbus's own city of Genoa, coincidentally. Both of these books were the product of an extraordinary era of unprecedented interactions among the peoples of Europe, Asia, and the Mediterranean world. And both became extraordinarily influential, inspiring generations of mercantile adventurers, ambitious pilgrims, and armchair travelers (see Chapter 12).

These narratives are representative of an era that seemed wide open to every sort of influence. This was a time when ease of communication and commercial exchange made Western civilizations part of an interlocking network that potentially spanned the globe. Although this network would prove fragile in the face of a large-scale demographic crisis, the Black Death, it created a lasting impression of infinite possibilities. Indeed, it was only *because* of the medieval network's connective channels that the Black Death was able to wreak such devastation in the years around 1350.

Europeans' integration with this widening world not only put them into contact with unfamiliar cultures and commodities, it opened up new ways of looking at the world they already knew. New artistic and intellectual responses are discernible in this era, as are a host of new inventions and technologies. At the same time, involvement in a wider world placed new pressures on long-term developments within Europe: notably the growing tensions among large territorial monarchies, and between these secular powers and the authority of the papacy. By the early fourteenth century, the papal court would literally be held hostage by the king of France. A few decades later, the king of England would openly declare his own claim to the French throne. The ensuing struggles for sovereignty would have a profound impact on the balance of power in Europe, and further complicate Europeans' relationships with one another and with their far-flung neighbors.

THE MONGOL EMPIRE AND THE REORIENTATION OF THE WEST

In our survey of Western civilizations, we have frequently noted the existence of strong links between the Mediterranean world and East Asia. Trade along the network of trails known as the Silk Road can be traced far back into antiquity, and we have seen that such overland networks were extended by Europe's waterways and by the sea. But it was not until the late thirteenth century that Europeans were able to establish direct connections with India, China, and the so-called Spice Islands of the Indonesian archipelago. For Europeans, these connections would prove profoundly important, as much for their impact on the European imagination as for their economic significance. For the peoples of Asia, however, the more frequent appearance of Europeans was less consequential than the events that made these journeys possible: the rise of a new empire that encompassed the entire continent.

The Expansion of the Mongol Empire

The Mongols were one of many nomadic peoples inhabiting the vast steppes of Central Asia. Although closely connected with Turkic peoples, the Mongols spoke their own distinctive language and had their own homeland, located to the north of the Gobi Desert in what is now known as Mongolia. Essentially, their daily lives and wealth depended on the sheep that provided shelter (sheepskin tents), woolen clothing, milk, and meat. But the Mongols were also highly accomplished horsemen and raiders. Indeed, it was to curtail their raiding ventures that the Chines had fortified their Great Wall, many centuries before. Primarily, though, China relied on the Mongols' tribal feuds, which kept their energies turned against each other.

In the late twelfth century, however, a Mongol leader named Temujin (c. 1162–1227) began to unite the various tribes under his rule. He did so by incorporating the warriors of each defeated tribe into his own army. In 1206, his supremacy over all these tribes was reflected in his new title: Genghis Khan, from the Mongol words meaning "universal ruler." This new name also revealed wider ambitions: in 1209, Genghis Khan began to direct his enormous army against the Mongols' neighbors.

Taking advantage of the fact that China was then divided into three warring states, Ghengis Khan launched an attack on the Chin Empire of the north, managing to penetrate deep into its interior by 1211. These initial attacks were probably looting expeditions rather than deliberate attempts at conquest, but the Mongols' aims were soon sharpened under Genghis Khan's successors. Shortly after his death in 1227, a full-scale invasion of both northern and western China was under way. In 1234, these regions also fell to the Mongols. By 1279, one of Genghis Khan's numerous grandsons, Kublai Khan, would complete the conquest by adding southern China to this empire.

For the first time in centuries, China was reunited—but under Mongol rule. And it was now connected to western and central Asia in ways unprecedented in its long history, since Genghis Khan had brought crucial commercial cities and Silk Road trading posts (Tashkent, Samarkand, and Bukhara) into his empire. One of his sons, Ögedei (*EHRG-uh-day*), building on these achievements, laid plans for an even more far-reaching expansion of Mongol influence. Between 1237 and 1240, the Mongols under his command conquered the capital of the Rus' at Kiev and then launched a two-pronged assault directed at the rich lands of the eastern European frontier. The smaller of the two Mongol armies swept through Poland toward Germany; the larger army went southwest toward Hungary. In April of 1241, the smaller Mongol force met a hastily assembled army of Germans and Poles at the battle of Liegnitz, where the two sides fought to a bloody standstill. Two days later, the larger Mongol army annihilated the Hungarian army at the river Sajo. It could have moved even deeper into

THE STATES OF THE MONGOL EMPIRE. Like Alexander's, Genghis Khan's empire was swiftly assembled and encompassed vast portions of Europe and Asia. ▪ *How many different Mongol khanates were there after 1260, when Kublai Khan came to power, and were these domains mapped onto older divisions within Western civilizations?* ▪ *How might the Mongol occupation of the Muslim world have aided the expansion of European trade?* ▪ *At the same time, why would it have complicated the efforts of crusader armies in the Holy Land?*

Europe after this important victory, but it withdrew when Ögedei Khan died in December of that same year.

Muscovy and the Mongol Khanate

As we have seen in previous chapters, the Rus' of Kiev had fostered crucial diplomatic and trading relations with both western Europe and Byzantium, as well as with the Islamic Caliphate at Baghdad. That dynamic changed with the arrival of the Mongols, who shifted the locus of power

from Kiev to their own camp on the lower Volga River. This became known as the Khanate of the Golden Horde. Its magnificent name evokes the impression made by tents that shone with wealth, some literally hung with cloth of gold. It derives from the Mongol word meaning "encampment" and the related Turkish word *ordu* ("army").

Initially, the Mongols ruled their westernmost territories directly, installing their own administrative officials and requiring local princes to show their obedience by traveling in person to the Mongol court in China. But after Kublai Khan's death in 1294, the Mongols began to tolerate the existence of several semi-independent principalities

A MONGOL ROBE IN CLOTH OF GOLD. The majestic term *Khanate of the Golden Horde* captures both the power and the splendor of the Mongol warriors who conquered Rus' and many other lands. The robe depicted here dates from the late thirteenth or early fourteenth century and was made from cloth of gold: silk woven with gold (and sometimes silver) thread, a precious but surprisingly durable material that was also used for banners and even tents. A robe similar to this one was sold at auction in 2011 for nearly a quarter of a million dollars.

from which they demanded regular tribute. Kiev never recovered its dominant position, but one of these newer principalities would eventually form the core of a state called Muscovy, centered on the duchy of Moscow. As the tribute-collecting center for the Mongol Khanate, Moscow's dukes were encouraged to absorb neighboring territories in order to increase Moscow's security.

Compared to Kiev, Moscow's location was less advantageous for forging commercial contacts with the Baltic and Black Sea regions. Its direct ties with western Europe were also less developed, but this had little to do with geography. The Moscovites were staunchly loyal to the Orthodox Church of Byzantium and had watched relations between the Latin West and the Greek East deteriorate drastically during the Crusades. They became openly hostile to western Europeans after Constantinople was captured and sacked by crusaders in 1204 (see Chapter 9), an event that led Moscovites to see themselves as the last remaining protectors of the Orthodox Church. Eventually, as we shall see in Chapter 12, they would claim to be the heirs of Roman imperial power.

The Making of the Mongol Ilkhanate

As Ögedei Khan moved into the lands of Rus' and eastern Europe, Mongol armies were also sent to subdue the vast territory that had been encompassed by the former Persian

Empire and then by the empires of Alexander and Rome. Indeed, the strongest state in this region was known as Rûm, the Arabic word for "Rome." This was a Sunni Muslim sultanate that had been founded by the Seljuq Turks in 1077, just prior to the launching of the First Crusade, and consisted of Anatolian provinces formerly belonging to the eastern Roman Empire. It had successfully withstood waves of crusading aggression while capitalizing on the misfortunes of Byzantium, taking over several key ports on the Mediterranean and the Black Sea while cultivating a flourishing overland trade as well.

But in 1243, the Seljuqs of Rûm were forced to surrender to the Mongols, who had already succeeded in occupying what is now Iraq, Iran, portions of Pakistan and Afghanistan, and the Christian kingdoms of Georgia and Armenia. Thereafter, the Mongols easily found their way into regions weakened by centuries of Muslim infighting and Christian crusading movements. Byzantium, as we noted in Chapter 9, had been fatally weakened by the Fourth Crusade: Constantinople was now controlled by the Venetians, and Byzantine states centered on Nicaea (in Anatolia) and Epirus (in northern Greece) were fragile. The capitulation of Rûm left remaining Byzantine possessions in Anatolia open to the Mongols.

In 1261, the emperor Michael VIII Palaeologus (r. 1259–82) managed to regain control of Constantinople and its immediate hinterland, but the depleted empire he ruled was surrounded by hostile neighbors. The crusader principality of Antioch, which had been founded in 1098, finally succumbed to the Mongols in 1268. The Mongols themselves were only halted in their drive toward Palestine by the Mamluk Sultanate of Egypt, established in 1250 and ruled by a powerful Muslim military caste.

All of these disparate territories came to be called the Ilkhanate, the "subordinate khanate," meaning that its Mongol rulers paid deference to the Great Khan. The first Ilkhan was Hulagu, brother of China's Kublai Khan. His descendants would rule this realm for another eighty years, eventually converting to Islam but remaining hostile toward the Mamluk Muslims, who remained their chief rivals.

The Pax Mongolica *and Its Price*

Although the Mongols' expansion of power into Europe had been checked in 1241, their combined conquests made them masters of territories that stretched from the Black Sea to the Pacific Ocean: one-fifth of the earth's surface, the largest land empire in history. Within this domain, no single Mongol ruler's power was absolute. Kublai Khan

THE MONGOL RULER OF MUSLIM PERSIA, HIS CHRISTIAN QUEEN, AND HIS JEWISH HISTORIAN. The *Compendium of Chronicles* by the Jewish-born Muslim polymath Rashid al-Din (1247–1318) exemplifies the pluralistic culture encouraged by Mongol rule: written in Persian (and often translated into Arabic), it celebrates the achievements of Hulagu Khan (1217–1265), a grandson of Genghis and brother of Kublai, who consolidated Persia and its neighboring regions into the Ilkhanate. But it also embeds those achievements within the long history of Islam. This image depicts Hulagu with his wife, Dokuz Khatun, who was a Turkic princess and a Christian.

■ *Why would Rashid al-Din have wanted to place the new Mongol dynasty in this historical context?*

(r. 1260–94), who took the additional title *khagan*, or "Great Khan," never claimed to rule all Mongol khanates directly. In his own domain of China and Mongolia, his power was highly centralized and built on the intricate (and ancient) imperial bureaucracy of China; but elsewhere, Mongol governance was directed at securing a steady payment of tribute from subject peoples, which meant that local rulers could retain much of their power.

This distribution of authority made Mongol rule flexible and adaptable to local conditions. Indeed, the Mongol khans differed from most contemporary rulers in being highly tolerant of all religious beliefs. This was an advantage in governing peoples who observed an array of Buddhist, Christian, and Muslim practices, not to mention Hindus, Jews, and the many itinerant groups and individuals whose languages and beliefs reflected a melding of many cultures.

This acceptance of cultural and religious difference, alongside the Mongols' encouragement of trade and love of rich things, created ideal conditions for some merchants and artists. Hence, the term *Pax Mongolica* ("Mongol Peace") is often used to describe the century from 1250 to 1350. No such term should be taken at face value, however: this peace was bought at a great price. Indeed, the artists whose varied talents created the gorgeous textiles, utensils, and illuminated books prized by the Mongols were not all willing participants. Many were captives or slaves subject to ruthless relocation. The Mongols would often transfer entire families and communities of craftsmen from one part of the empire to another. The result was an intensive period of cultural exchange that might combine Chinese, Persian, Venetian, and Slavic influences (among many others) in a single work of art.

The Mongol Peace was also achieved at the expense of many flourishing Muslim cities that had preserved the heritage of even older civilizations and that were devastated or crippled during the bloody process of Mongol expansion. The city of Herat, situated in one of Afghanistan's few fertile valleys and described by the Persian poet Rumi as "the pearl in the oyster," was entirely destroyed in 1221 and did not fully recover for centuries. Baghdad, the splendid capital of the Abbasid Caliphate and a haven for artists and intellectuals since the eighth century (Chapter 8), was savagely besieged and sacked in 1258. The capture of the city resulted in the destruction of the House of Wisdom, the library and research center where Muslim scientists, philosophers, and translators preserved classical knowledge and advanced cutting-edge scholarship in such fields as mathematics, engineering, and medicine. Baghdad's fall is held to mark the end of Islam's golden age, since the establishment of the Mongol Ilkhanate in Persia eradicated a continuous zone of Muslim influence that had blended cultures stretching from southern Spain and North Africa to India.

Bridging East and West

To facilitate the movement of people and goods within their empire, the Mongols began to control the caravan routes that led from the Mediterranean and the Black Sea through Central Asia and into China, policing bandits and making conditions safer for travelers. They also encouraged and streamlined trade by funneling many exchanges through the Persian city of Tabriz, on which both land and sea routes from China converged. These measures accelerated and intensified economic and cultural connections.

Prior to Mongol control, such networks had been inaccessible to most European merchants. The Silk Road was a tangle of trails and trading posts, and there were few outsiders who understood its workings. Now travelers at both ends of the route found their way smoothed. Among the first were Franciscan missionaries whose journeys were sponsored by European rulers. In 1253, William of Rubruck was sent by King Louis IX of France as his ambassador to the Mongol court, with instructions to make a full report of his findings. Merchants quickly followed. The most famous of these are three Venetians: the brothers Niccolò and Matteo Polo, and Niccolò's son, Marco (1254–1324).

Marco Polo's account of his travels (which began when he was seventeen) includes a description of his twenty-year sojourn in the service of Kublai Khan and the story of his journey home through the Spice Islands, India, and Persia. As we noted above, this book had an enormous effect on the European imagination; Christopher Columbus's copy still survives. Even more impressive in scope than Marco's

travels are those of the Muslim adventurer Ibn Battuta (1304–1368), who left his native Morocco in 1326 to go on the sacred pilgrimage to Mecca—but then kept going. By the time he returned home in 1354, he had been to China and sub-Saharan Africa as well as to the ends of both the Muslim and Mongolian worlds: a journey of over 75,000 miles.

The Disintegration of Mongol Rule

The window of opportunity that made such impressive journeys possible was relatively narrow. By the middle of the fourteenth century, hostilities among and within various components of the Mongol Empire were making travel along the Silk Road perilous. The Mongols of the Ilkhanate came into conflict with merchants from Genoa who controlled trade at the western ends of the Silk

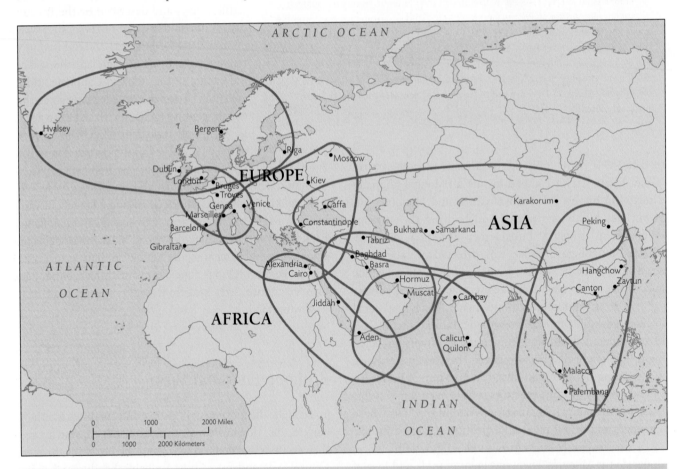

THE MEDIEVAL WORLD SYSTEM, c. 1300. At the turn of the fourteenth century, Western civilizations were more closely connected to one another and to the rest of the world than ever before. This map shows the major interlocking contact zones of the medieval world, showing how trade and travel within each zone could be extended to other zones and foster connections among all of them. ▪ *How has Europe's relationship with its neighbors changed as a result of its integration into this wider world?* ▪ *How might we need to see seemingly marginal territories (like Rus' or Hungary, Scotland or Norway) as central to one or more interlocking components of this system?*

THE EXTENSION OF EUROPEAN COMMERCE AND SETTLEMENT

VENETIAN AMBASSADORS TO THE GREAT KHAN. Around 1270, the Venetian merchants Niccolò and Matteo Polo returned to Europe after their first prolonged journey through the empire of the Great Khan, bearing with them an official letter to the Roman pope. This image, from a manuscript of Marco Polo's *Description of the World*, shows his father and uncle at the moment of their arrival in the Great Khan's court, to which they have seemingly brought a Christian cross and a Bible. ▪ *Based on what you've learned about the Mongols and the medieval world, is it plausible that the Polo brothers would have carried these items with them?*

Western civilizations' increased access to East Asia during the *Pax Mongolica* ran parallel to a number of ventures that were extending Europeans' presence in the Mediterranean and beyond it. These endeavors were both mercantile and colonial. Indeed, the language of crusading, with which we have become familiar, now came to be applied to these economic and political initiatives, whose often violent methods could be justified on the grounds that they were supporting Christian causes. To take one prominent example, the strategic goal of the Crusades that targeted North Africa in this era was to cut the economic lifelines that supported Muslim settlements in the Holy Land. Yet the only people who stood to gain from this were the merchants who dreamed of controlling the commercial routes that ran through Egypt: not only those that connected North Africa to the Silk Road, but the conduits of the sub-Saharan gold trade.

Road, especially in the transport depot of Tabriz. Mounting pressures finally forced the Genoese to abandon Tabriz, thereby breaking one of the major links in the commercial chain forged by the Mongol Peace. Then, in 1346, the Mongols of the Golden Horde besieged the Genoese colony at Caffa on the Black Sea. This event simultaneously disrupted trade while serving as a conduit for the Black Death, which passed from the Mongol army to the Genoese defenders, who returned with it to Italy (as will be discussed later).

Over the next few decades, the peoples of Eurasia and Africa would struggle to overcome the devastating effects of the massive depopulation caused by plague. In the meantime, in 1368, the last Mongol rulers of China were overthrown. Most Westerners were now denied access, while the remaining Mongol warriors were restricted to cavalry service in the imperial armies of the new Ming dynasty. The conditions that had enabled an integrated trans-Eurasian cultural and commercial network were no longer sustainable. Yet the view of the world that had been fostered by Mongol rule continued to exercise a lasting influence. European memories of the Far East would be preserved and embroidered, and the dream of reestablishing close connections between Europe and China would survive to influence a new round of commercial and imperial expansion in the centuries to come (Chapter 12).

The Quest for African Gold

The European trade in African gold was not new. It had been going on for centuries, facilitated by Muslim middlemen whose caravans brought a steady supply from the Niger River to the North African ports of Algiers and Tunis. In the early thirteenth century, rival bands of merchants from Catalonia and Genoa had established trading colonies in Tunis to expedite this process, exchanging woolen cloth from northern Europe for both North African grain and sub-Saharan gold.

But the medieval demand for gold accelerated during the late thirteenth and fourteenth centuries and could not be satisfied by these established trading relationships. The luxuries coveted by Europeans were now too costly to be bought solely with these goods. Although precious textiles (usually silk) were a form of wealth valued by the Mongols, the burgeoning economy of the medieval world demanded a reliable and abundant supply of more portable currency.

Silver production, which had enabled the circulation of coinage in Europe, fell markedly during the 1340s as Europeans reached the limits of their technological capacity to extract silver ore from deep mines. This would lead to a serious cash-flow problem, since more European silver was moving east than could now be replenished from existing sources. Gold therefore represented an obvious alternative currency for large transactions, and in the thirteenth century some European rulers began minting gold coins. But Europe itself had few natural gold reserves. To maintain and expand these currencies, new sources of gold were needed. The most obvious source was Africa, especially Mali and Ghana—which was called "the Land of Gold" by Muslim geographers.

Models of Mediterranean Colonization: Catalonia, Genoa, and Venice

The heightened European interest in the African gold trade, which engaged the seafaring merchants of Genoa and Catalonia in particular, coincided with these merchants' creation of entrepreneurial empires in the western Mediterranean. During the thirteenth century, Catalan adventurers conquered and colonized a series of western Mediterranean islands, including Majorca, Ibiza, Minorca, Sardinia, and Sicily. Except in Sicily, which already had a large and diverse population that included many Christians (see Chapter 8), the pattern of Catalan conquest was largely the same on all these islands: expulsion or extermination of the existing population, usually Muslim; the extension of economic concessions to attract new settlers; and a heavy reliance on slave labor to produce foodstuffs and raw materials for export.

These Catalan colonial efforts were mainly carried out by private individuals or companies operating under royal charters; they were not actively sponsored by the state. They therefore contrast strongly with the established colonial practices of the Venetian maritime empire, whose strategic ventures were focused mainly on the eastern Mediterranean, where the Venetians dominated the trade in spices and silks. Venetian colonies were administered directly by the city's rulers or their appointed colonial governors. These colonies included long-settled civilizations like Greece, Cyprus, and the cities of the Dalmatian coast, meaning that Venetian administration laid just another layer on top of many other economic, cultural, and political structures.

The Genoese, to take yet another case, also had extensive interests in the western Mediterranean, where they traded bulk goods such as cloth, hides, grain, and timber. They, too, established trading colonies, but these tended to consist of family networks that were closely integrated with the peoples among whom they lived, whether in North Africa, Spain, or the shores of the Black Sea.

From the Mediterranean to the Atlantic

For centuries, European maritime commerce had been divided between this Mediterranean world and a very different northeastern Atlantic world, which encompassed northern France, the Low Countries, the British Isles, and Scandinavia. Starting around 1270, however, Italian merchants began to sail through the Straits of Gibraltar and up to the wool-producing regions of England and the Low Countries. This was a step toward the extension of Mediterranean patterns of commerce and colonization into the Atlantic Ocean. Another step was the discovery (or possibly the rediscovery) of the Atlantic island chains known as the Canaries and the Azores, which Genoese sailors reached in the fourteenth century.

Efforts to colonize the Canary Islands, and to convert and enslave their inhabitants, began almost immediately. Eventually, the Canaries would become the focus of a new wave of colonial settlement sponsored by the Portuguese, and the base for Portuguese voyages down the west coast of Africa. They would be the point from which Christopher Columbus would sail westward across the Atlantic Ocean in the hope of reaching Asia (see Chapter 12).

There was also a significant European colonial presence in the northern Atlantic, as there had been for centuries. Viking settlers had begun to colonize Greenland in the late tenth century, and around 1000 they had established a settlement in a place they called Vinland: the coast of Newfoundland in present-day Canada. According to the sagas that tell the story of these explorations, written down in the late twelfth and thirteenth centuries, a band of adventurers led by Leif Eiriksson had intended to set up a permanent colony there. Numerous expeditions resulted in the construction of houses, a fortification, and even attempts to domesticate livestock transported from Scandinavia. Yet North America did not become home to a permanent European population at this time; the sagas report that relations with indigenous peoples were fraught, and there may have been other factors hindering settlement, such as malnutrition, disease, and the challenges of transatlantic travel.

However, Norse settlers did build a viable community on Greenland, which eventually formed part of the kingdom of Norway. This was facilitated by the warming of the earth's climate between 800 and 1300—the same

THE CHURCH AT HVALSEY, GREENLAND. Located on the southern tip of Greenland, Hvalsey was originally a farmstead established in the late tenth century by the uncle of Eirik the Red, father of the explorer Leif. The church at Hvalsey, pictured here, was built in the twelfth century and would have been roofed with turf. It was the site of the last documented event in the history of Norse settlement on the island, a wedding that took place in 1408. By that time, the population had largely died out due to starvation and disease.

phenomenon that partly enabled the agricultural revolution discussed in Chapter 8. For several centuries, these favorable climatic conditions made it possible to sustain some farming activities on the southern coastline of that huge island, supplemented by fishing, hunting, and foraging. But with the gradual cooling of the climate in the fourteenth century, which caused famines even in the rich farmlands of Europe, this fragile ecosystem was gradually eroded and the Greenlanders died out.

WAYS OF KNOWING AND DESCRIBING THE WORLD

The success of European commercial and colonial expansion in this era both drove and depended on significant innovations in measuring and mapping. It also coincided with intellectual, literary, and artistic initiatives that aimed to capture and describe the workings of this wider world.

Economic Tools: Balance Sheets, Banks, Charts, and Clocks

The economic boom that resulted from the integration of European and Asian commerce called for the refinement of existing business models and accounting techniques. New forms of partnership and the development of insurance contracts helped to minimize the risks associated with long-distance trading. Double-entry bookkeeping, widely used in Italy by the mid-fourteenth century, gave merchants a much clearer picture of their profits and losses by ensuring that both credits and debits were clearly laid out in parallel columns, a practice that facilitated the balancing of accounts. The Medici family of Florence established branches of their bank in each of the major cities of Europe and were careful that the failure of one would not bankrupt the entire firm. Banks also experimented with advanced credit techniques borrowed from Muslim and Jewish financiers, allowing their clients to transfer funds without any real money changing hands. Such transfers were carried out by written receipts: the direct ancestors of the check, the money order, and the currency transfer.

Other late medieval technologies kept pace in different ways with the demands for increased efficiency and accuracy. Eyeglasses, first invented in the 1280s, were perfected in the fourteenth century, extending the careers of those who made a living by reading, writing, and accounting. The use of the magnetic compass helped ships sail farther away from land, making longer-distance Atlantic voyages possible for the first time. And as more and more mariners began to sail waters less familiar to them, pilots began to make and use special charts that mapped the locations of ports. Called *portolani*, these charts also took note of prevailing winds, potential routes, good harbors, and known perils.

PORTOLAN CHART. Accurate mapping was essential to the success of maritime colonial ventures in the thirteenth and fourteenth centuries. The chart shown here is the oldest surviving example of a map used by mariners to navigate between Mediterranean ports. (The word *portolan* is used to describe such charts.) It dates from the end of the thirteenth century, and its shape clearly indicates that it was made from an animal hide. Although parchment was extremely durable, it would have slowly worn away owing to prolonged exposure to salt water and other elements—hence the rarity of this early example.

Vikings Encounter the Natives of North America

Although Norse voyagers had explored and settled the coast of Newfoundland around the year 1000, written accounts of these exploits were not made or widely circulated until the thirteenth century. The excerpt below comes from one of these narrative histories, the Grænlendinga Saga ("Greenlanders' Saga"). Its hero is Thorfinn Karlsefni, a Norwegian adventurer who arrives in Greenland and marries Gudrid, the twice-widowed sister-in-law of the explorer Leif Eiriksson. Leif had established the original colony of Vinland, but had since returned to Greenland.

 here was still the same talk about Vinland voyages as before, and everyone, including [his wife] Gudrid, kept urging Karlsefni to make the voyage. In the end he decided to sail and gathered a company of sixty men and five women. He made an agreement with his crew that everyone should share equally in whatever profits the expedition might yield. They took livestock of all kinds, for they intended to make a permanent settlement there if possible.

Karlsefni asked Leif if he could have the houses in Vinland; Leif said that he was willing to lend them, but not to give them away.

They put to sea and arrived safe and sound at Leif's Houses and carried their hammocks ashore. Soon they had plenty of good supplies, for a fine big rorqual* was driven ashore; they went down and cut it up, and so there was no shortage of food.

The livestock were put out to grass, and soon the male beasts became very frisky and difficult to manage. They had brought a bull with them.

Karlsefni ordered timber to be felled and cut into lengths for a cargo for the ship, and it was left out on a rock to season. They made use of all the natural resources of the country that were available, grapes and game of all kinds and other produce.

The first winter passed into summer, and then they had their first encounter with Skrælings,† when a great number of them came out of the wood one day. The cattle were grazing near by and the bull began to bellow and roar with great vehemence. This terrified the Skrælings and they fled, carrying their packs which contained furs and sables and pelts of all kinds. They made for Karlsefni's houses and tried to get inside, but Karlsefni had the doors barred against them. Neither side could understand the other's language.

Then the Skrælings put down their packs and opened them up and offered their contents, preferably in exchange for weapons; but Karlsefni forbade his men to sell arms. Then he hit on the idea of telling the women to carry milk out to the Skrælings, and when the Skrælings saw the milk they wanted to buy nothing else. And so the outcome of their trading expedition was that the Skrælings carried their purchases away in their bellies, and left their packs and furs with Karlsefni and his men.

After that, Karlsefni ordered a strong wooden palisade to be erected round the houses, and they settled in.

Among the many implements of modern daily life invented in this era, the most familiar and indispensable were clocks. Although mechanical clocks were too large and expensive for private purchase, prosperous towns vied with one another to install them in prominent public buildings, thus advertising municipal wealth and good governance. Mechanical timekeeping had two profound effects. One was the further stimulation of interest in complex machinery of all sorts, an interest already awakened by the widespread use of mills in the eleventh and twelfth centuries (see Chapter 8). More significant was the way that clocks regulated daily life. Until the advent of clocks, time was flexible. Although days had been *theoretically* divided into hours, minutes, and seconds since the time of the Sumerians (see Chapter 1), there had never been a way of mapping these temporal measurements onto an actual day. Now, clocks relentlessly divided time into exact units, giving rise to new expectations about labor and productivity. People were expected to start and end work "on time," to make the most of the time spent at work, and even to equate time with money. Like the improvements in bookkeeping, timekeeping made some

About this time Karlsefni's wife, Gudrid, gave birth to a son, and he was named Snorri.

Early next winter the Skrælings returned, in much greater numbers this time, bringing with them the same kind of wares as before. Karlsefni told the women, 'You must carry out to them the same produce that was most in demand last time, and nothing else.' . . .

But a Skræling was killed by one of Karlsefni's men for trying to steal some weapons. The Skrælings fled as fast as they could, leaving their clothing and wares behind. . . .

'Now we must devise a plan,' said Karlsefni, 'for I expect they will pay us a third visit, and this time with hostility and in greater numbers. This is what we must do: ten men are to go out on the headland here and make themselves conspicuous, and the rest of us are to go into the wood and make a clearing there, where we can keep our cattle when the Skrælings come out of the forest. We shall take our bull and keep him to the fore.'

The place where they intended to have their encounter with the Skrælings had the lake on one side and the woods on the other.

Karlsefni's plan was put into effect, and the Skrælings came right to the place that Karlsefni had chosen for the battle. The fighting began, and many of the Skrælings were killed. There was one tall and handsome man among the Skrælings and Karlsefni reckoned that he must be their leader. One of the Skrælings had picked up an axe, and after examining it for a moment he swung it at a man standing beside him, who fell dead at once. The tall man then took hold of the axe, looked at it for a moment, and then threw it as far as he could out into the water. Then the Skrælings fled into the forest as fast as they could, and that was the end of the encounter.

Karlsefni and his men spent the whole winter there, but in the spring he announced that he had no wish to stay there any longer and wanted to return to Greenland. They made ready for the voyage and took with them much valuable produce, vines and grapes and pelts. They put to sea and reached Eiriksfjord safely and spent the winter there.

*A kind of whale, the largest species of which is a blue whale.
†A Norse word meaning "savages," applied to the different indigenous peoples of Greenland and of North America.

Questions for Analysis

1. What policies do the Norse settlers adopt toward the native peoples they encounter on the coast of Newfoundland? How effective are they?

2. Given their extensive preparations for colonization and the success of their early efforts, why do you think that Karlsefni and his companions abandoned their settlement in North America? Are there clues discernible in the text?

3. Compare this encounter to the sources describing other interactions between Europeans and the indigenous inhabitants of the New World after 1492 (see Chapters 12 and 14). How do you account for any similarities? What are some key differences?

kinds of work more efficient, but it also created new tensions and obsessions.

Knowledge of the World and of God

In the mid-thirteenth century, Thomas Aquinas had constructed a theological view of the world as rational, organized, and comprehensible to the inquiring human mind (see Chapter 9). Confidence in this picture began to wane in the fourteenth century, even before the Black Death challenged it further. Philosophers such as William of Ockham (d.c. 1348), an English member of the Franciscan order, denied that human reason could prove fundamental theological truths such as the existence of God. He argued that human knowledge of God, and hence salvation, depends entirely on what God himself has chosen to reveal through scripture. At the same time, Ockham urged humans to investigate the natural world and to better understand its laws—without positing any necessary connection between the observable properties of nature and the unknowable essence of divinity.

This philosophical position, known as nominalism, had its roots in the philosophy of Plato (see Chapter 4) and has had an enormous impact on modern thought. The nominalists' distinction between the rational comprehensibility of the real world and the spiritual incomprehensibility of God encourages investigation of nature without reference to supernatural explanations; this is one of the most important foundations of the scientific method (see Chapter 16). Nominalism also encourages empirical observation, since it posits that knowledge of the world should rest on sensory experience rather than abstract theories. The philosophical principles laid down by these observers of the medieval world are thus fundamental to modern science.

Recreating God's World in Art

Just as a fascination with the natural world informed developments in medieval science, the artists of this era were also paying close attention to plants, animals, and human beings. Carvings of leaves and flowers were increasingly made from direct observation and are clearly recognizable to modern botanists as distinct species. Representations of humans also became more realistic in their portrayals of facial expressions and bodily proportions.

This trend toward naturalism extended to manuscript illumination and painting. The latter was a fast-developing art. As we saw in Chapter 1, wall paintings are among the oldest forms of artistic expression in human history, and throughout antiquity and the Middle Ages artists had decorated the walls of public and private buildings with frescoes (paintings executed on "fresh"—wet—plaster). But in addition to frescoes, Italian artists in the thirteenth century began to adapt the techniques used by icon painters in Byzantium, making freestanding pictures on pieces of wood or canvas using tempera (pigments mixed with water and natural gums). Because these devotional images and portraits were portable, they were also more commercial. As long as artists could afford the necessary materials, they did not have to wait for specific commissions. This meant that they had more freedom to choose their subject matter and to put an individual stamp on their work—one of the reasons why we know the names of many more artists from this era.

One of these, Giotto di Bondone of Florence (c. 1267–1337), painted both walls and portable wooden panels. Giotto (*gee-OHT-toh*) was preeminently an imitator of nature. Not only do his human beings and animals look lifelike, they seem to act naturally. When Christ enters Jerusalem on Palm Sunday, boys climb trees to get a better view; when the Virgin's parents, Joachim and Anna,

meet after a long separation, they embrace and kiss one another tenderly. Although many of the artists who came after Giotto moved away from naturalism, this style would become the norm by 1400. It is for this reason that Giotto is often regarded as the first painter of the Renaissance (see Chapter 11).

A Vision of the World We Cannot See

One of Giotto's exact contemporaries had a different way of capturing the spiritual world in a naturalistic way, and he worked in a different medium. Dante Alighieri (1265–1321) of Florence pioneered what he called a "sweet new style" of poetry in his native tongue, which was now so different from Latin that it had become a language in its own right. Yet as a scholar and devotee of classical Latin verse, Dante also strove to make this Italian vernacular an instrument for serious political and social critique. His great work, known in his own day as the *Comedy* (called by later admirers the *Divine Comedy*) was composed during the years he spent in exile from his beloved city after the political party he supported was ousted from power in 1301.

THE MEETING OF JOACHIM AND ANNA BY GIOTTO. According to legend, Anna and Joachim were an aged and infertile couple who were able to conceive their only child, Mary, through divine intervention. Hence, this painting may portray the moment of her conception—but it also portrays the affection of husband and wife. ● *What human characteristics and values does it convey to the viewer?*

The *Comedy* describes the poet's imaginary journey through hell, purgatory, and paradise, a journey beginning in a "dark wood": a metaphor for the personal and political crises that threatened Dante's faith and livelihood. In the poem, the narrator is led out of this forest and through the first two realms (hell and purgatory) by the Roman poet Virgil (see Chapter 5), who represents the best of classical culture. But Dante can only be guided toward knowledge of the divine by his deceased beloved, Beatrice, who symbolizes Christian wisdom. In the course of this visionary pilgrimage, Dante's narrator meets the souls of many historical personages and contemporaries, questioning them closely and inviting them to explain why they met their several fates: this is his ingenious way of commenting on current events and passing judgment on his enemies. In many ways, this monumental poem represents the fusion of classical and Christian cultures, Latin learning and vernacular artistry.

PAPAL POWER AND POPULAR PIETY

Dante's *Comedy* responded creatively to the political turmoil that engulfed Italy during his lifetime, a situation that was transforming the papacy in ways that he condemned. Indeed, many of the men whom Dante imaginatively placed in Hell were popes or men who had held high office in the Church, or foreign rulers (like the Holy Roman Emperor) who sought to subjugate Italian territories, or predatory Italian princes and factional leaders who were creating a state of permanent warfare among and within cities (like Dante's native Florence). But despite the weakening authority of the papal office, popular piety arguably achieved its strongest expressions during this era.

The Legacy of Innocent III

As we saw in Chapter 9, Innocent III's reign marked the height of papal power, but that power was not sustainable. The popes of the thirteenth century continued to centralize the government of the Church, as Innocent had done, but they simultaneously became involved in protracted political struggles that compromised the papacy's resources and credibility.

For example, because the Papal States bordered on the kingdom of Sicily—which comprised the important city of

Naples and southern Italy, too—subsequent popes came into conflict with its ruler, the emperor Frederick II. And instead of excommunicating him and calling for his deposition, the reigning pope called a crusade against him: an admission of crusading's overtly political motives. To implement this crusade, the papacy became preoccupied with finding a military champion to advance their cause. They found him in Charles of Anjou, the youngest brother of the French king Louis IX. But Charles made matters worse by antagonizing his own subjects, who transferred their allegiance to the king of Aragon. The pope then made Aragon the target of another crusade, which resulted in the death of the new French king, Philip III (r. 1270–85). In the wake of this debacle, Philip's son, Philip IV, resolved to punish the papacy for misusing its powers.

The Limits of Papal Propaganda

In 1300, Pope Boniface VIII (r. 1294–1303) celebrated a papal jubilee in Rome and offered a full crusader's indulgence to every pilgrim: the promise of absolution from all sins. It was a tacit recognition that Rome, not Jerusalem, was now the center of the Christian world—and also a tacit admission that the Crusades of the previous two centuries had failed.

But just nine years after this confident assertion of Rome's unassailable status, Rome had become obsolete. The new capital of Christendom was in France, because King Philip IV had challenged Boniface to a political duel

THE PAPAL PALACE AT AVIGNON. This great fortified palace was begun in 1339 and symbolizes the apparent permanence of the papal residence in Avignon. ■ *Why would it have been constructed as a fortress as well as a palace?*

Interpreting Visual Evidence

Seals: Signs of Identity and Authority

For much of human history, applying a seal to a document was the way to certify its legality and to identify the people who had ratified it. During antiquity and the early Middle Ages, this meant only powerful men—kings, bishops, heads of monasteries—and occasionally powerful women. But as participation in documentary practices became more and more common, corporations (like universities and crusading orders), towns, and many individual people also came to use seals. The devices (images) and legends (writing) on these seals were carefully chosen to capture central attributes of their owners' personality or status. Seals were made by pressing a deeply incised lead matrix onto hot wax or resin, which would quickly harden to form a durable impression. The images reproduced here are later engravings that make the features of the original seals easier to see.

A. Seal of the town of Dover, 1281. Dover has long been one of the busiest and most important port cities of England because of its strategic proximity to France; indeed, the Dover Strait that separates this town from Calais, just across the English Channel, is only twenty-one miles wide. In 1281, when this seal was used, ferries and other ships like the one depicted here (in a later engraving) would have made this crossing several times a day. The legend around the edges of the seal reads (in Latin): "Seal of the commune of barons of Dover." It reflects the extraordinary status accorded to the freemen of Dover by the English crown: because of their crucial role in the economy and defense of the kingdom, they were considered a corporate body and entitled to representation in Parliament alongside individual barons.

B. Personal seal of Charles II, king of Naples and Sicily, 1289.
Charles II (b. 1254, r. 1285–1309) was the son and heir of Charles of Anjou, who became King Charles I of Sicily in 1266 and died in 1285. This means that Charles II had succeeded his father and had reigned as king for four years before he used this seal to ratify an agreement to his own daughter's marriage in 1289. Yet the seal in image B was clearly made for him when he was a young man—probably when he was first knighted. It depicts him as count of Anjou (see the heraldic fleur-de-lys) and gives him his other princely titles, including "Son of King Charles of Sicily." Although he was thirty-five-years old, a king in his own right, and a father, he was still using this older seal!

Questions for Analysis

1. Medieval towns represented themselves in a variety of ways on their seals: sometimes showing a group portrait of town councilors, sometimes a local saint, sometimes a heraldic beast, sometimes distinctive architectural features. Why would Dover choose this image? What messages does this seal convey?

2. Think carefully about the mystery of Charles II's seal. Usually, an important agreement like a marriage contract (with the son of the French king, no less!) would have carried a king's official, royal seal. What are all the possible reasons why Charles would still have been using this outdated seal? What are the possible ramifications of this choice? In your role as historian-detective, how would you go about solving this mystery?

3. The seals of medieval women were almost always shaped like almonds (pointed ovals—the technical term is *vesica-shaped*). Yet Ingeborg's seal is round, like the seals of men and corporations. Why might that be the case?

4. In general, what are the value of seals for the study of history? What are the various ways in which they function as sources?

C. Seal of Ingeborg Håkansdotter, duchess of Sweden, 1321. Ingeborg (1301–1361) was the daughter of King Håkon V of Norway and was betrothed to a Swedish duke, Erick Magnusson, when she was only eleven years old. After a dramatic series of events that left her a young widow, she became the regent for her son, Magnus, who was elected king of both Norway and Sweden in 1319. Ingeborg herself was barely eighteen at the time. The legend on her seal (image C) reads "Ingeborg by the Grace of God Duchess of Norway"—her official title.

and won. The pretext was unimpressive: Boniface had protested against Philip's plan to bring a French bishop to trial on a charge of treason, thus violating the bishop's ecclesiastical immunity. Philip, who had probably anticipated this objection, accused Boniface of heresy and sent a troop of knights to arrest him. At the papal residence of Anagni in 1303, Boniface (then in his seventies) was so mistreated by Philip's thugs that he died a month later. Philip then pressed his advantage. He forced the new pope, Clement V, to thank him publicly for his zealous defense of the faith and then, in 1309, moved the entire papal court from Rome to Avignon (*AH-vee-nyon*), a French city near the southeastern border of his own realm.

The papacy's capitulation to French royal power illustrates the enormous gap that had opened up between rhetoric and reality in the centuries since the Investiture Conflict (see Chapter 8). Although Boniface was merely repeating an old claim—that kings ruled only by divine approval as recognized by the Church—the fact was that the Church now bowed to the superior power of a particular king.

The "Babylonian Captivity" of the Papacy

The papacy would remain in Avignon for nearly seventy years, until 1378 (see Chapter 11). This period is often called the "Babylonian Captivity" of the papacy, recalling the Jews' exile in Babylon during the sixth century B.C.E. (see Chapter 2). Even though the move was probably meant to be temporary, it was not reversed after Philip IV's death in 1314—perhaps because many found that doing business in Avignon was easier than doing business in Rome. Not only was Avignon closer to the major centers of power in northwestern Europe, it was now far removed from the tumultuous politics of Italy and safe from the aggressive attentions of the German emperors.

All of these considerations were important for a succession of popes who were closely allied with the aims of the French monarchy. In time, Avignon began to feel like home; in fact it *was* home for all of the popes elected there, who were natives of the region, as were nearly all the cardinals whom they appointed. This further cemented their loyalty to the French king. And the longer the papacy stayed in Avignon, the larger its bureaucracy grew and the harder it was to contemplate moving it.

Although the papacy never abandoned its claims to the overlordship of Rome and the Papal States, making good on these claims required decades of diplomacy and a great deal of money. The Avignon popes accordingly imposed new taxes and obligations on the wealthy dioceses of western and central Europe. Judicial cases from ecclesiastical courts also brought large revenues into the papal coffers. Most controversially, the Avignon popes claimed the right to appoint bishops and priests to vacant offices anywhere in Christendom, directly, therefore bypassing the rights of individual dioceses and allowing the papacy to collect huge fees from successful appointees.

By these and other measures, the Avignon popes further strengthened administrative control over the Church. But they also further weakened the papacy's moral authority. Stories of the court's unseemly luxury circulated widely, especially during the reign of the notoriously corrupt Clement VI (r. 1342–52), who openly sold spiritual benefits for money and insisted that his sexual transgressions were therapeutic. His reign coincided with the Black Death, whose terrifying and demoralizing effects were not alleviated by the quality of his leadership.

Uniting the Faithful: The Power of Sacraments

Despite the centralizing power of the papacy, most medieval Christians accessed the Church at a local level, within their communities. This was another of Innocent III's legacies: because he had insisted that all people should have direct access to religious instruction, nearly all of Europe was covered by a network of parish churches by the end of the thirteenth century. In these churches, parish priests not only taught the elements of Christian doctrine, they administered the sacraments ("holy rites") that conveyed the grace of God to individual Christians, marking significant moments in the life cycle of every person and significant times in the Christian calendar.

Medieval piety came to revolve around these seven sacraments: baptism, confirmation, confession (or penance), communion, marriage, extreme unction (last rites for the dying), and ordination (of priests). Baptism, a ceremony of initiation administered in the early centuries of Christianity to adults (see Chapter 6), had become a sacrament administered to infants as soon as possible after birth, to safeguard their souls in case of an early death. The confirmation of adolescents reaffirmed the promises made on a child's behalf at baptism by parents and godparents. Periodic confession of sins to a priest guaranteed forgiveness by God; for if a sinner did not perform appropriate acts of penance, atonement for sins would have to be completed in purgatory—that netherworld between heaven and hell, whose existence was made a matter of Church doctrine in 1274.

Marriage was a relatively new sacrament, increasingly emphasized but very seldom practiced as a ceremony; in reality, marriage in this period required only the exchange of solemn promises and was often formed simply by an act of sexual intercourse or the fact of cohabitation. Extreme unction refers to the holy oil with which the priest anointed the forehead of a dying person, signifying the final absolution of all sins and thus offering a final assurance of salvation. Like baptism, this rite could, in an emergency, be administered by any Christian believer. The other sacraments, however, could be administered only by a properly ordained priest—or, in the case of confirmation and ordination, by a bishop. Ordination was the only sacrament reserved for priests, and it conferred the special authority to share God's grace through the sacraments: a power that could never be lost, even by a priest who led an immoral life.

This sacramental system was the foundation on which the practices of medieval popular piety rested. Pilgrimages, for example, were a form of penance and could therefore lessen one's time in purgatory. Crusading was a kind of extreme pilgrimage that promised the complete fulfillment of all penances that the crusader might owe for all the sins of his life. Many other pious acts—saying the prayers of the rosary, for example, or giving alms to the poor—could also serve as penance for one's sins.

The Miracle of the Eucharist

Of these sacraments, the one was most central to the religious lives of medieval Christians was the communion ceremony of the Mass, also known as the Eucharist. As we noted in Chapter 9, the ritual power of the Mass was greatly enhanced in the twelfth century, when the Church began promoting the doctrine of transubstantiation. Christians attending Mass were taught that when the priest spoke the ritual words "This is my body" and "This is my blood," the substances of bread and wine on the altar were miraculously transformed into the body and blood of Jesus Christ. To consume one or both of these substances was to ingest holiness; and so powerful was this idea that most Christians received the sacramental bread just once a year, at Easter. Some holy men and women, however, attempted to sustain themselves by consuming only the single morsel of bread consecrated at daily Mass.

Yet, to share in the miracle of the Eucharist, one did not have to consume it. One had only to witness the elevation of the host, the wafer of bread raised up by the priest,

which "hosted" the real presence of Jesus Christ. Daily attendance at Mass simply to view the consecration of the host was therefore a common form of devotion, and this was facilitated by the practice of displaying a consecrated wafer in a special reliquary called a monstrance ("showcase"), which could be set up on an altar or carried through the streets. Believers sometimes attributed astonishing properties to the eucharistic host, feeding it to sick animals or rushing from church to church to see the consecrated bread as many times as possible in a day. Some of these practices were criticized as superstitious. Nevertheless, these expressions of popular piety were encouraged and fervently practiced by many.

"THIS IS MY BODY": THE ELEVATION OF THE HOST. This fresco from a chapel in Assisi was painted by Simone Martini in the 1320s. It shows the moment in the Mass when the priest raises the eucharistic host so that it can be seen by the faithful. The Latin phrase spoken at this moment, *Hoc est corpus meum* ("This is my body"), came to be regarded as a magical formula because it could transform one substance into another: *hocus pocus.* ▪ *Since medieval Christians believed that merely seeing the host was just as powerful as ingesting it, how would they have responded to this life-size image of the elevation?* ▪ *What does the appearance of angels (above the altar) signify?*

The Pursuit of Holiness

The fundamental theme of preachers in this era, that salvation was open to any Christian who strove for it, helps to explain the central place of the Mass and other sacraments in daily life. It also led many to seek out new paths that could lead to God. As we noted in Chapter 9, some believers who sought to achieve a mystical union with God were ultimately condemned for heresy because they would not subordinate themselves to the authority of the Church. But even less radical figures might find themselves treading on dangerous ground. For example, the German preacher Meister ("Master") Eckhart (c. 1260–1327), a Dominican friar, taught that there is a "spark" deep within every human soul and that God lives in this spark. Through prayer and self-renunciation, any person could therefore retreat into the inner recesses of her being and access divinity. This conveyed the message that a layperson might attain salvation through her own efforts, without the intervention of a priest. As a result, many of Eckhart's teachings were condemned. But views like these would find support in the teachings of popular preachers after the Black Death (see Chapter 11).

STRUGGLES FOR SOVEREIGNTY

When the French king Philip IV transplanted the papal court from Rome to Avignon, he was not just responding to previous popes' abuse of power: he was bolstering his own. By the middle of the thirteenth century, the growth of strong territorial monarchies had given some secular rulers a higher degree of power than any European ruler had wielded since the time of Charlemagne (see Chapter 7). Meanwhile, monarchs' willingness to support the Church's crusading efforts not only yielded distinct economic and political advantages, it also allowed them to assert their commitment to the moral and spiritual improvement of their realms. A king's authority in his own realm rested on the acquiescence of the aristocracy and on popular perceptions of his reputation for justice, piety, and regard for his subjects' prosperity. On the wider stage of the medieval world, it also rested on his successful assertion of his kingdom's sovereignty.

The Problem of Sovereignty

Sovereignty can be defined as inviolable authority over a defined territory. In Chapter 9, we noted that Philip

Augustus was the first monarch to call himself "king of France" and not "king of the French." In other words, he was defining his kingship in geographical terms, claiming that there was an entity called France and that he was king within that area.

But what was "France"? Was it the tiny "island" (Île-de-France) around Paris, which had been his father's domain? If so, then France was very small—and very vulnerable, which would make it hard to maintain any claim to sovereignty. Or did it comprise, rather, any region whose lord was willing to do homage to the French king, like Champagne or Normandy? In that case, the king would need to enforce these rights of lordship constantly and, if necessary, exert his rule directly. But what if some of France's neighboring lords ruled in their own right, as did the independent counts of Flanders, thus threatening the security of France's borders? In that case, the king would either need to forge an alliance with these borderlands or negate their independence. He would need to assert his sovereignty by absorbing these regions into an ever-growing kingdom.

The problem of sovereignty, then, is a zero-sum game: one state's sovereignty is won and maintained by diminishing that of other states. France and every other modern European state was being cobbled together in the medieval period through a process of annexation and colonization—just as the United States was assembled at the expense of the empires that had colonized North America and through the killing or displacement of autonomous native peoples.

The process of achieving sovereignty is thus an aggressive and often violent one. In Spain, the "Reconquest" of Muslim lands, which had accelerated in the twelfth century, continued apace in the thirteenth and fourteenth, much to the detriment of these regions' Muslim and Jewish inhabitants. German princes continued to push northward into the Baltic region and into Slavic lands, where native peoples' resistance to colonizing efforts was met with brutal force. Meanwhile, the Scandinavian kingdoms that had been forming in the eleventh and twelfth centuries were warring among themselves and their neighbors for the control of contested regions and resources. Italy and the Mediterranean also became a constant battleground, as we have observed. Among all emerging states, the two most strident in their assertion of sovereignty were France and England.

The Prestige of France: The Saintly Kingship of Louis IX

After the death of Philip Augustus in 1223, the heirs to the French throne continued to pursue an expansionist policy, pushing the boundaries of their influence out to the east and south. There were significant pockets of resistance, though, notably from the southwestern lands that the kings of England had inherited from Eleanor of Aquitaine (see Chapter 9) and from the independent towns of Flanders that had escaped French conquest. In 1302, citizen militias from several of these towns, fighting on foot with farming implements and other unconventional weapons, even managed to defeat a heavily armed French cavalry at the Battle of Courtrai (Kortrijk).

This defeat was a setback for Philip IV of France, but we have already observed that Philip had other ways of asserting the power of French sovereignty. Much of that power derived from his grandfather, Louis IX (r. 1226–70). Louis was famous for his piety and for his conscientious exercise of his kingly duties. Unlike most of his fellow princes, he not only pledged to go on crusade—he actually went. And while both of his campaigns were notorious failures (he died on the second, in 1270), they cemented Louis's saintly reputation.

Louis's willingness to risk his life (and that of his brothers) in the service of the Church would give him tremendous influence. Moreover, the necessity of ensuring the good governance of his kingdom during his years of absence prompted Louis to reform or invent many key aspects of royal governance, which made France the bureaucratic rival of England for the first time. Louis's first crusading venture was also seen as confirmation that the king of France had inherited the mantle of Charlemagne as the protector of the Church and the representative of Christ on earth. Although it was a military fiasco, this crusade found lasting artistic expression in the Sainte-Chapelle (Holy Chapel), a gorgeous jewel box of a church that Louis built in Paris for his collection of Passion relics—that is, artifacts thought to have been used for the torture and crucifixion of Christ. The most important of these was the Crown of Thorns, intended by Pilate as a mocking reference to "the king of the Jews" (see Chapter 6). Now that this holy crown belonged to Louis and was housed in Paris, it could be taken as a sign that Paris was the new Jerusalem.

Widely regarded as a saint in his lifetime, Louis was formally canonized in 1297—by the same Pope Boniface VIII who was brought down by Philip IV. Indeed, Boniface partly intended this gesture as a rebuke to the saint's grandson. Philip, however, turned it to his advantage. He even used his grandfather's pious reputation as a cloak for his frankly rapacious treatment of the Knights Templar, whose military order he suppressed in 1314 so that he could confiscate its extensive property and dissolve his own debts to the order. He had expelled the Jews from his realm in 1306 for similar reasons.

Castles and Control: Edward I and the Expansion of English Rule

The expulsion of Jews who depended on a king's personal protection had been a precedent set by Philip's contemporary and kinsman, Edward I of England (r. 1272–1307). Unlike Philip, Edward had to build up the sovereignty of his state almost from scratch. His father, Henry III (1216–1272), had a long but troubled reign. Inheriting the

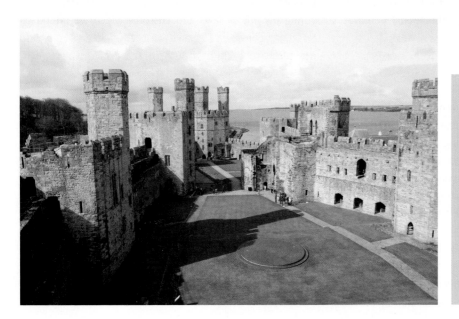

CAERNARVON CASTLE. One of many massive fortifications built by Edward I, this castle was the birthplace of the first English "Prince of Wales" and the site where the current Prince of Wales, Charles, was formally invested with that title in 1969. ▪ *Castles of this size and strength had been constructed in the Crusader States and on the disputed frontiers of Muslim and Christian Spain but never before in Britain (see the photo on page 233 of Chapter 9).* ▪ *What does their construction reveal about Edward's attitude toward the Welsh?*

A Declaration of Scottish Independence

In April of 1320, a group of powerful Scottish lords gathered at the abbey of Arbroath to draft a letter to Pope John XII in Avignon. The resulting "Declaration of Arbroath" petitioned the exiled pope (a Frenchman loyal to the French king) to recognize the Scots as a sovereign nation and to support their right to an independent kingdom that would be free from encroachment by the English. The Scots' elected king, Robert the Bruce, had been excommunicated by a previous pope, who had also upheld English claims to lordship in Scotland. The letter therefore makes a number of different arguments for the recognition of the Scots' right to self-governance.

e know, most holy father and lord, and have gathered from the deeds and books about men in the past, that . . . the nation of the Scots has been outstanding for its many distinctions. It journeyed from the lands of Greece and Egypt by the Tyrrhenian Sea and the Pillars of Hercules, . . . but could not be subdued anywhere by any peoples however barbaric. . . . It took possession of the settlements in the west which it now desires, after first driving out the Britons and totally destroying the Picts, and although often attacked by the Norwegians, Danes, and English. Many were its victories and innumerable its efforts. It has held these places always free of all servitude, as the old histories testify.

One hundred and thirteen kings of their royal lineage have reigned in their kingdom, with no intrusion by a foreigner.

If the noble qualities and merits of these men were not obvious for other reasons, they shine forth clearly enough in that they were almost the first to be called to his most holy faith by the King of Kings and Lord of Lords, our Lord Jesus Christ, after his Passion and Resurrection, even though they were settled on the most distant boundaries of the earth. . . .

Thus our people lived until now in freedom and peace . . . , until that mighty prince Edward [I] king of England (the father of the present king) in the guise of a friend and ally attacked our kingdom in hostile fashion, when it had no head and the people were not harbouring any evil

treachery, nor were they accustomed to wars or attacks. His unjust acts, killings, acts of violence, pillagings, burnings, imprisonments of prelates, burnings of monasteries, robbings and killings of regular clergy, and also innumerable other outrages, which he committed against the said people, sparing none on account of age or sex, religion or order—no one could write about them or fully comprehend them who had not been instructed by experience.

From these countless ills we have been set free, with the help of Him who follows up wounds with healing and cures, by our most energetic prince, king and lord Sir Robert [the Bruce, r. 1306–29]. . . . By divine providence his succession to his right according to our laws and customs which we intend to

throne as a young boy, shortly after his father John's loss of Normandy and capitulation to Magna Carta (see Chapter 9), Henry had to contend with factions among his regents and, later, the restive barons of his realm who rose against him on several occasions. His son Edward even sided with the rebels at one point, but later worked alongside his father to suppress them. When Edward himself became king in 1272, he took steps toward ensuring that there would be no further revolts on his watch; he tightened his control over the aristocracy and their lands, diffused their power by strengthening that of Parliament, and reformed the administration of the realm.

Having seen to the internal affairs of England, Edward looked to its borders. Since Welsh chieftains had been major backers of the barons who had rebelled against his father, Edward was determined to clean up the border region and bring "wild Wales" within the orbit of English sovereignty. He initially attempted to do this by making treaties with various Welsh princes, but none of these arrangements were stable or gave Edward the type of control he wanted. He accordingly embarked on an ambitious and ruthless campaign of castle-building, ringing the hilly Welsh country-side with enormous fortifications on a scale not seen in most of Europe; they were maintain to the death, together with the due consent and assent of us all, have made him our prince and king. . . . But if he should give up what he has begun, seeking to subject us or our kingdom to the king of the English, . . . we would immediately strive to expel him as our enemy and a subverter of his right and ours, and we would make someone else our king, who is capable of seeing to our defence. For as long as a hundred of us remain alive, we intend never to be subjected to the lordship of the English, in any way. For it is not for glory in war, riches, or honours that we fight, but only for the laws of our fathers and for freedom, which no good man loses except along with his life.

Therefore, most holy father and lord, we implore your holiness with all vehemence in our prayers that you . . . look with paternal eyes on the troubles and difficulties brought upon us and the church of God by the English. And that you deign to admonish and exhort the king of the English, who ought to be satisfied with what he has (since England was formerly enough for seven kings or more), to leave us Scots in peace, living as we do in the poor country of Scotland beyond which there is no dwelling place, and desiring nothing but our own. . . .

It is important for you, holy father, to do this, since you see the savagery of the heathen raging against Christians (as the sins of Christians require), and the frontiers of Christendom are being curtailed day by day, and you have seen how much it detracts from your holiness's reputation if (God forbid!) the church suffers eclipse or scandal in any part of it during your time. Let it then rouse the Christian princes who are covering up their true motivation when they pretend that they cannot go to the assistance of the Holy Land on account of wars with their neighbours. The real reason that holds them back is that in warring with their smaller neighbours they anticipate greater advantage to themselves and weaker resistance. . . .

But if your Holiness too credulously trusts the tales of the English fully, or does not leave off favouring the English to our confusion, then we believe that the Most High will blame you for the slaughter of bodies. . . . Dated at our monastery at Arbroath in Scotland 6 April 1320 in the fifteenth year of our said king's reign.

Source: Walter Bower, *Scotichronicon*, Vol. 7, ed. A. B. Scott and D. E. R. Watt (Aberdeen: 1996), pp. 4–9.

Questions for Analysis

1. On what grounds does this letter justify the political independence of the Scots? What different arguments does it make? Which one, in your view, is the most compelling?

2. Why does this letter mention crusading? What are the Scottish lords implying about the relationship between Europe's internal conflicts and the ongoing wars with external adversaries?

3. Imagine that you are an adviser to the pope. Based on your knowledge of the papacy's situation at this time, would you advise him to do as this letter asks? Why or why not?

---

more like crusader castles, and Edward certainly treated the Welsh (who were actually his fellow Christians) as infidels. Indeed, he treated conquered Wales like a crusader state, making it a settler colony and subjecting the Welsh to the overlordship of his own men. When his son, the future Edward II, was born in 1284 at the great castle he had built at Caernarvon, he gave the infant the title "Prince of Wales," a title usually borne by a Welsh chieftain.

Edward then turned to Scotland, England's northern frontier. Until now, control of Scotland had not been an English concern: the Scottish border had been peaceful for many years, and the Scottish kings did homage to the English king for some of their lands. In 1290, however, the succession to the Scottish throne was disputed among many rival claimants, none of whom had enough backing to secure election. Edward intervened, pressing his own claim and seemingly prepared to take Scotland by conquest. To avoid this, the Scots forged an alliance with the French, but this did not prevent Edward's army from fighting its way through to Scone Abbey in 1296.

Scone was a symbolic target: the site of the Stone of Destiny on which Scottish kings were traditionally enthroned. So Edward seized this potent symbol, brought it back to Westminster Abbey in London, and embedded it in the coronation chair of his namesake, Edward the Confessor (see Chapter 8). Save for a brief hiatus in 1950 (when the stone was stolen from the abbey by Scottish nationalists, students at the University of Glasgow) it would remain there until 1996 as a sign that England had sovereignty over Scotland. It will be temporarily returned to London when the next English monarch is crowned.

Edward called himself "the Hammer of the Scots," and when he died he charged his son Edward II (r. 1307–1327) with the completion of his task. But Edward, unlike his father, was not a ruthless and efficient advocate of English expansion. And he had to contend with a rebellion led by his own queen, Isabella of France, who eventually engineered his abdication and murder. Their son, Edward III (r. 1327–77), would renew his grandfather's expansionist policies—but his main target would be France, not Scotland. He would thus launch Europe's two biggest monarchies into a war that lasted over a hundred years.

The Outbreak of the Hundred Years' War

The Hundred Years' War was the largest, longest, and most wide-ranging military conflict since Rome's wars with Carthage (see Chapter 5). Although England and France were its principal antagonists, almost all of the major European powers became involved in it at some stage.

The most fundamental source of conflict was the fact that the kings of England held the duchy of Gascony as vassals of the French king; this had been part of Eleanor of Aquitaine's domain, added to the Anglo-Norman empire in 1154 (see Chapter 9). In the twelfth and thirteenth centuries, when the French kings had not absorbed this region into their domain, this was not an issue. But as Europe's territorial monarchies began to claim sovereignty based on the free exercise of power within the "natural" boundaries of their domains, the English presence in "French" Gascony became more and more problematic. That England also had close commercial links with Flanders—which consistently resisted French imperialism—added fuel to the fire. So did the French alliance with the Scots, who continued to resist English imperialism.

Complicating this volatile situation was the disputed succession of the French crown. In 1328, the last of Philip IV's three sons died without leaving a son to succeed him: the Capetian dynasty, founded by the Frankish warlord Hugh Capet in 987 (see Chapter 8), had finally exhausted itself. A new dynasty, the Valois, came to the throne—but only by insisting that women could neither inherit royal power nor pass it on. For otherwise, the heir to France was Edward III of England, whose ambitious mother, Isabella, was Philip IV's only daughter. When his claim was initially

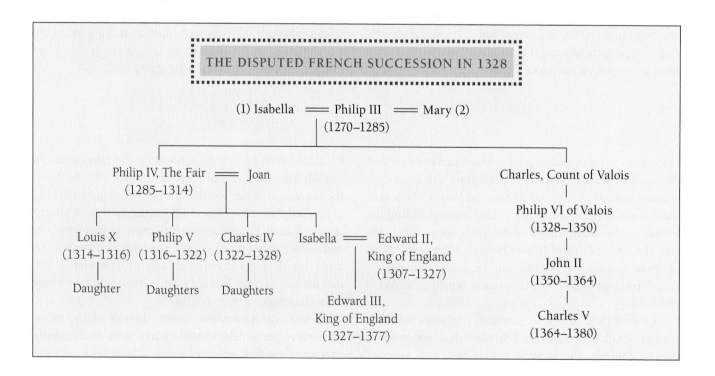

THE DISPUTED FRENCH SUCCESSION IN 1328

(1) Isabella === Philip III === Mary (2)
(1270–1285)

Philip IV, The Fair === Joan
(1285–1314)

Charles, Count of Valois

Philip VI of Valois
(1328–1350)

Louis X
(1314–1316)

Philip V
(1316–1322)

Charles IV
(1322–1328)

Isabella === Edward II,
King of England
(1307–1327)

John II
(1350–1364)

Daughter

Daughters

Daughters

Edward III,
King of England
(1327–1377)

Charles V
(1364–1380)

passed over, Edward was only fifteen and in no position to protest. In 1337, however, when the disputes over Gascony and Scotland erupted into war, Edward raised the stakes by claiming to be the rightful king of France, a claim that subsequent English kings would maintain until the eighteenth century.

Although France was richer and more populous than England by a factor of at least three to one, the English crown was more effective in mobilizing the entire population, for reasons that we discussed in Chapter 9. Edward III was therefore able to levy and maintain a professional army of seasoned and well-disciplined soldiers, cavalry, and archers. The huge but virtually leaderless armies assembled by the French proved no match for the tactical superiority of these smaller English forces. English armies pillaged the French countryside at will, while civil wars broke out between embattled French lords. A decade after the declaration of war, French knights were defeated in two humiliating battles, at Crécy (1346) and Calais (1347). The English seemed invincible. Yet they were no match for a new and deadly adversary approaching from the East Asia.

FROM THE GREAT FAMINE TO THE BLACK DEATH

By 1300, as we have seen, Europe was connected to Asia and the lands in between by an intricate network that fostered connections of all kinds. Yet Europe was also reaching its own ecological limits. Between 1000 and 1300, the population had tripled, and a sea of grain fields stretched, almost unbroken, from Ireland to the Ukraine. Forests had been cleared, marshes drained, and pastureland reduced by generations of peasants performing lifetimes of backbreaking labor. But still, Europe was barely able to feed its people. At the same time, the warming trend that had begun in the late eighth century reversed itself. Even a reduction of one or two degrees centigrade is enough to cause substantial changes in rainfall patterns, shorten growing seasons, and diminish agricultural productivity. So it did in Europe, with disastrous consequences.

Evil Times: The Seven Years' Famine

Between the years 1315 to 1322, the cooling climate caused nearly continuous adverse weather conditions in northern Europe. Winters were extraordinarily severe: in 1316, the Baltic Sea froze over and ships were trapped in the ice. Rains prevented planting in spring or summer, and when a crop did manage to struggle through it would be dashed by rain and hail in autumn. In the midst of these natural calamities, dynastic warfare continued in the sodden wheatfields of central Europe, as the princes of Scandinavia and the Holy Roman Empire fought for supremacy. In the once-fertile fields of Flanders, French armies slogged through mud in continued efforts to subdue the Flemish population. On the Scottish and Welsh borders, uprisings were ruthlessly suppressed and the paltry storehouses were pillaged to feed the English raiders.

The result was human suffering more devastating than that caused by any famine affecting Europe since that time: hence the name "Great Famine." Weakened by years of malnutrition, between 10 and 15 percent of the population of northern Europe perished. Many starved, and others fell victim to epidemic diseases that affected both animals and people. In southern Europe, around the shores of the Mediterranean, the effects of climate change were more muted and there were also different channels through which food could be distributed. Nonetheless, the overall health of this region suffered from the disruption of trade and the shortage of some staple goods, as well as from the highly unstable political situation we have already discussed.

Plans for future crops, which kept hope alive, would be dashed when spring arrived and seeds could not germinate in the flooded fields. Cold summers and autumns were spent foraging for food. Hunting was restricted to the nobility, but even those who risked the death penalty for poaching found little game. Wages did not keep pace with rising costs, and so those who lived in towns and depended on markets had less to spend on scarce provisions. Only a year after the famine began, people were dying of ailments that would not have been fatal in good years.

The effects were especially devastating for children, since even those who survived would be highly susceptible to disease, owing to the severe impairment of their immune systems. It may have been the Great Famine, then, that paved the way for the more transient (if more horrific) destruction caused by the Black Death.

A Crisis of Connectivity: Tracking the Black Death

The Black Death is the name given to a deadly pandemic that spread outward from Mongolia during the 1330s.

THE PROGRESS OF THE BLACK DEATH, FOURTEENTH CENTURY. ■ *What trajectories did the Black Death follow once it was introduced into Europe?* ■ *How might the growth of towns, trade, and travel have contributed to the spread of the Black Death?* ■ *Would such a rapid advance have been likely during the early Middle Ages or even in the ancient world?*

By 1346, the plague had reached the Black Sea, where it was transmitted to Genoese colonists (as we noted previously). From there, in 1347, Genoese ships inadvertently brought it to Sicily and northern Italy. From Italy, it spread westward, first striking seaports, then turning inland with the travelers who carried it. It moved with astonishing rapidity, advancing about two miles per day, summer or winter. By 1350, it had reached Scandinavia and the Baltic, then spread southward again until it linked up with the original waves of infection that had brought it from Central Asia. It continued to erupt in local epidemics for the next 300 years; some localities could expect a renewed outbreak every decade. The last Europe-wide eruption occurred between 1661 and 1669, although there were sporadic outbreaks in Poland and Russia until the end of the eighteenth century and continued threats of plague in Anatolia.

What caused the Black Death? In 2011, scientists were able to confirm that it can be traced to the deadly microbe

Past and Present

Global Pandemics

The image on the left shows citizens from the town of Tournai (now in Belgium) marching in a procession to ward off the plague. They are praying and doing penance for their sins by beating their own bodies with whips, a practice called *flagellation*. On the right, citizens of Mumbai (India) wear protective masks to ward off infection and stand in line to receive testing for the swine flu virus.

Watch related author videos on the Student Site
wwnorton.com/college/history/western-civilizationsBrief4

Yersinia pestis, and that it originated in western China on the Tibetan Plateau. *Y. pestis* actually causes several different kinds of contagion, including bubonic plague and its even deadlier cousins, septicemic plague and pneumonic plague. In its bubonic form, the microbe is carried by fleas that thrive in the fur of many animals; humans catch it only if they are bitten by an infected flea or come into direct contact with an animal host. Bubonic plague attacks the lymphatic system, producing enormous swellings (buboes) of the lymph nodes in the groin, neck, and armpits. Septicemic plague occurs when an infected flea introduces the microbe directly into the human bloodstream, causing death within hours, often before any symptoms of the disease can manifest themselves. Pneumonic plague, perhaps the most frightening variation, results when *Y. pestis* infects the lungs, allowing the contagion to spread silently and invisibly in the same ways as the common cold.

Part of what made the Black Death so terrifying, therefore, was that it manifested itself in several different ways.

Those afflicted by the hideous bubonic plague might actually recover, while others—seemingly untouched—might die suddenly, mysteriously. Immediate reactions understandably ranged from panic to resignation. Observers quickly realized that the plague was contagious, but precisely how it spread remained enigmatic. Some believed that it was caused by breathing "bad air" and so they urged people to flee from stricken areas, which caused the disease to spread even faster.

Others looked for scapegoats and revived old conspiracy theories that implicated Jews in the poisoning of wells. Scores of Jewish communities were attacked and thousands of their inhabitants massacred in the Rhineland, southern France, and Christian Spain. (No such attacks are known to have occurred in the Muslim world.) The papacy and some local authorities tried to halt these attacks, but these efforts were weak. Another response to the plague was the flagellant movement, so called because of the whips (*flagella*) with which traveling

From the Great Famine to the Black Death | 279

Competing Viewpoints

Responses to the Black Death

> Many chroniclers, intellectuals, and private individuals have left accounts of the plague in which they attempt to understand why it had occurred, how it spread, and how communities should respond to it.

The Spread of the Plague according to Gabriele de' Mussi (d. 1356), a Lawyer in Piacenza (Northern Italy)

Oh God! See how the heathen Tartar races, pouring together from all sides, suddenly infested the city of Caffa [on the Black Sea] and besieged the trapped Christians there for almost three years. . . . But behold, [in 1346] the whole army was affected by a disease which overran the Tartars and killed thousands upon thousands every day. It was as though arrows were raining down from heaven to strike and crush the Tartars' arrogance. All medical advice and attention was useless; the Tartars died as soon as the signs of disease appeared on their bodies: swellings in the armpit or groin caused by coagulating humours, followed by a putrid fever.

The dying Tartars, stunned and stupefied by the immensity of the disaster brought about by the disease, and realising that they had no hope of escape, lost interest in the siege. But they ordered corpses to be placed in catapults and lobbed into the city in the hope that the intolerable stench would kill everyone inside. What seemed like mountains of dead were thrown into the city, and the Christians could not hide or flee or escape from them, although they dumped as many of the bodies as they could in the sea. And soon the rotting corpses tainted the air and poisoned the water supply. . . . Moreover one infected man could carry the poison to others, and infect people and places with the disease by look alone. No one knew, or could discover, a means of defence.

Thus almost everyone who had been in the East . . . fell victim . . . through the bitter events of 1346 to 1348—the Chinese, Indians, Persians, Medes, Kurds, Armenians, Cilicians, Georgians, Mesopotamians, Nubians, Ethiopians, Turks, Egyptians, Arabs, Saracens, and Greeks. . . .

* * *

As it happened, among those who escaped from Caffa by boat were a few sailors who had been infected with the poisonous disease. Some boats were bound for Genoa, others went to Venice and to other Christian areas. When the sailors reached these places and mixed with the people there, it was as if they had brought evil spirits with them. . . .

* * *

Scarcely one in seven of the Genoese survived. In Venice, where an inquiry was held into the mortality, it was found that more than 70 percent of the people had died. . . . The rest of Italy, Sicily, and Apulia and the neighbouring regions maintain that they have been virtually emptied of inhabitants. . . . The Roman Curia at Avignon, the provinces on both sides of the Rhône, Spain, France, and the Empire cry up their griefs. . . .

* * *

Everyone has a responsibility to keep some record of the disease and the deaths, and because I am myself from Piacenza I have been urged to write more about what happened there in 1348. . . .

I don't know where to begin. Cries and laments arise on all sides. Day after day one sees the Cross and the Host

bands of penitents lashed themselves in order to appease the wrath of God. But the unruly and sometimes hysterical mobs that gathered around the flagellants aroused the concern of both ecclesiastical and secular authorities, and the movement was suppressed by papal order.

CONCLUSION

The century between 1250 and 1350 was a time of significant change within all Western civilizations and neighboring lands. The growing power of some monarchies led to encroachments on territories and cities that being carried about the city, and countless dead being buried. . . . The living made preparations for their [own] burial, and because there was not enough room for individual graves, pits had to be dug in colonnades and piazzas, where nobody had ever been buried before. It often happened that man and wife, father and son, mother and daughter, and soon the whole household and many neighbours, were buried together in one place. . . .

A Letter from the Town Council of Cologne to the Town Council of Strasbourg (Germany), 12 January 1349

Very dear friends, all sorts of rumours are now flying about against Judaism and the Jews prompted by this unexpected and unparalleled mortality of Christians. . . . Throughout our city, as in yours, many-winged Fame clamours that this mortality was initially caused, and is still being spread, by the poisoning of springs and wells, and that the Jews must have dropped poisonous substances into them. When it came to our knowledge that serious charges had been made against the Jews in several small towns and villages on the basis of this mortality, we sent numerous letters to you and to other cities and towns to uncover the truth behind these rumours, and set a thorough investigation in train. . . .

If a massacre of the Jews were to be allowed in the major cities (something which we are determined to prevent in our city, if we can, as long as the Jews are found to be innocent of these or similar actions) it could lead to the sort of outrages and disturbances which would whip up a popular revolt among the common people—and such revolts have in the past brought cities to misery and desolation. In any case we are still of the opinion that this mortality and its attendant circumstances are caused by divine vengeance and nothing else. Accordingly we intend to forbid any harassment of the Jews in our city because of these flying rumours, but to defend them faithfully and keep them safe, as our predecessors did—and we are convinced that you ought to do the same. . . .

Source: From Rosemary Horrox, ed. and trans., *The Black Death* (Manchester: 1994), pp. 16–21, 219–20.

Questions for Analysis

1. How does Gabriele de' Mussi initially explain the causes of the plague? How does his understanding of it change as he traces its movements from East to West—and closer to Italy?

2. Why does the Council of Cologne wish to quell violence against the Jews? How does this reasoning complement or challenge what we have learned so far about the treatment of Jews in medieval Europe?

3. In your view, do these two perspectives display a rational approach to the horrors of the Black Death? Why or why not?

had once been independent, and that fueled resistance to these internal acts of colonization. The papacy, whose power had seemed so secure at the turn of the thirteenth century, would itself become a pawn in the keeping of the French king by the beginning of the fourteenth. Rome thereby lost its last source of authority while the New Rome, Constantinople, struggled to rebuild its prestige in the face of Mongol expansion. Yet for the Mongol khans and the merchants they favored, for seafaring civilizations like Venice and Genoa, for ambitious students at the universities, and for men on the make, the opportunities for advancement and mobility were great

And there were still other factors at play during this era. Even in good times, Europe's population had outgrown its capacity to produce food, and when the climate grew cooler, years of cold summers and heavy rainfall took an enormous toll. Those regions most closely tied to the new global networks were also densely settled and urban, which made the shortage of food and the spread of disease more acute there. In short, the benefits and drawbacks of increased globalization were already beginning to manifest themselves in the early fourteenth century—700 years ago. The Black Death can be understood as the ultimate example of medieval connectivity.

The scale of mortality caused by this pandemic is almost unimaginable, as much to us as to those who survived it. At least a third, and probably half, of Europe's people died between 1347 and 1353. In the countryside, entire villages disappeared. Cities and

After You Read
This Chapter

 Go to **INQUIZITIVE** to see what you've learned—and learn what you've missed—with personalized feedback along the way.

REVIEWING THE OBJECTIVES

- The conquests of the Mongols had a significant impact on Europe. How?
- The expansion of commerce and communication between Eastern and Western civilizations created a new world system. What were some key characteristics of this system? What kinds of exchange did it enable?
- What were the short- and longer-term causes for the papacy's loss of prestige? Why was the papal court moved to Avignon? What were the consequences of this move?
- What is sovereignty? What were the effects of competition for sovereignty among European states?
- What caused the Black Death? In what sense can it be seen as a product of the new world system that began with the Mongol conquests?

towns, overcrowded and unsanitary, were particularly vulnerable to plague and, thereafter, to outbreaks of violence. The immediate social consequences were profound, and so were the economic ones. Crops rotted in the fields, manufacturing ceased, and trade came to a standstill in affected areas. Basic commodities became scarcer and prices rose, prompting ineffectual efforts to control prices and to force the remaining able-bodied laborers to work.

These were the short-term effects. How did the Black Death matter to those who survived it—including ourselves? According to Ibn Khaldun (1332–1406), a Muslim historian who is considered one of the founders of modern historical methods, it marked the end of the old world and the beginning of a new one that would require new systems of government, bodies of knowledge, and forms of art. Was he right? We will begin to answer that question in Chapter 11.

PEOPLE, IDEAS, AND EVENTS IN CONTEXT

- What accounts for the success of **GENGHIS KHAN** and his successors? What circumstances enabled **MARCO POLO**'s travels to China? To what extent does the term *PAX MONGOLICA* describe this era in history?

- How did seafaring communities like that of **GENOA** rise to prominence in this era? Why were new navigational aids like **PORTOLAN CHARTS** necessary?

- How do the paintings of **GIOTTO** capture contemporary attitudes toward the world? How does **DANTE**'s artistry respond to the religious and political trends of his day?

- What was at stake in the controversy between **BONIFACE VIII** and **PHILIP IV**? Why is the papacy's residency at **AVIGNON** called the **"BABYLONIAN CAPTIVITY"**? What are **SACRAMENTS**, and why were these rites so important?

- In what different ways did **LOUIS IX** of France and **EDWARD I** of England contribute to the sovereignty of their respective kingdoms? What was the relationship between claims to sovereignty and the causes of the **HUNDRED YEARS' WAR**?

- How did climate change contribute to the outbreak of the **GREAT FAMINE**?

- What were the long-term and short-term causes of the **BLACK DEATH**?

THINKING ABOUT CONNECTIONS

- If the Mongol khan Ögedei had not died in 1241, the Mongols could conceivably have continued their westward movement into Europe. Given what you have learned about Mongol rule, how might this have changed the history of the world?

- How do the patterns of conquest and colonization discussed in this chapter compare to those of earlier periods, particularly those of antiquity? How many of these developments were new in 1250–1350?

- We live in a world in which the global circulation of people, information, goods, and bacteria is rapid. How does the medieval system compare to ours? What features seem familiar?

Before You Read This Chapter

Rebirth and Unrest, 1350–1453

CORE OBJECTIVES

- **TRACE** the economic and social effects of the Black Death, and **EXPLAIN** their importance.

- **EXPLAIN** the relationship between the concepts of the Middle Ages and the Renaissance.

- **DESCRIBE** the intellectual, cultural, and technological innovations of this era.

- **DEFINE** the concept of national monarchy and **SUMMARIZE** its implications.

- **UNDERSTAND** the significance of the conciliar movement and its defeat by the papacy.

I n June 1381, thousands of English workers rose in rebellion against royal authorities. Most were peasants or craftsmen who were dismissed as ignorant by contemporary chroniclers, and yet their revolt was carefully coordinated. Plans were spread in coded messages circulated by word of mouth and by the followers of a renegade Oxford professor, John Wycliffe, who had called for the redistribution of Church property and taught that common people should be able to read the Bible in their own language. The rebellion's immediate catalyst had been a series of exorbitant taxes, but its fundamental cause was a pandemic that had occurred thirty years earlier. The Black Death had reduced the entire population of Europe by 30 to 50 percent and had drastically altered the world of those who survived it. In this new world, workers were valuable and could stand up to those who paid them poorly or treated them like slaves. Although the leaders of this rebellion were eventually captured and executed, it made the strength of the common people known.

The fourteenth century is often seen as a time of crisis. Famine and plague decimated the population and war was a brutally recurrent fact of life. But this was also a time of extraordinary opportunity. The exhausted land of Europe recovered from centuries of overfarming, while workers gained the economic edge; some even gained social and political power. Meanwhile, popular and intellectual movements sought to reform the Church. A host of intellectual, artistic, and scientific innovations contributed to all of these phenomena.

This time of rebirth and unrest has been called by two different names: the later Middle Ages and the Renaissance. But these are not two separate historical periods; rather they reflect two different ways of looking back at an era considered to be the precursor of modernity. To understand it, we need to study it holistically.

LIFE AFTER THE BLACK DEATH

By 1353, when plague began to loosen its death grip on Europe, the Continent had lost nearly half of its population within a half century, owing to a combination of famine and disease (Chapter 10). In the century to come, recurring outbreaks of the plague and frequent warfare in some regions would result in further losses. In Germany, some 400,000 villages disappeared. Around Paris, more than half of the farmland formerly under cultivation became pasture. Elsewhere, abandoned fields returned to woodland, increasing the forested areas of Europe by about a third.

Life after the Black Death would therefore be radically different for those who survived it, because this massive depopulation affected every aspect of existence. First and foremost, it meant a relative abundance of food. The price of grain fell, which made it more affordable. At the same time, the scarcity of workers made peasant labor more valuable, and wages rose accordingly. Ordinary people could now afford more bread and could also spend their surplus cash on dairy products, meat, fish, fruits, and wine. As a result, the people of Europe were better nourished than they had ever been—better than many are today. A recent study of fifteenth-century rubbish dumps has concluded that the people of Glasgow (Scotland) ate a healthier diet in 1405 than they did in 2005.

The Rural Impact

In the countryside, a healthier ecological balance was reestablished in the wake of the plague. Forests that

THE PLAGUE CLAIMS A VICTIM. A priest gives last rites to a bedridden plague victim as a smiling devil pierces the dying man with a spear and as Christ looks mercifully down from heaven. ▪ *What are the possible meanings of this image?* ▪ *What does it reveal about contemporary attitudes toward death by plague?*

had almost disappeared began to recover and expand. Meanwhile, the declining demand for grain allowed many farmers to expand their livestock herds, which also improved the fertility of the soil through manuring. Some farmers were even able to enlarge their holdings, because so much land had been abandoned.

Many of these innovations were made by small farmers, because many great lords—individuals as well as monasteries—were slower to adjust. But some large landholders responded to the shortage of workers by forcing their tenants to perform unpaid labor. In parts of eastern Europe, many free peasants became serfs for the first time: in Poland and Germany, and also in Castile, lords succeeded in imposing new forms of servitude.

In France and the Low Countries, by contrast, peasants experienced new freedoms. In England, where bondage had been common in some regions, serfdom eventually disappeared altogether. Although the Peasants' Revolt of 1381 was ultimately unsuccessful, increased economic opportunity allowed English workers to move to town or to the lands of a lord who offered more favorable terms, despite repeated attempts by Parliament to prevent this, as in the Statute of Labourers enacted in 1351. Geographical mobility and social mobility are, as we have often noted, intertwined.

The Urban Impact

Mortality rates were high in some of the crowded cities and towns of Europe, but not all cities were equally affected and many recovered quickly. In London and Paris, for example, immigration from the countryside reversed the short-term declines caused by the plague. Other urban areas suffered more from internal violence or warfare than from disease. In Florence, for example, the population rebounded quickly after the Black Death but was eventually depleted by civil unrest: by 1427, it had dropped from around 300,000 to about 100,000. In Toulouse (southwestern France), the population remained fairly stable until 1430, when it was reduced by a staggering 75 percent as a result of the ravages of the Hundred Years' War.

So while the overall population of Europe declined drastically because of the plague, a far larger percentage of all people were living in towns by 1500: approximately 20 percent as opposed to 10 or 15 percent prior to the Black Death. Fueling this urban growth was the increasing specialization of the late-medieval economy. With farmers under less pressure to produce grain in bulk, land could be devoted to livestock, dairy farming, and the production of a more diverse array of fruits and vegetables; and these could now be exchanged more efficiently on the open market.

Towns with links to extant trading networks benefited accordingly. In northern Germany, a group of entrepreneurial cities formed a coalition to build an entirely new mercantile corporation, the Hanseatic League, which came to control commerce from Britain and Scandinavia to the Baltic. In northern Italy, the increased demand for luxury goods—which even some peasants and urban laborers could now afford—brought renewed wealth to the spice- and silk-trading city of Venice and also to the fine-cloth manufacturers of Milan and the jewelers of Florence. Milan's armaments industry also prospered, supplying its warring neighbors and the armies of Europe.

Popular Revolts and Rebellions

Although the consequences of the Black Death were ultimately beneficial for many, survivors did not adjust easily to this new world. Established elites resisted the demands of newly powerful workers; and when these demands were not met, violence erupted. Between 1350 and 1425, hundreds of popular rebellions challenged the status quo in many regions. In 1358, peasants in northeastern France rose up, destroying property, burning buildings and crops, and even murdering targeted individuals. This incident is known as the Jacquerie Rebellion, because all French peasants were caricatured by the aristocracy as "Jacques" ("Jack").

In England, as we have already noted, a very different uprising occurred in June of 1381, far more organized and involving a much wider segment of society. Thousands of people marched on London, targeting the bureaucracies of the government and the Church, capturing and killing the archbishop of Canterbury, and meeting personally with the fourteen-year-old king, Richard II, to demand an end to serfdom and to call for the redistribution of property. In Florence, cloth-industry workers—known as the Ciompi (chee-OHM-pee)—protested high unemployment and mistreatment by the manufacturers who also ran the Florentine government. They seized control of the city and maintained power for a remarkable six weeks before their reforms were revoked.

The local circumstances behind each of these revolts were unique, but all of them exhibit certain common features. Those who took part were empowered by new economic conditions and wanted to enact even larger reforms. Some revolts were touched off by resistance to new and higher taxes. Others took place at moments when governments were weakened by factionalism and military defeat. The English revolt was also fueled by the widespread perception of corruption within the Church.

Behind this social and political unrest, therefore, lies the growing prosperity and self-confidence of village communities and urban laborers who were taking advantage of the changed circumstances that arose from the plague. This tradition of popular rebellion would remain an important feature of Western civilizations. It would eventually fuel the American War of Independence and the French Revolution (see Chapter 18), and it continues to this day.

Aristocratic Life in the Wake of the Plague

Although the elites of Europe did not adapt easily to "the world turned upside down" by the plague, many great families became far wealthier and more dominant than their ancestors had ever been. However, their situations did become more complex and uncertain.

Across Europe, noble families continued to derive much of their revenue from vast land holdings. Many also tried to increase their sources of income through investment in trading ventures. In Catalonia, Italy, Germany, and England, this became common practice. In France and Castile, however, direct involvement in commerce was regarded as socially demeaning. Commerce could still be a route to ennoblement in these kingdoms; but once aristocratic rank was achieved, one was expected to abandon these employments and adopt an appropriate way of life: acquiring a rural castle or urban palace surrounded by a lavish household, embracing the values and conventions of chivalry (engaging in the hunt, commissioning a family coat of arms), and serving the ruler at court and in war.

What it meant to be "noble" became, as a result, even more difficult to define than it had been during previous centuries. In countries where noble rank entailed clearly defined legal privileges—such as the right to be tried only in special courts—proven descent from noble ancestors might be sufficient. Legal nobility of this sort was, however, a somewhat less exclusive distinction than one might expect. In fifteenth-century Castile and Navarre,

10 to 15 percent of the total population had claims to be recognized as noble on these terms. In Poland, Hungary, and Scotland, the legally privileged nobility was closer to 5 percent.

Fundamentally, however, nobility was expressed by lifestyle and conspicuous consumption. This means that, in practice, the distinctions between noble and wealthy non-noble families were very hard to discern. Even on the battlefield, where the mark of nobility was to fight on horseback, the supremacy of mounted knights was being threatened by the growing importance of professional soldiers, archers, crossbowmen, and artillery experts. There were even hints of a radical critique of the aristocracy's claims to superiority. As the English rebels put it in 1381, "When Adam dug and Eve spun / Who then was a gentleman?"

Precisely because nobility was contested, those who claimed it took elaborate measures to assert their right to this status. This accounts, in part, for the extraordinary number, variety, and richness of the artifacts and artworks that survive from this period. Aristocrats—or those who wanted to be viewed as such—vied with one another in hosting lavish banquets, which required numerous costly utensils, special dining chambers, and the most exotic foods attainable. They dressed in rich and extravagant clothing: close-fitting doublets and hose with long pointed shoes for men, multilayered silk dresses with ornately festooned headdresses for women. They maintained enormous households: in France, around 1400, the Duke of Berry had 1,000 servants and 400 matched pairs of hunting dogs. They took part in elaborately ritualized tournaments, in which the participants pretended to be the heroes of chivalric romances. Noble status had to be constantly reasserted and displayed.

Rulers contributed to this process. Kings and princes across Europe competed in founding chivalric orders such as the Knights of the Garter in England and the Order of the Star in France. These orders honored men who had demonstrated the idealized virtues of knighthood. By exalting the nobility as a class, chivalric orders helped cement the links that bound the nobility to their kings and princes. These bonds were further strengthened by the gifts, pensions, offices, and marriage prospects that kings and princes could bestow.

Given the decline in the agricultural revenues of many noble estates, such rewards of princely service were critically important to maintaining noble fortunes. Indeed, the alliance that was forged in the fifteenth century between kings and their noble supporters would become one of the most characteristic features of Europe's ruling class. In France, this "Old Regime" (*ancien régime*) alliance lasted

A HUNTING PARTY. This fifteenth-century illustration shows an elaborately dressed group of noblemen and noblewomen setting out with falcons, accompanied by their servants and their dogs. Hunting, an activity restricted to the aristocracy, was an occasion for conspicuous consumption and display.

A NOBLE BANQUET. Uncle of the mad king Charles VI of France, the Duke of Berry left politics to his brothers, the Duke of Burgundy and the Duke of Anjou. In return, he received enormous subsidies from the royal government, which he spent on sumptuous buildings, festivals, and artworks, including the famous Book of Hours (prayer book, c. 1410), which includes this image. Here, the duke (seated at right, in blue) gives a New Year's Day banquet for his household, who exchange gifts while his hunting dogs dine on scraps from the table. In the background, knights confront one another in a tournament.

until the French Revolution of 1789. In Germany, Austria, central Europe, and Russia, it would last until the outbreak of World War I.

Capturing Reality in Writing

The writings of literary artists who survived the Black Death, or who grew up in the decades immediately following it, are characterized by intense observations of the world and their appeal to a far larger and more diverse audience than that of their predecessors. We have noted that vernacular languages were becoming powerful vehicles for poetry and narrative in the twelfth century (see Chapter 9). Now they were being used to critique changing social mores and regimes. Behind this phenomenon lie three interrelated developments: the growing identification between vernacular language and the community of a realm, the still-increasing accessibility of education, and the rise of

a substantial reading public. We can see these influences at work in three of the major authors who flourished during this period: Giovanni Boccaccio, Geoffrey Chaucer, and Christine de Pisan.

Boccaccio (*boh-KAHT-chee-oh*, 1313–1375) is best known for *The Decameron*, a collection of prose tales about sex, adventure, and trickery. He presents these stories as being told over a period of ten days (hence the title, which means "work of ten days") by a sophisticated group of young women and men who have fled to a country villa outside Florence in order to escape the Black Death. Boccaccio borrowed the outlines of these tales from many earlier sources, especially the fabliaux discussed in Chapter 9, but he couched them in colloquial Italian. Whereas Dante had used the same Florentine dialect to evoke the awesome landscape of sacred history in his *Divine Comedy* (Chapter 10), Boccaccio used it to capture the foibles of human beings in plainspoken prose.

The English poet Geoffrey Chaucer (c. 1340–1400) was highly influenced by Boccaccio. Chaucer was among the first generation of English authors whose compositions can be understood by modern readers of that language with relatively little effort. By the late fourteenth century, the Anglo-Saxon (Old English) tongue of England's preconquest inhabitants had mixed with the French dialect spoken by their Norman conquerors, to create the language which is the ancestor of our own: Middle English.

Chaucer's masterpiece is *The Canterbury Tales*. Like *The Decameron*, this is a collection of stories held together by a framing narrative. In this case, the stories are told by travelers on a pilgrimage from London to the shrine of Thomas Becket at Canterbury. But there are also significant differences between *The Decameron* and *The Canterbury Tales*. Chaucer's stories are in verse, for the most part, and they are recounted by people of all different classes—from a high-minded knight to a poor university student to a lusty widow. Each character tells a story that is particularly illustrative of his or her own outlook on the world, forming a kaleidoscopic human comedy.

The generation or so after the Black Death also saw the emergence of authors who made their livings through the patronage of the aristocracy and the publication of their works. One of the first of these literary professionals was Christine de Pisan (c. 1365–c. 1434). Although born in northern Italy, Christine spent her adult life in France, where her husband was a member of the king's household. When he died, the widowed Christine wrote to support herself and her children. She mastered a wide variety of literary genres, including treatises on chivalry and warfare, which she dedicated to King Charles VI of

CHRISTINE DE PISAN. One of the most prolific authors of the Middle Ages, Pisan used her influence to uphold the dignity of women and to celebrate their history and achievements. Here she is seen describing the prowess of an Amazon warrior who could defeat men effortlessly in armed combat.

France. She also wrote for a more popular audience. For example, her imaginative *Book of the City of Ladies* is an extended defense of the capacities and history of women, designed to help female readers refute their male detractors. Christine also took part in a vigorous pamphlet campaign that condemned the misogynistic claims made by influential male authors like Boccaccio. This debate became so famous that it was given a name: the *querelle des femmes*, "the debate over women." Remarkably, Christine also wrote a song in praise of Joan of Arc. Sadly, she probably lived long enough to learn that this other extraordinary woman had been put to death for behaving in a way that was considered dangerously unwomanly (as will be discussed later).

Visualizing Reality

Just as the desire to capture real experiences and emotions was a dominant trait of the literature produced after the Black Death, so it was in the visual arts. This is evident both in the older arts of manuscript illumination and in the new kinds of sculpture we discussed in Chapter 10. A further innovation in the early fifteenth century was the technique of painting in oils, a medium pioneered in Flanders, where artists found a ready market for their works among the nobility and wealthy merchants.

Oil paints were a revolutionary artistic development: because they do not dry as quickly as water-based pigments, a painter can work more slowly and carefully, taking time with difficult aspects of the work and making corrections as needed. Masterful practitioners of this technique include Rogier van der Weyden (c. 1400–1464), who excelled at communicating spiritual messages through the details of everyday life (see **Interpreting Visual Evidence** on page 293). Just as contemporary saints saw divinity in all things, so too an artist could portray the Virgin and Child against a background of ordinary life: people going about their business or a man urinating against a wall. This conveyed the profound message that sacred events are constantly present, here and now: Christ is our companion, such artworks suggest, not some distant figure irrelevant to us.

The same immediacy is also evident in medieval drama. Plays were often devotional exercises that involved the efforts of an entire community, but they also celebrated that community. In the English city of York, for example, an annual series of pageants reenacted the entire history of human salvation from the Creation to the Last Judgment in a single summer day, beginning at dawn and ending late at night. Each pageant was produced by a particular craft guild and showcased that guild's special talents: "The Last Supper" was performed by the bakers, whose bread was used to reenact the first Eucharist, while "The Crucifixion" was performed by the nail makers and painters, whose wares were thereby put on prominent display. In Italy, confraternities competed with one another to honor the saints with songs and processions. In Catalonia and many regions of Spain, elaborate dramas celebrated the life and miracles of the Virgin; one of these is still performed every year in the Basque town of Elche, and is the oldest European play in continuous production. In northern France, the Low Countries, and German-speaking lands, civic spectacles were performed over a period of several days, celebrating both local history and sacred history at once. But not all plays were pious. Some honored visiting kings and princes. Others celebrated the flouting of social conventions, featuring cross-dressing and the reversal of hierarchies. They were further expressions of the topsy-turvy world created by the Black Death.

THE BEGINNINGS OF THE RENAISSANCE IN ITALY

Rummaging through the old books in a cathedral library, an Italian bureaucrat attached to the papal court at Avignon was surprised to find a manuscript of Cicero's letters—letters

Why a Woman Can Write about Warfare

Christine de Pisan (c. 1365–c. 1434) was one of the West's first professional writers, best known today for her Book of the City of Ladies *and* The Treasure of the City of Ladies, *works that aimed to provide women with an honorable and rich history and to combat generations of institutionalized misogyny. But in her own time, Christine was probably best known for the work excerpted here,* The Book of the Deeds of Arms and of Chivalry, *a manual of military strategy and conduct written at the height of the Hundred Years' War, in 1410.*

s boldness is essential for great undertakings, and without it nothing should be risked, I think it is proper in this present work to set forth my unworthiness to treat such exalted matter. I should not have dared even to think about it, but although boldness is blameworthy when it is foolhardy, I should state that I have not been inspired by arrogance or foolish presumption, but rather by true affection and a genuine desire for the welfare of noble men engaging in the profession of arms. I am encouraged, in the light of my other writings, to undertake to speak in this book of the most honorable office of arms and chivalry. . . . So to this end I have gathered together facts and subject matter from various books to produce this present volume. But inasmuch as it is fitting for this matter to be discussed factually, diligently, and sensibly . . . and also in consideration of the fact that military and lay experts in the aforesaid art of chivalry are not usually clerks or writers who are expert in language,

I intend to treat the matter in the plainest possible language. . . .

As this is unusual for women, who generally are occupied in weaving, spinning, and household duties, I humbly invoke . . . the wise lady Minerva [Athena], born in the land of Greece, whom the ancients esteemed highly for her great wisdom. Likewise the poet Boccaccio praises her in his *Book of Famous Women*, as do other writers praise her art and manner of making trappings of iron and steel, so let it not be held against me if I, as a woman, take it upon myself to treat of military matters. . . .

O Minerva! goddess of arms and of chivalry, who, by understanding beyond that of other women, did find and initiate among the other noble arts and sciences the custom of forging iron and steel armaments and harness both proper and suitable for covering and protecting men's bodies against arrows slung in battle—helmets, shields, and protective covering having come first from you—you instituted and gave directions for drawing up a battle order, how to begin an assault and to engage in

proper combat. . . . In the aforementioned country of Greece, you provided the usage of this office, and insofar as it may please you to be favorably disposed, and I in no way appear to be against the nation from which you came, the country beyond the Alps that is now called Apulia and Calabria in Italy, where you were born, let me say that like you I am an Italian woman.

Source: From *The Book of the Deeds of Arms and of Chivalry*, ed. Charity Cannon Willard and trans. Sumner Willard (University Park, PA: 1999), pp. 11–13.

Questions for Analysis

1. Christine very cleverly deflects potential criticism for her "boldness" in writing about warfare. What tactics does she use?

2. The Greco-Roman goddess Athena (Minerva) was the goddess of wisdom, weaving, and warfare. Why does Christine invoke her aid? What parallels does she draw between her own attributes and those of Minerva?

---

that no living person had known to exist. They had probably been copied in the time of Charlemagne, and then forgotten for hundreds of years. How many other works of this great Roman orator had been lost to posterity? Clearly, thought Francesco Petrarca (1304–1374), he was living in an age of

ignorance. A great gulf seemed to open up between his own time and that of the ancients: a middle age that separated him from those well-loved models.

For centuries, Christian intellectuals had regarded "the dark ages" as the time between Adam's expulsion from

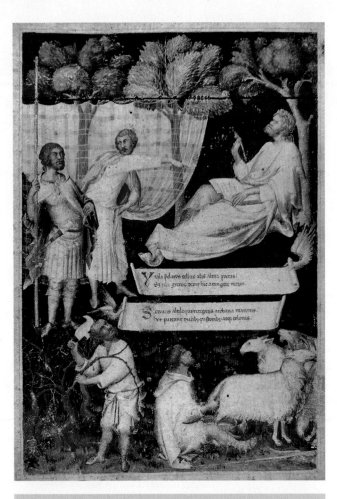

PETRARCH'S COPY OF VIRGIL. Petrarch's devotion to the classics of Roman literature prompted him to commission this new frontispiece for his treasured volume of Virgil's poetry. It was painted by the Sienese artist Simone Martini, who (like Petrarch) was attached to the papal court at Avignon. It is an allegorical depiction of Virgil (top right) and his poetic creations: the hero Aeneas (top left, wearing armor) and the farmer and shepherd whose humble labors are celebrated in Virgil's lesser-known works. The figure next to Aeneas is the fourth-century scholar Servius, who wrote a famous commentary on Virgil. He is shown drawing aside a curtain to reveal the poet in a creative trance. The two scrolls proclaim (in Latin) that Italy was the country that nourished famous poets and that Virgil helped it to rival the glories of classical Greece. ▪ *How does this image encapsulate and express Petrarch's devotion to the classical past?*

Petrarch was famous in his own day as an Italian poet, Latin stylist, and a tireless advocate for the resuscitation of the classics. The values that he and his followers began to espouse would give rise to a new intellectual and artistic movement in Italy, a movement strongly critical of the present and admiring of a past that had disappeared with the western Roman Empire and the end of Italy's greatness. We know this movement as "the Renaissance," from the French word for "rebirth" that was applied to it in the eighteenth century and popularized in the nineteenth, when the term "medieval" was also invented. It has since become shorthand for the epoch *following* the Middle Ages—but it was really part of the same era.

Renaissance Classicism

Talking about "the Renaissance," then, is a way of talking about some significant changes in education and artistic outlook that transformed the culture of northern Italy from the late fourteenth to the early sixteenth centuries and that eventually influenced the rest of Europe in important ways. The term has often been taken literally, as though the cultural accomplishments of antiquity had ceased to be appreciated and needed to be "reborn." Yet we have been tracing the enduring influence of classical civilization for many chapters, and we have constantly noted the reverence accorded to the heritage of antiquity, not to mention the persistence of Roman law and Roman institutions.

That said, one can certainly find traits that make the concept of "renaissance" newly meaningful in this era. For example, there was a significant quantitative difference between the ancient texts available to scholars in the first thousand years after Rome's fragmentation and those that became accessible in the fourteenth and fifteenth centuries. The discovery of "new" works by Livy, Tacitus, and Lucretius expanded the canon considerably, supplementing the well-studied works of Virgil, Ovid, and Cicero.

More important was the expanded access to ancient Greek literature in western Europe. In the twelfth and thirteenth centuries, as we have seen in Chapters 8 and 9, Greek scientific and philosophical works became available to western Europeans thanks to increased contact with Islam, via Latin translations of Arabic translations of the original Greek. Yet no Greek poems or plays were yet available in Latin translations, and neither were the major dialogues of Plato. Moreover, only a handful of western Europeans could read the language of classical Greece. But as the Mongols and, after them, the Ottoman Turks put increasing pressure on the shrinking borders of Byzantium

Eden and the birth of Christ. But now, Petrarch (the name by which English-speakers know him) redefined that concept. According to him, this age was not the pagan past but the time that separated him from direct communion with the classics. Yet this did not stop him from trying to bridge the gap. "I would have written to you long ago," he said in a Latin letter to the Greek poet Homer (dead for over 2,000 years), "had it not been for the fact that we lack a common language."

Interpreting Visual Evidence

Realizing Devotion

These two paintings by the Flemish artist Rogier van der Weyden (*FAN-der-VIE-den*, c. 1400–1464) capture some of the most compelling characteristics of late medieval art, particularly the trend toward realistic representations of holy figures and sacred stories. On the left (image A), the artist depicts himself as the evangelist Luke, regarded in Christian tradition as a painter of portraits; he sketches the Virgin nursing the infant Jesus in a town house overlooking a Flemish city. On the right (image B), van der Weyden imagines the entombment of the dead Christ by his followers, including the Virgin (left), Mary Magdalene (kneeling), and the disciple John (right). Here, he

makes use of a motif that became increasingly prominent in the later Middle Ages: Christ as the Man of Sorrows, displaying his wounds and inviting the viewer to share in his suffering. In both paintings, van der Weyden emphasizes the humanity of his subjects rather than their iconic status (see Chapter 7), and he places them in the urban and rural landscapes of his own world.

Questions for Analysis

1. How are these paintings different from the sacred images of the earlier Middle Ages (see, for example, page 169)? What messages does the artist convey by setting these events in his own immediate present?

2. In what ways do these paintings reflect broad changes in popular piety and medieval devotional practices? Why, for example, would the artist display the dead and wounded body of Christ—rather than depicting him as resurrected and triumphant, or as an all-seeing creator and judge?

3. In general, how would you use these images as evidence of the worldview of the fifteenth century? What do they tell us about people's attitudes, emotions, and values?

A. Saint Luke drawing the portrait of the Virgin.

B. The Deposition.

(to be discussed later), more and more Greek-speaking intellectuals fled to Italy, bringing their books and their knowledge with them.

Thanks to these developments, some Italian intellectuals had access to more classical texts and they also used these texts in new ways. For centuries, Christian scholars had worked to bring ancient writings and values into line with their own beliefs (Chapter 6). By contrast, the new reading methods pioneered by Petrarch and others fostered an awareness of the conceptual gap that separated the contemporary world from that of antiquity. This awakened a determination to recapture ancient worldviews and value systems. In the second half of the fifteenth century, classical models would also contribute to the strikingly distinctive artistic style that is most strongly associated with the Renaissance (something we will address in Chapter 12).

Another distinguishing feature of this new perspective on the classical past was the way that it became overtly materialistic and commercialized. The competition among and within Italian city-states fostered a culture that used the symbols and artifacts of ancient Rome as pawns in an endless power game. Meanwhile, the relative weakness of the Church contributed to the growth of claims to power based on classical models—even by Italian bishops and Church-sponsored universities. When the papacy was eventually restored to Rome, it too had to compete in this Renaissance arena by patronizing the artists and intellectuals who espoused these aesthetic and political ideals.

Renaissance Humanism

The most basic feature of this new intellectual and political agenda is summarized in the term *humanism*. This was a program of study that aimed to replace the scholastic emphasis on logic and theology—central to the curriculum of universities like Paris and Oxford—with the study of ancient literature, rhetoric, history, and ethics. The goal of a humanist education was the understanding of human experience through the lenses of the classical past, in the service of man's individual potential in the present. By contrast, a scholastic education filtered human experience through the teachings of scripture and the Church fathers, with the salvation of humankind as the ultimate goal.

Some intellectuals also believed that the university curriculum concentrated too much on abstract speculation rather than the achievement of virtue and ethical conduct. Petrarch felt that the true Christian thinker must cultivate literary eloquence and so inspire others to do good through the pursuit of beauty and truth. According

to him, the best models of eloquence were to be found in the classics of Latin literature, which were also filled with ethical wisdom. Petrarch dedicated himself, therefore, to rediscovering such texts and to writing his own poems and moral treatises in a Latin style modeled on that of classical authors.

Humanists therefore preferred ancient writings to those of more recent authors, including their own contemporaries. And although some early humanists wrote in Italian dialects as well as Latin, most regarded vernacular literature as a lesser diversion for the uneducated; serious scholarship and poetry could be written only in Latin (or Greek). Proper Latin, moreover, had to be the classical Latin of Cicero and Virgil, not the evolving language of their own day, which they derided as a barbarous departure from "correct" standards of Latin style.

But ironically, their determination to revive this older language eventually helped to kill the lively Latin that had continued to flourish in Europe. By insisting on outmoded standards of grammar, syntax, and vocabulary, they turned Latin into a fossilized discourse that ceased to have any relevance to real life. They thus contributed, unwittingly, to the ultimate triumph of the various European vernaculars they despised.

Because humanism was an educational program designed to produce able public men, it largely excluded women because women were largely excluded from Italian political life. Here again is a paradox: as more and more Italian city-states fell into the hands of autocratic rulers, the humanist educational curriculum lost its immediate connection to the republican ideals of ancient Rome. Nevertheless, humanists never lost their conviction that the study of the "humanities" (as the humanist curriculum came to be known) was the best way to produce leaders.

Why Italy?

These new attitudes toward education and the antique models were fostered in northern Italy for historically specific reasons. After the Black Death, this region was the most densely populated part of Europe; other urban areas, notably northeastern France and Flanders, had been decimated by the Great Famine as well as the plague. Northern Italy also differed from the rest of urbanized Europe because aristocratic families customarily lived in cities and consequently became more fully involved in public affairs than their counterparts north of the Alps. Moreover, many town-dwelling aristocrats were engaged in banking or mercantile enterprises, while many rich mercantile families imitated the manners of the aristocracy. The Florentine ruling family, the Medici, originally made their fortune in banking and commerce.

These factors help to explain the emergence of the humanist ideals described above. Newly wealthy families were not content to have their sons learn only the skills necessary to becoming successful businessmen; they sought teachers who would impart the knowledge and finesse that would enable them to cut a figure in society, mix with their noble neighbors, and speak with authority on public affairs. Consequently, Italy produced and attracted a large number of independent intellectuals who were not affiliated with monasteries, cathedral schools, or universities—many of whom served as schoolmasters for wealthy young men while acting as cultural consultants and secretaries for their families. These intellectuals advertised their learning by producing political and ethical treatises and works of literature that would attract the attention of patrons or reflect well on the patrons they already had. As a result, Italian schools and private tutors turned out the best-educated laymen in all of Europe, men who also constituted a new generation of wealthy, knowledgeable patrons ready to invest in the cultivation of new ideas and new forms of artistic expression.

A second reason why late-medieval Italy was the birthplace of the Renaissance movement has to do with its vexed political situation. Unlike France and England, or the kingdoms of Spain, Scandinavia, and central Europe, Italy had no unifying political institutions. Italians therefore looked to the classical past for their time of glory, dreaming of a day when Rome would be, again, the center of the world. They boasted that ancient Roman monuments were omnipresent in their landscape and that classical Latin literature referred to cities and sites they recognized as their own.

Italians were also intent on reappropriating their classical heritage because they were seeking to establish an independent cultural identity that could counter the intellectual and political supremacy of France. The removal of the papacy to Avignon (Chapter 10) had heightened antagonism between the city-states of Italy and the burgeoning kingdom beyond the Alps. This also explains the Italians' rejection of the scholasticism taught in northern Europe's universities and their embrace of models that could create an artistic alternative to the dominant French school of Gothic architecture.

Finally, this Italian Renaissance could not have occurred without the underpinning of Italian wealth gained through the commercial ventures described in Chapter 10. This wealth meant that talented men seeking employment and patronage were more likely to stay at home, fueling the artistic and intellectual competition that arose from the intensification of urban pride and the concentration of individual and family wealth in urban areas. Cities themselves became primary patrons of art and learning in this era.

The Renaissance of Civic Ideals

For the intellectuals of Florence, in particular, the goal of classical education was civic enrichment. Humanists such as Leonardo Bruni (c. 1370–1444) and Leon Battista Alberti (1404–1472) valued eloquence and classical literature, but they also taught that man's nature should be cultivated for service to the state—ideally a city-state after the Florentine model. Ambition and the quest for glory are noble impulses, but they ought to be encouraged and channeled toward these ends. They also argued that the history of human progress is inseparable from the human dominion of the earth and its resources.

Many of the humanists' civic ideals are expressed in Alberti's treatise *On the Family* (1443), in which the nuclear family is presented as the fundamental unit of the city-state and, as such, is to be governed in such a way as to further the state's political and economic goals. He therefore consigned women—who, in reality, governed the household—to childbearing, child rearing, and subservience to men even within this domestic realm. He asserted, furthermore, that women should play no role whatsoever in the public sphere. Although such dismissals of women's abilities were fiercely resisted by actual women, the humanism of the Renaissance was characterized by a pervasive denigration of women.

The Emergence of Textual Criticism

The humanists' project was aided by a number of Byzantine scholars who emigrated to Italy in the first half of the fifteenth century and who gave instruction in the ancient form of their own native language. Wealthy, well-connected Florentines also increasingly aspired to acquire Greek literary masterpieces for themselves, which often involved journeys back to Constantinople. In 1423, one adventurous bibliophile managed to bring back 238 manuscript books, among them rare works of Sophocles, Euripides, and Thucydides. These were quickly paraphrased in Latin and made accessible to western Europeans for the first time.

This influx of new classical texts spurred a new interest in textual criticism. A pioneer in this activity was

Lorenzo Valla (1407–1457). Born in Rome and active primarily as a secretary to the king of Naples and Sicily, Valla turned his skills to the painstaking analysis of Greek and Latin writings in order to show how the historical study of language could discredit old assumptions and even unmask some texts as forgeries. For example, some propagandists argued that the papacy's claim to secular power in Europe derived from rights granted to the bishop of Rome by the emperor Constantine in the fourth century, enshrined in a document known as "The Donation of Constantine." By analyzing the language of this spurious text, Valla proved that it could not have been written in the time of Constantine because it contained more recent Latin usages and vocabulary.

This demonstration not only discredited more traditional scholarly methods, it made the concept of anachronism (the detection of historical errors) central to all subsequent textual criticism and historical thought. Indeed, Valla even applied his expert knowledge of Greek to elucidating the meaning of Saint Paul's letters, which he believed had been obscured by Jerome's Latin translation (see Chapter 6). This work was to prove an important link between Italian Renaissance scholarship and the subsequent Christian humanism of the north, which in turn fed into the Reformation (see Chapter 13).

THE END OF THE EASTERN ROMAN EMPIRE

The Greek-speaking refugees who arrived in Italy after the Black Death were self-made exiles. They were responding to the succession of calamities that had reduced the once-proud eastern Roman Empire to a scattering of embattled provinces. As we've noted, when Constantinople fell to western crusaders in 1204, the surrounding territories of Byzantium were severed from the capital that had held them together (see Chapter 9). When the Latin presence in Constantinople was finally expelled in 1261, imperial power had been so weakened that it extended only into the immediate hinterlands of the city and parts of Greece. The rest of the empire had become a collection of small principalities in precarious alliance with the Mongols and dependant on the Pax Mongolica for survival (see Chapter 10). Then, with the coming of the Black Death, the imperial capital suffered the loss of half of its inhabitants and shrank still further. Meanwhile, the disintegration of the Mongol Empire laid the larger region of Anatolia open to a new set of invaders.

The Rise of the Ottoman Turks

Like the Mongols, the Turks were originally a nomadic people. When the Mongols arrived in northwestern Anatolia, the Turks were already established there and were being converted to Islam by the resident Muslim powers of the region: the Seljuq Sultanate of Rûm and the Abbasid Caliphate of Baghdad. But when the Mongols toppled these older powers, they eliminated the two traditional authorities that had kept Turkish border chieftains in check. Now they were free to raid, unhindered, along the soft frontiers of Byzantium. At the same time, the Turks remained far enough from the centers of Mongol authority to avoid being destroyed themselves. One of their chieftains, Osman Gazi (1258–1326), established his own independent kingdom. Eventually, his name was given to the Turkish dynasty that would control the most ancient lands of Western civilizations for six centuries: the Ottomans.

By the mid-fourteenth century, Osman's successors had captured a number of important cities. These successes brought the Ottomans to the attention of the Byzantine emperor, who hired a contingent of them as mercenaries in 1345. They were extraordinarily successful—so much so that the eastern Roman Empire could not control their movements. They then struck out on their own and began to extend their control westward. By 1370, their holdings stretched all the way to the Danube. In 1389, they defeated a powerful coalition of Serbian forces at the battle of Kosovo, which enabled them to begin subduing Bulgaria, the Balkans, and eventually Greece. In 1396, the Ottoman army even attacked Constantinople itself, although it withdrew to repel an ineffectual crusading force that had been hastily sent by the papacy.

In 1402, another attack on Constantinople was deflected—this time, by a more potent foe who had ambitions to match those of the Ottomans. Timur the Lame (Tamerlane, as he was called by European admirers) was born to a family of small landholders in the Mongol Khanate of Chagatai. While still a young man, he rose to prominence as a military leader and gained a reputation for tactical genius. He was no politician, though, and never officially assumed the title of khan in any of the territories he dominated. Instead, he moved ceaselessly from conquest to conquest, becoming the master of lands from the Caspian Sea to the Volga River, as well as most of Persia. For a time, it looked briefly as if the Mongol Empire might be reunited under his reign. But Timur died in 1405, on his way to invade China, and his various conquests fell into the hands of local rulers. Mongol influence continued in the Mughal Empire of India, but in Anatolia the Ottoman Turks were once again on the rise.

The Fall of Constantinople

During the 1420s and 1430s, Ottoman pressure on Constantinople escalated. Monasteries and schools that had been established since the fourth century found themselves in the path of an advancing army, and a steady stream of fleeing scholars strove to salvage a millennium's worth of Byzantine books—many of them preserving the heritage of ancient Greece and the Hellenistic world. Then, in 1451, the Ottoman sultan Mehmet II turned his full attention to the conquest of the imperial city. In 1453, after a brilliantly executed siege, his army succeeded in breaching its walls. The Byzantine emperor was killed in the assault, the city itself was plundered, and its remaining population was sold into slavery. The Ottomans then settled down to rule their new capital in a style reminiscent of their Byzantine predecessors.

The Ottoman conquest of Constantinople was an enormous shock to European Christians. Yet its actual political and economic impact on western and central Europe was minor. Ottoman control may have reduced some Europeans' access to the Black Sea, but Europeans got most of their spices and silks through Venice anyway. Moreover, as we saw in Chapter 10, Europeans already had colonial ambitions and significant trading interests in Africa and the Atlantic that connected them to far-reaching networks.

But the effects of the Ottoman conquest on the Turks themselves were transformative. Vast new wealth poured into Anatolia, which the Ottomans increased by carefully tending to the industrial and commercial interests of their new capital city, which they also called Istanbul—the Turkish pronunciation of the Greek phrase *eis tan polin* "in (to) the city." Trade routes were redirected to feed the capital, and the Ottomans became a naval power in the eastern Mediterranean as well as in the Black Sea. As a result, Constantinople's population grew rapidly, from fewer than 100,000 in 1453 to more than 500,000 by 1600, making it the largest city in the world outside of China.

Slavery and Social Advancement in the Ottoman Empire

Despite the Ottomans' new attention to commerce, their empire continued to rest on the spoils of conquest.

To manage its continual expansion, the size of the Ottoman army and administration grew exponentially, drawing more and more manpower from conquered territories. And because both army and bureaucracy were largely composed of slaves, the demand for more soldiers and administrators could best be met through further conquests, requiring a still larger army and even more extensive bureaucracy—and so the cycle continued. It mirrors, in many respects, the dilemma of the Roman Empire in the centuries of its rapid expansion beyond Italy (see Chapter 5), which also created an insatiable demand for slaves.

Not only were slaves the backbone of Ottoman government, they were critical to the lives of the Turkish upper class. Indeed, one of the important measures of status in Ottoman society was the number of slaves in one's household. After the capture of Constantinople, new wealth would permit some elites to maintain households in the thousands. By the sixteenth century, the sultan alone possessed more than 20,000 slave attendants, not including his bodyguard and elite infantry units, both of which also comprised of slaves.

Where did all of these slaves come from? Many were captured in war. Many others were taken on raiding forays into Poland and Ukraine and sold to Crimean slave merchants, who shipped their captives to the slave markets of Constantinople. But slaves were also recruited (some willingly, some by coercion) from rural areas of the Ottoman Empire itself. Because the vast majority of slaves were household servants and administrators rather than laborers, some men willingly accepted enslavement, believing that they would be better off as slaves in Constantinople than as impoverished peasants in the countryside. In the Balkans especially, many people were enslaved as children, handed over by their families to pay the "child tax" that the Ottomans imposed on rural areas too poor to pay a monetary tribute. Although an excruciating experience for families, this practice did open up opportunities for social advancement. Special academies were created at Constantinople to train the most able of the enslaved male children, some of whom rose to become powerful figures in the Ottoman Empire.

For this reason, slavery carried relatively little social stigma (the sultan himself was most often the son of an enslaved woman). And because Muslims were not permitted to enslave other Muslims, the vast majority of Ottoman slaves were Christian—although many eventually converted to Islam. And because so many of the elite positions within Ottoman government were held by these slaves, the paradoxical result was that Muslims, including the Turks themselves, were effectively excluded from the main avenues of social and political influence in the Ottoman Empire. Avenues to power were therefore remarkably open to men of ability and talent, most of them non-Muslim slaves.

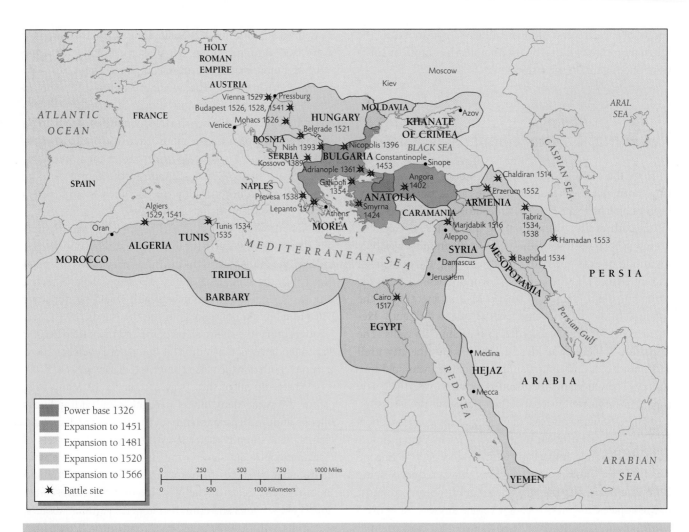

THE GROWTH OF THE OTTOMAN EMPIRE. Consider the patterns of Ottoman expansion revealed in this map. ▪ *Where is Constantinople, and how might the capture of Constantinople in 1453 have facilitated further conquests?* ▪ *Compare the extent of the Ottoman Empire in 1566 with that of the Byzantine Empire under Justinian (see the map on page 166). How would you account for their similarities?*

Nor was this power limited to the government and the army. Commerce and business also remained largely in the hands of non-Muslims, most frequently Greeks, Syrians, and Jews. Jews in particular found in the Ottoman Empire a welcome refuge from the persecutions that had characterized Jewish life in western Europe. After their expulsion from Spain in 1492 (see Chapter 12), more than 100,000 Spanish (Sephardic) Jews ultimately immigrated to the territories of the Ottoman Empire.

Because the Ottoman sultans were Sunni Muslims, they often dealt harshly with other Muslim sects. But they were tolerant of Christians and Jews. They organized the major religious groups of their empire into legally recognized units and permitted them considerable rights of self-government. They even promoted the authority of the Greek Orthodox patriarch of Constantinople. As a result, the Ottomans enjoyed staunch support from

their Orthodox Christian subjects for their wars with the Christians of western Europe.

Russia: "The Third Rome"

The Orthodox Church also received staunch support from the peoples of Rus' whose own Church had been founded by Byzantine missionaries (see Chapter 8) and whose written language was based on the Greek alphabet. Indeed, the emerging duchy of Muscovy (see Chapter 10) saw itself as the natural protector and ally of the eastern Roman Empire. After Constantinople fell to the Turks—predictably, without any help from Latin Christendom—the Russian Church emerged as the strongest proponent of Orthodoxy.

SULTAN MEHMET II, "THE CONQUEROR" (r. 1451–81). This portrait, executed by the Ottoman artist Siblizade Ahmed, exhibits features characteristic of both Central Asia and Europe. The sultan's pose—his aesthetic appreciation of the rose, his elegant handkerchief—are indicative of the former, as is the fact that he wears the white turban of a scholar and the thumb ring of an archer. But the subdued coloring and three-quarter profile may reflect the influence of Italian portraits. ▪ *What did the artist achieve through this blending of styles and symbols?* ▪ *What messages does this portrait convey?*

Muscovy's distrust of western Europe was increased by developments on its western borders. In the thirteenth century, the small kingdom of Poland had struggled to defend itself from absorption by German princes. When the Holy Roman Empire's strength waned after the death of Frederick the Great (see Chapter 9), Poland's situation grew more secure. In 1386, its female King, Jadwiga, strengthened its power when she married Jagiello, the grand duke of neighboring Lithuania. Lithuania had begun to carve out an extensive territory in the Baltic (modern-day Belarus and Ukraine) and this momentum increased after its union with Poland. In 1410, a combined Polish and Lithuanian force defeated the Teutonic Knights at the Battle of Tannenberg, crushing the military order that controlled a crucial region lying between the allied kingdoms. Thereafter, Poland-Lithuania began to push eastward toward Muscovy.

Although many of Lithuania's aristocratic families were Orthodox Christians, the established church in Poland was loyal to Rome, and Duke Jagiello was a pagan convert to Latin Christianity. For the rulers of Muscovy threatened by Poland-Lithuania, it therefore seemed expedient to take up the imperial mantle that had been abandoned when Constantinople fell, and to declare the Muscovite state the successor to Rome. To drive the point home, Muscovite dukes began to take the title of tsar, "caesar." "Two Romes have fallen," said a Muscovite chronicler, "the third is still standing, and a fourth there shall not be."

WARFARE AND NATION-BUILDING IN EUROPE

War has always been an engine for the development of new technologies. This is something we have noted since Chapter 1, but the pace and scale of warfare escalated to an unprecedented degree in the era after the Black Death. Although explosives had been invented in China, and were originally deployed in displays of fireworks, they were first put to devastating and destructive use in Europe. In fact, the earliest cannons were as dangerous to those who fired them as to those they targeted. But by the middle of the fifteenth century, they were reliable enough to revolutionize warfare. In 1453, heavy artillery played a leading role in the outcomes of two crucial conflicts: the Ottoman Turks breached the ancient defenses of Constantinople with cannon fire and the French captured the English-held city of Bordeaux, bringing an end to the Hundred Years' War.

Thereafter, cannons made it more difficult for rebellious aristocrats to hole up in their stone castles and consequently facilitated their subjugation by powerful monarchies. Cannons placed aboard ships made navies more effective. A handheld firearm, the pistol, was also invented in the fourteenth century, and around 1500 the musket ended forever the military dominance of heavily armored cavalry.

Indeed, there is a symbiotic relationship between warfare and politics as well as between warfare and technology. Because Europeans were almost constantly at war from the fourteenth century to the middle of the twentieth, governments claimed new powers to tax their subjects and to control their subjects' lives. Armies became larger, military technology deadlier. Wars became more destructive, society more militarized. As a result of these developments, the most successful European states were aggressively expansionist.

The Hundred Years' War Resumes

The hostilities that make up the Hundred Years' War can be divided into three main phases (see the maps on page 303). The first phase dates from the initial declaration of war in 1337 (Chapter 10), after which the English won a series of startling military victories. The war then resumed in 1356, with another English victory at Poitiers. Four years later, in 1360, Edward III decided to leverage his strong position: he renounced his larger claim to the French throne, and in return he was guaranteed full sovereignty over a greatly enlarged duchy of Gascony and the promise of a huge ransom for the king of France, whom he held captive.

But the terms of this treaty were never honored, nor did it resolve the underlying issues that had led to the war itself: namely, the problem of sovereignty in contested territory and the question of the English king's place in the French royal succession. The French king continued to treat the English king as his vassal, while Edward's heirs renewed their claim to the throne of France.

Although there were no pitched battles for two decades after this, a destabilizing proxy war developed during the 1360s and 1370s. Both the English troops (posted in Gascony) and the French troops (eager to avenge their losses) were organized into "Free Companies" of mercenaries and hired themselves out in the service of hostile factions in Castile and competing city-states in northern Italy. By 1376, when the conflict between England and France was reignited, the Hundred Years' War had become a Europe-wide phenomenon.

England's Disputed Throne and the Brief Victory of Henry V

In this second phase of the war, the tide quickly shifted in favor of France. The new king, Charles V (r. 1364–80), imposed a series of taxes to fund an army and disbanded the Free Companies, hiring the leader of one band as his commander. He thereby created a professional military that could match the English in discipline and tactics. By 1380, English territories in France had been reduced to a core area around the southwestern city of Bordeaux and the port of Calais in the extreme northeast.

Meanwhile, the aging Edward III has been succeeded by his nine-year-old grandson, Richard II (r. 1377–99), who was too young to prosecute a claim to the French crown. This was problematic, because the war had been extremely popular in England. And when Richard came

A FIFTEENTH-CENTURY SIEGE WITH CANNONS. Cannons were an essential element in siege warfare during the Hundred Years' War.

of age and showed no signs of martial ambition, many of his own aristocratic relatives turned against him. Richard retaliated against the ringleader of this faction, his cousin Henry of Lancaster, by sending him into exile and confiscating his property. Henry's supporters used this as pretext for rebellion. In 1399, Richard was deposed by Henry and eventually murdered.

As a usurper whose legitimacy was always in doubt, Henry IV (r. 1399–1413) struggled to maintain his authority. The best way to unite the country would have been to renew the war against France, but Henry was frequently ill and in no position to lead an army into combat. So when his son Henry V succeeded him in 1413, the new king immediately began to prepare for an invasion. His timing was excellent: the French royal government was foundering due to the insanity of the reigning king, Charles VI (r. 1380–1422). A brilliant diplomat as well as a capable soldier, Henry V sealed an alliance with the powerful Duke of Burgundy, who was allegedly loyal to France but stood to gain from its defeat. Henry also made a treaty with the German emperor, who agreed not to come to France's aid.

When he crossed the English Channel in the autumn of 1415, Henry V's troops thus faced a much-depleted French army that could not rely on reinforcements. Although it was still vastly larger and boasted hundreds of mounted knights, it was undisciplined. It was also severely hampered by bad weather and deep mud when the two armies clashed at Agincourt on October 25 of that year—conditions that favored the lighter English infantry. Henry's men managed to win a crushing victory.

Then, over the next five years, Henry conquered most of northern France. In 1420, the ailing Charles VI was forced to recognize him as heir to the throne of France, thereby disinheriting his own son. (This prince bore the ceremonial title of *dauphin*, "the dolphin," from the heraldic device of the borderland province he inherited.) Henry sealed the deal by marrying the French princess, Catherine, and fathering an heir to the joint kingdom of England and France.

Joan of Arc's Betrayal and Legacy

Unlike his great-grandfather Edward III, who has used his claim to the French throne as a bargaining chip to secure sovereignty over Gascony, Henry V honestly believed himself to be the rightful king of France. And his astonishing success in capturing the kingdom seemed to put the stamp of divine approval on that claim. But Henry's successes in France also transformed the nature of the war, turning it from a profitable war of conquest and plunder into an extended and expensive military occupation. It might have been sustainable had Henry been as long-lived as many of his predecessors. But he died early in 1422, just short of his thirty-sixth birthday. King Charles VI died only a few months later.

The new king of England and France, Henry VI (r. 1422–61), was only an infant, and yet the English armies under the command of his regents continued to press southward into territories held by the dauphin. Although it seemed unlikely that English forces would ever succeed in dislodging him, confidence in the French prince's right to the throne had been shattered by his own mother's declaration that he was illegitimate. It might have happened that England would once again rule an empire comprising much of France, as it had for a century and a half after the Norman conquest.

But this scenario fails to reckon with Joan of Arc. In 1429, a peasant girl from Lorraine (a territory only nominally part of France) made her way to the dauphin's court and announced that an angel had told her that he, Charles, was the rightful king, and that she, Joan, should drive the English out of France. The fact that she even got a hearing underscores the hopelessness of the dauphin's position, as does the extraordinary fact that he gave her a contingent of troops. With this force, Joan liberated the strategic city of Orléans, then under siege by the English, after which a series of victories culminated in Charles's coronation in the cathedral of Reims, the traditional site for crowning French kings.

Despite her miraculous success, Joan was an embarrassment whose very charisma made her dangerous. She was a peasant leading aristocrats, a woman leading men, and a commoner who claimed to have been commissioned by God. When, a few months later, the Burgundians captured her in battle and handed her over to the English, the king she had helped to crown did nothing to save her. Accused of witchcraft, condemned by the theologians of Paris, and tried for heresy by an English ecclesiastical court, Joan was burned to death in the market square at Rouen in 1431. She was nineteen years old.

The French forces whom Joan had inspired, however, continued on the offensive. In 1435, the duke of Burgundy withdrew from his alliance with England. When the young English king, Henry VI, proved first incompetent and then insane, a series of French military victories brought hostilities to an end with the capture of Bordeaux in 1453. English kings would threaten to renew the war for another century, and Anglo-French hostility would last until the defeat of Napoleon in 1815. But after 1453, English control over French territory would be limited to the port of Calais (which eventually fell, in 1558).

JOAN OF ARC. A contemporary sketch of Joan was drawn in the margin of this register documenting official proceedings at the Parlement of Paris in 1429.

The Long Shadow of the Hundred Years' War

The Hundred Years' War challenged the very existence of France. The disintegration of that kingdom glaringly revealed the fragility of the bonds that tied the king to

The Condemnation of Joan of Arc by the University of Paris, 1431

After Joan's capture by the Burgundians, she was handed over to the English and tried for heresy at an ecclesiastical court set up in Rouen. It was on this occasion that the theology faculty of Paris pronounced the following verdict on her actions.

You, Joan, have said that, since the age of thirteen, you have experienced revelations and the appearance of angels, of St. Catherine and St. Margaret, and that you have very often seen them with your bodily eyes, and that they have spoken to you. As for the first point, the clerks of the University of Paris have considered the manner of the said revelations and appearances. . . . Having considered all . . . they have declared that all the things mentioned above are lies, falsenesses, misleading and pernicious things and that such revelations are superstitions, proceeding from wicked and diabolical spirits.

Item: You have said that your king had a sign by which he knew that you were sent by God, for St. Michael, accompanied by several angels, some of which having wings, the others crowns, with St. Catherine and St. Margaret, came to you at the chateau of Chinon. All the company ascended through the floors of the castle until they came to the room of your king, before whom the angel bearing the crown bowed. . . . As for this matter, the clerks say that it is not in the least probable, but it is rather a presumptuous lie, misleading and pernicious, a false statement, derogatory of the dignity of the Church and of the angels. . . .

Item: you have said that, at God's command, you have continually worn men's clothes, and that you have put on a short robe, doublet, shoes attached by points, also that you have had short hair, cut around above the ears, without retaining anything on your person which shows that you are a woman, and that several times you have received the body of Our Lord dressed in this fashion, despite having been admonished to give it up several times, the which you would not do. You have said that you would rather die than abandon the said clothing, if it were not at God's command, and that if you were wearing those clothes and were with the king, and those of your party, it would be one of the greatest benefits for the kingdom of France. You have also said that not for anything would you swear an oath not to wear the said clothing and carry arms any longer. And all these things you say you have done for the good and at the command of God. As for these things, the clerics say that you blaspheme God and hold him in contempt in his sacraments; you transgress Divine Law, Holy Scripture, and canon law. You err in the faith. You boast in vanity. You are suspected of idolatry and you have condemned yourself in not wishing to wear clothing suitable to your sex, but you follow the custom of Gentiles and Saracens.

Source: Carolyne Larrington, ed. and trans., *Women and Writing in Medieval Europe* (New York: 1995), pp. 183–84.

Questions for Analysis

1. Paris was in the hands of the English when this condemnation was issued. Is there any evidence that its authors were coerced into making this pronouncement?

2. On what grounds was Joan condemned for heresy?

3. In what ways does Joan's behavior highlight larger trends in late medieval spirituality and popular piety?

---

the nobility, and the royal capital, Paris, to the kingdom's outlying regions. Nonetheless, the king's power was actually increased by the war's end, laying the foundations on which the power of early modern France would be built.

The Hundred Years' War also had dramatic effects on the English monarchy. When English armies in France were successful, the king rode a wave of popularity that fueled an emerging sense of patriotism. When the war turned against the English, however, defeats abroad undermined support for the monarch at home. Of the nine English kings who ruled England between 1307 and 1485, five were deposed and murdered by aristocratic factions.

England's peculiar form of kingship depended on the king's ability to mobilize popular support through

ENGLAND

London•

Crécy

English Channel

•Rouen

Paris•

Orléans•

FRANCE

•Poitiers

Lyons•

Bordeaux•

0   50   100 Miles

0 50 100 Kilometers

1328

◻ Under English influence

1429

◻ Under English influence

— Boundary of France, 1453

✳ Battle sites

ENGLAND

London•

Calais
✳1347

✳ **Crécy
1346**

•Rouen

Paris•

Orléans•

FRANCE

✳
**Poitiers
1356**

Lyons•

Bordeaux•

0   50   100 Miles

0 50 100 Kilometers

1360

◻ Under English influence

✳ Battle sites

THE PHASES OF THE HUNDRED YEARS' WAR. Here we see three snapshots of the political geography of France during the Hundred Years' War. ▪ *In what areas of France did England make its greatest territorial gains before 1360?* ▪ *How and why did this change in the period leading up to 1429?* ▪ *What geographic and strategic advantages did the French monarchy enjoy after 1429 that might help explain its success in recapturing the French kingdom from the English?*

Parliament while maintaining the support of his nobility through successful wars. Failure to maintain this balance was even more destabilizing than it would have been elsewhere, precisely because royal power was so centralized. In France, the nobility could endure the insanity of Charles VI because his government was not powerful enough to threaten them. In England, neither the nobility nor the nation could afford the weak kingship of Henry VI. The result was an aristocratic rebellion that led to a full-blown civil war: the Wars of the Roses, so called—by the novelist Sir Walter Scott (1771–1832)—because of the floral emblems, red and white, adopted by the two com-

peting noble families, Lancaster and York. It ended only when a Lancastrian claimant, Henry Tudor (r. 1485–1509), resolved the dynastic feud by marrying Elizabeth of York, ruling as Henry VII and establishing a new Tudor dynasty whose symbol was a rose with both white and red petals (see Chapter 13).

Despite England's ultimate defeat, the Hundred Years' War strengthened the English nation in several ways. First, it equated national strength with the power of the state and its king. Second, it fomented a strong anti-French sentiment that led to the triumph of the English vernacular for the first time since the Norman conquest over 300 years

Past and Present

Replacing "Retired" Popes

When Benedict XVI decided to retire from papal office in February 2013, pundits and theologians alike struggled to find a precedent for this extraordinary decision. Most reached back to the year 1417, when Pope Martin V was elected at the Council of Constance (left) to replace the "retired" Gregory XII. But in this case, the retirement was not voluntary—and it was accompanied by the enforced resignation of an additional rival pope and the excommunication of yet another. The installation mass of Pope Francis in March 2013 (right) was much more universally celebrated and much more public than that of his medieval predecessor.

Watch related author videos on the Student Site
wwnorton.com/college/history/western-civilizationsBrief4

earlier: the first English court to speak English was that of Richard II, a patron of Geoffrey Chaucer. Third, the loss of its continental possessions made England, for the first time, a self-contained island. This would later prove to be an advantage in many ways.

Conflict in the Holy Roman Empire and Italy

Elsewhere in Europe, a new trend toward perpetual warfare was even more destructive. In the lands of the Holy Roman Empire, armed conflict among territorial princes, and between these princes and the emperor, weakened all combatants. Periodically, a powerful emperor would emerge to play a major role, but the dissolution of power continued when German princes divided their territories among their

heirs while free cities and local lords strove to shake off the princes' rule. Only in the eastern regions of the empire were the rulers of Bavaria, Austria, and Brandenburg-Prussia able to strengthen their authority, mostly by supporting the efforts of the nobility to subject their peasants to serfdom and by conquering and colonizing new territories on their eastern frontiers.

In northern and central Italy, the last half of the fourteenth century was also marked by incessant conflict. With the papacy based in Avignon, the Papal States collapsed and Rome itself was riven by factional violence. Warfare among northern city-states added to the chaos. But around 1400, Venice, Milan, and Florence succeeded in stabilizing their differing forms of government. Venice was now ruled by an oligarchy of merchants; Milan by a family of despots; and Florence was a nominal republic dominated by the influence of a few wealthy clans, especially the Medici banking family. These three cities then began to expand their influence by subordinating other cities to their rule.

Eventually, almost all the towns of northern Italy were allied with one of these powers. An exception was Genoa, which had its own trading empire in the Mediterranean and Atlantic (see Chapter 10). The papacy, meanwhile, reasserted its control over central Italy when it was restored to Rome in 1377. The southern kingdom of Naples and Sicily persisted as a separate entity, though one riven by local warfare and poor government. Diplomacy and frequently shifting alliances did little to check the ambitions of any one state for further expansion, and it could not change the fact that none of these small-scale states could oppose the powers surrounded Italy.

The Growth of National Monarchies

In France and England, as well as in smaller kingdoms like Scotland and Portugal, the later Middle Ages saw the emergence of European states more cohesive than any that had existed before. The basic political patterns established in the formative twelfth and thirteenth centuries had made this possible, yet the active construction of a sense of shared identity in these territories was a new phenomenon. Forged by war and fueled by the growing cultural importance of vernacular languages, this fusion produced a new type of political organization: the national monarchy.

The advantages of these national monarchies when compared to older forms of political organization would become very evident. When the armies of France invaded the Italian peninsula at the end of the fifteenth century, neither the militias of the city-states nor the far-flung resources of Venice were a match for them. Germany and the Low Countries would suffer similar invasions and remain battlegrounds for competing armies until the middle of the nineteenth century. But the new national monarchies brought significant disadvantages, too. They guaranteed the prevalence of warfare in Europe as they continued their struggle for sovereignty and territory, and they would eventually transport their rivalry to every corner of the globe.

THE TRIALS OF THE ROMAN CHURCH

The century after the Black Death witnessed the papacy's return to Rome, as well as changes in the Church that would have far-reaching consequences.

The Great Western Schism

Calls for the papacy's return to Rome grew more insistent after the Black Death. Its return was eventually catalyzed by the letter-writing campaign of Catherine of Siena (1347–1380), a nun and influential mystic whose teasing but pious missives to Gregory XI (r. 1370–78) alternately shamed and coerced him into making the move.

But the papacy's restoration was short lived. Gregory died a year after his return to Rome, in 1377. His cardinals—many of them Frenchmen—struggled to interpret the wishes of the volatile Romans, and they would later claim to have capitulated to the Roman mob when they elected an Italian candidate, Urban VI. When Urban fell out with them soon afterward, the cardinals fled the city and, from a safe distance, declared his election invalid. They then elected a new pope, a Frenchman who took the name Clement VII. Urban retaliated by naming a new and entirely Italian College of Cardinals. The French pope and his cardinals withdrew ignominiously to the papal palace in Avignon, while the Italian pope remained in Rome.

The resulting rift is known as the Great Schism, or the Great Western Schism (to distinguish it from the ongoing schism between the Roman and Orthodox Churches). Between 1378 and 1417, the Roman Church was divided between two (and, ultimately, three) competing papacies, each claiming to be legitimate and each denouncing the heresy of the others. Europe's religious allegiances fractured along political lines: France and her allies Scotland, Castile, Aragon, and Naples recognized the pope in Avignon, whereas England, Germany, northern Italy, Scandinavia, Bohemia, Poland, and Hungary recognized the Roman pope. Nor was there any obvious way to end this embarrassing state of affairs. Finally, in 1409, some cardinals from both camps met at Pisa, where they declared the deposition of both popes and named a new one from among their number. But neither of the popes reigning in Rome and Avignon accepted that decision, so there were now three rival popes instead of two.

The Council of Constance and the Failure of the Conciliar Movement

This debacle was ultimately addressed between 1414 and 1418 at the Council of Constance, a city in southern Germany: it was the largest ecclesiastical gathering

Competing Viewpoints

Council or Pope?

The Great Schism spurred a fundamental and far-reaching debate about the nature of authority within the Church. Arguments for papal supremacy rested on traditional claims that the popes were the successors of Saint Peter, to whom Jesus Christ had delegated his own authority. Arguments for the supremacy of a general council had been advanced by many intellectuals throughout the fourteenth century, but it was only in the circumstances of the schism that these arguments found a wide audience. The following documents trace the history of the controversy, from the declaration of conciliar supremacy at the Council of Constance (Haec Sancta Synodus), *to the council's efforts to guarantee regular meetings of general councils thereafter* (Frequens), *to the papal condemnation of appeals to the authority of general councils issued in 1460* (Execrabilis).

Haec Sancta Synodus (1415)

This holy synod of Constance . . . declares that being lawfully assembled in the Holy Spirit, constituting a general council and representing the Catholic Church Militant, it has its power directly from Christ, and that all persons of whatever rank or dignity, even a Pope, are bound to obey it in matters relating to faith and the end of the Schism and the general reformation of the church of God in head and members.

Further, it declares that any person of whatever position, rank, or dignity, even a Pope, who contumaciously refuses to obey the mandates, statutes, ordinances, or regulations enacted or to be enacted by this holy synod, or by any other general council lawfully assembled, relating to the matters aforesaid or to other matters involved with them, shall, unless he repents, be . . . duly punished. . . .

Source: R. L. Loomis, ed. and trans., *The Council of Constance* (New York: 1961), p. 229.

Frequens (1417)

The frequent holding of general councils is the best method of cultivating the field of the Lord, for they root out the briars, thorns, and thistles of heresies, errors, and schisms, correct abuses, make crooked things straight, and prepare the Lord's vineyard for fruitfulness and rich fertility. Neglect of general councils sows the seeds of these evils and encourages their growth. This truth is borne in upon us as we recall times past and survey the present.

Therefore by perpetual edict we . . . ordain that henceforth general councils shall be held as follows: the first within the five years immediately following the end of the present council, the second within seven years from the end of the council next after this, and subsequently

---

since the Council of Nicea, over a thousand years earlier (see Chapter 6). Its chief mission was to remove all rival claimants for papal office before electing a new pope. But many of the council's delegates had even more far-reaching plans for the reform of the Church, ambitions that stemmed from the legal doctrine that gave the council power to depose and elect popes in the first place.

This doctrine, known as conciliarism, holds that supreme authority within the Church rests not with the pope but with a representative general council: not just the council at Constance but any future council. The delegates at Constance decreed that general councils should meet

regularly to oversee the governance of the Church, and to act as a check on papal power.

Had conciliarism triumphed, the Reformation of the following century might not have occurred. But, predictably, the newly elected pope Martin V did everything he could to undermine this doctrine. When the next general council met at Siena in 1423, Pope Martin duly sent representatives—who then turned around and went back to Rome. (The Council of Constance had specified frequent meetings but had not specified how long they should last.) A lengthy struggle for power ensued between the advocates of papal monarchy and the conciliarists who

306 | CHAPTER 11 *Rebirth and Unrest, 1350–1453*

every ten years forever.... Thus there will always be a certain continuity. Either a council will be in session or one will be expected at the end of a fixed period....

Source: R. L. Loomis, ed. and trans., *The Council of Constance* (New York: 1961), pp. 246–47.

Execrabilis (1460)

An execrable abuse, unheard of in earlier times, has sprung up in our period. Some men, imbued with a spirit of rebellion and moved not by a desire for sound decisions but rather by a desire to escape the punishment for sin, suppose that they can appeal from the Pope, Vicar of Jesus Christ—from the Pope, to whom in the person of blessed Peter it was said, "Feed my sheep" and "whatever you bind on earth will be bound in heaven"—from this Pope to a future council. How harmful this is to the Christian republic, as well as how contrary to canon law, anyone who is not ignorant of the law can understand. For ... who would not consider it ridiculous to appeal to something which does not now exist anywhere nor does anyone know when it will exist? The poor are heavily oppressed by the powerful, offenses remain unpunished, rebellion against the Holy See is encouraged, license for sin is granted, and all ecclesiastical discipline and hierarchical ranking of the Church are turned upside down.

Wishing therefore to expel this deadly poison from the Church of Christ, and concerned with the salvation of the sheep committed to us ... with the counsel and assent of our venerable brothers, the Cardinals of the Holy Roman Church, together with the counsel and assent of all those prelates who have been trained in canon and civil law who follow our Court, and with our own certain knowledge, we condemn appeals of this kind, reject them as erroneous and abominable, and declare them to be completely null and void. And we lay down that from now on, no one should dare ... to make such an appeal from our decisions, be they legal or theological, or from any commands at all from us or our successors....

Source: Reprinted by permission of the publisher from Gabriel Biel, *Defensorium Obedientiae Apostolicae et Alia Documenta*, ed. and trans. Heiko A. Oberman, Daniel E. Zerfoss, and William J. Courtenay (Cambridge, MA: 1968), pp. 224–27. Copyright © 1968 by the President and Fellows of Harvard College.

Questions for Analysis

1. On what grounds does *Haec Sancta Synodus* establish the authority of a council? Why would this be considered a threat to papal power?

2. Why was it considered necessary for councils to meet regularly (*Frequens*)? What might have been the logical consequences of such regular meetings?

3. On what grounds does *Execrabilis* condemn the appeals to future councils that have no specified meeting date? Why would it not have condemned the conciliar movement altogether?

were convened at Basel. Twenty-five years later, in 1449, the Council of Basel dissolved itself—dashing the hopes of those who thought it would lead to an internal reformation of the Church.

Spiritual Challenges

We have noted that the spiritual and social lives of medieval Christians were inextricably intertwined. The parish church stood literally at the center of their lives: churchyards were communal meeting places, and church buildings were a refuge from attack and a gathering place for business. The church's holidays marked the passage of the year, and the church's bells marked the hours of the day. The church was holy, but it was also essential to daily life. Yet, in the wake of the Black Death, when many parishes ceased to exist and many communities were decimated, an increasing number of people were not satisfied with these conventional forms of worship. Many are regarded today as saints, but this was not necessarily the case in their lifetimes. As Joan of Arc's predicament reveals, medieval women found it particularly challenging to find outlets for their piety.

Many therefore internalized their devotional practices or confined them to the domestic sphere—sometimes to the inconvenience of their families and communities. For example, the young Catherine of Siena refused to help support her working-class family; instead, she took over one of the house's two rooms for her own private prayers, confining her parents and a dozen siblings to the remaining room. Juliana of Norwich (1342–1416) withdrew from the world into a small cell built next to her local church, where she spent the rest of her life in prayer and contemplation. Her younger contemporary, the housewife Margery Kempe (c. 1372–c. 1439), resented the fact that she had a husband, several children, and a household to support. In later life, she renounced her duties and devoted her life to performing acts of histrionic piety, which alienated many who came into contact with her.

The extraordinary strength of such individuals could be inspiring, but it could also threaten the Church's control over

THE GREAT SCHISM, 1378–1417. During the Great Western Schism, the various territories of Europe were divided in their allegiances. ▪ *According to the map key, whom were they choosing between?* ▪ *What common interests would have united the supporters of the Avignon pope or of the Roman pope?* ▪ *Why would areas like Portugal and Austria waver in their support?*

religious life. More safely orthodox was the practical mysticism preached by Thomas à Kempis, whose *Imitation of Christ* (c. 1427) taught readers how to appreciate aspects of the divine in their everyday lives. Originally written in Latin, it was quickly translated into many languages and is now more widely read than any other Christian book except the Bible.

Popular Reform Movements

In the kingdoms of England and Bohemia (the modern Czech Republic), some popular religious movements posed serious challenges to papal authority. The key figure in both cases was John Wycliffe (c. 1330–1384), an Oxford

WYCLIFFE'S ENGLISH BIBLE. Although John Wycliffe was not directly responsible for this translation of the Bible, it was made in the later fourteenth century by his followers. Written in the same Middle English vernacular used by Geoffrey Chaucer for his popular works, it was designed to be accessible to lay readers who did not understand Latin. This page shows the beginning of the Gospel of John: "In ye bigynnyng was / ye word & ye word / was at god & god was the word. Yis was in ye bi / gynninge at god, all yingis weren maad bi him. . . ." ▪ *Compare this translation to a modern one. How different (or not) is this version of English?* ▪ *What might have been the impact of this language on readers and listeners in the late fifteenth century?* ▪ *How would translation have helped to further the reforming efforts of Wycliffe and his disciples?*

THE TEACHINGS OF JAN HUS. An eloquent religious reformer, Jan Hus was burned at the stake in 1415 after having been found guilty of heresy at the Council of Constance. This lavishly illustrated booklet of his teachings was published over a century later in his native Bohemia and includes texts in the Czech vernacular and in Latin. ▪ *What does its later publication suggest about the uses to which Hus's image and theology were put during the Protestant Reformation?*

theologian and powerful critic. Wycliffe concluded that the empty sacraments of a debased Church could not save anyone. He therefore urged the English king to confiscate the Church's wealth and to replace corrupt priests and bishops with men who would live by apostolic standards of poverty and piety.

Some of Wycliffe's followers, known to their detractors as Lollards ("mumblers" or "beggars"), went even further, dismissing the sacraments as fraudulent attempts to extort money from the faithful. Lollard preachers also promoted an English translation of the Bible sponsored by Wycliffe himself, to enable direct access to scripture. Wycliffe's teachings played an important role in the Peasants' Revolt of 1381, and the movement was even supported by a number of aristocratic families. But after a failed Lollard uprising in 1414, the movement and its supporters went underground.

In Bohemia and eastern Europe, however, Wycliffe's ideas lived on and struck even deeper roots. They were adopted by Jan Hus (c. 1373–1415), a charismatic teacher at the royal university in Prague. In contrast to the Lollards, Hus emphasized the centrality of the Eucharist. Indeed, he demanded that the laity be allowed to receive both the consecrated bread and the consecrated wine, which was usually reserved for priests. This demand became a rallying cry for the Hussite movement, which was also endorsed by influential nobles.

On behalf of his supporters, Hus traveled to the Council of Constance to urge the Church to undertake sweeping reforms. But rather than giving him a hearing, the other delegates convicted him of heresy and had him burned at the stake. Back home, Hus's supporters raised the banner of open revolt, and the aristocracy took advantage of the situation to seize Church property. Between 1420 and 1424, armed bands of fervent Hussites resoundingly defeated several armies and rallied to pursue goals of religious reform and social justice. In 1434, a more conservative arm of the Hussite movement was able to negotiate a settlement with Church officials. By the terms of this agreement, Bohemians could receive both the bread and wine of the Mass, which effectively separated the Bohemian religious establishment from Rome.

The English and Bohemian movements exhibit striking similarities. Both began in the university and then galvanized popular preaching and social activism. Both called for the clergy to live in simplicity and poverty, and both employed the vernacular (English and Czech) in opposition to the Latin of a "foreign" Church. In all these respects, they

After You Read This Chapter

🐰 Go to **INQUIZITIVE** to see what you've learned—and learn what you've missed— with personalized feedback along the way.

REVIEWING THE OBJECTIVES

- The Black Death had short-term and long-term effects on the economy and societies of Europe. What were some of the most important changes?
- The later "Middle Ages" and "the Renaissance" are often perceived to be two different periods, but the latter was actually part of the former. Explain why.
- What were some of the intellectual, cultural, and artistic innovations of this era in Italy and elsewhere in Europe?
- How were some European kingdoms becoming stronger and more centralized during this period? What are some examples of national monarchies?
- The conciliar movement sought to limit the power of the papacy. How? Why was this movement unsuccessful?

anticipated the much larger movement of the Protestant Reformation (see Chapter 13).

CONCLUSION

The century after the Black Death was a period of tremendous creativity and revolutionary change. The effects of the plague were catastrophic, but the resulting food surpluses and opportunities encouraged experimentation and opened up broad avenues for advancement. Europe's economy diversified and expanded; increasing wealth and access to education produced new forms of art and new ways of looking at the world. Women were still excluded from formal schooling but nevertheless became active—and in many cases dominant—participants in literary endeavors, cultural life, and religious movements. Average men and women not only became more active in cultivating their own worldly goals, they also took control of their spiritual destinies at a time when the institutional Church provided little leadership.

Meanwhile, some states were growing stronger while the rise of the Ottoman Empire absorbed the venerable Muslim caliphate at Baghdad, the western portions of the former Mongol Empire, and—above all—the surviving core of the eastern Roman Empire. Greek-speaking refugees streamed into Italy, many bringing with them classics of ancient Greek literature little known in Europe. Fueled by a fervid nostalgia for the past, Italians began to experiment with new ways of reading ancient texts, advocating a return to classical models while at the same time trying to counter the political and artistic authority of the more powerful kingdoms north of the Alps.

In contrast to Italy, these emerging national monarchies cultivated a common identity through the promotion of a shared vernacular language and allegiance to a more centralized state. These tactics would allow initially smaller kingdoms like Poland and Scotland to increase their territories and influence, and would also lead France and England into an epic battle for sovereignty and hegemony. The result, in all cases, was the escalation of armed conflict made possible by new technologies and more effective administration.

The generations who survived the calamities of famine, plague, and warfare seized the opportunities their new world presented to them, and they stood on the verge of an extraordinary period of global expansion.

PEOPLE, IDEAS, AND EVENTS IN CONTEXT

- Compare and contrast the **BLACK DEATH**'s effects on rural and urban areas.
- In what ways do rebellions like the **ENGLISH PEASANTS' REVOLT** reflect the changes brought about by the plague?
- How do the works of **GIOVANNI BOCCACCIO, GEOFFREY CHAUCER**, and **CHRISTINE DE PISAN** exemplify the culture of this era?
- What was **HUMANISM**? How was it related to the artistic and intellectual movement known as the **RENAISSANCE**?
- How did the **OTTOMAN EMPIRE** come to power? What were some consequences of its rise?
- On what grounds did **MUSCOVY** claim to be "the third Rome"? What is the significance of the title **TSAR**?
- What new military technologies were in use during the **HUNDRED YEARS' WAR**? How did this conflict affect other parts of Europe, beyond England and France? What role did **JOAN OF ARC** play?
- How did the **COUNCIL OF CONSTANCE** respond to the crisis of the **GREAT SCHISM**?
- Why did **CONCILIARISM** fail? How did **JOHN WYCLIFFE** and **JAN HUS** seek to reform the Church?

THINKING ABOUT CONNECTIONS

- In the year 2000, a group of historians was asked to identify the most significant historical figure of the past millennium. Rather than selecting a person (e.g., Martin Luther, Shakespeare, Napoleon, Adolf Hitler), they chose the microbe *Yersinia pestis*, the cause of the Black Death. Do you agree with this assessment? Why or why not?
- In your view, which was more crucial to the formation of the modern state: the political and legal developments we surveyed in Chapter 9 or the emergence of national monarchies discussed in this chapter? Why?
- Was the conciliar movement doomed to failure, given what we have learned about the history of the Roman Church? How far back does one need to go in order to trace the development of disputes over ecclesiastical governance?

STORY LINES

- The invention of the printing press accelerated the dissemination of information, including reports on the riches of the New World.

- Competition for power in Italy led to increased violence and to the increase of artistic patronage, providing opportunities to a new breed of Renaissance men.

- The humanist approach to education that had developed in Italy spread to other parts of Europe, influencing new approaches to biblical scholarship and political philosophies.

- Spain, the newest and most powerful European state, completed its "reconquest" of the Iberian Peninsula in 1492 and then looked to counter the successful colonial ventures of the Portuguese, which led, in turn, to the early beginnings of a Spanish empire in the Americas.

Before
You
Read
This
Chapter

CHRONOLOGY

1454–1455	Gutenberg's Bible completed
1488	Bartolomeu Dias rounds the Cape of Good Hope (Africa)
1492	Christopher Columbus embarks on his first transatlantic voyage
1494	The Treaty of Tordesillas divides the undiscovered world into Spanish and Portuguese hemispheres
1498	Vasco da Gama reaches India
1511	Portuguese ventures to Indonesia
1512	Michelangelo completes his painting of the Sistine Chapel's ceiling
1513	Niccolò Machiavelli's *The Prince* completed
	Vasco Núñez de Balboa reaches the Pacific Ocean
1516	Thomas More publishes *Utopia*
1519–1521	Aztec wars enable Cortés's conquest of Mexico
1519–1522	Magellan's fleet circumnavigates the globe
1531–1533	Pizarro's conquest of the Inca Empire

Innovation and Exploration, 1453–1533

CORE OBJECTIVES

- **UNDERSTAND** the relationship between Renaissance ideals and the political and economic realities of Italy.

- **IDENTIFY** the key characteristics of Renaissance arts and learning during this period, and **EXPLAIN** their significance.

- **DEFINE** the term *Reconquista* and its meaning in Spain.

- **DESCRIBE** the methods and motives of European colonization during this period.

- **EXPLAIN** why Europeans were able to dominate the peoples of the New World.

What if exact copies of an idea could circulate quickly, all over the world? What if the same could be done for the latest news, the oldest beliefs, the most beautiful poems, the most exciting—and deadly—discoveries? It would be doing for knowledge what the invention of coinage did for wealth: making it portable, easier to use and disseminate. Indeed, it's no accident that the man who developed such a technology, Johannes Gutenberg of Mainz (c. 1398–1468), was the son of a goldsmith who minted coins for the bishop of that German city. Both technologies were based on the same principle and used the same basic tools. Coins are metal disks stamped with identical words and images, impressed on them with a reusable matrix. The pages of the first printed books were stamped with ink spread on rows of movable type (lead or cast-iron letter forms and punctuation marks) slotted into frames to form lines of words. Once a set of pages was ready, a press could make hundreds of copies in a matter of hours, many hundreds of times faster than the same page could be copied by hand. Afterward, the type could be reused.

A major stimulus for this invention was the more wide-spread availability of paper. Parchment, northern Europe's chief writing material since the advent of the codex (see Chapter 6), was extremely expensive to manufacture and required special training on the part of those who used it—one reason why writing remained a specialized skill for much of the Middle Ages, while the ability to read was common. Paper, made from rags turned into pulp by mills, was both cheaper and far easier to use; accordingly, books became cheaper and written communication easier. Growing demand for books, in turn, led to experimentation with different methods of book production—and so to Gutenberg's breakthrough. By 1455, his workshop had printed multiple copies of the Latin Bible, of which forty-eight complete or partial volumes survive today. Although printing never entirely replaced traditional modes of publication via manuscript, it revolutionized the spread of information.

The printing press played a crucial role in many of the developments we study in this chapter. The artistic and intellectual experiments of the Italian Renaissance were rapidly exported to other parts of Europe; specifications for new weapons would be printed on the same presses that churned out humanist literature. News of Columbus's first voyage would spread via the same media as critiques of European imperialism. Printing not only increased the amount and rapidity of publication, it also made it more difficult for those in power to censor dissenting opinions.

But at the same time, the printing press also became an indispensable tool of power, making it possible for rulers to govern growing empires and increasingly centralized states. The "reconquest" of Spain and the extension of Spanish imperialism to the New World were both facilitated by the circulation of printed propaganda. The widespread availability of reading materials even helped to standardize national languages, by enabling governments to promote one official printed dialect over others. Hence the "king's English," the variety of the language spoken around London, was imposed as the only acceptable literary and bureaucratic language throughout the English realm. For these reasons, among others, many historians consider the advent of print to be both the defining event and the driving engine of modernity, and it coincided with another essentially modern development: the discovery of a "New World."

RENAISSANCE IDEALS— AND REALITIES

The intellectual and artistic movement that had begun in Italy during the fourteenth century (Chapter 11) was characterized by an intense interest in the classics and by a new type of curriculum: humanism. These Renaissance ideals—and the realities that under-girded them—were extended through the medium of the printing press. By the time the Ottoman conquest of Constantinople was complete, just a year before Gutenberg's Bible, hundreds of refugees from the eastern Roman Empire had been propelled into Italy. Many carried with them precious manuscripts of Greek texts: the epics of Homer, the works of Athenian dramatists, the dialogues of Plato. Prior to the invention of print, such manuscripts could be owned and studied by only a very few, very privileged men. Now printers in Venice and other European cities rushed to produce cheap editions, as well as Greek grammars and glossaries that could facilitate reading them.

In Florence, an informal "Platonic Academy" was convened. There, the work of intellectuals like Marsilio Ficino (1433–1499) and Giovanni Pico della Mirandola (1463–1494) was fostered by the patronage of the wealthy Cosimo de' Medici. Based on his reading of Plato, Ficino's philosophy moved away from the focus on civic life that had been such a feature of earlier humanist thought. He taught instead that the individual should look to free the immortal soul from its "always miserable" mortal body: a Platonic ideal compatible with much late-medieval piety. Ficino's great achievement was his translation of Plato's works into Latin. His disciple Pico also rejected the everyday world of public affairs, arguing that man (but not woman) can aspire to union with God through the exercise of his unique talents.

The Politics of Italy and the Philosophy of Machiavelli

Not all Florentines were galvanized by Platonic ideals, though. Indeed, the most influential philosopher of this era was a thoroughgoing realist who spent more time studying Roman history: Niccolò Machiavelli (1469–1527). Machiavelli's political writings reflect the unstable political situation of his home city as well as his wider aspirations for a unified Italy. We have observed that Italy had been in political disarray for centuries, a situation exacerbated by the "Babylonian Captivity" of the papacy and the controversies raging after its return to Rome (see Chapters 10 and 11). Now Italy was becoming the arena in which bloody international struggles were being played out. The monarchs of France and Spain both had imperial ambitions, and both claimed to be the rightful champions of the papacy. Both sent

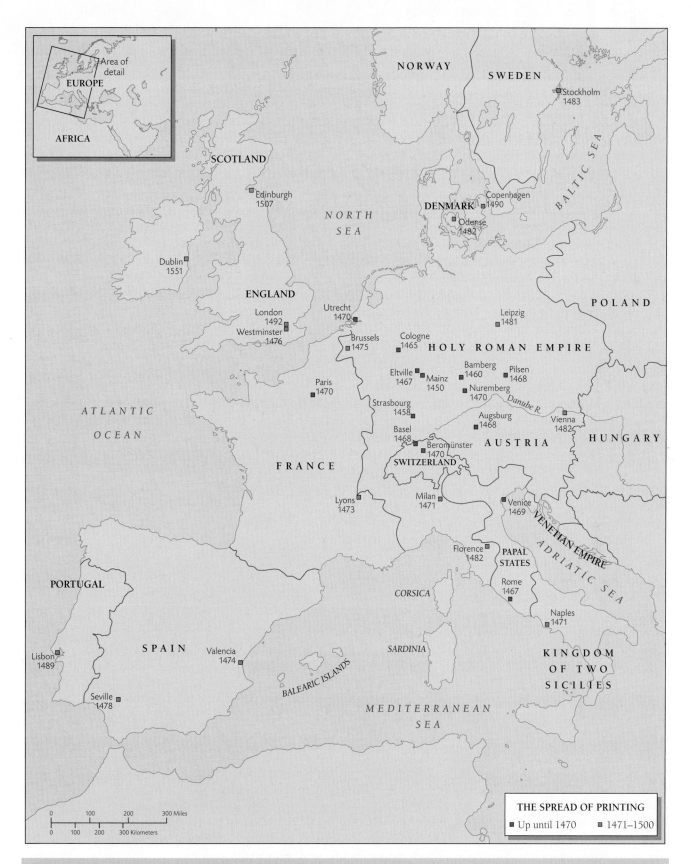

THE SPREAD OF PRINTING. This map shows how quickly the technology of printing spread throughout Europe between 1470 and 1500.
• *In what regions were printing presses most heavily concentrated?* • *What factors would have led to their proliferation in the Low Countries, northern Italy, and Germany—as compared to France, Spain, and England?*

Competing Viewpoints

Printing, Patriotism, and the Past

The printing press helped to create new communities of readers by standardizing national languages and even promoting patriotism. And while it enabled authors of new works to reach larger audiences, it also allowed printers to popularize older writings that had previously circulated in manuscript. The two sources presented here exemplify two aspects of this trend. The first is the preface to a version of the legend of King Arthur, which was originally written by an English soldier, Sir Thomas Malory, who completed it in 1470. It was printed for the first time in 1485, and it quickly became a best seller. The author of this preface was also the printer, William Caxton of London, who specialized in publishing books that glorified England's history and heritage. The second excerpt is from the concluding chapter of Machiavelli's treatise The Prince. *Like the book itself, these remarks were originally addressed to Lorenzo de' Medici, head of Florence's most powerful family. But when* The Prince *was printed in 1532, five years after Machiavelli's death, the author's passionate denunciation of foreign "barbarians" and his lament for Italy's lost glory would have resonated with a wider Italian-speaking public.*

William Caxton's preface to Thomas Malory's *Le Morte d'Arthur* ("The Death of Arthur"), 1485

After I had accomplished and finished diverse histories, both of contemplation and of other historical and worldly acts of great conquerors and princes, . . . many noble and diverse gentlemen of this realm of England came and demanded why I had not made and imprinted the noble history of the Holy Grail, and of the most renowned Christian king and worthy, King Arthur, which ought most to be remembered among us Englishmen before all other Christian kings. . . . The said noble gentlemen instantly required me to imprint the history of the said noble king and conqueror King Arthur, and of his knights, with the history of the Holy Grail . . . considering that he was a man born within this realm, and king and emperor of the same: and that there be, in French, diverse and many noble volumes of his acts, and also of his knights. To whom I answered that diverse men hold opinion that there was no such Arthur, and that all such books as have been made of him be feigned and fables, because some chronicles make of him no mention. . . . Whereto they answered, and one in

special said, that in him that should say or think that there was never such a king called Arthur might well be accounted great folly and blindness. . . . For in all places, Christian and heathen, he is reputed and taken for one of the Nine Worthies, and the first of the three Christian men. And also, he is more spoken of beyond the sea, and there are more books made of his noble acts than there be in England, as well in Dutch, Italian, Spanish, and Greek, as in French. . . . Wherefore it is a marvel why he is no more renowned in his own country. . . .

Then all these things aforesaid alleged, I could not well deny but that there was such a noble king named Arthur, reputed one of the Nine Worthies, and first and chief of the Christian men. And many noble volumes be made of him and of his noble knights in French, which I have seen and read beyond the sea, which be not had in our maternal tongue. . . . Wherefore, among all such [manuscript] books as have late been drawn out briefly into English I have . . . undertaken to imprint a book of the noble histories of the said King

Arthur, and of certain of his knights, after a copy unto me delivered—which copy Sir Thomas Malory did take out of certain books of French, and reduced it into English. And I, according to my copy, have done set it in print, to the intent that noble men may see and learn the noble acts of chivalry, the gentle and virtuous deeds that some knights used in those days, by which they came to honor, and how they that were vicious were punished and oft put to shame and rebuke; humbly beseeching all noble lords and ladies (with all other estates of what estate or degree they be) that shall see and read in this said book and work, that they take the good and honest acts to their remembrance, and follow the same. . . . For herein may be seen noble chivalry, courtesy, humanity, friendliness, hardiness, love, friendship, cowardice, murder, hate, virtue, and sin. Do after the good and leave the evil, and it shall bring you to good fame and renown.

Source: Sir Thomas Malory, *Le Morte d'Arthur* (London: 1485), (text and spelling slightly modernized).

From the conclusion of Niccolò Machiavelli's *The Prince* (completed 1513, printed 1533)

Reflecting on the matters set forth above and considering within myself where the times were propitious in Italy at present to honor a new prince and whether there is at hand the matter suitable for a prudent and virtuous leader to mold in a new form, giving honor to himself and benefit to the citizens of the country, I have arrived at the opinion that all circumstances now favor such a prince, and I cannot think of a time more propitious for him than the present. If, as I said, it was necessary in order to make apparent the virtue of Moses, that the people of Israel should be enslaved in Egypt, and that the Persians should be oppressed by the Medes to provide an opportunity to illustrate the greatness and the spirit of Cyrus, and that the Athenians should be scattered in order to show the excellence of Theseus, thus at the present time, in order to reveal the valor of an Italian spirit, it was essential that Italy should fall to her present low estate, more enslaved than the Hebrews, more servile than the Persians, more disunited than the Athenians, leaderless and lawless, beaten, despoiled, lacerated, overrun and crushed under every kind of misfortune. . . . So Italy now, left almost lifeless, awaits the coming of one who will heal her wounds, putting an end to the sacking and looting in Lombardy and the spoliation and extortions in the Realm of Naples and Tuscany, and cleanse her sores that have been so long festering. Behold how she prays God to send her someone to redeem her from the cruelty and insolence of the barbarians. See how she is ready and willing to follow any banner so long as there be someone to take it up. Nor has she at present any hope of finding her redeemer save only in your illustrious house [the Medici] which has been so highly exalted both by its own merits and by fortune and which has been favored by God and the church, of which it is now ruler. . . .

This opportunity, therefore, should not be allowed to pass, and Italy, after such a long wait, must be allowed to behold her redeemer. I cannot describe the joy with which he will be received in all these provinces which have suffered so much from the foreign deluge, nor with what thirst for vengeance, nor with what firm devotion, what solemn delight, what tears! What gates could be closed to him, what people could deny him obedience, what envy could withstand him, what Italian could withhold allegiance from him? THIS BARBARIAN OCCUPATION STINKS IN THE NOSTRILS OF ALL OF US. Let your illustrious house then take up this cause with the spirit and the hope with which one undertakes a truly just enterprise. . . .

Source: Niccolò Machiavelli, *The Prince*, ed. and trans. Thomas G. Bergin (Arlington Heights, IL: 1947), pp. 75–76, 78.

Questions for Analysis

1. What do these two sources reveal about the relationship between patriotism and the awareness of a nation's past? Why do you think that Caxton looks back to a legendary medieval king, whereas Machiavelli's references are all to ancient examples? What do both excerpts reveal about the value placed on history in the popular imagination?

2. How does Caxton describe the process of printing a book? What larger conclusions can we draw from this about the market for printed books in general?

3. Why might Machiavelli's treatise have been made available in a printed version, nearly twenty years after its original appearance in manuscript? How might his new audience have responded to its message?

invading armies into the peninsula while they competed for the allegiance of the various city-states, which were torn by internal dissension.

In 1498, Machiavelli became a prominent official in the government of a new Florentine republic, set up when a French invasion had led to the expulsion of the ruling Medici family. His duties largely involved diplomatic missions to other city-states. While in Rome, he became fascinated with the attempt of Cesare Borgia, son of Pope Alexander VI, to create his own principality in central Italy. He noted Cesare's ruthlessness and his complete subordination of personal ethics to political

ends. He remembered this example in 1512, when the Medici returned to overthrow the Florentine republic and Machiavelli was imprisoned, tortured, and exiled. He now devoted his energies to the articulation of a political philosophy suited to the times and to the family that had ousted him.

On the surface, Machiavelli's two great works of political analysis appear to contradict each other. In his *Discourses on Livy*, which drew on the works of that Roman historian (see Chapter 5), he praised the ancient Roman Republic as a model for his own time. There is little doubt that Machiavelli was a committed believer in the free city-state as the ideal form of human government. But Machiavelli also wrote *The Prince*, "a handbook for tyrants" in the eyes of his critics, and he dedicated this work to Lorenzo, son of Piero de' Medici, his old enemy.

Because *The Prince* has been so much more widely read than *Discourses*, it has often been interpreted as an endorsement of power for its own sake. Machiavelli's real position was quite different. In the political chaos of early-sixteenth-century Italy, he saw the likes of Cesare Borgia as the only hope for making Italy fit, eventually, for independence. Machiavelli never ceased to hope that his contemporaries would rise up, expel the French and Spanish occupying forces, and restore ancient traditions of liberty and equality. He regarded a period of despotism as a necessary step toward that end.

Yet Machiavelli continues to be a controversial figure. Some modern scholars represent him as amoral, interested solely in power. Others see him as an Italian patriot. Still others see him as a realist influenced by Saint Augustine (see Chapter 6), who understood that a ruler's good intentions do not guarantee good policies or results. Machiavelli argued that "the necessity of preserving the state will often compel a prince to take actions which are opposed to loyalty, charity, humanity, and religion." As we shall see in later chapters, many subsequent political philosophers would go even further: arguing that the preservation of the

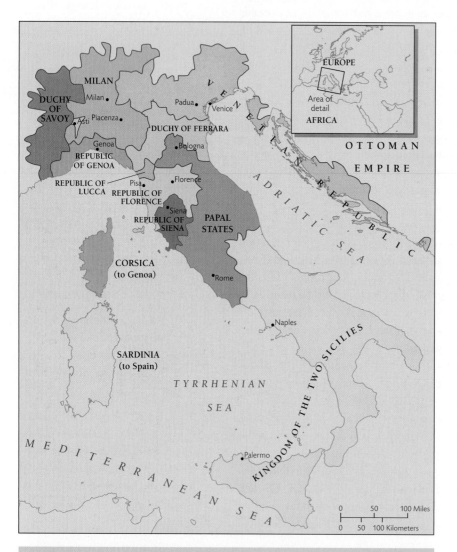

THE STATES OF ITALY, c. 1494. This map shows the divisions of Italy on the eve of the French invasion in 1494. Contemporary observers often described Italy as being divided among five great powers: Milan, Venice, Florence, the Papal States, and the united Kingdoms of Naples and Sicily. ▪ *Which of these powers would have been most capable of expanding their territories?* ▪ *Which neighboring states would have been most threatened by such attempts at expansion?* ▪ *Why would Florence and the Papal States so often find themselves in conflict with each other?*

state does indeed warrant the exercise of absolute power (see Chapters 14 and 15).

The Ideal of the Courtier

Machiavelli's political theories were informed by years of diplomatic service, and so was his engaging literary style. Indeed, he never abandoned his interest in the literary arts of the court and continued to write poems, plays, and adaptations of classical comedies. In this he resembled another poet-courtier, Ludovico Ariosto (1474–1533), who undertook diplomatic missions for the Duke of Ferrara and some of Rome's most powerful prelates. His lengthy verse narrative, *Orlando Furioso* ("The Madness of Roland"), was a comic retelling of the heroic exploits celebrated in the French *Song of Roland* (see Chapter 8)—but without the heroism. Although very different in form and tone from *The Prince*, it shared that work's skepticism of chivalric ideals. Instead, it sought to charm an audience that worshiped pleasure and beauty.

Thus a new Renaissance ideal was born, one that promoted the arts of pleasing the powerful princes who employed clever men like Machiavelli and Ariosto: the ideal of the courtier. This ideal was embodied by their contemporary, the diplomat and nobleman Baldassare Castiglione (*cah-stee-lee-OH-nay,* 1478–1529), who wrote a manual for those who wished to acquire these skills. If *The Prince* was a forerunner of modern self-help books, *The Book of the Courtier* was an early handbook of etiquette; and both stand in sharp contrast to the treatises on public virtue composed in the previous century, which taught the sober virtues of strenuous service on behalf of the city-state. Instead, Castiglione taught how to attain the elegant and seemingly effortless skills necessary for personal advancement.

Castiglione articulated and popularized the set of talents still associated with the "Renaissance man": accomplished, witty, cultured, and stylish. But in many ways, this new ideal actually represents a *rejection* of the older ideals associated with the rebirth of classical education for public men. Castiglione even rejected the misogyny of the humanists by stressing the ways in which ladies could rise to influence and prominence. Widely read throughout Europe, his *Courtier* set the standard for polite behavior until the early twentieth century.

The Dilemma of the Artist

Without question, the most enduring legacy of the Italian Renaissance has been the contributions of its artists. We have already noted (Chapter 11) the creative and economic opportunities afforded by painting on canvas or wood, which freed artists from having to work on site and on commission: such paintings are portable and can be displayed in different settings and reach different markets. We also saw that the use of oil paints, pioneered in Flanders, further revolutionized painting styles. To these benefits, the artists of Italy added an important technical ingredient: mastery of a vanishing (one-point) perspective that gave painting an illusion of three-dimensional space. They also experimented with effects of light and shade, and studied intently the anatomy and proportions of the human body. These techniques also influenced sculptors.

Behind all of the beautiful artworks created in this era—which led to the glorification of the artist as a new type of hero—lie the harsh political and economic realities within which these artists worked. Increasing private wealth and the growth of lay patronage opened up new markets and created a huge demand for buildings and objects that could increase the prestige of ambitious men. Portraiture was a direct result of this trend, since princes and merchants alike sought to glorify themselves and their families, and to compete with their neighbors and rivals.

THE IMPACT OF PERSPECTIVE. Masaccio's painting *The Trinity with the Virgin* illustrates the startling sense of depth made possible by observing the rules of one-point perspective.

An artist therefore had to study the techniques of the courtier as well as the new artistic techniques in order to succeed in winning a patron. He also had to be ready to perform other services: overseeing the building and decoration of palaces; designing tableware, furniture, fanciful liveries for servants and soldiers; and even decorating guns. Some artists, like Leonardo da Vinci, were prized as much for their capacity to invent deadly weapons as for their artworks.

New Illusions and the Career of Leonardo

For much of the fifteenth century, the majority of the great painters were Florentines who followed in the footsteps of the precocious Masaccio (1401–1428), who had died prematurely at the age of twenty-seven. His lasting legacy was the pioneering use of one-point perspective and dramatic lighting effects. Both are evident in his painting of the Trinity, where the body of the crucified Christ appears to be thrust forward by the impassive figure of God the Father, while the Virgin's gaze directly engages the viewer. Masaccio's

most obvious successor was Sandro Botticelli (1445–1510), who excelled in depicting graceful motion and the sensuous pleasures of nature.

The most adventurous and versatile artist of this period was Leonardo da Vinci (1452–1519). Leonardo personifies a Renaissance ideal: he was a painter, architect, musician, mathematician, engineer, and inventor. The illegitimate son of a notary, he set up an artist's shop in Florence by the time he was twenty-five and gained the patronage of the Medici ruler, Lorenzo the Magnificent. Yet Leonardo had a weakness: he worked slowly, and he had difficulty finishing anything. This naturally displeased Lorenzo and other Florentine patrons, who regarded artists as craftsmen who worked on their patrons' time—not their own. Leonardo, however, strongly objected to this view; he considered himself to be an inspired, independent innovator. He therefore left Florence in 1482 and went to work for the Sforza dictators of Milan, whose favor he courted by emphasizing his skills as a maker of bombs, heavy ordinance, and siege engines. He remained there until the French invasion of 1499; he then wandered about, finally accepting the patronage of the French king, under whose auspices he lived and worked until his death.

THE BIRTH OF VENUS. This painting was executed by Sandro Botticelli in Florence, and represents the artist's imaginative treatment of stories from ancient mythology. Here, he depicts the moment when Aphrodite, goddess of love, was spontaneously engendered from the foam of the sea by Chronos, the god of time.

Leonardo da Vinci Applies for a Job

Few sources illuminate the tensions between Renaissance ideals and realities better than the résumé of accomplishments submitted by Leonardo da Vinci to a prospective employer, Ludovico Sforza of Milan. In the following letter, Leonardo explains why he deserves to be appointed chief architect and military engineer in the duke's household administration. He got the job and moved to Milan in 1481.

1. I have the kind of bridges that are extremely light and strong, made to be carried with great ease, and with them you may pursue, and, at any time, flee from the enemy; . . . and also methods of burning and destroying those of the enemy.

2. I know how, when a place is under attack, to eliminate the water from the trenches, and make endless variety of bridges . . . and other machines. . . .

3. . . . I have methods for destroying every rock or other fortress, even if it were built on rock, etc.

4. I also have other kinds of mortars [bombs] that are most convenient and easy to carry. . . .

5. And if it should be a sea battle, I have many kinds of machines that are most efficient for offense and defense. . . .

6. I also have means that are noiseless to reach a designated area by secret and tortuous mines. . . .

7. I will make covered chariots, safe and unattackable, which can penetrate the enemy with their artillery. . . .

8. In case of need I will make big guns, mortars, and light ordnance of fine and useful forms that are out of the ordinary.

9. If the operation of bombardment should fail, I would contrive catapults, mangonels, trabocchi [trebuchets], and other machines of marvelous efficacy and unusualness. In short, I can, according to each case in question, contrive various and endless means of offense and defense.

10. In time of peace I believe I can give perfect satisfaction that is equal to any other in the field of architecture and the construction of buildings. . . . I can execute sculpture in marble, bronze, or clay, and also in painting I do the best that can be done, and as well as any other, whoever he may be.

Having now, most illustrious Lord, sufficiently seen the specimens of all those who consider themselves master craftsmen of instruments of war, and that the invention and operation of such instruments are no different from those in common use, I shall now endeavor . . . to explain myself to your Excellency by revealing to your Lordship my secrets. . . .

Source: Excerpted from Leonardo da Vinci, *The Notebooks,* in *The Italian Renaissance Reader,* ed. Julia Conaway and Mark Mosa (Harmondsworth, UK: 1987), pp. 195–96.

Questions for Analysis

1. Based on the qualifications highlighted by Leonardo in this letter, what can you conclude about the political situation in Milan and the priorities of its duke? What can you conclude about the state of military technologies in this period and the conduct of warfare?

2. What do you make of the fact that Leonardo mentions his artistic endeavors only at the end of the letter? Does this fact alter your opinion or impression of him? Why or why not?

Paradoxically, considering his skill in fashioning weapons, Leonardo was convinced of the essential divinity of all living things. He was a vegetarian—unusual at the time—and when he went to the marketplace to buy caged birds he released them to their native habitat when he had finished observing them. His approach to painting was that it should be the most accurate possible imitation of nature. He made careful studies: blades of grass, cloud formations, a waterfall. He obtained human corpses for dissection and reconstructed in drawing the minutest features of anatomy,

THE LAST SUPPER. This fresco on the refectory wall of the monastery of Santa Maria delle Grazie in Milan is a testament to both the powers and limitations of Leonardo's artistry. It skillfully employs the techniques of one-point perspective to create the illusion that Jesus and his disciples are actually dining at the monastery's head table; but because Leonardo had not mastered the techniques of fresco painting, he applied tempera pigments to a dry wall that had been coated with a sealing agent. As a result, the painting's colors began to fade just years after its completion. By the middle of the sixteenth century, it had seriously deteriorated. Large portions of it are now invisible.

carrying this knowledge over to his paintings. In *The Last Supper*, painted on the refectory walls of a monastery in Milan (and now in an advanced state of decay), he also displayed his keen studies of human psychology. In this image, a serene Christ has just announced to his disciples that one will betray him. The artist captures the mingled emotions of surprise, horror, and guilt on their faces as they gradually perceive the meaning of this. He also implicates the painting's viewers in this dramatic scene, since they too dined with Christ, in the very same room.

Renaissance Arts in Venice and Rome

By the end of the fifteenth century, Florentine artists had influenced a group of painters active in the wealthy city of Venice. Among them was Tiziano Vecellio, better known as Titian (c. 1490–1576). Many of Titian's paintings evoke the luxurious, pleasure-loving life of this thriving commercial center; for although they copied Florentine techniques, most Venetian painters showed little of that city's concerns for philosophical or religious allegory. They catered to patrons who wanted sumptuous portraits of the rich and powerful (see the portrait on page 347).

Rome, too, became a major artistic center in this era and a place where the Florentine school exerted a more potent influence. Among its eminent painters was Raffaello Sanzio (1483–1520), or Raphael. As we noted in Chapter 4, his fresco *The School of Athens* depicts

both the harmony and the differences of Platonic and Aristotelian thought (see page 90). It also includes a number of Raphael's contemporaries as models. The image of Plato is actually a portrait of Leonardo, while the architect Donato Bramante (c. 1444–1514) stands in for the geometer Euclid, and Michelangelo for the philosopher Heraclitus.

Michelangelo Buonarroti (1475–1564), who spent many decades in Rome in the service of the papacy, was another native of Florence. Like Leonardo, he was a polymath: painter, sculptor, architect, poet—and he expressed himself in all these forms with a similar power. At the center of all of his work, as at the center of Renaissance humanism, is the male figure: the embodied masculine mind.

Michelangelo's greatest achievements in painting appear in a single location, the Sistine Chapel of the Vatican palace; yet they are products of two different periods in the artist's life and consequently exemplify two different artistic styles and outlooks on the human condition. More famous are the extraordinary frescoes painted on the ceiling from 1508 to 1512, depicting scenes from the book of Genesis. All the panels in this series, including *The Creation of Adam*, exemplify the young artist's affirm the heroic qualities of humankind. But a quarter of a century later, when Michelangelo returned to work in the Sistine Chapel, both his style and mood had changed dramatically. In the enormous *Last Judgment*, a fresco completed on the chapel's altar wall in 1536, Michelangelo repudiated classical restraint and substituted a style that emphasized tension and distortion: a humanity wracked with fear, guilt, and frailty. He included himself in it—painting a grotesque self-portrait on the flayed skin of Saint Bartholomew, who was martyred by being skinned alive. Perhaps this was a metaphor for the challenges of working for the papal court.

Michelangelo and the Renaissance of Sculpture

Although sculpture was not a new medium for artists, as oil painting was, it too became an important area of Renaissance innovation. For the first time since late antiquity, monumental statues became figures "in the round" rather than sculptural elements incorporated into buildings or featured as effigies on tombs. By freeing sculpture from

SELF-PORTRAIT OF THE ARTIST AS A YOUNG MAN: DETAIL FROM *THE SCHOOL OF ATHENS*. We have already analyzed aspects of Raphael's famous group portrait of the Greek philosophers, with Plato and Aristotle at their center (see page 90). In addition to featuring his own contemporaries as models—including the artists Leonardo, Michelangelo, and the architect Bramante—Raphael put himself in the picture, too. ▪ *What messages does this choice convey?*

its bondage to architecture, the Renaissance reestablished it as a separate art form.

The first great master of Renaissance sculpture was Donatello (c. 1386–1466). His bronze statue of David, triumphant over the head of the slain Goliath, is the first freestanding nude of the period. Yet this *David* is clearly an agile adolescent rather than a muscular Greek athlete like that of Michelangelo's *David*, executed in 1501, as a public expression of Florentine civic life. Michelangelo regarded sculpture as the most exalted of the arts because it allowed the artist to imitate God most fully in re-creating human forms. He also insisted on working in marble—the "noblest" sculptural material—and on creating figures twice as large as life. By sculpting a serenely confident young man at the peak of physical fitness, Michelangelo celebrated the Florentine republic's own determination to resist tyrants and uphold ideals of civic justice.

Renaissance Architecture

To a much greater extent than either sculpture or painting, Renaissance architecture had its roots in the classical past. The Gothic style pioneered in northern France (see Chapter 9) had not found a welcome reception in Italy; most of the buildings constructed there were Romanesque ("Roman-like"), and the great architects influenced by the Renaissance movement generally adopted their building plans from these structures—some of which they believed (mistakenly) to be ancient. They also copied decorative devices from the authentic ruins of ancient Rome. Above all, they derived their influence from the writings of Vitruvius (fl. c. 60–15 B.C.E.), a Roman architect and engineer whose multivolume *On Architecture* was among the humanists' rediscovered ancient texts. The governing principles laid out by Vitruvius were popularized by Leon Battista Alberti in his own book, *On the Art of Building*, which began to circulate in manuscript around 1450.

In keeping with classical models, Renaissance buildings emphasized geometrical proportion. Architectural

THE CREATION OF ADAM. This is one of a series of frescoes painted on the ceiling of the Sistine Chapel of the Vatican palace in Rome, executed by Michelangelo over a period of many years and in circumstances of extreme physical hardship. It has since become an iconic image. ▪ *How might it be said to capture Renaissance ideals?*

THE GRACE AND POWER OF THE MALE BODY. Donatello's *David* (left) was the first freestanding nude executed since antiquity. It shows the Hebrew leader as an adolescent youth and is a little over five feet tall. The *David* by Michelangelo (center) stands thirteen feet high and was placed prominently in front of Florence's city hall to proclaim the city's power and humanistic values. ▪ *How does Michelangelo's representation of David—and the context in which this figure was displayed—compare to that of Donatello?*

ST. PETER'S BASILICA, ROME. This eighteenth-century painting shows the massive interior of the Renaissance building. But were it not for the perspective provided by the tiny human figures, the human eye would be fooled into thinking this a much smaller space.

values were also reinforced by the interest in Platonic philosophy, which taught that certain mathematical ratios reflect the harmony of the universe. For example, the proportions of the human body serve as the basis for the proportions of the quintessential Renaissance building: St. Peter's Basilica in Rome. Designed by some of the most celebrated architects of the time, including Bramante and Michelangelo, it is still one of the largest buildings in the world. Yet it seems smaller than a Gothic cathedral because it is built to mimic human proportions. The same artful proportions are evident in smaller-scale buildings too, as in the aristocratic country houses later designed by the northern Italian architect Andrea Palladio (1508–1580), who created secular miniatures of ancient temples (such as the Roman Pantheon) to glorify the aristocrats who dwelled within them.

THE RENAISSANCE NORTH OF THE ALPS

Despite Italian resentment of encroaching foreign monarchs, contacts between Italy and northern Europe were close throughout this period. Italian merchants and financiers were familiar figures in northern courts and cities; students from all over Europe studied at Italian universities such as Bologna or Padua; northern poets (including Geoffrey Chaucer: see Chapter 11) and their works traveled to and from Italy; and northern soldiers were frequent combatants in Italian wars. Yet only at the very end of the fifteenth century did the innovative artistry and learning of Italy begin to cross the Alps into northern Europe.

A variety of explanations have been offered for this delay. Northern European intellectual life in the later Middle Ages was dominated by universities in Paris, Oxford, Kraków, and Prague, where the curricula focused on the study of philosophical logic, Christian theology, and (to a lesser extent) medicine. In Italy, by contrast, universities were more often professional schools specializing in law and medicine and were more integrally tied to the nonacademic intellectual lives of the cities in which they were situated. As a result, a more secular, urban-oriented educational tradition took shape in Italy, as we saw in our previous discussion of humanism. In northern Europe, by contrast, those scholars who *were* influenced by Italian ideas usually worked outside the university system under the private patronage of kings and princes.

The Reputation of Richard III

England's king Richard III (r. 1483–1485) has been a byword for villainy since the time of his death, when Sir Thomas More and other propagandists working for his successor, Henry VII, alleged that his physically deformed body was matched by the depravity of his actions. For centuries, historians have debated the truth of these claims. Was Richard really a hunchback—and a murderer, too? In 2012, the stunning discovery of Richard's body (under a parking lot near the medieval battlefield where he died) confirmed that he had indeed suffered from severe scoliosis. The other claim has yet to be proven.

Watch related author videos on the Student Site
wwnorton.com/college/history/western-civilizationsBrief4

Before the turn of the sixteenth century, northern rulers were also less committed to patronizing artists and intellectuals than were the city-states and princes of Italy. In Italy, as we have seen, such patronage was an important arena for competition between political rivals. In northern Europe, however, political units were larger and political rivals were fewer. It was therefore less necessary to use art for political purposes—a major exception being the independent duchy of Burgundy, which surpassed even the French court in its magnificence. A statue erected in a central square of Florence would be seen by all the city's residents and visitors. In Paris, such a statue would be seen by only a tiny minority of the French king's subjects. But as royal courts became showcases for royal power, kings needed to impress townspeople, courtiers, and guests—and they consequently relied more on artists and intellectuals to advertise their wealth and taste.

Christian Humanism and the Career of Erasmus

In general, then, the Renaissance movement of northern Europe differed from that of Italy because it grafted certain Italian ideals onto preexisting traditions, rather than sweeping away older forms of knowledge. This can be seen very clearly in the case of the intellectual development known as Christian humanism. Although Christian humanists shared the Italian humanists' scorn for scholasticism's limitations, northern humanists were more committed to seeking ethical guidance from biblical and religious precepts, as well as from Cicero or Virgil. Like their Italian counterparts, they embraced the wisdom of antiquity, but the antiquity they favored was Christian as well as classical—the antiquity of the New Testament and the early Church. Similarly, northern artists were inspired by the accomplishments of Italian masters and copied their techniques, but they depicted classical subjects less frequently and almost never portrayed completely nude human figures.

Any discussion of Christian humanism must begin with the career of Desiderius Erasmus (c. 1469–1536). The illegitimate son of a priest, Erasmus was born near Rotterdam in the Netherlands. Forced into a monastery against his will when he was a teenager, the young Erasmus found little formal instruction there—but plenty of freedom to read what he liked. He devoured all the classics he could get his hands on, alongside the writings of the church fathers (see Chapter 6). When he was about thirty years old, he obtained permission to leave the monastery and enroll in the University of Paris, where he completed the requirements for a bachelor's degree in theology.

***ERASMUS* BY HANS HOLBEIN THE YOUNGER.** This is generally regarded as the most evocative portrait of the preeminent Christian humanist.

But Erasmus subsequently rebelled against what he considered the arid learning of Parisian academe. Nor did he ever serve actively as a priest. Instead, he made his living from teaching and writing. Ever on the lookout for new patrons, he traveled often to England, stayed for three years in Italy, and resided in several different cities in Germany and the Low Countries before settling finally, toward the end of his life, in Basel (Switzerland). By means of a voluminous correspondence with learned friends, Erasmus became the leader of a humanist coterie.

As a Latin prose stylist, Erasmus was unequaled since the days of Cicero. Extraordinarily eloquent and witty, he reveled in tailoring his mode of discourse to fit his subject, creating dazzling verbal effects and coining puns that took on added meaning if the reader knew Greek as well as Latin. Above all, Erasmus excelled in the deft use of irony, poking fun at everything, including himself. But although Erasmus's urbane Latin style and humor earned him a wide audience on those grounds alone, he intended everything he wrote to promote what he called the "philosophy of Christ." Accordingly, he offered his contemporaries three different kinds of writings: clever satires in which people could recognize their own foibles, serious moral treatises meant to offer guidance toward proper Christian behavior, and scholarly editions of basic Christian texts.

In the first category belong the works of Erasmus that are still widely read today: *The Praise of Folly* (1509), in which he ridiculed pedantry and dogmatism, ignorance and gullibility—even within the Church; and the *Colloquies* (1518), in which he held up contemporary religious practices for examination, couching a serious message in a playful tone. In these books, Erasmus let fictional characters do the talking so his own views on any given topic can only be determined by inference. But in his second mode, Erasmus spoke clearly in his own voice. In the *Handbook of the Christian Knight* (1503), he used the popular language of chivalry as a means to encourage a life of inward piety; in the *Complaint of Peace* (1517), he argued movingly for Christian pacifism. Erasmus's pacifism was one of his most deeply held values, and he returned to it again and again in his published works.

But Erasmus considered textual scholarship his greatest achievement. Revering the authority of the earliest church fathers, he brought out reliable printed editions of works by Saints Augustine, Jerome, and Ambrose (see Chapter 6). He also used his extraordinary command of Latin and Greek to produce a more accurate edition of the New Testament. Erasmus became convinced that nothing was more imperative than divesting the Christian scriptures of myriad errors in transcription and translation that had piled up over the course of preceding centuries. He therefore spent ten years comparing all the early Greek biblical manuscripts he could find in order to establish an authoritative text. When it finally appeared in 1516, Erasmus's Greek New Testament, published together with explanatory notes and his own new Latin translation, became one of the most important scholarly landmarks of all time.

The Influence of Erasmus

One of Erasmus's closest friends was the Englishman Sir Thomas More (1478–1535). In later life, following a successful career as a lawyer and politician. More was appointed lord chancellor of England in 1529. He was not long in this position, however, before he opposed King Henry VIII's plan to establish a national church under royal control that would deny the supremacy of the pope; see Chapter 13. Much earlier, however, in 1516, More published his most famous book, *Utopia* ("No Place").

Purporting to describe an ideal community on an imaginary island, *Utopia* is really an Erasmian critique of its own time: disparities between poverty and wealth, heresy, and war's senseless slaughter. In contrast to Europeans, the inhabitants of the fictional Utopia hold all their goods in common, work only six hours a day (so that all may have leisure for intellectual pursuits), and practice the virtues of moderation, fortitude, and justice.

Erasmus and More head a long list of energetic and eloquent northern humanists who made signal contributions to the collective enterprise of revolutionizing the study of early Christianity, and their achievements had a direct influence on Protestant reformers—as we shall see in the next chapter. Yet very few of them were willing to join Luther and other Protestant leaders in rejecting the fundamental principles on which the power of the Roman Church was based. Most tried to remain within its fold while espousing an ideal of inward piety and scholarly inquiry. But as the leaders of the Church grew less and less tolerant, even mild criticism came to seem like heresy. Erasmus himself died early enough to escape persecution, but several of his followers did not.

The Literature of the Northern Renaissance

Although Christian humanism would be severely challenged by the Reformation, the artistic Renaissance in the north would flourish. Poets in France and England vied with one another to adapt the elegant lyric forms pioneered by Petrarch (Chapter 11) and popularized by many subsequent poets, including Michelangelo. The sonnet was particularly influential and would become one of the verse forms embraced by William Shakespeare (1554–1616; see chapter 14). Another English poet, Edmund Spenser (c. 1552–1599), drew on the literary innovation of Ariosto's *Orlando Furioso;* his *Faerie Queene* is a similarly long chivalric romance that revels in sensuous imagery. Meanwhile, the more satirical side of Renaissance humanism was embraced by the French writer François Rabelais (*RAH-beh-lay,* c. 1494–1553).

Like Erasmus, whom he greatly admired, Rabelais began his career in the Church; but he soon left the cloister to study medicine. A practicing physician, Rabelais interspersed his professional activities with literary endeavors, the most enduring of which are the twin books *Gargantua* and *Pantagruel,* a series of "chronicles" describing the lives and times of giants whose fabulous size and gross appetites serve as vehicles for much lusty humor. Also like Erasmus, Rabelais satirized religious hypocrisy, scholasticism, superstition, and bigotry. But unlike Erasmus, who wrote in a highly cultivated classical Latin style, Rabelais chose to address a different audience by writing in extremely crude French and by glorifying every human appetite as natural and healthy.

Northern Architecture and Art

Although many architects in northern Europe continued to build in the flamboyant Gothic style of the later Middle Ages, the classical values of Italian architects can be seen in some of the splendid new castles constructed in France's Loire valley—*châteaux* too elegant to be defensible—and in the royal palace (now museum) of the Louvre in Paris, which replaced an old twelfth-century fortress. The influence of Renaissance ideals are also visible in the work of the German artist Albrecht Dürer (*DIRR-er,* 1471–1528). Dürer was the first northerner to master the techniques of proportion and perspective, and he shared with contemporary Italians a fascination with nature and the human body. He also took advantage of the printing press to circulate his work to a wide audience, making his delicate pencil drawings into engravings that could be mass produced.

But Dürer never really embraced classical subjects, drawing inspiration instead from more-traditional Christian legends and from the Christian humanism of

SAINT JEROME IN HIS STUDY BY DÜRER. Jerome, the biblical translator of the fourth century (see Chapter 6), was a hero to both Dürer and Erasmus: the paragon of inspired Christian scholarship. Note how the scene exudes contentment, even down to the sleeping lion, which seems more like an overgrown tabby cat than a symbol of Christ.

Erasmus. For example, Dürer's serenely radiant engraving of Saint Jerome seems to express the scholarly absorption that Erasmus would have enjoyed while working quietly in his study.

Tradition and Innovation in Music

Like the visual arts, the gorgeous music produced during this era was nourished by patrons' desire to surround themselves with beauty. Yet unlike painting and sculpture, musical practice did not reach back to classical antiquity but drew instead on well-established medieval conventions. Even before the Black Death, a musical movement called *ars nova* ("new art") was flourishing in France, and it had spread to Italy during the lifetime of Petrarch. Its outstanding composers had been Guillaume de Machaut (c. 1300–1377) and Francesco Landini (c. 1325–1397).

The madrigals (part-songs) and ballads composed by these musicians and their successors expanded on earlier genres of secular music, but their greatest achievement was a highly complicated yet delicate contrapuntal style adapted for the liturgy of the Church. Machaut was the first-known composer to provide a polyphonic (harmonized) version of the major sections of the Mass. In the fifteenth century, the dissemination of this new musical aesthetic combined with a host of French, Flemish, and Italian elements in the multicultural courts of Europe, particularly that of Burgundy. By the beginning of the sixteenth century, Franco-Flemish composers came to dominate many important courts and cathedrals, creating a variety of new forms and styles that bear a close affinity to Renaissance art and poetry.

Throughout Europe, the general level of musical proficiency in this era was very high. The singing of part-songs was a popular pastime in homes and at social gatherings, and the ability to sight-read a part was expected of the educated elite. Aristocratic women, in particular, were expected to display mastery of the new musical instruments that had been developed to add nuance and texture to existing musical forms, including the lute, the violin, and a variety of woodwind and keyboard instruments like the harpsichord.

Although most composers of this period were men trained in the service of the Church, they rarely made sharp distinctions between sacred and secular music. Like sculpture, music was coming into its own as a serious independent art. As such, it would become an important medium for the expression of both Catholic and Protestant ideals during the Reformation.

THE POLITICS OF CHRISTIAN EUROPE

We have already observed how the intellectual and artistic activity of the Renaissance movement was fueled by the political developments of the time—within Italy and throughout Europe. In 1453 France had emerged victorious in the Hundred Years' War, while England plunged into a further three decades of bloody civil conflict that touched every corner of that kingdom. The French monarchy was therefore able to rebuild its power and prestige while at the same time extending its control over regions that had long been controlled by the English crown. In 1494, the French king Charles VIII acted on a plan to expand his reach even further, into Italy. Leading an army of 30,000 well-trained troops across the Alps, he intended to claim the duchy of Milan and the kingdom of Naples. This effort solidified

Italian opposition to French occupation, as we noted above in our discussion of Machiavelli.

The rulers of Spain, whose territorial claims on Sicily also extended to Naples, were spurred by this French challenge to forge an uneasy alliance among the Papal States, some principalities of the Holy Roman Empire, Milan, and Venice. But the respite was brief. Charles's successor, Louis XII, launched a second invasion in 1499. For over a generation, until 1529, warfare in Italy was virtually uninterrupted. Alliances and counteralliances among city-states became further catalysts for violence and made Italy a magnet for mercenaries who could barely be kept in check by the generals who employed them.

Meanwhile, northern Italian city-states' virtual monopoly of trade with Asia, which had been one of the chief economic underpinnings of artistic and intellectual patronage, was being gradually eroded by the shifting of trade routes from the Mediterranean to the Atlantic (Chapters 10 and 11). It was also hampered by the increasing power of the Ottoman Empire, and even by the imperial pretensions of a new Russian ruler.

The Imperial Power of Ivan the Great

In previous chapters, we noted that the duchy of Muscovy had become the champion of the Orthodox Church. After the fall of Constantinople to the Ottomans, the Muscovite grand duke even assumed the imperial title *tsar* (caesar) and borrowed the Byzantine ideology of the ruler's divine election. These claims would eventually undergird the sacred position later ascribed to the tsars. But ideology alone could not have built a Muscovite empire. Behind its growth lay the steadily growing power of its rulers, especially that of Grand Duke Ivan III (1462–1505), known as Ivan the Great, the first to lay down a distinctive imperial agenda.

Ivan launched a series of conquests that annexed all the independent principalities lying between Moscow and the border of Poland-Lithuania. After invading Lithuania in 1492 and 1501, Ivan even succeeded in bringing parts of that domain (portions of modern Belarus and Ukraine) under his control. Meanwhile, he married the niece of the last Byzantine emperor, giving substance to the claim that Muscovy was "New Rome." He also rebuilt his fortified Moscow residence, known as the Kremlin, in magnificent Italianate style. He would later adopt, as his imperial insignia, the double-headed eagle of Rome and its legions. By the time of his death in 1505, Muscovy was firmly established as a dominant power. Indeed, the power of the tsar was more absolute in this period than was that of any European monarch.

Papal Politics and the Growth of National Churches

As Muscovy laid claim to the mantle of Roman imperial power, the papacy was pouring resources into the glorification of the original Rome and the aggrandizement of the papal office. But neither the city nor its rulers could keep pace with their political and religious rivals. Following the Council of Constance (see Chapter 11), the papacy's victory over the conciliarists proved to be a costly one. To win the support of Europe's kings and princes, various popes negotiated a series of religious treaties known as "concordats," which granted these rulers extensive authority over churches within their domains. The papacy thus secured its theoretical supremacy at the expense of its real power. For under the terms of these concordats, kings now received many of the revenues that had previously gone to the papacy. They also acquired new powers to appoint candidates to church offices. It was, in many ways, a drastic reversal of the hard-won reforms of the eleventh and twelfth centuries that had created such a powerful papacy in the first place.

Having given away so many sources of revenue and authority, the popes of the late fifteenth century became even more dependent on their own territories in central Italy. But to tighten their hold on the Papal States, they had to rule like other Italian princes: leading armies, jockeying for alliances, and undermining their opponents by every possible means—including covert operations, murder, and assassination. Judged by the secular standards of the day, these efforts paid off: the Papal States became one of the better-governed and wealthier principalities in Italy. But such methods did nothing to increase the popes' reputation for piety, and disillusionment with the papacy as a force for the advancement of spirituality became even more widespread.

With both papal authority and Rome's spiritual prestige in decline, kings and princes became the primary figures to whom both clergy and laity looked for religious and moral guidance. Many secular rulers responded to such expectations aggressively, closing scandal-ridden monasteries, suppressing alleged heretics, and regulating vice. By these and other such measures, rulers could present themselves as champions of moral reform while also strengthening their political power. The result was an increasingly close link between national monarchies and national churches, a link that would become even stronger after the Reformation.

THE EXPANSION OF MUSCOVITE RUSSIA TO 1505. The grand duchy of Moscow was the heart of what would become a Russian empire.
▪ With what other empires and polities did the Muscovites have to compete during this period of expansion? ▪ How did the relative isolation of Moscow, compared with early Kiev, allow for the growth of Muscovite power, on the one hand, and Moscow's distinctively non-Western culture, on the other? ▪ How might the natural direction of the expansion of Muscovite power until 1505 help to encourage attitudes often at odds with those of western European civilization?

The Triumph of the "Reconquista"

The kingdoms of the Iberian Peninsula were also in constant conflict during this period. In Castile, civil war and incompetent governance allowed the Castilian nobility to gain greater control over the peasantry and greater independence from the monarchy. In Aragon, royal government benefited from the extended commercial influence of Catalonia, which was under Aragonese authority.

But after 1458, Aragon too became enmeshed in a civil war, a war in which both France and Castile were involved.

A solution to the disputed succession that had caused the war in Aragon would ultimately lie in the blending of powerful royal families. In 1469, Prince Ferdinand of Aragon was recognized as the heir to that throne and, in the same year, secured this position by marrying Isabella, the heiress to Castile. Isabella became a queen in 1474,

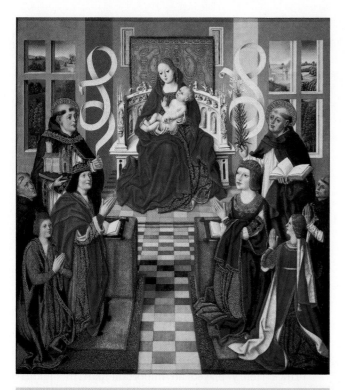

FERDINAND AND ISABELLA HONORING THE VIRGIN. In this Spanish painting, the royal couple are shown with two of their children and two household chaplains and in the company of the Blessed Virgin, the Christ Child, and saints from the Dominican order (the Dominicans were instrumental in conducting the affairs of the Spanish Inquisition). ▪ *How clear is the distinction between these holy figures and the royal family?* ▪ *What message is conveyed by their proximity?*

Ferdinand a king in 1479; and although Castile and Aragon continued to be ruled as separate kingdoms until 1714—there are tensions between the two former kingdoms even now—the marriage of Ferdinand and Isabella enabled the pursuit of several ambitious policies. In particular, their union allowed them to spend their combined resources on the creation of Europe's most powerful army, which was initially employed to conquer the last remaining principality of what had been al-Andalus: Muslim Spain. That principality, Granada, fell in 1492.

The End of the Convivencia and the Expulsion of the Jews

For more than seven centuries, Spain's Jewish communities had enjoyed the many privileges extended by their Muslim rulers, who were also relatively tolerant of their Christian subjects. Indeed, scholars often refer to this period of Spain's history as a time of *convivencia*—"living together" or "harmonious coexistence." While relations among various religious and ethnic groups were not always peaceful or positive, the policies of Muslim rulers in al-Andalus had enabled an extraordinary hybrid culture to flourish there.

The aims of the Spanish Reconquista were diametrically opposed to those of "living together." The crusading ideology of "reconquest" sought instead to forge a single, homogeneous community, based on the fiction that Spain had once been entirely Christian and should be restored to its former purity. The year 1492 therefore marks not only the end of Muslim rule in medieval Spain but also the culmination of a process of Jewish exclusion that had accelerated in western Europe (see Chapter 9). Within this history, the Spanish expulsion of the Jews stands out for the staggering scope of the displacements and destruction it entailed: at least 100,000 and possibly as many as 200,000 men, women, and children were deprived of their homes and livelihoods.

The Christian monarchs' motives for ordering this expulsion are still debated. Tens of thousands of Spanish Jews had converted to Christianity between 1391 and 1420, many as a result of coercion but some from sincere conviction. And for a generation or so, it seemed possible that these converts, known as *conversos*, might successfully assimilate into Christian society. But the same civil wars that led to the union of Ferdinand and Isabella made the *conversos* targets of discriminatory legislation. Conflict may also have fueled popular suspicions that these converts remained Jews in secret. To make "proper" Christians out of the *conversos*, the "Most Catholic" monarchs—as they were now called—may have concluded that they needed to remove any potentially seditious influences.

What became of the Spanish Jews? Some traveled north, to the Rhineland towns of Germany or to Poland, but most settled in Muslim regions of the Mediterranean and North Africa. Many found a haven in the Ottoman Empire. As we already noted, there were many opportunities for advancement in the Ottoman imperial bureaucracy, while the Ottoman economy benefited from the highly skilled labor of Jewish artisans and the intricate trading networks of Jewish merchants. In time, new forms and expressions of Jewish culture would emerge, and new communities would form. And although the extraordinary opportunities afforded by the *convivencia* could never be revived, the descendants of these Spanish Jews—known as Sephardic Jews, or Sephardim—still treasure the traditions and customs formed in Spain over a thousand years ago.

The Extension of the Reconquista

The victory over the Muslims of Granada and the expulsion of the Jews in 1492 were watershed events. They mark the beginning of a sweeping initiative to construct a new basis for the precariously united kingdoms of Aragon and Castile, one that could transcend rival regional affinities. Like other contemporary monarchs, Ferdinand and Isabella sought to strengthen their emerging nation-state by constructing an exclusively Christian identity for its people and by attaching that new identity to the crown and promoting a single national language, Castilian Spanish. They also succeeded in capturing and redirecting another language: the rhetoric of crusade.

The problem with the crusading ethos, as we have seen, is that it always seeks new outlets. Having created a new exclusively Christian Spanish kingdom through the defeat of all external enemies and internal threats, where were the energies harnessed by the Reconquista to be directed? The answer came from an unexpected quarter and had very unexpected consequences. Just a few months after Ferdinand and Isabella marched victoriously into Granada, the queen granted three ships to a Genoese adventurer who promised to reach India by sailing westward across the Atlantic Ocean, claiming any new lands he found for Spain. Columbus never reached India, but he did help to extend the tradition of reconquest to the New World—with far-reaching consequences.

NEW TARGETS AND TECHNOLOGIES OF CONQUEST

The Spanish monarchs' decision to underwrite a voyage of exploration was spurred by their desire to counter the successful Portuguese ventures of the past half century. For it was becoming clear that a tiny kingdom on the southwestern tip of the Iberian Peninsula would soon dominate the sea-lanes if rival entrepreneurs did not find alternate routes and establish equally lucrative colonies. This competition with its Iberian neighbor, Portugal, was another reason why Isabella turned to a Genoese sea captain—not to a Portuguese one.

Prince Henry the Navigator and Portuguese Colonial Initiatives

Although Portugal had been an independent Christian kingdom since the twelfth century (see Chapter 9), it was never able to compete effectively with its more powerful neighbors (Muslim or Christian) on land. But when the focus of European economic expansion began to shift toward the Atlantic (Chapter 10), Portuguese mariners were well placed to take advantage of the trend. A central figure in the history of Portuguese maritime imperialism is Prince Henry, later called "the Navigator" (1394–1460), a son of King João I of Portugal and his English queen, Philippa (sister of England's Henry IV).

Prince Henry was fascinated by the sciences of cartography and navigation, and he helped to ensure that Portuguese sailors had access to the latest charts and navigational instruments. He was also inspired by the stories told by John de Mandeville and Marco Polo (see Chapter 10)—particularly the legend of Prester John, a mythical Christian king dwelling somewhere at the end of the earth. More concretely, Prince Henry had ambitions to extend Portuguese control into the Atlantic, to tap into the burgeoning market for slaves in the Ottoman Empire and to establish direct links with sources of African gold.

Prince Henry played an important part in organizing the Portuguese colonization of Madeira, the Canary Islands, and the Azores—and in the process he pioneered the Portuguese slave trade, which almost entirely eradicated the population of the Canaries before targeting Africa. By the 1440s, Portuguese explorers had reached the Cape Verde Islands. In 1444, they landed on the African mainland in the area that became known as the Gold Coast, where they began to collect cargoes of gold and slaves for export back to Portugal. And in order to outflank the cross-Saharan gold trade, largely controlled by the Muslims of North Africa and mediated by the Genoese, Prince Henry decided to intercept this trade at its source by building a series of forts along the African coastline. This was also his main reason for colonizing the Canary Islands, which he saw as a staging ground for expeditions into the African interior.

From Africa to India and Beyond: An Empire of Spices

By the 1470s, Portuguese sailors had rounded the western coast of Africa and were exploring the Gulf of Guinea. In 1483, they reached the mouth of the Congo River. In 1488, the Portuguese captain Bartholomeu Dias was accidentally blown around the southern tip of Africa by a gale, after which he named the point "Cape of Storms." But King João II (r. 1481–95) took a more optimistic view of Dias's achievement: he renamed it the Cape of Good Hope and

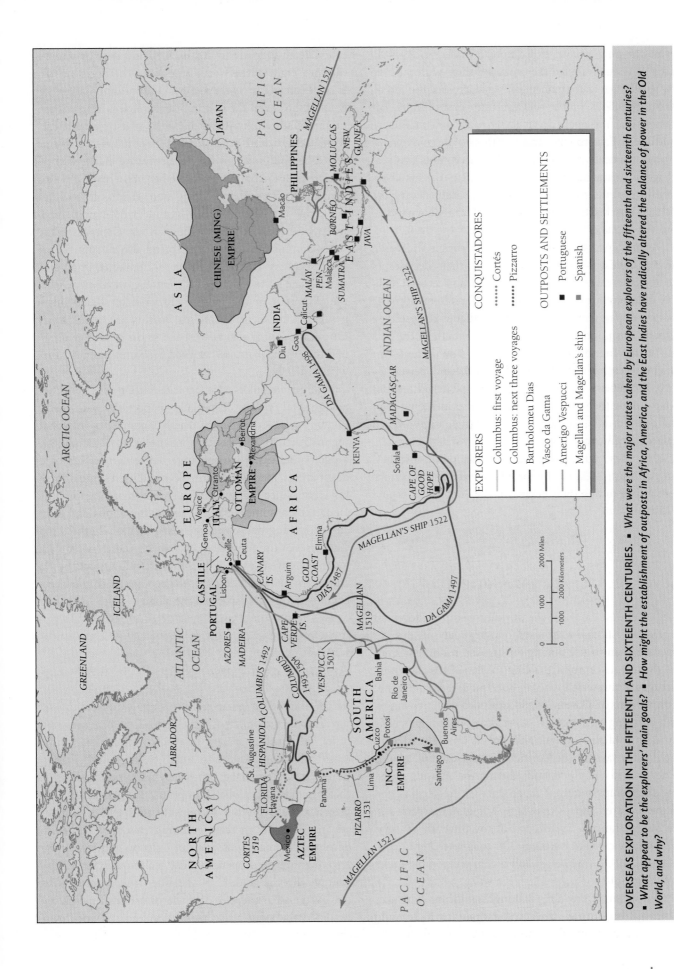

OVERSEAS EXPLORATION IN THE FIFTEENTH AND SIXTEENTH CENTURIES. ■ *What were the major routes taken by European explorers of the fifteenth and sixteenth centuries?* ■ *What appear to be the explorers' main goals?* ■ *How might the establishment of outposts in Africa, America, and the East Indies have radically altered the balance of power in the Old World, and why?*

began planning a naval expedition to India. In 1497–98, Vasco da Gama rounded the cape, and then, with the help of a Muslim navigator named Ibn Majid, crossed the Indian Ocean to Calicut, on the southwestern coast of India. For the first time, this opened a viable sea route between Europe and the Far Eastern spice trade. Although Vasco da Gama lost half his fleet and one-third of his men on his two-year voyage, his cargo of spices was so valuable that his losses were deemed insignificant. His heroism became legendary, and his story became the basis for the Portuguese national epic, the *Lusiads*.

As masters of the quickest route to riches in the world, the Portuguese swiftly capitalized on their decades of accomplishment. Not only did their trading fleets sail regularly to India, there were Portuguese efforts to monopolize the entire spice trade: in 1509, the Portuguese defeated an Ottoman fleet and then blockaded the mouth of the Red Sea, attempting to cut off one of the traditional routes by which spices had traveled to Alexandria and Beirut. By 1510, Portuguese military forces had established a series of forts along the western Indian coastline, including their headquarters at Goa. In 1511, Portuguese ships seized Malacca, a center of the spice trade on the Malay Peninsula. By 1515, they had reached the Spice Islands (East Indies) and the coast of China. By the 1520s, even the Venetians were forced to buy their pepper in the Portuguese capital of Lisbon.

Naval Technology and Navigation

The Portuguese caravel—the workhorse ship of those first voyages to Africa—was based on ship and sail designs that had been in use among Portuguese fishermen since the thirteenth century. Starting in the 1440s, however, Portuguese shipwrights began building larger caravels of about 50 tons displacement and equipped with two masts, each carrying a triangular (lateen) sail. Columbus's *Niña* was a ship of this design, although it was refitted with two square sails in the Portuguese-held Canary Islands to help it sail more efficiently during the Atlantic crossing. Such ships required much smaller crews than did the multi-oared galleys that were still commonly used in the Mediterranean. By the end of the fifteenth century, still larger caravels of around 200 tons were being constructed, with a third mast and a combination of square and lateen sails.

Europeans were also making significant advances in navigation during this era. Quadrants, which could calculate latitude in the Northern Hemisphere by measuring the height of the North Star above the horizon, were in widespread use by the 1450s. As sailors approached the equator, however, the quadrant became less and less useful, and navigators instead made use of astrolabes, which reckoned latitude by the height of the sun. Like quadrants, astrolabes had been in use for centuries. But it was not until the 1480s that the astrolabe became a really practical instrument for seaborne navigation, thanks to standard tables for the calculation of latitude whose preparation was sponsored by the Portuguese crown. Compasses, too, were coming into more widespread use during the fifteenth century. Longitude, however, remained impossible to calculate accurately until the eighteenth century, when the invention of the marine chronometer finally made it possible to keep time at sea. In this age of discovery, Europeans sailing east or west across the oceans generally had to rely on their skill at dead reckoning to determine where they were.

European sailors also benefited from new maps and navigational charts. Especially important were books known as *rutters* or *routiers*. These contained detailed sailing instructions and descriptions of the coastal landmarks a pilot could expect to encounter en route to a variety of destinations. Mediterranean sailors had used similar portolan charts since the thirteenth century, mapping the ports along the coastlines, tracking prevailing winds and tides, and indicating dangerous reefs and shallow harbors (see Chapter 10). In the fifteenth century, these mapmaking techniques were extended to the Atlantic Ocean; by the end of the sixteenth century, the accumulated knowledge contained in rutters spanned the globe.

Artillery and Empire

Larger, more maneuverable ships and improved navigational aids made it possible for the Portuguese and other European mariners to reach Africa, Asia, and—eventually—the Americas. But fundamentally, these European commercial empires were military achievements that capitalized on what Europeans had learned in their wars against each other. Perhaps the most critical military advance was the increasing sophistication of artillery, a development made possible not only by gunpowder but also by improved metallurgical techniques for casting cannon. By the middle of the fifteenth century, as we observed in Chapter 11, the use of artillery pieces had rendered the stone walls of medieval castles and towns obsolete, a fact brought home in 1453 by the successful French siege of Bordeaux (which ended the Hundred Years' War), and by the Ottoman siege of Constantinople (which ended the Byzantine Empire).

The new ship designs were important in part because their larger size made it possible to mount more-effective weaponry. European vessels were now conceived as floating artillery platforms, with scores of guns mounted in fixed positions along their sides and swivel guns mounted fore and aft. These guns were vastly expensive, as were the ships that carried them. For those rulers who could afford them, such ships made it possible to back mercantile ventures with military power: Vasco da Gama had been able to sail into the Indian Ocean in 1498, but the Portuguese did not gain control of that ocean until 1509, when they defeated combined Ottoman and Indian naval forces. Portuguese trading outposts in Africa and Asia were essentially fortifications, built not so much to guard against the attacks of native peoples as to ward off assaults from other Europeans. Without this essential military component, the European maritime empires that were emerging in this period could not have existed.

Atlantic Colonization and a New Regime of Slavery

Although slavery had effectively disappeared in much of northern Europe by the early twelfth century, it continued in parts of the Mediterranean world. But this slavery existed on a very small scale. There were no slave-powered factories or large-scale agricultural systems in this period. The only major slave markets and slave economies were in the Ottoman Empire, and there slaves ran the vast Ottoman bureaucracy and staffed the army. And in all these cases, as in antiquity, no aspect of slavery was racially based. In Italy and elsewhere in the medieval Mediterranean, slaves were often captives from an array of locales. In eastern Europe, they were functionally serfs. Most Ottoman slaves were European Christians, predominantly Poles, Ukrainians, Greeks, and Bulgarians. In the early Middle Ages, Germanic and Celtic peoples had been widely enslaved. Under the Roman Empire, slaves had come from every part of the known (and unknown) world.

What was new about the slavery of the late fifteenth century was its increasing racialization—an aspect of modern slavery that has made an indelible impact on our own society. To Europeans, African slaves were visible in ways that other slaves were not, and it became convenient for those who dealt in them to justify the mass deportation of entire populations by claiming their racial inferiority and their "natural" fitness for a life of bondage.

In Lisbon, which became a significant market for enslaved Africans during Prince Henry's lifetime, something on the order of 15,000 to 20,000 African captives were sold within a twenty-year period. In the following half century, by about 1505, the numbers amounted to 150,000. For the most part, the purchasers of these slaves regarded them as status symbols; it became fashionable to have African footmen, page boys, and ladies' maids. In the Atlantic colonies—Madeira, the Canaries, and the Azores—land was still worked mainly by European settlers and sharecroppers. Slave labor, if it was employed at all, was generally used only in sugar mills. But even sugar production did not lead to the widespread introduction of slavery on these islands.

However, a new kind of slave-based sugar plantation began to emerge in Portugal's eastern Atlantic colonies in the 1460s, starting on the Cape Verde Islands and then extending southward into the Gulf of Guinea. These islands were not populated when the Portuguese began to settle them, and their climate generally discouraged most Europeans from living there. They were ideally located, however, along the routes of slave traders venturing outward from the nearby West African coast. It was this plantation model that would be exported to Brazil by the Portuguese and to the Caribbean islands of the Americas by their Spanish conquerors, with incalculable consequences for the peoples of Africa, the Americas, and Europe (see Chapter 14).

EUROPEANS IN A NEW WORLD

Like his contemporaries, Christopher Columbus (1451–1506) understood that the world was a sphere. But he also thought it was much smaller than it actually is. It had long been accepted that there were only three continents: Europe, Asia, and Africa—hence Columbus's decision to reach Asia by sailing west, a plan that seemed even more plausible after the discovery and colonization of the Canary Islands and the Azores. The existence of these islands reinforced a new hypothesis that the Atlantic was dotted with similar lands all the way to Japan. This emboldened Columbus's royal patrons, who became convinced that the Genoese mariner could reach China in about a month, after a stop for provisions in the Canaries.

This turned out to be a kind of self-fulfilling prophecy, for when Columbus reached the Bahamas and the island of Hispaniola after only a month's sailing, he reported that he had reached the outer islands of Asia.

The Shock of Discovery

Of course, Columbus was not the first European to set foot on the American continents. As we have already learned, Viking sailors briefly settled present-day Newfoundland and Labrador around the year 1000 (see Chapter 8). But knowledge of Viking explorations had been forgotten or ignored outside of Iceland for hundreds of years. It wasn't until the 1960s that the stories of these expeditions were corroborated by archaeological evidence. Moreover, the tiny Norwegian colony on Greenland—technically part of the North American landmass—had been abandoned in the fifteenth century, when the cooling of the climate (Chapter 10) destroyed the fragile ecosystems that had barely sustained the lives of Norse settlers there.

Although Columbus brought back no spices to prove that he had found an alternate route to Asia, he did return with some small samples of gold and a few indigenous people—whose existence gave promise of entire tribes that might be "saved" by conversion to Christianity and whose lands could provide homes for Spanish settlers seeking new frontiers after the Reconquista. This provided sufficient incentive for the "Most Catholic" monarchs to finance three further expeditions by Columbus.

Meanwhile, the Portuguese, who had already obtained a papal charter granting them (hypothetical) ownership of all lands south of the Canaries, rushed to establish their own claims. After two years of wrangling and conflicting papal pronouncements, the Treaty of Tordesillas (1494) sought to demarcate Spanish and Portuguese possession of as-yet-undiscovered lands by dividing the globe longitudinally. The Spanish would ultimately emerge as the big winners in this gambling match: within a decade, the coasts of two hitherto unknown continents were identified, as were clusters of new islands, most on the Spanish side of the (disputed) meridian.

Gradually, Europeans reached the conclusion that the voyages of Columbus and his immediate successors had revealed an entirely "New World." And—shockingly—this world had not been foretold either by the teachings of Christianity or the wisdom of the ancients. Among the first to champion the fact of two new continents' existence was the Italian explorer and geographer Amerigo Vespucci (1454–1512), whose name was soon adopted as a descriptor for them. Eventually, those who came to accept this fact were forced to question the reliability of the key sources of knowledge on which Western civilizations had hitherto hinged (see Chapter 14).

At first, the realization that the Americas were not an outpost of Asia came as a disappointment to the Spanish: two major land masses and two vast oceans disrupted their plans to beat the Portuguese to the Spice Islands. But new possibilities gradually became clear. In 1513, the Spanish explorer Vasco Núñez de Balboa first viewed the Pacific Ocean from the Isthmus of Panama, and news of the narrow divide between two vast oceans prompted Ferdinand and Isabella's grandson to renew their dream. This young monarch, Charles V (1500–1556), ruled not only Spain but the huge patchwork of territories encompassed by the Holy Roman Empire (see Chapter 13). In 1519, he accepted Ferdinand Magellan's proposal to see whether a route to Asia could be found by sailing around South America.

Magellan's voyage demonstrated beyond question that the world was simply too large for any such plan to be feasible at that time. Of the five ships that left Spain under his command, only one returned, three years later, having been forced to circumnavigate the globe. Out of a crew of 265 sailors, only 18 survived. Most had died of scurvy or starvation; Magellan himself had been killed in a skirmish with native peoples in the Philippines.

This fiasco ended all hope of discovering an easy southwest passage to Asia—although the deadly dream of a northwest passage survived and motivated many European explorers of North America into the twentieth century. It has been revived today: in our age of global warming, the retreat of Arctic pack ice has led to the opening of new shipping lanes, and in 2008 the first commercial voyage successfully traversed the Arctic Ocean.

The Dream of Gold and the Downfall of Empires

Although the unforeseen size of the globe made a westward passage to Asia untenable, given the technologies then available, Europeans were quick to capitalize on the sources of wealth that the New World itself could offer. What chiefly fired the imagination were those small samples of gold that Columbus had initially brought back to Spain. While rather paltry in themselves, they nurtured hopes that gold might lie piled in ingots somewhere in these vast new lands, ready to enrich any adventurer who discovered them. Rumor fed rumor, until a few freelance Spanish soldiers really did strike it rich beyond their most avaricious imaginings.

Interpreting Visual Evidence

America as an Object of Desire

Under the influence of popular travel narratives that had circulated in Europe for centuries, Columbus and his fellow voyagers were prepared to find the New World full of cannibals. They also assumed that the indigenous peoples' custom of wearing little or no clothing—not to mention their "savagery"—would render their women sexually available. In a letter sent back home in 1495, one of Columbus's men recounted a notable encounter with a "cannibal girl" whom he had taken captive in his tent and whose naked body aroused his desire. He was surprised to find that she resisted his advances so fiercely that he had to tie her up—which of course made it easier for him to "subdue" her. In the end, he cheerfully reports, the girl's sexual performance was so satisfying that she might have been trained, as he put it, in a "school for whores."

The Flemish artist Jan van der Straet (1523–1605) would have heard many such reports of the encounters between (mostly male) Europeans and the peoples of the New World. This engraving, based on one of his drawings, is among the thousands of mass-produced images that circulated widely in Europe, thanks to the invention of printing. It imagines the first encounter between a male "Americus" (like Columbus or Amerigo Vespucci himself) and the New World, "America," depicted as a voluptuous, available woman. The Latin caption reads: "America rises to meet Americus; and whenever he calls her, she will always be aroused."

AMERICA.
Americen Americus retexit, & Semel vocauit inde semper excitam.

Questions for Analysis

1. Study the details of this image carefully. What does each symbolize, and how do they work together as an allegory of conquest and colonization?

2. On what stereotypes of indigenous peoples does this image draw? Notice, for example, the cannibalistic campfire of the group in the background or the posture of "America."

3. The New World itself—America—is imagined as female in this image. Why is this? What messages might this—and the suggestive caption—have conveyed to a European viewer?

Their success, though, had little to do with their own efforts. Within a generation after the landing of the first ships under Columbus's command, European diseases had spread rapidly among the indigenous peoples of the Caribbean and the coastlines of the Americas. These diseases—especially measles and smallpox—were not fatal to those who carried them, because many Europeans had developed immunities to them over many generations. But to the peoples of this New World, they were deadly in the extreme. For example, there were probably 250,000 people living on Hispaniola when Columbus arrived; within thirty years—a single generation—70 percent had perished from disease.

Moreover, the new waves of *conquistadores* (conquerors) were assisted by the complex political, economic, and military rivalries that already existed among the highly sophisticated societies they encountered. The Aztec Empire of Mexico rivaled any European state in its power, culture, and wealth—and like any successful empire it had subsumed many neighboring territories in the course of its own conquests. Its capital, Tenochtitlán (*ten-och-tit-LAN*, now Mexico City), amazed its European assailants, who had never seen anything like the height and grandeur of its buildings or the splendor of its public works. This splendor was itself evidence of the Aztecs' imperial might, which was resisted by many of the peoples whom they ruled.

The Aztecs' eventual conqueror, Hernán Cortés (1485–1547), had arrived in Hispaniola as a young man in the wake of Columbus's initial landing. He had received a land grant from the Spanish crown and acted as magistrate of one of the first towns established there. In 1519, he headed an expedition to the mainland, which had been the target of some earlier exploratory missions. But these had not resulted in any permanent settlements, owing largely to the tight control of the Aztecs.

When Cortés arrived on the coast of the Aztec realm, he formed an intimate relationship with a native woman known as La Malinche. She became his consort and interpreter in the Nahuatl language, which was a lingua franca among the many different ethnic groups within the empire. With her help, he discovered that some peoples subjugated by the Aztecs were rebellious, and so he began to form strategic alliances with their leaders. Cortés himself could only muster a force of a few hundred men, but his native allies numbered in the thousands.

These strategic alliances were crucial: although Cortés and his men had potentially superior weapons—guns and horses—these were more effective for their novelty than their utility. In fact, the guns were of inferior quality and their gunpowder was easily dampened by the humid climate; they had a tendency to misfire or fail altogether. So Cortés adopted the tactics and weaponry of his native allies in his dealings with the Aztec emperor, Montezuma II (r. 1502–1520), and in his assaults upon the fortification of Tenochtitlán. In the end, though, it was European bacteria (not European technology) that led to his victory: the Aztecs were devastated by an outbreak of the plague virus that had arrived along with Cortés and his men. In 1521, their empire fell.

In 1533, another lucky conquistador, Francisco Pizarro, would manage to topple the highly centralized empire of the Incas, based in what is now Peru, by similar lucky and involuntary means. In this case, he took advantage of an ongoing civil war that had weakened the reigning dynasty. He was

THE AZTEC CITY OF TENOCHTITLÁN. The Spanish conquistador Bernal Díaz del Castillo (1492–1585) took part in the conquest of the Aztec Empire and later wrote a historical account of his adventures. His admiring description of the Aztec capital at Tenochtitlán records that the Spaniards were amazed to see such a huge city built in the midst of a vast lake, with gigantic buildings arranged in a meticulous urban plan around a central square and broad causeways linking the city to the mainland. This hand-colored woodcut was included in an early edition of Hernán Cortés's letters to Emperor Charles V, printed at Nuremberg (Germany) in 1524.

also assisted by an epidemic of smallpox. Like Cortés, Pizarro promised his native allies liberation from an oppressive regime. Those formerly subject to the Aztecs and Incas would soon be able to judge how loaded these promises were.

The Costs of Conquest

The "conquests" of Mexico and Peru gave the conquistadors access to hoards of gold and silver that had been accumulated for centuries by Aztec and Inca rulers. Almost immediately, a search for the sources of these precious metals was launched by agents of the Spanish crown. The first gold deposits were discovered in Hispaniola, where surface mines were speedily established using native laborers, who were already dying in appalling numbers from disease and were now further decimated by brutality and overwork. The population quickly dwindled to a mere 10 percent of its Pre-Columbian size.

The loss of so many workers made the mines of Hispaniola uneconomical to operate, so European colonists turned instead to cattle ranching and sugar production. Modeling their sugarcane plantations on those of the

Analyzing Primary Sources

A Spanish Critique of New World Conquest

Not all Europeans approved of European imperialism or its "civilizing" effects on the peoples of the New World. One of the most influential contemporary critics was Bartolomé de las Casas (1484–1566). In 1502, when Bartolomé was eighteen years old, he and his father joined an expedition to Hispaniola. In 1510, he became the first ordained priest in the Americas and eventually became bishop of Chiapas (Mexico). Although he was a product of his times–he owned many slaves–he was also prescient in discerning the devastating effects of European settlement in the West Indies and Central America, and he particularly deplored the exploitation and extermination of indigenous populations. The following excerpt is from one of the many eloquent manifestos he published in an attempt to gain the sympathies of the Spanish crown and to reach a wide readership. It was printed in 1542 but draws on the impressions and opinions he had formed since his arrival in New Spain as a young man.

 od made all the peoples of this area, many and varied as they are, as open and as innocent as can be imagined. The simplest people in the world—unassuming, long-suffering, unassertive, and submissive—they are without malice or guile, and are utterly faithful and obedient both to their own native lords and to the Spaniards in whose service they now find themselves. . . . They are innocent and pure in mind and have a lively intelligence, all of which makes them particularly receptive to learning and understanding the truths of our Catholic faith and to being instructed in virtue; indeed, God has invested them with fewer impediments in this regard than any other people on earth. . . .

It was upon these gentle lambs . . . that from the very first day they clapped eyes on them the Spanish fell like ravening wolves upon the fold, or like tigers and savage lions who have not eaten meat for days. The pattern established at the outset has remained unchanged to this day, and the Spaniards still do nothing save tear the natives to shreds, murder them and inflict upon them untold misery, suffering and distress, tormenting, harrying and persecuting them mercilessly. . . .

When the Spanish first journeyed there, the indigenous population of the island of Hispaniola stood at some three million; today only two hundred survive.

The island of Cuba, which extends for a distance almost as great as that separating Valladolid from Rome, is now to all intents and purposes uninhabited; and two other large, beautiful and fertile islands, Puerto Rico and Jamaica, have been similarly devastated. Not a living soul remains today on any of the islands of the Bahamas . . . even though every single one of the sixty or so islands in the group . . . is more fertile and more beautiful than the Royal Gardens in Seville and the climate is as healthy as anywhere on earth. The native population, which once numbered some five hundred thousand, was wiped out by forcible expatriation to the island of Hispaniola, a policy adopted by the Spaniards in an endeavour to make up losses among the indigenous population of that island. . . .

At a conservative estimate, the despotic and diabolical behaviour of the Christians has, over the last forty years, led to the unjust and totally unwarranted deaths of more than twelve million souls, women and children among them. . . .

The reason the Christians have murdered on such a vast scale and killed anyone and everyone in their way is purely and simply greed. . . . The Spaniards have shown not the slightest consideration for these people, treating them (and I speak from first-hand experience, having been there from the outset) not as brute animals—indeed, I would to God they had done and had shown them the consideration they afford their animals—so much as piles of dung in the middle of the road. They have had as little concern for their souls as for their bodies, all the millions that have perished having gone to their deaths with no knowledge of God and without the benefit of the Sacraments. One fact in all this is widely known and beyond dispute, for even the tyrannical murderers themselves acknowledge the truth of it: the indigenous peoples never did the Europeans any harm whatever. . . .

Source: Bartolomé de las Casas, *A Short Account of the Destruction of the Indies*, trans. Nigel Griffin (Harmondsworth, UK: 1992), pp. 9–12.

Questions for Analysis

1. Given his perspective on the behavior of his countrymen, how might Bartolomé de las Casas have justified his own presence in New Spain (Mexico)? What do you think he may have hoped to achieve by publishing this account?

2. What comparisons does the author make between New Spain (Mexico) and the Old, and between indigenous peoples and Europeans? What is he trying to convey?

3. Compare this account with the engraving on page 337. What new light does this excerpt throw on that visual allegory? How might a reader-viewer of the time have reconciled these two very different pictures of European imperialism?

SPANISH CONQUISTADORS IN MEXICO. This sixteenth-century drawing of conquistadors slaughtering the Aztec aristocracy emphasizes the advantages that plate armor and steel weapons gave to the Spanish soldiers.

Cape Verde Islands and St. Thomas (São Tomé) in the Gulf of Guinea, colonists began to import thousands of African slaves to labor in the new industry. Sugar production was, by its nature, a capital-intensive undertaking. The need to import slave labor added further to its costs, guaranteeing that control over the new industry would fall into the hands of a few extremely wealthy planters and financiers.

Despite the establishment of sugar production in the Caribbean and cattle ranching on the Mexican mainland—whose devastating effects on the fragile ecosystem of Central America will be discussed in Chapter 14—it was mining that would shape the Spanish colonies most fundamentally in this period. If gold was the lure that had initially inspired the conquest, silver became its most lucrative export. Even before the discovery of vast silver deposits, the Spanish crown had taken steps to assume direct control over all colonial exports. It was therefore to the Spanish crown that the profits of empire were channeled. Europe's silver shortage, which had been acute for centuries, therefore came to an abrupt end.

Yet this massive infusion of silver into the European economy created more problems than it solved, because it accelerated an inflation of wages and prices that had already begun in the late fifteenth century. Initially, inflation had been driven by the renewed growth of the European population, an expanding colonial economy, and a relatively fixed supply of food. Thereafter, thanks to the influx of New World silver, inflation was driven by the hugely increased supply of coinage. As we shall see, this abundance of coinage led to the doubling and quadrupling of prices in the course of the sixteenth century and to the

After You Read This Chapter

Go to **INQUIZITIVE** to see what you've learned—and learn what you've missed—with personalized feedback along the way.

REVIEWING THE OBJECTIVES

- The artists of Italy were closely tied to those with political and military power. How did this relationship affect the kinds of work these artists produced?
- What aspects of Renaissance artistry and learning were adopted in northern Europe?
- What was the Reconquista, and how did it lead to a new way of thinking about Spanish identity?
- Europeans, especially the Portuguese, were developing new technologies and techniques that enabled exploration and colonial ventures in this period. What were they?
- The "discovery" of the New World had profound effects on the indigenous peoples and environment of the Americas. Describe some of these effects.

collapse of this inflated economy—paradoxically driving a wave of impoverished Europeans to settle in the New World in ever greater numbers.

CONCLUSION

The expansion of the Mediterranean world into the Atlantic, which had been ongoing since the thirteenth century, was the essential preliminary to Columbus's voyages and to the rise of European empires in Africa, India, the Caribbean, and the Americas. Other events and innovations that we have surveyed in this chapter played a key role, too: the relatively rapid communications facilitated by the printing press; the tussle for power in Italy that led to the development of ever deadlier weapons; the navigational and colonial initiatives of the Portuguese; and the success of the Spanish Reconquista, which displaced Spain's venerable Jewish community and spurred Spanish rulers and adventurers to seek their fortunes overseas.

For the indigenous peoples and empires of the Americas, the results were cataclysmic. Within a century of Europeans' arrival, between 50 and 90 percent of some native populations had perished from disease, massacre, and enslavement. Moreover, Europeans' capacity to further their imperial ambitions wherever ships could sail and guns could penetrate profoundly destabilized Europe, too, by sharpening the divisions among competing kingdoms and empires.

The ideals of the humanists and the artistry associated with the Renaissance often stand in sharp contrast to the harsh realities alongside which they coexisted and in which they were rooted. Artists could thrive in the atmosphere of competition and one-upmanship that characterized this period, but they could also find themselves reduced to the status of servants in the households of the powerful—or forced to subordinate their artistry to the demands of warfare and espionage.

Meanwhile, intellectuals and statesmen looked for inspiration to the precedents and glories of the past. But to which aspects of the past? Some humanists may have wanted to revive the principles of the Roman Republic, but many of them worked for ambitious despots who more closely resembled Rome's dictators. The theories that undergirded European politics and colonial expansion were being used to legitimize many different kinds of power, including that of the papacy. All of these trends would be carried forward in the sixteenth century and would have a role to play in the upheaval that shattered Europe's fragile religious unity. It is to this upheaval, the Reformation, that we turn in Chapter 13.

PEOPLE, IDEAS, AND EVENTS IN CONTEXT

- Why was **GUTENBERG**'s invention of the **PRINTING PRESS** such a significant development?
- How did **NICCOLÒ MACHIAVELLI** respond to Italy's political situation within Europe? In what ways do artists like **LEONARDO DA VINCI** and **MICHELANGELO BUONARROTI** exemplify the ideals and realities of the Renaissance?
- How did northern European scholars like **DESIDERIUS ERASMUS** and **THOMAS MORE** apply humanist ideas to Christianity? How were these ideas expressed in art?
- What is significant about **IVAN THE GREAT**'s use of the title **TSAR**? In what other ways did the Russian emperor claim to be the heir of Rome?
- How did **ISABELLA OF CASTILE** and **FERDINAND OF ARAGON** succeed in creating a unified Spain through the **RECONQUISTA**?
- How does **PRINCE HENRY THE NAVIGATOR** exemplify the motives for pursuing overseas expansion? Why were the Portuguese so successful in establishing colonies in this period?
- What were the expectations that launched **COLUMBUS**'s voyage? What enabled the Spanish **CONQUISTADORS** to subjugate the peoples of the **AMERICAS**?

THINKING ABOUT CONNECTIONS

- Phrases like "Renaissance man" and "a Renaissance education" are still part of our common vocabulary. Given what you have learned in this chapter, how has your understanding of such phrases changed? How would you explain their true meaning to others?
- How do the patterns of conquest and colonization discussed in this chapter compare to those of earlier periods, such as the era of the Crusades or the empires of antiquity? How many of these developments were new?
- Although the growth of the African slave trade would result in a new racialization of slavery in the Atlantic world, the justifications for slavery had very old roots. How might Europeans have used Greek and Roman precedents in defense of these new ventures? (See Chapters 4 and 5.)

Before
You
Read
This
Chapter

The Age of Dissent and Division, 1500–1564

CORE OBJECTIVES

- **DEFINE** the main ideas advanced by Martin Luther and understand their significance.

- **EXPLAIN** why Switzerland emerged as an important Protestant center.

- **IDENTIFY** the ways that family structures and values changed during the Reformation.

- **UNDERSTAND** the reasons behind England's unique kind of Protestantism.

- **DESCRIBE** the Catholic Church's response to the challenge of Protestant movements.

In 1517, on the night before the Feast of All Saints—All Hallows' Eve, or Halloween—a professor of theology at a small university in northern Germany published a series of debating points on the door of Wittenberg's All Saints' Church. (This church served as the university's chapel, and it was also called the "Castle church," because it was part of the palace recently built for the local ruler.) The act of nailing such a document to the church door was not a prank; it was the usual method of announcing a public disputation. Still, it is peculiarly appropriate that Martin Luther did this on a night associated with mischief-making. Although he cannot have anticipated the magnitude of mischief it would cause, the posting of these ninety-five theses was a subversive act. For one thing, the sheer number of propositions that Dr. Luther offered to debate was unusual. But what really caught the attention of his fellow scholars was their unifying theme: the corruption of the Church and, in particular, the office of the pope. It was a topic very much in vogue at the time, but it had seldom been dissected so clearly by a licensed theologian who was also a monk, an ordained priest, and a charismatic teacher.

Thanks to Luther's well-placed correspondents, this document and the debate it stimulated soon found audiences well beyond the university of Wittenberg. By the time the papacy formally retaliated, in 1520, dissent was widespread—and not only among academics. Many of Europe's kings and princes saw the political advantages of either defying or defending the pope, and they chose sides accordingly. Luther's own lord, Frederick III of Saxony, would spend the rest of his life shielding the man who had first expounded those theses in his own Castle church.

Martin Luther (1483–1546) had grown up in a largely peaceful Europe. After two centuries of economic, social, and political turmoil, its economy was expanding, its cities growing, and its major monarchies were secure. Europeans had also embarked on a new period of colonial expansion. Meanwhile, the Church had weathered the storms of the Avignon captivity and the Great Schism. In the struggle over conciliarism, the papacy had won the support of all major European rulers. At the local level, the devotion of ordinary Christians was strong and the parish a crucial site of community identity. To be sure, there were some problems. Reformers noted that too many priests were ignorant or neglectful of their duties. Monasticism seemed to have lost its spiritual fire, while popular religious enthusiasm sometimes led to superstition, or to movements that the Church considered heretical. Yet, on the whole, secular and ecclesiastical institutions were strong.

No one could have predicted that this coherence would be irreparably shattered in the course of a generation, or that the next century would witness an appallingly destructive series of wars. Nor could anyone have foreseen that the catalyst for these extraordinary events would be a university professor. The debate ignited by Martin Luther on that evening in 1517 would set off the chain reaction we know as the Reformation. Initially, it was intended as a call for another phase in the Church's long history of internal reforms; but Luther's teachings instead launched a revolution that would splinter western Christendom into a variety of Protestant ("dissenting") faiths, while prompting the Roman Church to reaffirm its status as the only true Catholic ("universal") religion. At the same time, these movements deepened existing divisions among peoples, rulers, and states. The result was a profound transformation that affected the lives of everyone in Europe—and everyone in the new European colonies.

MARTIN LUTHER'S CHALLENGE

To explain the impact of Martin Luther's ideas and actions, we must first ask how he arrived at his theological convictions. We then need to assess why so many Europeans were galvanized by his teachings, and why many rulers quickly adopted the Protestant faith within their territories.

As we shall see, Luther's message appealed to different types of people for different reasons. Many peasants hoped that the new religion would free them from the dominion of their lords; towns and princes thought it would allow them to consolidate their political independence; politicians thought it would liberate emerging states from the demands of foreign popes.

But what Luther's followers shared was a conviction that their new understanding of Christianity would lead to salvation, whereas the traditional religion of Rome would not. For this reason, *reformation* is a rather misleading term for the movement they initiated. Although Luther himself began as a reformer seeking to change the Church from within, he quickly developed into a committed opponent of its principles and practices. Many of his followers were even more radical. The movement that began with Luther therefore went beyond "reformation." It was a frontal assault on religious, political, and social institutions that had been in place for a thousand years.

Luther's Quest for Justice

Although Martin Luther became an inspiration to millions, he was a terrible disappointment to his father. The elder Luther was a Thuringian peasant who had prospered in business. Eager to see his clever son rise still further, he sent young Luther to the University of Erfurt to study law. In 1505, however, Martin shattered his father's hopes by becoming a monk of the Augustinian order. In some sense, though, Luther was a chip off the old block: throughout his life, he lived simply and expressed himself in the vigorous, earthy vernacular of the German peasantry.

As a monk, Luther zealously pursued all the traditional means for achieving holiness. Not only did he fast and pray continuously, but he reportedly confessed his sins so often that his exhausted confessor would sometimes jokingly suggest that he should do something really worthy of penance. Yet still Luther could find no spiritual peace; he feared that he could never perform enough good deeds to deserve salvation. But then an insight led him to a new understanding of God's justice.

For years, Luther had worried that it seemed unfair for God to issue commandments that he knew humans could not observe—and then to punish them with eternal damnation for breaking them. But after becoming a professor of

MARTIN LUTHER. This late portrait is by Lucas Cranach the Elder (1472–1553), court painter to the electors of Brandenburg and a friend of Luther.

theology at the University of Wittenberg, Luther's study of the Bible convinced him that God's justice lay in his mercy, not in the power of damnation. As Luther later wrote, "I began to understand the justice of God as that by which God makes *us* just, in his mercy and through faith . . . and at this I felt as though I had been born again, and had gone through open gates into paradise."

Lecturing at Wittenberg in the years immediately following this epiphany, which occurred around 1515, Luther pondered a passage in Paul's Letter to the Romans (1:17): "The just shall live by faith." From this, he derived his central doctrine of "justification by faith alone." By this, Luther meant that God's justice does not demand endless good works and religious rituals, because humans can never be saved entirely by their own weak efforts. Rather, humans are saved by God's grace, which God offers as an utterly undeserved gift to those whom he has selected (predestined) for salvation. Because this grace comes to humans through the gift of faith, men and women are "justified" (i.e., made worthy of salvation) by faith alone. While those whom God has justified through faith will manifest that fact by performing deeds of piety and charity, such works are not what saves them. Piety and charity are merely visible signs of each believer's invisible spiritual state, which is known to God alone.

The essence of this doctrine was not original to Luther. It had been central to the thought of Augustine (see Chapter 6), the patron saint of Luther's own monastic order. During the twelfth and thirteenth centuries, however, theologians such as Peter Lombard and Thomas Aquinas (see Chapter 9) had developed a very different understanding of salvation. They emphasized the role that the Church itself (through its sacraments) and the individual believer (through acts of piety and charity) could play in the process of salvation. Although none of these previous theologians claimed that a human being could earn his or her way to heaven by good works alone, the late medieval Church had encouraged this understanding by presenting the process of salvation in increasingly quantitative terms—declaring, for example, that by performing a specific action (such as a pilgrimage or a pious donation), a believer could reduce the amount of penance she or he owed to God by a specific number of days.

Since the fourteenth century, moreover, popes had claimed to dispense "special grace" from the so-called Treasury of Merits, a storehouse of surplus good works piled up by Christ and the saints in heaven. By the late fifteenth century, when Luther was a child, the papacy began to claim that the dead could receive this grace, too, and so speed their way through purgatory. In both cases, grace was said to be withdrawn from this "Treasury" through indulgences: special remissions of penitential obligations. When indulgences were first conceived in the eleventh and twelfth centuries, they could be earned only by demanding spiritual exercises, such as joining a crusade. By the end of the fifteenth century, however, indulgences were for sale.

To many, this looked like heresy, specifically simony: the sin of exchanging God's grace for cash. It had been a practice loudly condemned by Wycliffe and his followers (see Chapter 11), and it was even more widely criticized by reformers like Erasmus (see Chapter 12). But Luther's objection to indulgences rested on a set of theological premises that, taken to their logical conclusion, resulted in dismantling of much contemporary religious practice, including the authority and sanctity of the papacy. Luther himself does not appear to have realized these implications at first.

The Scandal of Indulgences

Luther's thinking on these issues developed in an academic setting, but in 1517 he was provoked into attacking actual practice. The worldly bishop Albert of Hohenzollern, youngest brother of the prince of Brandenburg, paid a large sum for papal permission to hold the lucrative bishoprics of Magdeburg and Halberstadt concurrently—even though, at twenty-three, he was not old enough to be a bishop at all. Moreover, when the prestigious archbishopric of Mainz fell vacant in the next year, Albert bought

SAINT PETER'S BASILICA, ROME. The construction of a new papal palace and monumental church was begun in 1506. This enormous complex replaced a modest, dilapidated Romanesque basilica that had replaced an even older church built on the site of the apostle Peter's tomb. ∎ *How might this building project have been interpreted in different ways, depending on one's attitude toward the papacy?*

that, too. Obtaining the necessary funds by taking out loans from a German banking firm, he then struck a bargain with Pope Leo X (r. 1513–21): Leo would authorize the sale of indulgences in Albert's ecclesiastical territories—where Luther lived—with the understanding that half of the income would go to Rome for the building of St. Peter's Basilica, the other half to Albert.

Luther did not know the sordid details of Albert's bargain, but he did know that a Dominican friar named Tetzel was soon hawking indulgences throughout much of the region, and that Tetzel was deliberately giving people the impression that an indulgence was an automatic ticket to heaven for oneself or loved ones in purgatory. For Luther, this was doubly offensive: not only was Tetzel violating Luther's conviction that people are saved by God's grace, he was misleading people into thinking that if they purchased an indulgence, they no longer needed to confess their sins. Tetzel was putting innocent souls at risk.

Accordingly, Luther's ninety-five theses were focused on dismantling the doctrine of indulgences. He published these points for debate in Latin, but they were soon translated into German and published even more widely. Suddenly, the hitherto obscure academic gained widespread notoriety. Tetzel and his powerful allies demanded that Luther withdraw his theses. Rather than backing down, however, Luther became even bolder. In 1519, at a public disputation held in Leipzig and attended by throngs of people, Luther defiantly maintained that the pope and all clerics were merely fallible men and that the highest authority for an individual's conscience was the truth of scripture.

Luther's year of greatest activity came in 1520, when he composed a series of pamphlets setting forth his three primary premises: justification by faith, the authority of scripture, and "the priesthood of all believers." We have already examined the meaning of the first premise. By the second, he meant that the reading of scripture took precedence over Church traditions—including the teachings of all theologians—and that beliefs (such as purgatory) or practices (such as prayers to the saints) not explicitly grounded in scripture should be rejected as human inventions. Luther also declared that Christian believers were spiritually equal before God, which meant denying that priests, monks, and nuns had any special qualities by virtue of their vocations: hence "the priesthood of all believers."

From these premises, a host of practical consequences logically followed. Because works could not lead to salvation, Luther declared fasts, pilgrimages, and the veneration of relics to be spiritually valueless. He also called for the dissolution of all monasteries and convents. He advocated a demystification of religious rites, proposing the substitution of German and other vernaculars for Latin and calling for a reduction in the number of sacraments from seven to two. In his view, the only true sacraments were baptism and the Eucharist, both of which had been instituted by Christ. (Later, he included penance, too.) Although Luther continued to believe that Christ was really present in the consecrated bread and wine of the Mass, he insisted that it was only through the faith of each individual believer that this sacrament could lead anyone to God; it was not a miracle performed by a priest.

To further emphasize that those who served the Church had no supernatural authority, Luther insisted on calling them "ministers" or "pastors" rather than priests. He also proposed to abolish the entire ecclesiastical hierarchy from popes to bishops on down. Finally, on the principle that no spiritual distinction existed between clergy and laity,

Luther argued that ministers could and should marry. In 1525, he himself took a wife, Katharina von Bora, one of a dozen nuns he had helped to escape from a Cistercian convent.

The Break with Rome

Widely disseminated by means of the printing press, Luther's polemical pamphlets electrified much of Europe, gaining him passionate popular support and touching off a revolt against the papacy. In highly colloquial German, Luther declared that "the cardinals have sucked Italy dry and now turn to Germany" and that, given Rome's corruption, "the reign of Antichrist could not be worse." As word of Luther's defiance spread, his pamphlets became a publishing sensation. Whereas the average press run of a printed book before 1520 had been 1,000 copies, the first run of *To the Christian Nobility* (1520) was 4,000—and it sold out in a few days. Many thousands of copies quickly followed. Even more popular were woodcut illustrations mocking the papacy and exalting Luther. These sold in the tens of thousands and could be readily understood even by those who could not read. (See **Interpreting Visual Evidence** on page 348.)

Luther's denunciations met with this popular response in part because they expressed longstanding and widespread public dissatisfaction with the corruption of the papacy. Pope Alexander VI (r. 1492–1503) had bribed cardinals to gain his office and had then used the money raised from the papal jubilee of 1500 to support the military campaigns of his illegitimate son. Julius II (r. 1503–13) devoted his reign to enlarging the Papal States through a series of wars. Leo X (r. 1513–21), Luther's opponent, was a member of the Medici family of Florence; an able administrator, he was also a self-indulgent connoisseur. In *The Praise of Folly*, first published in 1511 and frequently reprinted (see Chapter 12), Erasmus had declared that if the popes of his day were ever forced to lead Christlike lives, as their office actually required, they would be incapable of it. In *Julius Excluded*, published anonymously in 1517, he imagined a conversation between Saint Peter and Julius II, in which Peter refuses to admit the pope to heaven.

In Germany, resentment of the papacy ran especially high because there were no special agreements (concordats) limiting papal authority in its principalities, as there were in Spain, France, Bohemia, and England (see Chapter 12). As a result, papal taxes were high, and yet Germans

had almost no influence over papal policy. Frenchmen, Spaniards, and Italians dominated the College of Cardinals and the papal bureaucracy, and the popes were almost invariably Italian—as they would continue to be until 1978 and the election of the Polish cardinal Karel Wojtyla as John Paul II. As a result of these trends, graduates from the rapidly growing German universities almost never found employment in Rome. Instead, many joined the throngs of Luther's supporters to become leaders of the new religious movement.

Emperor Charles V and the Condemnation at Worms

In the year 1520, Leo X issued a papal edict condemning Luther's publications as heretical and threatening him with excommunication. This edict was of the most solemn kind, known as a *bulla,* or "bull," from the lead seal it bore. Luther's response was flagrantly defiant: rather than acquiescing to the pope's demand, he staged a public burning of the document. Thereafter, his heresy confirmed, he was formally given over for punishment to his lay overlord, Frederick III "the Wise" of Saxony.

THE EMPEROR CHARLES V. This portrait by the Venetian painter Titian depicts Europe's most powerful ruler sitting quietly in a chair, dressed in simple clothing of the kind worn by judges or bureaucrats. ■ *Why might Charles have chosen to represent himself in this way—rather than in the regalia of his many royal, imperial, and princely offices?*

Decoding Printed Propaganda

The printing press has been credited with helping to spread the teachings of Martin Luther, and so securing the success of the Protestant Reformation. But even before Luther's critiques were published, reformers were using the new technology to disseminate images that attacked the corruption of the Church. After Luther rose to prominence, both his supporters and detractors vied with one another in disseminating propaganda that appealed, visually, to a lay audience and that could be understood even by those who were unable to read.

The first pair of images below is really a single printed artifact datable to around 1500: an early example of a "pop-up" card. It shows Pope Alexander VI (r. 1492–1503) as stately pontiff (image A) whose true identity is concealed by a flap. When the flap is raised (image B), he is revealed as a devil. The Latin texts read: "Alexander VI, *pontifex maximus*" (image A) and "I am the pope" (image B).

The other two examples represent two sides of the debate as it had

A. Alexander as pontiff.

B. Alexander as a devil.

developed by 1530, and both do so with reference to the same image: the seven-headed beast mentioned in the Bible's Book of Revelation. On the left (image C), a Lutheran engraving shows the papacy as the beast, with seven heads representing seven orders of Catholic clergy. The sign on the cross (referring to the sign hung over the head of the crucified Christ) reads, in German: "For money, a sack full of indulgences." The Latin words on either side say "Reign of the Devil." On the right (image D), a Catholic engraving produced in Germany shows Luther as Revelation's beast, with its seven heads labeled:

"Doctor–Martin–Luther–Heretic–Hypocrite–Fanatic–Barabbas," the last alluding to the thief who should have been executed instead of Jesus, according to the Gospels.

Questions for Analysis

1. Given that this attack on Pope Alexander VI precedes Martin Luther's critique of the Church by nearly two decades, what can you conclude about its intended audience? To what extent can it be read as a barometer of popular disapproval? What might have been the reason(s) for the use of the concealing flap?

2. What do you make of the fact that both Catholic and Protestant propagandists were using the same imagery? What do you make of key differences: for example, the fact that the seven-headed beast representing the papacy sprouts out of an altar in which a Eucharistic chalice is displayed, while the seven-headed Martin Luther is reading a book?

3. All of these printed images also make use of words. Would the message of each image be clear without the use of texts? Why or why not?

C. The seven-headed papal beast.

D. The seven-headed Martin Luther.

Frederick, however, proved a supporter of Luther and a critic of the papacy. Rather than burning Luther at the stake, Frederick declared that Luther had not yet received a fair hearing. Early in 1521, he therefore brought him to the city of Worms to be examined by a select assembly known as a "diet."

At Worms, the diet's presiding officer was the newly elected Holy Roman Emperor, Charles V. As a member of the Habsburg family, Charles had been born and bred in his ancestral holding of Flanders, then part of the Netherlands. By 1521, however, through the unpredictable workings of dynastic inheritance, marriage, election, and luck, he had

THE EUROPEAN EMPIRE OF CHARLES V, c. 1526. Charles V ruled a vast variety of widely dispersed territories in Europe and the New World, and as Holy Roman Emperor he was also the titular ruler of Germany. ▪ *What were the main territories under his control?* ▪ *Which regions would have been most threatened by Charles's extraordinary power, and where might the rulers of these regions have turned for allies?* ▪ *How might the expansion of the Ottoman Empire have complicated political and religious struggles within Christian Europe?*

become not only the ruler of the Netherlands but also king of Germany and Holy Roman emperor, duke of Austria, duke of Milan, and ruler of Burgundy's Franche-Comté. And as the grandson of Ferdinand and Isabella on his mother's side, he was also king of Spain; king of Naples, Sicily, and Sardinia; and ruler of all the Spanish possessions in the New World. Governing such an extraordinary combination of territories posed enormous challenges. Charles's empire had no capital and no centralized administrative institutions; it shared no common language, no common culture, and no geographically contiguous borders. The only thing uniting its peoples was the Church.

Charles could not, therefore, tolerate threats to the fundamental institution of Catholicism—as the religion of Rome was coming to be called. Moreover, Charles was a faithful and committed servant of the Church, and he was deeply disturbed by the prospect of heresy within his empire. There was little doubt that the Diet of Worms, held under his jurisdiction, would condemn Martin Luther. But when Luther refused to back down, his lord Frederick the Wise once more intervened, this time arranging for Luther to be "kidnapped" and hidden for a year at the castle of the Wartburg, out of harm's way.

Although the Diet of Worms proclaimed Luther an outlaw, this edict was never enforced. Instead, Charles V left Germany in order to conduct a war with France, and in 1522 Luther returned in triumph to Wittenberg and his university supporters. When several German princes formally converted to Lutheranism, they brought their territories with them. In a little over a decade, a new form of Christianity had been established.

The German Princes and the Lutheran Church

But why did some German princes, secure in their own powers, choose to establish Lutheran religious practices within their territories? This is a crucial development, because popular or academic support for Luther would not have been enough to ensure the success of his teachings had they not been embraced by a number of powerful rulers and free cities. It was only in those territories where Lutheranism was formally established that this new religion could survive. Elsewhere in Germany, Luther's sympathizers were forced to flee, face death, or conform to Catholicism.

The power of individual rulers to control the practice of religion in their own territories reflects developments we have noted in previous chapters. Rulers had long sought to control appointments to Church offices in their own realms, to restrict the flow of money to Rome and to limit the independence of ecclesiastical courts. The monarchs of Europe had already taken advantage of the continuing struggles between the papacy and the conciliarists to extract many concessions from the embattled popes during the fifteenth century (see Chapters 11 and 12). But in Germany, as noted above, neither the emperor nor the princes were strong enough to secure specially negotiated concordats.

Hence the political and economic appeal of Luther's initiatives. Luther himself had recognized that he could never hope to institute new religious practices without the strong arms of princes, so he explicitly encouraged them to confiscate the wealth of the Church as an incentive. When some princes realized that Luther had enormous public support and that Charles V could not act swiftly enough to stop them, several moved to introduce Lutheranism into their territories. Personal religious conviction surely played a role in individual cases, but considerations of power and wealth were generally more decisive. Self-proclaimed "protestant" princes could consolidate authority by naming their own religious officials, stopping the payment of fees to Rome, and curtailing the jurisdiction of Church courts. They could also guarantee that the political and religious boundaries of their territories would now coincide: no longer would a rival ecclesiastical prince (such as a bishop or abbot) be able to use his spiritual position to undermine a secular prince's sovereignty.

Similar considerations also moved a number of free cities to adopt Lutheranism. Acting independently of any prince, town councils could establish themselves as the supreme governing authorities within their jurisdictions, cutting out local bishops or powerful monasteries. Given the added fact that, under Lutheranism, monasteries and convents could be shut down and their lands appropriated by the newly sovereign Protestant authorities, the practical and economic advantages of the new faith were overwhelming.

Once safely ensconced in Wittenberg under Protestant princely protection, Luther began to express ever more vehemently his own political and social views, which tended toward the strong, conservative support of the new political order. In a treatise of 1523, *On Temporal Authority*, he even insisted that even "ungodly" Protestant princes should never be targets of dissent. In 1525, when peasants throughout Germany rebelled against their landlords, Luther therefore responded with hostility. In his vituperative pamphlet *Against the Thievish, Murderous*

Hordes of Peasants, he urged readers to hunt the rebels down as though they were mad dogs. After the ruthless suppression of this revolt, which may have cost as many as 100,000 lives, the firm alliance of Lutheranism with state power helped preserve and sanction the existing social order.

In his later years, Luther concentrated on debating with younger, more radical religious reformers who challenged his reactionary political conservatism. Never tiring in his amazingly prolific literary activity, he wrote an average of one treatise every two weeks for twenty-five years.

CONFESSIONAL DIFFERENCES, c. 1560. The religious affiliations (confessions) of Europe's territories had become very complicated by the year 1560, roughly a generation after the adoption of Lutheranism in some areas. ■ *What major countries and kingdoms had embraced Protestantism by 1560?* ■ *To what extent do these divisions conform to political boundaries, and to what extent would they have complicated the political situation?* ■ *Why might Lutheranism have spread north into Scandinavia but not south into Bavaria?*

THE SPREAD OF PROTESTANTISM

Originating as a term applied to Lutherans who "protested" the Catholic authority of Charles V, the word *Protestant* was soon applied to a much wider range of dissenting Christianities. Lutheranism itself struck lasting roots in northern Germany and Scandinavia, where it became the state religion of Denmark, Norway, and Sweden as early as the 1520s. But some other early Lutheran successes in southern Germany, Poland, and Hungary were eventually rolled back. Elsewhere in Europe, meanwhile, competing forms of Protestantism soon emerged from the seeds that Luther had sown. By the 1550s, Protestantism had become a truly international movement and also an increasingly diverse and divisive one.

Protestantism in Switzerland

In the early sixteenth century, Switzerland was ruled neither by kings nor by territorial princes; instead, prosperous Swiss cities were either independent or on the verge of becoming so. Hence, when the leading citizens of a Swiss municipality decided to adopt Protestant reforms, no one could stop them. Although religious arrangements varied from city to city, three main forms of Protestantism emerged in Switzerland between 1520 to 1550: Zwinglianism, Anabaptism, and Calvinism.

Zwinglianism, founded by Ulrich Zwingli (*TSVING-lee*, 1484–1531) in Zürich, was the most theologically moderate form of the three. Zwingli had just begun his career as a Catholic priest when his humanist-inspired study of the Bible convinced him that Catholic theology and practice conflicted with the Gospels. His biblical studies eventually led him to condemn religious images and hierarchical authority within the Church. Yet he did not speak out publicly until Luther set a precedent. In 1522, accordingly, Zwingli began attacking the authority of the Catholic Church in Zürich. Soon, much of northern Switzerland had accepted his religious leadership.

Although Zwingli's reforms closely resembled those of the Lutherans in Germany, Zwingli differed from Luther on the theology of the Eucharist. Whereas Luther believed in the real presence of Christ's body in the sacrament, for Zwingli the Eucharist was simply a reminder and celebration of Christ's historical sacrifice. This fundamental disagreement prevented Lutherans and Zwinglians from uniting. When Zwingli died in battle against Catholic forces in 1531, his movement was absorbed by the more systematic Protestantism of John Calvin (as will be discussed later).

Before Calvinism prevailed, however, an even more radical form of Protestantism arose in Switzerland and parts of Germany. The first Anabaptists were members of Zwingli's circle in Zürich, but they broke with him around 1525 on the issue of infant baptism. Anabaptists were convinced that the sacrament of baptism was only effective if administered to willing adults who understood its significance, and so they required those who had been baptized as infants to be baptized again as adults (the term *Anabaptism* means "rebaptism"). This doctrine reflected the Anabaptists' fundamental belief that the true church was a small community of believers whose members had to make a deliberate, inspired decision to join it.

No other Protestant groups were prepared to go so far in rejecting the medieval Christian view of the Church as a single vast body to which all members of society belonged from birth. And in an age when almost everyone assumed that religious and secular authority were inextricably connected, Anabaptism was bound to be anathema to all established powers, both Protestant and Catholic. It was a movement that appealed to sincere religious piety in calling for pacifism, strict personal morality, and extreme simplicity of worship.

However, this changed when a group of Anabaptist extremists managed to gain control of the German city of Münster in 1534. These zealots were driven by millenarianism: the belief that God intends to institute a completely new order of justice and spirituality throughout the world before the end of time. Determined to help God bring about this goal, the extremists attempted to turn Münster into a new Jerusalem. A former tailor named John of Leyden assumed the title "king of the New Temple" and proclaimed himself the successor of the Hebrew king David. Under his leadership, Anabaptist religious practices were made obligatory, private property was abolished, and even polygamy was permitted on the grounds of Old Testament precedents. Such practices were deeply shocking to Protestants and Catholics alike. Accordingly, Münster was besieged and captured by Catholic forces little more than a year after the Anabaptist takeover. The new "King David," together with two of his lieutenants, was put to death by torture, and the three bodies were displayed in iron cases in the town square.

Thereafter, Anabaptists throughout Europe were ruthlessly persecuted on all sides. The few who survived banded together in the Mennonite sect, named for its founder, the Dutchman Menno Simons (c. 1496–1561). This sect, dedicated to pacifism and the simple "religion of the heart" of the original Anabaptist movement, is still particularly strong in the central United States.

John Calvin's Systematic Protestant Theology

A year after the events in Münster, a twenty-six-year-old Frenchman named John Calvin (1509–1564), published the first version of his *Institutes of the Christian Religion*, the most influential formulation of Protestant theology ever written. Born in Noyon, in northern France, Calvin had originally trained for the law; but by 1533, he was studying the Greek and Latin classics while living off the income from a priestly benefice. As he later wrote, he was "obstinately devoted to the superstitions of popery" until he experienced a miraculous conversion. He became a Protestant theologian and propagandist, eventually fleeing to the Swiss city of Basel to escape persecution.

Although some aspects of Calvin's early career resemble those of Luther's, the two men were very different. Luther was an emotionally volatile personality and a lover of controversy. He responded to theological problems as they arose or as the impulse struck him; he never attempted to systematize his beliefs. Calvin, however, had a coolly analytical legal mind and he was determined to set forth all the principles of Protestantism: comprehensively, logically, and systematically. As a result, after several revisions and enlargements (the definitive edition appeared in 1559), Calvin's *Institutes* became the Protestant equivalent of Thomas Aquinas's *Summa Theologiae* (see Chapter 9).

Calvin's austere and stoical theology started with the omnipotence of God. For Calvin, the entire universe depends utterly on the will of the Almighty, who created all things for his greater glory and who knows all things present and to come. Because of man's original fall from grace in Eden, all human beings are sinners by nature, bound to an evil inheritance they cannot escape. Yet God (for reasons of his own) has predestined some for eternal salvation and damned all the rest to the torments of hell. Nothing that individual humans may do can alter fate; all souls are stamped with God's blessing or condemnation before they are born. Nevertheless, Christians cannot be indifferent to their conduct on earth. If they are among the elect, God will implant in them the desire to live according to his laws. Upright conduct is thus a sign that an individual has been chosen for future glory. Membership in Calvin's Reformed Church was another presumptive sign of election to salvation, and Calvin charged his followers to work actively to fulfill God's commandments and stamp out sin—not because this would lead to anyone's salvation (which is predetermined by God alone), but because God's glory is diminished if sin is allowed to flourish.

Calvin always acknowledged a great debt to Luther, but his teachings diverged in several essential respects. First of all, Luther's attitude toward proper Christian conduct in the world was much more passive. For Luther, a Christian should endure the trials of life through suffering, whereas for Calvin the world was to be actively mastered through unceasing labor. Calvin's religion was also more controlling than Luther's. Luther, for example, insisted that his followers attend church on Sunday, but he did not demand that they refrain from all pleasure or work on that day. Calvin, on the other hand, forbade worldliness of any sort on the Sabbath and all sorts of minor self-indulgences even on other days.

The two men also differed on fundamental matters of church governance and worship. Although Luther had attacked the Roman church's hierarchy, Lutheran district superintendents exercised some of the same powers as bishops, including supervision of parish clergy. Luther also retained many features of traditional Christian worship, including altars, music, and ritual. Calvin, however, rejected everything that smacked of "popery." He argued that each congregation should elect its own ministers, and that assemblies of ministers and "elders" (laymen responsible for maintaining proper religious conduct) were to govern the Reformed Church as a whole. Calvin also insisted on the utmost simplicity in worship, prohibiting (among much else) rich vestments, processions, rituals, instrumental music, and religious images or any sort of church decoration. He also dispensed with all Catholic sacraments by making the sermon, rather than the Eucharist, the centerpiece of worship.

Calvinist Geneva

Calvin was intent on putting his religious teachings into practice. Sensing an opportunity in the French-speaking Swiss city of Geneva—then in the throes of political and religious upheaval—he moved there in 1536 and began preaching and organizing. In 1538, his activities caused him to be expelled by the city council, but in 1541 he returned and brought the city under his influence.

With Calvin's guidance, Geneva's government became a theocracy. Supreme authority was vested in a "consistory" composed of twelve lay elders and between ten and twenty pastors, whose weekly meetings Calvin dominated. In addition to passing legislation proposed by an assembly of ministers, the consistory's main function was to supervise morality, public and private. To this end, Geneva was divided into districts, and a committee of the consistory visited every household, without prior warning, to check on the behavior of its members. Dancing, card playing, attending the theater, and working or playing on the Sabbath: all were outlawed as works of the devil. Innkeepers were forbidden to allow anyone to consume food or drink without first saying grace, or to permit any patron to stay up after nine o'clock. Adultery, witchcraft, blasphemy, and heresy all became capital crimes. Even penalties for lesser crimes were severe. During the first four years after Calvin gained control in Geneva, there were no fewer than fifty-eight executions in this city with a total population of only 16,000.

As rigid as such a regime may seem today, Calvin's Geneva was a beacon of light to thousands of Protestants throughout Europe in the mid-sixteenth century. Calvin's disciple John Knox (c. 1514–1572), who brought the Reformed Church to Scotland, declared Geneva to be "the most perfect school of Christ that ever was on earth since the days of the Apostles." Converts flocked there for refuge or instruction and then returned home to become ardent proselytizers for the new religion. Geneva thus became the center of an international movement dedicated to spreading reformed religion to the rest of Europe through organized missionary activity and propaganda.

These efforts were remarkably successful. By the end of the sixteenth century, Calvinists were a majority in Scotland (where they were known as Presbyterians) and Holland (where they founded the Dutch Reformed Church). They were also influential in England (where they were known as Puritans), and there were substantial Calvinist minorities in France (where they were called Huguenots), Germany, Hungary, Lithuania, and Poland. By the end of the sixteenth century, Calvinism would spread to the New World.

The Beginnings of Religious Warfare

Less than a generation after Luther's challenge to the Church, wars erupted between Catholic and Protestant rulers. In Germany, Charles V attempted to reestablish Catholic unity by launching a military campaign against several German princes who had instituted Lutheran worship in their territories. But despite several notable victories, his efforts failed. In part, this was because Charles was also involved in wars against France; but primarily, it was because the Catholic princes of Germany worked against him, fearing that any suppression of Protestant princes might also diminish their own independence.

This regional warfare sputtered on and off until a compromise settlement was reached via the Peace of Augsburg in 1555. Its governing principle was *cuius regio, eius religio*: "as the ruler, so the religion." This meant that, in those principalities where Lutherans ruled, Lutheranism would be the sole state religion; but where Catholic princes ruled, the people of their territories would also be Catholic. For better and for worse, the Peace of Augsburg was a historical milestone. For the first time since Luther had been excommunicated, Catholic rulers were forced to acknowledge the legality of Protestantism. Yet the peace also set a dangerous precedent because it established the principle that no sovereign state can tolerate religious diversity. Moreover, it excluded Calvinism entirely and thus spurred German Calvinists to become aggressive opponents of the status quo. As a result, Europe would be riven by religious warfare for another century and would export sectarian violence to the New World (see Chapter 14).

THE DOMESTICATION OF REFORM

Within two decades, Protestantism had become a diverse movement whose radical claims for the spiritual equality of all Christians had the potential to undermine the political, social, and even gender hierarchies on which European society rested. Luther himself did not anticipate that his ideas might have such implications, and he was genuinely shocked when the rebellious German peasants and the radical Anabaptists at Münster interpreted his teachings in this way. And Luther was by no means the only staunchly conservative Protestant leader. None of the prominent early Protestants were social or political radicals; most depended on the support of existing elites. As a result, the Reformation movement was speedily "domesticated" in two senses. Its revolutionary potential was muffled—Luther himself rarely spoke about "the priesthood of all believers" after 1525—and there was an increasing emphasis on the patriarchal family as the central institution of reformed life.

Reform and Discipline

As we have seen, the desire to lead a more disciplined and godly life has been a frequent catalyst of religious reform movements. Since the Black Death (see Chapter 11), many of these efforts were actively promoted by princes and town councils, most famously perhaps in Florence, where the Dominican preacher Girolamo Savonarola led the city on an extraordinary but short-lived campaign of puritanism and moral reform between 1494 and 1498. And there are numerous other examples of rulers legislating against sin.

Competing Viewpoints

Marriage and Celibacy: Two Views

> These two selections illustrate the strongly contrasting views of the spiritual value of marriage versus celibacy that came to be embraced by Protestant and Catholic religious authorities. The first selection is part of Martin Luther's more general attack on monasticism, which emphasizes his contention that marriage is the natural and divinely intended state for all human beings. The second selection, from the decrees of the Council of Trent (1545–63), restates traditional Catholic teaching on the holiness of marriage but also emphasizes the spiritual superiority of virginity to marriage as well as the necessity of clerical celibacy.

Luther's Views on Celibacy (1535)

Listen! In all my days I have not heard the confession of a nun, but in the light of Scripture I shall hit upon how matters fare with her and know I shall not be lying. If a girl is not sustained by great and exceptional grace, she can live without a man as little as she can without eating, drinking, sleeping, and other natural necessities.

Nor, on the other hand, can a man dispense with a wife. The reason for this is that procreating children is an urge planted as deeply in human nature as eating and drinking. That is why God has given and put into the body the organs, arteries, fluxes, and everything that serves it. Therefore what is he doing who would check this process and keep nature from running its desired and intended course? He is attempting to keep nature from being nature, fire from burning, water from wetting, and a man from eating, drinking, and sleeping.

Source: E. M. Plass, ed., *What Luther Says*, vol. 2 (St. Louis, MO: 1959), pp. 888–89.

Canons on the Sacrament of Matrimony (1563)

Canon 1. If anyone says that matrimony is not truly and properly one of the seven sacraments . . . instituted by Christ the Lord, but has been devised by men in the Church and does not confer grace, let him be anathema [cursed].

Canon 9. If anyone says that clerics constituted in sacred orders or regulars [monks and nuns] who have made solemn profession of chastity can contract marriage . . . and that all who feel that they have not the gift of chastity, even though they have made such a vow, can contract marriage, let him be anathema, since God does not refuse that gift to those who ask for it rightly, neither does *he suffer us to be tempted above that which we are able.*

Canon 10: If anyone says that the married state excels the state of virginity or celibacy, and that it is better and happier to be united in matrimony than to remain in virginity or celibacy, let him be anathema.

Source: H. J. Schroeder, *Canons and Decrees of the Council of Trent* (St. Louis, MO: 1941), pp. 181–82.

Questions for Analysis

1. On what grounds does Luther attack the practice of celibacy? Do you agree with his basic premise?

2. How do the later canons of the Catholic Church respond to Protestant views like Luther's? What appears to be at stake in this defense of marriage and celibacy?

When Desiderius Erasmus called on secular authorities to think of themselves as abbots and of their territories as giant monasteries, he was sounding an already-familiar theme.

Protestant rulers, however, took the need to enforce godly discipline with particular seriousness, because the depravity of human nature was a fundamental tenet of Protestant belief. Like Saint Augustine at the end of the fourth century, Protestants believed that people would inevitably turn out bad unless they were compelled to be good. It was therefore the responsibility of secular and religious leaders to control the behavior of their people, because otherwise their evil deeds would anger God and destroy humanity.

Protestant godliness began with the discipline of children. Luther himself wrote two catechisms (instructional tracts) designed to teach children the tenets of their faith and the obligations—toward parents, masters, and rulers—that God imposed on them. Luther also insisted that all children, boys and girls alike, be taught to read the Bible in their own languages. Schooling thus became a characteristically Protestant preoccupation and rallying cry. Even the Protestant family was designated a "school of godliness," in which fathers were expected to instruct and discipline their wives, their children, and their servants.

But private life still left much to be desired in the eyes of Protestant reformers. Drunkenness, domestic violence, illicit sex, dancing, and blasphemy were frequent topics of reforming discourse. Various methods of discipline were attempted, including private counseling, public confessions of wrongdoing, public penances and shamings, exclusion from church services, and even imprisonment. All of these efforts met with varying, but generally modest, success. Creating godly Protestant families, and enforcing godly discipline on entire communities, was going to require the active cooperation of godly authorities.

Protestantism, Government, and the Family

The domestication of the Reformation in this wider sense took place principally in the free towns of Germany, Switzerland, and the Netherlands—and from there spread westward to North America. Protestant emphasis on the depravity of the human will, and the consequent need for discipline, resonated powerfully with guilds and town governments, which were anxious to maintain and increase the control exercised by urban elites (mainly merchants and master craftsmen) over the apprentices and journeymen who made up the majority of the male population. By eliminating the competing jurisdictional authority of the Roman Church, Protestantism allowed town governments to consolidate all authority within the city into their own hands.

Protestant governments reinforced the control of individual men over their own households by emphasizing the family as the basic unit of religious education. In place of a priest, an all-powerful father figure was expected to assume responsibility for his household. At the same time, Protestantism introduced a new religious ideal for women. No longer was the virginal nun the exemplar of female holiness; in her place now stood the married and obedient Protestant "goodwife." As one Lutheran prince wrote in 1527: "Those who bear children please God better than all the monks and nuns singing and praying." By declaring the holiness of marital sex, Protestantism relieved the tensions between piety and sexuality that had long characterized Christian teachings.

Yet this did not promote a new view of women's spiritual potential, nor did it elevate their social and political status. Quite the contrary: Luther regarded women as more sexually driven than men and less capable of controlling their lusts (reflecting the fact that Luther confessed himself incapable of celibacy). His opposition to convents rested on his belief that it was impossible for women to remain chaste, so sequestering them simply made illicit behavior inevitable. To prevent sin, it was necessary that all women should be married, preferably at a young age, and so placed under the governance of a godly husband.

For the most part, Protestant town governments were happy to cooperate in shutting down female monasteries. The convent's property went to the town, after all. But conflicts did arise over marriage and sexuality, especially over the reformers' insistence that both men and women should marry young as a restraint on lust. In many towns, men were traditionally expected to delay marriage until they had achieved the status of master craftsman. In theory, then, apprentices and journeymen were not supposed to marry. Instead, they were expected to frequent brothels, a legally sanctioned outlet for extramarital sexuality long viewed as necessary to men's physical well-being, but one that Protestant reformers now deemed morally abhorrent.

Towns responded in a variety of ways to these opposing pressures. Some instituted special committees to police public morals, of the sort we have noted in Calvin's Geneva. Some abandoned Protestantism altogether. Others, like the German town of Augsburg, alternated between forms of Protestantism and Roman Catholicism for several decades. Yet regardless of a town's final choice of religious allegiance, by the end of the sixteenth century a revolution had taken place with respect to governments' attitudes toward public morality. In their competition with each other, neither Catholics nor Protestants wished to be seen as soft on sin. The result was the widespread abolition of publicly licensed brothels, the outlawing of prostitution, and far stricter governmental supervision of many other aspects of private life.

Parental Control of Marriage

Protestantism also increased parents' control over their children's choice of marital partners. The medieval Church had defined marriage as a sacrament that did not require the involvement of a priest. The mutual free consent of two individuals, even if given without witnesses or parental approval, was enough to constitute a legally valid marriage in the eyes of the Church. Opposition to this doctrine had long come from many quarters, especially from families who stood to lose from this liberal stance: because marriage involved rights of inheritance to property, it was regarded as too important a matter to be left to the choice of adolescents. Instead, parents wanted the power to prevent unsuitable matches and, in some cases, to force their children to accept the marriage arrangements their families made for them.

Protestantism offered a welcome opportunity to achieve such control. Luther had declared marriage to be a purely secular matter, not a sacrament at all, and one that could be regulated however governing authorities thought best. Calvin largely followed suit. Even the Catholic Church was eventually forced to give way. Although it never abandoned its insistence that both members of a couple must freely consent to their marriage, by the end of the sixteenth century the Church required formal public notice of intent to marry and insisted on the presence of a priest at the actual wedding ceremony. Both were efforts to prevent elopements and so to allow families time to intervene before an unsuitable marriage was formed. Individual Catholic countries sometimes went even further in trying to assert parental control over their children's choice of partners. In France, for example, although couples might still marry without parental consent, those who did so now forfeited all of their rights to inherit their families' property. In somewhat different ways, both Protestantism and Catholicism thus moved to strengthen the control that parents could exercise over their children.

THE REFORMATION OF ENGLAND

In England, the Reformation took a rather different course than it did in continental Europe. Although a long tradition of popular reform had thrived there for centuries, the number of dissidents was usually too small and their influence too limited to play a significant role. Nor was England particularly oppressed by the papal exactions and abuses that roiled Germany. When the sixteenth century began, English monarchs already exercised close control over Church appointments; they also received the lion's share of the papal taxation collected within the realm. Why, then, did England become a Protestant country at all?

The King's "Great Matter"

In 1527, King Henry VIII of England had been married to Ferdinand and Isabella's daughter, Catherine of Aragon, for eighteen years. Yet all the offspring of this union had died in infancy, with the exception of a daughter, Mary. Catherine was now past the age of childbearing. And Henry needed a male heir to preserve the fragile succession to the throne: his father, Henry VII, had come to power after a time of civil war (Chapter 11), and resentment against the new Tudor dynasty still smoldered. Henry thus had strong political reasons to propose a change of wife. He also had more personal motives, having become infatuated with a lady-in-waiting named Anne Boleyn.

Henry therefore appealed to Rome to annul his marriage to Catherine, arguing that because she had previously been married to his older brother Arthur (who had died in adolescence), their marriage had been invalid from the beginning. As Henry's representatives pointed out, the Bible pronounced it "an unclean thing" for a man to take his brother's wife and cursed such a marriage with childlessness (Leviticus 20:21). Even a papal dispensation, which Henry and Catherine had long before obtained for their marriage, could not exempt them from such a clear prohibition—as the marriage's childlessness proved.

Henry's petition put Pope Clement VII (r. 1523–34) in an awkward position. Both Henry and Clement knew that popes in the past had granted annulments to reigning monarchs on far weaker grounds than the ones Henry was alleging. If, however, the pope granted Henry's annulment, he would cast doubt on the validity of all papal dispensations. More seriously, he would provoke the wrath of Emperor Charles V, Catherine of Aragon's nephew, whose armies were in firm command of Rome and who at that moment held the pope himself in captivity. Clement was trapped; all he could do was procrastinate and hope that the matter would resolve itself. For two years, he allowed Henry's case to proceed in England without ever reaching a verdict. Then, suddenly, he transferred the case to Rome, where the legal process began all over again.

Exasperated, Henry began to take matters into his own hands. In 1531, he compelled an assembly of English clergy to declare him "protector and only supreme head" of the Church in England. In 1532, he encouraged Parliament to produce an inflammatory list of grievances against the English clergy and used this threat to force them to concede his right, as king, to approve or deny all Church legislation. In January 1533, Henry married Anne Boleyn (already pregnant) even though his marriage to Queen Catherine had still not been annulled. The new archbishop of Canterbury, Thomas Cranmer, later provided the required annulment in May, acting on his own authority.

In September, Princess Elizabeth was born; her father, disappointed again in his hopes for a son, refused to attend her christening. Nevertheless, Parliament settled the succession to the throne on the children of Henry and Anne, redirected all papal revenues from England into the king's hands, prohibited appeals to the papal court, and formally declared "the King's highness to be Supreme Head of the Church of England." In 1536, Henry executed his former tutor and chancellor Sir Thomas More (see Chapter 12) for his refusal to endorse this declaration of supremacy, and took the first steps toward dissolving England's many monasteries. By the end of 1539, the monasteries and convents were gone and their lands and wealth confiscated by the king.

These measures, largely masterminded and engineered by Henry's brilliant Protestant adviser, Thomas Cromwell (c. 1485–1540), broke the bonds that linked the English Church to Rome. But they did not make England a formally Protestant country. Although certain traditional practices (such as pilgrimages and the veneration of relics) were prohibited, the English Church remained overwhelmingly Catholic in organization, doctrine, ritual, and language. The Six Articles promulgated by Parliament in 1539 at Henry VIII's behest left no room for doubt as to official orthodoxy: confession to priests, masses for the dead, and clerical celibacy were all confirmed; the Latin Mass continued; and Catholic Eucharistic doctrine was not only confirmed but denying it was made punishable by death. To most English people, only the disappearance of the monasteries and the king's own continuing matrimonial adventures (he married six wives in all) were evidence that their Church was no longer in communion with Rome.

The Reign of Edward VI

For truly committed Protestants, and especially those who had visited Calvin's Geneva, the changes Henry VIII enforced on the English Church did not go nearly far enough. In 1547, the accession of the nine-year-old king Edward VI (Henry's son by his third wife, Jane Seymour) gave them the opportunity to finish the task of reform. Encouraged by the apparent sympathies of the young king, Edward's government moved quickly to reform the doctrine and ceremonies of the English Church. Priests were permitted to marry; English services replaced Latin ones; the veneration of images was discouraged, and the images themselves were defaced or destroyed; prayers for the dead were declared useless, and endowments for such prayers were confiscated; and new articles of belief were drawn up, repudiating all sacraments except baptism and communion and affirming the Protestant creed of justification by faith alone. Most important, *The Book of Common Prayer*, authored by Archbishop Cranmer and considered one of the great landmarks of English literature, was published to define precisely how the new English-language services of the church were to be conducted. By 1553, when the youthful Edward died, England appeared to have become a distinctly Protestant kingdom.

Mary Tudor and the Restoration of Catholicism

Edward's successor, however, was his pious and much older half sister Mary (r. 1553–58), granddaughter of "the most Catholic monarchs" of Spain. Mary speedily reversed her half-brother's religious policies, restoring the Latin Mass and requiring married priests to give up their wives. She even prevailed on Parliament to vote a return to papal allegiance. Hundreds of Protestant leaders fled abroad, many to Geneva; others, including Archbishop Thomas Cranmer, were burned at the stake for refusing to deny their Protestant faith. Yet Mary's policies could not wipe out religious resistance. Nor could they do anything to restore monastic life in England: too many leading families had profited from her father's dissolution of the monasteries.

Mary's marriage to her cousin Philip, Charles V's son and heir to the Spanish throne, was another miscalculation. Although the marriage treaty stipulated that Philip could not succeed her in the event of her death, her English subjects never trusted him. When the queen allowed herself to be drawn into a war with France on Spain's

The Six Articles of the English Church

Although Henry VIII withdrew the Church of England from obedience to the papacy, he continued to reject most Protestant theology. Some of his advisers, most notably Thomas Cromwell, were committed Protestants; and the king allowed his son and heir, Edward VI, to be raised as a Protestant. But even after several years of rapid (and mostly Protestant) change in the English Church, Henry reasserted a set of traditional Catholic doctrines in the Six Articles of 1539. These would remain binding on the Church of England until the king's death in 1547.

First, that in the most blessed sacrament of the altar, by the strength and efficacy of Christ's mighty word, it being spoken by the priest, is present really, under the form of bread and wine, the natural body and blood of our Savior Jesus Christ, conceived of the Virgin Mary, and that after the consecration there remains no substance of bread or wine, nor any other substance but the substance of Christ, God and man;

Secondly, that communion in both kinds is not necessary for salvation, by the law of God, to all persons, and that it is to be believed and not doubted . . . that in the flesh, under the form of bread, is the very blood, and with the blood, under the form of wine, is the very flesh, as well apart as though they were both together;

Thirdly, that priests, after the order of priesthood received as afore, may not marry by the law of God;

Fourthly, that vows of chastity or widowhood by man or woman made to God advisedly ought to be observed by the law of God. . . .

Fifthly, that it is right and necessary that private masses be continued and admitted in this the king's English Church and congregation . . . whereby good Christian people . . . do receive both godly and goodly consolations and benefits; and it is agreeable also to God's law;

Sixthly, that oral, private confession is expedient and necessary to be retained and continued, used and frequented in the church of God.

Source: *Statutes of the Realm*, vol. 3 (London: 1810–28), p. 739 (modernized).

Questions for Analysis

1. Three of these six articles focus on the sacrament of the Eucharist (the Mass). Given what you have learned in this chapter, why would Henry have been so concerned about this sacrament? What does this reveal about his values and those of his contemporaries?

2. Given Henry's insistence on these articles, why might he have allowed his son to be raised a Protestant? What does this suggest about the political situation in England?

---

behalf—in which England lost Calais, its last foothold on the European continent—many people became highly disaffected. Ultimately, however, what doomed Mary's policies was the fact that she died childless, after only five years of rule. Her throne passed to her Protestant sister, Elizabeth.

The Elizabethan Compromise

As the daughter of Henry VIII and the Lutheran sympathizer Anne Boleyn, Elizabeth (r. 1558–1603) was predisposed in favor of Protestantism by the circumstances of her parents' marriage as well as by her upbringing. But Elizabeth and her advisers also recognized that supporting radical Protestantism in England might provoke bitter sectarian strife. Accordingly, she presided over what is often known as "the Elizabethan settlement." By a new Act of Supremacy (1559), Elizabeth repealed Mary's Catholic legislation, prohibiting foreign religious powers (i.e., the pope) from exercising any authority within England and declaring herself "supreme governor" of the English church—a more Protestant title than Henry VIII's "supreme head" (since most Protestants believed that Christ alone was the head of the Church). She also adopted many of the Protestant liturgical reforms instituted under

QUEEN MARY AND QUEEN ELIZABETH. The two daughters of Henry VIII were the first two queens regnant of England: the first women to rule in their own right. Despite the similar challenges they faced, they had strikingly different fates and have been treated very differently in popular histories. ▪ *How do these two portraits suggest differences in their personalities and their self-representation as rulers?*

her half-brother, Edward, including the revised version of *The Book of Common Prayer.* But she retained vestiges of Catholic practice, too, including bishops, church courts, and vestments for the clergy. On most doctrinal matters, Elizabeth's Thirty-Nine Articles of Faith (approved in 1562) struck a decidedly Protestant, even Calvinist, tone. But the prayer book was more moderate and, on the critical issue of the Eucharist, deliberately ambiguous. By combining Catholic and Protestant interpretations ("This is my body. . . . Do this in remembrance of me"), the prayer book permitted there to be competing interpretations of the service by priests and parishioners alike.

Yet religious tensions persisted in Elizabeth's England, not only between Protestants and Catholics but also between moderate and more extreme Protestants, the Puritans. Ultimately, what preserved "the Elizabethan settlement" was not this artful blurring of religious doctrines and ceremonies but the extraordinary length of Queen Elizabeth's reign, combined with the fact that for much of that time England was at war with Catholic Spain. Under Elizabeth, Protestantism and nationalism gradually fused together into a potent conviction that God himself had chosen England for greatness. After 1588, when English naval forces won an improbable victory over the Spanish Armada (see Chapter 14), Protestantism and Englishness became nearly indistinguishable to most of Elizabeth's subjects. Laws against Catholic practices became increasingly severe, and although an English Catholic tradition did survive, its adherents were a persecuted minority. Significant, too, was the situation in Ireland, where the vast majority

of the population remained Catholic despite the government's efforts to impose Protestantism on them. As a result, Irishness would be as firmly identified with Catholicism as Englishness was with Protestantism; but it was the Protestants who held power in both countries.

THE REBIRTH OF THE CATHOLIC CHURCH

So far, our discussion of the Reformation has cast the spotlight on Protestant reformers. But there was also a powerful reform movement within the Roman Church in these same decades, a reform which resulted in its rebirth. For some, this movement is the "Catholic Reformation"; for others, it is the "Counter-Reformation." Those who prefer the former name emphasize that the Roman Church of the sixteenth century was actually continuing a reforming movement that can be traced back to the eleventh century (see Chapter 8) and which gained new momentum in the wake of the Great Schism (see Chapter 11): in this view, reform is just a part of Catholic tradition. Others insist that most Catholic reformers of this period were reactionary, inspired primarily by the urgent need to resist Protestantism and to strengthen the power of the Roman Church in opposition to it: hence the "Counter-Reformation." Both perspectives are valid.

Catholic Reform and the Council of Trent

Long before Luther's challenge to Rome, as we have seen, there were movements for moral and institutional reform within the medieval Church. In the fifteenth century, however, while these efforts received strong support from several secular rulers, the papacy showed little interest in them. In Spain, for example, reforming activities directed by Cardinal Francisco Ximenes de Cisneros (1436–1517) led to the imposition of strict rules of behavior and the elimination of abuses prevalent among the clergy. Ximenes (*she-MEN-ez*) also helped to regenerate the spiritual life of the Spanish Church. In Italy, meanwhile, earnest clerics labored to make the Italian Church more worthy of its prominent position. But reforming existing monastic orders was a difficult task, not least because the papal court set such a poor example. Still, Italian reformers did

Past and Present

Controlling Consumption

Although laws regulating the conspicuous consumption of expensive commodities—especially status-conscious clothing—were common during the later Middle Ages, it was not until after the Reformation that both Protestant and Catholic leaders began to criminalize formerly acceptable bodily practices and substances. New theories of sensory perception, the availability of new products like coffee and tobacco, and a new concern to internalize reform led some authorities to outlaw prostitution (hitherto legal) and to ban normal social practices like drinking and dancing. The image on the left shows the militant Catholic League founded in sixteenth-century France, which combatted Protestantism and promoted strict religious observance. The image on the right shows Czech protesters calling for the decriminalization of marijuana.

Watch related author videos on the Student Site
wwnorton.com/college/history/western-civilizationsBrief4

manage to establish several new orders dedicated to high ideals of piety and social service. In northern Europe, Christian humanists such as Erasmus and Thomas More also played a role in this Catholic reform movement, not only by criticizing abuses and editing sacred texts but also by encouraging the laity to lead lives of sincere piety (as we saw in Chapter 12).

As a response to the challenges posed by Protestantism, however, these internal reforms proved inadequate. Starting in the 1530s, therefore, a more aggressive phase of reform began to gather momentum under a new style of vigorous papal leadership. The popes of this era—Paul III (r. 1534–49), Paul IV (r. 1555–59), Pius V (r. 1566–72), and Sixtus V (r. 1585–90)—were the most zealous reformers of the Church since the eleventh century. All led upright lives; some, indeed, were so grimly ascetic that contemporaries longed for the bad old days. And these popes were not merely holy men. They were also accomplished administrators who reorganized papal finances and filled ecclesiastical offices with bishops and abbots no less renowned for austerity and holiness than were the popes themselves.

Papal reform efforts intensified at the Council of Trent, a general council of the entire Church convened in 1545, which met at intervals thereafter until 1563. The decisions taken at Trent (a provincial capital of the Holy Roman Empire, located in modern-day Italy) provided the foundations on which a new Roman Catholic Church would be erected. Although the council began by debating some form of compromise with Protestantism, it ended by reaffirming all of the tenets challenged by Protestant critics. "Good works" were affirmed as necessary for salvation, and all seven sacraments were declared indispensable means of grace, without which salvation was impossible. Transubstantiation, Purgatory, the invocation of saints, and the rule of celibacy for the clergy were all confirmed as dogmas—essential elements—of the Catholic faith.

The Demands of Obedience

The necessity of obedience in the spiritual formation of monks and nuns can be traced back to the Rule *of Saint Benedict in the early sixth century, and beyond. In keeping with the mission of its founder, Ignatius of Loyola (1491–1556), the Society of Jesus brought a new militancy to this old ideal.*

Rules for Thinking with the Church

1. Always to be ready to obey with mind and heart, setting aside all judgment of one's own, the true spouse of Jesus Christ, our holy mother, our infallible and orthodox mistress, the Catholic Church, whose authority is exercised over us by the hierarchy.

2. To commend the confession of sins to a priest as it is practised in the Church; the reception of the Holy Eucharist once a year, or better still every week, or at least every month, with the necessary preparation. . . .

4. To have a great esteem for the religious orders, and to give the preference to celibacy or virginity over the married state. . . .

6. To praise relics, the veneration and invocation of Saints: also the stations, and pious pilgrimages, indulgences, jubilees, the custom of lighting candles in the churches, and other such aids to piety and devotion. . . .

9. To uphold especially all the precepts of the Church, and not censure them in any manner; but, on the contrary, to defend them promptly, with reasons drawn from all sources, against those who criticize them.

10. To be eager to commend the decrees, mandates, traditions, rites, and customs of the Fathers in the Faith or our superiors. . . .

11. That we may be altogether of the same mind and in conformity with the Church herself, if she shall have defined anything to be black which to our eyes appears to be white, we ought in like manner to pronounce it to be black. For we must undoubtingly believe, that the Spirit of our Lord Jesus Christ, and the Spirit of the Orthodox Church His Spouse, by which Spirit we are governed and directed to salvation, is the same. . . .

From the Constitutions of the Jesuit Order

Let us with the utmost pains strain every nerve of our strength to exhibit this virtue of obedience, firstly to the Highest Pontiff, then to the Superiors of the Society; so that in all things . . . we may be most ready to obey his voice, just as if it issued from Christ our Lord . . . leaving any work, even a letter, that we have begun and have not yet finished; by directing to this goal all our strength and intention in the Lord, that holy obedience may be made perfect in us in every respect, in performance, in will, in intellect; by submitting to whatever may be enjoined on us with great readiness, with spiritual joy and perseverance; by persuading ourselves that all things [commanded] are just; by rejecting with a kind of blind obedience all opposing opinion or judgment of our own. . . .

Source: Henry Bettenson, ed., *Documents of the Christian Church*, 2nd ed. (Oxford: 1967), pp. 259–61.

Questions for Analysis

1. How might Loyola's career as a soldier have inspired the language used in his "Rules for Thinking with the Church"?

2. In what ways do these Jesuit principles respond directly to the challenges of Protestant reformers?

The Bible (in its flawed Vulgate form, not the new humanist edition of Erasmus) and the tradition of apostolic teaching were held to be of equal authority as sources of Christian truth. Papal supremacy over every bishop and priest was expressly maintained, and the supremacy of the pope over any Church council was taken for granted, signaling a final defeat of the still-active conciliar movement. The Council of Trent even reaffirmed the doctrine of indulgences that had touched off the Lutheran revolt, although it condemned the worst abuses connected with their sale.

The legislation of Trent was not confined to matters of doctrine. To improve pastoral care of the laity, bishops

THE INSPIRATION OF SAINT JEROME BY GUIDO RENI (1635). The Council of Trent declared Saint Jerome's Latin translation of the Bible, the Vulgate, to be the official version of the Catholic Church. Since biblical scholars had known since the early sixteenth century that Saint Jerome's translation contained numerous mistakes, Catholic defenders of the Vulgate insisted that even his mistakes had been divinely inspired. ■ *How does Guido Reni's painting attempt to make this point?*

and priests were forbidden to hold more than one spiritual office. To address the problem of an ignorant priesthood, a theological seminary was to be established in every diocese. The council also suppressed a variety of local religious practices and saints' cults, replacing them with new cults authorized and approved by Rome. To prevent heretical ideas from corrupting the faithful, the council further decided to censor or suppress dangerous books. In 1564, a specially appointed commission published the first *Index of Prohibited Books* forbidden to faithful Catholics. Ironically, all of Erasmus's works were immediately placed on the *Index*, even though he had been a champion of the Church against Martin Luther only forty years before. A permanent agency known as the Congregation of the Index was later set up to revise the list, which was maintained until 1966, when it was abolished after the Second Vatican Council (1962–65). For centuries, the *Index* was symbolic of the doctrinal intolerance that characterized sixteenth-century Christianity, both in its Catholic and Protestant varieties.

Ignatius Loyola and the Society of Jesus

In addition to the concerted activities of popes and the legislation of the Council of Trent, a third main force propelling the

Church's response to Protestantism was the foundation of the Society of Jesus, commonly known as the Jesuits. In 1521, in the midst of a career as a mercenary, a young Spanish nobleman called Ignatius Loyola (1491–1556) was wounded in battle. While recuperating, he turned from the reading of chivalric romances to a romantic retelling of the life of Jesus—and the impact of this experience convinced him to become a spiritual soldier of Christ. This was the same year that Luther defied papal authority at the Diet of Worms.

For ten months, Ignatius lived as a hermit in a cave near the town of Manresa, where he experienced ecstatic visions and worked out the principles of his *Spiritual Exercises*. This manual, eventually completed in 1535 and first published in 1541, offered practical advice on how to master one's will and serve God through a systematic program of meditations on sin and the life of Christ. It eventually became the basic handbook for all Jesuits and has been widely studied by Catholic laypeople as well. Indeed, Loyola's *Spiritual Exercises* ranks alongside Calvin's *Institutes* as the most influential religious text of the sixteenth century.

The Jesuit order originated as a small group of six disciples who gathered around Loyola during his belated career as a student in Paris. They vowed to serve God in poverty, chastity, and missionary work and were formally constituted as a clerical order by Pope Paul III in 1540. By the time of Loyola's death, the Society of Jesus already numbered some 1,500 members. It was by far the most militant of the religious orders fostered by the Catholic reform movements of the sixteenth century—not merely a monastic society but a company of soldiers sworn to defend the faith. Their weapons were not bullets and swords but eloquence, persuasion, and instruction in correct doctrines; as a result, the Society also became accomplished in more worldly methods of exerting influence.

The activities of the Jesuits consisted primarily of proselytizing and promoting strict educational standards. This meant that they were ideal missionaries. Accordingly, Jesuits were soon dispatched to preach to non-Christians in India, China, and Spanish America. One of Loyola's closest associates, Francis Xavier (ZAY-vyer, 1506–1552), baptized thousands of people and traveled thousands of miles in South and East Asia.

Although Loyola had not conceived of his society as a batallion of "shock troops" in the global spread of Catholicism and the fight against Protestantism, that is what it primarily became. Through preaching and diplomacy—sometimes at the risk of their lives—Jesuits in the second half of the sixteenth century helped to colonize the world. In many places, they were instrumental in keeping rulers and their subjects loyal to Catholicism; in others, they met martyrdom; and in some others, notably Poland and parts of Germany and France, they succeeded in regaining territory previously lost to followers of Luther and Calvin. Wherever they were allowed to settle, they set up schools and colleges, on the grounds that only a vigorous Catholicism nurtured by widespread literacy and learning could combat Protestant errors.

A New Catholic Christianity

The greatest achievement of these reform movements was the revitalization of the Roman Church. Had it not been for such determined efforts, Catholicism would not have swept over the globe during the seventeenth and eighteenth centuries—or reemerged in Europe as a vigorous spiritual force. There were some other consequences as well. One was the rapid advancement of lay literacy in Catholic countries, as well as in Protestant ones. Another was the growth of intense concern for acts of charity; because Catholicism continued to emphasize good works as well as faith, charitable activities took on an extremely important role.

There was also a renewed emphasis on the role of religious women. Reformed Catholicism did not exalt marriage as a route to holiness to the same degree as did Protestantism, but it did encourage the piety of a female religious elite. For example, it embraced the mysticism of women like Saint Teresa of Avila (1515–1582) and established new orders of nuns, such as the Ursulines and the Sisters of Charity. Both Protestants and Catholics continued to exclude women from the priesthood or ministry, but Catholic women could pursue religious lives with at least some degree of independence, and the convent continued to be a route toward spiritual and even political advancement in Catholic countries.

The reformed Catholic Church did not, however, perpetuate the tolerant Christianity of Erasmus. Instead, Christian humanists lost favor with the papacy, and even scientists such as Galileo Galilei (1564–1642) were regarded with suspicion (see Chapter 16). Yet contemporary Protestantism was just as intolerant, and even more hostile to the cause of rational thought. Indeed, because Catholic theologians turned for guidance to the scholasticism of Thomas Aquinas, they tended to be much more committed to the dignity of human reason than were their Protestant counterparts, who emphasized the literal interpretation of the Bible and the importance of unquestioning faith. It is no coincidence that René Descartes (1596–1650), one of the pioneers of rational philosophy ("I think, therefore I am"), was educated by Jesuits.

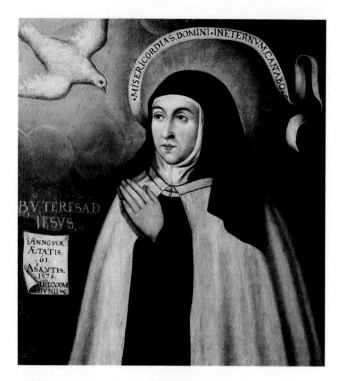

TERESA OF AVILA. Teresa of Avila (1515–1582) was one of many female religious figures who played an important role in the reformed Catholic Church. She was canonized in 1622. This image is dated 1576. The Latin wording on the scroll unfurled above Teresa's head reads: "I will sing forever of the mercy of the Holy Lord."

The Protestantism of this era cannot, therefore, be regarded as more progressive than Catholicism. Both were, in fact, products of the same troubled time. Each variety of Protestantism responded to specific historical conditions and to the needs of specific peoples in specific places, while carrying forward certain aspects of the Christian tradition considered valuable by those communities. The Catholic Church also responded to new spiritual, political, and social realities—to such an extent that it must be regarded as distinct from either the early Church of the later Roman Empire or even the oft-reformed Church of the Middle Ages. That is why the phrase "Roman Catholic Church" has not been used in this book prior to this chapter, because the Roman Catholic Church as we know it emerged for the first time in the sixteenth century.

CONCLUSION

The Reformation grew out of complex historical processes that we have been tracing in the last few chapters. Foremost among these was the increasing power of Europe's sovereign states. As we have seen, those German princes who embraced Protestantism were moved to do so by the desire for sovereignty. The kings of Denmark, Sweden, and England followed suit for many of the same reasons. Since Protestant leaders preached absolute obedience to godly rulers, and since the state in Protestant countries assumed direct control of its churches, Protestantism bolstered state power. Yet the power of the state had been growing for a long time prior to this, especially in such countries as France and Spain, where Catholic kings already exercised most of the same rights that were seized by Lutheran authorities, and by Henry VIII of England in the course of their own reformations. Those rulers who aligned themselves with Catholicism, then, had the same need to bolster their sovereignty and power.

Ideas of national identity, too, were already influential and thus available for manipulation by Protestants and Catholics alike. These religions, in turn, became new sources of both identity and disunity. Prior to the Reformation, peoples in the different regions of Germany spoke such different dialects that they had difficulty understanding each other. But Luther's German Bible gained such currency that it eventually became the linguistic standard for all these disparate regions, which eventually began to conceive of themselves as part of a single nation.

Elsewhere—as in the Netherlands, where Protestants fought successfully against a foreign, Catholic overlord—religion created a shared identity where politics could not. In England, membership in the Church of England became a new, but not uncontested, attribute of "Englishness." In every region of Europe, meanwhile, both Protestant and Catholic reformers called for new forms of morality, increased patriarchal control over family and

After You Read This Chapter

Go to **INQUIZITIVE** to see what you've learned—and learn what you've missed—with personalized feedback along the way.

REVIEWING THE OBJECTIVES

- The main premises of Luther's theology had religious, political, and social implications. What were these premises, and how did they affect real change?
- Swiss cities fostered a number of different Protestant movements. Why was this the case?
- The Reformation had a profound effect on the basic structures of family life and on attitudes toward marriage and morality. Describe these changes.
- The Church of England was established in response to a specific political situation. What was this, and how did the English Church continue to evolve in the course of the sixteenth century?
- How did the Catholic Church respond to the challenge of Protestantism?

community, strict disciplinary measures, and higher educational standards.

Ideals characteristic of the Renaissance also contributed something to the Reformation and the Catholic responses to it. The criticisms of Christian humanists helped to prepare Europe for the challenges of Lutheranism, and close textual study of the Bible led to the publication of the newer, more accurate editions used by Protestant reformers. For example, Erasmus's improved edition of the Latin New Testament enabled Luther to reach some crucial conclusions concerning the meaning of penance and became the foundation for Luther's own translation of the Bible. However, Erasmus was no supporter of Lutheran principles, and most other Christian humanists followed suit, shunning Protestantism as soon as it became clear to them what Luther was actually teaching. Indeed, in certain basic respects, Protestant doctrine was completely at odds with the principles, politics, and beliefs of most humanists, who became staunch supporters of the Catholic Church.

In the New World and Asia, both Protestantism and Catholicism became forces of imperialism and new catalysts for competition. The race to secure colonies and resources now became a race for converts, too, as missionaries of both faiths fanned out over the globe. In the process, the confessional divisions of Europe were mapped onto these regions, often with violent results. Over the course of the ensuing century, newly sovereign nation-states would struggle for hegemony at home and abroad, setting off a series of religious wars that would cause as much destruction as any plague. Meanwhile, Western civilizations' extension into the Atlantic would create new kinds of ecosystems, forms of wealth, and types of bondage.

PEOPLE, IDEAS, AND EVENTS IN CONTEXT

- How did **MARTIN LUTHER**'s attack on **INDULGENCES** tap into more widespread criticism of the papacy? What role did the printing press and the German vernacular play in the dissemination of his ideas?

- Why did many German principalities and cities rally to Luther's cause? Why did his condemnation at the **DIET OF WORMS** not lead to his execution on charges of heresy?

- How did the Protestant teachings of **ULRICH ZWINGLI**, **JOHN CALVIN**, and the **ANABAPTISTS** differ from one another and from those of Luther?

- What factors made some of Europe's territories more receptive to **PROTESTANTISM** than others? What was the meaning of the principle *CUIUS REGIO, EIUS RELIGIO*, established by the Peace of Augsburg?

- How did the **REFORMATION** alter the status and lives of women in Europe? Why did it strengthen male authority in the family?

- Why did **HENRY VIII** break with Rome? How did the **CHURCH OF ENGLAND** differ from other Protestant churches in Europe?

- What decisions were made at the **COUNCIL OF TRENT**? What were the founding principles of **IGNATIUS LOYOLA**'s **SOCIETY OF JESUS**, and what was its role in the **COUNTER-REFORMATION** of the **CATHOLIC CHURCH**?

THINKING ABOUT CONNECTIONS

- Our study of Western civilizations has shown that reforming movements are nothing new: Christianity has been continuously reformed throughout its long history. What made this Reformation so different?

- Was a Protestant break with the Roman Catholic Church inevitable, in your view? Why or why not?

- The political, social, and religious structures put in place during this era continue to shape our lives in such profound ways that we scarcely notice them—or we assume them to be inevitable and natural. In your view, what is the most far-reaching consequence of this age of dissent and division, and why? In what ways has it formed your own values and assumptions?

STORY LINES

- By the middle of the sixteenth century, the Atlantic Ocean became a zone of colonization, commerce, migration, and settlement, as the peoples of this Atlantic world confronted one another.

- In the wake of the Reformation, Europe itself remained politically unstable. Devastating religious wars were waged on the Continent. In England, mounting pressures caused a crisis that resulted in civil war and the execution of the reigning king.

- At the same time, competition in the wider Atlantic world exported these political and religious conflicts to Europe's new American colonies.

- This widening world and its pervasive violence caused many to question the beliefs of earlier generations and to seek new sources of authority.

CHRONOLOGY

1555	Peace of Augsburg
1562–1598	French wars of religion
1566–1609	Dutch wars with Spain
1588	Destruction of the Spanish Armada
1598	Edict of Nantes
1607	English colony of Jamestown founded
1608	French colony in Québec founded
1611	Shakespeare's play *The Tempest* is performed in London
1618	Thirty Years' War begins
1621	Dutch West India Company founded
1642–1649	English Civil War
1648	Beginning of the *Fronde* rebellions; the Thirty Years' War ends
1649	Execution of Charles I of England
1660	Restoration of the English monarchy

Before
You
Read
This
Chapter

Europe in the Atlantic World, 1550–1660

CORE OBJECTIVES

- **TRACE** the new linkages between Western civilizations and the Atlantic world, and **DESCRIBE** their consequences.

- **DESCRIBE** the different forms of unfree labor that developed in European colonies during this period, and **EXPLAIN** why each was created.

- **IDENTIFY** the monarchies that dominated Europe and the newer powers whose influence was expanding in the Atlantic.

- **EXPLAIN** the reasons for Europe's religious and political instability and its consequences.

- **UNDERSTAND** how artists and intellectuals responded to the crises and uncertainties of this era.

The Atlantic Ocean thrashes the shores of Europe and Africa with waves that have traveled thousands of miles from the American coasts. It links continents shaped by a wide variety of climates and diverse ecosystems. For most of human history, the limited movement of peoples on opposite sides of the ocean allowed these regions to nurture their own forms of plant and animal life, their own unique microbes and pathogens.

But in the sixteenth century, the Atlantic became an arena of cultural and economic exchange that broke down the isolation of these ecosystems. Humans, animals, and plants on once-remote shores came into intense contact. Europeans brought diseases that devastated the peoples of the Americas, along with gunpowder and a hotly divided Christianity. Meanwhile, the huge influx of silver from South America transformed (and eventually exploded) the cash-starved European economy, while the arrival of American luxury goods such as tobacco, sugar, and chocolate fostered new appetites. The need

369

for slaves to power the plantations that supplied these consumer products created a vast industry of human trafficking, which led to the forcible removal of nearly 11 million people from Africa over the course of three centuries. Colonial settlement in North and South America also created new social hierarchies and new regimes of inequality. Indigenous peoples and newly arrived settlers confronted one another, and all were affected by the profound upheavals of Europe. In response, intellectuals and artists strove to reassess Europeans' place in this expanding Atlantic world, and to make sense of the profound changes that were occurring in daily life.

THE EMERGENCE OF THE ATLANTIC WORLD

By the middle of the sixteenth century, Spanish and Portuguese ventures into Africa, the Caribbean, and South America were galvanizing other European kingdoms to launch imperial experiments of their own. In 1585, the Englishman Walter Raleigh attempted to start a colony just north of Spanish Florida. The settlement at Roanoke Island (present-day North Carolina) was intended to solidify English claims to the territory of Virginia, which was named for the "Virgin Queen" Elizabeth and originally encompassed the North American seaboard from South Carolina to Maine, as well as Bermuda.

Raleigh's ill-fated experiment ended with the disappearance of the first colonists, but it was followed by an English expedition to the Chesapeake Bay in 1606, funded by a private London firm called the Virginia Company. These English adventurers were not being sponsored by the crown, and they probably did not intend to remain permanently in the New World. Instead, their goal was to provide agricultural goods for the European market and to make their fortunes before returning home. Nevertheless, with the Spanish model much in mind, the English reserved the right to "conquer" any peoples who proved uncooperative. So when Native Americans of the Powhatan tribe killed one-third of the settlers during a raid in 1622, the colonists responded by crushing the Powhatans and seizing their lands.

For decades thereafter, the native populations of North America both threatened and nurtured the fragile settlements that were gaining a toehold on the continent. Especially in the early years of colonization, when the number of European immigrants was small, some Native American peoples sought to take advantage of these new contacts, in order to trade for goods otherwise unavailable to them. European settlers, for their part, often exhibited a combination of paternalism and contempt for the peoples they encountered. Some hoped to convert Americans to Christianity; others sought to use them as laborers. Ultimately, however, the balance was tipped by larger environmental, biological, and demographic factors that lay outside the control of individuals.

The Columbian Exchange

The accelerating rate of global connections in the sixteenth century precipitated an extraordinary movement of peoples, plants, animals, and diseases, known as the "Columbian exchange." Yet this exchange soon encompassed lands that lay far beyond the purview of Columbus and his contemporaries, including Australia and the Pacific Islands.

Because of its far-reaching effects, the Columbian exchange is considered a fundamental turning point in both human history and the history of the earth's ecology. It put new agricultural products into circulation, introduced new domesticated species of animals, and accidentally encouraged the spread of deadly diseases and the devastation caused by invasive plants and animals. Ecosystems around the world were destroyed or transformed. For example, the introduction of pigs and dogs to islands in the Atlantic and Pacific resulted in the extinction of indigenous animals and birds. The landscapes of Central America and southwestern North America were stripped of vegetation after Spanish settlers attempted large-scale ranching operations. European honeybees displaced native insect populations and encouraged the propagation of harmful plant species. Meanwhile, gray squirrels and raccoons from North America found their way to Europe, while insects from all over the world traveled to new environments and spread unfamiliar forms of bacteria and pollen.

Obviously, the transfer of human populations in the form of settlers, soldiers, merchants, sailors, indentured servants, and slaves accelerated the process of change. Some groups were wiped out through violence, forced resettlement, and unaccustomed illnesses. As much as 90 percent of the pre-Columbian population of the Americas died from communicable diseases such as smallpox, cholera, influenza, typhoid, measles, malaria, and plague—all brought from Europe. Syphilis, on the other hand, appears to have been brought to Europe from the Americas; some scholars

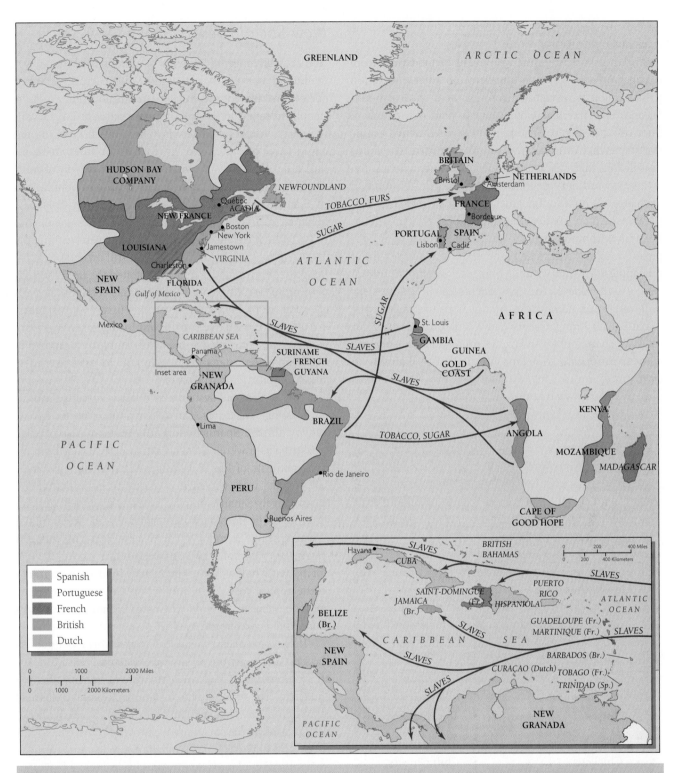

THE ATLANTIC WORLD. ▪ *Trace the routes of the triangular trade. What products did French and British colonies in North America provide to the European market?* ▪ *Which colonies would have been most dependent on slave labor?* ▪ *What did they produce, and how did these products enter into the triangle?*

have even asserted that it was Columbus's own sailors who transmitted the disease.

At the same time, the movement of foodstuffs from one part of the world to another, and their cultivation in new habitats, revolutionized the diets of local populations. The American potato, which could be grown in poor soil and stored for long periods, eventually became the staple diet of the European poor. Indeed, the foods and flavors that characterize today's iconic cuisines are, to an extraordinary degree, the result of the Columbian exchange. Who can imagine an English meal without potatoes? Italian food without tomatoes? Switzerland or Belgium without chocolate? Thai food without chili peppers? Or, on the other side of the Atlantic, Hawaii without pineapples? Florida without oranges? Colombia without coffee? Only one of the components of the quintessentially American hamburger is indigenous to America: the tomato. Everything else is Old World: beef, wheat for the bun, cucumber for the pickle, onion, lettuce. Even the name is European, a reference to the city of Hamburg in Germany.

THE COLUMBIAN EXCHANGE

The following list names just a few of the commodities and contagions that moved between the Old and New Worlds in this era.

Old World → New World	New World → Old World
• Wheat	• Corn
• Sugar	• Potatoes
• Bananas	• Beans
• Rice	• Squash
• Wine grapes	• Pumpkins
• Horses	• Tomatoes
• Pigs	• Avocados
• Chickens	• Chili peppers
• Sheep	• Pineapples
• Cattle	• Cocoa
• *Smallpox*	• Tobacco
• *Measles*	• *Syphilis*
• *Typhus*	

New Social Hierarchies in New Spain

The centralization of imperial power in New Spain was facilitated by the highly organized structure of Aztec society in Mexico and that of the Incas in Peru. Native peoples already lived, for the most part, in large, well-regulated villages and towns. The Spanish government could therefore work closely with local elites to maintain order. It did so by transplanting the system of *encomiendas* originally set up to manage Muslim populations in Spanish territories captured by Christian crusaders (Chapter 12). The Spanish verb *encomendar* means "to trust," which means that *encomenderos* were technically agents of the crown, overseeing land still owned by native peoples. But in practice, many exploited the land for their own profit, treating native workers like serfs. Some *encomenderos* were descendants of the first conquistadors; others were drawn from Aztec and Inca elites. Many were women: the daughters of the Aztec emperor Montezuma had been given extensive lands to hold in trust after their father's capitulation to Cortés.

The *encomienda* system was effective because it built on existing structures and did not attempt to uproot native cultures. Spanish efforts to convert native peoples to Catholicism were also successful because they built on basic patterns of life and indigenous religious practices. The result was widespread cultural assimilation by the relatively small numbers of (usually male) settlers, assisted by the normalcy of intermarriage between (male) colonizers and (female) colonial subjects. This pattern gave rise to a complex and distinctive caste system in New Spain, with a few "pure-blooded" Spanish immigrants at the top; a very large number of Creoles (peoples of mixed descent) in the middle; and indigenous peoples and Africans at the bottom.

In theory, these racial categories corresponded to class distinctions, but in practice race and class did not always coincide. Racial concepts were extremely flexible, and prosperous individuals or families of mixed descent often found ways to establish their "pure" Spanish ancestry by adopting the social practices of the Spanish colonial elites. The lingering effects of this complicated stratification are still evident in Latin America today.

Patterns of English Colonial Settlement

In the early decades of the seventeenth century, the English challenge to Spanish supremacy in the Atlantic began to bear fruit. But like the colonies of New Spain, England's North American settlements were private ventures, farmed either by individual landholders (as in Maryland and Pennsylvania) or managed by groups of investors (as in Virginia and the Massachusetts Bay Colony). Many English immigrants were motivated by a desire for religious and political freedom from England—hence the name we give to the "Pilgrims" who landed at Plymouth, Massachusetts, in 1620. These radical Protestants were known in England as Puritans and were almost as unwelcome as Catholics in a country whose church was an extension of the monarchy (Chapter 13). The number of early immigrants to English territories was also swelled by indentured servitude, a practice that brought thousands of "free" laborers from overpopulated cities across the Atlantic to work under terms that made them little different from slaves. Perhaps 75–80 percent of the people who arrived in the Chesapeake colony were indentured servants, and nearly a quarter of these were women.

Strikingly, English colonists showed little interest in trying to convert Native American peoples to Christianity, another thing that set them apart from their Spanish counterparts. Still another was the fact that many English colonists tended to emigrate with their families or even as part of entire communities. Because there were many women among the first waves of settlers, intermarriage with native populations was rare, which eventually created a nearly unbridgeable social and racial divide—again in stark contrast to the colonies of South America.

Building on their experience in Ireland, where colonies had been called "plantations," English settlers established plantations—planned communities—that attempted to replicate as many features of English life as possible. Geography largely dictated the locations of these settlements, which were scattered along the northern Atlantic coast and on rivers and bays that provided good harbors. Aside from the Hudson, there were no great rivers to lead colonists very far inland, so the English colonies clung to the shoreline and to each other. Today's densely populated corridor along the Atlantic seaboard is a direct result of these early settlement patterns.

The accumulation of wealth through the control of land was a new and exciting prospect for small- and medium-scale landholders in the new English colonies; at home in the Old World, most land was owned by royal and aristocratic families, or by the Church. This helps to explain their rural, agricultural character—in contrast to the great cities of New Spain. But this focus on agriculture also resulted from the demographic catastrophe that decimated native populations in this region: by the early seventeenth century, a great deal of rich land had been abandoned because there were so few native farmers left

PLYMOUTH PLANTATION. An English settlement was established at Plymouth in the Massachusetts Bay Colony in 1620. This image shows a reconstruction of the village as it might have looked in 1627 and captures something of the plantation's diminutive fragility and isolation.

alive. As a result, indigenous peoples who had not already succumbed to European diseases were now under threat from colonists who wanted complete control over their lands.

To this end, the English soon set out to eliminate, through expulsion and massacre, the former inhabitants of the region. There were a few exceptions; in the Quaker colony of Pennsylvania, colonists and Native Americans maintained friendly relations for more than half a century. But in the Carolinas there was widespread enslavement of native peoples, either for sale to the West Indies or to work on the rice plantations along the coast. Ultimately, however, the plantation system rendered its greatest profits through the use of African slaves.

Sugar, Slaves, and the Transatlantic Triangle

In contrast to the more than 7 million African slaves who were forced to labor and die on plantations across the Atlantic, only about 1.5 million Europeans came to the Americas in the two centuries after Columbus's first voyage. Although farming and ranching were encouraged in Central and South America, and later in Florida and California, the Spanish colonial economy was dominated by intensive extraction of mineral resources, which required a constant supply of fresh workers; conditions in the mines were terrible and

Enslaved Native Laborers at Potosí

Since the Spanish crown received one-fifth of all revenues from the mines of New Spain, while maintaining a monopoly over the mercury used to refine the ore into silver, it had an important stake in ensuring the mines' productivity. To this end, the crown granted colonial mine owners the right to conscript native peoples and gave them considerable freedom when it came to the treatment of the workers. This account, dated to about 1620, describes the conditions endured by these native laborers at Potosí (also discussed in Chapter 12).

 ccording to His Majesty's warrant, the mine owners on this massive range [at Potosí] have a right to the conscripted labor of 13,300 Indians in the working and exploitation of the mines, both those [mines] which have been discovered, those now discovered, and those which shall be discovered. It is the duty of the *Corregidor* [municipal governor] of Potosí to have them rounded up and to see that they come in from all the provinces between Cuzco . . . and as far as the frontiers of Tarija and Tomina. . . .

The conscripted Indians go up every Monday morning to the . . . foot of the range; the *Corregidor* arrives with all the provincial captains or chiefs who have charge of the Indians assigned him for his miner or smelter; that keeps him busy till 1 p.m., by which time the Indians are already turned over to these mine and smelter owners.

After each has eaten his ration, they climb up the hill, each to his mine, and go in, staying there from that hour until Saturday evening without coming out of the mine; their wives bring them food, but they stay constantly underground, excavating and carrying out the ore from which they get the silver. They all have tallow candles, lighted day and night; that is the light they work with, for as they are underground, they have need for it all the time. . . .

These Indians have different functions in the handling of the silver ore; some break it up with bar or pick, and dig down in, following the vein in the mine; others bring it up; others up above keep separating the good and the poor in piles; others are occupied in taking it down from the range to the mills on herds of llamas; every day they bring up more than 8,000 of these native beasts of burden for this task. These teamsters who carry the metal are not conscripted, but are hired.

Source: Antonio Vázquez de Espinosa, *Compendium and Description of the West Indies*, trans. Charles Upson Clark (Washington, DC: 1968), p. 62.

Questions for Analysis

1. From the tone of this account, what do you think was the narrator's purpose in writing? Who is his intended audience?

2. Reconstruct the conditions in which these laborers worked. What would you estimate to be the human costs of this week's labor? Why, for example, would a fresh workforce be needed every Monday?

---

mortality was high. In North America, plantation agriculture was also in need of a new labor supply. As we have seen, diseases and violence resulted in the deaths of millions of Native Americans in the space of only a few decades, and experiments in the use of indentured servants on plantations in tropical climates were unsuccessful. Moreover, the return of the plague in Europe, along with the devastation of religious warfare (as will be discussed later), meant that colonists could not look to Europe to satisfy their labor needs. Colonial agents thus began to import slaves from Africa to bolster the labor force and to produce the wealth they so avidly sought. And overwhelmingly, that wealth was derived from a new commodity for which there was an insatiable appetite in Europe: sugar.

Sugar was at the center of the "triangular trade" that linked markets in Africa, the Americas, and Europe—all of which were driven by slave labor. For example, ships that transported African slaves to the Caribbean might trade their human cargo for molasses made on the sugar

HOW SLAVES WERE STOWED ABOARD SHIP DURING THE MIDDLE PASSAGE. Men were "housed" on the right, women on the left, children in the middle. The human cargo was jammed onto platforms six feet wide without sufficient headroom to permit an adult to sit up. This diagram is from evidence gathered by English abolitionists and depicts conditions on the Liverpool slave ship *Brookes*.

plantations of the islands. These ships would then sail to New England, where the molasses would be used to make rum. Loaded with a consignment of rum, the ship would return to the African coast to repeat the process, bartering rum for human bodies. An alternative triangle might see cheap manufactured goods move from England to Africa, where they would be traded for slaves. Those slaves would then be shipped to Virginia and exchanged for tobacco, which would be shipped back to England.

Although the transatlantic slave trade was theoretically controlled by the governments of European colonial powers—Britain officially entered this trade in 1564, the year of William Shakespeare's birth—private entrepreneurs and working-class laborers were active at every stage of the supply chain: manning the ships, capturing human cargo, running the slave markets. Many other branches of the economy in Europe and the Americas were also linked to the slave trade: from the investors in Amsterdam, London, Lisbon, and Bordeaux who financed the slave trade, to the insurance brokers who protected these investments, to the

financial agents who offered credit. And this is to say nothing of the myriad ways in which the everyday lives of average people were bound to slavery. All those who bought the commodities produced by slave labor, or who manufactured the weapons that enabled enslavement, were also implicated. The slave trade was not driven by a few unscrupulous men. It was the engine of the modern globalized economy.

Counting the Human Cost of the Slave Trade

When the Portuguese began to transport African slaves to their sugarcane plantations in Brazil in the 1540s, slavery became crucial to the domestic economies of West African kingdoms. In the following decades, however, the ever-increasing demand for slaves would cause the permanent disintegration of political order in this region by creating an incentive for war and raiding among rival tribes. Moreover, the increased traffic in human beings called for more highly systematized and inhumane methods for corralling, sorting, and shipping them. At the end of the sixteenth century, accordingly, the Portuguese government established a fortified trading outpost on the central African coast (near what is now Angola). Additional trading posts were then established to assist in processing the captives.

Once on board ship, enslaved humans were shackled below decks in spaces barely wider than their own bodies, without sanitary facilities of any kind. It might seem surprising that the mortality rate on these voyages was relatively low: probably 10 or 11 percent. But this was only because the slaves chosen for the voyage were healthy to begin with, and traders were anxious to maintain their goods to sell at a profit. Those Africans who were transported were already the survivors of unimaginable hardships. In order to place the preceding statistic in a larger context, then, we need to consider how many would have died before they reached the ship. One historian has estimated that 36 out of every 100 people captured in the African interior would perish in the six-month-long forced march to the coast. Another dozen or so would die in the prisons there. Eventually, perhaps 57 of the original 100 captives would be taken on board a slave ship. Some 51 would survive the journey and be sold into slavery on arrival. If the destination was Brazil's sugar plantations, only 40 would still be alive after two years. In other words, the actual mortality rate was something like 60 percent—and this doesn't begin to account for life expectancy.

The people consigned to this fate struggled against it, and their initiatives helped to shape the emerging Atlantic world. When the opportunity presented itself, slaves banded together in revolt—a perpetual possibility that haunted slave owners and led to regimes of violence (as in ancient Rome: Chapter 5). There were other forms of resistance, among them suicide and infanticide. Above all, slaves sought to escape. Almost as soon as the slave trade escalated, there were communities of escaped slaves throughout the Americas. Many of these independent settlements were large enough to assert and defend their autonomy. One such community, founded in 1603 in the hinterlands of Brazil, persisted for over a century and had as many as 20,000 inhabitants. Others were smaller and more ephemeral, but their existence testifies to the limits of imperialism in the new American colonies.

CONFLICT AND COMPETITION IN EUROPE AND THE ATLANTIC WORLD

The colonization of the Americas seemed to guarantee European prosperity, providing an outlet for expansion and aggression. But in the second half of the sixteenth century, prolonged political, religious, and economic crises began to cripple Europe. These crises were the product of long-term developments within and between powerful states, but they were also exacerbated by these same states' imperial ambitions. Inevitably, then, European conflicts spread to European colonial holdings. Eventually, the outcome of these conflicts would determine which European powers were best positioned to enlarge their presence in the Atlantic world—and beyond.

New World Silver and Old World Economies

In the latter half of the sixteenth century, an unprecedented inflation in prices profoundly destabilized the European economy, leading to widespread financial panic. Although the twentieth century would see more dizzying inflations, skyrocketing prices were a terrifying novelty in this era, causing what some historians have termed a "price revolution."

Two developments underlay this phenomenon. The first was demographic. After the plague-induced decline of the fourteenth century (Chapter 11), Europe's population grew from roughly 50 million people in 1450 to 90 million in 1600: that is, it increased by nearly 80 percent in a relatively short span of time. Yet Europe's food supply remained nearly constant, meaning that food prices were driven sharply higher by the greater demand for basic commodities. Meanwhile, the enormous influx of silver and gold from Spanish America flooded Europe's previously cash-poor economy (Chapter 12). This sudden availability of ready coin drove prices higher still.

How? In just four years, from 1556 to 1560, about 10 million ducats' worth of silver passed through the Spanish port of Seville: roughly equivalent to 10 billion U.S. dollars in today's currency. (A single gold ducat, the standard unit of monetary exchange for long-distance trade, would be worth nearly a thousand dollars.) Consequently, the market was flooded with coins whose worth quickly

POPULATION DENSITY ▪ *What regions were most densely peopled?* ▪ *Why were many of these regions on the coasts?* ▪ *How would urbanization affect patterns of life and trade?*

became debased because there were so many of them. And still the silver poured in, cheapening the coinage even more: by 1580, the amount of imported silver had doubled; by 1595, it more than quadrupled. Because most of this money was used by the Spanish crown to pay its armies and the many creditors who had financed imperial ventures, a huge volume of coinage was put quickly into circulation through European banks, making the problem of inflation even more widespread. Since some people suddenly had more money to pay for goods and services, those who supplied these commodities could charge higher and higher prices. "I learned a proverb here," said a French traveler in Spain: "Everything costs a lot, except silver."

The New European Poor

In this economic climate, aggressive entrepreneurs profited from financial speculation, landholders from the rising prices of agricultural produce, and merchants from increasing demand for luxury goods. But laborers were caught in a vice. Prices were rising steeply, but wages were not keeping pace. As the cost of food staples rose, poor people had to spend an ever-greater percentage of their incomes on necessities. The overall cost of living in England, for example, more than doubled in Shakespeare's lifetime. When wars or bad harvests drove grain prices higher still, the poor starved to death.

The price revolution also placed new pressures on the sovereign states of Europe. Inflation depressed the real value of money, so fixed incomes derived from taxes and rents yielded less and less actual wealth. Governments were therefore forced to raise taxes merely to keep their revenues constant. Yet most states needed even more revenue than before, because they were engaging in more wars, and warfare was becoming increasingly expensive. The only recourse, then, was to raise taxes precipitously. Hence, governments faced continuous threats of defiance and even armed resistance from their citizens, who could not afford to foot these bills.

Although prices rose less rapidly after 1600, as both population growth and the flood of silver began to slow, the ensuing decades were a time of economic stagnation. A few areas—notably the Netherlands (as will be discussed later)—bucked the trend, but the laboring poor made no advances. Indeed, the lot of the poor deteriorated even further, as helpless civilians were plundered by predatory tax collectors, looting soldiers, and sometimes both. Peasants who had been dispossessed of property or driven off lands once held in common were branded as vagrants, and vagrancy itself became a criminal offense. It was this population of newly impoverished Europeans who became the indentured servants or deported criminals of the American colonies.

The Legacy of the Reformation: The French Wars of Religion

Compounding these economic problems were the wars that erupted within many European states. As we began to observe in Chapter 9, most medieval kingdoms were created through the colonization of smaller, traditionally autonomous territories—either by conquest or through marriage alliances among ruling families. Now these enlarged monarchies began to make ever-greater financial claims on their citizens while at the same time demanding religious uniformity among them. The result was regional and civil conflict, as local populations and even elites rebelled against the centralizing demands of monarchs who often embraced a different religion than that of their subjects. Although the Peace of Augsburg (1555) had established that each territory would follow the religion of its ruler (see Chapter 13), it was based on the premise that no state can tolerate religious diversity. This was a dangerous idea, and it poisoned European colonies in the New World as well.

France was the first to be enflamed by religious warfare. Calvinist missionaries from Geneva had made significant headway there in southern regions. By the 1560s, Calvinists—known as Huguenots (*HEW-guh-nohz*)—made up between 10 and 20 percent of the French population. But there was no open warfare until dynastic politics led factions within the government to break down along religious lines, pitting the (mostly southern) Huguenots against the (mostly northern) Catholic aristocracy. In 1572 the two sides almost brokered a truce: the presumptive heir to the throne, Prince Henry of Navarre—who had become a Protestant—was contracted to marry the Catholic sister of the reigning king, Henry III. But the compromise was undone by the Queen Mother, Catherine de Medici, whose Catholic faction plotted to kill all the Huguenot leaders when they assembled in Paris for her daughter's wedding. In the early morning of St. Bartholomew's Day (August 24), most of these Protestant aristocrats were murdered in their beds, and thousands of humble citizens were slaughtered when riots broke out in the city. When word of the Parisian massacre spread to the provinces, local atrocities proliferated.

Although Henry of Navarre and his bride escaped, religious warfare in France continued for more than two decades. Finally, Catherine's death in 1589 was followed by that of her son, Henry III, who had produced no heir to supplant Henry of Navarre. He became Henry IV, renouncing his Protestant faith in order to placate France's Catholic majority. Then, in 1598, Henry made a landmark effort to end conflict by issuing the Edict of Nantes, which recognized Catholicism as the official religion of the realm but enabled Protestants to practice their religion in specified places. This was an important step toward a policy of religious tolerance, and because the religious divide had a regional component, the edict also reinforced a tradition of regional autonomy in southwestern France. The success of this effort can be measured by the fact that peace was maintained in France even after Henry IV was assassinated by a Catholic in 1610.

The Revolt of the Netherlands and the Dutch Trading Empire

Warfare between Catholics and Protestants also broke out in the Netherlands during this period. Controlled for almost a century by the same Habsburg family that ruled Spain and its overseas empire, the Netherlands had prospered through intense involvement with trade in the

Atlantic world. Their inhabitants had the greatest per capita wealth in all Europe, and the metropolis of Antwerp was northern Europe's leading commercial and financial center. So when the Spanish king and emperor Philip II (r. 1556–98) attempted to tighten his hold there in the 1560s, the fiercely independent Dutch cities resented this imperial intrusion and were ready to fight it.

This conflict took on a religious dynamic because Calvinism had spread into the Netherlands from France. Philip, an ardent defender of the Catholic faith, could not tolerate this combination of political and religious disobedience. When crowds began ransacking and desecrating Catholic churches throughout the country, Philip dispatched an army of 10,000 Spanish soldiers to wipe out Protestantism in his Dutch territories. A reign of terror ensued, which further catalyzed the Protestant opposition.

In 1572, a Dutch aristocrat, William of Orange, emerged as the anti-Spanish leader and sought help from religious allies in France, Germany, and England. Organized fleets of Protestant privateers (that is, privately owned ships) began harassing the Spanish navy in the waters of the North Atlantic. William's Protestant army then seized control of the Netherlands' northern provinces. Although William was assassinated in 1584, his efforts were instrumental in forcing the Spanish crown to recognize the independence of a northern Dutch Republic in 1609. Once united, these seven northern provinces became wholly Calvinist; the southern region, still largely Catholic, remained under Spanish rule.

After gaining its independence, the new Dutch Republic began to build the most prosperous European commercial empire of the seventeenth century. Indeed, its reach extended well beyond the Atlantic world, targeting the Indian Ocean

and East Asia as well. This colonial project owed more to the strategic "fort and factory" model of expansion favored by the Portuguese than to the Spanish technique of territorial conquest and settlement. Many of its early initiatives were spurred by the establishment of the Dutch East India Company, a private mercantile corporation that came to control Sumatra, Borneo, and the Moluccas (the so-called Spice Islands). This meant that the Dutch had a lucrative monopoly on the European trade in spices. The company also secured an exclusive right to trade with Japan and maintained military and trading outposts in China and India, too.

In North America, the Dutch presence was limited to a single outpost: the colony known as New Amsterdam, until it was surrendered to the English in 1667, when it was renamed New York. The remaining Dutch territorial holdings in the Atlantic world were Dutch Guyana (present-day Suriname) on the coast of South America, and the islands of Curaçao and Tobago in the Caribbean. But if the Dutch did not match the Spanish or the English in their accumulation of land, the establishment of a second merchant enterprise, the Dutch

PROTESTANTS RANSACKING A CATHOLIC CHURCH IN THE NETHERLANDS. Protestant destruction of religious images provoked a stern response from Philip II. ■ *Why would Protestants have smashed statuary and other devotional artifacts?*

THE NETHERLANDS AFTER 1609. ■ *What were the two main divisions of the Netherlands?* ■ *Which was Protestant, and which was Catholic?* ■ *How could William of Orange and his allies use the geography of the northern Netherlands against the Spanish?*

West India Company, allowed them to dominate the Atlantic slave trade with Africa after 1621.

In constructing this new transoceanic empire of slaves and spices, the Dutch leveraged a new financial mechanism: the joint-stock company. The Dutch East and West India Companies were early examples, raising cash by selling shares to individual investors whose liability was limited to the sum of their investment and who were entitled to a comparable share in any profits. Originally, the Dutch East India Company intended to pay off its investors within ten years, but when the period was up, investors who wanted to realize their profits immediately were encouraged to sell their shares on the open market. The creation of a market in shares—we now call it a stock market—was an innovation that spread quickly. Stock markets now control the world's economy.

The Struggle of England and Spain

Religious strife could spark civil war, as in France, or political rebellion, as in the Netherlands. But it could also provoke warfare between sovereign states, as in the struggle between England and Spain. In this case, religious conflict was also entangled with dynastic claims and economic competition in the Atlantic world.

The dynastic strife came from the English royal family's division along confessional lines. The Catholic queen Mary (r. 1553–58), eldest daughter of Henry VIII and granddaughter of Ferdinand and Isabella of Spain (see Chapter 13), married her cousin Philip II of Spain in 1554 and ruled at a time of great tension between Catholics and Protestants in England. After Mary's death, her Protestant half-sister Elizabeth (r. 1558–1603) came to the throne, and relations with Spain rapidly declined. They deteriorated further when Catholic Ireland—an English colony—rose in rebellion in 1565, with Spain quietly supporting the Irish. Although it took almost thirty bloody years, English forces eventually suppressed the rebellion. Elizabeth then cemented the Irish defeat by encouraging extensive colonial settlement in Ireland, establishing the plantations that would provide models for those in North America. Indeed, she did so in conscious (and ironic) imitation of Spanish policy in Mexico, in the hopes of creating a colonial state with a largely English identity. Instead, these measures created the deep divisions that trouble Ireland to this day.

England's conflict with Spain, meanwhile, worsened because English economic interests were directly opposed to those of Spain. English traders were making steady inroads into Spanish commercial networks in the Atlantic, as English sea captains such as Sir Francis Drake plundered Spanish vessels on the high seas. In a particularly dramatic exploit lasting from 1577 to 1580, prevailing winds and a lust for booty propelled Drake all the way around the world, to return with stolen Spanish treasure worth twice as much as Queen Elizabeth's annual revenue.

After suffering numerous such attacks, Philip finally resolved to fight back when Elizabeth's government

THE "ARMADA PORTRAIT" OF ELIZABETH. This is one of several portraits that commemorated the defeat of the Spanish Armada in 1588. Through the window on the left (the queen's right hand), an English flotilla sails serenely on sunny seas; on the right, Spanish ships are wrecked by a "Protestant wind." Elizabeth's right hand rests protectively—and commandingly—on the globe. ▪ *How would you interpret this image?*

openly supported the Dutch rebellion against Spain in 1585. In 1588, he dispatched an enormous fleet, confidently called the "Invincible Armada," whose mission was to invade England. But the invasion never occurred. After a major battle, a fierce storm—hailed as a "Protestant wind" by the lucky English—drove the Spanish galleons off course, many of them wrecking on the Irish coast. The shattered flotilla eventually limped home and Elizabeth took credit for her country's miraculous escape. In subsequent years, continued threats from Spain nurtured a new sense of English nationalism and fueled anti-Catholic sentiment.

THE THIRTY YEARS' WAR AND THE RISE OF FRANCE

With the promulgation of the French Edict of Nantes, the end of open hostilities between England and Spain, and the truce between Spain and the Dutch Republic, religious warfare in Europe came briefly to an end. In 1618, however, a new series of conflicts broke out in some of the German-speaking lands that had felt the first divisive effects of the Reformation (Chapter 13). Not only was this period of warfare one of the longest in history, it was one of the bloodiest and most widespread, engulfing most of the European continent before it ended thirty years later, in 1648. Although it began as a religious war, it quickly became an international struggle for political dominance. In the end, some 8 million people died and entire provinces never recovered. Most of the great states involved were impoverished and weakened. The exception was France, which became a preeminent power in Europe for the first time.

The Beginnings of the Thirty Years' War

On one level, the Thirty Years' War was an outlet for tensions that had been building up since the Peace of Augsburg in 1555. On another, it grew out of even longer-standing disputes among rulers and territories (Catholic and Protestant) in the patchwork of provinces that made up the Holy Roman Empire, disputes into which allied powers were drawn. On still another, it was an opportunity for players on the fringes of power to come into prominence.

The catalyst came in 1618. In that year, the Habsburg (Catholic) prince of Austria, Ferdinand—who also ruled Hungary and Poland—was named heir to the throne of Protestant Bohemia. This prompted a rebellion among the Bohemian aristocracy. A year later, complex dynastic politics resulted in Ferdinand's election as Holy Roman Emperor. This gave him access to an imperial (Catholic) army, which he now sent in to crush the Protestant revolt. The Bohemians, meanwhile, were bolstered by the support of some Austrian elites, many of whom were also Protestant and who saw in the rebellion a way to recover power from the Habsburg ruling family.

In 1620, the war escalated further when the Ottoman Empire threw its support behind the Protestants. This touched off a war with the staunchly Catholic kingdom of Poland, whose borders the Muslim army would need to cross in order to get to Prague. The Poles won and the Ottomans retreated: a major Catholic victory. At the same time, Ferdinand's Habsburg cousin, the Spanish king and emperor Philip IV, had renewed hostilities with the Protestant Dutch Republic, so an alliance between the two Habsburg rulers made sense. This led to a major pitched battle between united Protestant forces and a Spanish-led Catholic army just outside of Prague. The Habsburgs were victorious, and Bohemia was forced to accept Ferdinand's Catholic rule.

The Tangled Politics and Terrible Price of War

The conflict, which had started in Bohemia, should have ended there. But it did not. Unrest between Catholics and Protestants now found outlets in other parts of Europe. France erupted into violence once again. Protestant Denmark, fearing that Catholic victories in neighboring parts of the Holy Roman Empire might threaten its sovereignty, was drawn into the fray—losing valuable territories before it was forced to concede defeat.

In this new phase of warfare, political expediency soon outweighed religious allegiances. When a confederation of Catholic princes seemed close to uprooting Protestantism throughout Germany, it found its way blocked by other German Catholic princes who were willing to ally with Protestants in order to preserve their own autonomy. Joining them was the (Protestant) king of Sweden, Gustavus Adolphus (r. 1611–32), who championed both the German Lutheran states and his own nation's sovereignty, but whose Protestant army was secretly subsidized by Catholic France, because France

The Devastation of the Thirty Years' War

The author of the following excerpt, Hans Jakob Christoph von Grimmelshausen (1621–1676), barely survived the horrors of the Thirty Years' War. His parents were killed, probably when he was thirteen years old, and he himself was kidnapped the following year and forced into the army. By age fifteen, he was a soldier. His darkly satiric masterpiece, Simplicissimus *("The Simpleton"), drew heavily on these experiences. Though technically a fictional memoir, it portrays with brutal accuracy the terrible realities of this era.*

 lthough it was not my intention to take the peaceloving reader with these troopers to my dad's house and farm, seeing that matters will go ill therein, yet the course of my history demands that I should leave to kind posterity an account of what manner of cruelties were now and again practised in this our German war: yes, and moreover testify by my own example that such evils must often have been sent to us by the goodness of Almighty God for our profit. For, gentle reader, who would ever have taught me that there was a God in Heaven if these soldiers had not destroyed my dad's house, and by such a deed driven me out among folk who gave me all fitting instruction thereupon? . . .

The first thing these troopers did was, that they stabled their horses: thereafter each fell to his appointed task: which task was neither more nor less than ruin and destruction. For though some began to slaughter and to boil and to roast so that it looked as if there should be a merry banquet forward, yet others there were who did but storm through the house above and below stairs. Others stowed together great parcels of cloth and apparel and all manner of household stuff, as if they would set up a frippery market. All that

they had no mind to take with them they cut in pieces. Some thrust their swords through the hay and straw as if they had not enough sheep and swine to slaughter: and some shook the feathers out of the beds and in their stead stuffed in bacon and other dried meat and provisions as if such were better and softer to sleep upon. Others broke the stove and the windows as if they had a never-ending summer to promise. Houseware of copper and tin they beat flat, and packed such vessels, all bent and spoiled, in with the rest. Bedsteads, tables, chairs, and benches they burned, though there lay many cords of dry wood in the yard. Pots and pipkins must all go to pieces, either because they would eat none but roast flesh, or because their purpose was to make there but a single meal.

Our maid was so handled in the stable that she could not come out, which is a shame to tell of. Our man they laid bound upon the ground, thrust a gag into his mouth, and poured a pailful of filthy water into his body: and by this, which they called a Swedish draught, they forced him to lead a party of them to another place where they captured men and beasts, and brought them back to our farm, in which company were my dad, my mother, and our Ursula.

And now they began: first to take the flints out of their pistols and in place of

them to jam the peasants' thumbs in and so to torture the poor rogues as if they had been about the burning of witches: for one of them they had taken they thrust into the baking oven and there lit a fire under him, although he had as yet confessed no crime: as for another, they put a cord round his head and so twisted it tight with a piece of wood that the blood gushed from his mouth and nose and ears. In a word each had his own device to torture the peasants, and each peasant his several tortures.

Source: Hans Jakob Christoph von Grimmelshausen, *Simplicissimus,* trans. S. Goodrich (New York: 1995), pp. 1–3, 8–10, 32–35.

Questions for Analysis

1. The first-person narrator here recounts the atrocities committed "in this our German war," in which both perpetrators and victims are German. How believable is this description? What lends it credibility?

2. Why might Grimmelshausen have chosen to publish his account as a satirical fiction rather than as a straightforward historical narrative or autobiography? How would this choice affect a reader's response to scenes such as this?

EUROPE AT THE END OF THE THIRTY YEARS' WAR. This map shows the fragile political checkerboard that resulted from the Peace of Westphalia in 1648. ▪ *When you compare this map to the map on page 350, what are the most significant territorial changes between 1550 and 1648?* ▪ *Which regions were weakened or endangered?* ▪ *Which would be in a strong position to dominate Europe?*

wanted to avoid being surrounded by a strong (Catholic) Habsburg alliance on its northern, eastern, and southern borders.

One of the great military commanders of all time, Gustavus had become king at age seventeen. Like another young general, Alexander the Great (see Chapter 4), he was not only an expert tactician but a splendid leader. His army became the best-trained and best-equipped fighting force of the era—what some have called the first modern army. When Gustavus died in battle in 1632, a month before his thirty-eighth birthday, Sweden had become one

of Europe's great powers, rivaling Spain and Russia in size and prestige.

In 1635, with Gustavus dead, Catholic France was compelled to join Protestant Sweden in declaring open war on the Catholic Habsburgs of Austria and Spain. In the middle lay the lands of Central Europe, already weakened by seventeen years of war and now a helpless battleground. In the next thirteen years, this region suffered more from warfare than at any time until the twentieth century. Several cities were besieged and sacked nine or ten times over, while soldiers from all nations, who had to sustain themselves by plunder, gave no quarter to defenseless civilians. Most horrifying was the loss of life in the final four years of the war, when the carnage continued even after peace negotiators arrived at broad areas of agreement.

The Peace of Westphalia and the Decline of Spain

The eventual adoption of the Peace of Westphalia in 1648 was a watershed in European history. It marked the emergence of France as the predominant power on the Continent, a position it would hold for the next two centuries. The greatest losers in the conflict (aside from the millions of victims) were the Austrian Habsburgs, who were forced to surrender all the territory they had gained. The Spanish Habsburgs were also substantially weakened and were no longer able to fall back on the wealth of their Atlantic empire. While war was raging in Europe, large portions of the Atlantic trade had been infiltrated by merchants from other countries, and the expansion of local economies in Spain's colonies had made them less dependent on trade with Spain itself.

In 1600, the Spanish Empire had been the mightiest power in the world. A half century later, this empire had begun to fall apart. As we've already noted, New Spain's great wealth had begun to turn into a liability when the infusion of silver spiked inflation and slowed economic development at home. Lacking both agricultural and mineral resources of its own, Spain might have developed its own industries and a balanced trading pattern, as some of its Atlantic rivals were doing. Instead, the Spanish used imperial silver to buy manufactured goods from other parts of Europe. When the river of silver began to slow down, Spain was plunged into debt. Meanwhile, the Spanish crown's commitment to supporting the Catholic Church meant costly wars, as did attempts to maintain Spain's international dominance.

Involvement in the Thirty Years' War was the last straw. The strains of warfare drove the kingdom, with its power base in Castile, to raise more money and soldiers from other Iberian provinces. First Catalonia and then Portugal (incorporated into Spain in 1580) rose in revolt, followed by the southern Italians who rebelled against their Castilian viceroys in Naples and Sicily. It was only by chance that Spain's greatest external enemies, France and England, could not act in time to take advantage of its plight. This gave the Castilian-based government time to put down the Italian revolts and bring Catalonia to heel. But Portugal retained its independence and Spain became increasingly isolated.

French Power in Europe and North America

Like Spain, France had grown over the course of the previous centuries by absorbing formerly independent principalities whose inhabitants were not always willing to cooperate with the royal government. The fact that France became more powerful as a result of this process, while Spain did not, can be attributed in part to France's greater natural resources and the greater prestige of the French monarchy, which can be traced back to the rule of Louis IX (later canonized as Saint Louis; see Chapter 10). Most subjects of the French king, including the Protestants whose welfare had been cultivated by Henry IV, were loyal to the crown. Moreover, France had enormous economic resiliency, owing primarily to its rich and varied agricultural productivity. Unlike Spain, which had to import food, France was able to feed itself. Moreover, Henry IV's government had financed the construction of roads, bridges, and canals to facilitate the flow of goods. Royal factories manufactured luxuries such as crystal, glass, and tapestries, and Henry also supported the production of silk, linen, and wool throughout the kingdom.

France thus emerged from the crisis of the Thirty Years' War with a stronger state, a more dynamic economy, and increased influence abroad. A decade before the war, royal patronage had also allowed the explorer Samuel de Champlain to claim parts of northeastern North America as France's first foothold in the New World. In 1608, Champlain founded the colony of Québec in the Saint Lawrence river valley. But whereas the English had limited colonial settlement to regions along the Atlantic coastline, the French set out to dominate the interior of the continent. In the ensuing centuries, French traders ranged far up and down the few Canadian rivers that led inland, exchanging furs and goods with the Native American groups they encountered, while French missionaries used the same arteries to spread Catholic Christianity from Québec to Louisiana. Eventually, French imperial ventures spread via the Great Lakes and the great river systems along the Mississippi to the prairies of America's Midwest.

These far-flung French colonies were established and administered as royal enterprises like those of Spain, a fact that distinguished them from the private commercial ventures put together by the English and the Dutch. Also like New Spain, the colonies of New France were overwhelmingly populated by men. The elite of French colonial society were military officers and administrators sent from Paris. Below their ranks were fishermen, fur traders, small farmers, and common soldiers who constituted the bulk of French settlers in North America. Because the fishing and fur trades relied on cooperative relationships with native peoples, a mutual economic interdependence grew up between the French colonists and the peoples of surrounding regions. Intermarriage between French traders and native women was common.

Yet in contrast to both Spanish and English colonies, these French colonies remained very dependent on the wages and supplies sent to them from the mother country. Only rarely did they become truly self-sustaining economic enterprises. Financial rewards were modest: furs, fish, and tobacco were exported to European markets, but it was not until the late seventeenth century that some French colonies began to realize large profits by building sugar plantations in the Caribbean islands of Guadeloupe, Martinique, and Saint-Domingue (the French portion of Hispaniola, now Haiti). By 1750, 500,000 slaves on Saint-Domingue were laboring under extraordinarily harsh conditions to produce 40 percent of the world's sugar and 50 percent of its coffee (see Chapter 15).

The Policies of Cardinal Richelieu

This expansion of French power can be credited, in part, to Henry IV's de facto successor, Cardinal Richelieu (REESH-eh-lyuh). The real king of France, Henry's son Louis XIII (r. 1610–43), had come to the throne at the age of nine; and so Richelieu, as his chief advisor, dominated his reign. His aim was to centralize royal bureaucracy while exploiting opportunities to foster French influence.

Within France, Richelieu amended the Edict of Nantes so that it no longer supported the political rights of the Huguenots. He also prohibited French Protestants from settling in Québec. Yet considering that he owed his political power (in part) to his ecclesiastical position in the Catholic Church, the fact that he allowed the edict to stand speaks to his larger interest in fostering a sense of French national identity that centered on the monarchy. In keeping with this policy, he also imposed direct taxation on powerful provinces that had retained their financial autonomy up to that point. Later, to make sure that taxes were efficiently collected, Richelieu instituted a new system of local government which empowered royal officials to put down provincial resistance.

These policies made the French royal government more powerful than any in Europe. It also doubled the crown's income, allowing France to engage in the Thirty Years' War, which in turn extended its power on the continent. Yet this increased centralization would provoke challenges to royal authority from aristocratic elites in the years after Richelieu's death. Eventually, the extreme centralization of royal authority in France would lead to the French Revolution (see Chapter 18).

The Challenge of the Fronde

One more immediate response to Richelieu's policies was a series of uncoordinated revolts known collectively as the *Fronde* (from the French word for a sling used to hurl stones). In 1643, just after the death of Richelieu, Louis XIII was succeeded by his five-year-old son, Louis XIV. The young king's regents were his mother, Anne of Austria, and her alleged lover, Cardinal Mazarin. Many powerful nobles hated them and also hated the way that Richelieu's government had curtailed their own authority. Popular resentments were aroused as well, so when cliques of nobles expressed their disgust they found some support. In 1648, the levy of a new tax had protesters on the streets of Paris, armed with slings and projectiles. Years later, when Louis XIV began to rule in his own right, the memory of these early years haunted him. He resolved never to let the aristocracy or their provinces get out of hand (see Chapter 15). Over the next five years, a series of insurrections challenged the authority of the French Parlement, while factional disputes and struggles for power divided the nobility. This period of civil warfare, coinciding with an ongoing war with Spain, threatened the very existence of the French throne and the sovereignty of its child occupant.

THE CRISIS OF MONARCHY IN ENGLAND

Of all the crises that shook Europe in this era, the most radical in its consequences was the English Civil War. The causes of this conflict were similar to those that had sparked trouble in other countries: hostilities between the component parts of a composite kingdom; religious animosities; struggles for power among competing factions; and the increasing costs of war. But in England, these developments led to the unprecedented criminal trial and execution of a

Analyzing Primary Sources

Cardinal Richelieu on the Common People of France

Armand Jean du Plessis, Duke of Richelieu and cardinal of the Roman Catholic Church, was the effective ruler of France from 1624 until his death in 1642. His Political Testament was assembled after his death from historical sketches and memoranda of advice which he prepared for King Louis XIII, the ineffectual monarch whom he ostensibly served. This book was eventually published in 1688, during the reign of Louis XIV.

All students of politics agree that when the common people are too well off it is impossible to keep them peaceable. The explanation for this is that they are less well informed than the members of the other orders in the state, who are much more cultivated and enlightened, and so if not preoccupied with the search for the necessities of existence, find it difficult to remain within the limits imposed by both common sense and the law.

It would not be sound to relieve them of all taxation and similar charges, since in such a case they would lose the mark of their subjection and consequently the awareness of their station. Thus being free from paying tribute, they would consider themselves exempted from obedience. One should compare them with mules, which being accustomed to work, suffer more when long idle than when kept busy. But just as this work should be reasonable, with the burdens placed upon these animals proportionate to their strength, so it is likewise with the burdens placed upon the people. If they are not moderate, even when put to good public use, they are certainly unjust. I realize that when a king undertakes a program of public works it is correct to say that what the people gain from it is returned by paying the *taille* [a heavy tax imposed on the peasantry]. In the same fashion it can be maintained that what a king takes from the people returns to them, and that they advance it to him only to draw upon it for the enjoyment of their leisure and their investments, which would be impossible if they did not contribute to the support of the state.

Source: *The Political Testament of Cardinal Richelieu*, trans. Henry Bertram Hill (Madison, WI: 1961), pp. 31–32.

Questions for Analysis

1. According to Cardinal Richelieu, why should the state undertake to subjugate the common people? What assumptions about the nature and status of "common people" underlie this argument?

2. What theory of the state emerges from this argument? What are the relationships between the king and the state and between the king and the people, according to Richelieu?

---

king, an event that sent shock waves throughout Europe and the Atlantic world.

The Origins of the English Civil War

The chain of events leading to this civil war can be traced to the last decades of Queen Elizabeth's reign. The expenses of defense against Spain, rebellion in Ireland, widespread crop failures, and the inadequacies of the antiquated English taxation system drove the government deeply into debt. When Elizabeth was succeeded by her cousin, James Stuart—King James VI of Scotland, James I of England—bitter factional disputes were complicated by the financial crisis. When the English Parliament rejected James's demands for more taxes, he raised what revenues he could without parliamentary approval, imposing new tolls and selling trading monopolies on colonial imports. These measures aroused resentment and made voluntary grants of taxation from Parliament even less likely.

James also struggled with religious divisions among his subjects. His own kingdom of Scotland had been firmly Calvinist since the 1560s. England was Protestant, too, but of a very different kind because the Church of England had retained many of the rituals, hierarchies, and doctrines of the medieval Catholic Church (see Chapter 13). A significant number of English Protestants, the Puritans, wanted to bring their church more firmly into line with Calvinist principles; a particularly zealous group of these Puritans took

CHARLES I. King Charles of England was a connoisseur of the arts and a patron of artists. He was adept at using portraiture to convey the magnificence of his tastes and the grandeur of his conception of kingship. ▪ *How does this portrait by Anthony Van Dyck compare to the engravings of the "martyred" king on page 390 in* **Interpreting Visual Evidence?**

subjects by marrying the Catholic sister of France's Louis XIII, and he launched a new war with Spain, straining his already slender financial resources. When Parliament refused to grant him funds, he demanded forced loans from his subjects and punished those who refused by lodging soldiers in their homes. Others were imprisoned without trial. Parliament responded by imposing the Petition of Right in 1628, which declared that taxes not condoned by Parliament were illegal, condemned arbitrary imprisonment, and prohibited the quartering of soldiers in private houses. Thereafter, Charles tried to rule England without Parliament—something not attempted since the establishment of that body 400 years earlier (see Chapter 9). He also ran into trouble with his Calvinist subjects in Scotland because he began to favor the most Catholic-leaning elements in the English Church. The Scots rebelled in 1640, and a Scottish army marched south into England to demand the withdrawal of Charles's "Catholicizing" measures.

To meet the Scottish threat, Charles was forced to summon Parliament, whose members were determined to impose radical reforms on the king's government before they would even consider granting him funds to raise an army. To avoid dealing with this difficult situation, Charles tried to arrest Parliament's leaders and force his own agenda. When this failed, he withdrew from London to raise his own army. Parliament responded by mustering a separate military force and voting itself the taxation to

refuge in North America and founded the Massachusetts Bay Colony when their efforts were criminalized in England. James also stirred up trouble in staunchly Catholic Ireland by encouraging thousands of Scottish Calvinists to settle in the northern Irish province of Ulster, exacerbating a situation that had already become violent under Elizabeth.

Parliament versus the King

This situation became more volatile in 1625, when James was succeeded by his son Charles. Charles alarmed his Protestant

OLIVER CROMWELL AS PROTECTOR OF THE COMMONWEALTH. This coin, minted in 1658, shows the lord protector wreathed with laurel garlands like a classical hero or a Roman consul, but it also proclaims him to be "by the Grace of God Protector of the Commonwealth." ▪ *What mixed messages does this coin convey?*

Competing Viewpoints

Debating the English Civil War

The English Civil War raised fundamental questions about political rights and responsibilities. Many of these are addressed in the two excerpts below. The first comes from a lengthy debate held within the General Council of Cromwell's army in October of 1647. The second is taken from the speech given by King Charles, moments before his execution in 1649.

The Army Debates, 1647

Colonel Rainsborough: Really, I think that the poorest man that is in England has a life to live as the greatest man, and therefore truly, sir, I think it's clear, that every man that is to live under a government ought first by his own consent to put himself under that government, and I do think that the poorest man in England is not at all bound in a strict sense to that government that he has not had a voice to put himself under . . . insomuch that I should doubt whether I was an Englishman or not, that should doubt of these things.

General Ireton: Give me leave to tell you, that if you make this the rule, I think you must fly for refuge to an absolute natural right, and you must deny all civil right, and I am sure it will come to that in the consequence. . . . For my part, I think it is no right at all. I think that no person has a right to an interest or share in the disposing of the affairs of the kingdom, and in determining or choosing those that shall determine what laws we shall be ruled by here, no person has a right to this that has not a permanent fixed interest in this kingdom, and those persons together are properly the represented of this kingdom who, taken together, and consequently are to make up the representers of this kingdom. . . .

We talk of birthright. Truly, birthright there is. . . . Men may justly have by birthright, by their very being born in England, that we should not seclude them out of England. That we should not refuse to give them air and place and ground, and the freedom of the highways and other things, to live amongst us, not any man that is born here, though he in birth or by his birth there come nothing at all that is part of the permanent interest of this kingdom to him. That I think is due to a man by birth. But that by a man's being born here he shall have a share in that power that shall dispose of the lands here, and of all things here, I do not think it is a sufficient ground.

Source: David Wootton, ed., *Divine Right and Democracy: An Anthology of Political Writing in Stuart England* (New York: 1986), pp. 286–87 (language modernized).

pay for it. By the end of 1642, open warfare had erupted between the English king and the English government: something inconceivable in neighboring France, where the king and the government were inseparable.

Arrayed on the king's side were most of England's aristocrats and large landholders, many of whom owned lands in the Atlantic colonies as well. The parliamentary forces were made up of smaller landowners, tradesmen, and artisans, many of whom were Puritan sympathizers. The king's royalist supporters were commonly known by the aristocratic name of Cavaliers. Their opponents, who cut their hair short in contempt for the fashionable custom of wearing curls, were derisively called Roundheads. After 1644, when the parliamentary army was efficiently reorganized,

the royalist forces were badly beaten and the king was compelled to surrender in 1646. Soon afterward, the episcopal hierarchy of the Church of England was abolished and a Calvinist-style church was mandated throughout England and Wales.

The struggle might have ended there, but Parliament was divided on the question of the monarch's role in the new government. The majority of its members were ready to restore Charles to the throne, with limited powers, and to impose a uniform Calvinist faith. But a radical minority of Puritans insisted on religious freedom for themselves and other Protestant dissenters. Their leader was Oliver Cromwell (1599–1658), commander of the parliamentary forces, which he had reconstituted as "the

Charles I on the Scaffold, 1649

I think it is my duty, to God first, and to my country, for to clear myself both as an honest man, a good king, and a good Christian.

I shall begin first with my innocence. In truth I think it not very needful for me to insist long upon this, for all the world knows that I never did begin a war with the two Houses of Parliament, and I call God to witness, to whom I must shortly make an account, that I never did intend to incroach upon their privileges. . . .

As for the people—truly I desire their liberty and freedom as much as anybody whatsoever. But I must tell you that their liberty and freedom consists in having of government those laws by which their lives and goods may be most their own. It is not for having share in government. That is nothing pertaining to them. A subject and a sovereign are clean different things, and therefore, until they

do that—I mean that you do put the people in that liberty as I say—certainly they will never enjoy themselves.

Sirs, it was for this that now I am come here. If I would have given way to an arbitrary way, for to have all laws changed according to the power of the sword, I needed not to have come here. And therefore I tell you (and I pray God it be not laid to your charge) that I am the martyr of the people.

Source: Brian Tierney, Donald Kagan, and L. Pearce Williams, eds., *Great Issues in Western Civilization* (New York: 1967), pp. 46–47.

Questions for Analysis

1. What fundamental issues are at stake in both of these excerpts? How do the debaters within the parliamentary army (first excerpt) define "natural" and "civil" rights?

2. How does Charles defend his position? What is his theory of kingship, and how does it compare to that of Cardinal Richelieu's (page 386)? How does it conflict with the ideas expressed in the army's debate?

3. It is interesting that none of the participants in these debates seems to have recognized the implications their arguments might have for the political rights of women. Why would that have been the case?

New Model Army." Ultimately, he became the new ruler of England, too.

The Fall of Charles Stuart and Oliver Cromwell's Commonwealth

Taking advantage of the dissension within Parliament, Charles renewed the war in 1648. But his royalists were forced to surrender after a brief campaign. In order to ensure that the Puritan agenda would be carried out, Cromwell ejected all the moderates from Parliament by force. This "Rump" (remaining) Parliament then put the king on trial, finding him guilty of treason against his own subjects. Charles Stuart

was publicly beheaded on January 30, 1649: the first time in history that a reigning king had been legally deposed and executed. Europeans reacted to his death with horror, astonishment, or rejoicing, depending on their own political convictions (see **Interpreting Visual Evidence** on page 390).

After the king's execution, his son Charles and his royalist supporters fled to France. Cromwell and his faction then abolished Parliament's hereditary House of Lords and declared England a Commonwealth. Technically, Parliament was the governing body; but Cromwell, with the army at his command, possessed the real power. By 1653 the "Commonwealth" had become a thinly disguised autocracy established under legislation drafted by officers of the army. Called the *Instrument of Government*, this text is the nearest

Interpreting Visual Evidence

The Execution of a King

This allegorical engraving (image A) accompanied a pamphlet called *Eikon Basilike* (*"The Kingly Image"*), which began to circulate in Britain just weeks after the execution of King Charles I. It purported to be an autobiographical account of the king's last days and a justification of his royal policies. It was intended to arouse widespread sympathy for the king and his exiled heir, Charles II, and it succeeded admirably: the cult of Charles "King and Martyr" became increasingly popular. Here, the Latin inscription on the shaft of light suggests that Charles's piety will beam "brighter through the shadows," while the scrolls at the left proclaim that "virtue grows beneath weight" and "unmoved, triumphant." Charles's earthly crown (on the floor at his side) is "splendid and heavy," while the crown of thorns he grasps is "bitter and light" and the heavenly crown is "blessed and eternal." Even people who could not read these and other Latin mottoes would have known that Charles's last words

were: "I shall go from a corruptible to an incorruptible Crown, where no disturbance can be."

A. King Charles I as a martyr.

At the same time, broadsides showing the moment of execution (image B) circulated in various European countries with

approximation to a written constitution England has ever had. Extensive powers were granted to Cromwell as Lord Protector, and his office was made hereditary.

The Restoration of the Monarchy

By this time, though, Cromwell's Puritan military dictatorship was growing unpopular, not least because it prohibited public recreation on Sundays and closed London's theatres. Many became nostalgic for the milder Church of England and began to hope for a restoration

of the old royalist regime. The opportunity came with Cromwell's death in 1658. His son Richard duly succeeded to the office of Lord Protector but was almost immediately removed from power by a royalist faction within the army. A new Parliament was organized, and, in April of 1660, it declared that King Charles II had been the ruler of England since his father's execution in 1649. Almost overnight, England became a monarchy again.

Charles II (r. 1660–85) revived the Church of England but was careful not to revive the contentious policies of his father. Quipping that he did not wish to "resume his travels," he agreed to respect Parliament and to observe the Petition of Right.

explanatory captions. This one was printed in Germany, and there are almost identical versions surviving from the Netherlands. It shows members of the crowd fainting and turning away at the sight of blood spurting from the king's neck while the executioner holds up the severed head.

B. The execution of King Charles I.

Questions for Analysis

1. How would you interpret the message of the first image? How might it have been read differently by Catholics and Protestants within Britain and Europe?

2. What would have been the political motives underlying the publication and display of these images? For example, would you expect the depiction of the king's execution to be intended as supportive of monarchy or as antiroyalist? Why?

3. Given what you have learned about political and religious divisions in Europe at the time of the king's execution, where do you think the first image would have found the most sympathetic audiences? Why might it be significant that the second circulated more in Germany and the Netherlands rather than in France or Spain?

He also accepted all the legislation passed by Parliament immediately before the outbreak of civil war in 1642, including the requirement that Parliament be summoned at least once every three years. England thus emerged from its civil war as a constitutional monarchy, and it remains so to this day.

The English Civil War and the Atlantic World

These tumultuous events had a significant influence on England's Atlantic colonies. While the landed aristocracy had sided with the king during this conflict, many colonists had applauded Parliament's protection of small landowners and civil liberties. Even after the restoration of the monarchy in 1660, colonial leaders retained an antimonarchist bias. Moreover, the twelve years of civil war had given the colonies a large degree of independence. As a result, efforts to re-establish royal control over colonial governance resulted in greater and greater friction (see Chapter 15). The bitter religious conflicts that had divided the more radical Puritans from the Church of England also forced the colonies to come to grips with the problem of religious diversity. Some, like Massachusetts, tried to impose their own brand of Puritanism on settlers. Others experimented with forms of tolerance that went beyond those of England.

Paradoxically, though, the spread of ideas about the protection of liberties and citizens' rights coincided with a rapid and considerable expansion of unfree labor in the colonies. The demand for workers was increasing rapidly, owing to the expansion of tobacco plantations in Virginia and sugar plantations in Barbados and Jamaica, which the British captured from the Spanish in 1655. These plantations, with their punishing conditions and high mortality rates, were insatiable in their demand for workers. Plantation owners thus sought to meet this demand by investing ever more heavily in indentured servants and African slaves. The social and political crisis unleashed by Europe's wars also led to the forced migration of paupers and political prisoners. These exiles, many without resources, swelled the ranks of the unfree and the very poor in the English colonies, creating new social hierarchies as earlier arrivals sought to distance themselves from newer immigrants regarded as inferiors. The crisis of kingship in England thus led to a substantial increase in the African slave trade and a sharpening of social and economic divisions in North America.

THE PROBLEM OF DOUBT AND THE ART OF BEING HUMAN

On the first day of November in 1611, a new play by William Shakespeare premiered in London, at the royal court. *The Tempest* takes place on a remote island, where an exiled duke has used his magical arts to subjugate the island's inhabitants. This plot drew on widespread reports from the new colonies in the Caribbean, where slaves were called Caribans—hence the name Shakespeare chose for the play's rebellious Caliban, who seeks revenge on his oppressive master. When reminded that he owes his knowledge of the English language to the civilizing influence of the magician's daughter, Caliban retorts: "You taught me language, and my profit on't is / I know how to curse." Shakespeare's audience was thus confronted with a spectacle of their own colonial ambitions gone awry.

The unrest caused by Europe's extension into the Atlantic world, and by its bitter decades of warfare, motivated many creative artists to document and critique contemporary trends. Another example of this artistic response is *Don Quixote*, which its Spanish author, Miguel de Cervantes (*sehr-VAHN-tehs*, 1547–1616), composed largely in prison.

This early novel recounts the adventures of an idealistic gentleman, Don Quixote of La Mancha, who becomes deranged by his constant reading of chivalric romances and sets off on delusional adventures of his own. His sidekick, Sancho Panza, is his exact opposite: a plain, practical man content with modest bodily pleasures. Together, they represent different facets of human nature. *Don Quixote* is both a devastating satire of Spain's decline and a sincere celebration of human optimism.

Throughout the long century between 1550 and 1660, Europeans confronted a world in which all they had once known was cast into confusion. Vast continents had been discovered, populated by millions of people whose existence challenged Western civilizations' former parameters and Europeans' most basic assumptions. Not even religion could be seen as an adequate foundation on which to build new certainties. Political allegiances were similarly under threat, as intellectuals and common people alike began to assert a right to resist princes with whom they disagreed. The foundations of morality and custom were beginning to seem arbitrary. Europeans responded to this pervasive climate of doubt by seeking new bases on which to construct some measure of certainty.

Witchcraft and the Power of the State

Contributing to the anxiety of this age was the widespread conviction that witchcraft was a new and increasing threat. Although belief in magic had always been common, it was not until the late fifteenth century that such powers were deemed to derive from some kind of satanic bargain. In 1484, papal inquisitors had been empowered to detect and eliminate witchcraft by any means. Predictably, torture increased the number of accused witches who "confessed" to their alleged crimes. And as more accused witches "confessed," more witches were "discovered," tried, and executed—even in places like England and Scotland, where torture was not legal and the Catholic Church had no influence. Both Luther and Calvin had also condoned the trial and execution of witches.

It was through this fundamental agreement between Catholics and Protestants, and with the complicity of modern secular states, that an early modern "witch craze" claimed tens of thousands of victims. The final death toll will never be known, but the vast majority were women. Accusations of witchcraft also became endemic in some colonies, as occurred in the English settlement of Salem in the Massachusetts Bay Colony. This hunt for witches resulted, in part, from fears that traditional religious remedies were no longer adequate to guard against the evils of the world. It also reflects Europeans' growing conviction that only the state had the power to protect them. In Catholic countries, where witchcraft prosecutions began in Church courts, these cases would be transferred to the state's courts for final judgment and punishment. In most Protestant countries, the entire process of detecting, prosecuting, and punishing suspected witches was carried out under state supervision.

The Search for a Source of Authority

The crisis of religious and political authority in Europe also led to more rational approaches to the problem of uncertainty. The French nobleman Michel de Montaigne (*mohn-TEHN-yeh*, 1533–1592), son of a Catholic father and a Huguenot mother of Jewish ancestry, applied a searching skepticism to all traditional ways of knowing the world and adopted instead a practice of profound introspection. His *Essays* (from the French word for "attempts" or "exercises") were composed during the wars of religion and proceed from the same basic question: "What do I know?" Their first premise is that every human perspective is limited: what may seem indisputably true to one group of people may seem absolutely false to another. From this follows Montaigne's second premise: the need for moderation. Because all people think they follow the true religion or have the best form of government, Montaigne concluded that no religion or government is really perfect, and consequently no belief is worth fighting or dying for.

Another French philosopher, Blaise Pascal (*pahs-KAHL*, 1623–1662), confronted the problem of doubt differently, by embracing an extreme form of Catholicism. Until his death, he worked on a highly ambitious philosophical-religious project meant to establish truth by appealing simultaneously to intellect and emotion. In his posthumously published work *Pensées* (*Thoughts*), Pascal argued that only faith could resolve the contradictions of the world. He argued that the awe an uncertainty we feel in the face of evil is evidence for the existence of God. Pascal's hope was that, on this foundation, some measure of confidence in the human capacity for self-knowledge could be rediscovered.

The Science of Politics

The French jurist Jean Bodin (*boh-DAN*, 1530–1596) took a more practical approach to the problem of uncertainty

and found a solution in the power of the state. Like his exact contemporary Montaigne, Bodin was troubled by religious upheaval. He had witnessed the St. Bartholomew's Day Massacre of 1572 and, in response, developed a theory of absolute sovereignty that would (he surmised) put an end to such catastrophes. His monumental *Six Books of the Commonwealth* (1576) argued that the state has its origins in the needs of families and that its paramount duty is to maintain order. He defined sovereignty as "the most high, absolute, and perpetual power over all subjects," which meant that a sovereign head of state could make and enforce laws without the consent of those governed: precisely what King Charles of England later argued when he tried to dispense with Parliament—and precisely what his subjects ultimately rejected. Even if the ruler proved a tyrant, Bodin insisted that the subject had no right to resist, for any resistance would open the door to anarchy, "which is worse than the harshest tyranny in the world."

In England, the experience of civil war led Thomas Hobbes (1588–1679) to propose a different theory of state sovereignty in his treatise *Leviathan* (1651). Whereas Bodin assumed that sovereign power should be vested in a monarch, Hobbes argued that any form of government capable of protecting its subjects' lives and property might act as an all-powerful sovereign. But Hobbes's convictions arose from a similarly pessimistic view of human nature. The "state of nature" that existed before government, he wrote, was a "war of all against all." Because man naturally behaves as "a wolf" toward other men, human life without government is "solitary, poor, nasty, brutish, and short." To escape such consequences, people must surrender their liberties in exchange for the state's obligation to keep the peace.

Bodin had seen the ultimate goal of the state as the protection of property; Hobbes saw it as the preservation of people's lives, even at the expense of their liberties. Both developed such theories in response to the breakdown of traditional authorities. Their different political philosophies thus reflect a shared, practical preoccupation with the observation and analysis of actual occurrences (empirical knowledge) rather than abstract or theological arguments. Because of this, they are seen as early examples of a new kind of discipline, what we now call "political science."

A similar preoccupation with observation and results was also emerging among those who sought to understand the physical universe. Historians have often referred to the rapid scientific developments of this era as the "scientific revolution," a phenomenon that actually had its beginnings in the later Middle Ages

Analyzing Primary Sources

Montaigne on Skepticism and Faith

The Essays of Michel de Montaigne (1533–1592) reflect the sincerity of his own attempts to grapple with the contradictions of his time, even if he could not resolve those contradictions. Here, he discusses the relationship between human knowledge and the teachings of religious authorities.

Perhaps it is not without reason that we attribute facility in belief and conviction to simplicity and ignorance, for . . . the more a mind is empty and without counterpoise, the more easily it gives beneath the weight of the first persuasive argument. That is why children, common people, women, and sick people are most subject to being led by the ears. But then, on the other hand, it is foolish presumption to go around disdaining and condemning as false whatever does not seem likely to us; which is an ordinary vice in those who think they have more than common ability. I used to do so once. . . . But reason has taught me that to condemn a thing thus, dogmatically, as false and impossible, is to assume the advantage of knowing the bounds and limits of God's will and of the power of our mother Nature, and that there is no more notable folly in the world than to reduce these things to the measure of our capacity and competence. . . .

It is a dangerous and fateful presumption, besides the absurd temerity that it implies, to disdain what we do not comprehend. For after you have established, according to your fine understanding, the limits of truth and falsehood, and it turns out that you must necessarily believe things even stranger than those you deny, you are obliged from then on to abandon these limits. Now what seems to me to bring as much disorder into our consciences as anything, in these religious troubles that we are in, is this partial surrender of their beliefs by Catholics. It seems to them that they are being very moderate and understanding when they yield to their opponents some of the articles in dispute. But, besides the fact that they do not see what an advantage it is to a man charging you for you to begin to give ground and withdraw, and how much that encourages him to pursue his point, those articles which they select as the most trivial are sometimes very important. We must either submit completely to the authority of our ecclesiastical government, or do without it completely. It is not for us to decide what portion of obedience we owe it.

Source: *Montaigne: Selections from the Essays*, ed. and trans. Donald M. Frame (Arlington Heights, IL: 1971), pp. 34–38.

Questions for Analysis

1. Why does Montaigne say that human understanding is limited? How do his assumptions compare to those of Richelieu's (page 386)?

2. What does Montaigne mean by the "partial surrender" of belief? If a Catholic should place his faith in the Church, what then is the purpose of human intellect?

(see Chapters 12 and 13). It will be treated at greater length in Chapter 16.

The World of Theater

In the late sixteenth century, the construction of public playhouses—enclosed theaters—made drama an especially effective mass medium for the formation of public opinion, the dissemination of ideas, and the discussion of the rapidly changing world. This was especially so in England during the last two decades of Elizabeth's reign and the two-decade reign of her successor, James.

Christopher Marlowe (1564–1593), who may have been a spy for Elizabeth's government and who was mysteriously murdered in a tavern brawl, was extremely popular in his own day. In plays such as *Doctor Faustus* and *Tamburlaine*— about the life of the Mongolian warlord Timur the Lame (see Chapter 12)— Marlowe created vibrant heroes who

Past and Present

Shakespeare's Popular Appeal

Although the plays of William Shakespeare are frequently described as elite entertainments, their enduring appeal can hardly be explained in those terms. In fact, Shakespeare wrote for a diverse audience—and a group of actors—who would have been more likely to see the inside of a prison than a royal court. His plays combine high politics, earthy comedy, and deeply human stories that still captivate and motivate audiences at the reconstructed Globe Theatre in London (left). They also lend themselves to inventive adaptations that comment on our own contemporary world, as in the recent film of *Coriolanus* (right).

Watch related author videos on the Student Site
wwnorton.com/college/history/western-civilizationsBrief4

pursue larger-than-life ambitions only to be felled by their own human limitations. In contrast to the heroic tragedies of Marlowe, Ben Jonson's (c. 1572–1637) dark comedies expose human vices and foibles. In the *Alchemist*, he balanced an attack on pseudo-scientific quackery with admiration for resourceful lower-class characters who cleverly take advantage of their social betters.

William Shakespeare (1564–1616) was born into the family of a tradesman in the provincial town of Stratford-upon-Avon, where he attained a modest education before moving to London at around the age of twenty. There, he composed or collaborated on an unknown number of plays, of which some forty survive in whole or in part. They owe their longevity to the author's unrivaled use of langauge, humor, and psychological insight. Those written during the playwright's early years reflect the political, religious, and social upheavals of the time. These include many history plays that recount episodes from England's medieval past and the struggles that established the Tudor dynasty

of Elizabeth's grandfather, Henry VII. They also include the lyrical tragedy *Romeo and Juliet* and a number of comedies that explore fundamental problems of identity, honor, ambition, and love. The plays from Shakespeare's second period are, like other contemporary artworks, characterized by a troubled searching into the meaning of human existence. They showcase the perils of indecisive idealism (*Hamlet*) and the abuse of power (*Macbeth*, *King Lear*). The plays composed toward the end of his career emphasize the possibilities of reconciliation and peace even after years of misunderstanding and violence: *The Tempest* is one of these.

The Artists of Southern Europe

The tensions of this age were also explored in the visual arts. In Italy and Spain, painters cultivated a highly dramatic style sometimes known as "Mannerism." The most

VIEW OF TOLEDO BY EL GRECO. This is one of many landscape portraits representing the hilltop city that became the artist's home in later life. Its supple Mannerist style defies historical periodization.

THE MAIDS OF HONOR (LAS MENINAS) BY DIEGO VELÁZQUEZ. The artist himself (at left) is shown working at his easel and gazing out at the viewer—or at the subjects of his double portrait, the Spanish king and queen, depicted in a distant mirror. But the real focus of the painting is the delicate, impish princess in the center, flanked by two young ladies-in-waiting, a dwarf, and another royal child. Courtiers in the background look on.

unusual of these artists was El Greco ("the Greek," c. 1541–1614). Born Domenikos Theotokopoulos on the Greek island of Crete, El Greco absorbed the style characteristic of Byzantine icon painting (see Chapter 7) before traveling to Italy and eventually settling in Spain. Many of his paintings were too strange to be appreciated in his own day and even now appear almost surreal. His *View of Toledo*, for example, is a transfigured landscape, mysteriously lit from within. The great Spanish master Diego Velázquez (*vay-LAH-skez*, 1599–1660), who served the Habsburg court in Madrid, was also conceptually thoughtful and daring. His painting *The Maids of Honor* is a masterpiece of multiple perspectives: it shows the artist himself at work on a double portrait of the Spanish king and queen, but the scene is dominated by the children and servants of the royal family.

In architecture and sculpture, the dominant artistic style was that of the Baroque, a school whose name has become a synonym for elaborate ornamentation. This style originated in Rome during the Counter-Reformation and promoted a glorified Catholic worldview. Its most influential figure was Gianlorenzo Bernini (1598–1680), a frequent employee of the Vatican who created a magnificent celebration of papal grandeur in the sweeping colonnades leading up to St. Peter's Basilica. Breaking

with the more serene classicism of Renaissance styles (Chapter 12), Bernini's work drew inspiration from the restless motion and artistic bravado of Hellenistic statuary (Chapter 4).

Dutch Painting in the Golden Age

Southern Europe's main rival in the visual arts was the Netherlands, where many painters explored the theme of man's greatness and wretchedness. Pieter Bruegel the Elder (*BROY-ghul*, c. 1525–1569) exulted in portraying the busy, elemental life of the peasantry. But later in his career, Bruegel became appalled by the intolerance and bloodshed he witnessed during the Spanish repression of the Netherlands. His work *The Massacre of the Innocents* looks, from a distance, like a snug scene of village life. In fact, however, soldiers are methodically breaking into homes and slaughtering helpless infants, as Herod's soldiers once did and as warring armies were doing in Bruegel's own day.

Another Dutch painter, Peter Paul Rubens (1577–1640), was inspired by very different politics. A native of

***THE MASSACRE OF THE INNOCENTS* BY BRUEGEL (c. 1525–1569).**
This painting shows how effectively art can be used as a means of
political and social commentary. Here, Bruegel depicts the suffering
of the Netherlands at the hands of the Spanish in his own day, with
reference to the biblical story of Herod's slaughter of Jewish children
after the birth of Jesus—thereby collapsing these two historical
incidents.

***THE HORRORS OF WAR* BY RUBENS (1577–1640).** In his old age,
Rubens took a far more critical view of war than he had done for most
of his earlier career. Here, the war-god Mars casts aside his mistress
Venus, goddess of love, and threatens humanity with death and
destruction.

SELF-PORTRAITS. Self-portraits became common during the sixteenth and seventeenth centuries, reflecting the intense introspection of the
period. Left: Rembrandt painted more than sixty self-portraits; this one, dating from around 1660, captures the artist's creativity, theatricality
(note the costume), and honesty of self-examination. Right: Judith Leyster was a contemporary of Rembrandt who pursued a successful career
during her early twenties, before she married. Respected in her own day, she was all but forgotten for centuries thereafter but is once again the
object of much attention.

Antwerp, still part of the Spanish Netherlands, Rubens was a staunch Catholic who supported the Habsburg regime. He reveled in the sumptuous extravagance of the Baroque style; he is most famous today for the pink and rounded flesh of his well-nourished nudes. But his late painting *The Horrors of War* captures what he called "the grief of unfortunate Europe."

Rembrandt van Rijn (*vahn-REEN*, 1606–1669) defies all attempts at easy characterization. Living across the border from the Spanish Netherlands in the staunchly Calvinist Dutch Republic, Rembrandt managed to put both realistic and Baroque traits to new uses. In his early career, he gained fame and fortune as a painter of biblical scenes and was also active as a portrait painter who knew how to flatter his subjects—to the great advantage of his purse. But his later portraits, including several self-portraits, are highly introspective. They can be contrasted with the frank, fearless gaze of Rembrandt's slightly younger contemporary,

Judith Leyster (1609–1660), who looks out of her own self-portrait with a refreshingly optimistic and good-humored expression.

CONCLUSION

The European states engaged in colonizing the Atlantic were riven by internal dissent and deadly competitions among themselves, all of which would be exported to the peoples of that world. Colonial initiatives, in turn, affected European politics and deepened divisions among Protestants and Catholics, causing waves of migration by persecuted minorities who replanted and propagated these rivalries across the Atlantic. Religion was not the only cause of conflict. Supporting colonial expansion in the Atlantic

After You Read This Chapter

🦉 Go to **INQUIZITIVE** to see what you've learned—and learn what you've missed—with personalized feedback along the way.

REVIEWING THE OBJECTIVES

- How were the peoples and ecosystems of the Americas, Africa, and Europe intertwined during this period? What were some consequences of these new linkages?

- Why did the colonies of the Spanish, the English, and the Dutch differ from one another? How did these differences affect the lives and labor of colonists, both free and unfree?

- Which European powers came to dominate the Atlantic world? What factors led to the decline of Spain and to the rise of France?

- What forms did religious and political conflict take in France, the Netherlands, and Germany? What were the causes of the English Civil War, and what impact did this event have on the English colonies?

- How do the arts and political philosophies of this period reflect the turmoil of Europe and the Atlantic world?

world and fighting wars within Europe were expensive projects, and they placed strain on traditional alliances and ideas. Intellectuals and artists strove to reassess Europeans' place in this expanding Atlantic world, to process the flood of new information and commodities, and to make sense of the profound changes in daily life.

It would take centuries for Europeans to adapt themselves to the changes brought about by their integration into the Atlantic world and to process its implications. Finding new lands and cultures unknown to the ancients and unmentioned in the Bible had exposed the limitations of Western civilizations' accumulated knowledge and called for new ways of knowing and explaining the world. The Columbian exchange of people, plants, livestock, and pathogens that had previously been isolated from one another had a profound and lasting effect on populations and ecosystems throughout the Atlantic zone. The distribution of new agricultural products transformed the lives of Europe's poor and rich alike. The transatlantic slave trade, which made all of this possible, brought Africans and their cultures into a world of growing global connections under the worst possible circumstances for those who were enslaved—yet this did not prevent them from helping to shape this new world.

Meanwhile, the influx of silver from New Spain precipitated the great price inflation of the sixteenth and seventeenth centuries, which bewildered contemporary observers and contributed to the atmosphere of crisis in post-Reformation Europe, already riven by religious and civil warfare. Political and moral philosophers also struggled to redefine the role of government in a world of religious pluralism, and to articulate new ideologies that did not necessitate violence among people of different faiths. The response was a trend toward stronger centralized states, justified by theories of absolute government. Led by the French monarchy of Louis XIV, these absolutist regimes would reach their apogee in the coming century.

PEOPLE, IDEAS, AND EVENTS IN CONTEXT

- What was the **COLUMBIAN EXCHANGE**? How did it affect the relations among the peoples of the Americas, Africa, and Europe during this period?

- What circumstances led to the development of the **TRIANGULAR TRADE**?

- What were the main sources of instability in Europe during the sixteenth century? How did the **PRICE REVOLUTION** exacerbate these?

- How did **HENRY IV** of France and **PHILIP II** of Spain deal differently with the religious conflict that beset Europe during these years?

- What were the origins of the **THIRTY YEARS' WAR**? Was it primarily a religious conflict?

- How did the policies of **CARDINAL RICHELIEU** strengthen the power of the French monarchy?

- What policies of England's **CHARLES I** were most detested by his subjects? Why was his execution so momentous?

- In what ways did the **WITCH CRAZE** of early modern Europe reveal the religious and social tensions of the sixteenth and seventeenth centuries?

- What were the differences between **JEAN BODIN**'s theory of absolute sovereignty and that of **THOMAS HOBBES**?

- How did philosophers like **MONTAIGNE** and **PASCAL** respond to the uncertainties of the age? How were contemporary trends reflected in the works of **SHAKESPEARE** and in the visual arts?

THINKING ABOUT CONNECTIONS

- The emergence of the Atlantic world can be seen as a *cause* of new developments and as the *result* of historical processes. What long-term political, economic, and demographic circumstances drove the expansion of European influence into the Atlantic? What subsequent historical developments can we attribute to the creation of this interconnected world?

- The political crises of this era reveal the tensions produced by sectarian religious disputes and by a growing rift between powerful centralizing monarchies and landholding elites unwilling to surrender their authority and independence. What other periods in history display similar tensions? How do those periods compare to the one we have studied in this chapter?

- The intellectual currents of this era reveal that a new generation was challenging the assumptions of its predecessors. In what other historical eras do we find a similar phenomenon? What social and political circumstances tend to produce consensus, and which tend to produce dissent, skepticism, and doubt?

STORY LINES

- After 1660, European rulers invoked an absolutist definition of sovereignty in order to expand the power of the monarchy. The most successful absolutist kings, such as Louis XIV of France or Peter the Great of Russia, limited the power of traditional aristocratic elites and the independence of religious institutions.

- Efforts by English monarchs to create an absolutist regime in England after the civil war were resisted by political opponents in Parliament. Though they agreed with the king that a strong state was needed, they demanded a different definition of sovereignty, in which the king would rule alongside Parliament.

- Absolutism reinforced the imperial ambitions of European monarchies and led to frequent wars that were increasingly fought both in Europe and in colonial spaces in other parts of the world. The pressures of war favored dynasties capable of building strong centralized states with reliable sources of revenue from trade and taxation.

CHRONOLOGY

1643–1715	Reign of Louis XIV of France
1660	Restoration of the Stuart kings in England
1683	Ottoman siege of Vienna
1685	Revocation of the Edict of Nantes
1688	Glorious Revolution in England
1688–1697	War of the League of Augsburg
1682–1725	Reign of Peter the Great of Russia
1690	Publication of John Locke's *Two Treatises of Government*
1702–1713	War of the Spanish Succession
1713	Treaty of Utrecht

Before
You
Read
This
Chapter

European Monarchies and Absolutism, 1660–1725

CORE OBJECTIVES

- **DEFINE** *absolutism*, **UNDERSTAND** its central principles as a theory of government, and **IDENTIFY** the major absolutist rulers in Europe during this period.

- **DEFINE** *mercantilism* and its relation to absolutist rule.

- **EXPLAIN** the alternatives to absolutism that emerged, most notably in England and the Dutch Republic.

- **DESCRIBE** how the wars between 1680 and 1713 changed the balance of power in Europe and in the colonial spheres of the Atlantic world.

In the mountainous region of south-central France known as the Auvergne in the 1660s, the Marquis of Canillac had a notorious reputation. His noble title gave him the right to collect minor taxes on special occasions, but he insisted that these small privileges be converted into annual tributes. To collect these payments, he housed in his castle twelve accomplices that he called his "apostles." Their other nicknames—one was known as "Break Everything"—gave a more accurate sense of their activities in the local villages. The marquis imprisoned those who resisted and forced their families to buy their freedom. In an earlier age, the marquis might have gotten away with this profitable arrangement. In 1662, however, he ran up against the authority of a king, Louis XIV, who was determined to demonstrate that the power of the central monarch was absolute. The marquis was brought up on charges before a special court of judges from Paris. He was found guilty and forced to pay a large fine. The king confiscated his property and had the marquis's castle destroyed.

Louis XIV's special court in the Auvergne heard nearly a thousand civil cases over four months in 1662. It convicted 692 people, and many of them, like the Marquis of Canillac, were noble.

401

The verdicts were an extraordinary example of Louis XIV's ability to project his authority into the remote corners of his realm and to do so in a way that diminished the power of other elites. During his long reign (1643–1715), Louis XIV systematically pursued such a policy on many fronts, asserting his power over the nobility, the clergy, and the provincial courts. Increasingly, these elites were forced to look to the crown to guarantee their interests, and their own power became more closely connected with the sacred aura of the monarchy itself. Louis XIV's model of kingship was so successful that it became known as absolute monarchy. In recognition of the success and influence of Louis XIV's political system, the period from around 1660 (when the English monarchy was restored and Louis XIV began his personal rule in France) to 1789 (when the French Revolution erupted) is traditionally known as the age of absolutism. This is a crucial period in the development of modern, centralized, bureaucratic states in Europe.

Absolutism was a political theory that encouraged rulers to claim complete sovereignty within their territories. An absolute monarch could make law, dispense justice, create and direct a bureaucracy, declare war, and levy taxation, without the approval of any other governing body. Assertions of absolute authority were buttressed by claims that rulers governed by divine right, just as fathers ruled over their households. After the chaos and religious wars of the previous century, many Europeans came to believe that it was only by exalting the sovereignty of absolute rulers that order could be restored to European life.

***THE DEFENSE OF CÁDIZ AGAINST THE ENGLISH* BY FRANCISCO ZURBARAN.** The rivalry between European powers that played out over the new colonial possessions further proved the decline of Spain, which lost the island of Jamaica and ships in the harbor of Cádiz to the English in the 1650s.

European monarchs also continued to project their power abroad during this period. By 1660, as we have seen, the French, Spanish, Portuguese, English, and Dutch had all established important colonies in the Americas and in Asia. These colonies created trading networks that brought profitable new consumer goods such as sugar, tobacco, and coffee to a wide public in Europe. They also encouraged the colonies' reliance on slavery to produce these goods. Rivalry among colonial powers to control the trade in slaves and consumer goods was intense and often led to wars that were fought both in Europe and in contested colonies. These wars, in turn, increased the motivation of absolutist rulers to extract as much revenue as they could from their subjects and encouraged the development of institutions that enhanced their power: armies, navies, tax systems, tariffs, and customs controls.

Absolutism was not universally successful during this period. The English monarchy, restored in 1660 after the turbulent years of the Civil War, attempted to impose absolutist rule but met with resistance from parliamentary leaders who insisted on more-inclusive institutions of government. After 1688, England, Scotland, the Dutch Republic, Switzerland, Venice, Sweden, and Poland-Lithuania were all either limited monarchies or republics. In Russia, on the other hand, an extreme autocracy emerged that gave the tsar a degree of control over his subjects' lives and property far beyond anything imagined by western European absolutists. Even in Russia, however, absolutism was never unlimited in practice. Even the most absolute monarchs could rule effectively only with the consent of their subjects (particularly the nobility). When serious opposition erupted, even powerful kings were forced to back down. King George III of Britain discovered this when his North American colonies declared their independence in 1776, creating the United States of America. In 1789, an even more sweeping revolution began in France, and the entire structure of absolutism came crashing to the ground (see Chapter 18).

THE APPEAL AND JUSTIFICATION OF ABSOLUTISM

Absolutism's promise of stability and order was an appealing alternative to the disorder of the sixteenth and seventeenth centuries (see Chapter 14). The early theorists of absolutism such as Jean Bodin and Thomas Hobbes looked to strong royal governments as an answer to the ever-present threat of religious war and civil conflict.

Absolutist monarchs sought control of the state's armed forces and its legal system, and they demanded the right to collect and spend the state's financial resources at will.

To achieve these goals, they also needed to create an efficient, centralized bureaucracy that owed its allegiance directly to the monarch. Creating and sustaining such a bureaucracy was expensive but necessary in order to weaken the special interests that hindered the free exercise of royal power. The nobility and the clergy, with their traditional legal privileges; the political authority of semiautonomous regions; and representative assemblies such as parliaments, diets, or estates-general were all obstacles—in the eyes of absolutists—to strong, centralized monarchical government. The history of absolutism is the history of kings who attempted to bring such institutions to heel.

In most Protestant countries, the power of the church had already been subordinated to the state when the age of absolutism began. Even where Roman Catholicism remained the state religion, such as in France, Spain, and Austria, absolutist monarchs now devoted considerable attention to bringing the Church and its clergy under royal control. Louis XIV took an active role in religious matters, appointing his own bishops and encouraging the repression of religious dissidents. Unlike his predecessors, however, he rarely appointed members of the clergy to offices within his administration.

The most important potential opponents of royal absolutism were not churchmen, however, but nobles. Louis XIV deprived the French nobility of political power in the provinces but increased their social prestige by making them live at his lavish court at Versailles. Peter the Great of Russia (1689–1725) forced his nobles into lifelong government service, and successive monarchs in Brandenburg-Prussia managed to co-opt the powerful aristocracy by granting them immunity to taxation and giving them the right to enserf their peasants. In exchange, they ceded administrative control to the increasingly bureaucratized Prussian state. In most European monarchies, including Spain, France, Prussia, and England, the nobility retained their preponderant role within the military.

Struggles between monarchs and nobles frequently affected relations between local and central government. In France, the requirement that nobles live at the king's court undermined the provincial institutions that the nobility used to exercise their political power. In Spain, the monarchy, based in Castile, battled the independent-minded nobles of Aragon and Catalonia. Prussian rulers asserted control over formerly "free" cities by claiming the right to police and tax their inhabitants. The Habsburg emperors tried, unsuccessfully, to suppress the largely autonomous nobility of Hungary. Rarely, however, was the path of confrontation between crown and nobility successful in the long run. The most effective absolutist monarchies of the eighteenth century continued to trade privileges for allegiance, so that nobles came to see their own interests as tied to those of the crown. For this reason, wary cooperation between kings and nobles was more common than open conflict during the eighteenth century.

THE ABSOLUTISM OF LOUIS XIV

In Louis XIV's state portrait, it is almost impossible to discern the human being behind the facade of the absolute monarch dressed in his coronation robes and surrounded by the symbols of his authority. That facade was artfully constructed by Louis, who recognized, more fully than any other early modern ruler, the importance of theater to effective kingship. Louis and his successors deliberately staged spectacular demonstrations of their sovereignty to enhance their position as rulers endowed with godlike powers.

Performing Royalty at Versailles

Louis's most elaborate staging of his authority took place at his palace at Versailles (ver-SY), outside of Paris. The main facade of the palace was a third of a mile in length. Inside, tapestries and paintings celebrated French military victories and royal triumphs; mirrors reflected shimmering light throughout the building. In the vast gardens outside, statues of the Greek god Apollo, god of the sun, recalled Louis's claim to be the "Sun King" of France. Noblemen vied to attend him when he arose from bed, ate his meals (usually stone cold after having traveled the distance of several city blocks from kitchen to table), strolled in his gardens (even the way the king walked was choreographed by the royal dancing master), or rode to the hunt. France's leading nobles were required to reside with Louis at Versailles for a portion of the year; the splendor of Louis's court was deliberately calculated to blind them to the possibility of disobedience while raising their prestige by associating them with himself. At the same time, the almost impossibly detailed rules of etiquette at court left these privileged nobles in constant suspense, forever fearful of offending the king by committing some trivial violation of proper manners.

Of course, the nobility did not surrender social and political power entirely. The social order was still hierarchical, and noblemen retained enormous privileges and rights over local peasants within their jurisdiction. The absolutist system forced the nobility to depend on the crown, but it did not seek to undermine their superior place in society. In this sense, the relationship between Louis XIV and the nobility was more of a negotiated settlement than a complete victory of the king over other powerful elites. Louis XIV understood this, and in a memoir that he prepared for his

Interpreting Visual Evidence

The Performance and Display of Absolute Power at the Court of Louis XIV

istorians studying the history of absolutism and the court of Louis XIV in particular have emphasized the Sun King's brilliant use of symbols and display to demonstrate his personal embodiment of sovereignty. Royal portraits, such as that painted by Hyacinthe Rigaud in 1701, vividly illustrate the degree to which Louis's power was based on a studied performance. His pose, with his exposed and shapely calf, was an important indication of power and virility, necessary elements of legitimacy for a hereditary monarch. In the

elaborate rituals of court life at Versailles, Louis often placed his own body at the center of attention, performing in one instance as the god Apollo in a ballet before his assembled courtiers. His movements through the countryside, accompanied by a retinue of soldiers, servants, and aristocrats, were another occasion for highly stylized ritual demonstrations of his quasi-divine status. Finally, of course, the construction of his palace at Versailles, with its symmetrical architecture and its sculpted gardens, was a demonstration that his power extended over the natural world as easily as it did over the lives of his subjects.

Questions for Analysis

1. Who was the intended audience for the king's performance of absolute sovereignty?

2. Who were Louis's primary competitors in this contest for eminence through the performance of power?

3. What possible political dangers might lie in wait for a regime that invested so heavily in the sumptuous display of semidivine authority?

A. Hyacinthe Rigaud's 1701 portrait of Louis XIV.

B. Louis XIV as the Sun King.

C. *The Royal Procession of Louis XIV*, 1664, by Adam Franz van der Meulen.

D. Louis XIV arrives at the Palace of Versailles.

Competing Viewpoints

Absolutism and Patriarchy

> These selections show how two political theorists justified royal absolutism by deriving it from the absolute authority of a father over his household. Bishop Jacques-Bénigne Bossuet (1627–1704) was a famous French preacher who served as tutor to the son of King Louis XIV of France before becoming bishop of Meaux. Sir Robert Filmer (1588–1653) was an English political theorist. Filmer's works attracted particular attention in the 1680s, when John Locke directed the first of his Two Treatises of Government to refuting Filmer's views on the patriarchal nature of royal authority.

Bossuet on the Nature of Monarchical Authority

There are four characteristics or qualities essential to royal authority. First, royal authority is sacred; Secondly, it is paternal; Thirdly, it is absolute; Fourthly, it is subject to reason.... All power comes from God.... Thus princes act as ministers of God, and his lieutenants on earth. It is through them that he exercises his empire.... In this way ... the royal throne is not the throne of a man, but the throne of God himself....

We have seen that kings hold the place of God, who is the true Father of the human race. We have also seen that the first idea of power that there was among men, is that of paternal power; and that kings were fashioned on the model of fathers. Moreover, all the world agrees that obedience, which is

due to public power, is only found ... in the precept which obliges one to honor his parents. From all this it appears that the name "king" is a father's name, and that goodness is the most natural quality in kings....

Royal authority is absolute. In order to make this term odious and insupportable, many pretend to confuse absolute government and arbitrary government. But nothing is more distinct, as we shall make clear when we speak of justice.... The prince need account to no one for what he ordains.... Without this absolute authority, he can neither do good nor suppress evil: his power must be such that no one can hope to escape him.... The sole defense of individuals against the public power must be their innocence....

One must, then, obey princes as if they were justice itself, without which there is neither order nor justice in affairs. They are gods, and share in some way in divine independence.... It follows from this that he who does not want to obey the prince ... is condemned irremissibly to death as an enemy of public peace and of human society.... The prince can correct himself when he knows that he has done badly; but against his authority there can be no remedy....

Source: Jacques-Bénigne Bossuet, *Politics Drawn from the Very Words of Holy Scripture*, (1709) trans. Patrick Riley (Cambridge: 1990), pp. 46–69 and 81–83.

---

son on the art of ruling he wrote, "The deference and the respect that we receive from our subjects are not a free gift from them but payment for the justice and the protection that they expect from us. Just as they must honor us, we must protect and defend them." In their own way, absolutists depended on the consent of those they ruled.

Administration and Centralization

Louis defined his responsibilities in absolutist terms: to concentrate royal power so as to produce domestic tranquility.

In addition to convincing the nobility to cede political authority, he also recruited the upper bourgeoisie as royal intendants, administrators responsible for running the thirty-six *generalités* into which France was divided. Intendants usually served outside the region where they were born and were thus unconnected with the local elites over whom they exercised authority. They held office at the king's pleasure and were clearly his men. Other administrators, often from families newly ennobled as a reward for their service, assisted in directing affairs of state from Versailles.

Louis's administrators devoted much of their time and energy to collecting the taxes necessary to finance the

Filmer on the Patriarchal Origins of Royal Authority

The first government in the world was monarchical, in the father of all flesh, Adam being commanded to multiply, and people the earth, and to subdue it, and having dominion given him over all creatures, was thereby the monarch of the whole world; none of his posterity had any right to possess anything, but by his grant or permission, or by succession from him.... Adam was the father, king, and lord over his family: a son, a subject, and a servant or a slave were one and the same thing at first....

I cannot find any one place or text in the Bible where any power ... is given to a people either to govern themselves, or to choose themselves governors, or to alter the manner of government at their pleasure. The power of government is settled and fixed by the commandment of "honour thy father"; if there were a higher power than the fatherly, then this commandment could not stand and be observed....

All power on earth is either derived or usurped from the fatherly power, there being no other original to be found of any power whatsoever. For if there should be granted two sorts of power without any subordination of one to the other, they would be in perpetual strife which should be the supreme, for two supremes cannot agree. If the fatherly power be supreme, then the power of the people must be subordinate and depend on it. If the power of the people be supreme, then the fatherly power must submit to it, and cannot be exercised without the licence of the people, which must quite destroy the frame and course of nature. Even the power which God himself exercises over mankind is by right of fatherhood: he is both the king and father of us all. As God has exalted the dignity of earthly kings ... by saying they are gods, so ... he has been pleased ... to humble himself by assuming the title of a king to express his power, and not the title of any popular government.

Source: Robert Filmer, "Observations upon Aristotle's Politiques," in *Divine Right and Democracy: An Anthology of Political Writing in Stuart England*, ed. David Wootton (Harmondsworth, UK: 1986), pp. 110–18. First published 1652.

Questions for Analysis

1. Bossuet's definition of *absolutism* connected the sacred power of kings with the paternal authority of fathers within the household. What consequences does he draw from defining the relationship between king and subjects in this way?

2. What does Filmer mean when he says, "All power on earth is either derived or usurped from the fatherly power"? How many examples does he give of paternal or monarchical power?

3. Bossuet and Filmer make obedience the basis for order and justice in the world. What alternative political systems did they most fear?

---

large standing army on which his aggressive foreign policy depended. Absolutism was fundamentally an approach to government by which ambitious monarchs could increase their own power through conquest and display. As such, it was enormously expensive. In addition to the *taille*, or land tax, which increased throughout the seventeenth century, Louis's government introduced a *capitation* (a head tax) and pressed successfully for the collection of indirect taxes on salt (the *gabelle*), wine, tobacco, and other goods. Because the nobility was exempt from the taille, its burden fell most heavily on the peasantry, whose local revolts Louis easily crushed.

Regional opposition was curtailed but not eliminated during Louis's reign. By removing the provincial nobility to Versailles, Louis cut them off from their local sources of power and influence. To restrict the powers of regional parlements, Louis decreed that members of any parlement who refused to approve and enforce his laws would be summarily exiled. The Estates-General, the French representative assembly that met at the king's pleasure to act as a consultative body for the state, had last been summoned in 1614. It did not meet at all during Louis's reign and, in fact, was not convened again until 1789.

Past and Present

The Persistence of Monarchies in a Democratic Age

In the past, monarchs such as Louis XIV (left) often ran roughshod over tradition as they sought ways to increase their power. Today, twelve European states still have reigning monarchs, such as Queen Elizabeth II (right), but their popularity would probably be diminished if they sought an active role in government.

Watch related author videos on the student site
wwnorton.com/college/history/western-civilizationsBrief4

Louis XIV's Religious Policies

Both for reasons of state and of personal conscience, Louis was determined to impose religious unity on France, regardless of the economic and social costs.

Although the vast majority of the French population was Roman Catholic, French Catholics were divided among Quietists, Jansenists, Jesuits, and Gallicans. Quietists preached retreat into personal mysticism, emphasizing a direct relationship between God and the individual human heart. Such doctrine, dispensing as it did with the intermediary services of the Church, was suspect in the eyes of absolutists wedded to the doctrine of *un roi, une loi, une foi* ("one king, one law, one faith"). Jansenism—a movement named for its founder Cornelius Jansen, a seventeenth-century bishop of Ypres—emphasized that original sin could only be overcome through divine grace, and they were committed to a doctrine of predestination that sounded like

a kind of Catholic Calvinism. Louis vigorously persecuted Quietists and Jansenists, offering them a choice between recanting and prison or exile. At the same time, he supported the Jesuits in their efforts to create a Counter-Reformation Catholic Church in France. Louis's support for the Jesuits upset the traditional Gallican Catholics of France, however, who desired a French church independent of papal, Jesuit, and Spanish influence. As a result of this dissension among Catholics, the religious aura of Louis's kingship diminished during the course of his reign.

Against the Protestant Huguenots, Louis waged unrelenting war. Protestant churches and schools were destroyed, and Protestants were banned from many professions. In 1685, Louis revoked the Edict of Nantes, the legal foundation of the toleration Huguenots had enjoyed since 1598. Protestant clerics were exiled, laymen were sent to the galleys as slaves, and their children were forcibly baptized as Catholics. Many families converted, but 200,000

Protestant refugees fled to England, Holland, Germany, and America, bringing with them their professional and artisanal skills. Huguenots fleeing Louis XIV's persecution established the silk industries of Berlin and London, for example. This migration was an enormous loss to France.

Colbert and Mercantilism

Louis's drive to unify France depended on a vast increase in royal revenues. Jean-Baptiste Colbert, the king's finance minister from 1664 to 1683, accomplished this by eliminating wherever possible the practice of tax farming (which permitted collection agents to retain for themselves a percentage of the taxes they gathered for the king). When Colbert assumed office, only about 25 percent of the taxes collected throughout the kingdom reached the treasury. By the time he died, that figure had risen to 80 percent. Under Colbert's direction, the state sold public offices, including judgeships and mayoralties, and guilds purchased the right to enforce trade regulations. Colbert also tried to increase the nation's income by controlling and regulating foreign trade. Colbert was a firm believer in the economic doctrine known as "mercantilism"—a theory that aimed to increase the wealth of the absolutist state by reducing imports and increasing exports (see **Analyzing Primary Sources** on page 410). He imposed tariffs on foreign goods imported into France and used state money to promote the domestic manufacture of formerly imported goods, such as silk, lace, tapestries, and glass. He was especially anxious to create domestic industries capable of producing the goods France would need for war. To encourage domestic trade, he improved France's roads, bridges, and waterways.

Despite Colbert's efforts to increase crown revenues, his policies ultimately foundered on the insatiable demands of Louis XIV's wars (see pages 413–14). Colbert himself foresaw this result when he lectured the king in 1680: "Trade is the source of public finance and public finance is the vital nerve of war. . . . I beg your Majesty to permit me only to say to him that in war as in peace he has never consulted the amount of money available in determining his expenditures." Louis, however, paid him no heed. By the end of Louis's reign, his aggressive foreign policy lay in ruins and his country's finances had been shattered by the unsustainable costs of war.

French Colonialism under Louis XIV

Finance minister Colbert regarded overseas expansion as an integral part of the French state's mercantilist economic policy, and with his guidance, Louis XIV's absolutist realm emerged as a major colonial power. Realizing the profits to be made in responding to Europe's growing demand for sugar, Colbert encouraged the development of sugar-producing colonies in the West Indies, the largest of which was Saint-Domingue (present-day Haiti). Sugar, virtually unknown in Christian Europe during the Middle Ages, became a popular luxury item in the late fifteenth century (see Chapter 14). It took the slave plantations of the Caribbean to turn sugar into a mass-market product. By 1750, slaves in Saint-Domingue produced 40 percent of the world's sugar and 50 percent of its coffee, exporting more sugar than Jamaica, Cuba, and Brazil combined. By 1700, France also dominated the interior of the North American continent, where French traders brought furs to the American Indians and missionaries preached Christianity in a vast territory that stretched from Quebec to Louisiana. The financial returns from North America were never large, however. Furs, fish, and tobacco were exported to European markets but never matched the profits from the Caribbean sugar colonies or from the trading posts that the French maintained in India.

Like the earlier Spanish colonies (see Chapter 14), the French colonies were established and administered as direct crown enterprises. French colonial settlements in North America were conceived mainly as military outposts and trading centers, and they were overwhelmingly populated by men. The elite of French colonial society were military officers and administrators sent from Paris. Below their ranks were fishermen, fur traders, small farmers, and common soldiers who constituted the bulk of French settlers in North America. Because the fishing and the fur trades relied on cooperative relationships with native peoples, a mutual economic interdependence grew up between the French colonies and the peoples of the surrounding region. Intermarriage, especially between French traders and native women, was common. These North American colonies remained dependent on the wages and supplies sent to them from the mother country. Only rarely did they become truly self-sustaining economic enterprises.

The phenomenally successful sugar plantations of the Caribbean had their own social structure, with slaves at the bottom, people of mixed African and European descent forming a middle layer, and wealthy European plantation owners at the top, controlling the lucrative trade with the outside world. Well over half of the sugar and coffee sent to France was resold and sent elsewhere to markets throughout Europe. Because the monarchy controlled the prices that colonial plantation owners

Analyzing Primary Sources

Mercantilism and War

Jean-Baptiste Colbert (1619–1683) served as Louis XIV's finance minister from 1664 until his death. He worked assiduously to promote commerce, build up French industry, and increase exports. However much Colbert may have seen his economic policies as ends in themselves, to Louis they were always means to the end of waging war. Ultimately, Louis's wars undermined the prosperity that Colbert tried so hard to create. This memorandum, written to Louis in 1670, illustrates clearly the mercantilist presumptions of self-sufficiency on which Colbert operated: every item needed to build up the French navy must ultimately be produced in France, even if it could be acquired at less cost from elsewhere.

 nd since Your Majesty has wanted to work diligently at reestablishing his naval forces, and since afore that it has been necessary to make very great expenditures, since all merchandise, munitions, and manufactured items formerly came from Holland and the countries of the North, it has been absolutely necessary to be especially concerned with finding within the realm, or with establishing in it, everything which might be necessary for this great plan.

To this end, the manufacture of tar was established in Médoc, Auvergne, Dauphiné, and Provence; iron cannons, in Burgundy, Nivernois, Saintonge, and Périgord; large anchors in Dauphiné, Nivernois, Brittany, and Rochefort; sailcloth for the Levant, in Dauphiné; coarse muslin, in Auvergne; all the implements for pilots and others, at Dieppe and La Rochelle; the cutting of wood suitable for vessels, in Burgundy, Dauphiné, Brittany, Normandy, Poitou, Saintonge, Provence, Guyenne, and the Pyrenees; masts, of a sort once unknown in this realm, have been found in Provence, Languedoc, Auvergne, Dauphiné, and in the Pyrenees. Iron, which was obtained from Sweden and Biscay, is currently manufactured in the realm. Fine hemp for ropes, which came from Prussia and from Piedmont, is currently obtained in Burgundy, Mâconnais, Bresse, Dauphiné; and markets for it have since been established in Berry and in Auvergne, which always provides money in these provinces and keeps it within the realm.

In a word, everything serving for the construction of vessels is currently established in the realm, so that Your Majesty can get along without foreigners for the navy and will even, in a short time, be able to supply them and gain their money in this fashion. And it is with this same objective of having everything necessary to provide abundantly for his navy and that of his subjects that he is working at the general reform of all the forests in his realm, which, being as carefully preserved as they are at present, will abundantly produce all the wood necessary for this.

Source: Charles W. Cole, *Colbert and a Century of French Mercantilism*, 2 vols. (New York: 1939), p. 320.

Questions for Analysis

1. Why would Colbert want to manufacture materials for supplying the navy within France rather than buying them from abroad?

2. From this example, does Colbert see the economy as serving any interest other than that of the state?

3. Was there a necessary connection between mercantilism and war?

---

could charge French merchants for their goods, traders in Europe who bought the goods for resale abroad could also make vast fortunes. Historians estimate that as many as 1 million of the 25 million inhabitants of France in the eighteenth century lived off the money flowing through this colonial trade, making the slave colonies of the Caribbean a powerful force for economic change in France. The wealth generated from these colonies added to the prestige of France's absolutist system of government.

ALTERNATIVES TO ABSOLUTISM

Although absolutism was the dominant model for seventeenth- and eighteenth-century European monarchs, it was by no means the only system by which Europeans governed themselves. A republican oligarchy continued to rule in Venice. In the Polish-Lithuanian commonwealth, the monarch was elected by the nobility and governed alongside a parliament that met every two years. In the Netherlands, the territories that had won their independence from Spain during the early seventeenth century combined to form the United Provinces, the only truly new country to take shape in Europe during the early modern era.

The Restoration in England and the Glorious Revolution of 1688

After the civil war of 1642–51 and the subsequent years of Oliver Cromwell's Commonwealth and Protectorate (see Chapter 14), England took a different path from that of France. By 1688, the English arrived at a constitutional settlement that gave a larger role to Parliament and admitted a degree of participation by non-nobles in the affairs of state. Arriving at this settlement was not easy, however, and two issues remained contentious between 1660 and 1688: the religious question and the relationship between Parliament and the king.

Following the Restoration of the Stuarts in 1660, Charles II (r. 1660–85) showed his affinity for Catholicism by bringing bishops back to the Church of England, but he also declared limited religious toleration for Protestant "dissenters." He comforted members of Parliament by promising to observe the Magna Carta and he accepted legislation stating that Parliament be summoned at least once every three years. England thus emerged from its civil war as a limited monarchy, with power exercised by the "king in Parliament."

During the 1670s, however, Charles began to openly model his kingship on the absolutism of Louis XIV. England's powerful elites became divided between Charles's supporters, known as "Tories" (a nickname for Irish Catholic bandits) and his opponents, called "Whigs" (a nickname for Scottish Presbyterian rebels). In fact, both sides feared both absolutism and the prospect of renewed civil war. What they could not agree on was which possibility frightened them more.

Charles's known sympathy for Roman Catholicism and his claim that he had the right to ignore parliamentary legislation worked to the advantage of his Whig opponents, who won a series of parliamentary elections between 1679 and 1681. Charles responded by moving aggressively against the Whig leadership, executing several on charges of treason. When he died in 1685, his power had been enhanced, but his divisive political and religious legacy was the undoing of his less able successor, his Roman Catholic brother, James II.

James's admiration of the French monarchy's Gallican Catholicism led him to seek ways of furthering the work of the Church by connecting it to the power of an absolutist state. His commitment to absolutism also led him to build up the English army and navy, which required increased taxation. He also took control of the country's new post office, making domestic surveillance routine and prosecutions of seditious speech frequent. For the Whigs, James's policies were

CHARLES II OF ENGLAND (r. 1660–85) IN HIS CORONATION ROBES. This full frontal portrait of the monarch, holding the symbols of his rule, seems to confront the viewer personally with the overwhelming authority of the sovereign's gaze. Compare this classic image of the absolutist monarch with the very different portraits of William and Mary, who ruled after the Glorious Revolution of 1688 (page 412). ▪ *What had changed between 1660, when Charles II came to the throne, and 1688, when the more popular William and Mary became the rulers of England?*

all that they had feared. The Tories, meanwhile, remained loyal to the Church of England and were alienated by James's Catholicism. When a son was unexpectedly born to the royal couple, and it was announced that he was to be raised a Catholic, events moved swiftly to a climax. A delegation of Whigs and Tories crossed the channel to Holland to invite James's much older Protestant daughter Mary Stuart and her Protestant husband, William of Orange, to cross to England with an invading army to preserve English Protestantism and English liberties by summoning a new Parliament.

Following the invasion, James fled for exile in France. Parliament declared the throne vacant, allowing William and Mary to succeed him as joint sovereigns in 1688. Parliament passed a Bill of Rights, which reaffirmed English civil liberties such as trial by jury, habeas corpus (a guarantee that no one could be imprisoned unless charged with a crime) and the right to petition the monarch through Parliament. The Bill of Rights also declared the monarchy subject to the law. The Act of Toleration of 1689 granted Protestant dissenters the right to worship freely, and in 1701, the Act of Succession ordained that every future English monarch must be a member of the Church of England.

The English referred to the events of 1688–89 as the "Glorious Revolution" because it established England as a mixed monarchy governed by the "king in Parliament" according to the rule of law. After 1688, no English monarch ever again attempted to govern without Parliament, which has met annually ever since, while strengthening its control over taxation and expenditure. Although Parliament never codified the legal provisions of this form of monarchy into one constitutional document, historians consider 1688 as a founding moment in the development of a constitutional monarchy in Britain.

Yet the revolution of 1688 was not all glory. It was not bloodless, and it was accompanied by violence in many parts of England, Scotland, and Ireland. Also, it consolidated the position of large property holders, whose control over local government had been threatened by the centralizing absolutist policies of Charles II and James II. It thus reinforced the power of a wealthy class of English elites who would soon become even wealthier from government patronage and the profits of war. The 1688 revolution also brought misery to the Catholic minority in Scotland and the Catholic majority in Ireland. After 1690, power in Ireland would lie firmly in the hands of a "Protestant Ascendancy," whose dominance over Irish society would last until modern times.

The Glorious Revolution nevertheless favored the growth and political power of the English commercial classes, especially the growing number of people concentrated in English cities whose livelihood depended on commerce in the Atlantic world and beyond. Whigs in Parliament became the voice of this newly influential pressure group of commercial entrepreneurs; the Whigs called for revisions to the tax code that would benefit those engaged in manufacturing and trade. In 1694, the Whigs established the Bank of England, which aimed to promote English power through the generation of wealth, inaugurating a financial revolution that would make London the center of a vast network of banking and investment in the eighteenth century.

John Locke and the Contract Theory of Government

The Glorious Revolution was the product of unique circumstances, but it also reflected antiabsolutist theories of politics that were taking shape in the late seventeenth century. Chief among these opponents of absolutism was the Englishman John Locke (1632–1704), whose *Two Treatises of Government* were written before the Glorious Revolution but published for the first time in 1690.

Locke maintained that humans had originally lived in a state of nature characterized by absolute freedom and equality, with no government of any kind. The only law was the law of nature (which Locke equated with the law of reason), by which individuals enforced for themselves their natural rights to life, liberty, and property. Soon, however, humans perceived that the inconveniences of the state of nature outweighed its advantages. Accordingly, they agreed first to establish a civil society based on absolute equality and then to set up a government to arbitrate the disputes that might arise within this civil society. But they did not make government's powers absolute. All powers not expressly surrendered to the government were reserved to the people themselves; as a result, governmental authority was both contractual and conditional. If a government exceeded or abused the authority granted to it, society had the right to dissolve that government and create another.

Locke condemned absolutism in every form. He denounced absolute monarchy, but he was also critical of

WILLIAM AND MARY. In 1688, William of Orange and his wife, Mary Stuart, became Protestant joint rulers of England in a bloodless coup that took power from her father, the Catholic James II. Compare this contemporary print with the portraits of Louis XIV (page 404) and Charles II (page 411). ▪ *What relationship does it seem to depict between the royal couple and their subjects?* ▪ *What is the significance of the gathered crowd in the public square in the background?* ▪ *How is this different from the spectacle of divine authority projected by Louis XIV or the image of Charles II looking straight at the viewer?*

claims for the sovereignty of parliaments. Government, he argued, had been instituted to protect life, liberty, and property; no political authority could infringe these natural rights. The law of nature was therefore an automatic and absolute limitation on every branch of government.

In the late eighteenth century, Locke's ideas would resurface as part of the intellectual background of both the American and French Revolutions. Between 1690 and 1720, however, they served a far less radical purpose. The landed gentry who replaced James II with William and Mary read Locke as a defense of their conservative revolution. Rather than protecting their liberty and property, James II had threatened both; hence, the magnates were entitled to overthrow the tyranny he had established and replace it with a government that would defend their interests by preserving these natural rights. English government after 1689 would be dominated by Parliament; Parliament in turn was controlled by a landed aristocracy who were firm in the defense of their common interests, and who perpetuated their control by determining that only men possessed of substantial property could vote or run for office. During the beginning of the eighteenth century, then, both France and Britain had solved the problem of political dissent and social disorder in their own way. The emergence of a limited monarchy in England after 1688 contrasted vividly with the absolutist system developed by Louis XIV, but in fact both systems worked well enough to balance the competing interests of royal authority and powerful landed nobles.

The Dutch Republic

Another exception to absolutist rule in Europe was the Dutch Republic of the United Provinces, which had gained its independence from Spanish rule in 1648 (see Chapter 14). The seven provinces of the Dutch Republic (also known as the Netherlands) preserved their autonomy with a federal legislature known as the States General. The inhabitants of the republic worked hard to prevent the reestablishment of hereditary monarchy in the Dutch Republic. They were all the more jealous of their independence because several Catholic provinces of the southern Low Countries, including present-day Belgium and Luxembourg, remained under Spanish control.

The princes of the House of Orange served the Dutch Republic with a special title, *stadtholder*, or steward. The stadtholder did not technically rule and had no power to make laws, though he did exercise some influence over the appointments of officials and military officers. Powerful merchant families in the United Provinces exercised real authority, through their dominance of the legislature. It was from the Dutch Republic that the stadtholder William

of Orange launched his successful bid to become the king of England in the Glorious Revolution of 1688.

By 1670, the prosperity of the Dutch Republic was strongly linked to trade: grains and fish from eastern Europe and the Baltic Sea; spices, silks, porcelains, and tea from the Indian Ocean and Japan; slaves, silver, coffee, sugar, and tobacco from the Atlantic world. With a population of nearly 2 million and a capital, Amsterdam, that served as an international hub for goods and finance, the Dutch Republic's commercial network was global (see Chapter 14). Trade brought with it an extraordinary diversity of peoples and religions, as Spanish and Portuguese Jews, French Huguenots, English Quakers, and Protestant dissidents from central Europe all sought to take advantage of the relative spirit of toleration that existed in the Netherlands. This toleration did have limits. Jews were not required to live in segregated neighborhoods, as in many other European capitals, but they were prohibited from joining guilds or trade associations. Tensions between Calvinists and Catholics were also a perennial issue.

The last quarter of the seventeenth century witnessed a decline in Dutch power. The turning point came in 1672, when the French king, Louis XIV, put together a coalition that quickly overran all but two of the Dutch provinces. Popular anger at the failures of Dutch leadership turned violent, and in response the panicked assemblies named William of Orange the new stadtholder of Holland, giving him the power to organize the defense of the republic and to quell internal dissent. William opened the dikes that held back the sea, and the French armies were forced to retreat in the face of rising waters. After the Glorious Revolution of 1688 in England, which brought William of Orange to the English throne, the Dutch joined an alliance with the English against the French. This alliance protected the republic against further aggression from France, but it also forced the Dutch into heavy expenditures on fortifications and defense and involved them in a series of costly wars (as will be discussed later). As a result, the flexible political institutions that had been part of the strength of the Dutch Republic became more rigid over time. Meanwhile, both the French and the British continued to pressure the Dutch commercial fleet at sea. In the eighteenth century, the Dutch no longer exercised the same influence abroad.

WAR AND THE BALANCE OF POWER, 1661–1715

By the beginning of the eighteenth century, then, Europe was being reshaped by wars whose effects were also felt far beyond Europe's borders. The initial causes of these wars lay in the French monarchy's efforts to challenge France's main European rivals, the Habsburg powers in Spain, the Spanish Netherlands, and the Holy Roman Empire. Through his continued campaigns in the Low Countries, Louis XIV expanded his territory, eventually taking Strasbourg (1681), Luxembourg (1684), and Cologne (1688). In response, William of Orange organized the League of Augsburg, which over time included Holland, England, Spain, Sweden, Bavaria, Saxony, the Rhine Palatinate, and the Austrian Habsburgs. The resulting Nine Years' War between France and the League extended from Ireland to India to North America (where it was known as King William's War), demonstrating the broadening imperial reach of European dynastic regimes and the increasing significance of French and English competition in the Atlantic world.

These wars were a sign both of the rising power of Europe's absolutist regimes and of a growing vulnerability. Financing the increasingly costly wars of the eighteenth century would prove to be one of the central challenges faced by all of Europe's absolutist regimes, and the pressure to raise revenues from royal subjects through taxation would eventually strain European society to a breaking point. By the end of the eighteenth century, popular unrest and political challenges to absolutist and imperial states were widespread, both on the European continent and in the colonies of the Atlantic world.

From the League of Augsburg to the War of the Spanish Succession

The League of Augsburg reflected the emergence of a new diplomatic goal in western and central Europe: the preservation of a balance of power. This goal would animate European diplomacy for the next 200 years, until the balance of power system collapsed with the outbreak of the First World War. The main proponents of balance of power diplomacy were England, the United Provinces (Holland), Prussia, and Austria. By 1697, the League forced Louis XIV to make peace, because France was exhausted by war and famine. Louis gave back much of his recent gains but kept his eyes on the real prize: a French claim to succeed to the throne of Spain and thus to control of the Spanish Empire in the Americas, Italy, the Netherlands, and the Philippines.

In the 1690s, it became clear that King Charles II of Spain (r. 1665–1700) would soon die without a clear heir, and both Louis XIV of France and Leopold I of Austria (r. 1658–1705) were interested in promoting their own relatives to succeed him. Either solution would have upset the balance of power in Europe, and several schemes to divide the Spanish realm between French and Austrian candidates

were discussed. Meanwhile, King Charles II's advisers sought to avoid partition by passing the entire Spanish Empire to a single heir: Louis XIV's grandson, Philip of Anjou. Philip was to renounce any claim to the French throne in becoming king of Spain, but the terms of this were kept secret. When Charles II died, Philip V (r. 1700–46) was proclaimed king of Spain and Louis XIV rushed troops into the Spanish Netherlands while also sending French merchants into the Spanish Americas to break their monopoly on trade from the region. Immediately a war broke out, known as the War of the Spanish Succession, pitting England, the United Provinces, Austria, and Prussia against France, Bavaria, and Spain. Although the English king, William of Orange, died in 1702, just as the war was beginning, his generals led an extraordinary march deep into the European continent, inflicting a devastating defeat on the French and their Bavarian allies at Blenheim in southern Germany (1704). Soon after, the English captured Gibraltar, establishing a commercial foothold in the Mediterranean. The costs of the campaign nevertheless created a chorus of complaints from English and Dutch merchants, who feared the damage that was being done to trade and commerce. Queen Anne of England (Mary's sister and William's successor) gradually grew disillusioned with the war, and her government sent out peace feelers to France.

In 1713, the war finally came to an end with the Treaty of Utrecht. Its terms were reasonably fair to all sides. Philip V, Louis XIV's grandson, remained on the throne of Spain and retained Spain's colonial empire intact. In return, Louis agreed that France and Spain would never be united under the same ruler. Austria gained territories in the Spanish Netherlands and Italy, including Milan and Naples. The Dutch were guaranteed protection of their borders against future invasions by France, but the French retained both Lille and Strasbourg. The most significant consequences of the settlement, however, were played out in the Atlantic world, as the balance of powers among Europe's colonial empires underwent a profound shift.

Imperial Rivalries after the Treaty of Utrecht

The fortunes of Europe's colonial empires changed dramatically owing to the wars of the late seventeenth and early eighteenth centuries. Habsburg Spain proved unable to defend its early monopoly over colonial trade, and by 1700, although Spain still possessed a substantial empire, it lay at the mercy of its more dynamic rivals. Portugal, too, found it impossible to prevent foreign penetration of its colonial empire. In 1703, the English signed a treaty with

Portugal allowing English merchants to export woolens duty-free into Portugal and allowing Portugal to ship its wines duty-free into England. Access to Portugal also led British merchants to trade with the Portuguese colony of Brazil, an important sugar producer and the largest of all the American markets for African slaves.

The 1713 Treaty of Utrecht opened a new era of colonial rivalries. The French retained Quebec and other territories in North America, as well as their small foothold in India. The biggest winner by far was Great Britain, as the combined kingdoms of England and Scotland were known after 1707. The British acquired large chunks of French territory in the New World, including Newfoundland, mainland Nova Scotia, the Hudson Bay, and the Caribbean island of St. Kitts. Even more valuable, however, Britain also extracted from Spain the right to transport and sell African slaves in Spanish America. As a result, the British were now poised to become the principal slave merchants and the dominant colonial and commercial power of the eighteenth-century world.

The Treaty of Utrecht thus reshaped the balance of power in the Atlantic world in fundamental ways. Spain's collapse was already precipitous; by 1713, it was complete. Spain would remain the "sick man of Europe" for the next two centuries. The Dutch decline was more gradual, but by 1713 Dutch merchants' inability to compete with the British in the slave trade diminished their economic clout. In the Atlantic, Britain and France were now the dominant powers. Although they would duel for another half century for control of North America, the balance of colonial power tilted decisively in Britain's favor after Utrecht. Within Europe, the myth of French military supremacy had been shattered. Britain's navy, not France's army, would rule the new imperial and commercial world of the eighteenth century.

THE REMAKING OF CENTRAL AND EASTERN EUROPE

The decades between 1680 and 1720 were also decisive in reshaping the balance of power in central and eastern Europe. As Ottoman power waned, the Austro-Hungarian Empire of the Habsburgs emerged as the dominant power in central and southeastern Europe. To the north, Brandenburg-Prussia was also a rising power. The most dramatic changes, however, occurred in Russia, which emerged from a long war with Sweden as the dominant power in the Baltic Sea and would soon threaten the combined kingdom of Poland-Lithuania. Within these regimes, the main tension came from ambitious monarchs who sought to increase the power of the centralized state at the expense of other elites, especially

aristocrats and the religious institutions. In Brandenburg-Prussia and in Tsarist Russia, these efforts were largely successful, whereas in Habsburg Austria, regional nobilities retained much of their influence.

The Austrian Habsburg Empire

In the second half of the seventeenth century, as Louis XIV of France demonstrated the power of absolutism in western Europe, the Austrian Habsburg Empire must have seemed increasingly like a holdover from a previous age. Habsburg Austria was the largest state within what remained of the medieval Holy Roman Empire, a complex federal association of nearly 300 nominally autonomous dynastic kingdoms, principalities, duchies, and archbishoprics that had been created to protect and defend the papacy. Some, such as the kingdom of Bavaria, were large and had their own standing armies. Each Holy Roman emperor was chosen by seven "electors" who were either of noble rank or archbishops—in practice, nevertheless, the emperor was always from the Habsburg family. Through strategic marriages with other royal lines, earlier generations of Habsburg rulers had consolidated their control over a substantial part of Europe, including Austria, Bohemia, Moravia, and Hungary in central Europe; the Netherlands and Burgundy in the west; and, if one included the Spanish branch of the Habsburg family, Spain and its vast colonial empire as well. After 1648, when the Treaty of Westphalia granted individual member states within the Holy Roman Empire the right to conduct their own foreign policy, the influence of the Austrian Habsburgs waned at precisely the moment that they faced challenges from France to the west and the Ottoman Empire to the east.

The complicated structure of the Holy Roman Empire limited the extent to which a ruler such as Leopold I of Austria could emulate the absolutist rule of Louis XIV in France. Every constituent state within the empire had its own local political institutions and its own entrenched nobilities. Each state had a strong interest in resisting attempts to centralize taxation or the raising of armies. Even if direct assertion of absolutist control was impossible, however, Habsburg rulers found ways of increasing their authority. In Bohemia and Moravia, the Habsburgs encouraged landlords to produce crops for export by forcing peasants to provide three days per week of unpaid work for their lords. In return, the landed elites of these territories permitted the emperors to reduce the political independence of their traditional legislative estates. In Hungary, however, the powerful and independent nobility resisted such compromises. When the Habsburgs began a campaign against Hungarian Protestants in 1679, an insurrection broke out that forced Leopold to

EUROPE AFTER THE TREATY OF UTRECHT (1713). ▪ *What were the major Habsburg dominions?* ▪ *What geographical disadvantage faced the kingdom of Poland as Brandenburg-Prussia grew in influence and ambition?* ▪ *How did the balance of power change in Europe as a result of the Treaty of Utrecht?*

grant concessions to Hungarian nobles in exchange for their assistance in restoring order. When the Ottoman Empire sought to take advantage of this disorder by pressing an attack against Austria from the east, the Habsburgs survived only by enlisting the help of a Catholic coalition led by the Polish king John Sobieski (r. 1674–96).

In 1683 the Ottomans launched their last assault on Vienna, but after their failure to capture the Habsburg capital, Ottoman power in southeastern Europe declined rapidly. By 1699, Austria had reconquered most of Hungary from the Ottomans; by 1718, it controlled all of Hungary and also Transylvania and Serbia. In 1722, Austria acquired the territory of Silesia from Poland. With Hungary now a buffer state between Austria and the Ottomans, Austria became one of the arbiters of the European balance of

power. The same obstacles to the development of centralized absolutist rule persisted, however, and Austria was increasingly overshadowed in central Europe by the rise of another German-speaking state: Prussia.

The Rise of Brandenburg-Prussia

After the Ottoman collapse, the main threat to Austria came from the rising power of Brandenburg-Prussia. Like Austria, Prussia was a composite state made up of several geographically divided territories acquired through inheritance by a single royal family, the Hohenzollerns. Their two main holdings were Brandenburg, centered on its capital city, Berlin, and the duchy of East Prussia. Between these two territories lay Pomerania (claimed by Sweden) and an important part of the kingdom of Poland, including the port of Gdansk (Danzig). The Hohenzollerns' aim was to unite their state by acquiring these intervening territories. Over the course of more than a century of steady state building, they finally succeeded in doing so. In the process, Brandenburg-Prussia became a dominant military power and a key player in the balance-of-power diplomacy of the mid-eighteenth century.

The foundations for Prussian expansion were laid by Frederick William, the "Great Elector" (r. 1640–88). He obtained East Prussia from Poland in exchange for help in a war against Sweden. Behind the Elector's diplomatic triumphs lay his success in building an army and mobilizing the resources to pay for it. He gave the powerful nobles of his territories (known as "Junkers" [YUN-kurs]) the right to enserf their peasants and guaranteed them immunity from taxation. In exchange, they staffed the officer corps of his army and supported his highly autocratic taxation system. Secure in their estates and made increasingly wealthy in the grain trade, the Junkers surrendered management of the Prussian state to the Elector's newly reformed bureaucracy, which set about its main task: increasing the size and strength of the Prussian army.

By supporting Austria in the War of the Spanish Succession, the Great Elector's son, Frederick I (r. 1688–1713) earned the right to call himself king of Prussia from the Austrian emperor. He too was a crafty diplomat, but his main attention was devoted to developing the cultural life of his new royal capital, Berlin. His son, Frederick William I (r. 1713–40) focused, like his grandfather, on building the army. During his reign, the Prussian army grew from 30,000 to 83,000 men, becoming the fourth largest army in Europe, after France, Austria, and Russia. To support his army, Frederick William increased taxes and shunned the luxuries of court life. For him, the theater of absolutism was not the palace but the office, where he personally supervised his army and the growing bureaucracy that sustained it. Frederick William's son, known as Frederick the Great, would take this Prussian army and the bureaucracy that sustained it and transform the kingdom into a major power in central Europe after 1740 (see Chapter 17).

Thus, in both Prussia and Habsburg Austria, the divided nature of the respective realms and the entrenched strength of local nobilities forced the rulers in each case to grant significant concessions to noble landowners in exchange for incremental increases in the power of the centralized state. Whereas the nobility in France increasingly sought to maximize their power by participating in the system of absolutist rule at the court of Louis XIV, and wealthy landowners in England sought to exercise their influence through Parliament, the nobilities of Prussia and Habsburg Austria had more leverage to demand something in return for their cooperation. Often, what they demanded was the right to enserf or coerce labor from the peasantry in their domains. In both eastern and western Europe, therefore, the state became stronger. In eastern Europe, however, this increase in state power often came at the expense of an intensification of feudal obligations that the peasantry owed to their local lords.

AUTOCRACY IN RUSSIA

An even more dramatic transformation took place in Russia under Tsar Peter I (1672–1725). Peter's official title was "autocrat of all the Russias" but he was soon known as Peter the Great. His imposing height—he was six feet eight inches tall—and his mercurial personality—jesting one moment, raging the next—added to the outsize impression he made on his contemporaries. Peter was not the first tsar to bring his country into contact with western Europe, but his policies were decisive in making Russia a great European power.

THE CITY OF STETTIN UNDER SIEGE BY THE GREAT ELECTOR FREDERICK WILLIAM IN THE WINTER OF 1677–78 (c. 1680). This painting depicts the growing sophistication and organization of military operations under the Prussian monarchy. Improvements in artillery and siege tactics forced cities to adopt new defensive strategies, especially the zone of battlements and protective walls that became ubiquitous in central Europe during this period. ▪ *How might these developments have shaped the layout of Europe's growing towns and cities?* ▪ *How might this emphasis on the military and its attendant bureaucracy have affected the relationship between the monarchy and the nobility or between the king and his subjects?*

The Early Years of Peter's Reign

Since 1613, Russia had been ruled by members of the Romanov dynasty, who had attempted to restore political stability after the chaotic "time of troubles" that followed the death of the bloodthirsty, half-mad tsar Ivan the Terrible in 1584. The Romanovs faced a severe threat to their rule between 1667 and 1671, when a Cossack leader (the Russian Cossacks were semiautonomous bands of peasant cavalrymen) named Stenka Razin led a rebellion in southeastern Russia. This uprising found widespread support, not only from oppressed serfs but also from non-Russian tribes in the lower Volga region who longed to cast off the domination of Moscow. Ultimately Tsar Alexis I (r. 1645–76) and the Russian nobility were able to defeat Razin's zealous but disorganized bands of rebels, slaughtering more than 100,000 of them in the process.

Like Louis XIV of France, Peter came to the throne as a young boy, and his minority was marked by political dissension and court intrigue. In 1689, however, at the age of seventeen, he overthrew the regency of his half sister Sophia and assumed personal control of the state. Determined to make Russia into a great military power, the young tsar traveled to Holland and England during the 1690s to study shipbuilding and to recruit skilled foreign workers to help him build a navy. While he was abroad, however, his elite palace guard (the *streltsy*) rebelled, attempting to restore Sophia to the throne. Peter quickly returned home from Vienna and crushed the rebellion with striking savagery. About 1,200 suspected conspirators were summarily executed, many of them gibbeted outside the walls of the Kremlin, where their bodies rotted for months as a graphic reminder of the fate awaiting those who dared challenge the tsar's authority.

The Transformation of the Tsarist State

Peter is most famous as the tsar who attempted to westernize Russia by imposing a series of social and cultural reforms on the traditional Russian nobility: ordering noblemen to cut off their long beards and flowing sleeves; publishing a book of manners that forbade spitting on the floor and eating with one's fingers; encouraging polite conversation between the sexes; and requiring noblewomen to appear, together with men, in Western garb at weddings, banquets, and other public occasions. The children of Russian nobles were sent to western European courts for their education. Thousands of western European experts were brought to Russia to staff the new schools and academies Peter built; to design the new buildings he constructed; and to serve in the tsar's army, navy, and administration.

These measures were important, but the tsar was not primarily motivated by a desire to modernize or westernize Russia. Peter's policies transformed Russian life in fundamental ways, but his real goal was to make Russia a great military power, not to remake Russian society. His new taxation system (1724), for example, which assessed taxes on individuals rather than on households, rendered many of the traditional divisions of Russian peasant society obsolete. It was created, however, to raise more money for war. His Table of Ranks, imposed in 1722, had a similar impact on the nobility. By insisting that all nobles must work their way up from the (lower) landlord class to the (higher) administrative class and to the (highest) military class, Peter reversed the traditional hierarchy of Russian noble society, which had valued landlords by birth above administrators and soldiers who had risen by merit. But he also created a powerful new incentive to lure his nobility into administrative and military service to the tsar.

As "autocrat of all the Russias," Peter the Great was the absolute master of his empire to a degree unmatched elsewhere in Europe. After 1649, Russian peasants were legally the property of their landlords; by 1750, half were serfs and the other half were state peasants who lived on lands owned by the tsar himself (by comparison, many peasants in western Europe owned their own land and very few were serfs). State peasants could be conscripted to serve as soldiers in the tsar's army, as workers in his factories (whose

EXECUTION OF THE *STRELTSY* (1698). A contemporary woodcut showing how Peter the Great ordered the public hanging of guard regiments who had rebelled against his authority. How does this display of autocratic power compare with the spectacle of power so carefully orchestrated by Peter's contemporary, Louis XIV of France?

The Revolt of the Streltsy and Peter the Great

The streltsy were four regiments of Moscow guards that became involved in a conspiracy in support of Peter the Great's older sister, Sophia, who had earlier made claim to the throne while Peter was still a child. Approximately 4,000 of the rebels were defeated in June 1698 by troops loyal to Peter. Peter himself was abroad during the fighting, and although his officers had already tortured many of the streltsy to determine the involvement of other nobles, Peter ordered a more far-reaching investigation on his return. Over 1,000 of the streltsy were executed after being tortured again. Afterward, their bodies were placed on display in the capital. Johann Georg Korb, an Austrian diplomat in Moscow, recorded his observations of the power wielded by the Russian autocrat.

ow sharp was the pain, how great the indignation to which the Czar's Majesty was mightily moved, when he knew of the rebellion of the Strelitz [*streltsy*], betrayed openly a mind panting for vengeance.... Going immediately to Lefort (the only person almost that he condescended to treat with intimate familiarity), he thus indignantly broke out: "Tell me, Francis, son of James, how I can reach Moscow, by the shortest way, in a brief space, so that I may wreak vengeance on this great perfidy of my people, with punishments worthy of their flagitious crime. Not one of them shall escape with impunity. Around my royal city, of which, with their impious efforts, they meditated the destruction, I will have gibbets and gallows set upon the walls and ramparts, and each and every of them will I put to a direful death." ...

His first anxiety, after his arrival [in Moscow] was about the rebellion. In what it consisted? What the insurgents meant? Who had dared to instigate such a crime? And as nobody could answer accurately upon all points, and some pleaded their own ignorance, others the obstinacy of the Strelitz, he began to

have suspicions of everybody's loyalty, and began to cogitate about a fresh investigation. The rebels that were kept in custody ... were all brought in by four regiments of the guards, to a fresh investigation and fresh tortures. Prison, tribunal, and rack, for those that were brought in, was in Bebraschentsko. No day, holy, or profane, were the inquisitors idle; every day was deemed fit and lawful for torturing. As many as there were accused there were knouts, and every inquisitor was a butcher. Prince Feodor Jurowicz Romadonowski showed himself by so much more fitted for his inquiry, as he surpassed the rest in cruelty. He put the interrogatories, he examined the criminals, he urged those that were not confessing, he ordered such Strelitz as were more pertinaciously silent, to be subjected to more cruel tortures; those that had already confessed about many things were questioned about more; those who were bereft of strength and reason, and almost of their senses, by excess of torment, were handed over to the skill of the doctors, who were compelled to restore them to strength, in order that they might be broken down by fresh excruciations. The whole month of October was spent in butchering the

backs of the culprits with knout and with flames: no day were those that were left alive exempt from scourging or scorching, or else they were broken upon the wheel, or driven to the gibbet, or slain with the axe—the penalties which were inflicted upon them as soon as their confessions had sufficiently revealed the heads of the rebellion.

Source: Johann Georg Korb, *Diary of an Austrian Secretary of Legation at the Court of Czar Peter the Great*, trans. Count MacDonnell (London: 1863), pp. 2:85–87.

Questions for Analysis

1. Why was it important for Korb to begin this description with the monarch's pain?

2. What does this episode reveal about Peter's conception of his own person and of the loyalty that his subjects owed him? Does it show that his power was fragile, immense, or both?

3. What does it mean to describe torture as an "investigation" even while it is also being described as "vengeance?"

productive capacity increased enormously during Peter's reign), or as forced laborers in his building projects. Serfs could also be taxed by the tsar and summoned for military service, as could their lords. All Russians, of whatever rank, were expected to serve the tsar, and all Russia was considered in some sense to belong to him. Russia's autocracy thus surpassed even the absolutism of Louis XIV.

To further consolidate his power, Peter replaced the Duma—the nation's rudimentary national assembly—with a handpicked senate, a group of nine administrators who supervised military and civilian affairs. In religious matters, he took direct control over the Russian Orthodox Church by appointing an imperial official to manage its affairs. To cope with the demands of war, he also fashioned a new, larger, and more efficient administration, for which he recruited both nobles and non-nobles. But rank in the new bureaucracy did not depend on birth. One of his principal advisers, Alexander Menshikov, began his career as a cook and finished as a prince. This degree of social mobility would have been impossible in any contemporary western European country. In Russia, more so than in western Europe, noble status depended on governmental service, with all nobles expected to participate in Peter's army or administration. Peter was not entirely successful in enforcing this requirement, but the administrative machinery he devised furnished Russia with its ruling class for the next 200 years.

Russian Imperial Expansion

The goal of Peter's foreign policy was to secure year-round ports for Russia on the Black Sea and the Baltic Sea. In the Black Sea, his enemy was the Ottomans. Here, however, he had little success; although he captured the port of Azov in 1696, he was forced to return it in 1711. Russia would not secure its position in the Black Sea until the end of the eighteenth century. Nevertheless, Peter continued to push against the Ottoman Empire in the North Caucasus region throughout his reign. This mountainous area on Russia's southern flank became important sites for Russia's experiments in colonial expansion into central Asia, which began during the sixteenth century and would later mirror the process of colonial conquest undertaken by European powers and the United States in North and South America. Like France and Britain, the Russian state bureaucracy was built during a period of ambitious colonialism; and like Spain, the monarchy's identity was shaped by a long contest with Muslim power on its borders.

Since the late sixteenth century, successive Russian leaders had extended their control over bordering territories of central Asia to the south and east. Although merchants

PETER THE GREAT CUTS THE BEARD OF AN OLD BELIEVER. This woodcut depicts the Russian emperor's enthusiastic policy of westernization, as he pushed everybody in Russia who was not a peasant to adopt Western styles of clothes and grooming. The Old Believer (a member of a religious sect in Russia) protests that he has paid the beard tax and should therefore be exempt. ▪ *Why would an individual's choices about personal appearance be so politically significant in Peter's Russia?* ▪ *What customs were the target of Peter's reforms?*

helped fund early expeditions into Siberia, this expansion was primarily motivated by geopolitical concerns; the tsar sought to gain access to the populations of Russia's border areas and bring them into the service of the expanding Russian state. In this sense, Russian colonialism during this period differed from western European expansion into the Atlantic world, which had primarily been motivated by hopes of commercial gain. Nevertheless, tsarist Russia's colonization of central Asia was similar to the process of European colonial expansion elsewhere in some respects. Like European colonizers in the Americas, Russian expansion brought Russian troops into contact with a variety of peoples with different religious beliefs and their own political structures. Some, such as the Muslim Kumyks of northern Dagestan, had a highly centralized government. Others, such as the Kabardinians or the Chechens, were more fragmented politically.

Russia in 1584
Acquisitions, 1584–1700
Acquisitions, 1700–1772 (primarily by Peter the Great)
Acquisitions, 1772–1796 (by Catherine the Great)
Area of Pugachev rebellion, 1773–1775
Ottoman Empire, c. 1800
Qing Empire, c. 1850
✳ Battle sites

THE GROWTH OF THE RUSSIAN EMPIRE. ▪ *How did Peter the Great expand the territory controlled by Russia?* ▪ *What neighboring dynasties would have been the most affected by Russian expansion?* ▪ *How did the emergence of a bigger, more powerful Russia affect the European balance of power?*

In its early stages, as successive Russian emperors moved Russian troops into the region, they relied on a process of indirect rule, often seeking to co-opt local elites. Later in the eighteenth century, they had more success settling Russians in border regions who ruled over local populations directly. Religion also provided a cover for expansion, and Peter and his successors funded missionary work by Georgian Christians among Muslims in the Caucasus. Efforts to convert Muslim populations to Orthodox Christianity had little effect, and in fact the opposite occurred: the region's commitment to Islam was continuously renewed through contact with different strains of Islamic practice coming from neighboring Ottoman lands and Persia.

Peter could point to more concrete success to the north. In 1700, he began what would become a twenty-one-year war with Sweden, then the dominant power in the Baltic Sea. By 1703, Peter had secured a foothold on the Gulf of Finland and immediately began to build a new capital city there, which he named St. Petersburg. After 1709, when Russian armies, supported by Prussia, decisively defeated the Swedes at the battle of Poltava, work on Peter's new

capital city accelerated. An army of serfs was now conscripted to build the new city, whose centerpiece was a royal palace designed to imitate and rival Louis XIV's Versailles.

The Great Northern War with Sweden ended in 1721 with the Peace of Nystad. This treaty marks a realignment of power in eastern Europe comparable to that effected by the Treaty of Utrecht in the West. Sweden lost its North Sea territories to Hanover and its Baltic German territories to Prussia. Its eastern territories, including the entire Gulf of Finland, Livonia, and Estonia, passed to Russia. Sweden was now a second-rank power in the northern European world. Poland-Lithuania survived but it too was a declining power; by the end of the eighteenth century, the kingdom would disappear altogether, its territories swallowed up by its more powerful neighbors (see Chapter 17).

The victors at Nystad were the Prussians and the Russians. These two powers secured their position along the Baltic coast, positioning themselves to take advantage of the lucrative eastern European grain trade with western Europe. Peter's accomplishments came at enormous cost. Direct taxation in Russia increased 500 percent during his reign, and his army in the 1720s numbered more than 300,000 men. Peter made Russia a force to be reckoned with on the European scene; but in so doing, he also aroused great resentment, especially among his nobility. Peter's only son and heir, Alexis, became the focus for conspiracies against the tsar, until finally Peter had him arrested and executed in 1718. As a result, when Peter died in 1725, he left no son to succeed him. A series of ineffective tsars followed, mostly creatures of the palace guard, under whom the resentful nobles reversed many of Peter the Great's reforms. In 1762, however, the crown passed to Catherine the Great, a ruler whose ambitions and determination were equal to those of her great predecessor (see Chapter 17).

CONCLUSION

By the time of Peter the Great's death in Russia in 1725, the power of Europe's absolutist regimes to reinvigorate European political institutions was visible to all. Government had become more bureaucratic, state service had been more professionalized, administrators loyal to the king had become more numerous, more efficient, and more demanding. Despite the increasing scope of government, however, the structure and principles of government changed relatively little. Apart from Great Britain and the Dutch Republic, the great powers of eighteenth-century Europe were still governed by rulers who styled themselves as absolutist monarchs in the mold of Louis XIV, who claimed an authority that came directly from God and who ruled over a society where social hierarchies based on birth were taken for granted.

These absolutist regimes could not hide the fact, however, that their rule depended on a kind of negotiated settlement with other powerful elites within European society, in particular with landed aristocrats and with religious leaders. Louis XIV used his power to curb the worst excesses of nobles who abused their position, and he defended Catholic orthodoxy against dissident Catholics and Protestants. However, his power depended on a delicate exchange of favors—French aristocrats would surrender their political authority to the state in exchange for social and legal privileges and immunity from many (but not all) forms of taxation. The Church made a similar bargain. Peter the Great's autocratic rule in Russia worked out a slightly different balance of powers between his state and the Russian aristocracy, one that tied aristocrats more closely to an ideal of state service, a model that also worked well for the rulers of Brandenburg-Prussia. Even in England, the establishment of a limited constitutional monarchy and a king who

After You Read This Chapter

 Go to **INQUIZITIVE** to see what you've learned—and learn what you've missed—with personalized feedback along the way.

REVIEWING THE OBJECTIVES

- Absolutist rulers claimed a monopoly of power and authority within their realms. Who were the most important absolutist rulers, how did they justify their innovations, and what did they do to achieve their goals?
- Mercantilism was an economic doctrine that guided the policies of absolutist rulers. What did mercantilists believe?
- Between 1660 and 1688, political leaders in England continued to debate the nature of the state, the role of Parliament, and religious divisions. What was the significance of these dates, and what was the outcome of these debates?
- What circumstances led to the decline of the Dutch Republic's power in this period?
- The wars begun by Louis XIV after 1680 drove his opponents to ally with one another to achieve a balance of power. What was the result of these conflicts in Europe and in the Atlantic world?

ruled alongside Parliament was not really a radical departure from the European absolutist model. It was merely a different institutional answer to the same problem—what relationship should the monarchical state have with other elites within society?

The demands of state building during this period required that kings raise enormous revenues—for the sumptuous displays of their sovereignty in royal residences like Louis XIV's palace at Versailles, for the sponsorship of royal academies and the patronage of artists, but most of all, for war. Territorial expansion within Europe and holding on to colonial empires in the Atlantic world was costly. Distributing the burden of taxation to pay for these endeavors became an intensely fought political issue for European monarchs during this period, and the financing of royal debt became an increasingly sophisticated art. Colbert's mercantilist policy was an attempt to harness the full power of the economy for the benefit of royal government, and the competition among Spain, Holland, England, and France to control the revenue flows coming from the Atlantic world forced Europe's monarchs to recognize that the "balance of powers" was increasingly being played out on a global stage.

These themes—the expansion of state powers; conflicts between the monarchy and the aristocracy or with religious dissidents; the intensification of the tax burden on the population; and the opening up of Europe to ever more frequent interactions with other peoples in the Atlantic world, the Indian Ocean, and eventually, the Pacific—prompted many in eighteenth-century Europe to reflect on the consequences of these developments. What were the limits to state power, and by what criteria were the actions of rulers to be judged? What was the proper measure of economic prosperity, and who was it for? Could a well-ordered society tolerate religious diversity? Given Europe's growing awareness of cultures in other parts of the world with different religions, different political systems, and different ways of expressing their moral and ethical values, how might Europeans justify or take the measure of their own beliefs and customs? The intellectuals who looked for answers to these questions were similar to earlier generations of scientific researchers in their respect for reason and rational thought, but they turned their attention beyond problems of natural philosophy and science to the messy world of politics and culture. Their movement—known as the Enlightenment—reached its peak in the middle decades of the eighteenth century, and created the basis for a powerful critique of Europe's absolutist regimes. The Enlightenment itself emerged slowly from a revolution in scientific thinking that had begun earlier in the early modern period, and it is to this history that we now turn.

PEOPLE, IDEAS, AND EVENTS IN CONTEXT

- What did **LOUIS XIV** of France and **PETER THE GREAT** of Russia have in common? How did they deal with those who resisted their attempts to impose absolutist rule?

- Compare the religious policies of **LOUIS XIV** of France with the religious policies of the English Stuart kings **CHARLES II** and **JAMES II**. In what way did religious disagreements limit their ability to rule effectively?

- How did European monarchies use the economic theory known as **MERCANTILISM** to strengthen the power and wealth of their kingdoms, and how did this theory influence **FRENCH COLONIALISM**?

- What was the **CONTRACT THEORY OF GOVERNMENT** according to the English political thinker **JOHN LOCKE**?

- What limits to royal power were recognized in Great Britain as a result of the **GLORIOUS REVOLUTION**?

- What was significant about the new **BALANCE OF POWERS** that developed in Europe as a result of **LOUIS XIV**'s wars?

- What does the **TREATY OF UTRECHT** (1713) tell us about the diminished influence of Spain and the corresponding rise of Britain and France as European and colonial powers?

- What was different about the attempts by rulers in Habsburg Austria and Brandenburg-Prussia to impose **ABSOLUTISM** in central Europe?

- What innovations did **PETER THE GREAT** bring to Russia?

THINKING ABOUT CONNECTIONS

- What makes absolutism different from earlier models of kingship in earlier periods?

- Was the absolutist monarchs' emphasis on sumptuous displays of their authority something new? Is it different from the way that political power is represented today in democratic societies?

Before
You
Read
This
Chapter

STORY LINES

- After c. 1550, new sciences in Europe questioned older beliefs about the physical universe. New methods of inquiry led to the development of astronomy, physics, biology, and chemistry, as well as new institutions that supported scientific research and education.

- The scientific revolution entailed both theoretical breakthroughs in explaining the physical universe and advances in the practical knowledge of artisans who built mechanical devices such as telescopes. This combination of scientific inquisitiveness and craft techniques encouraged technological developments that would later be useful in industrialization.

- The new sciences did not mark a clean rupture with older traditions of religious thinking. Most scientists in the 1600s remained essentially religious in their worldview, and in any case, their work was only accessible to a small, literate minority who had access to books.

CHRONOLOGY

1543	Nicolaus Copernicus (1473–1543) publishes *On the Revolutions of the Heavenly Spheres*
1576	Tycho Brahe sets up Uraniborg observatory
1609	Johannes Kepler (1571–1643) publishes *Astronomia nova*
1610	Galileo (1564–1642) publishes *Starry Messenger*
1620	Francis Bacon (1561–1626) publishes *Novum Organum*
1632	Galileo publishes *Dialogue Concerning the Two Chief World Systems*
1633	Galileo's trial
1637	René Descartes (1596–1650) publishes *Discourse on Method*
1660	Royal Society of London founded
1666	French Academy of Sciences founded
1687	Isaac Newton (1642–1727) publishes *Principia Mathematica*

The New Science of the Seventeenth Century

Doubt thou the stars are fire,
Doubt that the sun doth move,
Doubt truth to be a liar,
But never doubt I love.

SHAKESPEARE, HAMLET, II.2

oubt thou the stars are fire" and "that the sun doth move." Was Shakespeare alluding to controversial ideas about the cosmos that contradicted the teachings of medieval scholars? *Hamlet* (c. 1600) was written more than fifty years after Copernicus had suggested, in his treatise *On the Revolutions of the Heavenly Spheres* (1543), that the sun did not move and that the earth did, revolving around the sun. Shakespeare probably knew of such theories, although they circulated only among small groups of learned Europeans. As Hamlet's love-torn speech to Ophelia makes clear, they were considered conjecture—or strange mathematical hypotheses. These theories were not exactly new—a heliocentric (sun-centered) universe had been proposed as early as the second century B.C.E. by ancient Greek astronomers. But they flatly contradicted the consensus that had set in after Ptolemy proposed a geocentric (earth-centered) universe in the second century C.E., and to Shakespeare's contemporaries they defied common sense and observation. Learned philosophers, young lovers, shepherds, and sailors alike could watch the sun and the stars move from one horizon to the other each day and night, or so they thought.

Still, a small handful of thinkers did doubt. Shakespeare was born in 1564, the same year as Galileo Galilei. By the time the English playwright and the Italian natural philosopher were working, the long process of revising knowledge about the universe, and discovering a new set of rules that explained how the universe worked, was under way. By the end of the seventeenth century a hundred years later, the building blocks of the new view had been put in place. This intellectual transformation brought sweeping changes to European philosophy and to Western views of the natural world and of humans' place in it.

Science entails at least three things: a body of knowledge, a method or system of inquiry, and a community of practitioners and the institutions that support them and their work. The *scientific revolution* of the seventeenth century (usually understood to have begun in the mid-sixteenth century and to have culminated in 1687 with Newton's *Principia*) involved each of these three realms. As far as the content of knowledge is concerned, the scientific revolution saw the emergence and confirmation of a heliocentric view of the planetary system, which displaced the earth—and humans—from the center of the universe. Even more fundamental, it brought a new mathematical physics that described and confirmed such a view. Second, the scientific revolution established a method of inquiry for understanding the natural world: a method that emphasized the role of observation, experiment, and the testing of hypotheses. Third, *science* emerged as a distinctive branch of knowledge. During the period covered in this chapter, people referred to the study of matter, motion, optics, or the circulation of blood variously as natural philosophy, experimental philosophy, medicine, and—increasingly—science. The growth of societies and institutions dedicated to what we now commonly call scientific research was central to the changes at issue here. Science required not only brilliant thinkers but patrons, states, and communities of researchers; the scientific revolution was thus embedded in other social, religious, and cultural transformations.

The scientific revolution was not an organized effort. Brilliant theories sometimes led to dead ends, discoveries were often accidental, and artisans grinding lenses for telescopes played a role in the advance of knowledge just as surely as did great abstract thinkers. Educated women also claimed the right to participate in scientific debate, but their efforts were met with opposition or indifference.

Old and new worldviews often overlapped as individual thinkers struggled to reconcile their discoveries with their faith or to make their theories (about the earth's movements, for instance) fit with received wisdom. Science was slow to work its way into popular understanding. It did not necessarily undermine religion, and it certainly did not intend to; figures like Isaac Newton thought their work confirmed and deepened their religious beliefs. In short, change came slowly and fitfully. But as the new scientific method began to produce radical new insights into the workings of nature, it eventually came to be accepted well beyond the small circles of experimenters, theologians, and philosophers with whom it began.

THE INTELLECTUAL ORIGINS OF THE SCIENTIFIC REVOLUTION

The scientific revolution marks one of the decisive breaks between the Middle Ages and the modern world. For all its novelty, however, it was rooted in earlier developments. Medieval artists and intellectuals had been observing and illustrating the natural world with great precision since at least the twelfth century. Medieval sculptors carved plants and vines with extraordinary accuracy, and fifteenth-century painters and sculptors devoted the same careful attention to the human face and form. Nor was the link among observation, experiment, and invention new to the sixteenth century. The magnetic compass had been known in Europe since the thirteenth century; gunpowder since the early fourteenth; printing, which permeated the intellectual life of the period and opened new possibilities—disseminating ideas quickly, collaborating more easily, buying books, and building libraries—since the middle of the fifteenth. "Printing, firearms, and the compass," wrote Francis Bacon, "no empire, sect, or star appears to have exercised a greater power and influence on human affairs than these three mechanical discoveries." A fascination with light, which was a powerful symbol of divine illumination for medieval thinkers, encouraged the study of optics and, in turn, new techniques for grinding lenses. Lens grinders laid the groundwork for the seventeenth-century inventions of the telescope and microscope, creating reading glasses along the way. Astrologers were also active in the later Middle Ages, charting the heavens in the firm belief that the stars controlled the fates of human beings.

Behind these efforts to understand the natural world lay a nearly universal conviction that the natural world had been created by God. Religious belief spurred scientific study.

One school of thinkers (the Neoplatonists) argued that nature was a book written by its creator to reveal the ways of God to humanity. Convinced that God's perfection must be reflected in nature, Neoplatonists searched for the ideal and perfect structures they believed must lie behind the "shadows" of the everyday world. Mathematics, particularly geometry, were important tools in this quest.

Renaissance humanism also helped prepare the grounds for the scientific revolution. Humanists revered the authority of the ancients. Yet the energies the humanists poured into recovering, translating, and understanding classical texts (the source of conceptions of the natural world) made many of those important works available for the first time, and to a wider audience. Previously, Arabic sources had provided Europeans with the main route to ancient Greek learning; Greek classics were translated into Arabic by Islamic scholars who often knew them better than Europeans. Later they returned to Europe through the work of medieval scholars in Spain and Sicily. The humanists' return to the texts themselves—and the fact that the new texts could be more easily printed and circulated—encouraged new study and debate. The humanist rediscovery of works by Archimedes—the great Greek mathematician who had proposed that the natural world operated on the basis of mechanical forces, like a great machine, and that these forces could be described mathematically—profoundly impressed important late-sixteenth- and seventeenth-century thinkers, including the Italian scientist Galileo, and shaped mechanical philosophy in the 1600s.

The Renaissance also encouraged collaboration between artisans and intellectuals. Twelfth- and thirteenth-century thinkers had observed the natural world, but they rarely tinkered with mechanical devices and they had little contact with artisans who constructed machines for practical use. During the fifteenth century, however, these two worlds began to come together. Renaissance artists such as Leonardo da Vinci were accomplished craftsmen; they investigated the laws of perspective and optics, they worked out geometric methods for supporting the weight of enormous architectural domes, they studied the human body, and they devised new and more effective weapons for war. The Renaissance brought a vogue for alchemy and astrology; wealthy amateurs built observatories and measured the courses of the stars. These social and intellectual developments laid the groundwork for the scientific revolution.

What of the voyages of discovery? Sixteenth-century observers often linked the exploration of the globe to new knowledge of the cosmos. An admirer wrote to Galileo that he had kept the spirit of exploration alive: "The memory of Columbus and Vespucci will be renewed through you, and with even greater nobility, as the sky is more worthy than the earth." In truth, Columbus had not been driven by an interest in science, and the links between the voyages of discovery and breakthroughs in science were largely indirect and slow to develop. The discoveries made the most immediate impact in the field of natural history, which was vastly enriched by travelers' detailed accounts of the flora and fauna of the Americas. Finding new lands and cultures in Africa and Asia and the revelation of the Americas, a world unknown to the ancients and unmentioned in the Bible, also laid bare gaps in Europeans' inherited body of knowledge. In this sense, the exploration of the New World dealt a blow to the authority of the ancients.

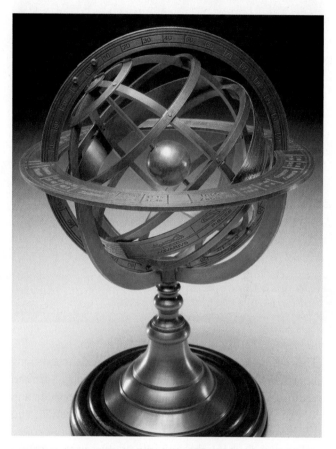

PTOLEMAIC ASTRONOMICAL INSTRUMENTS. Pictured here is an armillary sphere, 1560s, built to facilitate the observation of planetary positions relative to the earth, in support of Ptolemy's theory of an earth-centered universe. In the sphere, seven concentric rings rotated about different axes. When the outermost ring was set to align with a north–south meridian, and the next ring was set to align with the celestial pole (the North Star, or the point around which the stars seem to rotate), one could determine the latitude of the place where the instrument was placed. The inner rings were used to track the angular movements of the planets, key measurements in validating the Ptolemaic system. ▪ *What forms of knowledge were necessary to construct such an instrument?* ▪ *How do they relate to the breakthrough that is known as the scientific revolution?*

Has Science Replaced Religion?

Galileo recanted his claims about the movement of heavenly bodies when challenged by the Church (left); but physicists persisted in their research, leading eventually to the development of modern particle accelerators like the one located in this lab in Grenoble, France (right). Few would say, however, that science has replaced religion in the modern world.

Watch related author videos on the student site
wwnorton.com/college/history/western-civilizationsBrief4

In sum, the late-medieval recovery of ancient texts long thought to have been lost, the expansion of print culture and reading, the turmoil in the Church and the fierce wars and political maneuvering that followed the Reformation, and the discovery of a new world across the oceans to explore and exploit all shook the authority of older ways of thinking. What we call the scientific revolution was part of the intellectual excitement that surrounded these challenges, and, in retrospect, the scientific revolution enhanced and confirmed the importance of these other developments.

THE COPERNICAN REVOLUTION

Medieval cosmologists, like their ancient counterparts and their successors during the scientific revolution, wrestled with the contradictions between ancient texts and the evidence of their own observations. Their view of a geocentric universe was particularly influenced by the teachings of Aristotle (384–322 B.C.E.), especially as they were systematized by Ptolemy of Alexandria (100–178 C.E.). In fact, Ptolemy's vision of an earth-centered universe contradicted an earlier proposal by Aristarchus of Samos (310–230 B.C.E.), who had deduced that the earth and other planets revolve around the sun. Like the ancient Greeks, Ptolemy's medieval followers used astronomical observations to support their theory, but the persuasiveness of the model for medieval scholars also derived from the ways that it fit with their Christian beliefs (see Chapter 4). According to Ptolemy, the heavens orbited the earth in a carefully organized hierarchy of spheres. Earth and the heavens were fundamentally different, made of different matter and subject to different laws of motion. The sun, moon, stars, and planets were formed of an unchanging (and perfect) quintessence or ether. The earth, by contrast, was composed of four elements (earth, water, fire, and air), and each of these elements had its natural place: the heavy elements (earth and water) toward the center and the lighter ones farther out. The heavens—first the planets, then the stars—traced perfect circular paths around the stationary earth. The motion of these celestial bodies was produced by a prime mover, whom Christians identified as God. The view fit Aristotelian physics, according to which objects could move only if acted on by an external force, and it fit with a belief that each fundamental element of the universe had a natural place. Moreover, the view both followed from and confirmed belief in the purposefulness of God's universe.

By the late Middle Ages astronomers knew that this cosmology, called the "Ptolemaic system," did not correspond exactly to what many had observed. Orbits did not conform to the Aristotelian ideal of perfect circles. By the early fifteenth century, the efforts to make the observed motions of the planets fit into the model of perfect circles in a geocentric cosmos had produced astronomical charts that were mazes of complexity. Finally, the Ptolemaic system proved unable to solve serious difficulties with the calendar. That practical crisis precipitated Copernicus's intellectual leap forward.

Realizing that the old Roman calendar was significantly out of alignment with the movement of the heavenly bodies, Catholic authorities consulted mathematicians and astronomers all over Europe. One of these was a Polish church official and astronomer, Nicolaus Copernicus (1473–1543). Educated in Poland and northern Italy, he was a man of diverse talents. He was trained in astronomy, canon law, and medicine. He read Greek. He was well versed in ancient philosophy. He was also a careful mathematician and a devout Catholic who did not believe that God's universe could be as messy as the one in Ptolemy's model. His proposed solution, based on mathematical calculations, was simple and radical: Ptolemy was mistaken; the earth was neither stationary nor at the center of the planetary system; the earth rotated on its axis and orbited with the other planets around the sun. Reordering the Ptolemaic system simplified the geometry of astronomy and made the orbits of the planets comprehensible.

Copernicus was in many ways a conservative thinker. He did not consider his work to be a break with either the Church or with the authority of ancient texts. He believed, rather, that he had restored a pure understanding of God's design, one that had been lost over the centuries. Still, the implications of his theory troubled him. His ideas contradicted centuries of astronomical thought, and they were hard to reconcile with the observed behavior of objects on earth. If the earth moved, why was that movement imperceptible? How did people and objects remain standing?

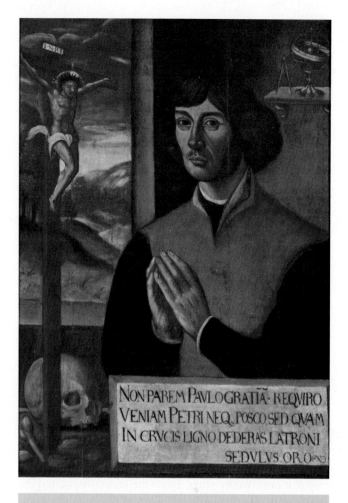

NICOLAUS COPERNICUS. This anonymous portrait of Copernicus characteristically blends his devotion and his scientific achievements. His scholarly work (behind him in the form of an early planetarium) is driven by his faith (as he turns toward the image of Christ triumphant over death). ▪ *What relationship between science and religion is evoked by this image?*

Copernicus was not a physicist. He tried to refine, rather than overturn, traditional Aristotelian physics, but his effort to reconcile that physics with his new model of a sun-centered universe created new problems and inconsistencies that he could not resolve. These frustrations and complications dogged Copernicus's later years, and he hesitated to publish his findings. Just before his death, he consented to the release of his major treatise, *On the Revolutions of the Heavenly Spheres* (*De Revolutionibus*), in 1543. To fend off scandal, the Lutheran scholar who saw his manuscript through the press added an introduction to the book declaring that Copernicus's system should be understood as an abstraction, a set of mathematical tools for doing astronomy and not a dangerous claim about the nature of heaven and earth. For decades after 1543, Copernicus's ideas were taken in just that sense—as useful but not realistic mathematical hypotheses. In the long run, however, as one historian puts it, Copernicanism represented the first "serious and systematic" challenge to the Ptolemaic conception of the universe.

TYCHO'S OBSERVATIONS AND KEPLER'S LAWS

Within fifty years, Copernicus's cosmology was revived and modified by two astronomers also critical of the Ptolemaic model of the universe: Tycho Brahe (*TI-koh BRAH-hee*, 1546–1601) and Johannes Kepler (1571–1630). Each was considered the greatest astronomer of his day. Tycho was born into the Danish nobility, but he abandoned his family's military and political legacy to pursue his passion for astronomy. Like Copernicus, he sought to correct the contradictions in traditional astronomy. Unlike Copernicus, who was a theoretician, Tycho championed observation and believed careful study of the heavens would unlock the secrets of the universe. He first made a name for himself by observing a completely new star, a "nova," that flared into sight in 1572. The Danish king Friedrich II, impressed by Tycho's work, granted him the use of a small island, where he built a castle specially designed to house an observatory. For over twenty years, Tycho meticulously charted the movements of each significant object in the night sky, compiling the finest set of astronomical data in Europe.

Tycho was not a Copernican. He suggested that the planets orbited the sun and the whole system then orbited a stationary earth. This picture of cosmic order, though clumsy, seemed to fit the observed evidence better than the Ptolemaic system, and it avoided the upsetting theological implications of the Copernican model. In the late 1590s, Tycho moved his work and his huge collection of data to Prague, where he became court astronomer to the Holy Roman emperor Rudolph II. In Prague, he was assisted by a young mathematician from a troubled family, Johannes Kepler. Kepler was more impressed with the Copernican model than was Tycho, and Kepler combined study of Copernicus's work with his own interest in mysticism, astrology, and the religious power of mathematics.

Kepler believed that everything in creation, from human souls to the orbits of the planets, had been created according to mathematical laws. Understanding those laws would thus allow humans to share God's wisdom and penetrate the inner secrets of the universe. For Kepler, then, mathematics was God's language. His search for patterns of mathematical perfection took him through musical harmonies, nested geometric shapes inside the planets' orbits, and

numerical formulas. After Tycho's death, Kepler inherited Tycho's position in Prague, as well as his trove of observations and calculations. That data demonstrated to Kepler that two of Copernicus's assumptions about planetary motion simply did not match observations. Copernicus, in keeping with Aristotelian notions of perfection, had believed that planetary orbits were circular. Kepler calculated that the planets traveled in elliptical orbits around the sun; this finding became his First Law. Copernicus held that planetary motion was uniform; Kepler's Second Law stated that the speed of the planets varied with their distance from the sun. Kepler also argued that magnetic forces between the sun and the planets kept the planets in orbital motion, an insight that paved the way for Newton's law of universal gravitation formulated nearly eighty years later, at the end of the seventeenth century.

Kepler's version of Copernicanism fit with remarkable accuracy the best observations of the time (which were Tycho's). Kepler's search for rules of motion that could account for the earth's movements in its new position was also significant. Even more than Copernicus, Kepler broke down the distinction between the heavens and the earth that had been at the heart of Aristotelian physics.

NEW HEAVENS, NEW EARTH, AND WORLDLY POLITICS: GALILEO

Kepler had a friend deliver a copy of his *Cosmographic Mystery* to the "mathematician named Galileus Galileus," then teaching mathematics and astronomy at Padua, near Venice. Galileo (1564–1642) thanked Kepler in a letter that nicely illustrates the Italian's views at the time (1597).

> So far I have only perused the preface of your work, but from this I gained some notion of its intent, and I indeed congratulate myself of having an associate in the study of Truth who is a friend of Truth. . . . I adopted the teaching of Copernicus many years ago, and his point of view enables me to explain many phenomena of nature which certainly remain inexplicable according to the more current hypotheses. I have written many arguments in support of him and in refutation of the opposite view—which, however, so far I have not dared to bring into the public light. . . . I would certainly dare to publish my reflections at once if more people like you existed; as they don't, I shall refrain from doing so.

Kepler replied, urging Galileo to "come forward!" Galileo did not answer.

At Padua, Galileo couldn't teach what he believed; Ptolemaic astronomy and Aristotelian cosmology were the established curriculum. By the end of his career, however, Galileo had provided powerful evidence in support of the Copernican model and laid the foundation for a new physics. What was more, he wrote in the vernacular (Italian) as well as in Latin. Kepler's work was abstruse and bafflingly mathematical. (So was Copernicus's.) By contrast, Galileo's writings were widely translated and widely read, raising awareness of changes in natural philosophy across Europe. Ultimately, Galileo made the case for a new relationship between religion and science, challenging in the process some of the most powerful churchmen of his day.

Galileo became famous by way of discoveries with the telescope. In 1609, he heard reports from Holland of a lens grinder who had made a spyglass that could magnify very distant objects. Excited, Galileo quickly devised his own telescope; trained it first on earthly objects to demonstrate that it worked; and then, momentously, pointed it at the night sky. Galileo studied the moon, finding on it mountains, plains, and other features of an earthlike landscape. His observations suggested that celestial bodies resembled the earth, a view at odds with the conception of the heavens as an unchanging sphere of heavenly perfection, inherently and necessarily different from the earth. He saw moons orbiting Jupiter, evidence that earth was not at the center of all orbits. He saw spots on the sun. Galileo published these results, first in *The Starry Messenger* (1610) and then in *Letters on Sunspots* in 1613, a work that declared his Copernicanism openly.

A seventeenth-century scientist needed powerful and wealthy patrons. As a professor of mathematics, Galileo chafed at the power of university authorities who were subject to Church control. Princely courts offered an inviting alternative. The Medici family of Tuscany, like others, burnished its reputation and bolstered its power by surrounding itself with intellectuals as well as artists. Persuaded he would be freer at its court than in Padua, Galileo took a position as tutor to the Medicis and flattered and successfully cultivated the family. He was rewarded with the title of chief mathematician and philosopher to Cosimo de' Medici, the grand duke of Tuscany. Now well positioned in Italy's networks of power and patronage, Galileo was able to pursue

his goal of demonstrating that Copernicus's heliocentric (sun-centered) model of the planetary system was correct.

In 1614, however, an ambitious and outspoken Dominican friar denounced Galileo's ideas as dangerous deviations from biblical teachings. Other philosophers and churchmen began to ask Galileo's patrons, the Medicis, whether their court mathematician was teaching heresy.

Disturbed by the murmurings against Copernicanism, Galileo penned a series of letters to defend himself, arguing that one could be a sincere Copernican and a sincere Catholic (see **Analyzing Primary Sources** on page 434). The Church, Galileo said, did the sacred work of teaching scripture and saving souls. Accounting for the workings of the physical world was a task better left to natural philosophy, grounded in observation and mathematics. For the Church to take a side in controversies over natural science might compromise the Church's spiritual authority and credibility. Galileo envisioned natural philosophers and theologians as partners in a search for truth, but with very different roles. In a brilliant rhetorical moment, he quoted Cardinal Baronius in support of his own argument: the purpose of the Bible was to "teach us how to go to heaven, not how heaven goes."

Nevertheless, in 1616, the Church moved against Galileo. The Inquisition ruled that Copernicanism was "foolish and absurd in philosophy and formally heretical." Copernicus's *De Revolutionibus* was placed on the Index

GALILEO GALILEI BEFORE THE INQUISITION BY FRANÇOIS FLEURY-RICHARD. This nineteenth-century painting of Galileo before the Holy Office dramatizes the conflict between science and religion and depicts the Italian natural philosopher as defiant. In fact, Galileo submitted to the Church but continued his work under house arrest and published, secretly, in the Netherlands. ▪ *Would Galileo himself have subscribed to the message of this much later painting, that religion and science were opposed to one another?*

Interpreting Visual Evidence

Astronomical Observations and the Mapping of the Heavens

One (often-repeated) narrative about the scientific revolution is that it marked a crucial break separating modern science from an earlier period permeated by an atmosphere of superstition and theological speculation. In fact, medieval scholars tried hard to come up with empirical evidence for beliefs that their faith told them must be true, and without these traditions of observation, scientists like Copernicus would never have been led to propose alternative cosmologies (see "Ptolemaic Astronomical Instruments" on page 427).

The assumption, therefore, that the "new" sciences of the seventeenth century marked an extraordinary rupture with a more ignorant or superstitious past is thus not entirely correct. It would be closer to the truth to suggest that works such as that of Copernicus or Galileo provided a new context for assessing the relationship between observations and knowledge that came from other sources. Printed materials provided opportunities for early modern scientists to learn as much from each other as from more ancient sources.

The illustrations here are from scientific works on astronomy both before and after the appearance of

A. The Ptolemaic universe, as depicted in Peter Apian, *Cosmographia* (1540).

B. The Copernican universe (1543).

of Prohibited Books, and Galileo was warned not to teach Copernicanism.

For a while, he did as he was asked. But when his Florentine friend and admirer Maffeo Barberini was elected pope as Urban VIII in 1623, Galileo believed the door to Copernicanism was (at least half) open. He drafted one of his most famous works, *A Dialogue Concerning the Two Chief World*

Systems, published in 1632. The *Dialogue* was a hypothetical debate between supporters of the old Ptolemaic system, represented by a character he named Simplicio (simpleton), on the one hand, and proponents of the new astronomy, on the other. Throughout, Galileo gave the best lines to the Copernicans. At the very end, however, to satisfy the letter of the Inquisition's decree, he had them capitulate to Simplicio.

Copernicus's work. All of them were based on some form of observation and claimed to be descriptive of the existing universe. Compare the abstract illustrations of the Ptolemaic (image A) and Copernican (image B) universes with Tycho Brahe's (image C) attempt to reconcile heliocentric observations with geocentric assumptions or with Galileo's illustration of sunspots (image D) observed through a telescope.

Questions for Analysis

1. What do these illustrations tell us about the relationship between knowledge and observation in sixteenth- and seventeenth-century science? What kinds of knowledge were necessary to produce these images?

2. Are the illustrations A and B intended to be visually accurate, in the sense that they represent what the eye sees?

Can one say the same of D? What makes Galileo's illustration of the sunspots different from the others?

3. Are the assumptions about observation contained in Galileo's drawing of sunspots (D) applicable to other sciences such as biology or chemistry? How so?

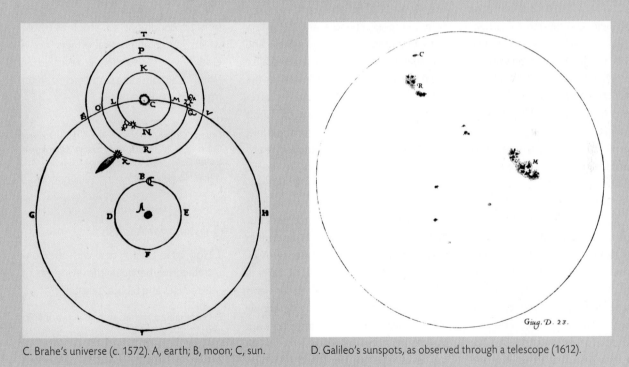

C. Brahe's universe (c. 1572). A, earth; B, moon; C, sun.

D. Galileo's sunspots, as observed through a telescope (1612).

The Inquisition banned the *Dialogue* and ordered Galileo to stand trial in 1633. Pope Urban, provoked by Galileo's scorn and needing support from Church conservatives during a difficult stretch of the Thirty Years' War, refused to protect his former friend. The verdict of the secret trial shocked Europe. The Inquisition forced Galileo to repent his Copernican position, banned him from working on or even discussing Copernican ideas, and placed him under house arrest for life. According to a story that began to circulate shortly afterward, as he left the court for house arrest he stamped his foot and muttered defiantly, looking down at the earth: "Still, it moves."

The Inquisition could not put Galileo off his life's work. He refined the theories of motion he had begun to

Galileo on Nature, Scripture, and Truth

One of the clearest statements of Galileo's convictions about religion and science comes from his 1615 letter to the Grand Duchess Christina, mother of Galileo's patron, Cosimo de' Medici, and a powerful figure in her own right. Galileo knew that others objected to his work. The Church had warned him that Copernicanism was inaccurate and impious; it could be disproved scientifically, and it contradicted the authority of those who interpreted the Bible. Thoroughly dependent on the Medicis for support, he wrote to the Grand Duchess to explain his position. In this section of the letter, Galileo sets out his understanding of the parallel but distinct roles of the Church and natural philosophers. He walks a fine line between acknowledging the authority of the Church and standing firm in his convictions.

ossibly because they are disturbed by the known truth of other propositions of mine which differ from those commonly held, and therefore mistrusting their defense so long as they confine themselves to the field of philosophy, these men have resolved to fabricate a shield for their fallacies out of the mantle of pretended religion and the authority of the Bible....

Copernicus never discusses matters of religion or faith, nor does he use arguments that depend in any way upon the authority of sacred writings which he might have interpreted erroneously. He stands always upon physical conclusions pertaining to the celestial motions, and deals with them by astronomical and geometrical demonstrations, founded primarily upon sense experiences and very exact observations. He did not ignore the Bible, but he knew very well that if his doctrine were proved, then it could not contradict the Scriptures when they were rightly understood....

I think that in discussions of physical problems we ought to begin not from the authority of scriptural passages, but from sense-experiences and necessary demonstrations; for the holy Bible and the phenomena of nature proceed alike from the divine Word, the former as the dictate of the Holy Ghost and the latter as the observant executrix of God's commands. It is necessary for the Bible, in order to be accommodated to the understanding of every man, to speak many things which appear to differ from the absolute truth so far as the bare meaning of the words is concerned. But Nature, on the other hand, is inexorable and immutable; she never transgresses the laws imposed upon her, or cares a whit whether her abstruse reasons and methods of operation are understandable to men. For that reason it appears that nothing physical which sense-experience sets before our eyes, or which necessary demonstrations prove to us,

ought to be called in question (much less condemned) upon the testimony of biblical passages which may have some different meaning beneath their words. For the Bible is not chained in every expression to conditions as strict as those which govern all physical effects; nor is God any less excellently revealed in Nature's actions than in the sacred statements of the Bible....

Source: Galileo, "Letter to the Grand Duchess Christina," in *The Discoveries and Opinions of Galileo Galilei*, ed. Stillman Drake (Garden City, NY: 1957), pp. 177–83.

Questions for Analysis

1. How does Galileo deal with the contradictions between the evidence of his senses and biblical teachings?

2. For Galileo, what is the relationship between God, man, and nature?

3. Why did Galileo need to defend his views in a letter to Christina de' Medici?

develop early in his career. He proposed an early version of the theory of inertia, which held that an object's motion stays the same until an outside force changes it. He calculated that objects of different weights fall at almost the same speed and with a uniform acceleration. He argued that the motion of objects follows regular mathematical laws. The same laws that govern the motions of objects

on earth (which could be observed in experiments) could also be observed in the heavens—again a direct contradiction of Aristotelian principles and an important step toward a coherent physics based on a sun-centered model of the universe. Compiled under the title *Two New Sciences* (1638), this work was smuggled out of Italy and published in Protestant Holland.

Among Galileo's legacies, however, was exactly the rift between religion and science that he had hoped to avoid. Galileo believed that Copernicanism and natural philosophy in general need not subvert theological truths, religious belief, or the authority of the Church. But his trial seemed to show the contrary, that natural philosophy and Church authority could not coexist. Galileo's trial silenced Copernican voices in southern Europe, and the Church's leadership retreated into conservative reaction. It was therefore in northwest Europe that the new philosophy Galileo had championed would flourish.

METHODS FOR A NEW PHILOSOPHY: BACON AND DESCARTES

As the practice of the new sciences became concentrated in Protestant northwest Europe, new thinkers began to spell out standards of practice and evidence. Sir Francis Bacon and René Descartes (*deh-KAHRT*) loomed especially large in this development, setting out the methods or rules that should govern modern science. Bacon (1561–1626) lived at roughly the same time as Kepler and Galileo—and Shakespeare; Descartes (1596–1650) was a generation younger. Both Bacon and Descartes came to believe that theirs was an age of profound change, open to the possibility of astonishing discovery. Both were persuaded that knowledge could take the European moderns beyond the ancient authorities. Both set out to formulate a philosophy to encompass the learning of their age.

"Knowledge is power." The phrase is Bacon's and captures the changing perspective of the seventeenth century and its new confidence in the potential of human thinking. Bacon trained as a lawyer, served in Parliament and, briefly, as lord chancellor to James I of England. His abiding concern was with the assumptions, methods, and practices that he believed should guide natural philosophers and the progress of knowledge. The authority of the ancients should not constrain the ambition of modern thinkers. Deferring to accepted doctrines could block innovation or obstruct understanding. "There is but one course left . . . to try the whole thing anew upon a better plan, and to commence a total reconstruction of sciences, arts, and all human knowledge, raised upon the proper foundations." To pursue knowledge did not mean to think abstractly and leap to conclusions; it meant observing, experimenting, confirming ideas, or demonstrating points. If thinkers will

FRONTISPIECE TO BACON'S *NOVUM ORGANUM* (1620). The illustration suggests that scientific work is like a voyage of discovery, similar to a ship setting out through uncharted waters. Is it a voyage of conquest? ■ *What metaphors and allegorical imagery did scientists use during this period to characterize the significance of their work?*

be "content to begin with doubts," Bacon wrote, "they shall end with certainties." We thus associate Bacon with the gradual separation of scientific investigation from philosophical argument.

Bacon advocated an *inductive* approach to knowledge: amassing evidence from specific observations to draw general conclusions. In Bacon's view, many philosophical errors arose from beginning with assumed first principles. The traditional view of the cosmos, for instance, rested on the principles of a prime mover and the perfection of circular motion for planets and stars. The inductive method required accumulating data (just as Tycho had done) and then, after careful review and experiment, drawing appropriate conclusions. Bacon argued that scientific knowledge was best tested through the cooperative efforts of researchers performing experiments that could be repeated and verified. The knowledge thus gained would be predictable and useful to philosophers and artisans alike, contributing to a wide range of endeavors, from astronomy to shipbuilding.

René Descartes was French, though he lived all over Europe. Descartes's *Discourse on Method* (1637), for which he is best known, began simply as a preface to three essays on optics, geometry, and meteorology. It is personal, recounting Descartes's dismay at the "strange and unbelievable" theories he encountered in his traditional education. His first response, as he described it, was to systematically doubt everything he had ever known or been taught. Better to clear the slate, he believed, than to build an edifice of knowledge on received assumptions. His first rule was "never to receive anything as a truth which [he] did not clearly know to be such." He took the human ability to think as his point of departure, summed up in his famous and enigmatic *Je pense, donc je suis*, later translated into Latin as *cogito ergo sum* and into English as "I think, therefore I am." As the phrase suggests, Descartes's doubting led (quickly, by our standards) to self-assurance and truth: the thinking individual existed, reason existed, God existed. For Descartes, then, doubt was a ploy, or a piece that he used in an intellectual chess game to defeat skepticism. Certainty, not doubt, was the centerpiece of the philosophy he bequeathed to his followers.

Descartes, like Bacon, sought a "fresh start for knowledge" or the rules for understanding of the world as it was. Unlike Bacon, Descartes emphasized *deductive* reasoning, proceeding logically from one certainty to another. "So long as we avoid accepting as true what is not so," he wrote in *Discourse on Method*, "and always preserve the right order of deduction of one thing from another, there can be nothing too remote to be reached in the end, or too well hidden to be discovered." For Descartes, mathematical thought expressed the highest standards of reason, and his work contributed greatly to the authority of mathematics as a model for scientific reasoning.

Descartes made a particularly forceful statement for *mechanism*, a view of the world shared by Bacon and Galileo and one that came to dominate seventeenth-century scientific thought. As the name suggested, mechanical philosophy proposed to consider nature as a machine. It rejected the traditional Aristotelian distinction between the works of humans and those of nature and the view that nature, as God's creation, necessarily

FROM RENÉ DESCARTES, *L'HOMME* (1729; ORIGINALLY PUBLISHED AS *DE HOMINI*, 1662). Descartes's interest in the body as a mechanism led him to suppose that physics and mathematics could be used to understand all aspects of human physiology, and his work had an important influence on subsequent generations of medical researchers. In this illustration, Descartes depicts the optical properties of the human eye. ▪ *How might such a mechanistic approach to human perception have been received by proponents of Baconian science, who depended so much on the reliability of human observations?*

belonged to a different—and higher—order. In the new picture of the universe that was emerging from the discoveries and writings of the early seventeenth century, it seemed that all matter was composed of the same material and all motion obeyed the same laws. Descartes sought to explain everything, including the human body, mechanically. As he put it firmly, "There is no difference between the machines built by artisans and the diverse bodies that nature alone composes." Nature operated according to regular and predictable laws and was thus accessible to human reason. This belief guided, indeed inspired, much of the scientific experiment and argument of the seventeenth century.

The Power of Method and the Force of Curiosity: Seventeenth-Century Experimenters

For nearly a century after Bacon and Descartes, most of England's natural philosophers were Baconian, and most of their colleagues in France, Holland, and elsewhere in northern Europe were Cartesians (followers of Descartes). The English Baconians concentrated on performing experiments in many different fields, producing results that could then be debated and discussed. The Cartesians turned instead toward mathematics and logic. Descartes himself pioneered analytical geometry. Blaise Pascal (1623–1662) worked on probability theory and invented a calculating machine before applying his intellectual skills to theology. The Cartesian thinker Christian Huygens (1629–1695) from Holland combined mathematics with experiments to understand problems of impact and orbital motion. The Dutch Cartesian Baruch Spinoza (1632–1677) applied geometry to ethics and believed he had gone beyond Descartes by proving that the universe was composed of a single substance that was both God and nature.

English experimenters pursued a different course. They began with practical research, putting the alchemist's tool, the laboratory, to new uses. They also sought a different kind of conclusion: empirical laws or provisional generalizations, based on evidence, rather than absolute statements of deductive truth. Among the many English laboratory scientists of the era were the physician William Harvey (1578–1657), the chemist Robert Boyle (1627–1691), and the inventor and experimenter Robert Hooke (1635–1703).

Harvey's contribution was enormous: he observed and explained that blood circulated through the arteries, heart, and veins. To do this, he was willing to dissect living animals (vivisection) and experiment on himself. Boyle performed experiments and established a law (known as Boyle's law) showing that at a constant temperature the volume of a gas decreases in proportion to the pressure placed on it. Hooke introduced the microscope to the experimenter's tool kit. The compound microscope had been invented in Holland early in the seventeenth century. But it was not until the 1660s that Hooke and others demonstrated its potential by using it to study the cellular structure of plants. Like the telescope before it, the microscope revealed an unexpected dimension of material phenomena. Examining even the most ordinary objects revealed detailed structures of perfectly connected smaller parts and persuaded many that with improved instruments they would uncover even more of the world's intricacies.

The microscope also provided what many regarded as new evidence of God's existence. The way each minute structure of a living organism, when viewed under a microscope, corresponded to its purpose testified not only to God's existence but to God's wisdom as well. The mechanical philosophy did not exclude God but rather could be used to confirm his presence. If the universe was a clock, after all, there must be a clockmaker. Hooke himself declared that only imbeciles would believe that what they saw under the microscope was "the production of chance" rather than of God's creation.

The State, Scientific Academies, and Women Scientists

Seventeenth-century state building (see Chapter 14) helped secure the rise of science. In 1660, England's monarchy was restored after two decades of revolution and civil war. The newly crowned King Charles II granted a group of natural philosophers and mathematicians a royal charter (1662) to establish the Royal Society of London, for the "improvement of natural knowledge" through experimentation and collaborative work among natural philosophers. The founders of the Royal Society, in particular Boyle, believed it could serve a political as well as an intellectual purpose. The Royal Society would pursue Bacon's goal of collective research in which members would conduct formal experiments, record the results, and share them with other members. These members would in turn study the methods,

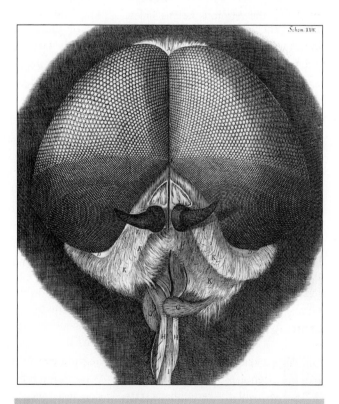

ROBERT HOOKE'S *MICROGRAPHIA*. Hooke's diagram of a fly's eye as seen through a microscope seemed to reveal just the sort of intricate universe the mechanists predicted. ▪ *Compare this image with that of Galileo's sunspots (page 433). What do these two images have in common?*

The New Science and The Foundations of Certainty

Francis Bacon (1561–1626) and René Descartes (1596–1650) were both enthusiastic supporters of science in the seventeenth century, but they differed in their opinions regarding the basis for certainty in scientific argumentation. Bacon's inductive method emphasized the gathering of particular observations about natural phenomena, which he believed could be used as evidence to support more general conclusions about causes, regularity, and order in the natural world. Descartes, on the other hand, defended a deductive method: he believed that certainty could be built only by reasoning from first principles that one knew to be true and was less certain of the value of evidence that came from the senses alone.

Aphorisms from Francis Bacon's *Novum Organum*

XXXI

It is idle to expect any advancement in science from the super-inducing and engrafting of new things upon old. We must begin anew from the very foundations, unless we would revolve forever in a circle with mean and contemptible progress. . . .

XXXVI

One method of delivery alone remains to us which is simply this: we must lead men to the particulars themselves, and their series and order; while men on their side must force themselves for a while to lay their notions by and begin to familiarize themselves with facts. . . .

XLV

The human understanding of its own nature is prone to suppose the existence of more order and regularity in the world than it finds. And though there be many things in nature which are singular and unmatched, yet it devises for them parallels and conjugates and relatives which do not exist. Hence the fiction that all celestial bodies move in perfect circles. . . . Hence too the element of fire with its orb is brought in, to make up the square with the other three which the sense perceives. . . . And so on of other dreams. And these fancies affect not dogmas only, but simple notions also. . . .

XCV

Those who have handled sciences have been either men of experiment or men of dogmas. The men of experiment are like the ant, they only collect and use; the reasoners resemble spiders, who make cobwebs out of their own substance. But the bee takes a middle course: it gathers its material from the flowers of the garden and of the field, but transforms and digests it by a power of its own. Not unlike this is the true business of philosophy; for it neither relies solely or chiefly on the powers of the mind, nor does it take the matter which it gathers from natural history and mechanical experiments and lay it up in the memory whole . . . but lays it up in the understanding altered and digested. Therefore, from a closer and purer league between these two faculties, the experimental and the rational (such as has never yet been made), much may be hoped. . . .

Source: Michael R. Matthews, ed., *The Scientific Background to Modern Philosophy: Selected Readings* (Indianapolis, IN: 1989), pp. 47–48, 50–52.

From *A Discourse on Method*

Just as a great number of laws is often a pretext for wrongdoing, with the result that a state is much better governed when, having only a few, they are strictly observed; so also I came to believe that in the place of the great number of precepts that go to make up logic, the following four would be sufficient for my purposes, provided that I took a firm but unshakeable decision never once to depart from them.

The first was never to accept anything as true that I did not *incontrovertibly* know to be so; that is to say, carefully to avoid both *prejudice* and premature conclusions; and to include nothing in my judgments other than that which presented itself to my mind so *clearly* and *distinctly*, that I would have no occasion to doubt it.

The second was to divide all the difficulties under examination into as many parts as possible, and as many as were required to solve them in the best way.

The third was to conduct my thoughts in a given order, beginning with the *simplest* and most easily understood objects, and gradually ascending, as it were step by step, to the knowledge of the most *complex*; and *positing* an order even on those which do not have a natural order of precedence.

The last was to undertake such complete enumerations and such general surveys that I would be sure to have left nothing out.

The long chain of reasonings, every one simple and easy, which geometers habitually employ to reach their most difficult proofs had given me cause to suppose that all those things which fall within the domain of human understanding follow on from each other in the same way, and that as long as one stops oneself taking anything to be true that is not true and sticks to the right order so as to deduce one thing from another, there can be nothing so remote that one cannot eventually reach it, nor so hidden that one cannot discover it. . . .

Because I wished . . . to concentrate on the pursuit of truth, I came to think that I should . . . reject as completely false everything in which I could detect the least doubt, in order to see if anything thereafter remained in my belief that was completely indubitable. And so, because our senses sometimes deceive us, I decided to suppose that nothing was such as they lead us to imagine it to be. And because there are men who make mistakes in reasoning, even about the simplest elements of geometry, and commit logical fallacies, I judged that I was as prone to error as anyone else, and I rejected as false all the reasoning I had hitherto accepted as valid proof. Finally, considering that all the same thoughts which we have while awake can come to us while asleep without any one of them then being true, I resolved to pretend that everything that had ever entered my head was no more true than the illusions of my dreams. But immediately afterwards I noted that, while I was trying to think of all things being false in this way, it was necessarily the case that I, who was thinking them, had to be something; and observing this truth: *I am thinking therefore I exist*, was so secure and certain that it could not be shaken by any of the most extravagant suppositions of the sceptics, I judged that I could accept it without scruple, as the first principle of the philosophy I was seeking.

Source: René Descartes, *A Discourse on the Method*, trans. Ian Maclean (New York: 2006), pp. 17–18, 28.

Questions for Analysis

1. Descartes's idea of certainty depended on a "long chain of reasonings" that departed from certain axioms that could not be doubted and rejected evidence from the senses. What science provided him with the model for this idea of certainty? What was the first thing that he felt he could be certain about? Did he trust his senses?

2. Bacon's idea of certainty pragmatically sought to combine the benefits of sensory knowledge and experience (gathered by "ants") with the understandings arrived at through reason (cobwebs constructed by "spiders"). How would Descartes have responded to Bacon's claims? According to Bacon, was Descartes an ant or a spider?

3. What do these two thinkers have in common?

reproduce the experiment, and assess the outcome. The enterprise would give England's natural philosophers a common sense of purpose and a system to reach reasoned, gentlemanly agreement on "matters of fact." By separating systematic scientific research from the dangerous language of politics and religion that had marked the civil war, the Royal Society could also help restore a sense of order and consensus to English intellectual life.

The society's journal, *Philosophical Transactions*, reached out to professional scholars and experimenters throughout Europe. Similar societies began to appear elsewhere.

The French Academy of Sciences was founded in 1666 and was also tied to seventeenth-century state building, in this case French absolutism (see Chapter 15). Scientific societies reached rough agreement about what constituted legitimate research. They established the modern scientific custom of crediting discoveries to those who were first to publish results. They enabled information and theories to be exchanged more easily across national boundaries, although philosophical differences among Cartesians, Baconians, and traditional Aristotelians remained very difficult to bridge. Science began to take shape as a discipline.

Gassendi on the Science of Observation and the Human Soul

Pierre Gassendi (1592–1655) was a seventeenth-century French Catholic priest and philosopher. A contemporary of Descartes's, Gassendi was part of a group of intellectuals in France who sought a new philosophy of nature that could replace the traditional teachings of Aristotle that had been so severely criticized by Copernicus and his followers. Gassendi had no doubt that his faith as a Christian was compatible with his enthusiasm for the new sciences of observation, but in order to demonstrate this to his contemporaries he had to show that the mechanical explanations of the universe and the natural world did not necessarily lead to a heretical materialism or atheism. In the following passage, taken from his posthumously published work Syntagma Philosophicum *(1658), Gassendi attempted to demonstrate that one might infer the existence of the human soul, even if it was not accessible to the senses.*

 here are many such things for which with the passage of time helpful appliances are being found that will make them visible to the senses. For example, take the little animal the mite, which is born under the skin; the senses perceived it as a certain unitary little point without parts; but since, however, the senses saw that it moved by itself, reason had deduced from this motion as from a perceptible sign that this little body was an animal and because its forward motion was somewhat like a turtle's, reason added that it must get about by the use of certain tiny legs and feet. And although this truth would have been hidden to the senses, which never perceived these limbs, the microscope was recently invented by which sight could perceive that matters were actually as predicted. Likewise, the question had been raised what the galaxy in the sky with the name of the Milky Way was. Democritus, concerning whom it was said that even when he did not know something he was knowing, had deduced from the perceptible sign of its filmy whiteness that it was nothing more than an innumerable multitude of closely packed little stars which could not be seen separately, but produced that effect of spilt milk when many of them were joined together. This truth had become

known to him, and yet had remained undisclosed to the senses until our day and age, until the moment that the telescope, recently discovered, made it clear that things were in fact what he had said. But there are many such things which, though they were hidden from the ancients, have now been made manifest for our eyes. And who knows but a great many of those which are concealed in our time, which we perceive only through the intelligence, will one day also be clearly perceived by the senses through the agency of some helpful appliance thought up by our descendants? . . .

Secondly, if someone wonders whether a certain body is endowed with a soul or not, the senses are not at all capable of determining that by taking a look as it were at the soul itself; yet there are operations which when they come to the senses' notice, lead the intellect to deduce as from a sign that there is some soul beneath them. You will say that this sign belongs to the empirical type, but it is not at all of that type, for it is not even one of the indicative signs since it does not inform us of something that the senses have ever perceived in conjunction with the sign, as they have seen fire with smoke, but informs us instead of something that has always been impenetrable to the senses themselves, like our skin's pores or the mite's feet before the microscope.

You will persist with the objection that we should not ask so much whether there is a soul in a body as what its nature is, if it is the cause of such operations, just as there is no question that there is a force attracting iron in a magnet or that there is a tide in the sea, but there are questions over what their nature is or what they are caused by. But let me omit these matters which are to be fully treated elsewhere, and let it be enough if we say that not every truth can be known by the mind, but at least some can concerning something otherwise hidden, or not obvious to the senses themselves. And we bring up the example of the soul both because vital action is proposed by Sextus Empiricus as an example of an indicative sign and because even though it pertains not so much to the nature of the soul as to its existence, still a truth of existence of such magnitude as this, which it is most valuable for us to know, is made indisputable. For when among other questions we hear it asked if God is or exists in the universe, that is a truth of existence which it would be a great service to establish firmly even if it is not proven at the same time what he is or what his nature is. Although God is such that he can no more come under the perusal of the senses than the soul can, still we infer that the soul exists in the body from the actions that occur before the senses and are so peculiarly appropriate to a soul that if one were not present, they would not be, either. In the same way we deduce that God exists in the universe from his effects perceived by the senses, which could not be produced by anything but God and which therefore would not be observed unless God were present in the world, such as the great order of the universe, its great beauty, its grandeur, its harmony, which are so great that they can only result from a sovereignly wise, good, powerful, and inexhaustible cause. But these things will be treated elsewhere at greater length.

Source: Craig B. Brush, ed., *The Selected Works of Pierre Gassendi* (New York: 1972), pp. 334–36.

Questions for Analysis

1. What is the relationship between new knowledge and new scientific tools (the microscope and the telescope) in Gassendi's examples of the mite and the Milky Way? Is he a Baconian or a Cartesian?

2. What are the limitations of the senses when it comes to questions of the human soul, according to Gassendi?

3. Given these limitations, does Gassendi conclude that science will never be able to say anything about his religious faith?

The early scientific academies did not have explicit rules barring women, but with few exceptions they contained only male members. This did not mean that women did not practice science, though their participation in scientific research and debate remained controversial. In some cases, the new science could itself become a justification for women's inclusion, as when the Cartesian philosopher François Poullain de la Barre used anatomy to declare in 1673 that "the mind has no sex." Since women possessed the same physical senses as men and the same nervous systems and brains, Poullain asked, why should they not equally occupy the same roles in society? In fact, historians have discovered more than a few women who taught at European universities in the sixteenth and seventeenth centuries, especially in Italy. Elena Cornaro Piscopia received her doctorate of philosophy in Padua in 1678, the first woman to do so. Laura Bassi became a professor of physics at the University of Bologna after receiving her doctorate there in 1733, and based on her exceptional contributions to mathematics she became a member of the Academy of Science in Bologna. Her papers—including titles such as "On the Compression of Air" (1746), "On the Bubbles Observed in Freely Flowing Fluid" (1747), "On Bubbles of Air That Escape from Fluids" (1748)—gained her a stipend from the academy.

Italy appears to have been an exception in allowing women to get formal recognition for their education and research in established institutions. Elsewhere, elite women could educate themselves by associating with learned men. The aristocratic Margaret Cavendish (1623–1673), a natural philosopher in England, gleaned the information necessary to start her career from her family and their friends, a network that included Thomas Hobbes and, while she was in exile in France in the 1640s, René Descartes. These connections were not enough to overcome the isolation she felt working in a world of letters that was still largely the preserve of men, but this did not prevent her from developing her own speculative natural philosophy and using it to critique those who would exclude her from scientific debate. The "tyrannical government" of men over women, she wrote, "hath so dejected our spirits, that we are become so stupid, that beasts being but a degree below us, men use us but a degree above beasts. Whereas in nature we have as clear an understanding as men, if we are bred in schools to mature our brains."

The construction of observatories in private residences enabled some women living in such homes to work their way into the growing field of astronomy. Between 1650 and 1710, 14 percent of German astronomers were women, the most famous of whom was Maria Winkelmann (1670–1720). Winkelmann had worked with her husband, Gottfried Kirch, in his observatory, and when he died she had already done significant work, discovering a comet and preparing calendars for the Berlin Academy of Sciences. When Kirch died, she petitioned the academy to be granted her husband's place in the prestigious body but was rejected. Gottfried Leibniz, the academy's president, explained, "Already during her husband's lifetime the society was burdened with ridicule because its calendar was prepared by a woman. If she were now to be kept on in such capacity, mouths would gape even wider." In spite of this rejection, Winkelmann continued to work as an

FROM MARIA SYBILLA MERIAN, *METAMORPHOSIS OF THE INSECTS OF SURINAM* (1705). Merian, the daughter of a Frankfurt engraver, learned in her father's workshop the skills necessary to become an important early entomologist and scientific illustrator who conducted her research on two continents.

astronomer, training both her son and two daughters in the discipline.

Like Winkelmann, the entomologist Maria Sibylla Merian (1647–1717) also made a career based on observation. And like Winkelmann, Merian was able to carve out a space for her scientific work by exploiting the precedent of guild women who learned their trade in family workshops. Merian was the daughter of an engraver and illustrator in Frankfurt, and she served as an informal apprentice to her father before beginning her own career as a scientific illustrator, specializing in detailed engravings of insects and plants. Traveling to the Dutch colony of Surinam, Merian supported herself and her two daughters by selling exotic insects and animals she collected and brought back to Europe. She endured the colony's sweltering climate and overcame malaria to publish her most important scientific work, *Metamorphosis of the Insects of Surinam*, which detailed the life cycles of Surinam's insects in sixty ornate

illustrations. Merian's *Metamorphosis* was well received in her time; in fact, Peter I of Russia proudly displayed Merian's portrait and books in his study.

"AND ALL WAS LIGHT": ISAAC NEWTON

Sir Isaac Newton's work marks the culmination of the scientific revolution. Galileo, peering through his telescope in the early 1600s, had come to believe that the earth and the heavens were made of the same material. And Galileo's experiments with pendulums aimed to discover the laws of motion, and he proposed theories of inertia. But it was Newton who articulated those laws and presented a coherent, unified vision of how the universe worked. All bodies in the universe, Newton said, whether on earth or in the heavens, obeyed the same basic laws. One set of forces and one pattern, which could be expressed mathematically, explained why planets orbited in ellipses and why (and at what speed) apples fell from trees. An Italian mathematician later commented that Newton was the "greatest and most fortunate of mortals"—because there was only one universe, and he had discovered its laws.

Isaac Newton (1642–1727) was born on Christmas Day to a family of small landowners. His father died before his birth, and it fell to a succession of relatives, family friends, and schoolmasters to spot, and then encourage, his genius. In 1661, he entered Trinity College in Cambridge University, where he would remain for the next thirty-five years, first as a student, then as the Lucasian Professor of Mathematics.

Newton's first great burst of creativity came at Cambridge in the years from 1664 to 1666, "the prime of my age for invention." During these years, Newton broke new ground in three areas. The first was optics. Descartes believed that color was a secondary quality produced by the rotational speed of particles but that light itself was white. Newton, using prisms he had purchased at a local fair, showed that white light was composed of different-colored rays (see image on page 443). The second area in which Newton produced innovative work during these years was in mathematics. In a series of brilliant insights, he invented both integral calculus and differential calculus, providing mathematical tools to model motion in space. The third area of his creative genius involved his early works on gravity. Newton later told different versions of the same story: the idea about gravity had come to him when he was in a "contemplative mood" and was "occasioned by the fall of an apple." Why did the apple "not go sideways or upwards, but constantly to the earth's

NEWTON'S EXPERIMENTS WITH LIGHT (1672). Newton's own sketch (left) elegantly displays the way he proved that white light was made up of differently colored light rays. Earlier scientists had explained the color spectrum produced by shining sunlight through a prism by insisting that the colors were a by-product of contaminating elements within the prism's glass. Newton disproved this theory by shining the sunlight through two consecutive prisms. The first produced the characteristic division of light into a color spectrum. When one of these colored beams passed through a second prism, however, it emerged on the other side unchanged, demonstrating that the glass itself was not the cause of the dispersal. He was not yet thirty when he published the results of this experiment.

center? . . . Assuredly the reason is, that the earth draws it. There must be a drawing power in matter." Voltaire, the eighteenth-century French essayist, retold the story to dramatize Newton's simple brilliance. But the theory of gravity rested on mathematical formulations, it was far from simple, and it would not be fully worked out until Newton published his *Principia*, more than twenty years later.

Newton's work on the composite nature of white light led him to make a reflecting telescope, which used a curved mirror rather than lenses. The telescope earned him election to the Royal Society (in 1672) and drew him out of his sheltered obscurity at Cambridge. Encouraged by the Royal Society's support, he wrote a paper describing his theory of optics and allowed it to be published in *Philosophical Transactions*. Astronomers and scientists across Europe applauded the work. Robert Hooke, the Royal Society's curator of experiments, did not. Hooke was not persuaded by Newton's mode of argument; he found Newton's claims that science had to be mathematical both dogmatic and high-handed; and he objected—in a series of sharp exchanges with the reclusive genius—that Newton had not provided any physical explanation for his results. Stung by the conflict with Hooke and persuaded that few natural philosophers could understand his theories, Newton

withdrew to Cambridge and long refused to share his work. Only the patient effort of friends and fellow scientists like the astronomer Edmond Halley (1656–1742), already well known for his astronomical observations in the Southern Hemisphere (and the person for whom Halley's Comet is named), convinced Newton to publish again.

Newton's *Principia Mathematica* (Mathematical Principles of Natural Philosophy) was published in 1687. It was prompted by a visit from Halley, in which the astronomer asked Newton for his ideas on a question being discussed at the Royal Society: was there a mathematical basis for the elliptical orbits of the planets? Halley's question inspired Newton to expand calculations he had made earlier into an all-encompassing theory of celestial—and terrestrial—dynamics. Halley not only encouraged Newton's work but supervised and financed its publication (though he had less money than Newton); and on several occasions he had to persuade Newton, enraged again by reports of criticism from Hooke and others, to continue with the project and to commit his findings to print.

Principia was long and difficult—purposefully so, for Newton said he did not want to be "baited by little smatterers in mathematics." Its central proposition was that gravitation was a universal force and one that could be expressed mathematically. Newton built on Galileo's work on inertia, Kepler's findings concerning the elliptical orbits of planets, the work of Boyle and Descartes, and even his rival Hooke's work on gravity. He once said, "If I have seen further, it is by standing on the shoulders of giants." But Newton's universal theory of gravity, although it drew on work of others before him, formulated something entirely new. His synthesis offered a single, descriptive account of mass and motion. "All bodies whatsoever are endowed with a principle of mutual gravitation." The law of gravitation was stated in a mathematical formula and supported by observation and experience; it was, literally, universal.

The scientific elite of Newton's time were not uniformly persuaded. Many mechanical philosophers, particularly Cartesians, objected to the prominence in Newton's theory of forces acting across empty space. Such attractions smacked of mysticism (or the occult); they seemed to lack any driving mechanism. Newton responded to these criticisms in a note entitled *General Scholium*, added to the next edition of the *Principia* in 1713. He did not know what *caused* gravity, he said, and he did not "feign hypotheses." "For whatever is not deduced from the phenomena must be called hypothesis," he wrote, and has "no place in the experimental philosophy." For Newton, certainty and objectivity lay in the precise mathematical characterization of phenomena—"the mathematization of the universe," as one historian puts it. Science could not, and need not, always uncover causes. It did describe natural phenomena and accurately predict the behavior of objects as confirmed by experimentation.

Other natural philosophers immediately acclaimed Newton's work for solving long-standing puzzles. Thinkers persuaded that the Copernican version of the universe was right had been unable to piece together the physics of a revolving earth. Newton made it possible to do so. Halley provided a poem to accompany the first edition of *Principia*. "No closer to the gods can any mortal rise," he wrote of the man with whom he had worked so patiently. Halley did have a financial as well as an intellectual interest in the book, and he also arranged for it to be publicized and reviewed in influential journals. John Locke (whose own *Essay Concerning Human Understanding* was written at virtually the same time, in 1690) read *Principia* twice and summarized it in French for readers across the Channel. By 1713, pirated editions of *Principia* were being published in Amsterdam for distribution throughout Europe. By the time Newton died, in 1727, he had become an English national hero and was given a funeral at Westminster Abbey. The poet Alexander Pope expressed the awe that Newton inspired in some of his contemporaries in a famous couplet:

> Nature and nature's law lay hid in night;
> God said, "Let Newton be!" and all was light.

Voltaire, the French champion of the Enlightenment (discussed in the next chapter), was largely responsible for Newton's reputation in France. In this, he was helped by a woman who was a brilliant mathematician in her own right, Emilie du Châtelet. Du Châtelet coauthored a book with Voltaire introducing Newton to a French audience; and she translated *Principia*, a daunting scientific and mathematical task and one well beyond Voltaire's mathematical abilities. Newton's French admirers and publicists disseminated Newton's findings. In their eyes, Newton also represented a cultural transformation, a turning point in the history of knowledge.

NEWTON AND SATIRE. The English artist and satirist William Hogarth mocking both philosophy and "Newton worship" in 1763. The philosophers' heads are being weighed on a scale that runs from "absolute gravity" to "absolute levity" or "stark fool."

Science and Cultural Change

From the seventeenth century on, science stood at the heart of what it meant to be "modern." It grew increasingly central to the self-understanding of Western culture, and scientific and technological power became one of the justifications for the expansion of Western empires and the subjugation of other peoples. For all these reasons, the scientific revolution was and often still is presented as a thoroughgoing break with the past, a moment when Western culture was recast. But, as one historian has written, "no house is ever built of entirely virgin materials, according to a plan bearing no resemblance to old patterns, and no body of culture is able to wholly reject its past. Historical change is not like that, and most 'revolutions' effect less sweeping changes than they advertise or than are advertised for them."

To begin with, the transformation we have canvassed in this chapter involved elite knowledge. Ordinary people inhabited a very different cultural world. Second, natural philosophers' discoveries—Tycho's mathematics and Galileo's observations, for instance—did not undo the authority of the ancients in one blow, nor did they seek to do so. Third, science did not subvert religion. Even when traditional concepts collapsed in the face of new discoveries, natural philosophers seldom gave up on the project of restoring a picture of a divinely ordered universe. Mechanists argued that the intricate universe revealed by the discoveries of Copernicus, Kepler, Galileo, Newton, and others was evidence of God's guiding presence. Robert Boyle's will provided the funds for a lecture series on the "confutation of atheism" by scientific means. Isaac Newton was happy to have his work contribute to that project. "Nothing," he wrote to one of the lecturers in 1692, "can rejoice me more than to find [*Principia*] usefull for that purpose." The creation of "the Sun and Fixt stars," "the motion which the Planets now have could not spring from any naturall cause alone but were imprest with a divine Agent." Science was thoroughly compatible with belief in God's providential design, at least through the seventeenth century.

The greatest scientific minds were deeply committed to beliefs that do not fit present-day notions of science. Newton, again, is the most striking case in point. The great twentieth-century economist John Maynard Keynes was one of the first to read through Newton's private manuscripts. On the three hundredth anniversary of Newton's birth (the celebration of which was delayed because of the Second World War), Keynes offered the following reappraisal of the great scientist:

> I believe that Newton was different from the conventional picture of him. . . .
>
> In the eighteenth century and since, Newton came to be thought of as the first and greatest of the modern age of scientists, a rationalist, one who taught us to think on the lines of cold and untinctured reason.
>
> I do not see him in this light. I do not think that any one who has pored over the contents of that box which he packed up when he finally left Cambridge in 1696 and which, though partly dispersed, have come down to us, can see him like that. Newton was not the first of the age of reason. He was the last of the magicians, the last of the Babylonians and Sumerians, the last great mind which looked out on the visible and intellectual world with the same eyes as those who began to build our intellectual inheritance rather less than 10,000 years ago.

Like his predecessors, Newton saw the world as God's message to humanity, a text to be deciphered. Close reading and study would unlock its mysteries. This same impulse led Newton to read accounts of magic, investigate

ESTABLISHMENT OF THE ACADEMY OF SCIENCES AND FOUNDATION OF THE OBSERVATORY, 1667. The 1666 founding of the Academy of Sciences was a measure of the new prestige of science and the potential value of research. Louis XIV sits at the center, surrounded by the religious and scholarly figures who offer the fruits of their knowledge to the French state. ▪ *What was the value of science for absolutist rulers like Louis?*

alchemist's claims that base metals could be turned into gold, and to immerse himself in the writings of the Church Fathers and in the Bible, which he knew in intimate detail. If these activities sound unscientific from the perspective of the present, it is because the strict distinction between rational inquiry and belief in the occult or religious traditions simply did not exist in his time. Such a distinction is a product of the long history of scientific developments after the eighteenth century. Newton, then, was the last representative of an older tradition, and also, quite unintentionally, the first of a new one.

What, then, did the scientific revolution change? Seventeenth-century natural philosophers had produced new answers to fundamental questions about the physical world. Age-old questions about astronomy and physics had been recast and, to some extent (although it was not yet clear to what extent), answered. In the process, there had developed a new approach to amassing and integrating information in a systematic way, an approach that helped yield more insights into the workings of nature as time went on. In this period, too, the most innovative scientific work moved out of the restrictive environment of the Church and the universities. Natural philosophers began talking to and working with each other in lay organizations that developed standards of research. England's Royal Society spawned imitators in Florence and Berlin and later in Russia. The French Royal Academy of Sciences had a particularly direct relationship with the monarchy and the French state. France's statesmen exerted control over the academy and sought to share in the rewards of any discoveries its members made.

New, too, were beliefs about the purpose and methods of science. The practice of breaking a complex problem down into parts made it possible to tackle more and different questions in the physical sciences. Mathematics assumed a more central role in the new science. Finally, rather than simply confirming established truths, the new methods were designed to explore the unknown and provide

After You Read This Chapter

Go to **INQUIZITIVE** to see what you've learned—and learn what you've missed—with personalized feedback along the way.

REVIEWING THE OBJECTIVES

- The scientific revolution marked a shift toward new forms of explanation in descriptions of the natural world. What made the work of scientists during this period different from earlier forms of knowledge or research?

- The scientific revolution nevertheless depended on earlier traditions of philosophical thought. What earlier traditions proved important in fostering a spirit of scientific investigation?

- Astronomical observations played a central role in the scientific revolution. What technological innovations made new astronomical work possible, and what conclusions did astronomers reach using these new technologies?

- Central to the scientific revolution was the rejection of the Ptolemaic view of the universe and its replacement by the Copernican model. What was this controversy about?

- Francis Bacon and René Descartes had contrasting ideas about scientific method. What approach to science did each of these natural philosophers defend?

means to discover new truths. As Kepler wrote to Galileo, "How great a difference there is between theoretical speculation and visual experience, between Ptolemy's discussion of the Antipodes and Columbus's discovery of the New World." Knowledge itself was reconceived. In the older model, to learn was to read: to reason logically, to argue, to compare classical texts, and to absorb a finite body of knowledge. In the newer one, to learn was to discover, and what could be discovered was boundless.

CONCLUSION

The pioneering natural philosophers remained circumspect about their abilities. Some sought to lay bare the workings of the universe; others believed humans could only catalog and describe the regularities observed in nature. By unspoken but seemingly mutual agreement, the question of first causes was left aside. The new science did not say *why*, but *how*. Newton, for one, worked toward explanations that would reveal the logic of creation laid out in mathematics. Yet, in the end, he settled for theories explaining motions and relationships that could be observed and tested.

The eighteenth-century heirs to Newton were much more daring. Laboratory science and the work of the scientific societies largely stayed true to the experimenters' rules and limitations. But as we will see in the next chapter, the natural philosophers who began investigating the human sciences cast aside some of their predecessors' caution. Society, technology, government, religion, even the individual human mind seemed to be mechanisms or parts of a larger nature waiting for study. The scientific revolution overturned the natural world as it had been understood for a millennium; it also inspired thinkers more interested in revolutions in society.

PEOPLE, IDEAS, AND EVENTS IN CONTEXT

- How did the traditions of **NEOPLATONISM, RENAISSANCE,** and **HUMANISM** contribute to a vision of the physical world that encouraged scientific investigation and explanation?
- In what way did the work of **NICOLAUS COPERNICUS, TYCHO BRAHE, JOHANNES KEPLER,** and **GALILEO GALILEI** serve to undermine the intellectual foundations of the **PTOLEMAIC SYSTEM**? Why did their work largely take place outside of the traditional centers of learning in Europe, such as universities?
- What differences in scientific practice arose from **FRANCIS BACON**'s emphasis on observation and **RENÉ DESCARTES**'s insistence that knowledge could only be derived from unquestionable first principles?
- What were **ISAAC NEWTON**'s major contributions to the scientific revolution? Why have some suggested that Newton's interests and thinking were not all compatible with modern conceptions of scientific understanding?
- What was important about the establishment of institutions such as the British **ROYAL SOCIETY** or the French **ACADEMY OF SCIENCES** for the development of scientific methods and research?
- What prevented women from entering most of Europe's scientific academies? How did educated women such as **LAURA BASSI, MARGARET CAVENDISH, MARIA WINKELMANN,** and **MARIA SYBILLA MERIAN** gain the skills necessary to participate in scientific work?

THINKING ABOUT CONNECTIONS

- How did ideas about the value of ancient scholarship and philosophy change after the development of new sciences of observation in the seventeenth century?
- What possible connections might be made between the intellectual developments in scientific thinking during the seventeenth century and the Reformation of the sixteenth century? Was the new science incompatible with religious faith?

Rulers of Principal States

THE CAROLINGIAN DYNASTY

Pepin of Heristal, Mayor of the Palace, 687–714
Charles Martel, Mayor of the Palace, 715–741
Pepin III, Mayor of the Palace, 741–751; King, 751–768
Charlemagne, King, 768–814; Emperor, 800–814
Louis the Pious, Emperor, 814–840

West Francia

Charles the Bald, King, 840–877; Emperor, 875–877
Louis II, King, 877–879
Louis III, King, 879–882
Carloman, King, 879–884

HOLY ROMAN EMPERORS

Saxon Dynasty

Otto I, 962–973
Otto II, 973–983
Otto III, 983–1002
Henry II, 1002–1024

Franconian Dynasty

Conrad II, 1024–1039
Henry III, 1039–1056
Henry IV, 1056–1106
Henry V, 1106–1125
Lothair II (Saxony), 1125–1137

Hohenstaufen Dynasty

Conrad III, 1138–1152
Frederick I (Barbarossa), 1152–1190
Henry VI, 1190–1197
Philip of Swabia, 1198–1208 ⎫
Otto IV (Welf), 1198–1215 ⎭ Rivals

Middle Kingdoms

Lothair, Emperor, 840–855
Louis (Italy), Emperor, 855–875
Charles (Provence), King, 855–863
Lothair II (Lorraine), King, 855–869

East Francia

Ludwig, King, 840–876
Carloman, King, 876–880
Ludwig, King, 876–882
Charles the Fat, Emperor, 876–887

Frederick II, 1220–1250
Conrad IV, 1250–1254

Interregnum, 1254–1273

Emperors from Various Dynasties

Rudolf I (Habsburg), 1273–1291
Adolf (Nassau), 1292–1298
Albert I (Habsburg), 1298–1308
Henry VII (Luxemburg), 1308–1313
Ludwig IV (Wittelsbach), 1314–1347
Charles IV (Luxemburg), 1347–1378
Wenceslas (Luxemburg), 1378–1400
Rupert (Wittelsbach), 1400–1410
Sigismund (Luxemburg), 1410–1437

Habsburg Dynasty

Albert II, 1438–1439
Frederick III, 1440–1493

Maximilian I, 1493–1519
Charles V, 1519–1556
Ferdinand I, 1556–1564
Maximilian II, 1564–1576
Rudolf II, 1576–1612
Matthias, 1612–1619
Ferdinand II, 1619–1637
Ferdinand III, 1637–1657

Leopold I, 1658–1705
Joseph I, 1705–1711
Charles VI, 1711–1740
Charles VII (not a Habsburg), 1742–1745
Francis I, 1745–1765
Joseph II, 1765–1790
Leopold II, 1790–1792
Francis II, 1792–1806

RULERS OF FRANCE FROM HUGH CAPET

Capetian Dynasty

Hugh Capet, 987–996
Robert II, 996–1031
Henry I, 1031–1060
Philip I, 1060–1108
Louis VI, 1108–1137
Louis VII, 1137–1180
Philip II (Augustus), 1180–1223
Louis VIII, 1223–1226
Louis IX (St. Louis), 1226–1270
Philip III, 1270–1285
Philip IV, 1285–1314
Louis X, 1314–1316
Philip V, 1316–1322
Charles IV, 1322–1328

Valois Dynasty

Philip VI, 1328–1350
John, 1350–1364
Charles V, 1364–1380
Charles VI, 1380–1422
Charles VII, 1422–1461
Louis XI, 1461–1483
Charles VIII, 1483–1498
Louis XII, 1498–1515
Francis I, 1515–1547

Henry II, 1547–1559
Francis II, 1559–1560
Charles IX, 1560–1574
Henry III, 1574–1589

Bourbon Dynasty

Henry IV, 1589–1610
Louis XIII, 1610–1643
Louis XIV, 1643–1715
Louis XV, 1715–1774
Louis XVI, 1774–1792

After 1792

First Republic, 1792–1799
Napoleon Bonaparte, First Consul, 1799–1804
Napoleon I, Emperor, 1804–1814
Louis XVIII (Bourbon dynasty), 1814–1824
Charles X (Bourbon dynasty), 1824–1830
Louis Philippe, 1830–1848
Second Republic, 1848–1852
Napoleon III, Emperor, 1852–1870
Third Republic, 1870–1940
Pétain regime, 1940–1944
Provisional government, 1944–1946
Fourth Republic, 1946–1958
Fifth Republic, 1958–

RULERS OF ENGLAND

Anglo-Saxon Dynasty

Alfred the Great, 871–899
Edward the Elder, 899–924
Ethelstan, 924–939
Edmund I, 939–946
Edred, 946–955
Edwy, 955–959
Edgar, 959–975

Edward the Martyr, 975–978
Ethelred the Unready, 978–1016
Canute, 1016–1035 (Danish Nationality)
Harold I, 1035–1040
Hardicanute, 1040–1042
Edward the Confessor, 1042–1066
Harold II, 1066

House of Normandy

William I (the Conqueror), 1066–1087
William II, 1087–1100
Henry I, 1100–1135
Stephen, 1135–1154

House of Plantagenet

Henry II, 1154–1189
Richard I, 1189–1199
John, 1199–1216
Henry III, 1216–1272
Edward I, 1272–1307
Edward II, 1307–1327
Edward III, 1327–1377
Richard II, 1377–1399

House of Lancaster

Henry IV, 1399–1413
Henry V, 1413–1422
Henry VI, 1422–1461

House of York

Edward IV, 1461–1483
Edward V, 1483
Richard III, 1483–1485

House of Tudor

Henry VII, 1485–1509
Henry VIII, 1509–1547
Edward VI, 1547–1553
Mary, 1553–1558
Elizabeth I, 1558–1603

House of Stuart

James I, 1603–1625
Charles I, 1625–1649

Commonwealth and Protectorate, 1649–1659

House of Stuart Restored

Charles II, 1660–1685
James II, 1685–1688
William III and Mary II, 1689–1694
William III alone, 1694–1702
Anne, 1702–1714

House of Hanover

George I, 1714–1727
George II, 1727–1760
George III, 1760–1820
George IV, 1820–1830
William IV, 1830–1837
Victoria, 1837–1901

House of Saxe-Coburg-Gotha

Edward VII, 1901–1910
George V, 1910–1917

House of Windsor

George V, 1917–1936
Edward VIII, 1936
George VI, 1936–1952
Elizabeth II, 1952–

RULERS OF AUSTRIA AND AUSTRIA-HUNGARY

*Maximilian I (Archduke), 1493–1519
*Charles V, 1519–1556
*Ferdinand I, 1556–1564
*Maximilian II, 1564–1576
*Rudolf II, 1576–1612
*Matthias, 1612–1619
*Ferdinand II, 1619–1637
*Ferdinand III, 1637–1657
*Leopold I, 1658–1705
*Joseph I, 1705–1711
*Charles VI, 1711–1740
Maria Theresa, 1740–1780

*Joseph II, 1780–1790
*Leopold II, 1790–1792
*Francis II, 1792–1835 (Emperor of Austria as Francis I after 1804)
Ferdinand I, 1835–1848
Francis Joseph, 1848–1916 (after 1867 Emperor of Austria and King of Hungary)
Charles I, 1916–1918 (Emperor of Austria and King of Hungary)
Republic of Austria, 1918–1938 (dictatorship after 1934)
Republic restored, under Allied occupation, 1945–1956
Free Republic, 1956–

*Also bore title of Holy Roman Emperor

RULERS OF PRUSSIA AND GERMANY

*Frederick I, 1701–1713
*Frederick William I, 1713–1740
*Frederick II (the Great), 1740–1786
*Frederick William II, 1786–1797
*Frederick William III,1797–1840
*Frederick William IV, 1840–1861
*William I, 1861–1888 (German Emperor after 1871)
Frederick III, 1888

*Kings of Prussia

*William II, 1888–1918
Weimar Republic, 1918–1933
Third Reich (Nazi Dictatorship), 1933–1945
Allied occupation, 1945–1952
Division into Federal Republic of Germany in west and
    German Democratic Republic in east, 1949–1991
Federal Republic of Germany (united), 1991–

RULERS OF RUSSIA

Ivan III, 1462–1505
Vasily III, 1505–1533
Ivan IV, 1533–1584
Theodore I, 1534–1598
Boris Godunov, 1598–1605
Theodore II,1605
Vasily IV, 1606–1610
Michael, 1613–1645
Alexius, 1645–1676
Theodore III, 1676–1682
Ivan V and Peter I, 1682–1689
Peter I (the Great), 1689–1725
Catherine I, 1725–1727
Peter II, 1727–1730

Anna, 1730–1740
Ivan VI, 1740–1741
Elizabeth, 1741–1762
Peter III, 1762
Catherine II (the Great), 1762–1796
Paul, 1796–1801
Alexander I,1801–1825
Nicholas I, 1825–1855
Alexander II,1855–1881
Alexander III, 1881–1894
Nicholas II, 1894–1917
Soviet Republic, 1917–1991
Russian Federation, 1991–

RULERS OF UNIFIED SPAIN

Ferdinand { and Isabella, 1479–1504
{ and Philip I, 1504–1506
{ and Charles I, 1506–1516
Charles I (Holy Roman Emperor Charles V), 1516–1556
Philip II, 1556–1598
Philip III, 1598–1621
Philip IV, 1621–1665
Charles II, 1665–1700
Philip V, 1700–1746
Ferdinand VI, 1746–1759
Charles III, 1759–1788
Charles IV, 1788–1808

Ferdinand VII, 1808
Joseph Bonaparte, 1808–1813
Ferdinand VII (restored), 1814–1833
Isabella II, 1833–1868
Republic, 1868–1870
Amadeo, 1870–1873
Republic, 1873–1874
Alfonso XII, 1874–1885
Alfonso XIII, 1886–1931
Republic, 1931–1939
Fascist Dictatorship, 1939–1975
Juan Carlos I, 1975–

RULERS OF ITALY

Victor Emmanuel II, 1861–1878
Humbert I, 1878–1900
Victor Emmanuel III, 1900–1946

Fascist Dictatorship, 1922-1943 (maintained in northern
    Italy until 1945)
Humbert II, May 9–June 13, 1946
Republic, 1946–

PROMINENT POPES

Silvester I, 314–335
Leo I, 440–461
Gelasius I, 492–496
Gregory I, 590–604
Nicholas I, 858–867
Silvester II, 999–1003
Leo IX, 1049–1054
Nicholas II, 1058–1061
Gregory VII, 1073–1085
Urban II, 1088–1099
Paschal II, 1099–1118
Alexander III, 1159–1181
Innocent III, 1198–1216
Gregory IX, 1227–1241
Innocent IV, 1243–1254
Boniface VIII, 1294–1303
John XXII, 1316–1334
Nicholas V, 1447–1455
Pius II, 1458–1464

Alexander VI, 1492–1503
Julius II, 1503–1513
Leo X, 1513–1521
Paul III, 1534–1549
Paul IV, 1555–1559
Sixtus V, 1585–1590
Urban VIII, 1623–1644
Gregory XVI, 1831–1846
Pius IX, 1846–1878
Leo XIII, 1878–1903
Pius X, 1903–1914
Benedict XV, 1914–1922
Pius XI, 1922–1939
Pius XII, 1939–1958
John XXIII, 1958–1963
Paul VI, 1963–1978
John Paul I, 1978
John Paul II, 1978–2005
Benedict XVI, 2005–2013
Francis, 2013–

Further Readings

CHAPTER 1

Aldred, Cyril. *The Egyptians*. 3d ed. London, 1998. An indispensable, lively overview of Egyptian culture and history by one of the great masters of Egyptology.

Baines, J., and J. Málek. *Atlas of Ancient Egypt*. Rev. ed. New York, 2000. A reliable, well-illustrated survey, with excellent maps.

Bottéro, Jean. *Everyday Life in Ancient Mesopotamia*. Trans. Antonia Nevill. Baltimore, MD, 2001. A wide-ranging, interdisciplinary account.

Bottéro, Jean. *Religion in Ancient Mesopotamia*. Chicago, 2001. An accessible, engaging survey.

Dodson, Aidan. *Amarna Sunset: Nefertiti, Tutankhamun, Ay, Horemheb, and the Egyptian Counter-Reformation*. Cairo, 2009. A provocative study of the resistance to Akhenaten's religious "reformation," this book argues that Nefertiti was not only queen but also a kind of "joint-pharaoh," the mother of Tutankhamun, and the leader of the movement toward a return to traditional forms of worship.

Foster, Benjamin R. and Karen Polinger Foster. *Civilizations of Ancient Iraq*. Princeton, 2011. A critically-acclaimed survey that charts the history of this region from the earliest Sumerian civilization to the Arab conquests of the seventh c. C.E.

Geller, Markham J. *Ancient Babylonian Medicine: Theory and Practice*. Malden, MA, 2010. Makes use of previously unstudied cuneiform sources to tell a new story about the relationship between medicine and magic.

George, Andrew, trans. *The Epic of Gilgamesh: A New Translation. The Babylonian Epic Poem and Other Texts in Akkadian and Sumerian*. New York and London, 1999. A reliable translation which carefully distinguishes the chronological "layers" of this famous text; also includes many related texts.

Hodder, Ian. *The Leopard's Tale:Revealing the Mysteries of Çatalhöyük*. London and New York, 2006. The most up-to-date account of this fascinating archaeological site, written for general readers by the director of the excavation.

Kemp, Barry. *The City of Akhenaten and Nefertiti: Armana and Its People*. London, 2012. A cutting-edge study of this ancient site, based on decades of archeological research.

Leick, Gwendolyn. *The Babylonians: An Introduction*. London and New York, 2002. A wide-ranging survey of Babylonian civilization across the centuries.

McDowell, A. G. *Village Life in Ancient Egypt: Laundry Lists and Love Songs*. Oxford, 1999. A fascinating collection of translated texts recovered from an Egyptian peasant village, dating from 1539 to 1075 B.C.E.

McGregor, Neil. *A History of the World in 100 Objects*. London, 2011. Based on an acclaimed BBC Radio program, this book features a range of artifacts from the collections British Museum, embeds them in their historical contexts, and explores the ways that that still hold meaning today.

Pollock, Susan. *Ancient Mesopotamia*. Cambridge, 1999. An advanced textbook that draws on theoretical anthropology to interpret Mesopotamian civilization up to 2100 B.C.E.

Redford, Donald B., ed. *The Oxford Encyclopedia of Ancient Egypt*. 3 vols. New York, 2001. An indispensible reference work, intended for both specialists and beginners.

Roaf, Michael. *Cultural Atlas of Mesopotamia and the Ancient Near East*. New York, 1990. An informative, authoritative, and lavishly illustrated guide, with excellent maps.

Robins, Gay. *The Art of Ancient Egypt*. London, 1997. An excellent survey, now the standard account.

Shafer, Byron E., ed. *Religion in Ancient Egypt: Gods, Myths, and Personal Practice*. London, 1991. A scholarly examination of Egyptian belief and ritual, with contributions from leading authorities.

Shaw, Ian, ed. *The Oxford History of Ancient Egypt*. Oxford, 2000. An outstanding collaborative survey of Egyptian history from the Stone Age to c. 300 C.E., with excellent bibliographical essays.

Shryock, Andrew and Daniel Lord Smail. Berkeley, 2012. *Deep History: The Architecture of Past and Present*. A fascinating fusion of historical, anthropological, and scientific research on what it means to be human.

Smail, Daniel Lord. *On Deep History and the Brain*. Berkeley, 2008. A pioneering introduction to the historical uses of neuroscience and evolutionary biology.

Snell, Daniel C., ed. *A Companion to the Ancient Near East*. Oxford, 2005. A topical survey of recent scholarly work, particularly strong on society, economy, and culture.

Wengrow, David. *The Archaeology of Early Egypt: Social Transformations in North-East Africa, 10,000 to 2650 B.C.* Cambridge, 2006. An authoritative account of archeological evidence and its interpretation.

CHAPTER 2

Aubet, Maria Eugenia. *Phoenicia and the West: Politics, Colonies, and Trade*. Trans. Mary Turton. Cambridge, 1993. An intelligent and thought-provoking examination of Phoenician civilization and its influence.

Boardman, John. *Assyrian and Babylonian Empires and Other States of the Near East from the Eighth to the Sixth Centuries B.C.* New York, 1991. Scholarly and authoritative.

———. *Persia and the West.* London, 2000. A great book by a distinguished scholar, with a particular focus on art and architecture as projections of Persian imperial ideologies.

Boyce, Mary. *Textual Sources for the Study of Zoroastrianism.* Totowa, NJ, 1984. An invaluable collection of documents.

Bryce, Trevor. *The Kingdom of the Hittites.* Oxford, 1998. And *Life and Society in the Hittite World.* Oxford, 2002. An extraordinary synthesis, now the standard account of Hittite political, military, and daily life.

Curtis, John. *Ancient Persia.* Cambridge, MA, 1990. Concise, solid, reliable.

Dever, William. *Who Were the Early Israelites and Where Did They Come From?* Grand Rapids, MI, 2003. A balanced, fair-minded account with excellent bibliographical guidance to recent work.

Dickinson, O. T. P. K. *The Aegean Bronze Age.* Cambridge, 1994. An excellent summary of archaeological evidence and scholarly argument concerning Minoan, Mycenaean, and other cultures of the Bronze Age Aegean basin.

Dothan, Trude, and Moshe Dothan. *Peoples of the Sea: The Search for the Philistines.* New York, 1992. The essential starting point for understanding Philistine culture and its links to the Aegean basin.

Drews, Robert. *The End of the Bronze Age: Changes in Warfare and the Catastrophe ca. 1200 B.C.* Princeton, NJ, 1993. A stimulating analysis and survey, with excellent bibliographies.

Finkelstein, Israel, and Nadav Na'aman, eds. *From Nomadism to Monarchy: Archaeological and Historical Aspects of Early Israel.* Jerusalem, 1994. Scholarly articles on the Hebrews' transformation from pastoralists to a sedentary society focused on the worship of Yahweh.

Fitton, J. Lesley. *Minoans: Peoples of the Past* (British Museum Publications). London, 2002. A careful, reliable debunking of myths about the Minoans, written for nonspecialists.

Kamm, Antony. *The Israelites: An Introduction.* New York, 1999. A short, accessible history of the land and people of Israel up to 135 C.E., aimed at students and general readers.

Kuhrt, Amélie. *The Ancient Near East, c. 3000–330 B.C.* 2 vols. London and New York, 1995. An outstanding survey, written for students, that includes Egypt and Israel as well as Mesopotamia, Babylonia, Assyria, and Persia.

Marinatos, Nannos. *Minoan Kingship and the Solar Goddess: A Near Eastern Koine.* Champaign, IL, 2010. A rich new interpretation of Minoan culture and its wider connections and influence within the world of the late Bronze Age.

Metzger, Bruce M., and Michael D. Coogan, eds. *The Oxford Companion to the Bible.* New York, 1993. An outstanding reference work, with contributions by leading authorities.

Niditch, Susan. *Ancient Israelite Religion.* New York, 1997. A short introduction designed for students, emphasizing the diversity of Hebrew religious practices.

Prezioso, Donald and Louise A. Hitchcock. *Aegean Art and Architecture.* Oxford, 2000. Archaic Greek artistic forms in their broader geographic and cultural context, from the fourth millennium to 1000 B.C.E.

Redford, Donald B. *Egypt, Canaan, and Israel in Ancient Times.* Princeton, NJ, 1992. An overview of the interactions between these peoples from about 1200 B.C.E. to the beginning of the Common Era.

Renfrew, Colin. *Archaeology and Language: The Puzzle of Indo-European Origins.* Cambridge, 1987. A masterful but controversial work by one of the most creative archaeologists of the twentieth century.

Sandars, Nancy K. *The Sea Peoples: Warriors of the Ancient Mediterranean.* Rev. ed. London, 1985. An introductory account for students and scholars.

Tubb, Jonathan N., and Rupert L. Chapman. *Archaeology and the Bible.* London, 1990. A good starting point for students that clearly illustrates the difficulties in linking archeological evidence to biblical accounts of early Hebrew history and society.

Wood, Michael. *In Search of the Trojan War.* New York, 1985. Aimed at a general audience, this carefully researched and engagingly written book is an excellent introduction to the late–Bronze Age context of the Trojan War.

CHAPTER 3

Penguin Classics and the Loeb Classical Library both offer reliable translations of Greek literary, philosophical, and historical texts.

Beard, Mary. *The Parthenon.* Cambridge, MA, 2003. A book that traces the successive stages of this monument's construction, deconstruction, reconstruction, and restoration.

Boardman, John, Jaspar Griffin, and Oswyn Murray, eds. *Greece and the Hellenistic World.* Oxford, 1988. A reprint of the Greek and Hellenistic chapters from *The Oxford History of the Classical World,* originally published in 1986. Excellent, stimulating surveys, accessible to a general audience.

Brunschwig, Jacques, and Geoffrey E. R. Lloyd. *Greek Thought: A Guide to Classical Knowledge.* Translated by Catherine Porter. Cambridge, MA, 2000. An outstanding work of reference.

Buckley, Terry, ed. *Aspects of Greek History, 750–323 B.C.: A Source-Based Approach.* London, 1999. An outstanding collection of source materials.

Cartledge, Paul A. *The Spartans: An Epic History.* New York, 2003. A lively and authoritative history of Sparta from its origins to the Roman conquest.

Dover, Kenneth J. *Greek Homosexuality.* Cambridge, MA, 1978. The standard account of an important subject.

Fantham, Elaine, Helene Foley, Natalie Kampen, Sarah B. Pomeroy, and H. A. Shapiro. *Women in the Classical World: Image and Text.* Oxford, 1994. Wide-ranging analysis drawing on both visual and written sources, covering both the Greek and the Roman periods.

Fornara, Charles W., and Loren J. Samons II. *Athens from Cleisthenes to Pericles.* Berkeley, CA, 1991. An excellent narrative history of Athenian politics during the first half of the fifth century B.C.E.

Garlan, Yvon. *Slavery in Ancient Greece*. Ithaca, NY, 1988. Now the standard account.

Hanson, Victor Davis. *The Other Greeks: The Family Farm and the Agrarian Roots of Western Civilization*. New York, 1995. Polemical and idiosyncratic, but convincing in its emphasis on smallholding farmers as the backbone of Greek urban society.

Havelock, Eric A. *The Literate Revolution in Greece and Its Cultural Consequences*. Princeton, 1982. A now-classic account of the wide-ranging effects of writing on Greek society.

Jones, Nicholas F. *Ancient Greece: State and Society*. Upper Saddle River, NJ, 1997. A concise survey from the Minoans up to the end of the Classical Period that emphasizes the connections between the social order and politics.

Krentz, Peter. *The Battle of Marathon*. New Haven, 2011. A fresh analysis of this landmark battle, paying special attention to the conditions in which hoplite warriors fought.

Lefkowitz, Mary, and Maureen Fant. *Women's Life in Greece and Rome: A Source Book in Translation*. 3rd ed. Baltimore, MD, 2005. A remarkably wide-ranging collection, topically arranged, invaluable to students.

Nevett, Lisa C. *Domestic Space in Classical Antiquity*. Cambridge, 2010. Reassesses what we can know about the architecture of households in antiquity through a fresh assessment of archeological evidence and material culture.

Pomeroy, Sarah B., Stanley M. Burstein, Walter Donlan, and Jennifer Tolbert Roberts. *Ancient Greece: A Political, Social, and Cultural History*. Oxford, 1999. An outstanding textbook; clear and lively.

Pomeroy, Sarah. *Goddesses, Whores, Wives, and Slaves: Women in Classical Antiquity*. New York, 1995. The first historical survey of antiquity to place women at the center of the narrative, and still unrivaled in scope.

Price, Simon. *Religions of the Ancient Greeks*. Cambridge, 1999. Concise and authoritative, this survey extends from the Archaic Period up to the fifth century C.E.

Seaford, Richard. *Money and the Greek Mind: Homer, Philosophy, Tragedy*. Cambridge, 2004. A provocative study of portable wealth and its far-reaching effects.

Strassler, Robert B., ed. *The Landmark Thucydides*. New York, 1996. Reprints the classic Richard Crawley translation with maps, commentary, notes, and appendices by leading scholars.

Thomas, Carol G., and Craig Conant. *Citadel to City-State: The Transformation of Greece, 1200–700 B.C.E.* Bloomington, IN, 1999. A lucid and accessible study that examines developments at a number of different Dark Age sites.

Thomas, Rosalind. *Oral Tradition and Written Record in Classical Athens*. Cambridge, 1989. A fascinating look at how oral epic, lyric, and drama were transmitted over time.

CHAPTER 4

Penguin Classics and the Loeb Classical Library both offer reliable translations of scores of literary and historical texts from this period. Particularly important are historical works by Arrian (*Anabasis of Alexander*), Plutarch (*Life of Alexander*), and Polybius (*The Histories*).

Austin, M. M. *The Hellenistic World from Alexander to the Roman Conquest: A Selection of Ancient Sources in Translation*. Cambridge, 1981. A good collection of primary documents.

Bagnall, R. S., and P. Derow. *Greek Historical Documents: The Hellenistic Period*. Chico, CA, 1981. Another useful collection.

Borza, Eugene N. *In the Shadow of Olympus: The Emergence of Macedon*. Princeton, NJ, 1990. The standard account of the rise of Macedon up to the accession of Philip II.

Bosworth, A. B. *Conquest and Empire: The Reign of Alexander the Great*. Cambridge, 1988. A political and military analysis of Alexander's career that strips away the romance, maintaining a clear vision of the ruthlessness and human cost of his conquests.

———. *The Legacy of Alexander: Politics, Warfare, and Propaganda under the Successors*. Oxford, 2002. The most recent survey of the half century following Alexander's death and of the people who created the Hellenistic kingdoms of Egypt, Persia, and Macedon.

Burstein, Stanley M., ed. and trans. *The Hellenistic Age from the Battle of Ipsos to the Death of Kleopatra VII*. Cambridge, 1985. An excellent collection, with sources not found elsewhere.

Cartledge, Paul. *Agesilaus and the Crisis of Sparta*. Baltimore, MD, 1987. A thorough but readable analysis of the social and political challenges besetting Sparta in the fourth century B.C.E.

———. *Alexander the Great: The Hunt for a New Past*. Woodstock, NY, 2004. A compelling account of Alexander's life, times, and influences.

Green, Peter. *Alexander to Actium: The Historical Evolution of the Hellenistic Age*. Berkeley, CA. 1990. An outstanding, comprehensive, and wide-ranging history of the period.

———. *Alexander of Macedon, 356–323 B.C.* Berkeley, CA, 1991. Revised edition of the author's earlier biography; entertainingly written, rich in detail and insight.

———. *The Hellenistic Age: A Short History*. New York, 2007. An authoritative synthesis that carries the history of Greek influence into the fourth century C.E.

Hansen, Mogens H. *The Athenian Democracy in the Age of Demosthenes*. Oxford, 1991. An examination of the political institutions of Athens in the fourth century B.C.E.

Holt, Frank. L. *Into the Land of Bones: Alexander the Great in Afghanistan*. Berkeley, 2012 repr. ed. A vivid, charged narrative that places the beginning of a current war in the distant past.

Lloyd, Geoffrey, and Nathan Sivin. *The Way and the Word: Science and Medicine in Early China and Greece*. New Haven, CT, 2002. An extraordinary comparative study.

McGing, Brian. *Polybius' Histories*. Oxford, 2010. A critical dissection of this influential ancient historian's techniques and historical philosophy.

Nicholas, G. L. *The Genius of Alexander the Great*. Chapel Hill, NC, 1998. A clear, authoritative, admiring account, distilling a lifetime of research on the subject.

Ober, Josiah. *Mass and Elite in Democratic Athens: Rhetoric, Ideology, and the Power of the People*. Princeton, NJ, 1989. An excellent study of the ideology of democracy in Athens that borrows from the insights of modern social science.

Pollitt, Jerome J. *Art in the Hellenistic Age*. New York, 1986. The standard account, blending cultural history with art history.

Sherwin-White, Susan, and Amélie Kuhrt. *From Samarkhand to Sardis: A New Approach to the Seleucid Empire*. London, 1993. A stimulating examination of the relationship between rulers and ruled in the vast expanses of the Seleucid Empire.

Shipley, Graham. *The Greek World after Alexander, 323–30 B.C.* New York and London, 2000. A study of the social, intellectual, and artistic changes in the Hellenistic era.

Thomas, Carol G. *Alexander the Great in His World*. Oxford and Malden, MA, 2007. A study of the contexts—familial, political, and social—that shaped Alexander's career.

Tripolitis, Antonia. *Religions of the Hellenistic-Roman Age*. Grand Rapids, MI, 2002. Survey of the variety of religious experience, ritual, and belief in the centuries before the emergence of Christianity.

Tritle, Lawrence A., ed. *The Greek World in the Fourth Century: From the Fall of the Athenian Empire to the Successors of Alexander*. New York, 1997. A wide-ranging collection of scholarly essays.

CHAPTER 5

Translations of Roman authors are available in both the Penguin Classics series and in the Loeb Classical Library.

Arnason, Johann P. and Kurt A. Raaflaub, eds. *The Roman Empire in Context: Historical and Comparative Perspectives*. Malden, MA, 2011. One of the few books to place the formation of the Roman Empire in a comparative, global perspective.

Barker, Graeme, and Tom Rasmussen. *The Etruscans*. Oxford and Malden, MA, 1998. A fine survey, from the Blackwell *Peoples of Europe* series.

Beard, Mary. *Pompeii: The Life of a Roman Town*. A fascinating, cutting-edge study of daily life.

Boardman, John, Jasper Griffin, and Oswyn Murray. *The Oxford History of the Roman World*. Oxford, 1990. Reprint of relevant portions of the excellent *Oxford History of the Classical World* (1986). Stimulating, accessible topical chapters by British specialists.

Cornell, T. J. *The Beginnings of Rome: Italy and Rome from the Bronze Age to the Punic Wars (c. 1000–264 B.C.)*. London, 1995. An ambitious survey of the archaeological and historical evidence for early Rome.

Crawford, Michael. *The Roman Republic*, 2d ed. Cambridge, MA, 1993. A lively, fast-paced survey of republican Rome. An excellent place to start.

Fantham, Elaine, Helene Peet Foley, Natalie Boymel Kampen, Sarah B. Pomeroy, and H. Alan Shapiro. *Women in the Classical World*. Oxford, 1994. An expert survey of both Greece and Rome.

Garnsey, Peter, and Richard Saller. *The Roman Empire: Economy, Society, and Culture*. Berkeley, CA, 1987. A straightforward short survey.

Gruen, Erich S. *The Hellenistic World and the Coming of Rome*. 2 vols. Berkeley, CA, 1984. A massive survey, focused on the unpredictable rise of Rome to a position of dominance within the Mediterranean world.

Harris, William V. *War and Imperialism in Republican Rome, 327–70 B.C.* Oxford, 1979. A challenging study arguing that Rome's need for military conquest and expansion was deeply embedded in the fabric of Roman life.

Krebs, Christopher. *A Most Dangerous Book: Tacitus's "Germania" from the Roman Empire to the Third Reich*. A history of this ancient ethnography's transmission and reception, and especially the political uses to which was put in Nazi Germany.

Lancel, Serge. *Carthage: A History*. Trans. Antonia Nevill. Oxford, 1995. An account of Rome's great rival for control of the Mediterranean world.

Millar, Fergus G. B. *The Emperor in the Roman World, 31 B.C.–A.D. 337*. London, 1977. A classic work that showed (among much else) the importance of emperor worship to the religious outlook of the Roman Empire.

———. *The Crowd in Rome in the Late Republic*. Ann Arbor, MI, 1999. A revisionist account that emphasizes the reality of Roman democracy in the late republic, against those who would see the period's politics as entirely under the control of aristocratic families.

Ward, Allen M., Fritz Heichelheim, and Cedric A. Yeo. *A History of the Roman People*, 3d ed. Upper Saddle River, NJ, 1999. An informative, well-organized textbook covering Roman history from its beginnings to the end of the sixth century C.E.

Watkin, David. *The Roman Forum*. London, 2009. A history of the successive buildings and archeological excavations of this central Roman space.

Wells, Colin. *The Roman Empire*, 2d ed. Cambridge, MA, 1992. An easily readable survey from the reign of Augustus to the mid-third century C.E., particularly useful for its treatment of the relationship between the Roman central government and its Italian provinces.

Wiseman, T. P. *Remembering the Roman People*. Oxford, 2009. A collection of studies devoted to popular politics in the late republic.

Woolf, Greg. *Becoming Roman: The Origins of Provincial Civilization in Gaul*. Cambridge, 1998. An exemplary study of how provincial elites made themselves "Roman."

———. *Rome: An Empire's Story*. Oxford, 2012. A masterful account of Rome's reconfiguration of the ancient world and enduring impact; critically acclaimed by scholars and general readers.

———. *Tales of the Barbarians: Ethnography and Empire in the Roman West*. Malden, MA, 2011. Applies modern ethnographic methodologies to a dissection of Romans applied their own ethnographic theories to contemporary "others."

CHAPTER 6

Augustine. *The City of God*. Trans. Henry Bettenson. Baltimore, MD, 1972.

———. *Confessions*. Trans. Henry M. Chadwick. Oxford, 1991.

———. *On Christian Doctrine*. Trans. D. W. Robertson Jr. New York, 1958.

Boethius. *The Consolation of Philosophy*. Trans. R. Green. Indianapolis, IN, 1962.

Bowersock, G. W., Peter Brown, and Oleg Grabar. *Late Antiquity: A Guide to the Postclassical World*. Cambridge, MA, 1999. An authoritative compilation. The first half is devoted to essays on the cultural features of the period; the second half is organized as an encyclopedia.

Brown, Peter. *Augustine of Hippo*. Berkeley, CA, 1967. A great biography by the great scholar of late antiquity.

———. *The Body and Society: Men, Women and Sexual Renunciation in Early Christianity*. New York, 1988. A revealing study of the fundamental transformations wrought by Christianity in the late antique world.

———. *Power and Persuasion in Late Antiquity: Toward a Christian Empire*. Madison, WI, 1992. An important account of Christianity's effects on the political culture of the later Roman Empire.

———. *The Rise of Western Christendom: Triumph and Diversity, 200–1000*, 2d ed. Oxford, 2002. An evocative picture of Christianity's spread eastward and northward from the Mediterranean world.

———. *The World of Late Antiquity*. New York, 1971. Still the best short survey of the period, with excellent illustrations.

———. *Through the Eye of a Needle: Wealth, the Fall of Rome, and the Making of Christianity in the West, 350–550 AD*. Princeton, NJ, 2012. The most recent of this historian's magisterial dissections of late antiquity, focused on the relationship between religion, culture, power, and wealth (or its lack).

Cameron, Averil. *The Later Roman Empire*, A.D. *284–430*. London, 1993. Now the standard account of its period, with an emphasis on imperial politics.

———. *The Mediterranean World in Late Antiquity*, A.D. *395–600*. London, 1993. Masterful, with excellent, succinct bibliographical essays.

Cassiodorus. *An Introduction to Divine and Human Readings*. Trans. L. W. Jones. New York, 1946.

Chadwick, Henry M. *Augustine*. Oxford, 1986. A short introduction to Augustine's thought.

———. *Boethius*. Oxford, 1981. An intellectual biography of this important thinker.

Clark, Gillian. *Christianity and Roman Society*. Cambridge, 2004. A short, stimulating survey that places early Christianity firmly in its Roman social context.

———. *Women in Late Antiquity*. Oxford, 1993. A clear, compact account of an important subject.

Coogan, Michael, ed. *The Oxford History of the Biblical World*. Oxford, 1998. A reliable but rather traditional account of the historical events recounted in the Hebrew Bible and the New Testament.

Ehrman, Bart D. *The New Testament: A Historical Introduction to the Early Christian Writings*, 4th ed. Oxford, 2008. The standard textbook by a leading authority.

Ehrman, Bart D. and Zlatko Pleše, eds. *The Aprocryphal Gospels: Texts and Translations* Oxford, 2011. The first scholarly edition and translation of all the apocryphal gospels, including Latin, Greek, and Coptic texts.

Eusebius. *The History of the Church*. Trans. G. A. Williamson. Baltimore, MD, 1965. A contemporary account of Constantine's reign, written by one of his courtier-bishops.

———. *Eusebius' Life of Constantine*. Trans. Averil Cameron and Stuart Hall. Oxford, 1999. An admiring biography that reflects Constantine's own vision of his religious authority.

Hopkins, Keith. *A World Full of Gods: The Strange Triumph of Christianity*. New York, 1999. An imaginative study of religious pluralism in the Roman world and the context in which Christianity emerged.

Kulikowski, Michael. *Rome's Gothic Wars: From the Third Century to Alaric*. Cambridge, 2007. An authoritative and critical account.

Lawrence, Clifford Hugh. *Medieval Monasticism*, 3d ed. London, 2000. Concise, perceptive survey of monasticism from its beginnings to the end of the Middle Ages.

Pagels, Elaine. *The Gnostic Gospels*. New York, 1979. A pathbreaking study of the noncanonical gospels and the history of their exclusion from the Bible.

Potter, David. *The Roman Empire at Bay*, A.D. *180–395*. London and New York, 2004. The most up-to-date account of the empire's reorganization and transformation in this era.

Rebillard, Éric. *Christians and Their Many Identities in Late Antiquity, North Africa, 200–450 CE*. Ithaca, 2012. In this book, as in his earlier works, the author argues that there was no special importance attached to being a "Christian" in late antiquity, and that religious identities are better understood as fluid and hybrid.

Sanders, E. P. *The Historical Figure of Jesus*. London and New York, 1993. A fine study of Jesus in his first-century Jewish context.

Shanks, Hershel, ed. *Christianity and Rabbinic Judaism: A Parallel History of Their Origins and Early Development*. Washington, DC, 1992. Accessible chapters written by top authorities, describing both Jewish and Christian developments from the first to the sixth centuries C.E.

Sherwin-White, A. N. *Roman Society and Roman Law in the New Testament*. Oxford, 1963. A fascinating reading of the New Testament in its historical context.

Traina, Giusto. *428 AD: An Ordinary Year at the End of the Roman Empire*. Princeton, NJ, 2011. An enlightening glimpse into the world of late antiquity, from the vantage point of a single "average" year.

Wallace-Hadrill, John Michael. *The Barbarian West*, 3d ed. London, 1966. A classic analysis of the hybrid culture of the late Roman West.

Whittaker, C. R. *Frontiers of the Roman Empire: A Social and Economic Study*. Baltimore, MD, 1994. A convincing picture of the frontiers of the Roman Empire as zones of intensive cultural interaction.

Williams, Stephen. *Diocletian and the Roman Recovery*. New York, 1997. Thorough and authoritative.

CHAPTER 7

Bede. *A History of the English Church and People*. Trans. Leo Sherley-Price. Baltimore, MD., 1955. The fundamental source for early Anglo-Saxon history.

Campbell, James, ed. *The Anglo-Saxons*. Oxford, 1982. An authoritative and splendidly illustrated volume.

Collins, Roger. *Early Medieval Europe, 300–1000*. 2d ed. New York, 1999. Dry and detailed, but a useful textbook nonetheless.

Conant, Jonathan. *Staying Roman: Conquest and Identity in Africa and the Mediterranean, 439–700.* Cambridge, 2012. An exploration of what it meant to be "Roman" and the sources of identity in this tumultuous period.

Donner, Fred. *The Early Islamic Conquests.* Princeton, NJ, 1981. A scholarly but readable narrative and analysis.

Einhard and Notker the Stammerer. *Two Lives of Charlemagne.* Trans. Lewis Thorpe. Baltimore, MD, 1969. Lively and entertaining works of contemporary biography.

Fletcher, Richard A. *The Barbarian Conversion: From Paganism to Christianity.* Berkeley, CA, 1999. Slow paced but informative and perceptive.

———. *Moorish Spain.* Berkeley, CA, 1993. The best short survey in English.

Geanakoplos, Deno John, ed. *Byzantium: Church, Society and Civilization Seen through Contemporary Eyes.* Chicago, 1984. An outstanding source book.

Gregory, Timothy E. A *History of Byzantium.* Malden, MA, and Oxford, 2005. The most accessible of the recent textbooks on Byzantium. An excellent place to start.

Herrin, Judith. *Byzantium: The Surprising Life of a Medieval Empire.* Princeton, 2009. An accessible and comprehensive history of the eastern Roman Empire.

———. *The Formation of Christendom.* Princeton, NJ, 1987. A synthetic history of the Christian civilizations of Byzantium and western Europe from 500 to 800, written by a prominent historian.

Hodges, Richard, and David Whitehouse. *Mohammed, Charlemagne and the Origins of Europe.* London, 1983. A critical analysis of the "Pirenne thesis," reexaming the relationship between the Mediterranean world and northern Europe.

Hourani, Albert. *A History of the Arab Peoples.* New York, 1992. A sympathetic and clear survey written for nonspecialists.

Kazhdan, Alexander P., ed. *The Oxford Dictionary of Byzantium.* 3 vols. Oxford, 1991. An authoritative reference work.

Kennedy, Hugh. *The Prophet and the Age of the Caliphates.* 2d ed. Harlow, UK, 2004. A lucid introduction to the political history of the Islamic world from the sixth through the eleventh centuries.

Krautheimer, Richard. *Early Christian and Byzantine Architecture.* 4th ed. New York, 1986. A classic work by one of the greatest Byzantine art historians of the twentieth century.

Little, Lester K., ed., *Plague and the End of Antiquity: The Pandemic of 541–750.* Cambridge, 2006. The first full-length scholarly history of the first global pandemic.

Mango, Cyril, ed. *The Oxford History of Byzantium.* Oxford and New York, 2002. Full of sharp judgments and attractively illustrated.

McCormick, Michael. *The Origins of the European Economy: Communications and Commerce A.D. 300–900.* Cambridge, 2002. An astonishing reinterpretation of the evidence for the myriad contacts between Christian Europe and Islam.

McKitterick, Rosamond. *Charlemagne: The Formation of a European Identity.* Cambridge, 2008. A history of Charlemagne's career and its lasting impact by an eminent scholar of the Carolingian world.

———, ed. *The Uses of Literacy in Early Medieval Europe.* New York, 1990. A superb collection of essays.

McNamara, Jo Ann, and John E. Halborg, eds. *Sainted Women of the Dark Ages.* Durham, NC, 1992. Translated saints' lives from Merovingian and Carolingian Europe.

Murray, A. C., ed. *From Roman to Merovingian Gaul: A Reader.* Toronto, 2000. An excellent collection of sources.

Pelikan, Jaroslav. *The Christian Tradition.* Vol. II, *The Spirit of Eastern Christendom.* Chicago, 1974. An outstanding synthetic treatment of the doctrines of Byzantine Christianity.

Procopius. *The Secret History.* Trans. G. A. Williamson. Baltimore, MD, 1966. An "unauthorized" account of Justinian's reign, written by the emperor's offical historian.

Reuter, Timothy. *Germany in the Early Middle Ages, 800–1056.* New York, 1991. The best survey in English.

Treadgold, Warren. *A History of the Byzantine State and Society.* Stanford, CA, 1997. A massive, encyclopedic narrative of the political, economic, and military history of Byzantium from 284 until 1461.

Wallace-Hadrill, John Michael. *Early Germanic Kingship in England and on the Continent.* Oxford, 1971. A classic analysis of changing ideas about kingship in early medieval Europe, emphasizing the links between Anglo-Saxon and Carolingian cultures.

———. *The Frankish Church.* Oxford, 1983. A masterful account that links the Merovingian and Carolingian churches.

Watt, W. Montgomery. *Islamic Philosophy and Theology,* 2d ed. Edinburgh, UK, 1985. The standard English account.

Wemple, Suzanne Fonay. *Women in Frankish Society: Marriage and the Cloister, 500–900.* Philadelphia, PA, 1981. An influential account of changing attitudes toward marriage among the early Franks.

Whittow, Mark. *The Making of Orthodox Byzantium, 600–1025.* London, 1996. Emphasizes the centrality of orthodoxy in shaping Byzantine history. Particularly good on Byzantine relations with the peoples outside the empire.

Wickham, Chris. *Framing the Middle Ages: Europe and the Mediterranean, 400–800.* Oxford, 2007. An eye-opening history that spans the transitional periods of late antiquity and the early Middle Ages, paying careful attention to regional differences.

Wood, Ian. *The Merovingian Kingdoms, 450–751.* New York, 1994. A detailed study, but difficult for beginners.

CHAPTER 8

Amt, Emily, ed. *Women's Lives in Medieval Europe: A Sourcebook.* New York, 1993. An excellent collection of primary texts.

The Song of Roland. Trans. Robert Harrison. Penguin, 1970. A lively translation.

Arnold, Benjamin. *Princes and Territories in Medieval Germany.* Cambridge and New York, 1991. The best such survey in English.

Blumenthal, Uta-Renate. *The Investiture Controversy.* Philadelphia, 1988. A clear review of a complicated subject.

Boswell, John E. *Christianity, Social Tolerance, and Homosexuality: Gay People in Western Europe from the Beginning of the Christian Era to the Fourteenth Century.* Chicago, 1980. A pioneering account, hotly debated but highly respected.

Burman, Thomas E. *Reading the Qur'ān in Latin Christendom, 1140–1560*. Philadelphia, 2007. A fascinating account of the Qu'ran's reception in medieval Europe.

Colish, Marcia. *Medieval Foundations of the Western Intellectual Tradition, 400–1400*. New Haven, CT, 1997. An encyclopedic work, best used as a reference.

Dunbabin, Jean. *France in the Making, 843–1180,* 2d ed. Oxford and New York, 2000. An authoritative survey of the disparate territories that came to make up the medieval French kingdom.

Dyer, Christopher. *Making a Living in the Middle Ages: The People of Britain 850–1520*. New Haven, 2002. A splendid new synthesis that combines social, economic, and archaeological evidence.

Fossier, Robert. *The Ax and the Oath: Ordinary Life in the Middle Ages*. Princeton, 2010. A quirky, personal, and often insightful look at the daily lives and worldview of this era by a leading French historian.

Frankopan, Peter. *The First Crusade: The Call from the East*. Cambridge, MA, 2012. Analyzes the causes and catalysts of the crusading movement.

Hicks, Carola. *The Bayeux Tapestry: The Life Story of Masterpiece*. London, 2006. An art historian's engrossing account of the making, reception, and interpretation of this amazing artifact.

Horden, Peregrine and Nicholas Purcell. *The Corrupting Sea: A Study of Mediterranean History*. Malden, MA, 2000. An extraordinary attempt to encompass the history of the Mediterranean World over a span of three millennia.

Leyser, Henrietta. *Medieval Women: A Social History of Women in England, 440–1500*. New York, 1995. Although limited to one country, this is the best of the recent surveys treating medieval women.

McLaughlin, Megan. *Sex, Gender, and Episcopal Authority in an Age of Reform, 1000–1122*. Cambridge, 2010. A new interpretation of gendered discourse and politics during the Investiture Controversy.

Miller, Maureen C. *Power and the Holy in the Age of the Investiture Conflict. A Brief History with Documents*. Boston, 2005. A stimulating approach to the eleventh-century conflicts over temporal and spiritual power, with many newly translated sources.

Moore, Robert I. *The First European Revolution, c. 970–1215*. Oxford and Cambridge, MA, 2000. A remarkable description of the ways in which European society was fundamentally reshaped during the eleventh and twelfth centuries.

Peters, F. E. *Aristotle and the Arabs*. New York, 1968. Well written and engaging.

Raffensperger, Christian. *Reimagining Europe: Kievan Rus' in the Medieval World*. Cambridge, MA, 2012. An exciting new study of early Rus' and its neighbors.

Reilly, Bernard F. *The Medieval Spains*. New York, 1993. A succinct account that covers the entire Iberian peninsula from 500 to 1500.

Reynolds, Susan. *Fiefs and Vassals: The Medieval Evidence Reinterpreted*. Oxford and New York, 1994. A detailed revisionist history of "feudalism."

Rubenstein, Jay. *Armies of Heaven: The First Crusade and the Quest for Apocalypse*. New York, 2011. An accessible narrative of the First Crusade, written for a general audience and arguing for a new interpretation of crusaders' motives.

Sawyer, Peter, ed. *The Oxford Illustrated History of the Vikings*. Oxford, 1997. The best one-volume account, lavishly illustrated.

Sheingorn, Pamela, trans. *The Book of Sainte Foy*. Philadelphia, 1995.

Stillman, Norman A. *The Jews of Arab Lands: A History and Source Book*. Philadelphia, PA, 1979. An essential resource.

Stow, Kenneth R. *Alienated Minority: The Jews of Medieval Latin Europe*. Cambridge, MA, 1992. An excellent survey.

Tierney, Brian. *The Crisis of Church and State, 1050–1300*. Toronto, 1988. An indispensable collection for both teachers and students.

Winroth, Anders. *The Conversion of Scandinavia: Vikings, Merchants, and Missionaries in the Remaking of Northern Europe*. New Haven, 2012. Argues that the peoples of Scandinavia were active participants in the cultural, economic, and political processes that accompanied their conversion to Christianity.

CHAPTER 9

Abelard and Heloise. *The Letters and Other Writings*. Trans. William Levitan. Indianapolis, 2007. A beautiful and accurate translation of the correspondence and related documents, with a full introduction and notes.

Abulafia, David. *Frederick II: A Medieval Emperor*. London and New York, 1988. A reliable biography that strips away much of the legend that has hitherto surrounded this monarch.

Baldwin, John W. *The Government of Philip Augustus*. Berkeley and Los Angeles, CA, 1986. A landmark scholarly account.

Barber, Malcolm. *The Crusader States*. New Haven, 2012. A new and comprehensive history by an esteemed historian.

Bartlett, Robert. *The Making of Europe: Conquest, Colonization and Cultural Change, 950–1350*. Princeton, NJ, 1993. A wide-ranging examination of the economic, social, and religious expansion of Europe, full of stimulating insights.

Bisson, Thomas N. *The Crisis of the Twelfth Century: Power, Lordship, and the Origins of European Government*. Princeton, NJ, 2009. A new interpretation of the evidence.

Bynum, Caroline Walker. *Holy Feast and Holy Fast: The Religious Significance of Food to Medieval Women*. Berkeley and Los Angeles, 1988. One of the most influential and important works of scholarship published in the late twentieth century.

Camille, Michael. *Gothic Art: Glorious Visions*. New York, 1996. A succinct and beautifully illustrated introduction.

Chrétien de Troyes. *Arthurian Romances*. Trans. W. W. Kibler. New York, 1991.

Clanchy, Michael T. *Abelard: A Medieval Life*. Oxford and Cambridge, MA, 1997. A great biography.

———. *From Memory to Written Record: England, 1066–1307*. Oxford, 1992. A fascinating and hugely influential account of this revolutionary shift.

Cobban, Alan B. *The Medieval Universities*. London, 1975. The best short treatment in English.

Fassler, Margot. *Gothic Song: Victorine Seqeunces and Augustinian Reform in Twelfth-Century Paris*. Cambridge, UK, 1993. The emergence of new musical genres and their cultural context.

Gillingham, John. *The Angevin Empire,* 2d ed. Oxford and New York, 2001. The best treatment by far of its subject, brief but full of ideas.

Gottfried von Strassburg. *Tristan.* Trans. A. T. Hatto. Baltimore, MD, 1960.

Hallam, Elizabeth, and Judith Everard. *Capetian France, 987–1328,* 2d ed. New York, 2001. A clear and well-organized account.

Haskins, Charles Homer. *The Renaissance of the Twelfth Century.* Cambridge, MA, 1927. A classic and influential study.

Jones, P. J. *The Italian City-State: From Commune to Signoria.* Oxford and New York, 1997. A fundamental reinterpretation of the evidence.

Jordan, William C. *Europe in the High Middle Ages: The Penguin History of Europe.* Vol. III. New York and London, 2003. An outstanding new survey.

Kaeuper, Richard W. *Chivalry and Violence in Medieval Europe.* Oxford and New York, 1999. A darker view of chivalry than Keen's.

Keen, Maurice. *Chivalry.* New Haven, CT, 1984. A comprehensive treatment of chivalry from its origins to the sixteenth century.

Lawrence, Clifford Hugh. *The Friars: The Impact of the Early Mendicant Movement on Western Society.* London and New York, 1994. The best short introduction to the early history of the Franciscans and the Dominicans.

Leclerq, Jean. *The Love of Learning and the Desire for God,* 3d ed. New York, 1982. A beautiful interpretation of twelfth-century monastic culture and the influence of Bernard of Clairvaux.

Little, Lester. *Religious Poverty and Profit Economy in Medieval Europe.* Ithaca, 1978. A fascinating study of the relationship between religious practice and economic reality.

Lopez, Robert S., and Irving W. Raymond, eds. *Medieval Trade in the Mediterranean World.* New York, 1990. A pathbreaking collection of source material.

Madden, Thomas F. *The New Concise History of the Crusades.* New York, 2005. An acclaimed and accessible survey for students.

Marie de France. *Lais.* Trans. Glyn S. Burgess and Keith Busby. Harmondsworth, UK, 1999. A compelling and entertaining prose translation.

Moore, R. I. *The War on Heresy.* Cambridge, MA, 2012. A courageous and searching revisionist history, based on decades of research and reflection. Moore argues for a radical reassessment of what "heresy" consisted of, and why those branded as "heretics" were persecuted during the Middle Ages.

Morris, Colin. *The Papal Monarchy: The Western Church from 1050 to 1250.* Oxford, 1989. An excellent scholarly survey; part of the Oxford History of the Christian Church series.

Newman, Barbara, ed. *Voice of the Living Light: Hildegard of Bingen and Her World.* Berkeley and Los Angeles, CA, 1998. An introduction to Hildegard's life and work.

Otto, Bishop of Freising. *The Deeds of Frederick Barbarossa.* Trans. C. C. Mierow. New York, 1953. A contemporary chronicle interesting enough to read from start to finish.

Smalley, Beryl. *The Study of the Bible in the Middle Ages,* 3d ed. Oxford, 1983. The standard work, gracefully written and illuminating.

Strayer, Joseph R. *On the Medieval Origins of the Modern State.* With new forewords by Charles Tilly and William Chester Jordan. Princeton, 2005. This new edition of Strayer's series of lectures places them in their scholarly context.

Swanson, R. N. *The Twelfth-Century Renaissance.* Manchester, UK, 1999. An updated survey of the intellectual developments of the twelfth century.

Symes, Carol. *A Common Stage: Theater and Public Life in Medieval Arras.* Ithaca, NY, 2007. A study of a vibrant cultural hub.

Wakefield, Walter, and Austin P. Evans, eds. and trans. *Heresies of the High Middle Ages.* New York, 1969, 1991. A comprehensive collection of sources.

Wilhelm, James J., ed. and trans. *Medieval Song: An Anthology of Hymns and Lyrics.* New York, 1971. An excellent collection of sacred and secular poetry that illustrates the connections between them.

Wolfram von Eschenbach. *Parzival.* Trans. H. M. Mustard and C. E. Passage. New York, 1961.

CHAPTER 10

Abu-Lughod, Janet L. *Before European Hegemony: The World System A.D. 1250–1350.* Oxford and New York, 1989. A study of the trading links among Europe, the Middle East, India, and China, with special attention to the role of the Mongol Empire; extensive bibliography.

Allsen, Thomas T. *Culture and Conquest in Mongol Eurasia.* Cambridge and New York, 2001. A synthesis of the author's earlier studies, emphasizing Mongol involvement in the cultural and commercial exchanges that linked China, Central Asia, and Europe.

Christian, David. *A History of Russia, Central Asia and Mongolia.* Vol. 1, *Inner Eurasia from Prehistory to the Mongol Empire.* Oxford, 1998. The authoritative English-language work on the subject.

Cole, Bruce. *Giotto and Florentine Painting, 1280–1375.* New York, 1976. A clear and stimulating introduction.

Crummey, Robert O. *The Formation of Muscovy, 1304–1613.* New York, 1987. The standard account.

Dante Alighieri. *The Divine Comedy.* Trans. Mark Musa. 3 vols. Baltimore, MD, 1984–86.

Dunn, Ross E. *The Adventures of Ibn Battuta: A Muslim Traveler of the Fourteenth Century.* Berkeley, rev. ed. 2005. Places the writings and experiences of this far-reaching Muslim traveler in their historical and geographical contexts.

Dyer, Christopher. *Standards of Living in the Later Middle Ages: Social Change in England, c. 1200–1520.* Cambridge and New York, 1989. Detailed but highly rewarding.

Foltz, Richard. *Religions of the Silk Road: Premodern Patterns of Globalization.* New York, 2nd ed. 2010. A compelling and thought-provoking study of the varieties of religious experience and cross-cultural interaction in medieval Eurasia.

The History and the Life of Chinggis Khan: The Secret History of the Mongols. Trans. Urgunge Onon. Leiden, 1997. A newer version of *The Secret History,* now the standard English version of this important Mongol source.

Horrox, Rosemary, ed. *The Black Death.* New York, 1994. A fine collection of documents reflecting the impact of the Black Death, especially in England.

Jackson, Peter. *The Mongols and the West, 1221–1410*. Harlow, UK, 2005. A well-written survey that emphasizes the interactions among the Mongol, Latin Christian, and Muslim worlds.

Jordan, William Chester. *The Great Famine: Northern Europe in the Early Fourteenth Century*. Princeton, NJ, 1996. An outstanding social and economic study.

Keen, Maurice, ed. *Medieval Warfare: A History*. Oxford and New York, 1999. The most attractive introduction to this important subject. Lively and well illustrated.

Kitsikopoulos, Harry, ed. *Agrarian Change and Crisis in Europe, 1200–1500*. London, 2011. An up-to-date collection of scholarly essays that addresses a classic and complicated set of historical questions.

Komaroff, Linda and Stefano Carboni, eds. *The Legacy of Ghenghis Khan: Courtly Art and Culture in Western Asia, 1256–1353*. New York, 2002. An informative and lavishly illustrated catalog of an acclaimed exhibition.

Larner, John. *Marco Polo and the Discovery of the World*. New Haven, CT, 1999. A study of the influence of Marco Polo's *Travels* on Europeans.

Mandeville's Travels. Ed. M. C. Seymour. Oxford, 1968. An edition of the *Book of Marvels* based on the Middle English version popular in the fifteenth century.

Memoirs of a Renaissance Pope: The Commentaries of Pius II. Abridged ed. Trans. F. A. Gragg, New York, 1959. Remarkable insights into the mind of a particularly well-educated mid-fifteenth-century pope.

Nicholas, David. *The Transformation of Europe, 1300–1600*. Oxford and New York, 1999. The best textbook presently available.

Rossabi, M. *Khubilai Khan: His Life and Times*. Berkeley, CA, 1988. The standard English biography.

Swanson, R. N. *Religion and Devotion in Europe, c. 1215–c. 1515*. Cambridge and New York, 1995. An excellent study of late-medieval popular piety; an excellent complement to Oakley.

The Travels of Marco Polo. Ed. Peter Harris. London, 2008 repr. A new edition of a classic translation.

Vaughan, Richard. *Valois Burgundy*. London, 1975. A summation of the author's four-volume study of the Burgundian dukes.

CHAPTER 11

Alberti, Leon Battista. *The Family in Renaissance Florence (Della Famiglia)*. Trans. Renée Neu Watkins. Columbia, SC, 1969.

Allmand, Christopher T., ed. *Society at War: The Experience of England and France During the Hundred Years' War*. Edinburgh, 1973. An outstanding collection of documents.

———. *The Hundred Years' War: England and France at War, c. 1300–c. 1450*. Cambridge and New York, 1988. Still the best analytic account of the war; after a short narrative, the book is organized topically.

Boccaccio, Giovanni. *The Decameron*. Trans. Mark Musa and P. E. Bondanella. New York, 1977.

Brucker, Gene. *Florence, the Golden Age, 1138–1737*. Berkeley and Los Angeles, CA, 1998. The standard account.

Bruni, Leonardo. *The Humanism of Leonardo Bruni: Selected Texts*. Trans. Gordon Griffiths, James Hankins, and David Thompson. Binghamton, NY, 1987. Excellent translations, with introductions, to the Latin works of a key Renaissance humanist.

Burke, Peter. *The Renaissance*. New York, 1997. A brief introduction by an influential modern historian.

Burkhardt, Jacob. *The Civilization of the Renaissance in Italy*. Many editions. The nineteenth-century work that first crystallized an image of the Italian Renaissance, and with which scholars have been wrestling ever since.

Canning, Joseph. *Ideas of Power in the Late Middle Ages, 1296–1417*. Cambridge, 2011. An old fashioned but nonetheless original synthesis.

Cassirer, Ernst, et al., eds. *The Renaissance Philosophy of Man*. Chicago, 1948. Important original works by Petrarch, Ficino, and Pico della Mirandola, among others.

Chaucer, Geoffrey. *The Canterbury Tales*. Trans. Nevill Coghill. New York, 1951. A modern English verse translation, lightly annotated.

Cohn, Samuel K., Jr. *Lust for Liberty: The Politics of Social Revolt in Medieval Europe, 1200–1425. Italy, France, and Flanders*. Cambridge, MA, 2006. An important new study.

Coles, Paul. *The Ottoman Impact on Europe*. London, 1968. An excellent introductory text, still valuable despite its age.

Dobson, R. Barrie. *The Peasants' Revolt of 1381*, 2d ed. London, 1983. A comprehensive source collection, with excellent introductions to the documents.

Fernández-Armesto, Felipe. *Before Columbus: Exploration and Colonisation from the Mediterranean to the Atlantic, 1229–1492*. London, 1987. An indispensible study of the medieval background to the sixteenth-century European colonial empires.

Froissart, Jean. *Chronicles*. Trans. Geoffrey Brereton. Baltimore, MD, 1968. A selection from the most famous contemporary account of the Hundred Years' War to about 1400.

Goffman, Daniel. *The Ottoman Empire and Early Modern Europe*. Cambridge and New York, 2002. A revisionist account that presents the Ottoman Empire as a European state.

Hankins, James. *Plato in the Italian Renaissance*. Leiden and New York, 1990. A definitive study of the reception and influence of Plato on Renaissance intellectuals.

———, ed. *Renaissance Civic Humanism: Reappraisals and Reflections*. Cambridge and New York, 2000. An excellent collection of scholarly essays reassessing republicanism in the Renaissance.

Hobbins, Daniel, ed. and trans. *The Trial of Joan of Arc*. Cambridge, MA, 2007. A new and excellent translation of the transcripts of Joan's trial.

Inalcik, Halil. *The Ottoman Empire: The Classical Age, 1300–1600*. London, 1973. The standard history by the dean of Turkish historians.

———, ed. *An Economic and Social History of the Ottoman Empire, 1300–1914*. Cambridge, 1994. An important collection of essays, spanning the full range of Ottoman history.

John Hus at the Council of Constance. Trans. M. Spinka, New York, 1965. The translation of a Czech chronicle with an expert introduction and appended documents.

Kafadar, Cemal. *Between Two Worlds: The Construction of the Ottoman State*. Berkeley and Los Angeles, 1995. An important study of

Ottoman origins in the border regions between Byzantium, the Seljuk Turks, and the Mongols.

Kempe, Margery. *The Book of Margery Kempe*. Trans. Barry Windeatt. New York, 1985. A fascinating personal narrative by an early-fifteenth-century Englishwoman who hoped she might be a saint.

Lane, Frederic C. *Venice: A Maritime Republic*. Baltimore, MD, 1973. An authoritative account.

Morgan, David. *The Mongols*. 2d ed. Oxford, 2007. An accessible introduction to Mongol history and its sources, written by a noted expert on medieval Persia.

Ormrod, W. Mark. *Edward III*. New Haven, 2012. A new biography of this English monarch by a leading social historian.

Saunders, J. J. *The History of the Mongol Conquests*. London, 1971. Still the standard English-language introduction; somewhat more positive about the Mongols' accomplishments than is Morgan.

Shirley, Janet, trans. *A Parisian Journal, 1405–1449*. Oxford, 1968. A marvelous panorama of Parisian life recorded by an eyewitness.

Sumption, Jonathan. *The Hundred Years' War*. Vol. 1: *Trial by Battle*. Vol. 2: *Trial by Fire*. Philadelphia, 1999. The first two volumes of a massive narrative history of the war, carrying the story up to 1369.

The Four Voyages: Christopher Columbus. Trans. J. M. Cohen. New York, 1992. Columbus's own self-serving account of his four voyages to the Indies.

CHAPTER 12

Baxandall, Michael. *Painting and Experience in Fifteenth-Century Italy*. Oxford, 1972. A classic study of the perceptual world of the Renaissance.

Castiglione, Baldassare. *The Book of the Courtier*. Many editions. The translations by C. S. Singleton (New York, 1959) and by George Bull (New York, 1967) are both excellent.

Cellini, Benvenuto. *Autobiography*. Trans. George Bull. Baltimore, MD, 1956. This Florentine goldsmith (1500–1571) is the source for many of the most famous stories about the artists of the Florentine Renaissance.

Erasmus, Desiderius. *The Praise of Folly*. Trans. J. Wilson. Ann Arbor, MI, 1958.

Fernández-Armesto, Felipe. *1492: The Year the World Began*. London, 2010. A panoramic view of the world in a pivotal year, putting the voyage of Columbus in a broad historical perspective.

Flint, Valerie I. J. *The Imaginative Landscape of Christopher Columbus*. Princeton, NJ, 1992. A short, suggestive analysis of the intellectual influences that shaped Columbus's geographical ideas.

Fox, Alistair. *Thomas More: History and Providence*. Oxford, 1982. A balanced account of a man too easily idealized.

Grafton, Anthony, and Lisa Jardine. *From Humanism to the Humanities: Education and the Liberal Arts in Fifteenth- and Sixteenth-Century Europe*. London, 1986. An account that presents Renaissance humanism as the elitist cultural program of a self-interested group of pedagogues.

Grendler, Paul, ed. *Encyclopedia of the Renaissance*. New York, 1999. A valuable reference work.

Jardine, Lisa. *Worldly Goods*. London, 1996. A revisionist account that emphasizes the acquisitive materialism of Italian Renaissance society and culture.

Kanter, Laurence, Hilliard T. Goldfarb, and James Hankins. *Botticelli's Witness: Changing Style in a Changing Florence*. Boston, 1997. This catalog for an exhibition of Botticelli's works, at the Gardner Museum in Boston, offers an excellent introduction to the painter and his world.

King, Margaret L. *Women of the Renaissance*. Chicago, 1991. Deals with women in all walks of life and in a variety of roles.

Kristeller, Paul O. *Renaissance Thought: The Classic, Scholastic, and Humanistic Strains*. New York, 1961. Very helpful in defining the main trends of Renaissance thought.

Machiavelli, Niccolò. *The Discourses* and *The Prince*. Many editions. These two books must be read together if one is to understand Machiavelli's political ideas properly.

Mallett, Michael and Christine Shaw. *The Italian Wars, 1494–1559: War, State, and Society in Early Modern Europe*. Boston, 2012. Argues that the endemic warfare of this period within Italy revolutionized European military tactics and technologies.

Mann, Charles. C. *1491: New Revelations of the Americas Before Columbus*. New York, 2006.

———. *1493: Uncovering the New World Columbus Created*. New York, 2012. Written for a popular audience, these are also engaging and well-informed syntheses of historical research.

Martines, Lauro. *Power and Imagination: City-States in Renaissance Italy*. New York, 1979. Insightful account of the connections among politics, society, culture, and art.

More, Thomas. *Utopia*. Many editions.

Olson, Roberta, *Italian Renaissance Sculpture*. New York, 1992. The most accessible introduction to the subject.

Parker, Geoffrey. *The Military Revolution: Military Innovation and the Rise of the West (1500–1800)*. 2d ed. Cambridge and New York, 1996. A work of fundamental importance for understanding the global dominance achieved by early modern Europeans.

Perkins, Leeman L. *Music in the Age of the Renaissance*. New York, 1999. A massive new study that needs to be read in conjunction with Reese.

Phillips, J. R. S. *The Medieval Expansion of Europe*. 2d ed. Oxford, 1998. An outstanding study of the thirteenth- and fourteenth-century background to the fifteenth-century expansion of Europe. Important synthetic treatment of European relations with the Mongols, China, Africa, and North America. The second edition includes a new introduction and a bibliographical essay; the text is the same as in the first edition (1988).

Phillips, William D., Jr., and Carla R. Phillips. *The Worlds of Christopher Columbus*. Cambridge and New York, 1991. The first book to read on Columbus: accessible, engaging, and scholarly. Then read Fernández-Armesto's biography.

Rabelais, François. *Gargantua and Pantagruel*. Trans. J. M. Cohen. Baltimore, MD, 1955. A robust modern translation.

Reese, Gustave. *Music in the Renaissance*, rev. ed. New York, 1959. A great book; still authoritative, despite the more recent work by Perkins, which supplements but does not replace it.

Rice, Eugene F., Jr., and Anthony Grafton. *The Foundations of Early Modern Europe, 1460–1559,* 2d ed. New York, 1994. The best textbook account of its period.

Rowland, Ingrid D. *The Culture of the High Renaissance: Ancients and Moderns in Sixteenth-Century Rome.* Cambridge and New York, 2000. Beautifully written examination of the social, intellectual, and economic foundations of the Renaissance in Rome.

Russell, Peter. *Prince Henry "The Navigator": A Life.* New Haven, CT, 2000. A masterly biography by a great historian who has spent a lifetime on the subject. The only book one now needs to read on Prince Henry.

Scammell, Geoffrey V. *The First Imperial Age: European Overseas Expansion, 1400–1715.* London, 1989. A useful introductory survey, with a particular focus on English and French colonization.

CHAPTER 13

Bainton, Roland. *Erasmus of Christendom.* New York, 1969. Still the best biography in English of the Dutch reformer and intellectual.

Benedict, Philip. *Christ's Churches Purely Reformed: A Social History of Calvinism.* New Haven, CT, 2002. A wide-ranging recent survey of Calvinism in both western and eastern Europe.

Bossy, John. *Christianity in the West, 1400–1700.* Oxford and New York, 1985. A brilliant, challenging picture of the changes that took place in Christian piety and practice as a result of the sixteenth-century reformations.

Bouwsma, William J. *John Calvin: A Sixteenth-Century Portrait.* Oxford and New York, 1988. The best biography of the magisterial reformer.

Dixon, C. Scott, ed. *The German Reformation: The Essential Readings.* Oxford, 1999. A collection of important recent articles.

Duffy, Eamon. *The Stripping of the Altars: Traditional Religion in England, c. 1400–c. 1550.* A brilliant study of religious exchange at the parish level.

———. *The Voices of Morebath: Reformation and Rebellion in an English Village.* New Haven, 2003. How the crises of this period affected and are reflected in the history of a single parish.

Hart, D. G. *Calvinism: A History.* New Haven, 2013. A new survey of this leading Protestant movement from its beginnings to the present day.

John Calvin: Selections from His Writings, ed. John Dillenberger. Garden City, NY, 1971. A judicious selection, drawn mainly from Calvin's *Institutes.*

Koslofksy, Craig. *The Reformation of the Dead: Death and Ritual in Early Modern Germany.* Basingstoke, 2000. How essential rituals and responses to death were reshaped in this period.

Loyola, Ignatius. *Personal Writings.* Trans. by Joseph A. Munitiz and Philip Endean. London and New York, 1996. An excellent collection that includes Loyola's autobiography, his spiritual diary, and some of his letters, as well as his *Spiritual Exercises.*

Luebke, David, ed. *The Counter-Reformation: The Essential Readings.* Oxford, 1999. A collection of nine important recent essays.

MacCulloch, Diarmaid. *Reformation: Europe's House Divided, 1490–1700.* London and New York, 2003. A definitive new survey; the best single-volume history of its subject in a generation.

Martin Luther: Selections from His Writings, ed. John Dillenberger. Garden City, NY, 1961. The standard selection, especially good on Luther's theological ideas.

McGrath, Alister E. *Reformation Thought: An Introduction.* Oxford, 1993. A useful explanation, accessible to non-Christians, of the theological ideas of the major Protestant reformers.

Mullett, Michael A. *The Catholic Reformation.* London, 2000. A sympathetic survey of Catholicism from the mid-sixteenth to the eighteenth century that presents the mid-sixteenth-century Council of Trent as a continuation of earlier reform efforts.

Murray, Linda. *High Renaissance and Mannerism.* London, 1985. The place to begin a study of fifteenth- and sixteenth-century Italian art.

Oberman, Heiko A. *Luther: Man between God and the Devil.* Trans. by Eileen Walliser-Schwarzbart. New Haven, CT, 1989. A biography stressing Luther's preoccupations with sin, death, and the devil.

O'Malley, John W. *The First Jesuits.* Cambridge, MA, 1993. A scholarly account of the origins and early years of the Society of Jesus.

———. *Trent and All That: Renaming Catholicism in the Early Modern Era.* Cambridge, MA, 2000. Short, lively, and with a full bibliography.

———. *Trent: What Happened at the Council.* Cambridge, MA, 2012. A clear and comprehensive narrative of the Church council that gave birth to the modern Catholic Church.

Pettegree, Andrew, ed. *The Reformation World.* New York, 2000. An exhaustive multi-author work representing the most recent thinking about the Reformation.

Pelikan, Jaroslav. *Reformation of Church and Dogma, 1300–1700.* Vol. 4 of *A History of Christian Dogma.* Chicago, 1984. A masterful synthesis of Reformation theology in its late-medieval context.

Roper, Lyndal. *The Holy Household: Women and Morals in Reformation Augsburg.* Oxford, 1989. A pathbreaking study of Protestantism's effects on a single town, with special attention to its impact on attitudes toward women, the family, and marriage.

Shagan, Ethan H. *Popular Politics and the English Reformation.* Cambridge, 2002. Argues that the English Reformation reflects an ongoing process of negotiation, resistance, and response.

Tracy, James D. *Europe's Reformations, 1450–1650.* 2d ed. Lanham, MD, 2006. An outstanding survey, especially strong on Dutch and Swiss developments, but excellent throughout.

Williams, George H. *The Radical Reformation.* 3d ed. Kirksville, MO, 1992. Originally published in 1962, this is still the best book on Anabaptism and its offshoots.

CHAPTER 14

Bonney, Richard. *The European Dynastic States, 1494–1660.* Oxford and New York, 1991. An excellent survey of continental Europe during the "long" sixteenth century.

Briggs, Robin. *Early Modern France, 1560–1715*, 2d ed. Oxford and New York, 1997. Updated and authoritative, with new bibliographies.

———. *Witches and Neighbors: The Social and Cultural Context of European Witchcraft*. New York, 1996. An influential recent account of Continental witchcraft.

Cervantes, Miguel de. *Don Quixote*. Trans. Edith Grossman. New York, 2003. A splendid new translation.

Clarke, Stuart. *Thinking with Demons: The Idea of Witchcraft in Early Modern Europe*. Oxford and New York, 1999. By placing demonology into the context of sixteenth- and seventeenth-century intellectual history, Clarke makes sense of it in new and exciting ways.

Cochrane, Eric, Charles M. Gray, and Mark A. Kishlansky. *Early Modern Europe: Crisis of Authority*. Chicago, 1987. An outstanding source collection from the University of Chicago Readings in Western Civilization series.

Elliot, J. H. *The Old World and the New, 1492–1650*. Cambridge, 1992 repr. A brilliant and brief set of essays on the ways that the discovery of the Americas challenged European perspectives on the world and themselves.

———. *Empires of the Atlantic World: Britain and Spain in America, 1492–1830*. An illuminating comparative study. New Haven, 2007.

Hibbard, Howard. *Bernini*. Baltimore, MD, 1965. The basic study in English of this central figure of Baroque artistic activity.

Hirst, Derek. *England in Conflict, 1603–1660: Kingdom, Community, Commonwealth*. Oxford and New York, 1999. A complete revision of the author's *Authority and Conflict* (1986), this is an up-to-date and balanced account of a period that has been a historical battleground over the past twenty years.

Hobbes, Thomas. *Leviathan*. Ed. Richard Tuck. 2d ed. Cambridge and New York, 1996. The most recent edition, containing the entirety of *Leviathan*, not just the first two parts.

Holt, Mack P. *The French Wars of Religion, 1562–1629*. Cambridge and New York, 1995. A clear account of a confusing time.

Kors, Alan Charles, and Edward Peters. *Witchcraft in Europe, 400–1700: A Documentary History*, 2d ed. Philadelphia, 2000. A superb collection of documents, significantly expanded in the second edition, with up-to-date commentary.

Kingdon, Robert. *Myths about the St. Bartholomew's Day Massacres, 1572–1576*. Cambridge, MA, 1988. A detailed account of this pivotal moment in the history of France.

Levack, Brian P. *The Witch-Hunt in Early Modern Europe*, 2d ed. London and New York, 1995. The best account of the persecution of suspected witches; coverage extends from Europe in 1450 to America in 1750.

Levin, Carole. *The Heart and Stomach of a King: Elizabeth I and the Politics of Sex and Power*. Philadelphia, PA, 1994. A provocative argument for the importance of Elizabeth's gender for understanding her reign.

Limm, Peter, ed. *The Thirty Years' War*. London, 1984. An outstanding short survey, followed by a selection of primary-source documents.

Lynch, John. *Spain, 1516–1598: From Nation-State to World Empire*. Oxford and Cambridge, MA, 1991. The best book in English on Spain at the pinnacle of its sixteenth-century power.

MacCaffrey, Wallace. *Elizabeth I*. New York, 1993. An outstanding traditional biography by an excellent scholar.

Martin, Colin, and Geoffrey Parker. *The Spanish Armada*. London, 1988. Incorporates recent discoveries from undersea archaeology with more traditional historical sources.

Mattingly, Garrett. *The Armada*. Boston, 1959. A great narrative history that reads like a novel; for more recent work, however, see Martin and Parker.

McGregor, Neil. *Shakespeare's Restless World*. London, 2013. Based on an acclaimed BBC Radio program, this book illuminates Shakespeare's life, times, and plays with reference to specific objects in the British Museum.

Newson, Linda A. and Susie Minchin. *From Capture to Sale: The Portuguese Slave Trade to Spanish South America in the Early Seventeenth Century*. London, 2007. Makes use of slave traders' own rich archives to track the process of human trafficking.

Parker, Geoffrey. *The Dutch Revolt*, 2d ed. Ithaca, NY, 1989. The standard survey in English on the revolt of the Netherlands.

———. *Philip II*. Boston, 1978. A fine biography by an expert in both the Spanish and the Dutch sources.

———, ed. *The Thirty Years' War*, rev. ed. London and New York, 1987. A wide-ranging collection of essays by scholarly experts.

Pascal, Blaise. *Pensées* (French-English edition). Ed. H. F. Stewart. London, 1950.

Pestana, Carla. *Protestant Empire: Religion and the Making of the British Atlantic World*. Philadelphia, 2010. How the Reformation helped to drive British imperial expansion.

Roberts, Michael. *Gustavus Adolphus and the Rise of Sweden*. London, 1973. Still the authoritative English-language account.

Russell, Conrad. *The Causes of the English Civil War*. Oxford, 1990. A penetrating and provocative analysis by one of the leading "revisionist" historians of the period.

Schmidt, Benjamin. *Innocence Abroad: The Dutch Imagination and the New World, 1570–1670*. Cambridge, 2006. A cultural history of Europeans' encounter with the Americas that highlights the perspective and experience of Dutch merchants, colonists, and artists.

Tracy, James D. *Holland under Habsburg Rule, 1506–1566: The Formation of a Body Politic*. Berkeley and Los Angeles, CA, 1990. A political history and analysis of the formative years of the Dutch state.

CHAPTER 15

Beik, William. *A Social and Cultural History of Early Modern France*. Cambridge, UK, 2009. A broad synthesis of French history from the end of the Middle Ages to the French Revolution, by one of the world's foremost authorities on absolutism.

Clark, Christopher, *Iron Kingdom: The Rise and Downfall of Prussia, 1600–1947*. Cambridge, MA, 2009. A definitive account of Prussian history over nearly four centuries.

Jones, Colin. *The Great Nation: France From Louis XV to Napoleon*. New York, 2002. An excellent and readable scholarly account that argues that the France of Louis XV in the eighteenth century was even more dominant than the kingdom of Louis XIV in the preceding century.

Kishlansky, Mark A. *A Monarchy Transformed: Britain, 1603–1714.* London, 1996. An excellent survey that takes seriously its claims to be a "British" rather than merely an "English" history.

Klein, Herbert S. *The Atlantic Slave Trade.* Cambridge and New York, 1999. An accessible survey by a leading quantitative historian.

Lewis, William Roger, gen. ed. *The Oxford History of the British Empire.* Vol. I: *The Origins of Empire: British Overseas Enterprise to the Close of the Seventeenth Century,* ed. Nicholas Canny. Vol. II: *The Eighteenth Century,* ed. Peter J. Marshall. Oxford and New York, 1998. A definitive, multiauthor account.

Locke, John. *Two Treatises of Government.* Ed. Peter Laslett. Rev. ed. Cambridge and New York, 1963. Laslett has revolutionized our understanding of the historical and ideological context of Locke's political writings.

Massie, Robert. *Peter the Great, His Life and World.* New York, 1980. Prize-winning and readable narrative account of the Russian tsar's life.

Monod, Paul K. *The Power of Kings: Monarchy and Religion in Europe, 1589–1715.* New Haven, CT, 1999. A study of the seventeenth century's declining confidence in the divinity of kings.

Quataert, Donald. *The Ottoman Empire, 1700–1822.* Cambridge and New York, 2000. Well balanced and intended to be read by students.

Riasanovsky, Nicholas V., and Steinberg, Mark D. *A History of Russia.* 7th ed. Oxford and New York, 2005. Far and away the best single-volume textbook on Russian history: balanced, comprehensive, intelligent, and with full bibliographies.

Saint-Simon, Louis. *Historical Memoirs.* Many editions. The classic source for life at Louis XIV's Versailles.

Snyder, Timothy, *The Reconstruction of Nations: Poland, Ukraine, Lithuania, Belarus, 1569–1999.* New Haven, CT, 2004. Essential account of nation building and state-collapse in Eastern Europe with significant relevance to the region's contemporary situation.

Thomas, Hugh. *The Slave Trade: The History of the Atlantic Slave Trade, 1440–1870.* London and New York, 1997. A survey notable for its breadth and depth of coverage and for its attractive prose style.

Tracy, James D. *The Rise of Merchant Empires: Long-Distance Trade in the Early Modern World, 1350–1750.* Cambridge and New York, 1990. Important collection of essays by leading authorities.

White, Richard. *The Middle Ground: Indians, Empires and Republics in the Great Lakes Region, 1650–1815.* Cambridge, UK, 1991. A path-breaking account of interactions between Europeans and Native Americans during the colonial period.

CHAPTER 16

Biagioli, Mario. *Galileo, Courtier.* Chicago, 1993. Emphasizes the importance of patronage and court politics in Galileo's science and career.

Cohen, I. B. *The Birth of a New Physics.* New York, 1985. Emphasizes the mathematical nature of the revolution; unmatched at making the mathematics understandable.

Daston, Lorraine, and Elizabeth Lunbeck, eds. *Histories of Scientific Observation.* Chicago, IL, 2011. Field-defining collection of essays on the history of scientific observation from the seventeenth to the twentieth centuries.

Daston, Lorraine. *Wonders and the Order of Nature, 1150–1750.* Cambridge, MA, 2001. Erudite sweeping account of the history of science in the early modern period, emphasizing the natural philosopher's awe and wonder at the marvelous, the unfamiliar, and the counter-intuitive.

Dear, Peter. *Revolutionizing the Sciences: European Knowledge and Its Ambitions, 1500–1700.* Princeton, NJ, 2001. Among the best short histories.

Drake, Stillman. *Discoveries and Opinions of Galileo.* Garden City, NY, 1957. The classic translation of Galileo's most important papers by his most admiring modern biographer.

Feingold, Mardechai, *The Newtonian Moment: Isaac Newton and the Making of Modern Culture.* New York, 2004. An engaging essay on the dissemination of Newton's thought, with excellent visual material.

Gaukroger, Stephen. *Descartes: An Intellectual Biography.* Oxford, 1995. Detailed and sympathetic study of the philosopher.

Gleick, James. *Isaac Newton.* New York, 2003. A vivid and well-documented brief biography.

Grafton, Anthony. *New Worlds, Ancient Texts: The Power of Tradition and the Shock of Discovery.* Cambridge, MA, 1992. Accessible essay by one of the leading scholars of early modern European thought.

Jacob, Margaret. *Scientific Culture and the Making of the Industrial West.* Oxford, 1997. A concise examination of the connections between developments in science and the Industrial Revolution.

Kuhn, Thomas. *The Structure of Scientific Revolutions.* Chicago, 1962. A classic and much-debated study of how scientific thought changes.

Pagden, Anthony, *European Encounters with the New World.* New Haven, CT, and London, 1993. Subtle and detailed on how European intellectuals thought about the lands they saw for the first time.

Scheibinger, Londa. *The Mind Has No Sex? Women in the Origins of Modern Science.* Cambridge, MA, 1989. A lively and important recovery of the lost role played by women mathematicians and experimenters.

Shapin, Steven. *The Scientific Revolution.* Chicago, 1996. Engaging, accessible, and brief—organized thematically.

Shapin, Steven, and Simon Schaffer. *Leviathan and the Air Pump.* Princeton, NJ, 1985. A modern classic, on one of the most famous philosophical conflicts in seventeenth-century science.

Stephenson, Bruce. *The Music of the Heavens: Kepler's Harmonic Astronomy.* Princeton, NJ, 1994. An engaging and important explanation of Kepler's otherworldly perspective.

Thoren, Victor. *The Lord of Uraniborg: A Biography of Tycho Brahe.* Cambridge, 1990. A vivid reconstruction of the scientific revolution's most flamboyant astronomer.

Westfall, Richard. *The Construction of Modern Science.* Cambridge, 1977.

———. *Never at Rest: A Biography of Isaac Newton.* Cambridge, 1980. The standard work.

Wilson, Catherine. *The Invisible World: Early Modern Philosophy and the Invention of the Microscope.* Princeton, NJ, 1995. An important study of how the "microcosmic" world revealed by technology reshaped scientific philosophy and practice.

Zinsser, Judith P. *La Dame d'Esprit: A Biography of the Marquise Du Châtelet.* New York, 2006. An excellent cultural history. To be issued in paper as *Emilie du Châtelet: Daring Genius of the Enlightenment* (2007).

Glossary

1973 OPEC oil embargo Some leaders in the Arab-dominated Organization of the Petroleum Exporting Countries (OPEC) wanted to use oil as a weapon against the West in the Arab-Israeli conflict. After the 1972 Arab-Israeli war, OPEC instituted an oil embargo against Western powers. The embargo increased the price of oil and sparked spiraling inflation and economic troubles in Western nations, triggering in turn a cycle of dangerous recession that lasted nearly a decade. In response, Western governments began viewing the Middle Eastern oil regions as areas of strategic importance.

Abbasid Caliphate (750–930) The Abbasid family claimed to be descendants of Muhammad, and in 750 they successfully led a rebellion against the Umayyads, seizing control of Muslim territories in Arabia, Persia, North Africa, and the Near East. Establishing a new capital at Baghdad, the Abbasids modeled their behavior and administration on that of the Persian princes and their rule on that of the Persian Empire.

Peter Abelard (1079–1142) Highly influential philosopher, theologian, and teacher, often considered the founder of the University of Paris.

absolutism Form of government in which one body, usually the monarch, controls the right to make war, tax, judge, and coin money. The term was often used to refer to the state monarchies in seventeenth- and eighteenth-century Europe. In other countries the end of feudalism is often associated with the legal abolition of serfdom, as in Russia in 1861.

abstract expressionism Mid-twentieth-century school of art based in New York that included Jackson Pollock, Willem de Kooning, and Franz Kline. It emphasized form, color, gesture, and feeling instead of figurative subjects.

Academy of Sciences French institute of scientific inquiry founded in 1666 by Louis XIV. France's statesmen exerted control over the academy and sought to share in the rewards of any discoveries its members made.

Aeneas Mythical founder of Rome, Aeneas was a refugee from the city of Troy whose adventures were described by the poet Virgil in the *Aeneid*, which mimicked the oral epics of Homer.

Aetolian and Achaean Leagues Two alliances among Greek poleis formed during the Hellenistic period in opposition to the Antigonids of Macedonia. Unlike the earlier defensive alliances of the classic period, each league represented a real attempt to form a political federation.

African National Congress (ANC) Multiracial organization founded in 1912 whose goal was to end racial discrimination in South Africa.

Afrikaners Descendants of the original Dutch settlers of South Africa; formerly referred to as Boers.

agricultural revolution Numerous agricultural revolutions have occurred in the history of Western civilizations. One of the most significant began in the tenth century C.E., and increased the amount of land under cultivation as well as the productivity of the land. This revolution was made possible through the use of new technology, an increase in global temperatures, and more-efficient methods of cultivation.

AIDS Acquired Immunodeficiency Syndrome. AIDS first appeared in the 1970s and has developed into a global health catastrophe; it is spreading most quickly in developing nations in Africa and Asia.

Akhenaten (r. 1352–1336 B.C.E.) Pharaoh whose attempt to promote the worship of the sun god, Aten, ultimately weakened his dynasty's position in Egypt.

Alexander the Great (356–323 B.C.E.) Macedonian king whose conquests of the Persian Empire and Egypt created a new Hellenistic world.

Tsar Alexander II (1818–1881) After the Crimean War, Tsar Alexander embarked on a program of reform and modernization, which included the emancipation of the serfs. A radical assassin killed him in 1881.

Alexius Comnenus (1057–1118) Byzantine emperor who requested Pope Urban II's help in raising an army to recapture Anatolia from the Seljuk Turks. Instead, Pope Urban II called for knights to go to the Holy Land and liberate it from its Muslim captors, which launched the First Crusade.

Algerian War (1954–1962) War between France and Algerians seeking independence. Led by the National Liberation Front (FLN), guerrillas fought the French army in the mountains and desert of Algeria. The FLN also initiated a campaign of bombing and terrorism in Algerian cities that led French soldiers to torture many Algerians, attracting world attention and international scandal.

Dante Alighieri (c. 1265–1321) Florentine poet and intellectual whose *Divine Comedy* was a pioneering work in the Italian vernacular and a vehicle for political and religious critique.

Allied Powers First World War coalition of Great Britain, Ireland, Belgium, France, Italy, Russia, Portugal, Greece, Serbia, Montenegro, Albania, and Romania.

al Qaeda Radical Islamic organization founded in the late 1980s by former mujahidin who had fought against the Soviet Union in Afghanistan. Al Qaeda carried out the 9/11 terrorist attacks and is responsible as well for attacks in Africa, Southeast Asia, Europe, and the Middle East.

Ambrose (c. 340–397) One of the early "Fathers" of the Church, he helped to define the relationship between the sacred authority of bishops and other Church leaders and the secular authority of worldly rulers. He believed that secular rulers were a part of the Church and therefore subject to it.

Americanization The fear of many Europeans, since the 1920s, that U.S. cultural products, such as film, television, and music, exerted too much influence. Many of the criticisms centered on America's emphasis on mass production and organization. The fears about Americanization were not limited to culture. They extended to corporations, business techniques, global trade, and marketing.

Americas The name given to the two great landmasses of the New World, derived from the name of the Italian geographer Amerigo Vespucci. In 1492, Christopher Columbus reached the Bahamas and the island of Hispaniola, which began an era of Spanish conquest in North and South America. Originally, the Spanish sought a route to Asia. Instead they discovered two continents whose wealth they decided to exploit. They were especially interested in gold and silver, which they either stole from indigenous peoples or mined using the labor of indigenous peoples. Silver became Spain's most lucrative export from the New World.

Amnesty International Nongovernmental organization formed in 1961 to defend "prisoners of conscience"—those detained for their beliefs, color, sex, ethnic origin, language, or religion.

Anabaptists Protestant movement that emerged in Switzerland in 1521; its adherents insisted that only adults could be baptized Christians.

anarchists Nineteenth-century political movement with the aim of establishing small-scale, localized, and self-sufficient democratic communities that could guarantee a maximum of individual sovereignty. Renouncing parties, unions, and any form of modern mass organization, the anarchists fell back on the tradition of conspiratorial violence.

Anti–Corn Law League Organization that successfully lobbied Parliament to repeal Britain's Corn Laws in 1846. The Corn Laws of 1815 had protected British landowners and farmers from foreign competition by establishing high tariffs, which kept bread prices artificially high for British consumers. The league saw these laws as unfair protection of the aristocracy and pushed for their repeal in the name of free trade.

anti-Semitism Hostility toward Jewish people. Religious forms of anti-Semitism have a long history in Europe, but in the nineteenth century anti-Semitism emerged as a potent ideology for mobilizing new constituencies in the era of mass politics. Playing on popular conspiracy theories about alleged Jewish influence in society, anti-Semites effectively rallied large bodies of supporters in France during the Dreyfus Affair, and then again during the rise of National Socialism in Germany after the First World War. The Holocaust would not have been possible without the acquiescence or cooperation of many thousands of people who shared anti-Semitic views.

apartheid The racial segregation policy of the Afrikaner-dominated South African government. Legislated in 1948 by the Afrikaner National Party, it existed in South Africa for many decades.

appeasement Policy pursued by Western governments in the face of German, Italian, and Japanese aggression leading up to the Second World War. The policy, which attempted to accommodate and negotiate peace with the aggressive nations, was based on the belief that another global war like the First World War was unimaginable, a belief that Germany and its allies had been mistreated by the terms of the Treaty of Versailles, and a belief that fascist Germany and its allies protected the West from the spread of Soviet communism.

Thomas Aquinas (1225–1274) Dominican friar and theologian whose systematic approach to Christian doctrine was influenced by Aristotle.

Arab-Israeli conflict Between the founding of the state of Israel in 1948 and the present, a series of wars has been fought between Israel and neighboring Arab nations: the war of 1948 when Israel defeated attempts by Egypt, Jordon, Iraq, Syria, and Lebanon to prevent the creation of the new state; the 1956 war between Israel and Egypt over the Sinai peninsula; the 1967 war, when Israel gained control of additional land in the Golan Heights, the West Bank, the Gaza strip, and the Sinai; and the Yom Kippur War of 1973, when Israel once again fought with forces from Egypt and Syria. A particularly difficult issue in all of these conflicts has been the situation of the 950,000 Palestinian refugees made homeless by the first war in 1948 and the movement of Israeli settlers into the occupied territories (outside of Israel's original borders). In the late 1970s, peace talks between Israel and Egypt inspired some hope of peace, but an ongoing cycle of violence between Palestinians and the Israeli military has made a final settlement elusive.

Arab nationalism During the period of decolonization, secular forms of Arab nationalism, or pan-Arabism, found a wide following in many countries of the Middle East, especially in Egypt, Syria, and Iraq.

Arianism Variety of Christianity condemned as a heresy by the Roman Church; it derives from the teaching of a fourth-century priest called Arius, who rejected the idea that Jesus could be the divine equal of God.

aristocracy From the Greek word meaning "rule of the best." By 1000 B.C.E., the accumulated wealth of successful traders in Greece had created a new type of social class, which was based on wealth rather than warfare or birth. These men saw their wealth as a reflection of their superior qualities and aspired to emulate the heroes of old.

Aristotle (384–322 B.C.E.) Student of Plato whose philosophy was based on the rational analysis of the material world. In contrast to his teacher, he stressed the rigorous investigation of real phenomena, rather than the development of universal ethics. He was, in turn, the teacher of Alexander the Great.

Asiatic Society Cultural organization founded in 1784 by British Orientalists who lauded native cultures but believed in colonial rule.

Assyrians Semitic-speaking people who moved into northern Mesopotamia around 2400 B.C.E.

Athens Athens emerged as the Greek polis with the most markedly democratic form of government through a series of political struggles during the sixth century B.C.E. After its key role in the defeat of two invading Persian forces, Athens became the preeminent naval power of ancient Greece and the exemplar of Greek culture. But it antagonized many other poleis and became embroiled in a war with Sparta and her allies in 431 B.C.E. Called the Peloponnesian War, this bloody conflict lasted until Athens was defeated in 404 B.C.E.

atomic bomb In 1945, the United States dropped atomic bombs on Hiroshima and Nagasaki in Japan, ending the Second World War. In 1949, the Soviet Union tested its first atomic bomb, and in 1953 both superpowers demonstrated their new hydrogen bombs. Strategically, the nuclearization of warfare polarized the world. Countries without nuclear weapons found it difficult to avoid joining either the Soviet or American military pacts. The nuclearization of warfare encouraged "proxy wars" between client nations of the superpowers. Culturally, the hydrogen bomb came to symbolize the age as well as humanity's power and vulnerability.

Augustine (c. 354–397) One of the most influential theologians of all time, Augustine described his conversion to Christianity in his autobiographical *Confessions* and articulated a new Christian worldview in *The City of God*, among other works.

Augustus (63 B.C.E.–14 C.E.) Born Gaius Octavius, this grandnephew and adopted son of Julius Caesar came to power in 27 B.C.E. His reign signals the end of the Roman Republic and the beginning of the Principate, the period when Rome was dominated by autocratic emperors.

Auschwitz-Birkenau Nazi concentration camp in Poland designed to systematically murder Jews and Gypsies. Between 1942 and 1944 over 1 million people were killed in Auschwitz-Birkenau.

Austro-Hungarian Empire Dual monarchy established by the Habsburg family in 1867; it collapsed at the end of the First World War.

authoritarianism Centralized and dictatorial form of government, proclaimed by its adherents to be superior to parliamentary democracy. Authoritarian governments claim to be above the law, do not respect individual rights, and do not tolerate political opposition. Authoritarian regimes that have developed a central ideology such as fascism or communism are sometimes termed "totalitarian."

Avignon City in southeastern France that became the seat of the papacy between 1305 and 1377, a period known as the "Babylonian Captivity" of the Roman Church.

Aztecs An indigenous people of central Mexico; their empire was conquered by Spanish conquistadors in the sixteenth century.

baby boom (1950s), The post–Second World War upswing in U.S. birth rates it reversed a century of decline.

Babylon Ancient city between the Tigris and Euphrates Rivers, which became the capital of Hammurabi's empire in the eighteenth century B.C.E. and continued to be an important administrative and commercial capital under many subsequent imperial powers, including the Neo-Assyrians, Chaldeans, Persians, and Romans. It was here that Alexander the Great died in 323 B.C.E.

Babylonian captivity Reference to both the Jews' exile in Babylon during the sixth century B.C.E. and the period from 1309 to 1378, when papal authority of the Roman Catholic Church was subjugated to the French crown and the papal court was moved from Rome to the French city of Avignon.

Francis Bacon (1561–1626) British philosopher and scientist who pioneered the scientific method and the systematic use of inductive reasoning. In other words, he argued that thinkers should amass many observations and then draw general conclusions or propose theories on the basis of these data.

balance of powers Principle that no single country should be powerful enough to destabilize international relations. Starting in the seventeenth century, this goal of maintaining balance influenced diplomacy in western and central Europe for two centuries until the system collapsed with the onset of the First World War.

Balfour Declaration Letter of November 2, 1917, by Lord Arthur J. Balfour, British foreign secretary, promising a homeland for the Jews in Palestine.

Laura Bassi (1711–1778) Italian mathematician; her acceptance into the Academy of Science in Bologna for her work in mathematics made her one of the few women to be welcomed into a scientific academy in the seventeenth century.

Bastille Royal fortress and prison in Paris. In June 1789, a revolutionary crowd attacked the Bastille to show support for the newly created National Assembly. The fall of the Bastille was the first instance of the people's role in revolutionary change in France.

Bay of Pigs (1961) Site of the unsuccessful invasion of Cuba by Cuban exiles, supported by the U.S. government. The rebels intended to incite an insurrection in Cuba and overthrow the communist regime of Fidel Castro.

Cesare Beccaria (1738–1794) Influential Enlightenment-era writer who advocated for legal reforms. Beccaria believed that the only legitimate rationale for punishments was to maintain social order and to prevent other crimes. He argued for the greatest-possible leniency compatible with deterrence and opposed the use of torture and the death penalty.

Beer Hall Putsch (1923) Early attempt by the Nazi party to seize power, in Munich; Adolf Hitler was imprisoned for a year after the incident.

Benedict of Nursia (c. 480–c. 547) Italian abbot regarded as the patron saint of Europe; his "rule" for monks formed the basis of western monasticism and is still observed in monasteries all over the world.

Benedictine Monasticism Form of monasticism developed by Benedict of Nursia; its followers adhere to a defined cycle of daily prayers, lessons, communal worship, and manual labor.

Berlin airlift (1948) Transport of vital supplies to West Berlin by air, primarily under U.S. auspices, in response to a blockade of the city that had been instituted by the Soviet Union to force the Allies to abandon West Berlin.

Berlin Conference (1884) Conference of the leading colonial powers that met and established ground rules for the partition of Africa by European nations. By 1914, 90 percent of African territory was under European control. The Berlin Conference ceded control of the Congo region to a private company run by King Leopold II of Belgium. They agreed to make the Congo valleys open to free trade and commerce, to end the slave trade in the region, and to establish a Congo Free State. In reality, King Leopold II's company established a regime so brutal in its treatment of local populations that in 1908 an international scandal forced the Belgian state to take over the colony.

Berlin Wall Wall built in 1961 by East German communists to prevent citizens of East Germany from fleeing to West Germany; it was torn down in 1989.

birth control pill Oral contraceptive that became widely available in the mid-1960s. For the first time, women had a simple method of birth control that they could take themselves.

Otto von Bismarck (1815–1898) Prime minister of Prussia and later first chancellor of a unified Germany: Bismarck was the architect of German unification and helped to consolidate the new nation's economic and military power.

Black Death Epidemic of bubonic plague that ravaged Europe, Asia, and North Africa in the fourteenth century, killing one third to one half of the population.

Black Jacobins Nickname for the rebels in Saint-Domingue, including Toussaint L'Ouverture, a former slave who in 1791 led the slaves of this French colony in the largest and most successful slave insurrection.

Blackshirts Troops of Mussolini's fascist regime; the squads received money from Italian landowners to attack socialist leaders.

Black Tuesday (October 29, 1929) Day on which the U.S. stock market crashed, plunging U.S. and international trading systems into crisis and leading the world into the Great Depression.

William Blake (1757–1827) English writer who criticized industrial society and factories; Blake championed the imagination and poetic vision, seeing both as transcending the limits of the material world.

Blitzkrieg German "lightning war" strategy used during the Second World War; the Germans invaded Poland, France, Russia, and other countries with fast-moving and well-coordinated attacks using aircraft, tanks, and other armored vehicles, followed by infantry.

Bloody Sunday On January 22, 1905, the Russian tsar's guards killed 130 demonstrators who were protesting the tsar's mistreatment of workers and the middle class.

Giovanni Boccaccio (1313–1375) Florentine author best known for his *Decameron*, a collection of prose tales about sex, adventure, and trickery, written in the Italian vernacular after the Black Death.

Jean Bodin (1530–1596) French political philosopher whose *Six Books of the Commonwealth* advanced a theory of absolute sovereignty, on the grounds that the state's paramount duty is to maintain order and that monarchs should therefore exercise unlimited power.

Boer War (1898–1902) Conflict between the British army and ethnically European Afrikaners in South Africa, with terrible casualties on both sides.

Boethius (c. 480–524) Roman scholar who sought to preserve aspects of ancient learning by compiling a series of handbooks and anthologies appropriate for Christian readers. His translations of Greek philosophers provided a crucial link between classical Greek thought and the early intellectual culture of Christianity.

Bolsheviks Former members of the Russian Social Democratic Party who advocated the destruction of capitalist political and economic institutions and started the Russian Revolution. In 1918, the Bolsheviks changed their name to the Russian Communist Party. Prominent Bolsheviks included Vladimir Lenin, Joseph Stalin, and Leon Trotsky.

Napoleon Bonaparte (1769–1821) Corsican-born French general who seized power and ruled as dictator from 1799 to 1814. After the successful conquest of much of Europe, he was defeated by Russian, British, and Prussian forces and died in exile.

Boniface VIII Pope (r.1294–1303) whose repeated claims to papal authority were challenged by King Philip IV of France. When Boniface died in 1309 (at the hands of Philip's thugs), the French king moved the papal court from Rome to the French city of Avignon, where it remained until 1378.

Sandro Botticelli (1445–1510) Italian painter devoted to the blending of classical and Christian motifs by using ideas associated with the pagan past to illuminate sacred stories.

bourgeoisie Term for the middle class, derived from the French word for a town-dweller, *bourgeois*.

Boxer Rebellion (1899–1900) Chinese peasant movement that opposed foreign influence, especially that of Christian missionaries; it was finally put down after the Boxers were defeated by a foreign army composed mostly of Japanese, Russian, British, French, and American soldiers.

Tycho Brahe (1546–1601) Danish astronomer who believed that the careful study of the heavens would unlock the secrets of the universe. For over twenty years, he charted the movements of significant objects in the night sky, compiling the finest set of astronomical data in Europe.

British Commonwealth of Nations Formed in 1926, the Commonwealth conferred "dominion status" on Britain's white settler colonies in Canada, Australia, and New Zealand.

Bronze Age (3200–1200 B.C.E.) Name given to the era characterized by the discovery of techniques for smelting bronze (an alloy of copper and tin), which was then the strongest known metal.

Brownshirts German paramilitary troops who dedicated themselves to the Nazi cause in the early 1930s, holding street marches and mass rallies. They engaged in beatings of Jews and confronted anyone who opposed the Nazis.

Lord Byron (1788–1824) Writer and poet whose life helped give the Romantics their reputation as rebels against conformity; Byron was known for his love affairs, his defense of working-class movements, and his passionate engagement in politics, which led to his death in the war for Greek independence.

Byzantium Originally a small settlement located at the mouth of the Black Sea and at the crossroads between Europe and Asia, it was chosen by Constantine as the site for his new imperial capital of Constantinople in 324. Modern historians use this name to refer to the eastern Roman Empire that persisted in this region until 1453, but the inhabitants of that empire referred to themselves as Romans.

Julius Caesar (100–44 B.C.E.) Roman general who conquered the Gauls, invaded Britain, and expanded Rome's territory in Asia Minor. He became the dictator of Rome in 46 B.C.E. His assassination led to the rise of his grandnephew and adopted son, Gaius Octavius Caesar, who ruled the Roman Empire as Caesar Augustus.

caliphs Islamic rulers who claim descent from the prophet Muhammad.

John Calvin (1509–1564) French-born theologian and reformer whose radical form of Protestantism was adopted in many Swiss cities, notably Geneva.

Canary Islands Islands off the western coast of Africa that were colonized by Portugal and Spain in the mid-fifteenth century, after which they became bases for further expeditions around the African coast and across the Atlantic.

Carbonari Underground organization that opposed the Concert of Europe's restoration of monarchies. They flourished in southern Europe during the 1820s, especially in Italy.

Carolingian Derived from the Latin name Carolus (Charles), this term refers to the Frankish dynasty that began with the rise to power of Charles Martel (r. 718–41). At its height under his grandson, Charlemagne (Charles the Great), the dynasty controlled what is now France, Germany, northern Italy, Catalonia, and portions of central Europe. The Carolingian Empire collapsed under the combined weight of Viking raids, economic disintegration, and the growing power of local lords.

Carolingian Renaissance Cultural and intellectual flowering that took place around the court of Charlemagne in the late eighth and early ninth centuries.

Carthage Great maritime empire that grew out of Phoenician trading colonies in North Africa and eventually rivaled the power of Rome. Its wars with Rome, collectively known as the Punic Wars, ended in the destruction of Carthage in 146 B.C.E.

Cassiodorus (c. 490–c. 583) Member of an old Roman family, he was largely responsible for introducing classical learning into the monastic curriculum and for turning monasteries into centers for the collection, preservation, and transmission of knowledge. His *Institutes*, an influential handbook of classical literature for Christian readers, was intended as a preface to more-intensive study of theology and the Bible.

Catholic Church The "universal" (catholic) Christian church based in Rome; it was redefined in the sixteenth century when the Counter-Reformation resulted in the rebirth of the Catholic faith at the Council of Trent.

Margaret Cavendish (1623–1673) English aristocrat and scientist who developed her own speculative natural philosophy and critiqued those who sought to exclude her from scientific debate.

Camillo Benso di Cavour (1810–1861) Prime minister of Piedmont-Sardinia and founder of the Italian Liberal party; he played a key role in the movement for Italian unification under the Piedmontese king, Victor Emmanuel II.

Central Powers First World War alliance between Germany, Austria-Hungary, Bulgaria, and Turkey.

Charlemagne (742–814) As king of the Franks (767–813), Charles "the Great" consolidated much of western Europe under his rule. In 800, he was crowned emperor by the pope in Rome, establishing a problematic precedent that would have wide-ranging consequences for western Europe's relationship with the eastern Roman Empire in Byzantium and for the relationship between the papacy and secular rulers.

Charles I (r. 1625–49) The second Stuart king of England, Charles attempted to rule without the support of Parliament, sparking a controversy that erupted into civil war in 1642. The king's forces were ultimately defeated and Charles himself was executed by act of Parliament, the first time in history that a reigning king was legally deposed and executed by his own government.

Charles II (1630–1685) Nominally King of England, Ireland, and Scotland after his father Charles I's execution in 1649, Charles II lived in exile until he was restored to the throne in 1660. Influenced by his cousin, King Louis XIV of France, he presided over an opulent royal court until his death.

Chartists Working-class movement in Britain that called for reform of the British political system during the 1840s. They were supporters of the "People's Charter," which had six demands: universal white male suffrage, secret ballots, an end to property qualifications as a condition of public office, annual parliamentary elections, salaries for members of the House of Commons, and equal electoral districts.

Geoffrey Chaucer (1340–1400) English poet whose collection of versified stories, *The Canterbury Tales*, features characters from a variety of different classes.

Christine de Pisan (c. 1364–c. 1431) Born in Italy, Christine spent her adult life attached to the French court and, after her husband's death, became the first laywoman to earn her living by writing. She is the author of treatises on warfare and chivalry as well as of books and pamphlets that challenge long-standing misogynistic claims.

Church of England Protestant denomination founded by Henry VIII in the 1530s as a consequence of his break with the authority of the Roman pope.

Winston Churchill (1874–1965) British prime minister who led the country during the Second World War. He also coined the phrase "Iron Curtain" in a speech at Missouri's Westminster College in 1946.

Cicero (106–43 B.C.E.) Influential Roman senator, orator, Stoic philosopher, and prose stylist; his published writings still form the basis of instruction in classical Latin grammar and usage.

Cincinnatus (519–c. 430 B.C.E.) Legendary citizen-farmer of Rome who reluctantly accepted an appointment as dictator. After defeating Rome's enemies, he is said to have left his political office and returned to his farm.

Civil Constitution of the Clergy Charter issued by the French National Assembly in 1790. It decreed that all bishops and priests should be subject to the authority of the state. Their salaries were to be paid out of the public treasury, and they were required to swear allegiance to the new state, making it clear they served France rather than Rome. The Assembly's aim was to make the Catholic Church of France a truly national and civil institution.

civilizing mission Argument made by Europeans to justify colonial expansion in the nineteenth century. Supporters of this idea believed that Europeans had a duty to impose Western ideas of economic and political progress on the indigenous peoples they ruled over in their colonies. In practice, the colonial powers often found that ambitious plans to impose European practices on colonial subjects led to unrest that threatened the stability of colonial rule, and by the early twentieth century most colonial powers were more cautious in their plans for political or cultural transformation.

Civil Rights Movement The Second World War increased African American migration from the American South to northern cities, intensifying a drive for rights, dignity, and independence. By 1960, civil rights groups had started organizing boycotts and demonstrations directed at discrimination against blacks in the South. During the 1960s, civil rights laws passed under President Lyndon B. Johnson did bring African Americans some equality with regard to voting rights and, to a much lesser degree, school desegregation. However, racism continued in areas such as housing, job opportunities, and the economic development of African American communities.

Civil War (1861–1865) Conflict between the northern and southern states of America that cost over 600,000 lives; this struggle led to the abolition of slavery in the United States.

classical learning Study of ancient Greek and Latin texts. After Christianity became the only legal religion of the Roman Empire, scholars needed to find a way to make classical learning applicable to a Christian way of life. Christian monks played a significant role in resolving this problem by reinterpreting the classics for a Christian audience.

Cluny Powerful Benedictine monastery, founded in 910, whose enormous wealth and prestige would derive from its independence from secular authorities as well as from its wide network of daughter houses (priories).

Cold War (1945–1991) Ideological, political, and economic conflict in which the USSR and Eastern Europe opposed the United States and Western Europe in the decades after the Second World War. The Cold War's origins lay in the breakup of the wartime alliance between the United States and the Soviet Union in 1945 and resulted in a division of Europe into two spheres: the West, commited to market capitalism, and the East, which sought to build socialist republics in areas under Soviet Control. The Cold War ended with the collapse of the Soviet Union in 1991.

collectivization Stalin's plan for nationalizing agricultural production in the USSR, begun in 1929. Twenty-five million peasants were forced to give up their land and join 250,000 large collective farms. Many who resisted were deported to labor camps in the Far East, and Stalin's government cut off food rations to those areas most resistant to collectivization. In the ensuing man-made famines, millions of people starved to death.

Columbian Exchange The widespread exchange of peoples, plants, animals, diseases, goods, and culture between the African and Eurasian landmass (on the one hand) and the region that encompasses the Americas, Australia, and the Pacific Islands (on the other); precipitated by the first voyage of Columbus in 1492.

Christopher Columbus (1451–1506) Genoese sailor who persuaded King Ferdinand and Queen Isabella of Spain to fund his expedition across the Atlantic, with the purpose of discovering a new trade route to Asia. His miscalculations landed him in the Bahamas and the island of Hispaniola in 1492.

Commercial Revolution A period of economic development in Europe lasting from c. 1500 to c. 1800. Advances in agriculture and handicraft production, combined with the expansion of trade networks in the Atlantic world, brought new wealth and new kinds of commercial activity to Europe. The commercial revolution prepared the way for the industrial revolution of the 1800s.

Committee of Public Safety Political body during the French Revolution that was controlled by the Jacobins, who defended the revolution by executing thousands during the Reign of Terror (September 1793–July 1794).

commune Community of individuals who have banded together in a sworn association, with the aim of establishing their independence and setting up their own form of representative government. Many medieval towns originally founded by lords or monasteries gained their independence through such methods.

The Communist Manifesto Radical pamphlet by Karl Marx (1818–1883) and Friedrich Engels (1820–1895) that predicted the downfall of the capitalist system and its replacement by a classless egalitarian society. Marx and Engels believed that this revolution would be accomplished by industrial and agricultural workers (the proletariat).

Compromise of 1867 Agreement between the Habsburgs and the peoples living in Hungarian parts of the empire that re-established Hungarian sovereignty, thus creating the Austro-Hungarian Empire.

Concert of Europe (1814–1815) Series of diplomatic agreements, designed primarily by Austrian minister Klemens von Metternich between 1814 and 1848 and supported by other European powers until 1914, to maintain a balance of power on the Continent and to prevent destabilizing social and political change in Europe.

conciliarism Doctrine developed in the thirteenth and fourteenth centuries to counter the growing power of the papacy; conciliarism holds that papal authority should be subject to a council of the Church at large. Conciliarists emerged as a dominant force after the Council of Constance (1414–18) but were eventually outmatched by a rejuvenated papacy.

Congress of Vienna (1814–15) International conference to reorganize Europe after the downfall of Napoleon and the French Revolution. European monarchies restored the Bourbon family to the French throne, and agreed to respect each other's borders and to cooperate in guarding against future revolutions and wars.

conquistador Spanish term for "conqueror," applied to the mercenaries and adventurers who campaigned against indigenous peoples in central and southern America.

conservatives In the nineteenth century, European conservatives aimed to legitimize and solidify the monarchy's authority and the hierarchical social order. They believed that change had to be slow, incremental, and managed so that the structures of authority were strengthened.

Constantine (275–337) The first emperor of Rome to convert to Christianity, Constantine came to power in 312. In 324, he founded a new imperial capital, Constantinople, on the site of a maritime settlement in Asia Minor known as Byzantium.

Constantinople City founded by the emperor Constantine on the site of a village called Byzantium; it became the new capital of the Roman Empire in 324 and continued to be the seat of imperial power after its capture by the Ottoman Turks in 1453. It is now known as Istanbul.

contract theory of government Theory developed by Englishman John Locke (1632–1704) which posits that government authority is both contractual and conditional; therefore, if a government has abused its given authority, society has the right to dissolve it and create another.

Nicholaus Copernicus (1473–1543) Polish astronomer who advanced the idea that the earth revolves around the sun.

cosmopolitanism Stemming from the Greek word meaning "universal city," the culture characteristic of the Hellenistic world challenged and transformed the more narrow worldview of the Greek polis.

cotton gin Invented by Eli Whitney in 1793, this device mechanized the process of separating cotton seeds from the cotton fiber, which sped up the production of cotton and reduced its price. This change made slavery profitable in the United States.

Council of Constance (1417–20) A meeting of clergy and theologians in an effort to resolve the Great Schism within the Roman Church. The council deposed all rival papal candidates and elected a new pope, Martin V, but it also adopted the doctrine of conciliarism, which holds that the supreme authority within the Church rests with a representative general council and not with the pope. However, Martin V himself was an opponent of this doctrine and refused to be bound by it.

Council of Trent Name given to a series of meetings held in the Italian city of Trent (Trento) between 1545 and 1563, when leaders of the Roman Church reaffirmed Catholic doctrine and instituted internal reforms.

Counter-Reformation Movement to counter the Protestant Reformation, initiated by the Catholic Church at the Council of Trent in 1545.

coup d'état French term for the overthrow of an established government by a group of conspirators, usually with military support.

Crimean War (1854–56) War waged by Russia against Great Britain and France. Spurred by Russia's encroachment on Ottoman territories, the conflict revealed Russia's military weakness when Russian forces fell to British and French troops.

Cuban missile crisis (1962) Diplomatic standoff between the United States and the Soviet Union that was provoked by the Soviet Union's attempt to base nuclear missiles in Cuba; it brought the world closer to nuclear war than ever before or since.

Cuius regio, eius religio A Latin phrase meaning "as the ruler, so the religion." Adopted as a part of the settlement of the Peace of Augsburg in 1555, it meant that those principalities ruled by Lutherans would have Lutheranism as their official religion and those ruled by Catholics would practice Catholicism.

cult of domesticity Concept associated with Victorian England that idealized women as nurturing wives and mothers.

cult of the Virgin Beliefs and practices associated with the veneration of Mary, the mother of Jesus, which became increasingly popular in the twelfth century.

cuneiform Early writing system that began to develop in Mesopotamia in the fourth millennium B.C.E. By 3100 B.C.E., its distinctive markings were impressed on clay tablets using a wedge-shaped stylus.

Cyrus the Great (c. 585–529 B.C.E.) As architect of the Persian Empire, Cyrus extended his dominion over a vast territory stretching from the Persian Gulf to the Mediterranean and incorporating the ancient civilizations of Mesopotamia. His successors ruled this Persian Empire as "Great Kings."

Darius (521–486 B.C.E.) The Persian emperor whose conflict with Aristagoras, the Greek ruler of Miletus, ignited the Persian Wars. In 490 B.C.E., Darius sent a large army to punish the Athenians for their intervention in Persian imperial affairs, but this force was defeated by Athenian hoplites on the plain of Marathon.

Charles Darwin (1809–1882) British naturalist who wrote *On the Origin of Species* (1859) and developed the theory of natural selection to explain the evolution of living organisms.

D-Day (June 6, 1944) Date of the Allied invasion of Normandy, under General Dwight Eisenhower, to liberate Western Europe from German occupation.

Decembrists Russian army officers who were influenced by events in France and formed secret societies that espoused liberal governance. They were put down by Tsar Nicholas I in December 1825.

Declaration of Independence (1776) Historic document stating the principles of government on which the United States was founded.

Declaration of the Rights of Man and of the Citizen (1789) French charter of liberties formulated by the National Assembly during the French Revolution. The seventeen articles later became the preamble to the new constitution, which the assembly finished in 1791.

democracy In ancient Greece, the form of government that allowed a class of propertied male citizens to participate in the governance of their polis, but excluded women, slaves, and citizens without property from the political process. As a result, the ruling class amounted to only a small percentage of the entire population.

René Descartes (1596–1650) French philosopher and mathematician who emphasized the use of deductive reasoning.

Denis Diderot (1713–1784) French philosophe and author who was the guiding force behind the publication of the *Encyclopedia*, which showed how reason could be applied to nearly all realms of thought; it aimed to be a compendium of all human knowledge.

Dien Bien Phu (1954) Defining battle in the war between French colonialists and the Viet Minh that secured North Vietnam for Ho Chi Minh and his army and left the south to form its own government, to be supported by France and the United States.

Diet of Worms The select council of the Roman Catholic Church that convened in the German city of Worms and condemned Martin Luther on a charge of heresy in 1521.

Diocletian (245–316) As emperor of Rome from 284 to 305, Diocletian recognized that the empire could not be governed by one man in one place. His solution was to divide the empire into four parts, each with its own imperial ruler, but he himself remained the dominant ruler of the resulting tetrarchy (rule of four). He also initiated the Great Persecution, a time when many Christians became martyrs to their faith.

Directory (1795–1799) Executive committee that governed revolutionary France after the fall of Robespierre and held control until the coup of Napoleon Bonaparte.

Discourse on Method Philosophical treatise by René Descartes (1596–1650) proposing that the path to knowledge was through logical deduction, beginning with one's own self: "I think, therefore I am."

Dominican Order Also called the Order of Preachers, it was founded by Dominic of Osma (1170–1221), a Castilian preacher and theologian, and approved by Innocent III in 1216. The order was dedicated to the rooting out of heresy and the conversion of Jews and Muslims. Many of its members held teaching positions in European universities and contributed to the development of medieval philosophy and theology. Others became the leading administrators of the Inquisition.

Dominion in the British Commonwealth Canadian promise to maintain their fealty to the British crown, even after their independence in 1867; later applied to Australia and New Zealand.

Dreyfus Affair The 1894 French scandal surrounding accusations that a Jewish captain, Alfred Dreyfus, had sold military secrets to the Germans. Convicted, Dreyfus was sentenced to solitary confinement for life. However, after public outcry, it was revealed that the trial documents were forgeries, and Dreyfus was pardoned after a second trial in 1899. In 1906, he was fully exonerated and reinstated in the army. The affair revealed the depths of popular anti-Semitism in France.

Alexander Dubček (1921–1992) Communist leader of the Czechoslovakian government who advocated for "socialism with a human face." He encouraged debate within the party, academic and artistic freedom, and less censorship, which led to the "Prague spring" of 1968. People in other parts of Eastern Europe began to demonstrate in support of Dubček and to demand their own reforms. When Dubček tried to democratize the Communist party and failed to attend a meeting of the Warsaw Pact, the Soviets sent tanks and troops into Prague and ousted Dubček and his allies.

Duma The Russian parliament, created in response to the revolution of 1905.

Dunkirk French port on the English Channel where the British and French forces retreated after sustaining heavy losses against the German military early in World War II. Between May 27 and June 4, 1940, the Royal Navy evacuated over 300,000 troops using commercial and pleasure boats.

Eastern Front Battlefront between Germany and the Soviet Union during the First and Second World Wars.

East India Company (1600–1858) British charter company created to outperform Portuguese and Spanish traders in the Far East; in the eighteenth century the company became, in effect, the ruler of a large part of India. There was also a Dutch East India Company.

Edict of Nantes (1598) Proclamation issued by Henry IV of France in an effort to end religious violence; it declared France to be a Catholic country but tolerated some forms of Protestant worship.

Edward I of England King of England from 1272 to his death in 1307, Edward presided over the creation of new legal and bureaucratic institutions in his realm, violently subjugated the Welsh, and attempted to colonize Scotland. He expelled English Jews from his domain in 1290.

Eleanor of Aquitaine (1122–1204) Ruler of the wealthy province of Aquitaine and wife of Louis VII of France, Eleanor had her marriage annulled in order to marry the young count of Anjou, Henry Plantagenet, who became King Henry of England a year later. Mother of two future kings of England, she was an important patron of the arts.

Elizabeth I (1533–1603) Protestant daughter of Henry VIII and his second wife, Anne Boleyn, Elizabeth succeeded her sister Mary as the second queen regnant of England (r. 1558–1603).

emancipation of the serfs (1861) The abolition of serfdom was central to Tsar Alexander II's program of modernization and reform, but it produced a limited amount of change. Former serfs now had legal rights. However, farmland was granted to the village communes instead of to individuals. Most of this land was of poor quality and the former serfs had to pay for it in installments to the village commune.

emperor Originally the term for any conquering commander of the Roman army whose victories merited celebration in an official triumph; after Augustus seized power in 27 B.C.E., it was the title born by the sole ruler of the Roman Empire.

empire Centralized political entity consolidated through the conquest and colonization of other nations or peoples in order to benefit the ruler and/or his homeland.

Enabling Act (1933) Emergency act passed by the Reichstag (German parliament) that helped transform Hitler from Germany's chancellor, or prime minister, into a dictator, following the suspicious burning of the Reichstag building and a suspension of civil liberties.

enclosure Long process of privatizing what had been public agricultural land in eighteenth-century Britain; it helped to stimulate the development of commercial agriculture and forced many people in rural areas to seek work in cities during the early stages of industrialization.

The Encyclopedia Joint venture of French philosophe writers, led by Denis Diderot (1713–1784), which proposed to summarize all modern knowledge in a multivolume, illustrated work with over 70,000 articles.

Friedrich Engels (1820–1895) German social and political philosopher who collaborated with Karl Marx on *The Communist Manifesto* and many other publications.

English Civil War (1642–49) Conflicts between the English Parliament and King Charles I erupted into civil war, which ended in the defeat of the royalists and the execution of Charles on charges of high treason. A short time later, Parliament abolished the monarchy and hereditary House of Lords, and England was declared a Commonwealth.

English Navigation Act of 1651 English law stipulating that only English ships could carry goods between the mother country and its colonies.

Enlightenment Intellectual movement in eighteenth-century Europe marked by a belief in human betterment through the application of reason to solve social, economic, and political problems.

Epicureanism Philosophical position articulated by Epicurus of Athens (c. 342–270 B.C.E.), who rejected the idea of an ordered universe governed by divine forces; instead, he emphasized individual agency and proposed that the highest good is the pursuit of pleasure.

Desiderius Erasmus (c. 1469–1536) Dutch-born scholar, social commentator, and Catholic humanist whose new translation of the Bible influenced the theology of Martin Luther.

Estates-General Representative body of the three estates in France. In 1789, King Louis XVI summoned the Estates-General to meet for the first time since 1614 because it seemed to be the only solution to France's worsening economic crisis and financial chaos.

Etruscans Settlers of the Italian peninsula who dominated the region from the late Bronze Age until the rise of the Roman Republic in the sixth century B.C.E.

Euclid (fl. 300 B.C.E.) Hellenistic mathematician whose *Elements of Geometry* forms the basis of modern geometry.

eugenics Greek term, meaning "good birth," referring to the project of "breeding" a superior human race. Eugenics was popularly championed by scientists, politicians, and social critics in the late nineteenth and early twentieth centuries.

European Common Market (1957) The Treaty of Rome created the European Economic Community (EEC), or Common Market. The original members were France, West Germany, Italy, Belgium, Holland, and Luxembourg. The EEC sought to abolish trade barriers between its members and it pledged itself to common external tariffs, the free movement of labor and capital among the member nations, and uniform wage structures and social security systems to create similar working conditions in all member countries.

European Union (EU) Successor organization to the European Economic Community or European Common Market, formed by the Maastricht Treaty, which took effect in 1993. Currently twenty-eight member states compose the EU, which has a governing council, an international court, and a parliament. Over time, member states of the EU have relinquished some of their sovereignty, and cooperation has evolved into a community with a single currency, the euro.

Exclusion Act of 1882 U.S. congressional act prohibiting nearly all immigration from China to the United States; it was fueled by animosity toward Chinese workers in the American West.

existentialism Philosophical movement that arose out of the Second World War and emphasized the absurdity of the human condition. Led by Jean-Paul Sartre and Albert Camus, existen-

tialists encouraged humans to take responsibility for their own decisions and dilemmas.

expulsion of the Jews European rulers began to expel their Jewish subjects from their kingdoms beginning in the 1280s, mostly due to their inability to repay the money they had extorted from Jewish money-lenders but also as a result of escalating anti-Semitism in the wake of the Crusades. Jews were also expelled from the Rhineland in the fourteenth century and from Spain in 1492.

fascism Doctrine propounded by Italian dictator Benito Mussolini, which emphasized three main ideas: statism ("nothing above the state, nothing outside the state, nothing against the state"), nationalism, and militarism. Its name derives from the Latin *fasces*, a symbol of Roman imperial power adopted by Mussolini.

Fashoda Incident (1898) Disagreements between the French and the British over land claims in North Africa led to a standoff between armies of the two nations at the Sudanese town of Fashoda. The crisis was resolved diplomatically. France ceded southern Sudan to Britain in exchange for a stop to further expansion by the British.

The Feminine Mystique Groundbreaking book by feminist Betty Friedan (1921–2006), which offered various definitions of *femininity* and explored how women internalized those definitions.

Franz Ferdinand (1863–1914) Archduke of Austria and heir to the Austro-Hungarian Empire; his assassination led to the beginning of the First World War.

Ferdinand (1452–1516) **and Isabella** (1451–1504) In 1469, Ferdinand of Aragon married the heiress to Castile, Isabella. Their union allowed them to pursue several ambitious policies, including the conquest of Granada, the last Muslim principality in Spain, and the expulsion of Spain's large Jewish community. In 1492, Isabella granted three ships to Christopher Columbus of Genoa (Italy), who went on to claim portions of the New World for Spain.

Fertile Crescent Region of fertile land in what is now Syria, Israel, Turkey, eastern Iraq, and western Iran that was able to sustain settlements due to its wetter climate and its suitability for agriculture. Some of the earliest known civilizations emerged there between 9000 and 4500 B.C.E.

feudalism Problematic modern term that attempts to explain the diffusion of power in medieval Europe and the many different kinds of political, social, and economic relationships that were forged through the giving and receiving of fiefs (*feoda*). But because it is anachronistic and inadequate, this term has been rejected by most historians of the medieval period.

First Crusade (1095–1099) Campaign launched by Pope Urban II in response to a request from the Byzantine emperor Alexius Comnenus, who had asked for a small contingent of knights to assist him in fighting Turkish forces in Anatolia; Urban instead directed the crusaders' energies toward the Holy Land and the recapture of Jerusalem, promising those who took up the cross (*crux*) that they would merit eternal salvation if they died in the attempt. This crusade prompted attacks against Jews throughout Europe and resulted in six subsequent—and ultimately unsuccessful—military campaigns.

First World War A total war from August 1914 to November 1918, involving the armies of Britain, France, and Russia (the Allies), who eventually prevailed against Germany, Austria-Hungary, and the Ottoman Empire (the Central Powers). Italy joined the Allies in 1915, and the United States joined them in 1917, helping to tip the balance in favor of the Allies, who also drew upon the populations and raw materials of their colonial possessions. Also known as the Great War and World War I.

Five Pillars of Islam Muslim doctrine that salvation is only assured through observance of five basic precepts: submission to God's will as described in the teachings of Muhammad (the Qur'an), frequent prayer, ritual fasting, the giving of alms, and an annual pilgrimage to Mecca (the Hajj).

Five-Year Plan Soviet effort launched under Stalin in 1928 to replace the free-market economy with a state-owned and state-managed economy in order to promote rapid economic development over a five-year period and thereby "catch and overtake" the leading capitalist countries. The First Five-Year Plan was followed by the Second Five-Year Plan (1933–37) and so on, until the collapse of the Soviet Union in 1991.

fly-shuttle Invented by John Kay in 1733, this device sped up the process of weaving.

Fourteen Points President Woodrow Wilson's proposal for a diplomatic foundation on which to build peace in the world after the First World War. The Fourteen Points called for an end to secret treaties, "open covenants, openly arrived at," freedom of the seas, the removal of international tariffs, the reduction of arms, the "self-determination of peoples," and the establishment of a League of Nations to settle international conflicts.

Franciscan Order Also known as the Order of the Friars Minor. The earliest Franciscans were followers of Francis of Assisi (1182–1226) and strove, like him, to imitate the life and example of Jesus. The clerical order was formally established by Pope Innocent III in 1209. Its special mission was the care and instruction of the urban poor.

Frankfurt Parliament (1848–49) Failed attempt to create a unified Germany under constitutional principles. In 1849, the assembly offered the crown of a new German nation to Frederick William IV of Prussia, but he refused the offer and suppressed a brief protest. The delegates went home disillusioned.

Frederick the Great (1712–1786) Prussian ruler (r. 1740–86) who engaged the nobility in maintaining a strong military and bureaucracy and led Prussian armies to notable military victories. He also encouraged Enlightenment rationalism and artistic endeavors.

French Revolution of 1789 In 1788, a severe financial crisis forced the French monarchy to convene an assembly known as the Estates General, representing the three estates of the realm: the clergy, the nobility, and the commons (known as the Third Estate). When the Estates General met in 1789, representatives of the Third Estate demanded major constitutional changes, and when the king and his government proved uncooperative, these delegates broke with the other two estates and renamed themselves the National Assembly, demanding a written constitution. The position of the National Assembly was confirmed by a popular uprising in Paris, and the king was forced to accept the transformation of France into a constitutional monarchy. This constitutional phase of the revolution lasted until 1792, when the pressures of foreign invasion and the emergence of a more-radical revolutionary movement led to the collapse of the monarchy and the establishment of a republic.

French Revolution of 1830 French popular revolt against Charles X's July Ordinances of 1830, which dissolved the French Chamber of Deputies and restricted suffrage to exclude almost everyone except the nobility. After several days of violence, Charles abdicated the throne and was replaced by a constitutional monarch, Louis Philippe.

French Revolution of 1848 Revolution overthrowing Louis-Philippe in February, 1848, leading to the formation of the Second Republic (1848–52). Initially enjoying broad support from both the middle classes and laborers in Paris, the new government became more conservative after elections in which the French peasantry participated for the first time. A workers' revolt was violently repressed in June 1848, and in December 1848, Napoleon Bonaparte's nephew, Louis-Napoleon Bonaparte, was elected president. In 1852, Louis-Napoleon declared himself emperor and abolished the republic.

Sigmund Freud (1856–1939) Austrian physician who founded the discipline of psychoanalysis and suggested that human behavior was largely motivated by unconscious and irrational forces.

Galileo Galilei (1564–1642) Italian physicist and inventor; the implications of his ideas raised the ire of the Catholic Church, and he was forced to retract most of his findings.

Gallipoli (1915) In the First World War, a combined force of French, British, Australian and New Zealand troops tried to invade Turkey's Gallipoli Peninsula, in the first large-scale amphibious attack in history, and seize it from the Turks. After seven months of fighting, the Allies had lost 200,000 soldiers. Defeated, they withdrew.

Mohandas K. (Mahatma) Gandhi (1869–1948) Indian leader who advocated nonviolent noncooperation to protest colonial rule and helped win home rule for India in 1947.

Giuseppe Garibaldi (1807–1882) Italian revolutionary leader who led the fight to free Sicily and Naples from the Habsburg Empire; the lands were then peaceably annexed by Sardinia to produce a unified Italy.

Gaul Region of the Roman Empire that was home to the Celtic people of that name, comprising modern France, Belgium, and western Germany.

Geneva Conference (1954) International conference to restore peace in Korea and Indochina. The chief participants were the United States, the Soviet Union, Great Britain, France, the People's Republic of China, North Korea, South Korea, Vietnam, the Viet Minh party, Laos, and Cambodia. The conference resulted in the division of North and South Vietnam.

Genoa Maritime city on Italy's northwestern coast; the Genoese were active in trading ventures along the Silk Road and in the establishment of trading colonies in the Mediterranean. They were also involved in the world of finance and backed the commercial ventures of other powers, especially Spain's.

German Democratic Republic Communist nation founded from the Soviet zone of occupation of Germany after the Second World War; also known as East Germany.

German Social Democratic party Founded in 1875, it was the most powerful socialist party in Europe before 1917.

Gilgamesh Sumerian ruler of the city of Uruk around 2700 B.C.E.; Gilgamesh became the hero of one of the world's oldest epics, which circulated orally for nearly a millennium before being written down.

Giotto (c. 1266–1337) Florentine painter and architect who is often considered a forerunner of the Renaissance.

glasnost Introduced by Soviet leader Mikhail Gorbachev in June 1987, *glasnost* was one of the five major policies that constituted *perestroika* ("Restructuring"). Often translated into English as "openness," *glasnost* called for transparency in Soviet government and institutional activities by reducing censorship in mass media and lifting significant bans on the political, intellectual, and cultural lives of Soviet civilians.

globalization Term used to describe political, social, and economic networks that span the globe. Such global exchanges are not limited to nation-states and in recent decades are associated with new technologies such as the Internet. Globalization is not new, however, as human cultures and economies have been in contact with one another for centuries.

Glorious Revolution The overthrow of King James II of England and the installation of his Protestant daughter, Mary Stuart, and her husband, William of Orange, to the throne in 1688 and 1689. It is widely regarded as the founding moment in the development of a constitutional monarchy in Britain, while also establishing a more favorable climate for the economic and political growth of the English commercial classes.

Gold Coast Name that European mariners and merchants gave to that part of West Equatorial Africa from which gold and slaves were exported. Originally controlled by the Portuguese, this area later became the British colony of the Gold Coast (present-day Ghana).

Mikhail Gorbachev (b. 1931) Soviet leader who attempted to reform the Soviet Union through his programs of glasnost and perestroika in the late 1980s. He encouraged open discussions in other countries in the Soviet bloc, which helped inspire "velvet" revolutions throughout Eastern Europe. Eventually the political, social, and economic upheaval he had unleashed would lead to the breakup of the Soviet Union.

Gothic style Type of graceful architecture emerging in twelfth- and thirteenth-century England and France. The style is characterized by pointed arches, delicate decoration, and large windows.

Olympe de Gouges (1748–1793) French political radical and feminist whose *Declaration of the Rights of Woman and the Female Citizen* demanded an equal place for women in France.

Great Depression Global economic crisis following the U.S. stock market crash on October 29, 1929, and ending with the onset of the Second World War.

Great Famine Period of terrible hunger and deprivation in Europe that peaked between 1315 and 1317, caused by a cooling of the climate and by environmental degradation due to over-farming. It is estimated to have reduced the population of Europe by 10–15 percent.

Great Fear (1789) Following the outbreak of revolution in Paris, fear spread throughout the French countryside, as rumors circulated that armies of brigands or royal troops were coming. The peasants and villagers organized into militias, while others attacked and burned the manor houses in order to destroy the records of manorial dues.

Great Schism (1378–1417) Also known as the Great Western Schism, to distinguish it from the longstanding rupture between the Greek East and Latin West. During the schism, the Roman Church was divided between two (and, ultimately, three) competing popes. Each pope claimed to be legitimate and each denounced the heresy of the others.

Great Terror (1936–38) The systematic murder of nearly a million people and the deportation of another million and a half to labor camps by Stalin's regime in an attempt to consolidate power and eliminate perceived enemies.

Greek East After the founding of Constantinople, the eastern Greek-speaking half of the Roman Empire grew more populous, prosperous, and central to imperial policy. Its inhabitants considered themselves to be the true heirs of Rome, and their own Orthodox Church to be the true manifestation of Jesus's ministry.

Greek independence Nationalists in Greece revolted against the Ottoman Empire and fought a war that ended with Greek independence in 1827. They received crucial help from British, French, and Russian troops as well as widespread sympathy throughout Europe.

Pope Gregory I (r. 590–604) Also known as Gregory the Great, he was the first bishop of Rome to successfully negotiate a more universal role for the papacy. His political and theological agenda widened the rift between the western Latin (Catholic) Church and the eastern Greek (Orthodox) Church in Byzantium. He also articulated the Church's official position on the status of Jews, promoted affective approaches to religious worship, encouraged the Benedictine monastic movement, and sponsored missionary expeditions.

Guernica Basque town bombed by German planes in April 1937 during the Spanish Civil War. Guernica is also the subject of Pablo Picasso's famous painting from the same year.

guilds Professional organizations in commercial towns that regulated business and safeguarded the privileges of those practicing a particular craft. Often identical to confraternities ("brotherhoods").

Gulag Vast system of forced labor camps under the Soviet regime; it originated in 1919 in a small monastery near the Arctic Circle and spread throughout the Soviet Union. Penal labor was required of both ordinary criminals and those accused of political crimes. Tens of millions of people were sent to the camps between 1928 and 1953; the exact figure is unknown.

Gulf War (1991) Armed conflict between Iraq and a coalition of thirty-two nations, including the United States, Britain, Egypt, France, and Saudi Arabia. The war was prompted Iraq's invasion of Kuwait on August 2, 1990.

Johannes Gutenberg (c. 1398–1468) European inventor of the printing press; his shop in Mainz produced the first printed book—a Bible—between the years 1453 and 1455.

Habsburg Dynasty Powerful European dynasty that first came to power in the eleventh century in a region now part of Switzerland. Early generations of Habsburgs consolidated their control over neighboring German-speaking lands; through strategic marriages with other royal lines, later rulers eventually controlled a substantial part of Europe—including much of central Europe, the Netherlands, and even Spain and all its colonies for a time. In practice, the Holy Roman Emperor was chosen from a member of the Habsburg lineage. By the latter half of the seventeenth century, the Austrian Habsburg Empire was made of up nearly 300 nominally autonomous dynastic kingdoms, principalities, duchies, and archbishoprics.

Hagia Sophia Enormous church dedicated to "Holy Wisdom," built in Constantinople at the behest of the emperor Justinian in the sixth century C.E. When Constantinople fell to Ottoman forces in 1453, it became an important mosque.

Haitian Revolution (1802–4) In 1802, Napoleon sought to reassert French control of the colony of Saint-Domingue, but stiff resistance and yellow fever crushed the French army. In 1804, Jean-Jacques Dessalines, a general in the army of former slaves, declared the independent state of Haiti. (See **slave revolt in Saint-Domingue**.)

Hajj The annual pilgrimage to Mecca; an obligation for Muslims.

Hammurabi Ruler of Babylon from 1792 to 1750 B.C.E.; Hammurabi issued a collection of laws that were greatly influential in the Near East and which constitute the world's oldest surviving legal code.

Harlem Renaissance Cultural movement in the 1920s that was based in Harlem, a part of New York City with a large African American population. The movement gave voice to black novelists, poets, painters, and musicians, many of whom used their art to protest racial subordination.

Hatshepsut (r. 1479–1458 C.E.) As Egyptian pharaoh during the New Kingdom, she launched several successful military campaigns and extended trade and diplomacy. She was an ambitious builder who probably constructed the first tomb in the Valley of the Kings. Though she never pretended to be a man, she was routinely portrayed with a masculine figure and a ceremonial beard.

Hebrews Originally a pastoral people divided among several tribes, the Hebrews were briefly united under the rule of David and his son, Solomon, who promoted the worship of a single god, Yahweh, and constructed the first temple at the new capital city of Jerusalem. After Solomon's death, the Hebrew tribes were divided between the two kingdoms of Israel and Judah, which were eventually conquered by the Neo-Assyrian and Chaldean empires. It was in captivity that the Hebrews came to define themselves through worship of Yahweh and to develop a religion, Judaism, that could exist outside of Judea. They were liberated by the Persian king Cyrus the Great in 539 B.C.E.

Hellenistic art The art of the Hellenistic period bridged the tastes, ideals, and customs of classical Greece and those that would be more characteristic of Rome. Striving to emulate Hellenistic city planning and civic culture, the Romans thereby exported Hellenistic culture to their own far-flung colonies in western Europe.

Hellenistic culture The "Greek-like" culture that dominated the ancient world in the wake of Alexander's conquests.

Hellenistic kingdoms Following the death of Alexander the Great, his vast empire was divided into three separate states: Ptolemaic Egypt (under the rule of the general Ptolemy and his successors), Seleucid Asia (ruled by the general Seleucus and his heirs) and Antigonid Greece (governed by Antigonus of Macedonia). Each state maintained its independence, but the shared characteristics of Greco-Macedonian rule and a shared Greek culture and heritage bound them together in a united cosmopolitan world.

Hellenistic world The various Western civilizations of antiquity that were loosely united by shared Greek language and culture, especially around the eastern Mediterranean.

Heloise of Argentevil (c. 1090–1164) One of the foremost scholars of her time, she became the pupil and the wife of the philosopher and teacher Peter Abelard. In later life, she was the founder of a new religious order for women.

Henry IV of Germany King of Germany and Holy Roman Emperor from 1056—when he ascended the throne at the age of six years old—until his death in 1106. Henry's reign was first weakened by conflict with the Saxon nobility and later marked by the Investiture Controversy with Pope Gregory VII.

Henry VIII (1491–1547) King of England from 1509 until his death, Henry rejected the authority of the Roman Church in 1534 when the pope refused to annul his marriage to his queen, Catherine of Aragon; he became the founder of the Church of England.

Henry of Navarre (1553–1610) Crowned King Henry IV of France, he renounced his Protestantism but granted limited toleration for Huguenots (French Protestants) by the Edict of Nantes in 1598.

Prince Henry the Navigator (1394–1460) A brother of the king of Portugal, Henry encouraged the exploration and conquest of western Africa and the trade in gold and slaves.

hieroglyphs Writing system of ancient Egypt, based on a complicated series of pictorial symbols. It fell out of use when Egypt was absorbed into the Roman Empire and was only deciphered after the discovery of the Rosetta Stone in the early nineteenth century.

Hildegard of Bingen (1098–1179) A powerful German abbess, theologian, scientist, musician, and visionary who claimed to receive regular revelations from God. Although highly influential in her own day, she was never officially canonized by the Church, in part because her strong personality no longer accorded with the shifting ideal of female piety.

Hiroshima Japanese port devastated by an atomic bomb on August 6, 1945.

Adolf Hitler (1889–1945) Author of *Mein Kampf* and leader of the National Socialists (Nazis) who became chancellor of Germany in 1933. Hitler and his National Socialists Nazi regime started the Second World War and orchestrated the systematic murder of over 6 million Jews.

Hitler-Stalin Pact (1939) Treaty between Nazi Germany and the Soviet Union, which promised the USSR a share of Poland, Finland, the Baltic States, and Bessarabia in the event of a

German invasion of Poland, which began shortly thereafter, on September 1, 1939.

HIV epidemic The first cases of HIV-AIDS appeared in the late 1970s. As HIV-AIDS became a global crisis, international organizations recognized the need for an early, swift, and comprehensive response to future outbreaks of disease.

Thomas Hobbes (1588–1679) English political philosopher whose *Leviathan* (1651) argued that any form of government capable of protecting its subjects' lives and property might act as an all-powerful sovereign. This government should be allowed to trample over both liberty and property for the sake of its own survival and that of its subjects. For in his natural state, Hobbes argued, man was like "a wolf" toward other men.

Holy Roman Empire Loosely allied collection of lands in central and western Europe ruled by the kings of Germany (and later Austria) from the twelfth century until 1806. Its origins are usually identified with the empire of Charlemagne, the Frankish king who was crowned emperor of Rome by the pope in 800.

homage Ceremony in which an individual becomes the "man" (French: *homme*) of a lord.

Homer (fl. eighth century B.C.E.) Greek rhapsode ("weaver" of stories) credited with merging centuries of poetic tradition in the epics known as the *Iliad* and the *Odyssey*.

hoplite Greek foot-soldier armed with a spear or short sword and protected by a large round shield (*hoplon*). In battle, hoplites stood shoulder to shoulder in a close formation called a phalanx.

Huguenots French Protestants who endured severe persecution in the sixteenth and seventeenth centuries.

humanism Program of study associated with the movement known as the Renaissance; humanism aimed to replace the scholastic emphasis on logic and philosophy with the study of ancient languages, literature, history, and ethics.

human rights Principle that all people have the right to legal equality, freedom of religion and speech, and the right to participate in government. Human rights laws prohibit torture, cruel punishment, and slavery.

David Hume (1711–1776) Scottish writer who applied Newton's method of scientific inquiry and skepticism to the study of morality, the mind, and government.

Hundred Years' War (1337–1453) Series of wars between England and France, fought mostly on French soil and prompted by the territorial and political claims of English monarchs.

Jan Hus (c. 1373–1415) Czech reformer who adopted many of the teachings of the English theologian John Wycliffe, and who also demanded that the laity be allowed to receive both the consecrated bread and wine of the Eucharist. The Council of Constance burned him at the stake for heresy. In response, his supporters, the Hussites, revolted against the Church.

Saddam Hussein (1937–2006) Former dictator of Iraq who invaded Iran in 1980 and started the eight-year-long Iran-Iraq War; invaded Kuwait in 1990, which led to the Gulf War of 1991; and was overthrown when the United States invaded Iraq in 2003. Involved in Iraqi politics since the mid-1960s, Hussein became the official head of state in 1979.

Iconoclast Controversy (717–87) Serious and often violent theological debate that raged in Byzantium after Emperor Leo III ordered the destruction of religious art on the grounds that any image representing a divine or holy personage is prone to promote idol worship and blasphemy. Iconoclast means "breaker of icons." Those who supported the veneration of icons were called iconodules, "adherents of icons."

Il-khanate Mongol-founded dynasty in thirteenth-century Persia.

Indian National Congress Indian political party formed in 1885 to achieve Indian independence from British colonial control. The Congress was led by Mohandas Gandhi in the 1920s and 1930s.

Indian Rebellion of 1857 Uprising that began near Delhi when the military disciplined a regiment of Indian soldiers employed by the British for refusing to use rifle cartridges greased with pork fat—unacceptable to either Hindus or Muslims. Rebels attacked law courts and burned tax rolls, protesting debt and corruption. The mutiny spread through large areas of northwest India before being violently suppressed by British troops.

Indo-Europeans Group of people speaking variations of the same language who moved into the Near East and Mediterranean region shortly after 2000 B.C.E.

indulgences Grants exempting Catholic Christians from the performance of penance, either in life or after death. The abusive trade in indulgences was a major catalyst of the Protestant Reformation.

Incas People of the highly centralized South American empire that was toppled by the Spanish conquistador Francisco Pizarro in 1533.

Innocent III (1160/61–1216) Pope who wanted to unify all of Christendom under papal hegemony; he furthered this goal at the Fourth Lateran Council of 1215, which defined one of the Church's dogmas as the acknowledgment of papal supremacy. The council also took an unprecedented interest in the religious education and habits of every Christian.

Inquisition Tribunal of the Roman Catholic Church that aims to combat heresy by enforcing religious orthodoxy and conformity.

International Monetary Fund (IMF) Established in 1945 to ensure international cooperation regarding currency exchange and monetary policy, the IMF is a specialized agency of the United Nations.

Investiture Conflict Name given to a series of disputes over the limitations of spiritual and secular power in Europe during the eleventh and early twelfth century; it came to a head when Pope Gregory VII and Emperor Henry IV of Germany both claimed the right to appoint and invest bishops with the regalia of office. After years of diplomatic and military hostility, the conflict was partially settled by the Concordat of Worms in 1122.

Irish potato famine Period of agricultural blight from 1845 to 1849 whose devastating results produced widespread starvation and led to mass immigration to America.

Iron Curtain Term coined by Winston Churchill in 1946 to refer to the borders of Eastern European nations that lay within the zone of Soviet control.

Italian invasion of Ethiopia (1896) Italy invaded Ethiopia, which was the last major independent African kingdom. Menelik II, the Ethiopian emperor, soundly defeated them.

Ivan the Great (1440–1505) Russian ruler who annexed neighboring territories and consolidated his empire's position as a European power.

Jacobins Radical French political group during the French Revolution that took power after 1792, executed the French king, and sought to remake French culture.

Jacquerie Violent 1358 peasant uprising in northern France, incited by disease, war, and taxes.

James I (1566–1625) Monarch who ruled Scotland as James VI, and who succeeded Elizabeth I as king of England in 1603. He oversaw the English vernacular translation of the Bible known by his name.

James II of England King of England, Ireland, and Scotland (r. 1685–88) whose commitment to absolutism and the restoration of Roman Catholicism led to his exile to France in the Glorious Revolution of 1688.

Janissaries Corps of enslaved soldiers recruited as children from the Christian provinces of the Ottoman Empire and brought up to display intense personal loyalty to the Ottoman sultan, who used these forces to curb local autonomy and serve as his personal bodyguards.

Jerome (c. 340–420) One of the early "Fathers" of the Church; Jerome translated the Bible from Hebrew and Greek into a popular form of Latin—hence the name by which this translation is known: the Vulgate, or "vulgar" (popular) Bible.

Jesuits Religious order formally known as the Society of Jesus, founded in 1540 by Ignatius Loyola to combat the spread of Protestantism. The Jesuits would become active in politics, education, and missionary work.

Jesus (c. 4 B.C.E.–c. 30 C.E.) Jewish preacher and teacher in the rural areas of Galilee and Judea who was arrested for seditious political activity, tried, and crucified by the Romans. After his execution, his followers claimed that he had been resurrected from the dead and taken up into heaven. They began to teach that Jesus had been the divine representative of God, the Messiah (Christ) foretold by ancient Hebrew prophets, and that he had suffered for the sins of humanity and would return to judge all the world's inhabitants at the end of time.

Joan of Arc (c. 1412–1431) Peasant girl from the province of Lorraine who claimed to have been commanded by God to lead French forces against the English occupying army during the Hundred Years' War. Successful in her efforts, she was betrayed by the French king and handed over to the English, who condemned her to death for heresy. Her reputation underwent a process of rehabilitation, but she was not officially canonized as a saint until 1920.

Judaism Religion of the Hebrews as it developed in the centuries after the establishment of the Hebrew kingdoms under David and Solomon, especially during the period of Babylonian Captivity.

Justinian (527–565) Emperor of Rome who unsuccessfully attempted to reunite the eastern and western portions of the empire. Also known for his important codification of Roman law, in the *Corpus Juris Civilis.*

Justinian's Code of Roman Law Formally known as the *Corpus Juris Civilis* or "body of civil law," this compendium consisted of a systematic compilation of imperial statutes, the writings of Rome's great legal authorities, a textbook of legal principles, and the legislation of Justinian and his immediate successors. As the most authoritative collection of Roman law, it formed the basis of canon law (the legal system of the Roman Church) and became essential to the developing legal traditions of every European state as well as of many countries around the world.

Das Kapital (*Capital*) Book by Karl Marx that outlined the theory behind historical materialism and attacked the socioeconomic inequities of capitalism (1867).

Johannes Kepler (1571–1630) Mathematician and astronomer who elaborated on and corrected Copernicus's theory of a heliocentric solar system and is chiefly remembered for his discovery of the three laws of planetary motion that bear his name.

Keynesian Revolution Postdepression economic ideas developed by the British economist John Maynard Keynes (1883–1946), whereby the state took a greater role in managing the economy, stimulating it by increasing the money supply and creating jobs.

KGB Soviet political police and spy agency, first formed as the Cheka not long after the Bolshevik coup in October 1917. It grew to more than 750,000 operatives with military rank by the 1980s.

Genghis Khan (c. 1167–1227) "Oceanic Ruler," the title adopted by the Mongol chieftain Temujin, founder of a dynasty that conquered much of southern Asia.

Khanate Major political unit of the vast Mongol Empire. There were four Khanates, including the Yuan Empire in China, forged by Genghis Khan's grandson Kubilai in the thirteenth century.

Ruhollah Khomeini (1902–1989) Iranian Shi'ite religious leader who led the revolution in Iran after the abdication of the shah in 1979. His government allowed some limited economic and political populism combined with strict constructions of Islamic law, restrictions on women's public life, and the prohibition of ideas or activities linked to Western influence.

Nikita Khrushchev (1894–1971) Leader of the Soviet Union during the Cuban missile crisis, Khrushchev came to power after Stalin's death in 1953. His reforms and criticisms of the excesses of the Stalin regime led to his fall from power in 1964.

Kremlin Once synonymous with the Soviet government, the name *Kremlin* refers to Moscow's walled city center and the palace originally built by Ivan the Great.

Kristallnacht Known as the "Night of Broken Glass," an organized attack by Nazis and their supporters on the Jews of Germany following the assassination of a German embassy official by a Jewish man in Paris. Throughout Germany, thousands of stores, schools, cemeteries, and synagogues were attacked on November 9, 1938. Dozens of people were killed, and tens of thousands of Jews were arrested and held in camps, where many were tortured and killed in the ensuing months.

Labour party Party founded in Britain in 1900 to represent workers and promote socialist principles.

Latin West After the founding of Constantinople, the western Latin-speaking half of the Roman Empire became poorer and more peripheral, but it also fostered the emergence of new barbarian kingdoms. At the same time, the Roman pope claimed to have inherited both the authority of Jesus and the essential elements of Roman imperial authority.

League of Nations International organization founded after the First World War to solve international disputes through arbitration; it was dissolved in 1946 and its assets were transferred to the United Nations.

Leonardo da Vinci (1452–1519) Florentine inventor, sculptor, architect, and painter whose breadth of interests typifies the ideal of "the Renaissance man."

Vladimir Lenin (1870–1924) Leader of the Bolshevik Revolution in Russia (1917) and the first leader of the Soviet Union.

Leviathan Book by Thomas Hobbes (1588–1679) that recommended a ruler have unrestricted power (1651).

liberalism Political and social theory that judges the effectiveness of a government in terms of its ability to protect individual rights. Liberals support representative forms of government, free trade, and freedom of speech and religion. In the economic realm, liberals believe that individuals should be free to engage in commercial or business activities without interference from the state or their community.

lithograph Art form that involves incising writing or design on stone and producing printed impressions.

John Locke (1632–1704) English philosopher and political theorist known for his contributions to liberalism. Locke had great faith in human reason and believed that just societies were those that infringed the least on the natural rights and freedoms of individuals. This led him to assert that a government's legitimacy depended on the consent of the governed, a view that had a profound effect on the authors of the United States' Declaration of Independence.

Louis IX of France King of France from 1226 to his death on crusade in 1270, Louis was renowned for his piety and for his close attention to the administration of law and justice in his realm. He was officially canonized as Saint Louis in 1297.

Louis XIV (1638–1715) Called the "Sun King," he was known for his success at strengthening the institutions of the French absolutist state.

Louis XVI (1754–1793) Well-meaning but ineffectual king of France, finally deposed and executed during the French Revolution.

Ignatius Loyola (1491–1556) Spanish founder of the Society of Jesus (the Roman Catholic religious order commonly known as the Jesuits), whose members vow to serve God through poverty, chastity, and missionary work. He abandoned his first career as a mercenary after reading an account of Christ's life.

Lucretia According to Roman legend, Lucretia was a virtuous Roman wife who was raped by the son of Rome's last king and who virtuously committed suicide in order to avoid bringing shame on her family.

Luftwaffe Literally "air weapon," the name of the German air force, which was founded during the First World War, disbanded in 1945, and reestablished when West Germany joined NATO in 1950.

Lusitania British passenger liner that was sunk by a German U-boat (submarine) on May 7, 1915. Public outrage over the sinking contributed to the U.S. decision to enter the First World War.

Martin Luther (1483–1546) German monk and professor of theology whose critique of the papacy launched the Protestant Reformation.

ma'at Egyptian term for the serene order of the universe, with which the individual soul (*ka*) must remain in harmony. The power of the pharaoh was linked to *ma'at*, insofar as it ensured the prosperity of the kingdom. After the upheavals of the First Intermediate Period, the perception of the pharaoh's relationship with *ma'at* was revealed to be conditional, something that had to be earned.

Niccolò Machiavelli (1469–1527) As the author of *The Prince* and the *Discourses on Livy*, he looked to the Roman past for paradigms of greatness while at the same time hoping to win the patronage of contemporary rulers who would restore Italy's political independence.

Magna Carta Regarded now as a landmark in the development of constitutional government, the "Great Charter" of 1215 was enacted during the reign of King John of England in order to limit his powers. In its own time, its purpose was to restore the power of great lords.

Magyar nationalism National movement in the Hungarian region of the Habsburg Empire led by Lajos Kossuth, calling for national independence for Hungary in 1848. With the support of Russia, Habsburg troops crushed the movement and all other revolutionary activities in the empire. Kossuth fled into exile.

Moses Maimonides (c. 1137–1204) Jewish scholar, physician, and scriptural commentator whose *Mishneh Torah* is a fundamental exposition of Jewish law.

Thomas Malthus (1766–1834) British political economist who believed that populations inevitably grew faster than the available food supply. Societies that could not control their population growth would be checked only by famine, disease, poverty, and infant malnutrition. He argued that governments could not alleviate poverty. Instead, the poor had to exercise "moral restraint," postpone marriage, and have fewer children.

Nelson Mandela (1918–2013) South African opponent of apartheid who led the African National Congress and was imprisoned from 1962 until 1990. After his release from prison, he worked with Prime Minister Frederik Willem De Klerk to establish majority rule. Mandela became the first black president of South Africa in 1994.

Manhattan Project Secret U.S. government research project to develop the first nuclear bomb. The vast project involved dozens of sites across the United States, including New Mexico, Tennessee, Illinois, California, Utah, and Washington. The first test of a nuclear bomb was conducted near Alamogordo, New Mexico, on July 16, 1945.

manor Common farmland worked collectively by the inhabitants of an entire village, sometimes on their own initiative, sometimes at the behest of a lord.

Mao Zedong (1893–1976) Leader of the Chinese Revolution who defeated the Nationalists in 1949 and established the communist People's Republic of China.

Marne River in France and site of major battle of the First World War in September 1914, which halted the German invasion of France and led to protracted trench warfare on the war's Western Front.

Marshall Plan Economic aid package given to Europe by the United States after the Second World War to promote reconstruction and economic development and to secure Western European countries from a feared communist takeover.

Karl Marx (1818–1883) German philosopher and economist who believed that a revolution of the working classes would overthrow the capitalist order and create a classless society. Author of *Das Kapital* and co-author of *The Communist Manifesto*.

Marxists Followers of the socialist political economist Karl Marx who called for workers everywhere to unite and create an independent political force. Marxists believed that industrialization produced an inevitable struggle between laborers and the class of capitalist property owners, and that this struggle would culminate in a revolution that would abolish private property and establish a society committed to social equality.

Mary See **cult of the Virgin**.

Mary I (1516–1558) Catholic daughter of Henry VIII and his first wife, Catherine of Aragon, Mary Tudor was the first queen regnant of England. Her attempts to reinstitute Roman Catholicism in England met with limited success, and after her early death she was labeled "Bloody Mary" by the Protestant supporters of her half sister and successor, Elizabeth I.

mass culture The spread of literacy and public education in the nineteenth century created a new audience for print entertainment and a new class of entrepreneurs in the media to cater to this audience. The invention of radio, film, and television in the twentieth century carried this development to another level, as millions of consumers were now accessible to the producers of news, information, and entertainment. The rise of this "mass culture" has been celebrated as an expression of popular tastes but also criticized as a vehicle for the manipulation of populations through clever and seductive propaganda.

Mayans Native American peoples whose culturally and politically sophisticated empire encompassed lands in present-day Mexico and Guatemala.

Giuseppe Mazzini (1805–1872) Founder and ideological leader of the Italian nationalist movement Young Italy.

Mecca Center of an important commercial network of the Arabian Peninsula and birthplace of the prophet Muhammad. It is now considered the holiest site in the Islamic world.

Medici Powerful fourteenth- to eighteenth-century dynasty of Florentine bankers and politicians whose ancestors were originally apothecaries ("medics").

Meiji Empire Empire created under the leadership of Mutsuhito, emperor of Japan from 1868 until 1912. During the Meiji period Japan became a world industrial and naval power.

Mensheviks Within the Russian Social Democratic Party, the Mensheviks advocated slow changes and a gradual move toward socialism, in contrast with the Bolsheviks, who wanted to push for a proletarian revolution. Mensheviks believed that a proletarian revolution in Russia was premature and that the country needed to complete its capitalist development first.

mercantilism Theory and policy for directing the economy of monarchical states between 1600 and 1800 based on the assumption that wealth and power depended on a favorable balance of trade (more exports and fewer imports) and the accumulation of precious metals. Mercantilists advocated forms of economic protectionism to promote domestic production.

Maria Sybilla Merian (1647–1717) Scientific illustrator and an important early entomologist; Merian conducted research on two continents and published the well-received *Metamorphosis of the Insects of Surinam*.

Merovingian Frankish dynasty that claimed descent from a legendary ancestor called Merovic; the Merovingians were the only powerful family to establish a lasting kingdom in western Europe during the fifth and sixth centuries.

Mesopotamia Literally the "land between the Tigris and the Euphrates rivers" (Greek), where the civilization of Sumer, the first urban society, flourished.

Klemens von Metternich (1773–1859) Austrian foreign minister whose primary goals were to bolster the legitimacy of monarchies and, after the defeat of Napoleon, to promote a balance of power that would prevent another large-scale war in Europe. At the Congress of Vienna, he opposed social and political change and wanted to check Russian and French expansion.

Michelangelo Buonarroti (1475–1564) Virtuoso Florentine sculptor, painter, and poet who spent much of his career in the service of the papacy. He is best known for the decoration of the Sistine Chapel and for his monumental sculptures.

Middle Kingdom of Egypt (2055–1650 B.C.E.) Period following the First Intermediate Period of dynastic warfare, which ended with the reassertion of pharonic rule under Mentuhotep II.

Miletus Greek polis and Persian colony on the Ionian coast of Asia Minor. Influenced by the cultures of Mesopotamia, Egypt, and Lydia, it produced several of the ancient world's first scientists and sophist philosophers. Thereafter, a political conflict between the ruler of Miletus, Aristagoras, and the Persian Emperor, Darius, sparked the Persian Wars with Greece.

John Stuart Mill (1806–1873) English liberal philosopher whose faith in human reason led him to support a broad variety of civic and political freedoms for men and women, including the right to vote and the right to free speech.

Slobodan Milosevic (1941–2006) Serbian nationalist politician who became president of Serbia and whose policies during the Balkan wars of the early 1990s led to the deaths of thousands of Croatians, Bosnian Muslims, Albanians, and Kosovars. After leaving office in 2000, he was arrested and tried for war crimes at the International Court in The Hague. The trial ended before a verdict when he died in 2006.

Minoan Crete Maritime empire based at Knossos on the Greek island of Crete and named for the legendary King Minos. The Minoans dominated the Aegean for much of the second millennium B.C.E.

Modernism In the late-nineteenth and early twentieth centuries there were several different modernist movements in art and literature, but they shared three key characteristics. First, they had a sense that the world had radically changed and that this change should be embraced. Second, they believed that traditional aesthetic values and assumptions about creativity were ill-suited to the present. Third, they developed a new conception of what art could do that emphasized expression over representation and insisted on the value of novelty, experimentation, and creative freedom.

Mongols A nomadic people from the steppes of Central Asia who were united under the ruler Genghis Khan. His conquest of China was continued by his grandson Kubilai and his great-grandson son Ogedei, whose army also seized southern Russia and then moved through Hungary and Poland toward eastern Germany. The Mongol armies withdrew from eastern Europe after the death of Ogedei, but his descendants continued to rule his vast empire for much of the thirteenth century.

Michel de Montaigne (1533–1592) French philosopher and social commentator, best known for his *Essays*.

Montesquieu (1689–1755) French aristocrat and Enlightenment philosophe whose most influential work was *The Spirit of Laws*, in which he analyzed structures that shaped law and categorized governments into three types: republics, monarchies, and despotisms. His ideas about the separation of powers among the executive, the legislative, and the judicial branches of government influenced the authors of the U.S. Constitution.

Thomas More (1478–1535) Christian humanist, English statesman, and author of *Utopia*. In 1529, he was appointed lord chancellor of England but resigned because he opposed King Henry VIII's plans to establish a national church under royal control. He was eventually executed for refusing to take an oath acknowledging Henry to be the head of the Church of England and has since been canonized by the Roman Catholic Church.

mos maiorum Literally "the code of the elders" or "the custom of ancestors" (Latin). This unwritten code governed the lives of Romans under the Republic and stressed the importance of showing reverence to ancestral tradition. *Mos maiorum* was sacrosanct and essential to Roman identity, and an important influence on Roman culture, law, and religion.

Wolfgang Amadeus Mozart (1756–1791) Austrian composer, famous at a young age as a concert musician and later celebrated as a prolific composer of instrumental music and operas that are seen as the apogee of the Classical style in music.

Muhammad (570–632 C.E.) The founder of Islam, regarded by his followers as God's last and greatest prophet.

Munich Conference (1938) Hitler met with the leaders of Britain, France, and Italy and negotiated an agreement that gave Germany a major slice of Czechoslovakia. British prime minister Chamberlain believed that the agreement would bring peace to Europe. Instead, Germany invaded and seized the rest of Czechoslovakia.

Muscovy Duchy centered on Moscow whose dukes saw themselves as heirs to the Roman Empire. In the early fourteenth century, Moscow was under the control of the Mongol Khanate. After the collapse of the Khanate, the Muscovite grand duke, Ivan III, conquered all the Russian principalities between Moscow and the border of Poland-Lithuania, and then Lithuania itself. By the time of his death in 1505, Ivan had established Muscovy as a dominant power.

Muslim learning and culture The Crusades brought the Latin West into contact with the Islamic world, which affected European culture in myriad ways. Europeans adapted Arabic numerals and mathematical concepts as well as Arabic and Persian words. Through Arabic translations, Western scholars gained access to Greek learning, which had a profound influence on Christian theology. European scholars also learned from the Islamic world's accomplishments in medicine and science.

Benito Mussolini (1883–1945) Italian founder of the Fascist party who came to power in Italy in 1922 and allied himself with Hitler and the Nazis during the Second World War.

Mycenaean Greece (1600–1200 B.C.E.) Term used to describe the civilization of Greece in the late Bronze Age, when territorial kingdoms like Mycenae formed around a king, a warrior caste, and a palace bureaucracy.

Nagasaki Second Japanese city on which the United States dropped an atomic bomb. The attack took place on August 9, 1945; the Japanese surrendered shortly thereafter, ending the Second World War.

Napoleon III (1808–1873) Nephew of Napoleon Bonaparte, Napoleon III was elected president of the French Second Republic in 1848 and made himself emperor of France in 1852. During his reign (1852–70), he rebuilt the French capital of Paris. Defeated in the France-Prussian War of 1870, he went into exile.

Napoleonic Code Legal code drafted by Napoleon in 1804 and based on Justinian's *Corpus Iuris Civilis*; it distilled different legal traditions to create one uniform law. The code confirmed the abolition of feudal privileges of all kinds and set the conditions for exercising property rights.

Napoleon's military campaigns In 1805, the Russians, Prussians, Austrians, Swedes, and British attempted to contain Napoleon's French army, but he defeated them. Following his victories, Napoleon created a new empire of France and affiliated states. In 1808, he invaded Spain, but fierce resistance prevented Napoleon from achieving a complete victory. In 1812, Napoleon invaded Russia, and his army was decimated as it retreated from Moscow during the winter. After the Russian campaign, the united European powers defeated Napoleon and forced him into exile. He escaped and reassumed command of his army, but the European powers defeated him for the final time at the Battle of Waterloo in 1815.

Gamal Abdel Nasser (1918–1970) Former president of Egypt and the most prominent spokesman for secular pan-Arabism. He became a target for Islamist critics, such as Sayyid Qutb and the Muslim Brotherhood, who were angered by the Western-influenced policies of his regime.

National Assembly of France Governing body of France that succeeded the Estates General in 1789 during the French Revolution. It was composed of, and defined by, the delegates of the Third Estate.

National Association for the Advancement of Colored People (NAACP) U.S. civil rights organization founded in 1910 and dedicated to ending inequality and segregation for black Americans.

National Convention Governing body of France from September 1792 to October 1795. It declared France a republic and then tried and executed the French king. The Convention also confiscated the property of the enemies of the revolution, instituted a policy of de-Christianization, changed marriage and inheritance laws, abolished slavery in its colonies, placed a cap on the price of necessities, and ended the compensation of nobles for their lost privileges.

nationalism Movement to unify a country under one government based on perceptions of the population's common history, customs, and social traditions.

nationalism in Yugoslavia In the 1990s, Slobodan Milosevic and his allies reignited Serbian nationalism in the former Yugoslavia, which led non-Serb republics in Croatia and Slovenia to seek independence. The country erupted into war, with the worst violence taking place in Bosnia, a multi-ethnic region with Serb, Croatian, and Bosnian Muslim populations. European diplomats proved powerless to stop attempts by Croatian and Serbian military and paramilitary forces to claim territory through ethnic cleansing and violent intimidation. Atrocities were committed on all sides, but pro-Serb forces were responsible for the most deaths.

NATO The North Atlantic Treaty Organization, a 1949 military agreement among the United States, Canada, Great Britain, and eight Western European nations, which declared that an armed attack against any one of the members would be regarded as an attack against all. Created during the Cold War in the face of the Soviet Union's control of Eastern Europe, NATO continues to exist today and the current membership of twenty-eight states includes former members of the Warsaw Pact as well as Albania and Turkey.

Nazi party Founded in the early 1920s, the National Socialist German Workers' Party (NSDAP) gained control over Germany under the leadership of Adolf Hitler in 1933 and continued in power until Germany was defeated in 1945.

Nazism Political movement in Germany led by Adolf Hitler, which advocated a violent anti-Semitic, anti-Marxist, pan-German ideology.

Neo-Assyrian Empire (883–859 B.C.E.–612–605 B.C.E.) Assurnasirpal II laid the foundations of the Neo-Assyrian Empire through military campaigns against neighboring peoples. Eventually, the empire stretched from the Mediterranean Sea to western Iran. A military dictatorship governed the empire through its army, which it used to frighten and oppress both its subjects and its enemies. The empire's ideology was based on waging holy war in the name of its principal god, Assur, and the exaction of tribute through terror.

Neoliberalism Ideology emphasizing free markets, profit incentives, and restraints on both budget deficits and social welfare programs as the best guarantee of individual liberties. Beginning in the 1980s, neoliberal theory was used to structure the policy of financial institutions like the International Monetary Fund and the World Bank, which turned away from interventionist policies in favor of market-driven models of economic development.

Neolithic Revolution The "New" Stone Age, which began around 11,000 B.C.E., saw new technological and social developments, including managed food production, the beginnings of permanent settlements, and the rapid intensification of trade.

Neoplatonism School of thought based on the teachings of Plato and prevalent in the Roman Empire, which had a profound effect on the formation of Christian theology. Neoplatonists argued that nature is a book written by its creator to reveal the ways of God to humanity. Convinced that God's perfection must be reflected in nature, neoplatonists searched for the ideal and perfect structures that they believed must lie behind the "shadows" of the everyday world.

New Deal President Franklin Delano Roosevelt's package of government reforms that were enacted during the depression of the 1930s to provide jobs for the unemployed, social welfare programs for the poor, and security for the financial markets.

New Economic Policy In 1921, the Bolsheviks abandoned war communism in favor of the New Economic Policy (NEP). Under NEP, the state still controlled all major industrial and financial concerns, while individuals could own private property, trade freely within limits, and farm their own land for their own benefit. Fixed taxes replaced grain requisition. The policy successfully helped Soviet agriculture recover from the civil war but was later abandoned in favor of collectivization.

Isaac Newton (1642–1727) One of the foremost scientists of all time, Newton was an English mathematician and physicist; he is noted for his development of calculus, work on the properties of light, and theory of gravitation.

Tsar Nicholas II (1868–1918) The last Russian tsar, who abdicated the throne in 1917; he and his family were executed by the Bolsheviks on July 17, 1918.

Friedrich Nietzsche (1844–1900) German philosopher who denied the possibility of knowing absolute "truth" or "reality," since all knowledge comes filtered through linguistic, scientific, or artistic systems of representation. He also criticized Judeo-Christian morality for instilling a repressive conformity that drained civilization of its vitality.

nongovernmental organizations (NGOs) Private organizations like the Red Cross that play a large role in international affairs.

Novum Organum Treatise by English statesman and scientist Francis Bacon (1561–1626) that advanced a philosophy of study through observation.

October Days (1789) The high price of bread and the rumor that the king was unwilling to cooperate with the assembly caused the women who worked in Paris's large central market to march to Versailles along with their supporters to address the king, Louis XVI. Not satisfied with their initial reception, they broke through the palace gates and called for the king to return to Paris from Versailles, which he did the following day.

Old Kingdom of Egypt (c. 2686–2160 B.C.E.) During this time, the pharaohs controlled a powerful and centralized bureaucratic state whose vast human and material resources are embodied by the pyramids of Giza. This period came to an end as the pharaoh's authority collapsed, leading to a period of dynastic warfare and localized rule.

OPEC (Organization of the Petroleum Exporting Countries) Organization created in 1960 by oil-producing countries in the Middle East, South America, and Africa to regulate the production and pricing of crude oil.

Operation Barbarossa Codename for Hitler's invasion of the Soviet Union in 1941.

Opium Wars (1839–42 and 1856–60) Wars fought between the British and Qing-era China to protect British trade in opium; the wars resulted in the ceding of Hong Kong to the British.

Oracle at Delphi The most important shrine in ancient Greece. The priestess of Apollo who attended the shrine was believed to have the power to predict the future.

Ottoman Empire (c.1300–1923) During the thirteenth century, the Ottoman dynasty established itself as leader of the Turks. From the fourteenth to sixteenth centuries, they conquered Anatolia, Armenia, Syria, and North Africa as well as parts of southeastern Europe, the Crimea, and areas along the Red Sea. Portions of the Ottoman Empire persisted up to the time of the First World War, but it was dismantled in the following years.

Reza Pahlavi (1919–1980) The Western-friendly shah of Iran who was installed during a 1953 coup supported by Britain and the United States. After a lengthy economic downturn, public unrest, and personal illness, he retired from public life under popular pressure in 1979.

Pan-African Conference Assembly in London in 1900 that sought to draw attention to the sovereignty of African people and their mistreatment by colonial powers.

Panhellenism The "all Greek" culture that allowed ancient Greek colonies to maintain a connection to their homeland and to each other through their shared language and heritage. These colonies also exported their culture into new areas and created new Greek-speaking enclaves, which permanently changed the cultural geography of the Mediterranean world.

pan-Slavism Cultural movement that sought to unite native Slavic peoples within the Russian and Habsburg Empires under Russian leadership.

Partition of India (1947) At independence, British India was partitioned into the nations of India and Pakistan. The majority of the population in India was Hindu and the majority of the population in Pakistan was Muslim. The process of partition brought brutal religious and ethnic warfare. More than 1 million Hindus and Muslims died and 12 million became refugees.

Blaise Pascal (1623–1662) Catholic philosopher who wanted to establish the truth of Christianity by appealing simultaneously to intellect and emotion. In his *Pensées*, he argued that faith alone can resolve the world's contradictions and that his own awe in the face of evil and uncertainty must be evidence of God's existence.

Paul of Tarsus Originally known as Saul, Paul was a Greek-speaking Jew and Roman citizen who underwent a miraculous conversion experience and became the most important exponent of Christianity in the 50s and 60s C.E.

Pax Romana (27 B.C.E.–180 C.E.) Literally translated as "the Roman Peace." During this time, the Roman world enjoyed an unprecedented period of peace and political stability.

Peace of Augsburg Settlement negotiated in 1555 among factions within the Holy Roman Empire; it formulated the principle *cuius regio, eius religio* ("he who rules, his religion"), meaning that the inhabitants of any given territory should follow the religion of its ruler, whether Catholic or Protestant.

Peace of Paris The 1919 Paris Peace Conference established the terms to end the First World War. Great Britain, France, Italy, and the United States signed five treaties with each of the defeated nations: Germany, Austria, Hungary, Turkey, and Bulgaria. The settlement is notable for the territory that Germany had to give up, including large parts of Prussia to the new state of Poland, and Alsace and Lorraine to France; the disarming of Germany; and the "war guilt" provision, which required Germany and its allies to pay massive reparations to the victors.

Peace of Westphalia (1648) Agreement reached at the end of the Thirty Years' War that altered the political map of Europe. France emerged as the predominant power on the Continent, while the Austrian Habsburgs had to surrender all the territories they had gained and could no longer use the office of the Holy Roman Emperor to dominate central Europe. Spain was marginalized and Germany became a volatile combination of Protestant and Catholic principalities.

Pearl Harbor American naval base in Hawaii that was bombed by the Japanese on December 7, 1941, bringing the United States into the Second World War.

peasantry Term used in continental Europe to refer to rural populations that lived from agriculture. Some peasants were free and could own land. Serfs were peasants who were legally bound to the land and subject to the authority of the local lord.

Peloponnesian War Name given to the series of wars fought between Sparta (on the Greek Peloponnesus) and Athens from 431 B.C.E. to 404 B.C.E., and which ended in the defeat of Athens and the loss of her imperial power.

perestroika Introduced by Soviet leader Mikhail Gorbachev in June 1987, *perestroika* (Russian for "restructuring") was the name given to economic and political reforms begun earlier in his tenure. It restructured the state bureaucracy, reduced the privileges of the political elite, and instituted a shift from the centrally planned economy to a mixed economy, combining planning with the operation of market forces.

Periclean Athens Following his election as *strategos* in 461 B.C.E., Pericles pushed through political reforms in Athens which gave poorer citizens greater influence in politics. He promoted Athenians' sense of superiority through ambitious public works projects and lavish festivals to honor the gods, thus ensuring his continual reelection. But eventually, Athens' growing arrogance and aggression alienated it from the rest of the Greek world.

Pericles (c. 495–429 B.C.E.) Athenian politician who occupied the office of *strategos* for thirty years and who presided over a series of civic reforms, building campaigns, and imperialist initiatives.

Persian Empire Consolidated by Cyrus the Great in 559, this empire eventually stretched from the Persian Gulf to the Mediterranean and also encompassed Egypt. Persian rulers were able to hold this empire together through a policy of tolerance and a mixture of local and centralized governance. This imperial model of government would be adopted by many future empires.

Persian Wars (490–479 B.C.E.) In 501 B.C.E., a political conflict between the Greek ruler of Miletus, Aristagoras, and the Persian Emperor, Darius, sparked the first of the Persian Wars when Darius sent an army to punish Athens for its intervention on the side of the Greeks. Despite being heavily outnumbered, Athenian hoplites defeated the Persian army at the plain of

Marathon. In 480 B.C.E., Darius's son Xerxes invaded Greece but was defeated at sea and on land by combined Greek forces under the leadership of Athens and Sparta.

Peter the Great (1672–1725) Energetic tsar who transformed Russia into a leading European country by centralizing government, modernizing the army, creating a navy, and reforming education and the economy.

Francesco Petrarca (Petrarch) (1304–1374) Italian scholar who revived interest in classical writing styles and was famed for his vernacular love sonnets.

pharaoh Term meaning "household" which became the title borne by the rulers of ancient Egypt. The pharaoh was regarded as the divine representative of the gods and the embodiment of Egypt itself. The powerful and centralized bureaucratic state ruled by the pharaohs was more stable and long-lived than any another civilization in world history, lasting (with few interruptions) for approximately 3,000 years.

Pharisees Group of Jewish teachers and preachers who emerged in the third century B.C.E. They insisted that all of Yahweh's (God's) commandments were binding on all Jews.

Philip II (382–336 B.C.E.) King of Macedonia and father of Alexander, he consolidated the southern Balkans and the Greek city-states under Macedonian domination.

Philip II of Spain King of Spain (r. 1556–98) and briefly king of England and Ireland during his marriage to Queen Mary I of England. As a staunch Catholic, Philip responded with military might to the desecration of Catholic churches in the Spanish Netherlands in the 1560s. When commercial conflict with England escalated, Philip sent the Spanish Armada (Navy) to conquer England in 1588, but it was largely destroyed by stormy weather.

Philip II Augustus (1165–1223) The first French ruler to use the title "king of France" rather than "king of the French." After he captured Normandy and its adjacent territories from the English, he built an effective system of local administration, which recognized regional diversity while promoting centralized royal control. This administrative pattern would characterize French government until the French Revolution.

Philip IV of France King of France from 1285 until his death, Philip's conflict with Pope Boniface VIII led to the transfer of the papal court to Avignon from 1309 to 1378.

Philistines Descendants of the Sea Peoples who fled to the region that now bears their name, Palestine, after their defeat at the hands of the pharaoh Ramses III. They dominated their neighbors, the Hebrews, who used writing as an effective means of discrediting them (the Philistines themselves did not leave a written record to contest the Hebrews' views).

philosophe During the Enlightenment, this French word referred to an intellectual whose reflections were unhampered by the constraints of religion or dogma.

Phoenicians A Semitic people known for their trade in exotic purple dyes and other luxury goods, they originally settled in present-day Lebanon around 1200 B.C.E. and from there established commercial colonies throughout the Mediterranean, notably Carthage.

Plato (429–349 B.C.E.) Student of Socrates who dedicated his life to transmitting his teacher's legacy through the writing of dialogues on philosophical subjects, in which Socrates himself plays the major role. The longest and most famous of these, known as the *Republic*, describes an idealized polis governed by a superior group of individuals chosen for their natural attributes of intelligence and character, who rule as "philospher-kings."

Plotinus (204–270 C.E.) Neoplatonist philosopher who taught that everything in existence has its ultimate source in the divine, and that the highest goal of life should be the mystic reunion of the soul with this divine source, something that can be achieved through contemplation and asceticism. This outlook blended with that of early Christianity and was instrumental in the spread of that religion within the Roman Empire.

poleis One of the major political innovations of the ancient Greeks was the *polis*, or city-state (plural *poleis*). These independent social and political entities began to emerge in the ninth century B.C.E., each one organized around an urban center and fostering markets, meeting places, and religious worship; frequently, poleis also controlled some surrounding territory.

Marco Polo (1254–1324) Venetian merchant who traveled through Asia for twenty years and published his observations in a widely read memoir.

population growth In the nineteenth century, Europe experienced dramatic population growth. During this period, the spread of rural manufacturing allowed men and women to begin marrying younger and raising families earlier, which increased the size of the average family. As the population grew, the portion of young and fertile people also increased, which reinforced the population growth. By 1900, population growth was strongest in Britain and Germany, and slower in France.

portolan charts Also known as *portolani*, these special charts were invented by medieval mariners during the fourteenth century and were used to map locations of ports and sea routes, while also taking note of prevailing winds and other conditions at sea.

Potsdam (1945) At this conference, Truman, Churchill, and Stalin met to discuss issues that would be raised by the conclusion of the Second World War, including making territorial changes to Germany and its allies and the question of war reparations.

Prague spring Period of political liberalization in Czechoslovakia between January and August 1968 that was initiated by Alexander Dubček, the Czech leader. This period of expanding freedom and openness in this Eastern-bloc nation ended on August 20, when the USSR and Warsaw Pact countries invaded with 200,000 troops and 5,000 tanks.

pre-Socratics Group of philosophers in the Greek city of Miletus, who raised questions about humans' relationship with the natural world and the gods and who formulated rational theories to explain the physical universe they observed. Their name reflects the fact that they flourished prior to the lifetime of Socrates.

price revolution An unprecedented inflation in prices in the latter half of the sixteenth century, resulting in part from the enormous influx of silver bullion from Spanish America.

principate Modern term for the centuries of autocratic rule by the successors of Augustus, who seized power in 27 B.C.E.

and styled himself *princeps* or Rome's "first man." See **Roman Republic**.

printing press Introduced in Europe by Johannes Gutenberg of Mainz in 1453–55, this new technology quickly revolutionized communication and played a significant role in political, religious, and intellectual revolutions.

Protestantism Name given to the many dissenting varieties of Christianity that emerged during the Reformation in sixteenth-century western Europe. While Protestant beliefs and practices differed widely, all were united in their rejection of papal authority and the dogmas of the Roman Catholic Church.

provisional government After the collapse of the Russian monarchy in July 1917, leaders in the Duma organized this government and hoped to establish a democratic system under constitutional rule. They also refused to concede military defeat in the war against Germany, but it found impossible to institute domestic reforms and fight a war at the same time. As conditions worsened, the Bolsheviks gained support. In October 1917, they attacked the provisional government and seized control.

Claudius Ptolomeus, called Ptolemy (c. 85–165 C.E.) Greek-speaking geographer and astronomer active in Roman Alexandria, he rejected the findings of previous Hellenistic scientists in favor of the erroneous theories of Aristotle, publishing highly influential treatises that promulgated these errors and suppressed, for example, the accurate findings of Aristarchus (who had posited the Heliocentric universe) and Erathosthenes (who had calculated the circumference of the earth).

Ptolemaic system Ptolemy of Alexandria promoted Aristotle's understanding of cosmology. In this system, the heavens orbit the earth in an organized hierarchy of spheres, and the earth and the heavens are made of different matter and subject to different laws of motion. A prime mover (usually understood to be God) produces the motion of the celestial bodies.

Ptolemy (c. 367–c. 284 B.C.E.) One of Alexander the Great's trusted generals (and possibly his half brother), he became pharaoh of Egypt and founded a new dynasty that lasted until that kingdom's absorption into the Roman Empire in 30 B.C.E.

public sphere Between the official realm of state activities and the private realm of the household and individual, lies the "public sphere." The public sphere has a political dimension—it is the space of debate, discussion, and expressions of popular opinion. It also has an economic dimension—it is where business is conducted, where commercial transactions take place, where people enter into contracts, search for work, or hire employees.

Punic Wars (264–146 B.C.E.) Three periods of warfare between Rome and Carthage, two maritime empires who struggled for dominance of the Mediterranean. Rome emerged as the victor, destroyed the city of Carthage and took control of Sicily, North Africa, and Hispania (Spain).

pyramids Constructed in Egypt during the third millennium B.C.E., these structures were monuments to the power and divinity of the pharaohs entombed inside them.

Qur'an (often Koran) Islam's principal holy scriptures, comprised of the prophecies revealed to Muhammad and redacted during and after his death.

Raphael (Raffaelo Sanzio) (1483–1520) Italian painter active in Rome, his works include *The School of Athens*.

realism Artistic and literary style which emerged in the late nineteenth century and sought to portray common situations as they would appear in reality.

Realpolitik German term for a Political strategy based on advancing power for its own sake.

reason The human capacity to solve problems and discover truth in ways that can be verified intellectually. Philosophers distinguish the knowledge gained from reason from the teachings of instinct, imagination, and faith, which are verified according to different criteria.

Reformation Religious and political movement in sixteenth-century Europe that led to a break between dissenting forms of Christianity and the Roman Catholic Church; notable figures include Martin Luther and John Calvin.

Reich Term for the German state. The First Reich corresponded to the Holy Roman Empire (9th c.–1806), the Second Reich was from 1871 to 1919, and the Third Reich lasted from 1933 through May 1945.

Renaissance From the French word meaning "rebirth," this term came to be used in the nineteenth century to describe the artistic, intellectual, and cultural movement that emerged in Italy after 1300 and that sought to recover and emulate the heritage of the classical past.

Restoration period (1815–1848) European movement after the defeat of Napoleon to restore Europe to its pre–French Revolution status and to prevent the spread of revolutionary or liberal political movements.

Cardinal Richelieu (1585–1642) First minister to King Louis XIII, he is considered by many to have ruled France in all but name, centralizing political power and suppressing dissent.

Roman army Under the Republic, the Roman army was made up of citizen-soldiers who were required to serve in wartime. As Rome's empire grew, the need for more fighting men led to the extension of citizenship rights and, eventually, to the development of a vast, professional, standing army that numbered as many as 300,000 by the middle of the third century B.C.E. By that time, however, citizens were not themselves required to serve, and many legions were made up of paid conscripts and foreign mercenaries.

Roman citizenship The rights and responsibilities of Rome's citizens were gradually extended to the free (male) inhabitants of other Italian provinces and later to most provinces in the Roman world. In contrast to slaves and non-Romans, Romans had the right to be tried in an imperial court and could not be legally subjected to torture.

Roman Republic The Romans traced the founding of their republic to the overthrow of their last king and the establishment of a unique form of constitutional government, in which the power of the aristocracy (embodied by the Senate) was checked by the executive rule of two elected consuls and the collective will of the people. For hundreds of years, this balance of power provided the Republic with a measure of political stability and prevented any single individual or clique from gaining too much power.

Romanticism Beginning in Germany and England in the late eighteenth century and continuing up to the end of the nineteenth century, Romanticism was a movement in art, music, and literature that countered the rationalism of the Enlightenment by placing greater value on human emotions and the power of nature to stimulate creativity.

Jean-Jacques Rousseau (1712–1778) French philosopher and radical political theorist whose *Social Contract* attacked privilege and inequality. One of the primary principles of Rousseau's political philosophy is that politics and morality should not be separated.

Royal Society Scientific organization founded in Britain in 1660 with the goal of pursuing collective research. Members would conduct experiments, record the results, and share them with their peers, who would study the methods, reproduce the experiment, and assess the results. The arrangement gave English scientists a sense of common purpose as well as a system for reaching a consensus on facts.

Russian Revolution of 1905 After Russia's defeat in the Russo-Japanese War, Russians began clamoring for political reforms. Protests grew over the course of 1905, and the autocracy lost control of entire towns and regions as workers went on strike, soldiers mutinied, and peasants revolted. Forced to yield, Tsar Nicholas II issued the October Manifesto, which pledged individual liberties and provided for the election of a parliament (the Duma). The most radical of the revolutionary groups were put down with force, and the pace of political change remained very slow in the aftermath of the revolution.

Russo-Japanese War (1904–5) Japanese and Russian expansion collided in Mongolia and Manchuria. Russia was humiliated after the Japanese navy sank its fleet, which helped provoke a revolt in Russia and led to an American-brokered peace treaty.

sacrament Sacred rite. In the Roman Catholic tradition, the administration of the sacraments is considered necessary for salvation.

Saint Bartholomew's Day Massacre The mass murder of French Protestants (Huguenots) instigated by the French queen, Catherine de' Medici, and carried out by Catholics. It began in Paris on August 24, 1572, and spread to other parts of France, continuing into October of that year. More than 70,000 people were killed.

salons In the eighteenth century, informal gatherings of intellectuals and aristocrats devoted to discourse about Enlightenment ideas.

Sappho (c. 620–c. 550 B.C.E.) One of the most celebrated Greek poets, she was revered as "the Tenth Muse" and emulated by many male poets. Ironically, though, only two of her poems survive intact, and the rest must be pieced together from fragments quoted by later poets.

Sargon the Great (r. 2334–2279 B.C.E.) The Akkadian ruler who consolidated power in Mesopotamia.

SARS epidemic (2003) The successful containment of severe acute respiratory syndrome (SARS) is an example of how international health organizations can effectively work together to recognize and respond to a disease outbreak. The disease itself, however, is a reminder of the dangers that exist in a globalized economy with a high degree of mobility of both populations and goods.

Schlieffen Plan Devised by German general Alfred von Schlieffen in 1905 to avoid the dilemma of a two-front war against France and Russia. The Schlieffen Plan required that Germany attack France first through Belgium and secure a quick victory before wheeling to the east to meet the slower armies of the Russians on the Eastern Front. The Schlieffen Plan was put into operation on August 2, 1914, at the outset of the First World War.

scientific revolution of antiquity The Hellenistic period was the most brilliant age in the history of science before the seventeenth century C.E. Aristarchus of Samos posited the existence of a heliocentric universe. Eratosthenes of Alexandria accurately calculated the circumference of the earth. Archimedes turned physics into its own branch of experimental science. Hellenistic anatomists became the first to practice human dissection, greatly improving their understanding of human physiology. Ironically, most of these discoveries were suppressed by pseudo-scientists who flourished under the Roman Empire during the second century C.E., notably Claudius Ptolomaeus (Ptolemy) and Aelius Galenus (Galen).

second industrial revolution The technological developments in the last third of the nineteenth century, which included new techniques for refining and producing steel; increased availability of electricity for industrial, commercial, and domestic use; advances in chemical manufacturing; and the creation of the internal combustion engine.

Second World War Worldwide war that began in September 1939 in Europe, and even earlier in Asia (the Japanese invasion of Manchuria began in 1931), principally pitting Britain, the United States, and the Soviet Union (the Allies) against Nazi Germany, Italy, and Japan (the Axis). The war ended in 1945 with the defeat of Germany and Japan.

Seleucus (d. 280 B.C.E.) The Macedonian general who ruled the Persian heartland of the empire created by Alexander the Great.

Semitic The Semitic language family has the longest recorded history of any linguistic group and is the root for most languages of the Middle and Near East. Ancient Semitic languages include ancient Babylonian and Assyrian, Phoenician, the classical form of Hebrew, early dialects of Aramaic, and the classical Arabic of the Qur'an.

Sepoy Mutiny of 1857 See **Indian Rebellion of 1857**.

serfdom Peasant labor. Unlike slaves, serfs are "attached" to the land they work, and are not supposed to be sold apart from that land.

William Shakespeare (1564–1616) English playwright who flourished during the reigns of Elizabeth I and James I; Shakespeare received a basic education in his hometown of Stratford-upon-Avon and worked in London as an actor before achieving success as a dramatist and poet.

Shi'ites An often-persecuted minority within Islam, Shi'ites believe that only descendants of Muhammad's successor Ali and his wife Fatimah (Muhammad's daughter) can have any authority over the Muslim community. Today, Shi'ites constitute the ruling party in Iran and are numerous in Iraq but otherwise comprise only 10 percent of Muslims worldwide.

Abbé Sieyès (1748–1836) In 1789, he wrote the pamphlet "What is the Third Estate?" in which he posed fundamental questions about the rights of the Third Estate (the commons) and helped provoke its secession from the Estates-General. He was a leader at the Tennis Court Oath, but he later helped Napoleon seize power.

Sinn Féin Irish revolutionary organization that formed in 1900 to fight for Irish independence.

Sino-Japanese War (1894–95) Conflict over the control of Korea in which China was forced to cede the province of Taiwan to Japan.

slave revolt in Saint-Domingue (1791–1804) In September of 1791, the largest slave rebellion in history broke out in Saint-Domingue, the largest and most important French colony in the Caribbean. In 1794, the revolutionary government in France abolished slavery in the colonies, though this act was essentially only recognizing the liberty that the slaves had seized by their own actions. Napoleon reestablished slavery in the French Caribbean in 1802, but failed in his attempt to reconquer Saint-Domingue. Armies commanded by former slaves succeeded in winning independence for a new nation, Haiti, in 1804, making the revolt in Saint-Domingue the first successful slave revolt in history.

slavery The practice of subjugating people to a life of bondage, and of selling or trading these unfree people. For most of human history, slavery had no racial or ethnic basis, and was widely practiced by all cultures and civilizations. Anyone could become a slave, for example, by being captured in war or by being sold for the payment of a debt. It was only in the fifteenth century, with the growth of the African slave trade, that slavery came to be associated with particular races and peoples.

Adam Smith (1723–1790) Scottish economist and liberal philosopher who proposed that competition between self-interested individuals led naturally to a healthy economy. He became famous for his influential book, *The Wealth of Nations* (1776).

Social Darwinism Belief that Charles Darwin's theory of natural selection (evolution) was applicable to human societies and justified the right of the ruling classes or countries to dominate the weak.

social democracy Belief that democracy and social welfare go hand in hand and that diminishing the sharp inequalities of class society is crucial to fortifying democratic culture.

socialism Political ideology that calls for a classless society with collective ownership of all property.

Society of Jesus See **Jesuits**.

Socrates (469–399 B.C.E.) Athenian philosopher and teacher who promoted the careful examination of all inherited opinions and assumptions on the grounds that "the unexamined life is not worth living." A veteran of the Peloponnesian War, Socrates was tried and condemned by his fellow citizens for engaging in allegedly seditious activities and was executed in 399 B.C.E. His most influential pupils were the philosopher Plato and the historian and social commentator Xenophon.

Solon (d. 559 B.C.E.) Elected archon in 594 B.C.E., this Athenian aristocrat enacted a series of political and economic reforms that formed the basis of Athenian democracy.

Somme (1916) River in France and site of a battle of the First World War in which Allied forces attempted to take entrenched German positions from July to mid-November of 1916. Neither side was able to make any real gains despite massive casualties: 500,000 Germans, 400,000 British, and 200,000 French.

Soviet bloc International alliance that included the East European countries of the Warsaw Pact as well as the Soviet Union; it also came to include Cuba.

soviets Local councils elected by workers and soldiers in Russia. Socialists started organizing these councils in 1905, and the Petrograd soviet in the capital emerged as one of the centers of power after the Russian monarchy collapsed in 1917 in the midst of World War I. The soviets became increasingly powerful and pressed for social reform and the redistribution of land, and called for Russian withdrawal from the war against Germany.

Spanish-American War (1898) War between the United States and Spain in Cuba, Puerto Rico, and the Philippines. It ended with a treaty in which the United States took over the Philippines, Guam, and Puerto Rico; Cuba won partial independence.

Spanish Armada Supposedly invincible fleet of warships sent against England by Philip II of Spain in 1588 but vanquished by the English fleet and bad weather in the English Channel.

Sparta Region of Greece in the Peloponnesian peninsula; around 650 B.C.E., after the suppression of a slave revolt, Spartan rulers militarized their society in order to prevent future rebellions and to protect Sparta's superior position in Greece, orienting their society toward the maintenance of their army. Sparta briefly joined forces with Athens and other poleis in the second war with Persia in 480–479 B.C.E., but these two rivals ultimately fell out again in 431 B.C.E. when Sparta and her Peloponnesian allies went to war against Athens and her allies. This bloody conflict lasted until Athens was defeated in 404 B.C.E., after Sparta received military aid from the Persians.

Spartiate A full citizen of Sparta, hence a professional soldier of the hoplite phalanx.

spinning jenny Device invented by James Hargreaves (c. 1720–1774) that revolutionized the British textile industry by allowing a worker to spin much more thread than was possible on a hand spinner.

SS (Schutzstaffel) Formed in 1925 to serve as Hitler's personal security force and to guard Nazi party (NSDAP) meetings, the SS grew into a large militarized organization notorious for their participation in carrying out Nazi policies.

Joseph Stalin (1879–1953) Bolshevik leader who succeeded Lenin as the leader of the Soviet Union and ruled until his death in 1953.

Stalingrad (1942–43) The turning point on the Eastern Front during the Second World War came when the German army tried to take the city of Stalingrad in an effort to break the back of Soviet industry. The German and Soviet armies fought a bitter battle in which more than a half million German, Italian, and Romanian soldiers were killed and the Soviets suffered over a million casualties. The German army surrendered after more than five months of fighting. After Stalingrad, the Soviet army launched a series of attacks that pushed the Germans back.

Stoicism Ancient philosophy derived from the teachings of Zeno of Athens (fl. c. 300) and widely influential within the Roman Empire; it also affected the development of Christianity. Stoics believed in the essential orderliness of the cosmos, and that everything that occurs is for the best. Since everything is determined in accordance with rational purpose, no individual is master of his or her fate, and the only agency that human beings have consists in their responses to good fortune or adversity.

Sumerians The ancient inhabitants of southern Mesopotamia (modern Iraq and Kuwait) whose sophisticated civilization emerged around 4000 B.C.E.

Sunnis Proponents of Islam's customary religious practices (*sunna*) as they developed under the first two caliphs to succeed Muhammad, his father-in-law Abu-Bakr and his disciple Umar. Sunni orthodoxy is dominant within Islam but is opposed by the Shi'ites (from the Arabic word *shi'a*, "faction").

syndicalism Nineteenth-century political movement that embraced a strategy of strikes and sabotage by workers. Their hope was that a general strike of all workers would bring down the capitalist state and replace it with workers' syndicates or trade associations. Their refusal to participate in politics limited their ability to command a wide influence.

tabula rasa Term used by John Locke (1632–1704) to describe the human mind before it acquires ideas as a result of experience; Latin for "clean slate."

Tennis Court Oath (1789) Oath taken by representatives of the Third Estate in June 1789, in which they pledged to form a National Assembly and write a constitution limiting the powers of the king.

Reign of Terror (1793–94) Campaign at the height of the French Revolution in which violence, including systematic executions of opponents of the revolution, was used to purge France of its "enemies" and to extend the revolution beyond its borders; radicals executed as many as 40,000 persons who were judged to be enemies of the state.

Tetrarchy The result of Diocletian's political reforms of the late third century C.E., which divided the Roman Empire into four quadrants.

Theban Hegemony Term describing the period when the polis of Thebes dominated the Greek mainland, which reached its height after 371 B.C.E., under leadership of the Theban general Epaminondas. It was in Thebes that the future King Philip II of Macedon spent his youth, and it was the defeat of Thebes and Athens at the hands of Philip and Alexander—at the Battle of Chaeronea in 338—that Macedonian hegemony was forcefully asserted.

theory of evolution Darwin's theory that linked biology to history. Darwin believed that competition between different organisms and struggle with the environment were fundamental and unavoidable facts of life. In this struggle, those individuals who were better adapted to their environment survived, whereas the weak perished. This produced a "natural selection," or favoring of certain adaptive traits over time, leading to a gradual evolution of different species.

Third Estate The population of France under the Old Regime was divided into three "estates"—corporate bodies that determined an individual's rights or obligations under royal law. The clergy constituted the First Estate, the nobility the Second, and the commoners (the vast bulk of the population) made up the Third Estate.

Third Reich The German state from 1933 to 1945 under Adolf Hitler and the Nazi party.

Third World Nations—mostly in Asia, Latin America, and Africa—that are not highly industrialized.

Thirty Years' War (1618–48) Beginning as a conflict between Protestants and Catholics in Germany, this series of skirmishes escalated into a general European war fought on German soil by armies from Sweden, France, and the Holy Roman Empire.

Timur the Lame (1336–1405) Also known as Tamerlane, he was the last ruler of the Mongol Khans' Asian empire.

Marshal Tito (1892–1980) Yugoslavian communist and resistance leader who became the leader of Yugoslavia and fought to keep his government independent of the Soviet Union. In response, the Soviet Union expelled Yugoslavia from the communist countries' economic and military pacts.

towns Centers for markets and administration. Historically, towns have existed in a symbiotic relationship with the countryside, providing markets for surplus food from outlying farms as well as producing manufactured goods. In the Middle Ages, towns tended to grow up around a castle or monastery which afforded protection.

Treaty of Brest-Litovsk (1918) Separate peace between imperial Germany and the new Bolshevik regime in Russia. The treaty acknowledged the German victory on the Eastern Front and withdrew Russia from the war.

Treaty of Utrecht (1713) Resolution to the War of Spanish Succession that reestablished a balance of power in Europe, to the benefit of Britain and to the disadvantage of Spain, Holland, and France.

Treaty of Versailles Signed on June 28, 1919, this peace settlement ended the First World War and required Germany to surrender a large part of its most valuable territories and to pay huge reparations to the Allies.

trench warfare Weapons such as barbed wire and the machine gun gave a tremendous advantage to defensive positions in World War I, leading to prolonged battles between entrenched armies in fixed positions. The trenches eventually consisted of 25,000 miles of holes and ditches that stretched across the Western Front in northern France, from the Atlantic coast to the Swiss border. On the eastern front, the large expanse of territories made trench warfare less significant.

triangular trade The eighteenth-century commercial Atlantic shipping pattern that took rum from New England to Africa, traded it for slaves taken to the West Indies, and brought sugar back to New England to be processed into rum.

Triple Entente Alliance developed before the First World War that eventually included Britain, France, and Russia.

Truman Doctrine (1947) Declaration promising U.S. economic and military intervention to counter any attempt by the Soviet Union to expand its influence. Often cited as a key moment in the origins of the Cold War.

tsar Russian word for "emperor," derived from the Latin *caesar* and similar to the German *kaiser*, it was the title claimed by the rulers of medieval Muscovy and of the later Russian Empire.

Ubaid culture Early civilization that flourished in Mesopotamia between 5500 and 4000 B.C.E., it was characterized by large village settlements and temple complexes: a precursor to the more urban civilization of the Sumerians.

Umayyad Caliphate (661–930) The Umayyad family resisted the authority of the first two caliphs who succeeded Muhammad but eventually placed a member of their own family in that position of power. The Umayyad Caliphate ruled the Islamic world from 661 to 750, modeling their administration on that of the Roman Empire. After a rebellion led by the rival Abbasid family, the power of the Umayyad Caliphate was confined to their territories in al-Andalus (southern Spain).

Universal Declaration of Human Rights (1948) United Nations declaration that laid out the rights to which all human beings are entitled.

University of Paris The reputation of Peter Abelard and his students attracted many intellectuals to Paris in the twelfth century; some of them began offering instruction to aspiring scholars. By 1200, this loose association of teachers had formed themselves into a *universitas*, or corporation. They began collaborating in the higher academic study of the liberal arts, with a special emphasis on theology.

Pope Urban II (1042–1099) Instigator of the First Crusade (1096–99), who promised that anyone who fought or died in the service of the Church would receive absolution from sin.

urban populations During the nineteenth century, urban populations in Europe increased sixfold. For the most part, urban areas had medieval infrastructures that where overwhelmed by new populations and industries. As a result, many European cities became overcrowded and unhealthy.

Utopia Title of a semi-satirical social critique by the English statesman Sir Thomas More (1478–1535); the word derives from the Greek "best place" or "no place."

Lorenzo Valla (1407–1457) One of the first practitioners of scientific philology (the historical study of language), Valla's analysis of the so-called Donation of Constantine showed that the document could not possibly have been written in the fourth century C.E., but must have been forged centuries later.

vassal A person who pledges to be loyal and subservient to a lord in exchange for land, income, or protection.

velvet revolutions Peaceful political revolutions throughout Eastern Europe in 1989.

Verdun (1916) Site in France of a battle between German and French forces that lasted for ten months during the First World War. The Germans saw the battle as a chance to break French morale through a war of attrition, and the French believed the battle to be a symbol of France's strength. In the end, over 400,000 lives were lost and the German offensive failed.

Versailles Conference (1919) Peace conference following the First World War; it resulted in the Treaty of Versailles, which forced Germany to pay reparations and to give up territories to the victors.

Queen Victoria (1819–1901) Influential monarch who reigned from 1837 until her death; she presided over the expansion of the British Empire as well as the evolution of British politics and social and economic reforms.

Viet Cong Vietnamese communist group formed in 1954; committed to overthrowing the government of South Vietnam and reunifying North and South Vietnam.

Vikings (c. 800–c. 1000) The collapse of the Abbasid Caliphate disrupted Scandinavian commercial networks and turned traders into raiders (the word *viking* describes the activity of raiding). These raids often escalated into invasions that contributed to the collapse of the Carolingian Empire, resulted in the devastation of settled territories, and ended with the establishment of Viking colonies. By the tenth century, Vikings controlled large areas of eastern England, Scotland, Ireland, Iceland, Greenland, and parts of northern France. They had also established the beginnings of the kingdom that became Russia and made exploratory voyages to North America, founding a settlement at Newfoundland (Canada).

A Vindication of the Rights of Woman Book by Mary Wollstonecraft (1759–1797), English republican who applied Enlightenment political ideas to issues of gender.

Virgil (70–19 B.C.E.) Influential Roman poet who wrote under the patronage of the emperor Augustus. His *Aeneid* was modeled on the ancient Greek epics of Homer and told the mythical tale of Rome's founding by the Trojan refugee Aeneas.

Visigoths The tribes of "west" Goths who sacked Rome in 410 C.E. and later established a kingdom in the Roman province of Hispania (Spain).

Voltaire Pseudonym of French philosopher, deist, and satirist François Marie Arouet (1694–1778), who championed the cause of human dignity against state and church oppression in works such as the novel *Candide*.

Lech Wałęsa (b. 1943) Leader of the Polish labor movement Solidarity, which organized a series of strikes across Poland in 1980 to protest working conditions, shortages, and high prices. Above all, Solidarity demanded an independent labor union. Its leaders were imprisoned and the union banned, but a new series of strikes in 1988 led to the legalization of Solidarity and open elections.

war communism The Russian Civil War forced the Bolsheviks to take a more radical economic stance. They requisitioned grain from the peasantry and outlawed private trade in consumer goods as "speculation." They also militarized production facilities and abolished money.

Wars of the Roses Fifteenth-century civil conflict between the English dynastic houses of Lancaster and York, each of which was symbolized by the heraldic device of a rose (red and white, respectively). It was ultimately resolved by the accession of the Lancastrian king Henry VII, who married Elizabeth of York.

Warsaw Pact (1955–91) Military alliance between the USSR and other communist states that was established as a response to the creation of the NATO alliance.

The Wealth of Nations Treatise published in 1776 by Adam Smith, whose laissez-faire ideas predicted the economic boom of the Industrial Revolution.

Weimar Republic The government of Germany between 1919 and the rise of Hitler and the Nazi party.

Western Front Military front that stretched from the English Channel through Belgium and France to the Alps during the First World War.

Whites Term for the Russian "counterrevolutionaries" of the Bolshevik Revolution (1918–21) who fought the Bolsheviks (the "Reds"); they included former supporters of the tsar, Social Democrats, and large independent peasant armies.

William the Conqueror (1027–1087) Duke of Normandy who claimed the throne of England; in 1066, William invaded England and defeated the Anglo-Saxon king Harold at the Battle of Hastings. He and his Norman followers imposed imperial rule in England through a brutal campaign of military conquest, surveillance, and the suppression of the indigenous Anglo-Saxon (Old English) language.

William of Ockham (d. 1349) English philosopher and Franciscan friar who denied that human reason could prove fundamental theological truths, such as the existence of God; he argued that there is no necessary connection between the observable laws of nature and the unknowable essence of divinity. His theories, derived from the work of earlier scholastics, form the basis of the scientific method.

Woodrow Wilson (1856–1924) U.S. president who requested and received a declaration of war from Congress so that America could enter the First World War. After the war, his prominent role in the Paris Peace Conference signaled the rise of the United States as a world power. He also proposed the Fourteen Points, which influenced the peace negotiations.

Maria Winkelmann (1670–1720) German astronomer who worked with her husband in his observatory. Despite discovering a comet and preparing calendars for the Berlin Academy of Sciences, the academy would not let her take her husband's place within the Academy after he died.

witch craze Rash of persecutions against so-called witches that took place in both Catholic and Protestant countries of early modern Europe and their colonies, facilitated by both secular governments and religious authorities.

women's associations Because European women were excluded from the workings of parliamentary and mass politics, some women formed organizations to press for political and civil rights. Some groups focused on establishing educational opportunities for women while others, "suffragettes," campaigned energetically for the vote.

William Wordsworth (1770–1850) English Romantic poet whose central themes were nature, simplicity, and feeling. He considered nature to be man's most trustworthy teacher and source of sublime power that nourished the human soul.

World Bank International agency established in 1944 to provide economic assistance to war-torn nations in need of economic development.

John Wycliffe (c. 1330–1384) Professor of theology at the University of Oxford who urged the English king to confiscate ecclesiastical wealth and to replace corrupt priests and bishops with men who would live according to the apostolic standards of poverty and piety. Wycliffe advocated direct access to the scriptures and promoted an English translation of the Bible. His teachings played an important role in the Peasants' Revolt of 1381 and inspired the even more radical initiatives of a group known as Lollards.

Xerxes (c. 519–465 B.C.E.) Xerxes succeeded his father, Darius, as Great King of Persia. Seeking to avenge his father's shame and eradicate any future threats to Persian hegemony, he launched his own invasion of Greece in 480 B.C.E. An allied Greek army defeated his forces in 479 B.C.E.

Yalta Accords Meeting among U.S. president Franklin D. Roosevelt, British prime minister Winston Churchill, and Soviet premier Joseph Stalin that was held in the Crimea in 1945 shortly before the end of the Second World War to plan for the postwar order.

Young Turks Turkish reformist movement in 1908 that aimed to modernize the Ottoman Empire, restore parliamentary rule, and depose Sultan Abdul Hamid II.

ziggurats Temples constructed under the Dynasty of Ur in what is now Iraq, beginning around 2100 B.C.E.

Zionism Political movement dating to the end of the nineteenth century holding that the Jewish people constitute a nation and are entitled to a national homeland. Zionists rejected a policy of Jewish assimilation and advocated the reestablishment of a Jewish homeland in Palestine.

Zollverein Customs union, started by Prussia in 1834, which established free trade among the German states and a uniform tariff against the rest of the world. By the 1840s, the union included almost all of the German states except German Austria. It is considered an important forerunner of the political unification of Germany, which was completed in 1870 under Prussian leadership.

Zoroastrianism One of the three major universal faiths of the ancient world, alongside Judaism and Christianity; it was derived from the teachings of the Persian Zoroaster around 600 B.C.E. Zoroaster redefined religion as an ethical practice common to all, rather than as a set of rituals and superstitions unique to a particular group of people. Zoroastrianism teaches that there is one supreme god in the universe, Ahura-Mazda (Wise Lord), but that his goodness will be constantly assailed by the forces of evil until the arrival of a final "judgment day." Proponents of this faith should therefore help good to triumph over evil by leading a good life and by performing acts of compassion and charity. Zoroastrianism exercised a profound influence over many early Christians, including Augustine.

Ulrich Zwingli (1484–1531) Former priest from the Swiss city of Zurich who joined Luther and Calvin in attacking the authority of the Roman Catholic Church.

Text Credits

Aristophanes: 300 words from *Aristophanes: Lysistrata and Other Plays* translated with an introduction and notes by Alan H. Sommerstein (Penguin Books, 2002). Copyright © Alan H. Sommerstein, 2002. Reproduced by permission of Penguin Books Ltd.

Arrian: 365 words from *The Campaigns of Alexander* by Arrian, translated by Aubrey de Sélincourt, revised with an introduction and notes by J. R. Hamilton (Penguin Classics 1958, Revised edition 1971). Copyright © the Estate of Aubrey de Sélincourt, 1958. Introduction and Notes copyright © J.R. Hamilton, 1971. Reproduced by permission of Penguin Books Ltd.

Bernard of Angers: "A Miracle of St. Faith," by Bernard of Angers, from *Readings in Medieval History,* 2nd Edition, edited by Patrick J. Geary (Toronto, Ontario: University of Toronto Press, 2003). Copyright © 2003. Reprinted with permission of the publisher.

Henry Bettenson (ed.): "Obedience as a Jesuit Hallmark" from *Documents of the Christian Church*, 2nd Edition. Copyright © 1967, Oxford University Press. Reprinted by permission of Oxford University Press.

Gabriel Biel: "Execrabilis." Reprinted by permission of the publisher from *Defensorium Obedientiae Apostolicae Et Alia Documenta* by Gabriel Biel, edited and translated by Reiko A. Oberman, Daniel E. Zerfoss and William J. Courtenay, pp. 224–227, Cambridge, Mass.: The Belknap Press of Harvard University Press, Copyright © 1968 by the President and Fellows of Harvard College.

Walter Bower: "A Declaration of Scottish Independence," from *Scotichronicon*, Volume 7, by Walter Bower. Edited by B. Scott and D. E. R. Watt. Reprinted by permission of Birlinn Limited.

Jean Baptiste Colbert: "Mercantilism and War" from *Colbert and a Century of French Mercantilism*, edited by Charles W. Cole. Copyright © 1939 Columbia University Press. Reprinted with permission of the publisher.

Anna Comnena: pp. 308–311 from *The Alexiad of Anna Comnena*, translated by E.R.A. Sewter (Penguin Classics, 1969). Copyright © E.R.A. Sewter, 1969. Reproduced by permission of Penguin Books Ltd.

Marie de France: "Equitan" (pp. 56–57) from *The Lais of Marie de France*, by Marie de France, translated by Glyn S. Burgess and Keith Busby (Penguin Classics 1986, Second edition 1999). Copyright © Glyn S Burgess and Keith Busby, 1986, 1999. Reproduced by permission of Penguin Books Ltd.

Bartolome de las Casas: 500 words from *A Short Account of the Destruction of the Indies* by Bartolome de las Casas, edited and translated by Nigel Griffin, introduction by Anthony Pagden (Penguin Classics, 1992). Translation and Notes copyright © Nigel Griffin, 1992. Introduction copyright © Anthony Pagden 1992. Reproduced by permission of Penguin Books Ltd.

Michel de Montaigne: From *Montaigne: Selections from the Essays*, translated and edited by Donald M. Frame (Harlan Davidson, Inc., 1973), pp. 34–38.

René Descartes: From *A Discourse on the Method of Correctly Conducting One's Reason*, trans. Ian Maclean. Copyright © Ian Maclean 2006. Reprinted by permission of Oxford University Press.

Armand J. du Plessis: "Cardinal Richelieu on the Common People of France," pp. 31–32 from Hill, Henry Bertram, *The Political Testament of Cardinal Richelieu*. © 1961 by the Board of Regents of the University of Wisconsin System. Reprinted by permission of The University of Wisconsin Press.

Ecumenical Councils: "Epitome of the Definition of the Iconoclastic Conciliabulum" from *A Select Library of Nicene and Post-Nicene Fathers of the Christian Church, Vol. XIV*, eds. Schaff & Wace (Grand Rapids, MI: Wm. B. Eerdmans Publishing Company, 1955), pp. 543–544.

Robert Filmer: "Observations upon Aristotle's Politiques" (1652), in *Divine Right and Democracy: An Anthology of Political Writing in Stuart England*, edited by David Wootton. Pp 110–118. Copyright © 1986. Reproduced by permission of Hackett Publishing Company, Inc.

Galileo Galilei: From *Discoveries and Opinions of Galileo* by Galileo Galilei, translated by Stillman Drake, copyright © 1957 by Stillman Drake. Used by permission of Doubleday, an imprint of the Knopf Doubleday Publishing Group, a division of Penguin Random House LLC. All rights reserved.

Pierre Gassendi: From *The Selected Works of Pierre Gassendi*, Edited by Craig B. Brush. (New York: Johnson Reprint Corporation, 1972) pp. 334–336.

Homer: *Iliad*, translated by Stanley Lombardo, selections from pp. 115–118. Copyright © 1997 by Hackett Publishing Company, Inc. Reprinted by permission of Hackett Publishing Company, Inc. All rights reserved.

Rosemary Horrox (ed.): From *The Black Death*, by Horrox (Trans., Ed.), 1994, Manchester University Press, Manchester, UK. Reprinted with permission.

Juvenal: 224 words (pp. 138–139) from *The Sixteen Satires* by Juvenal, translated by Peter Green (Penguin Classics 1967, Revised edition 1974). Copyright © Peter Green 1967, 1974. Reproduced by permission of Penguin Books Ltd.

Chapter 1: pp. 2–3: The Louve, Paris. Giraudon/Art Resource, NY; p. 5: The Bridgeman Art Library; p. 8: © INTERFOTO/Alamy; p. 9 (left): Ashmolean Museum, University of Oxford, UK /The Bridgeman Art Library; p. 9 (right): British Museum; p. 11: Bettmann Corbis; p. 14 (left): The Granger Collection, NYC; p. 14 (right): © Arterra Picture Library/Alamy; p. 16 (top): © World Religions Photo Library/Bridgeman Art Library; p. 16 (bottom): © INTERFOTO/Alamy; p. 19 (left): © RMN-Grand Palais/Art Resource, NY; p. 19 (right): © RMN-Grand Palais/Art Resource, NY; p. 22 (left): Scala/Art Resource; p. 22 (right): Scala/Art Resource; p. 23: Bettmann/Corbis; p. 24: © Gian Berto Vanni/Corbis; p. 25: Charles & Josette Lenars/Corbis.

Chapter 2: pp. 30–31: Erich Lessing/Art Resource, NY; p. 35: Erich Lessing/Art Resource, NY; p. 36 (left): PCL/Alamy; p. 36 (right): Ian M Butterfield (P)/Alamy; p. 37 (left): Sebastian Bergmann/Flickr/ Creative Commons; p. 37 (right): Jim Henderson/Alamy; p. 40: Erich Lessing/Art Resource, NY; p. 41: Gianni Dagli Orti/Corbis; p. 43 (left): Nimatallah/Art Resource, NY; p. 43 (right): Bloomberg via Getty Images; p. 47: British Museum, London, Great Britain, photo: Erich Lessing/Art Resource, NY; p. 51: The Art Gallery Collection/ Alamy; p. 54: Courtesy of Zev Radovan; p. 55: Bildarchiv Preussischer Kulturbesitz/Art Resource, NY.

Chapter 3: pp. 58–59: Erich Lessing/Art Resource, NY; p. 60: Nagelestock.com/Alamy; p. 64: Wikimedia Commons; p. 65: De Agostini Picture Library/The Bridgeman Art Library; p. 68: Carol Symes; p. 73 (left): ©Paul Lipke/Trireme Trust, Montague, MA; p. 73 (right): National Museums of Scotland/Bridgeman Art Library; p. 75 (left): Clip Art ETC; p. 75 (right): Vanni/Art Resource, NY; p. 76 (left): DeA Picture Library/The Granger Collection; p. 76 (right): COMEDY CENT/MAD COW PROD/THE KOBAL COLLECTION/ART RESOURCE; p. 77 (left): Foto Marburg/Art Resource, NY; p. 77 (center): Gianni Dagli Orti/The Art Archive at Art Resource, NY; p. 77 (right): Nimatallah/Art Resource, NY; p. 81: Erich Lessing/Art Resource, NY.

Chapter 4: pp. 86–87: Erich Lessing/Art Resource, NY; p. 90: Scala/ Art Resource, NY; p. 91 (left): Marie-Lan Nguyen/Ludovisi Collection/Wikimedia; p. 91 (right): Vanni/Art Resource, NY; p. 92: © Gianni Dagli Ortie/Corbis; p. 93: Erin Babnik/Alamy; p. 94: Wikimedia Commons; p. 96: Erich Lessing/Art Resource, NY; p. 99 (left): The Trustees of the British Museum; p. 99 (right): Bildarchiv Preussischer Kulturbesitz/Art Resource, NY; p. 101 (left): The Granger Collection, New York; p. 101 (right): © Reuters/CORBIS; p. 106 (left): INTERFOTO/Alamy; p. 106 (right): Scala/Art Resource, NY; p. 107 (left): akg-images/CDA/Guillemot; p. 107 (right): Scala/Art Resource, NY.

Chapter 5: pp. 110–11: © Cultura Creative/Alamy; p. 113: Statue of Cincinnatus, Cincinnati, OH, 2010, by Rick Dikeman; p. 116: Scala/Art Resource, NY; p. 120 (left): The Print Collector/Alamy; p. 120 (right):

JAY DIRECTO/AFP/Getty Images/Newscom; p. 124 (left): Sandro Vannini/Corbis; p. 124 (right): Yale University Art Gallery/Art Resource, NY; p. 125: The Granger Collection, New York; p. 127: Courtesy of Carol Symes; p. 130: Silver Stock/Alamy; p. 133 (top): Vanni/Art Resource, NY; p. 133 (bottom): © Images & Stories/Alamy.

Chapter 6: pp. 138–39: Alinari/Art Resource, NY; p. 145: TopFoto/The Image Works; p. 148 (left): The Trustees of the British Museum; p. 148 (right): The Four Tetrarchs (porphyry), Italian School/Basillica di San Marco, Venice, Italy/The Bridgeman Art Library; p. 151 (left) Wikipedia Commons; p. 151 (right): Wikipedia Commons; p. 153: The Trustees of the British Museum; p. 154: Erich Lessing/Art Resource, NY; p. 158 (left): © julie woodhouse/Alamy; p. 158 (right): JAY DIRECTO/AFP/ Getty Images/Newscom; p. 159: akg-images/ullstein bild; p. 161: Scala/ Art Resource, NY.

Chapter 7: pp. 164–65: akg-images; p. 169: Wikipedia Commons; p. 172: Vanni/Art Resource, NY; p. 176 (left): Frédéric Soltan/Sygma/ Corbis; p. 176 (right): Bildarchiv Preussischer Kulturbesitz/Art Resource, NY; p. 178 (left): Galerie Bilderwelt/Getty Images; p. 178 (right): NeocoreGames/Wikimedia; p. 181: The Granger Collection, New York; p. 182 (left): Birmingham Museums & Art Gallery; p. 182 (right): The Trustees of the British Museum/Art Resource, NY; p. 183 (top): The Trustees of the British Museum; p. 183 (left): The Trustees of the British Museum; p. 183 (right): The Trustees of the British Museum; p. 187: Bibliotheque Nationale, Paris, France /The Bridgeman Art Library.

Chapter 8: pp. 192–93: Bayerische Staatsbibliothek/Art Resource; p. 195: Berig/Wikimedia Commons; p. 198 (left): Wikimedia Commons; p. 198 (right): Bayerische Staatsbibliothek/Art Resource; p. 200: From David Nicholas, *Urban Europe, 1100–1700* (Palgrave MacMillan, 2003, p.74 fig 3.3); p. 203: Wikimedia Commons; p. 204 (top): French School/The Bridgeman Art Library/Getty Images; p. 204 (bottom): French School/The Bridgeman Art Library/Getty Images; p. 206: The Granger Collection, New York; p. 208: Erich Lessing/ Art Resource, NY; p. 214: HIP/Art Resource, NY; p. 216 (left): The Bridgeman Art Library/Getty; p. 216 (right): STEPHEN JAFFE/AFP/ Newscom; p. 219 (left): Sites & Photos/akg-images; p. 219 (right): Album/Art Resource, NY.

Chapter 9: pp. 222–23: The Granger Collection, New York; p. 224: Giraudon/Art Resource, NY; p. 231 (left): The Granger Collection, New York; p. 231 (right): The Art Archive/Archivo de la Corona de Aragon Barcelona/Laurie Platt Winfrey; p. 233: Gianni Dagli Orti/The Art Archive at Art Resource, NY; p. 237: Erich Lesser/Art Resource, NY; p. 238: © The Metropolitan Museum of Art/Art Resource, NY; p. 239: Sueddeutsche Zeitung Photo/The Image Works; p. 247: akg-images; p. 248 (left): Scala/ White Images/Art Resource, NY; p. 248 (right): Lucasfilm Ltd./Twentieth Century Fox Film Corp./Photofest; p. 251 (left): Richard List/Corbis; p. 251 (right): Richard List/Corbis.

Index

Florence
    after Black Death, 287, 289
    Ciompi revolt, 287
    and classical education during Renaissance,
        295, 314
    literature, 289
    Renaissance in, 295, 322
    stabilization of government in late 1300s, 304–5
    trade, 287
forum, 113
Fourth Lateran Council (Lateran IV), 234–36, 240,
    246
France
    and Black Death, 287–90
    Capetian dynasty of, 197, 226
    colonialism and, 409–10
    Edict of Nantes and, 408–9
    expansionism under Louis IX, 272–73
    expansion of monarchic power in, 225, 226–27
    and Great Famine, 277
    Huguenots and, 355
    and Hundred Years' War, 276, 277, 300–302, 305
    Italian War (1494–1498), 328–29
    Jacquerie Rebellion, 287
    literature, 289–90
    Merovingian dynasty of, 180, 184
    in Nine Years' War, 414
    and papacy, 267, 270
    royal tax collection, 409
    scientific revolution and, 441, 445
    and sovereignty, 272
    and Thirty Years' War, 381, 383–85
    Treaty of Utrecht and, 415
    and War of the Spanish Succession, 414
    wars of religion in, 378
Francis, Pope, 304
Franciscans (Order of the Friars Minor), 240
Francis of Assisi, Saint, 240, 242–43
Franks, Kingdom of, 156–57, 180, 197
Frederick I, King of Prussia, 417
Frederick I (Barbarossa), Holy Roman Emperor, 227,
    232, 233, 239
Frederick II, Holy Roman Emperor, 227, 229, 267
Frederick II (the Great), King of Prussia, 417
Frederick III (the Wise), Elector of Saxony, 343, 347,
    350, 351
Frederick William (the Great Elector), Elector of
    Prussia, 417
Frederick William I, King of Prussia, 417
Free Companies, 300
French Academy of Sciences, 441
Frequens, 306–7
frescoes, 266
Friedrich II, King of Denmark, 430
Fronde, 385
Fulbert, 223
Fulcoer of Chartres, 212

Gabriele de' Mussi, 280
Gaius, 135, 137
Galen, 106–7
Galerius, Emperor of Rome, 148, 149, 150
Galilei, Galileo, 365, 426, 430–35, 433
    church and, 431–35
    Kepler and, 430–31, 447
    telescope and, 431
Galileo Galilei before the Inquisition (Fleury-Richard),
    431
Gallilee, 140
Gama, Vasco da, 334, 335
Ganelon, 193
Gargantua and Pantagruel (Rabelais), 327
Gascony, 276, 277, 300
Gassendi, Pierre, 440–41
Gath, 44
Gaza, 44
gender issues. See women
Genesis, Book of, 3, 54
Genghis Khan, 256

Genoa, 305
    abandonment of Tabriz, 261
    and African gold trade, 261
    and Black Death, 261, 278
    Mediterranean colonization in Middle Ages, 262
George III, King of England, 402
Germania (Tacitus), 132
Germany
    after Black Death, 286
    church and state power in, 205–6
    dissolution of Holy Roman Empire, 229
    Hanseatic League in, 287
    Ottonian dynasty in, 192, 192–93, 196, 198, 203
    and Thirty Years' War, 381
Ghana, 262
Gibbon, Edward, 163
Gilgamesh, Epic of, 11–13, 48
Giotto di Bondone, 266, 266
global economic crisis (2007–2010), 43
global pandemics, 279
Glorious Revolution, 411–12
gold
    African, European trade in, 261–62
    and colonization of New World, 335–41
    and inflation, 376–77
    Portuguese trade in, 332
Gold Coast, 332
Golden Horde Khanate, 257–58, 258, 261
Goliath, 44
Gothic architecture, 251, 252–53
Goths, 155–56
Gottfried von Strassburg, 249
Gracchus, Gaius, 110, 122–23
Gracchus, Tiberius, 110, 122
Gratian, 230, 245
Great Britain. See also England
    colonialism and, 372–73, 415
    Treaty of Utrecht and, 415
Great Famine (1315–1322), 277, 294
Great Northern War, 421
Great Umayyad Mosque at Damascus, 176
Great Western Schism, 305–7
    and Council of Constance, 305–7
    territorial allegiances in, 308
Greece, Archaic, 59–74
    architecture in, 60, 72
    aristocracy and, 64–65, 67, 68
    art of, 62, 64
    Athenian pre-eminence in, 62, 69
    codification of law in, 68
    coinage in, 49, 71
    colonization by, 61, 62, 63, 69, 71–72
    commerce of, 60–62, 71
    democracy in, 65–69
    foreign influences on, 62, 71
    heroic ideal in, 61
    hoplites of, 62–63, 65, 69, 72, 73
    literature and language in, 61, 65–67, 66
    naval power of, 61, 73, 73, 74
    Near Eastern influence on, 71
    organization and government of, 61, 64–69, 75
    Panhellenism in, 60, 62, 72
    in Persian Wars, 50, 72–74, 74
    philosophy in, 72
    polis in, 61, 62, 64, 67–74
    pottery of, 60, 68
    slavery in, 68, 69
    social structure of, 60–61, 64–65
    types of government in, 64–69
    tyrants and, 65, 68
    warfare in, 62–63, 65, 69, 70
    women in, 64
Greece, Classical
    architecture in, 75, 78
    art of, 77, 77–78, 88, 90, 91
    Athenian pre-eminence in, 75
    Corinthian War in, 88
    democracy in, 75, 84, 85
    foreign influences on, 77

hoplites of, 84, 88, 93, 95
legacy of, 85
literature in, 75–77, 88–90
naval power of, 80, 81
Peloponnesian War in, 58, 79, 79–81, 86, 88, 108
philosophy in, 62, 72, 77, 81–85, 88, 90, 90, 92,
    100–105, 170
polis in, 80, 85, 88, 90, 99, 100, 115
slavery in, 78–79, 85
theater in, 75, 75–76, 88, 90
women in, 78, 85
Greece, Hellenistic. See Hellenistic world
Greece, modern, 296
Greek fire, 168
Greek language, 294
Greek literature, 292, 294
Greenland, 263
    Norse settlers in, 262–63
    Viking colonization of, 262
Gregory I (the Great), Pope, 164, 181–83
Gregory of Tours, 178–79
Gregory VII, Pope, 192, 206, 206, 209–10, 236, 237
Gregory XI, Pope, 305
Gregory XII, Pope, 304
Gregory XIII, Pope, 26, 124
Grimmelshausen, Hans Jakob von, 382
Gustavus Adolphus, King of Sweden, 381, 383
Gutenberg, Johannes, 313, 314

Habsburg dynasty, 350, 414–17
    and Peace of Westphalia, 384
    and Thirty Years' War, 381, 383
hadith, 177
Hadrian, Emperor of Rome, 127, 130, 145
Hadrian's Wall, 127, 127, 146
Haec Sancta Synodus, 306
Hagia Sophia, Church of, 171–72, 172
Halley, Edmund, 443
Hamlet (Shakespeare), 425
Hammurabi, King of Babylon, 15–19, 19, 48, 96, 99
Handbook of the Christian Knight (Erasmus), 326
Hannibal, 118
Hanseatic League, 287
Harold II (Godwinson), King of England, 204, 205
Harun al-Rashid, Umayyad Caliph, 176, 178, 188
Harvey, William, 437
Haskins, Charles Homer, 253
Hastings, battle of, 204, 205
Hatshepsut, Queen of Egypt, 33–34, 36, 36, 37, 37
Hattusilis III, King of the Hittites, 39
Hebrews, Kingdom of, 44–47, 46, 53–57
    Babylonian captivity of, 55–56
    commerce in, 47
    consolidation of, 46
    development of monotheism in, 53–56
    early religion in, 53–54
    forced labor in, 47
    Jerusalem as capital of, 46
    Jerusalem temple in, 46–47
    organization of, 45
Hecataeus of Miletus, 71, 72
Hector, 61, 66, 94
Heliogabalus, Emperor of Rome, 147
Hellenic League, 73–74
Hellenistic world, 94, 96, 98, 98–100
    agriculture in, 100
    architecture in, 107
    Christianity in, 142, 144, 144
    cities and, 100, 107, 109
    commerce in, 100
    dual cultures of, 98
    Greek diaspora in, 100, 101
    literature in, 108
    religion in, 102–3, 142, 144
    Roman conquest of, 119–20
    sculpture in, 106, 107, 107
    warfare in, 99
    women in, 104–5
Heloise, 222, 223, 224, 239, 241, 251

Thomas à Kempis, 309
Thomas Aquinas, Saint, 240, 246, 265, 345, 354, 365
Thomas of Celano, 242
1001 Nights, 176
Thucydides, 38, 62, 77, 78, 80, 108, 170
Thutmose I, Pharaoh of Egypt, 33
Thutmose II, Pharaoh of Egypt, 33, 37, *37*
Thutmose III, Pharaoh of Egypt, 34, 37
Tiber River, 112–14, 150
Tigris River, 4, 8, 14, 190
time measurement
    Egyptian, 26
    in late Middle Ages, 264–65
    Roman, 124
Timur the Lame (Tamburlane), Mongol conqueror,
    296–97
Tirhakoh, Pharaoh of Egypt, 52
Tissaphernes, 89
Titian, 322, 347
Titus, Emperor of Rome, 130, *130*
tobacco trade, 375
Tordesillas, Treaty of, 336
Tories, 411
Toulouse, France, 287
trade, trade routes. *See* commerce
Trajan, Emperor of Rome, 110, 127, 145–47
transatlantic triangle. *See* triangular trade
transnational networks, late Bronze Age, 36–38
transubstantiation, *237*, 238
Treasury of Merits, 345
Trent, Council of, 361–64
triangular trade, *371*, 373–75, *375*
Tribonian, 167
tribunes, 115
Trinity with the Virgin, The (Masaccio), *319*
Tripoli, 233
Tristan (Gottfried), 249
triumph, Roman, 124
triumvirate, 123
Trojan War, 38
Trojan Women, The (Euripides), 76
Troy (Ilium), 38, 39
Tudor dynasty, 303
Tunis, 261
Tutankhamun (Tutankhaten), Pharaoh of Egypt, 35
Twelve Tables, Law of the, 110, 115–17, 135
Two New Sciences (Galileo), 434
Two Treatises on Government (Locke), 412
Tyre, 47
Tyrtaeus, 67

Ubaid peoples, 8
Ugarit, 38, 42
ulamas, 177
Ulpian, 135, 137
Umar, Caliph, 173, 175
Umar Khayyam, 219
Umayyad dynasty, 164, 176
universities
    Bologna, 244
    classical thought and Christian theology in, 246
    Paris, 226–27, 244
    rise of, 224, 241, 244–46, *245*
Ur, 15, 16, *16*
Urban II, Pope, 211–14, 232
urban planning
    Hellenistic, 100, 107, 109
    medieval, 199–200, *200*
    Roman, 121, 130, 133–35
Urban VI, Pope, 305
Urban VIII, Pope (Maffeo Barberini), 432
Ur-Nammu, King of Amorites, 15

Urraca, Queen of León-Castile, 249
Uruk, 8, *8*, 20
Uthman, Umayyad Caliph, 175
Utnapishtim, 12, 32
Utopia (More), 327
Utrecht, Treaty of, 414–15, *416*

Valla, Lorenzo, 296
Valley of the Kings, 34
Valois dynasty, 276
Vandals, 155–56, 160
van der Straet, Jan, 337
van der Weyden, Rogier, 290, 293
Van Dyke, Anthony, *387*
vanishing perspective, 319
vassal, 205
Velázquez, Diego, 396, *396*
Venice
    and Fourth Crusade, 235–36
    Mediterranean colonization in Middle Ages, 262
    Renaissance art in, 322
    stabilization of government in late 1300s, 304
    trade in aftermath of Black Death, 287
Venus, 116
Versailles, 403–6, *405*
Vespucci, Amerigo, 336, 427
Vesuvius, Mount, 110
View of Toledo (El Greco), 396, *396*
Vikings, 164, 188–90, *189*, 194–97, 199, 203, 210
    conversion to Christianity, 188
    and Native North Americans, 264–65
    New World and, 336
Vinland, 262
Virgil, 108, 112, 131, 161, 267, 292
Virginia Colony, 370
Virgin Mary, *238*, 238–39
Visigoths, 138, 156, 167
    conquest of kingdom by Umayyads, 174
    establishment of Iberian kingdom of, 156
visual arts, 290
Vitruvius, 323
Vladimir, Prince of Kiev, 210
Voltaire, 444

Wagner, Richard, 249
Waldensians, 240
Waldo (Waldes), Peter, 240, 242
Wales, 274–75, 277
Walid, Caliph al-, 176
warfare, 36–38. *See also specific wars*
    Akkadians and, 15
    artillery and, 334–35, 426
    between Catholic and Protestant rulers, 355
    chariots in, 13, 32
    Christine de Pisan's writings, 291
    Egyptians and, 28, 34
    in Europe after Black Death, 299–305
    Greek, 62–63, 69, 70
    Hebrew kingdom and, 46
    in Hellenistic world, 99
    Hittites and, 32
    holy war doctrine in, 48, 217
    hoplites and, 62–63, *65*, 69, 72, *73*, 84, 88, *93*, 95
    horses in, 33, 115
    Kassites and, 36
    knights in, 203, 213–14, 247
    medieval, 210–14, 215
    mercantilism and, 410
    Mycenaeans and, 40–41
    and national monarchies, 305
    Neo-Assyrians and, 47, 48
    in Neolithic Age, 4

Papal States and, 347
    phalanx and, 63, 69, 93, *93*, 114
    Philistines and, 44
    religious, 355
    Romans and, 114, 118–20, 122, 123
    Sumerians and, 9, 12, 13, 15
    wealth and, 179
War of the Spanish Succession, 414
Wars of the Roses, 303
Washday, 44
water power, early uses of, 198
Westphalia, Peace of, 384, 415
wheat, 277
wheel, *11*, 12–13
Whigs, 411, 412
White Temple at Uruk, 8, *8*
William I (the Conqueror), King of England, 192,
    203–5
William III, King of England, 411–12, 414
William of Ockham, 265
William of Orange (the Silent), Dutch Prince, 379,
    413
William of Rubruck, 260
Winged Victory of Samothrace (sculpture), 107, *107*
Winkelmann, Maria, 441–42
witchcraft, 392–93
Wittenberg, Germany, 343–44
Wolfram von Eschenbach, 249
women
    in ancient Egypt, 26–28
    in ancient Greece, 64, 78, 85, 92, 104–5
    in ancient Rome, 112–13, 117, 121, 131, 137
    Aristotle on, 92, 154
    astronomy and, 441–42
    in Byzantine Empire, 171
    Catholic Church and, 239, 307–9, 365
    in Christianity, 142, 144, 150, 153, 159
    in courtly literature, 248–49
    Etruscan, 112
    in Islam, 177
    in literature after Black Death, 290
    medieval literacy of, 241
    in monasteries, 180–81, 239
    Plato on, 104–5
    Reformation and, 357
    in Renaissance, 295
    scientific revolution and, 441–42
Worms, Concordat of, 210
writing. *See* alphabets and writing
Wycliffe, John, 285, 309–10, 345

Xavier, Saint Francis, 364
Xenophanes, 72
Xenophon, 62, 86–89, 92, 114
Xerxes, King of Persia, 50, 73–74
Ximenes de Cisneros, Cardinal Francisco, 361

Yahweh, 46, 47, 53–56, 141, 172
Yersinia pestis, 279
York, England, 290
York Castle, *203*

Zarathustra. *See* Zoroaster, Zoroastrianism
Zealots, 141
Zeno, Eastern Roman Emperor, 157
Zeno of Citium, 101
Zeus, 41, 62, 94
Ziggurat of Ur, 2, 15, 16, *16*
Zoroaster, Zoroastrianism, 51, 55, 57, 103,
    142, 149
Zurbaran, Francisco, *402*
Zwingli, Ulrich, 353

NORTH POLAR REGION inset:

NORTH
AMERICA

ARCTIC
OCEAN

North
Magnetic Pole

North Pole

New Siberian Islands

East
Siberian
Sea

Laptev
Sea

ASIA

Victoria
Island

Baffin
Bay

Svalbard

Novaya
Zemlya

Iceland

ARCTIC CIRCLE

GREENLAND

**Main map labels:**

ARCTIC

Longitude West of Greenwich

QUEEN
ELIZABETH
ISLANDS

GREENLAND

Baffin
Bay

Ireland

ARCTIC CIRCLE

Great Slave
Lake

Hudson
Bay

Island of
Newfoundland

NORTH

AMERICA

Lake
Winnipeg

Lake
Superior

L. Michigan

L. Huron

L. Ontario

L. Erie

Gulf of
St. Lawrence

NORTH

PACIFIC

OCEAN

NORTH

ATLANTIC

OCEAN

ALEUTIAN TRENCH

Hawaii

TROPIC OF CANCER

GULF OF
MEXICO

CENTRAL
AMERICA

CARIBBEAN
SEA

P
O
L
Y
N
E
S
I
A

EQUATOR

Amazon
Basin

MID-ATLANTIC RIDGE

ANDES

SOUTH

AMERICA

Samoa
Islands

SOUTH

ATLANTIC

OCEAN

Tahiti

TROPIC OF CAPRICORN

PERU-CHILE TRENCH

SOUTH

PACIFIC

OCEAN

ANDES

SOUTH

ATLANTIC

OCEAN

Falkland Islands

Cape Horn

Drake Passage

ANTARCTIC
PENINSULA

ANTARCTIC CIRCLE

WEDDELL
SEA

Ellsworth Land

Marie Byrd Land

ANTA

GLOBAL SATELLITE MOSAIC

The beauty and complexity of Earth's landscapes—above and below the
oceans—is revealed with the Global Satellite Mosaic. The mosaic was created
for the National Geographic Society by NASA's Jet Propulsion Laboratory from
more than 500 satellite images from the National Oceanic and Atmospheric
Administration. The cloud-free images show Earth in its natural colors as it might be
seen from space. One can easily identify the world's major glaciers, deserts, mountain
ranges, and rain forests. For example, follow the green ribbon of lush vegetation along
the Nile into the stark, dry Sahara. The mountain ranges seem to rise off the map thanks
to digital elevation databases from the Department of Defense. The deepest areas of the
ocean realm are colored dark blue in contrast to the light blue areas highlighting
continental shelves, submarine ridges, and underwater mountains.

BIOSPHERE

Thousands of satellite images were
combined to show a picture of biological
productivity in the oceans and on land.
In the oceans, red, yellow, and
green indicate waters rich in phytoplankton; dark blue to
green areas show high potential plant productivity; tan to
suffer from productivity limitations due to aridity and temperature.

THE W
SATEL

SOUTH POLAR
REGION

ANTARCTICA

THE NEED FOR SATELLITES

SURFACE
TEMPERATURE

ORLD
MAP